High Performance Parallelism Pearls

Multicore and Many-core Programming Approaches

High Performance Parallelism Pearls
Multicore and Many-core Programming Approaches

James Reinders

Jim Jeffers

Intel Corporation, United States

AMSTERDAM • BOSTON • HEIDELBERG • LONDON
NEW YORK • OXFORD • PARIS • SAN DIEGO
SAN FRANCISCO • SINGAPORE • SYDNEY • TOKYO
Morgan Kaufmann is an imprint of Elsevier

Acquiring Editor: *Todd Green*
Editorial Project Manager: *Lindsay Lawrence*
Project Manager: *Priya Kumaraguruparan*
Designer: *Maria Inês Cruz*
Cover Photo of: Stampede Supercomputer, courtesy of Texas Advanced Computing Center, *Sean Cunningham*.

Morgan Kaufmann is an imprint of Elsevier
225 Wyman Street, Waltham, MA, 02451, USA

Library of Congress Cataloging-in-Publication Data
A catalogue record for this book is available from the Library of Congress.

British Library Cataloguing-in-Publication Data
A catalogue record for this book is available from the British Library.

For information on all Morgan Kaufmann publications
visit our website at http://store.elsevier.com/

ISBN: 978-0-12-802118-7

Working together
to grow libraries in
developing countries

www.elsevier.com • www.bookaid.org

Contents

v

Contributors

Mustafa AbdulJabbar

King Abdullah University of Science and Technology, Saudi Arabia

Mustafa is a PhD candidate in the Extreme Computing Research Center at KAUST. He works on optimization of high-scale algorithms such as FMM and is interested in closing the gap between RMI-based execution models and real applications in molecular dynamics and fluid mechanics.

Jefferson Amstutz

SURVICE Engineering Company, USA

Jefferson is a Software Engineer in the Applied Technology Operation of SURVICE. He explores interactive visualization and high-performance computing in support of applications for the Army Research Laboratory; he works to solve a variety of physics-based simulation problems in domains such as ballistic vulnerability analysis, radio frequency propagation, and soft-body simulation.

Cédric Andreolli

Intel Corporation, France

Cédric is an application engineer in the Energy team at Intel Corporation. He helps optimize applications running on Intel platforms for the Oil and Gas industry.

Edoardo Aprà

Pacific Northwest National Laboratory, USA

Edoardo is a Chief Scientist at the Environmental Molecular Sciences Laboratory within PNNL. His research focus is on high-performance computational algorithm and software development especially for chemical applications. He is the main developer of the molecular density functional theory (DFT) module in the NWChem package.

Nikita Astafiev

Intel Corporation, Russia

Nikita is a senior software engineer in the Numerics team at Intel. He works on highly optimized math functions. His key areas of interest include automated floating-point error analysis and low-level optimizations.

Troy Baer

National Institute for Computational Sciences, The University of Tennessee and Oak Ridge National Laboratory, USA

Troy leads the HPC systems team for the NICS Systems and Operations group. He has been involved large system deployments including Beacon, Nautilus, and Kraken. In April 2014, Troy received the Adaptive Computing Lifetime Achievement award for contributions in scheduling and resource management using Moab.

Carsten Benthin

Intel Corporation, Germany

Carsten is a Graphics Research Scientist at Intel Corporation. His research interests include all aspects of ray tracing and high-performance rendering, throughput and high-performance computing, low-level code optimization, and massively parallel hardware architectures.

Per Berg

Danish Meteorological Institute, Denmark

Per applies his mathematical modeling and scientific computing education to develop modeling software for applications in water environments (estuaries, ocean). Working for both private companies and public institutes, Per has been involved in numerous projects that apply models to solve engineering and scientific problems.

Vincent Betro

National Institute for Computational Sciences, The University of Tennessee and Oak Ridge National Laboratory, USA

Vincent focuses his research on porting and optimizing applications for several architectures, especially the Intel Xeon Phi, and developing Computational Fluid Dynamics codes. He is also the training manager for the XSEDE project, and he has emphasized Xeon Phi Coprocessor training material development for Stampede and Beacon in this role.

Leonardo Borges

Intel Corporation, USA

Leo is a Senior Staff Engineer and has been engaged with the Intel Many Integrated Core program from its early days. He specializes in HPC applying his background in numerical analysis and in developing parallel numerical math libraries. Leo is focused on optimization work related to the Oil & Gas industry.

Ryan Braby

Joint Institute for Computational Sciences, The University of Tennessee and Oak Ridge National Laboratory, USA

Ryan is the Chief Cyberinfrastructure Officer for JICS. Ryan has been directly involved in the administration and/or deployment of 2 systems that ranked #1 on the Top 500 list, one system that ranked #1 on the Green 500 list, and 18 systems that were ranked in the top 50 on the Top 500 list.

Glenn Brook

Joint Institute for Computational Sciences, The University of Tennessee and Oak Ridge National Laboratory, USA

Glenn currently directs the Application Acceleration Center of Excellence (AACE) and serves as the Chief Technology Officer at JICS. He is the principal investigator for the Beacon Project, which is funded by NSF and UT to explore the impact of emerging computing technologies such as the Intel Xeon Phi coprocessor on computational science and engineering.

Ilya Burylov
Intel Corporation, Russia

Ilya is a senior software engineer in the Numerics team at Intel Corporation. His background is in computation optimizations for statistical, financial, and transcendental math functions algorithms. Ilya focuses on optimization of computationally intensive analytics algorithms and data manipulation steps for Big Data workflows within distributed systems.

Ki Sing Chan
The Chinese University of Hong Kong, Hong Kong

Ki Sing is an undergraduate student at the Chinese University of Hong Kong majoring in Mathematics and Information Engineering with a minor in Computer Science. His first research experience took place in the Oak Ridge National Laboratory in Tennessee during the summer break in 2013. His research focuses on the implementation of a Cholesky Factorization algorithm for large dense matrix.

Gilles Civario
Irish Centre for High-End Computing (ICHEC), Ireland

Gilles is a Senior Software Architect focused on designing and implementing tailored hardware and software solutions to users of the National Service and to ICHEC's technology transfer client companies.

Guillaume Colin de Verdière

Commissariat à l'Energie Atomique et aux Energies Alternatives (CEA), France

Guillaume is a senior expert at CEA. His current focus is on novel architectures especially the Intel Xeon Phi, a very promising technology that might potentially get us to an exascale machine. As a direct consequence of this focus, he is actively studying the impact of such novel technologies on legacy code evolution.

Eduardo D'Azevedo

Computational Mathematics Group at the Oak Ridge National Laboratory, USA

Eduardo is a staff scientist with research interests that include developing highly scalable parallel solvers. He contributes to projects in materials science and fusion in the Scientific Discovery through Advanced Computing (SciDAC) program. He has developed out-of-core and compact storage extensions for the ScaLAPACK library and made fundamental contributions in optimal mesh generation.

Jim Dempsey

QuickThread Programming, LLC, USA

Jim is a consultant specializing in high-performance computing (HPC) and optimization of embedded systems. Jim is the President of QuickThread Programming, LLC. Jim's expertise includes high efficiency programming and optimization for Intel Xeon and Intel Xeon Phi processors.

Alejandro Duran
Intel Corporation, Spain

Alejandro is an Application Engineer working with customers to help optimize their codes. He has been part of the OpenMP Language committee since 2005.

Manfred Ernst
Intel Corporation, now at Google Incorporated, USA

Manfred is a member of the Chromium team at Google. Prior to joining Google, he was a Research Scientist at Intel Labs, where he developed the Embree Ray Tracing Kernels. His primary research interests are photorealistic rendering, acceleration structures for ray tracing, sampling, and data compression.

Kerry Evans
Intel Corporation, USA

Kerry is a software engineer working primarily with customers on optimization of medical imaging software on Intel Xeon processors and Intel Xeon Phi coprocessors.

Rob Farber
TechEnablement.com, USA

Rob is a consultant with an extensive background in HPC and a long history of working with national labs and corporations engaged in HPC optimization work. Rob has authored/edited several books on GPU programming and is the CEO/Publisher of TechEnablement.com.

Louis Feng
Intel Corporation, USA

Louis is a software engineer working on high-performance graphics in collaboration with DreamWorks Animation. His current research interests include ray tracing, photorealistic image synthesis on highly parallel architectures, and parallel programming models.

Evgeny Fiksman
Intel Corporation, USA

Evgeny works on optimization of video enhancement algorithms for ×86 platforms. He was the lead architect and engineer for the Intel's implementation of an OpenCL runtime for both Intel CPUs and the Intel Xeon Phi coprocessors. His current focus area is the optimization of financial applications as a customer facing application engineer.

Jeff Hammond
Intel Corporation, USA

Jeff is a Research Scientist in the Parallel Computing Lab at Intel Labs. His research interests include one-sided and global view programming models, load balancing for irregular algorithms, and shared- and distributed-memory tensor contractions.

Michael Hebenstreit
Intel Corporation, USA

Michael is a senior cluster architect and tech lead for the Endeavor HPC benchmarking datacenter. He helped the datacenter to serve as a key HPC benchmarking resource. He created the very first Intel Xeon Phi cluster and was instrumental in integration of Intel Xeon Phi co-processors into Endeavour.

Christopher Hughes
Intel Corporation, USA

Christopher is a researcher at Intel Labs. His research interests are emerging workloads and computer architecture. He is currently helping to develop the next generation of microprocessors for compute- and data-intensive applications, focusing on wide SIMD execution and memory systems for processors with many cores.

Sverre Jarp

CERN honorary staff member, Norway

Sverre worked in IT at CERN for over 40 years, promoting advanced, but cost-effective, large-scale computing. In 2002, he was appointed as CTO of the CERN openlab, a position he held until his retirement in 2014. Today, as honorary staff at CERN, he retains an unabated interest in high-throughput computing and application scalability based on vector and parallel programming.

Jim Jeffers

Intel Corporation, USA

Jim is a Principal Engineer and engineering manager in Intel's Technical Computing Group. Jim coauthored *Intel Xeon Phi Coprocessor High Performance Programming* (Morgan Kaufmann, 2013). Jim currently leads Intel's technical computing visualization team.

Gregory S. Johnson

Intel Corporation, USA

Greg is a computer graphics researcher at Intel. His areas of interests include real-time and photorealistic rendering, visibility algorithms, spatial data structures, and graphics hardware architectures.

Vadim Karpusenko

Colfax International, USA

Vadim is a Principal HPC Research Engineer at Colfax International. His research interests include physical modeling with HPC clusters, highly parallel architectures, and code optimization.

Michael Klemm

Intel Corporation, Germany

Michael is a Senior Application Engineer in Intel's Software and Services Group. His focus is on high-performance and high-throughput computing. Michael is an Intel representative to the OpenMP Language Committee and leads the efforts to develop error-handling features for OpenMP.

Karol Kowalski

Pacific Northwest National Laboratory, USA

Karol is a Chief Scientist at the Environmental Molecular Sciences Laboratory within PNNL. His research focuses on the development of accurate electronic structure methods and their highly scalable implementations. His methods have been applied to describe a wide spectrum of many-body systems ranging from nuclei and molecules, to the systems being at the cross-road between molecular- and nanoscience.

Michael Lysaght

Irish Centre for High-End Computing (ICHEC), Ireland

Michael leads the Novel Technologies Activity and the Intel Parallel Computing Centre, at the Irish Centre for High End Computing (ICHEC). He is focused on supporting the Irish scientific user community and Irish industry in the exploitation of emerging multicore and many-core technologies. He leads the WP7 "Exploitation of HPC Tools and Techniques" activity as part of the EU's PRACE 3IP project.

Anton Malakhov

Intel Corporation, Russia

Anton is a senior software development engineer working on Intel Threading Building Blocks (TBB). He optimized the TBB task scheduler for the Intel Xeon Phi coprocessor and invented a few scheduling algorithms that improved the performance of Intel OpenCL runtime on the MIC architecture. He is currently responsible for productization of several TBB components including task_arena and affinity_partitioner.

Tim Mattson

Intel Corporation, USA

Tim is a Principal Engineer in Intel's Parallel Computing Laboratory where he conducts research on software infrastructure for Big Data applications and execution models for exascale computers. He has over 30 years of experience in parallel computing and helped create both OpenMP and OpenCL. His books include *Patterns for Parallel Programming*, *An Introduction to Concurrency in Programming Languages*, and *OpenCL Programming Guide*.

Simon McIntosh-Smith

University of Bristol, United Kingdom

Simon leads the HPC research group at the University of Bristol. He cofounded ClearSpeed and has pioneered the use of accelerators for BLAS/LAPACK and FFT libraries. His research focuses on many-core algorithms and performance portability, and fault tolerant software techniques to reach exascale. He actively contributes to the Khronos OpenCL heterogeneous programming standard.

Larry Meadows

Intel Corporation, USA

Larry is a Principal Engineer and has worked on compilers, tools, and applications software for HPC since 1982. He was a founding member of The Portland Group and has been working for Intel Corporation in Oregon since 2004.

Karl Meerbergen

KU Leuven, Belgium

Karl is a professor at the department of Computer Science, KU Leuven, Belgium. His research focuses on large-scale numerical linear algebra.

Iosif Meyerov

Lobachevsky State University of Nizhni Novgorod, Russia

Iosif is the vice-head of Software department at Lobachevsky State University of Nizhni Novgorod (UNN), principal investigator in several R&D projects. His research interests include high-performance computing, scientific computing, performance analysis and optimization, system programming, and applied mathematics.

Kent Milfeld

Texas Advanced Computing Center (TACC), USA

Kent has been an instructor, scientist, and HPC programmer at the Center for High Performance Computing at UT since its earliest days. His expert training, for the TACC user community, exposes methods of mapping programming paradigms to hardware that are efficient and seek to obtain the highest possible performance.

Paul Peltz, Jr.

National Institute for Computational Sciences, The University of Tennessee and Oak Ridge National Laboratory, USA

Paul is an HPC Systems Administrator for the National Institute for Computational Sciences at Oak Ridge National Laboratory at the University of Tennessee. He is the lead Administrator on the Beacon Cluster and is the operations mentor for the NICS Student Cluster Challenge team at SC.

Simon John Pennycook

Intel Corporation, United Kingdom

John is an application engineer focused on enabling developers to fully utilize the current generation of Intel Xeon Phi coprocessors. His previous research focused on the optimization of scientific applications for a wide range of different microarchitectures and hardware platforms, as well as the issues surrounding performance portability.

Jacob Weismann Poulsen

Danish Meteorological Institute, Denmark

Jacob is an HPC and scientific programming consultant for the research groups at DMI with expertise in analyzing and optimizing applications within the meteorological field.

Karthik Raman

Intel Corporation, USA

Karthik is a Software Architect at Intel focusing on performance analysis and optimization of HPC workloads for Intel Xeon Phi. He focuses on analyzing for optimal compiler code generation, vectorization and assessing key architectural features for performance. He helps deliver transformative methods and tools to expose new opportunities and insights.

James Reinders

Intel Corporation, USA

James promotes increased use of parallel programming throughout the industry. His projects have included both the world's first TeraFLOP/s supercomputer (ASCI Red) and the world's first TeraFLOP/s microprocessor (Intel Xeon Phi coprocessor). James coauthored *Intel Xeon Phi Coprocessor High Performance Programming* as well as several other books related to high-performance programming.

Alexander Reinefeld

Zuse Institute Berlin and Humboldt University, Germany

Alexander is the head of the Computer Science Department at ZIB and a professor at the Humboldt University of Berlin. His research interests include distributed computing, high-performance computer architecture, scalable and dependable computing, and peer-to-peer algorithms.

Dirk Roose

KU Leuven, Belgium

Dirk is a professor at the department of Computer Science, KU Leuven, Belgium. His research focuses on numerical methods for computational science and engineering and on algorithms for parallel scientific computing.

Carlos Rosales-Fernandez

Texas Advanced Computing Center (TACC), USA

Carlos is a co-director of the Advanced Computing Evaluation Laboratory at the Texas Advanced Computing Center, where his main responsibility is the evaluation of new computer architectures relevant to high-performance computing. He is the author of the open-source mplabs code.

Karl Schulz

Intel Corporation, USA

Karl leads a Cluster-Maker team working on future generation HPC software products for the Technical Computing Group at Intel.

Jason Sewall

Intel Corporation, USA

Jason is a researcher in the Data Center Group focused on Intel Xeon Phi. His interests include graphics, physically based modeling, parallel and high-performance computing, databases, computational finance, and graph algorithms.

Gregg Skinner

Intel Corporation, USA

Gregg specializes in porting and optimizing science and engineering applications on parallel computers. Gregg joined Intel Corporation Software and Services Group in 2011.

Mikhail Smelyanskiy

Intel Corporation, USA

Mikhail is a Principal Engineer at Intel's Parallel Computing Lab. His focus is on design, implementation, and analysis of parallel algorithms and workloads for the current and future generation parallel processor systems. His research interests include medical imaging, computational finance and fundamental high-performance compute kernels.

Thomas Steinke

Zuse Institute Berlin, Germany

Thomas is head of the Supercomputer Algorithms and Consulting group at the Zuse Institute Berlin (ZIB). His research interest is in high-performance computing, heterogeneous systems for scientific and data analytics applications, and parallel simulation methods. Thomas cofounded the OpenFPGA initiative in 2004, and he leads the Intel Parallel Computing Center (IPCC) at ZIB.

Shi-Quan Su

The University of Tennessee, USA

Shi-Quan is an HPC Consultant focused on helping users migrate the codes to the novel platforms available. His works include state-of-art large-scale Quantum Monte Carlo simulation for the high transition temperature superconductive materials.

Alexander Sysoyev

Lobachevsky State University of Nizhni Novgorod, Russia

Alexander is an associate professor of Software department at Lobachevsky State University of Nizhni Novgorod (UNN), principal investigator in several R&D projects. His research interests include high-performance computing, global optimization, performance analysis and optimization, system programming, applied mathematics.

Philippe Thierry

Intel Corporation, France

Philippe leads the Intel Energy Engineering Team supporting end users and software vendors in the energy sector. His work includes profiling and tuning of HPC applications for current and future platforms as well as for super-computer definition with respect to the applications behaviors. His research activity is devoted to performance extrapolation and application characterization and modeling toward exascale computing.

Antonio Valles
Intel Corporation, USA

Antonio is a Senior Software Engineer focused on performance analysis and optimizations for the Intel Xeon Phi coprocessors. Antonio has analyzed and optimized software at Intel spanning client, mobile, and HPC segments. Antonio loves to code and has written multiple internal post-Si and pre-Si tools to help analyze and optimize applications.

Jerome Vienne
Texas Advanced Computing Center (TACC), USA

Jerome is a Research Associate of the Texas Advanced Computing Center (TACC) at the University of Texas at Austin. His research interests include performance analysis and modeling, high-performance computing, high-performance networking, benchmarking and exascale computing.

Andrey Vladimirov
Colfax International, USA

Andrey is the Head of HPC Research at Colfax International. His research is focused on the application of modern computing technologies to computationally demanding scientific problems.

Ingo Wald

Intel Corporation, USA

Ingo is a Research Scientist at Intel. His research interests revolve around all aspects of ray tracing and lighting simulation, real-time graphics, parallel computing, and general visual/high-performance computing.

Florian Wende

Zuse Institute Berlin, Germany

Florian is a part of the Scalable Algorithms workgroup, in the Distributed Algorithms and Supercomputing department, at Zuse Institute Berlin (ZIB). He is interested in accelerator and many-core computing with applications in Computer Science and Computational Physics. His focus is on load balancing of irregular parallel computations and on close-to-hardware code optimization.

Kwai Lam Wong

Joint Institute for Computational Sciences at the University of Tennessee, USA

Kwai is the deputy director of the Campus Programs group at JICS. He is the director of the CFD Laboratory in the Mechanical, Aerospace, and Biomedical Engineering at the University of Tennessee, Knoxville. His interests include numerical linear algebra, parallel computing, computational fluid dynamics, and finite element method.

Sven Woop

Intel Corporation, Germany

Sven is a Graphics Research Scientist at Intel Corporation where he develops the Embree Ray Tracing Kernels. His research interests include computer graphics, hardware design, and parallel programming.

Claude Wright

Intel Corporation, USA

Claude is an Engineer at Intel working on Power Analysis and Green 500 tuning for systems using the Intel Xeon Phi coprocessor.

Rio Yokota

King Abdullah University of Science and Technology, Saudi Arabia

Rio is a Research Scientist in the Extreme Computing Research Center at KAUST. He is the main developer of the FMM library ExaFMM. He was part of the team that won the Gordon Bell prize for price/performance in 2009 using his FMM code on 760 GPUs. He is now optimizing his ExaFMM code on architectures such as Titan, Mira, Stampede, K computer, and TSUBAME 2.5.

Charles Yount

Intel Corporation, USA

Chuck is a Principal Engineer in the Software and Services Group, at Intel Corporation, where he has been employed since 1995. His research interests are computer performance analysis and optimization (pre-Si and post-Si), object-oriented software design, machine learning, and computer architecture.

Albert-Jan Nicholas Yzelman

KU Leuven, Belgium

Albert-Jan is a postdoctoral researcher at the department of Computer Science, KU Leuven, Belgium. He works within the ExaScience Life Lab on sparse matrix computations, high-performance computing, and general parallel programming.

Weiqun Zhang

Lawrence Berkeley National Laboratory, USA

Weiqun is a member of the Center for Computational Sciences and Engineering at Lawrence Berkeley National Laboratory. His research interests lie in high-performance computing, numerical methods for partial differential equations, and applications to science and engineering fields including combustion and astrophysics.

Acknowledgments

This book was only possible because of the dedicated software developers who took time away from coding to share their experiences. This book is the result of hard-working contributors to whom we are grateful. Their names are listed at the start of the chapters to which they contributed. In the preceding pages you will find some additional information about each contributor. We thank all the contributors for their perseverance and understanding as provided feedback and as we dotted i's and crossed t's together.

Thank you to our mutual friends Sverre Jarp for sharing his unique insights in the preface and Joe Curley for encouraging us to reach toward the impossible and make it happen.

Special thanks from James Reinders to his wife Susan Meredith. Her support was essential to making this book a possibility. James also thanks his daughter Katie and son Andrew who supported more than they can know. Finally, my coauthor and friend, Jim Jeffers, who was again the perfect partner in working together on a book.

Special thanks from Jim Jeffers to his wife Laura for her continued support and encouragement. Jim also thanks his children (including their spouses) Tim, Patrick, Colleen, Sarah, Jon, and especially Hannah, his new granddaughter, for providing inspiration whenever needed. Finally, many thanks to my friend and coauthor, James Reinders for his expertise, guidance and stalwart commitment to the success of this book from concept to completion.

For their support, guidance, and feedback, we thank Joe Curley, Bob Burroughs, Herb Hinstorff, Rob Farber and Nathan Schultz.

We appreciate the hard work by the entire Morgan Kaufmann team including the three people we worked with directly: Todd Green, Lindsay Lawrence, and Priya Kumaraguruparan.

Numerous colleagues offered information, advice, and vision. There are certainly many people who have helped directly and indirectly to whom we are very grateful for the support. We thank *all* those who helped and we apologize for any who helped us and we failed to mention.

Thank you all.

Jim Jeffers & James Reinders

Foreword

I am extremely honored by the invitation to write the foreword to this book for two reasons: first, the Intel® Xeon Phi™ coprocessor is a really thrilling "compute brick" that CERN and the High Energy Physics (HEP) community can leverage to help satisfy our humongous computing needs. Of course, many other scientific, and engineering endeavors around the world will benefit for similar reasons. Secondly, this book represents a magnificent set of examples that can teach programmers and scientists how to get the most from multicore and many-core processors.

HUMONGOUS COMPUTING NEEDS: SCIENCE YEARS IN THE MAKING

CERN began to prepare for the Large Hadron Collider (LHC), in the early 2000s, to be capable of reaching high energy ranges never before seen in particle accelerators.

The endeavor reached far beyond building the particle accelerator itself. Four new experiments had already been formed and scientists were beavering away on a broad set of activities. Experiments ALICE, ATLAS, CMS, and LHCb had thousands of participating physicists. Activities ranged from detector design and construction, to the design and development of the large-scale software reconstruction frameworks necessary to process petabytes of experimental data. All in the quest for ground breaking discoveries.

OPEN STANDARDS

Standards are important to the industry, and investing in open standards has always been a goal for CERN. We found that this aligned with philosophies at Intel as well. In collaboration with hundreds of scientific institutes and laboratories from the HEP community, we decided to establish the LHC Computing Grid (LCG) based on commodity x86 servers. In 2001, CERN established the CERN openlab, an entity that would investigate upcoming technologies potentially relevant to the LCG. Intel joined as an industrial partner from the very beginning. In openlab, we were involved in futuristic R&D efforts where the outcomes might be formidable successes or dramatic failures. This was, and still is, a very real R&D laboratory!

Our keen interest in open standards also led to our encouragement for Intel to move to Linux for the Intel Xeon Phi coprocessors. Intel succeeded in delivering a very stable Linux-based system and provided their implementation in open source to encourage innovation.

KEEN ON MANY-CORE ARCHITECTURE

A decade ago, the Intel Xeon processor family was quickly evolving into powerful *multicore* processors. This was a godsend for the HEP community since each physics *event* (the full picture of all particles resulting from a collision) is independent of all others and a large set of events can be computed using trivial parallelism. At openlab, we strive to ensure the best possible throughput for each new system generation.

Developments at Intel gave us new options in our quest to feed our insatiable appetite for more computing power. In 2008, we found ourselves extremely enthusiastic about the "Larrabee" project at Intel. Although it was initially touted as a graphics processor, its essence was really the world's first SMP-cluster-on-a-chip. This was indeed its destiny. It was easy to imagine how to run standard programs, or program kernels, on the device. At the time there was no hardware but articles such as Michael Abrash's "*First Look at the Larrabee New Instructions*" described a very sophisticated set of vector extensions to the standard x86 instruction set. With the help of Pradeep Dubey and his team from Intel Labs, we saw promising results by simulating code snippets. The hundreds of x86 threads that could be active in parallel had caught our imagination. The common programming models, languages and tooling would prove quite valuable.

Intel's initial performance targets had been completely focused on single precision (SP) floating-point, a good fit for graphics but not enough for computational physics. Our resulting critique regarding our need for high performance double precision (DP) floating-point proved influential in the Intel Xeon Phi product.

Imagine our excitement when we were the first group outside Intel to receive a Knights Ferry (KNF) card in 2009! While this was too soon to incorporate all our critiques, Intel was already working on the product that would. In the meantime, with KNF in hand, we looked to port some of the LHC experiments. ALICE, a heavy-ion experiment, had scientists collaborating with other heavy-ion experiments on a new version of the software called the "Trackfitter." This code reconstructs entire tracks, or particle trajectories, from the coordinates of the sensors that light up in a given particle collision. In openlab, we had already ported it to Intel Xeon processors, so it was ported to KNF literally in a matter of hours. We were very excited by the minimal effort, measured in days, that was needed to get to outstanding results.

XEON PHI IS BORN: MANY CORES, EXCELLENT VECTOR ISA

I received a flattering invitation to share our early results at the International Supercomputing Conference (ISC) in May 2010 where Kirk Skaugen, responsible for the Datacenter and Connected Systems Group at Intel, announced the Knights Corner as the first production-level many-core device. Soon after, the official name became Intel® Xeon Phi™ indicating that this would be a family of processors just like Intel® Xeon®.

You might ask: *Why we were so enthusiastic?* What we saw in the design of the Intel Xeon Phi included an excellent vector instruction set architecture (ISA). By having vector mask registers separate from the vector data registers, the architecture was able to handle both data flow and control flow in programs in a much more optimal way. Intel has been pleased by strong community enthusiasm; their recent announcement of the AVX-512 instruction set will push this vector architecture into their multicore processors as well.

Additionally, we were attracted to the many-core design. Our programs have limited Instruction-Level Parallelism (ILP), so running many of them in parallel, on a core that would consume only a few watts, is a great idea. We demonstrated the advantage of this approach by working with the developers of the detector simulation software, Geant 4, so that we could run an entire detector simulation process with hundreds of threads on a single Xeon Phi coprocessor. The future will tell whether small cores, big cores, or a mix will be the best option. Our aim is to be ready for all likely combinations. Our strong results with this many-core approach led to a desire to see this type of design in a pure processor instead of just a coprocessor; we look forward to bootable systems based on stand-alone many-core processors using the next generation of Intel Xeon Phi, known by as the Knights Landing (KNL) processor.

LEARN HIGHLY SCALABLE PARALLEL PROGRAMMING

The explosion in core count, both in the Intel Xeon and Intel Xeon Phi families, has been a blessing for the HEP community where parallelism is inherent in the science. The really exciting challenges are scaling to many cores and vectorization. CERN openlab has helped in this effort by teaching vectorization and parallelization in a series of workshops and schools for almost a decade, reaching over one thousand students. I am so pleased to be able to introduce and motivate reading this book; I hope that many, many readers will learn how to improve the performance of their programs by using what we call the "performance dimensions" of a modern microprocessor.

FUTURE DEMANDS GROW: PROGRAMMING MODELS MATTER

The Large Hadron Collider will continue running for two more decades. There is an ambitious plan to increase both the energy and the luminosity that will lead to increases in the complexity of the events and therefore increase our computational needs. Consequently, we must gain efficiency from vectorization.

The challenge in reconstructing physics events is to capture every single detail of each interaction. With Intel's help, a project called "Geant V" is writing vectorized software to meet these new challenges. With inspiration from lessons learned, such as those in this book, we are more likely to have even higher performance solutions in the near future.

This book will make it much easier in general to exploit high levels of parallelism including programming optimally for the Intel Xeon Phi products. The common programming methodology between the Intel Xeon and Intel Xeon Phi families is good news for the entire scientific and engineering community; the same programming can realize parallel scaling and vectorization for both multicore and many-core. LHC will be operating for a very long time and it will be fantastic to see the Intel Xeon Phi family of processors evolving alongside to provide our humongous computing needs.

Sverre Jarp
CERN Honorary Staff Member

Preface

This book draws on 69 authors who share how their parallel programming, inspired by the highly parallel Intel® Xeon Phi™ coprocessors, unlocks performance on both processors and coprocessors. In doing so, many of the most critical challenges and techniques in parallel programming are explored with exciting results. Most chapters show how to scale and vectorize well, which will help extract more performance from multicore processors as well as the many-core Intel Xeon Phi coprocessors. Other chapters shed light on harnessing neo-heterogeneous systems that combine Intel® Xeon® processors and Intel Xeon Phi coprocessors in a system offering their common programming models. We have also included chapters with expert advice on the unique aspects of deploying, managing, monitoring, and working with these neo-heterogeneous systems and clusters.

Inspired by 61 cores: A new era in programming

What has been more remarkable to us than the obvious success of the Intel® Xeon Phi™ coprocessors has been experiencing the awakening that the Intel Xeon Phi coprocessor has brought to parallel programming. The coprocessor has truly brought us all the dawn of a critical new chapter in programming. We have seen that the appeal of parallel programming for as many as 61 cores is far higher than the parallel programming for four or eight cores. It has been awakening both interest in adding parallel programming techniques into applications for the first time as well as enhancing already parallel applications. It is encouraging parallel programming that truly scales instead of merely limping along with "okay," sometimes marginal, performance improvements that was seen when targeting only a small amount of parallelism such as on a quad-core processor.

Intel Xeon Phi coprocessors have given an evolutionary path to parallelism that includes explosive opportunities for those who are willing to learn to unlock them. This has been done without requiring new programming models, new languages, or new tools. This book offers insights into unlocking the explosive potential by highlighting parallel programming that works, and ideas on how to rethink old techniques in light of the possibilities of neo-heterogeneous programming.

While we thank the authors with an earlier section dedicated to acknowledgements, we cannot thank them enough. The authors of the chapters found inside this book spent precious time away from their influential work of programming these inspirational and powerful machines, in order to explain their work so we might all learn from their successes. We hope you enjoy and benefit from their shared efforts, and we hope that leads to your own successes in this new era of parallel computing.

Jim Jeffers and James Reinders
Intel Corporation
November 2014

INTRODUCTION

James Reinders
Intel Corporation

We should "create a cookbook" was a common and frequent comment that Jim Jeffers and I heard after *Intel® Xeon Phi™ Coprocessor High-Performance Programming* was published. Guillaume Colin de Verdière was early in his encouragement to create such a book and was pleased when we moved forward with this project. Guillaume matched action with words by also coauthoring the first contributed chapter with Jason Sewall, *From "correct" to "correct & efficient": a Hydro2D case study with Godunov's scheme*. Their chapter reflects a basic premise of this book that the sharing of experience and success can be highly educational to others. It also contains a theme familiar to those who program the massive parallelism of the Intel Xeon Phi family: running code on Intel Xeon Phi coprocessors is easy. This lets you quickly focus on optimization and the achievement of high performance—but we do need to tune for parallelism in our applications! Notably, we see such optimization work improves the performance on processors *and* coprocessors. As the authors note, "a rising tide lifts all boats."

LEARNING FROM SUCCESSFUL EXPERIENCES

Learning from others is what this book is all about. This book brings together the collective work of numerous experts in parallel programming to share their work. The examples were selected for their educational content, applicability, and success—**and**—you can download the codes and try them yourself! All the examples demonstrate successful approaches to parallel programming, but not all the examples scale well enough to make an Intel Xeon Phi coprocessor run faster than a processor. In the real world, this is what we face and reinforces something we are not bashful in pointing out: a common programming model matters a great deal. You see that notion emerge over and over in real-life examples including those in this book.

We are indebted to the many contributors to this book. In this book, you find a rich set of examples and advice. Given that this is the introduction, we offer a little perspective to bind it together somewhat. Most of all, we encourage you to dive into the rich examples, found starting in Chapter 2.

CODE MODERNIZATION

It is popular to talk about "code modernization" these days. Having experienced the "inspired by 61 cores" phenomenon, we are excited to see it has gone viral and is now being discussed by more and more people. You will find lots of "modernization" shown in this book.

Code modernization is reorganizing the code, and perhaps changing algorithms, to increase the amount of thread parallelism, vector/SIMD operations, and compute intensity to optimize performance on modern architectures. Thread parallelism, vector/SIMD operations, and an emphasis on temporal data reuse are all critical for high-performance programming. Many existing applications were written before these elements were required for performance, and therefore, such codes are not yet optimized for modern computers.

MODERNIZE WITH CONCURRENT ALGORITHMS

Examples of opportunities to rethink approaches to better suit the parallelism of modern computers are scattered throughout this book. Chapter 5 encourages using barriers with an eye toward more concurrency. Chapter 11 stresses the importance of not statically decomposing workloads because neither workloads nor the machines we run them on are truly uniform. Chapter 18 shows the power of not thinking that the parallel world is flat. Chapter 26 juggles data, computation, and storage to increase performance. Chapter 12 increases performance by ensuring parallelism in a heterogeneous node. Enhancing parallelism across a heterogeneous cluster is illustrated in Chapter 13 and Chapter 25.

MODERNIZE WITH VECTORIZATION AND DATA LOCALITY

Chapter 8 provides a solid examination of data layout issues in the quest to process data as vectors. Chapters 27 and 28 provide additional education and motivation for doing data layout and vectorization work.

UNDERSTANDING POWER USAGE

Power usage is mentioned in enough chapters that we invited Intel's power tuning expert, Claude Wright, to write Chapter 14. His chapter looks directly at methods to measure power including creating a simple software-based power analyzer with the Intel MPSS tools and also the difficulties of measuring idle power since you are not idle if you are busy measuring power!

ISPC AND OPENCL ANYONE?

While OpenMP and TBB dominate as parallel programming solutions in the industry and this book, we have included some mind-stretching chapters that make the case for other solutions.

SPMD programming gives interesting solutions for vectorization including data layout help, at the cost of dropping sequential consistency. Is it that okay? Chapters 6 and 21 include usage of ispc and its SPMD approach for your consideration. SPMD thinking resonates well when you approach vectorization, even if you do not adopt ispc.

Chapter 22 is written to advocate for OpenCL usage in a heterogeneous world. The contributors describe results from the BUDE molecular docking code, which sustains over 30% of peak floating point performance on a wide variety of systems.

INTEL XEON PHI COPROCESSOR SPECIFIC

While most of the chapters move algorithms forward on processors and coprocessors, three chapters are dedicated to a deeper look at Intel Xeon Phi coprocessor specific topics. Chapter 15 presents current best practices for managing Intel Xeon Phi coprocessors in a cluster. Chapters 16 and 20 give valuable insights for users of Intel Xeon Phi coprocessors.

MANY-CORE, NEO-HETEROGENEOUS

The adoption rate of Intel Xeon Phi coprocessors has been steadily increasing since they were first introduced in November 2012. By mid-2013, the cumulative number of FLOPs contributed by Intel Xeon Phi coprocessors in TOP 500 machines exceeded the combined FLOPs contributed by all the graphics processing units (GPUs) installed as floating-point accelerators in the TOP 500 list. In fact, the only device type contributing more FLOPs to TOP 500 supercomputers was Intel Xeon® processors.

As we mentioned in the Preface, the 61 cores of an Intel Xeon Phi coprocessor have inspired a new era of interest in parallel programming. As we saw in our introductory book, *Intel Xeon Phi Coprocessor High-Performance Programming*, the coprocessors use the same programming languages, parallel programming models, and the same tools as processors. In essence, this means that the challenge of programming the coprocessor is largely the same challenge as parallel programming for a general-purpose processor. This is because the design of both processors and the Intel Xeon Phi coprocessor avoided the restricted programming nature inherent in heterogeneous programming when using devices with restricted programming capabilities.

The experiences of programmers using the Intel Xeon Phi coprocessor time and time again have reinforced the value of a common programming model—a fact that is independently and repeatedly emphasized by the chapter authors in this book. The take-away message is clear that the effort spent to tune for scaling and vectorization for the Intel Xeon Phi coprocessor is time well spent for improving performance for processors such as Intel Xeon processors.

NO "XEON PHI" IN THE TITLE, NEO-HETEROGENEOUS PROGRAMMING

Because the key programming challenges are generically parallel, we knew we needed to emphasize the applicability to both multicore and many-core computing instead of focusing only on Intel Xeon Phi coprocessors, which is why "Xeon Phi" does not appear in the title of this book.

However, systems with coprocessors and processors combined do usher in two unique challenges that are addressed in this book: (1) Hiding the latency of moving data to and from an attached device, a challenge common to any "attached" device including GPUs and coprocessors. Future Intel Xeon Phi products will offer configurations that eliminate the data-movement challenge by being offered as processors instead of being packaged coprocessors. (2) Another unique and broader challenge lies in programming heterogeneous systems. Previously, heterogeneous programming referred to systems that combined incompatible computational devices. Incompatible in that they used programming methods different enough to require separate development tools and coding approaches. The Intel Xeon Phi products changed all that. Intel Xeon Phi coprocessors offer compatible coding methods for parallel programming with those used by all processors. Intel customers have taken to calling this "neo-heterogeneity" to stress that the sought after value of heterogeneous systems can finally be obtained without the programming being heterogeneous. This gives us the highly desirable homogeneous programming on neo-heterogeneous hardware (e.g., use of a common programming model across the compute elements, specifically the processors and coprocessors).

THE FUTURE OF MANY-CORE

Intel has announced that it is working on multiple future generations of Intel Xeon Phi devices, and has released information about the second generation product, code named *Knights Landing*.

The many continued dividends of Moore's Law are evident in the features of Knights Landing. The biggest change is the opportunity to use Knights Landing as a processor. The advantages of being available as a processor are numerous, and include more power efficient systems, reduction in data movement, a large standard memory footprint, and support for Intel® AVX-512 (a processor-compatible vector capability nearly identical to the vector capabilities found in the first-generation Intel Xeon Phi coprocessor).

Additional dividends of Moore's Law include use of a very modern out-of-order low-power core design, support for on-package high-bandwidth memory, and versions that integrate fabric support (inclusion of a Network Interface Controller).

The best way to prepare for Knights Landing is to be truly "inspired by 61 cores." Tuning for today's Intel Xeon Phi coprocessor is the best way to be sure an application is on track to make good use of Knight Landing. Of course, since Knights Landing promises to be even more versatile it is possible that using a processor-based system with more than 50 cores is a better choice to get your application ready. We say more than 50 because we know from experience that a small number of cores does not easily inspire the level of tuning needed to be ready to utilize high levels of parallelism.

We can logically conclude that the future for many-core is bright. Neo-heterogeneous programming is already enabling code modernization for parallelism, while trending to get easier in each generation of Intel Xeon Phi devices. We hope the "recipes" in this book provide guidance and motivation for modernizing your applications to take advantage of highly parallel computers.

DOWNLOADS

During the creation of this book, we specifically asked chapter authors to focus on important code segments that highlight the key concepts in their chapters. In addition, we required that chapters include complete examples, which are available for download from our Web site http://lotsofcores.com or project web sites. Section "For more information" at the end of each chapter will steer you to the right place to find the code.

Instructors, and all who create presentations, can appreciate the value in being able to download all figures, diagrams and photos used in this book from http://lotsofcores.com. Please reuse them to help teach and explain parallel programming to more software developers! We appreciate being mentioned when you attribute the source of figures but otherwise we will place no onerous conditions on their reuse.

FOR MORE INFORMATION

Some additional reading worth considering includes:

- Downloads associated with this book: http://lotsofcores.com.
- Web site sponsored by Intel dedicated to parallel programming: http://go-parallel.com.
- Intel Web site for information on the Intel Xeon Phi products: http://intel.com/xeonphi.
- Intel Web site for information on programming the Intel Xeon Phi products: http://intel.com/software/mic.
- Intel Xeon Phi Users Group Web site: https://www.ixpug.org.
- Advanced Vector Instructions information: http://software.intel.com/avx.

FROM "CORRECT" TO "CORRECT & EFFICIENT": A HYDRO2D CASE STUDY WITH GODUNOV'S SCHEME

2

Jason D. Sewall*, Guillaume Colin de Verdière†

Intel, United States, †CEA, France

How can a given physical process be simulated on a computer efficiently? The answer is reliably complicated; physical phenomena are subtle and intricate, and modern computer systems sophisticated. The details of how best to achieve efficient simulation for even apparently similar phenomena—for example, the motion of waves in the ocean and the wake from a powerboat—vary greatly, and the evolving state of computing environments adds an additional dimension of complexity to the matter.

Computer environments today are rife with performance-minded features—several varieties of parallelism among them—and any efficient realization of a physical process on these contemporary systems must account for these features at some level.

In this chapter, we explore a real-world scientific code for gas dynamics that delivers useful and correct results but with (initially) unsatisfactory performance. By examining what the code implements and seeing how it may be mapped to modern architectural features, we will see its performance improve dramatically.

SCIENTIFIC COMPUTING ON CONTEMPORARY COMPUTERS

Numerical analysis and scientific interests have driven the development of computers long before the *electronic* computers even existed. From the abacus to Napier's bones, to the difference and analytical engines, the recognition that large quantities of arithmetic could describe nearly everything that surrounds us—to some accuracy—impelled the development of techniques and devices that could perform these basic mathematical operations reliably, quickly, and with known precision.

The role of scientific computing in the development of the computing field at large has hardly diminished in the modern world; supercomputers are built for weather simulations, material testing, and exploring the universe. The microchips that power supercomputers, laptops, and even phones are themselves judged by their ability to "crunch numbers" in contexts derived from scientific computing.

The persistent role scientific computing has played in the evolution and development of computing at large is due in part to the unmitigated need for larger and more detailed models and problems. Given the resources, a chemist would gladly add more atoms to their molecular dynamics simulation, an oceanographer would happily use more grid cells to describe the ocean, and an astrophysicist surely has no trouble in imagining include more stellar bodies to their model. The universe may be finite, but it is still very large.

The correctness challenge In addition to demanding large computational resources, any developer of numerical codes is keenly aware of the challenge of ensuring that their work is being performed as intended. Digital arithmetic is approximate, and many notions that are beautiful mathematical constructs in the abstract need careful shepherding into the discrete world to be useful, while many others are entirely unsuitable.

There are enough "moving parts" to a developing scientific code that tremendous patience and discipline must be exercised to ensure correctness throughout: is the mathematical model of the phenomena suitable in the first place? Is it numerically stable? Were the correct parameters chosen? Is the code that implements it correct? Is the hardware reliable?

In some cases, buggy code will still produce the correct answer, but much slower than a correct code would—anathema to the optimizer!

Specialized tools Software developers have long understood the benefit of standardized tools that deliver correct behavior and (hopefully) performance, but software libraries must by nature be specialized. While LAPACK/BLAS is an incredibly useful tool, not all codes (e.g. the subject of this chapter) are suitable for expression in terms of their operators.

Fortunately, compiler technology (perhaps the most generally applicable of software tools) has continued to advance with progressively sophisticated hardware. Increasingly, it is sufficient for a developer to convey how portions of the code should behave with respect to various architectural features, and the low-level details—for example, what vector instructions are used, how threads are marshaled—are handled automatically.

MODERN COMPUTING ENVIRONMENTS

The compiler is an important part of the "computing environment" that surrounds the codes we develop. This environment includes:

Hardware: the micro/macroarchitecture of the processor, plus I/O and communication interfaces and cluster-level considerations

Runtime: the operating system and runtime software that manages the hardware's resources and provides some manner of abstraction to the user.

Development tools: The compiler, debugger, and analysis tools that help the programmer translate their ideas into correct and efficient code.

Each part of the computing environment has a large role in the way code is developed, maintained, and how it performs. New technologies and ideas continue to develop and be adopted in the search for better performance and more expressive tools.

The scientist-programmer's dilemma Scientific codes are often written by domain experts who understand the theory well. These scientist-coders are usually familiar with the continually evolving state of computing environments, but not always intimately so. Development of a given scientific codebase might span a decade (or three!), and the task of both adapting to new methodologies and continuing to support legacy users can be nearly impossible.

In view of these challenges and the task of achieving correct results, the code is sometimes sub-optimal in performance in ways that the developers are aware of, and ways that they are not. The oft-considerable difference in performance between a "straightforward" implementation that is accessible and quick to write, and what can be achieved by an expert over several months is sometimes called the "ninja gap." The magnitude of this performance disparity—and how legible the shinobi's program is—is of keen interest to computer builders, compiler writers, and developers alike; it indicates the wide usability of performance features in processors and the quality of compilers. The "ninja gap" exists for all codes, but as this chapter shows, just a few hours in the dojo can do wonders.

CEA'S HYDRO2D

The subject of this case study is a modest-sized code called Hydro2D, that is developed in CEA—i.e., Commissariat à l'énergie atomique et aux énergies alternatives, a French governmental agency that performs both civilian and military research and development. This code was developed as a "proxy" for an internal astrodynamic code; such proxy codes are intended to expose the essential computational characteristics of their "base" applications while being manageable in size (thousands of lines of code instead of hundreds of thousands, or millions) and (sometimes) protecting IP in the original code as well.

The reference Hydro2D is about 5000 lines of C/C++ that solves "shock hydrodynamics" problems; essentially, high-energy gas motion in two dimensions. In addition to its applicability to astrodynamics, the techniques in the code are very similar to that used in the astronautics community.

The original code is relatively compact, easy to follow, and delivers correct results; unfortunately, its performance is disappointing on multicore and many-core architectures. As we will see, some of performance troubles are due to a desire to ensure clarity and simplicity in the code, while others are due to some performance-oriented features of the code being ignored. A few aspects of the reference code suffer from performance troubles because of misconceptions about how certain features of the runtime and hardware behave.

Chapter organization In the rest of this chapter, we will cover some background on the reference code and the problem it solves, discuss some of the more important features of modern computer environments, and we will explore how this code can be transformed into a highly tuned evolution of that code.

We will quantify the improvements in performance gained with each modification. We focus on single-node performance on modern many-core hardware, and we examine the consequences of "false starts" and optimizations made with erroneous or incomplete models of hardware. We shall see that careful treatment of various elements of the computing environment deliver a **3-10** × improvement over the reference implementation, for several architectures across a variety of problem sizes.

A NUMERICAL METHOD FOR SHOCK HYDRODYNAMICS

Before we dive into the code itself and how it can be optimized, it is useful to understand a little about what sort of problems the code aims to solve and to understand the high-level algorithm being used.

EULER'S EQUATION

Euler's equation (or more precisely, Euler's system of equations) is system of partial differential equations (PDEs) that is a special case of the general Navier-Stokes equations of fluid dynamics wherein the fluid is *inviscid*: viscosity is treated as having a negligible effect of the dynamics. In two dimensions (which we consider in this chapter) it takes the form:

$$\frac{\partial}{\partial t}\begin{bmatrix} \rho \\ \rho u \\ \rho v \\ E \end{bmatrix} + \frac{\partial}{\partial x}\begin{bmatrix} \rho u \\ \rho u^2 + p \\ \rho uv \\ (E + p)u \end{bmatrix} + \frac{\partial}{\partial y}\begin{bmatrix} \rho v \\ \rho uv \\ \rho v^2 + p \\ (E + p)v \end{bmatrix} = 0 \tag{2.1}$$

with

$$E = \frac{p}{\gamma - 1} + \frac{1}{2}\rho(u^2 + v^2) \tag{2.2}$$

Here ρ is the density, u and v are the x- and y-components of velocity, E is the total energy, and p is the pressure. Note that there are only four PDEs (Eq. (2.1)), but the system is not underdetermined; the *equation of state* (Eq. (2.2)) closes the system and expresses the dependent nature of the five variables present in the system. γ is the *adiabatic* constant for the fluid, typically set at 1.4 for air.

Eq. (2.1) might look peculiar because it is in *conservation form*; each equation represents a conserved quantity (namely, mass, momentum, and energy). With the proper discretization, conservation form allows for useful physical properties to be maintained in the solutions found.

The Euler system has several important applications. It is suitable for describing the motion of gases in many situations and easily lends itself to the study of basic shock dynamics. It also results in a much simpler system than full Navier-Stokes while preserving important nonlinear behavior, and mathematically, the elimination of the viscosity term changes the nature of the PDE to be fully *hyperbolic*, which has profound implications on how the solution may be advanced in time.

We should note that the equation of state used here (2.2) is the ideal-gas law. Much more sophisticated equations of state have been developed for specialized applications, but they ultimately have a relatively small impact on the performance of the method (the locality of access is no different than what we have used here).

GODUNOV'S METHOD

The context in which Euler's equations are usually used—in the study of shocks—informs the choice of numerical scheme that should be used in computing solutions. Hydro2D is a *shock-capturing* code, and uses Godunov's method to compute solutions to initial boundary-value problems (IBVP) posed by the user.

Godunov's method was developed in 1959 by the Soviet mathematician Godunov; because the derivatives in Eq. (2.1) are not well-defined in the presence of shocks, it uses the integral form of the PDE: each discrete cell tracks an average value for each of its unknowns. In each timestep, we compute the average *flux* between each adjacent cells that occurs over said timestep; this flux is simply the flow of quantities between cells. The solution is advanced forward in time by updating cells by the total amount of flux that enters and leaves it. See Figure 2.1 for a diagram of a one-dimensional Godunov method.

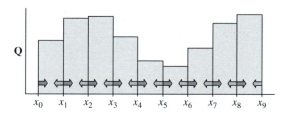

FIGURE 2.1

1D Godunov scheme with (possibly vector-valued) unknown **Q**. The x_i represent the boundaries between cells, and the cell volumes represent the discrete averages stored in each cell. The arrows represent the fluxes exchanged between cells.

Slope limiting Adopting an average-value representation has some useful properties for handling shocks, but it can be limiting at times as well—without modification, it acts as a piecewise-constant scheme and limits spatial accuracy to the first order.

Numerous techniques have been developed to address this and deliver higher-order of accuracy. These techniques must be constructed carefully so as to preserve discontinuities in the solution and to avoid introducing nonphysical dispersion phenomena.

One of these accuracy improvement techniques is known as *flux limiting* and it modifies the way the integration is carried out by considering a small neighborhood of fluxes before advancing the solution. Hydro2D uses an alternate technique known as *slope limiting* that uses a neighborhood of cell values to estimate a slope for the value of each cell at the interfaces where fluxes are computed.

The Riemann problem The core of Godunov's method lies in how fluxes are computed; given two cells sharing an edge, we must determine the average fluxes between them over a timestep. A more general way of posing this is: Given two piecewise-constant states that meet in space, how do they evolve in time subject to the governing equations? This is known as the Riemann problem, and for non-linear systems of equations, its evolution can be quite complicated; new intermediate states can arise between the two and impinge upon the left state, the right state, both, and even each other! These new states may contain sharp, fast-moving shocks and slow, smoothly-varying *rarefaction fans*.

We must solve a distinct Riemann problem for each pair of cells that share an edge—in a $n \times n$ grid, that is $2n(n-1)$ each timestep! The development of specialized and efficient Riemann solvers for computing the solutions to these Riemann problems has long been a subject of interest.

Hydro2D uses localized nonlinear solvers for its Riemann problems; in the case of the 2D Euler equations, the significant intermediate state can be determined through a nonlinear but scalar equation for the pressure between the left and right states. A number of Newton-Raphson iterations are performed on this equation to yield a suitable value for computing the fluxes.

Integration The 2D Euler equations form a *hyperbolic* system of equations and thus are often integrated using explicit techniques. Hydro2D performs temporal integration using the explicit Euler method; this is a simple scheme that works well in the presence of shocks.

One additional consideration with computational ramifications is stability; for any given state of the cells (meaning the **Q** and cell spacing Δx), there is a maximum allowable timestep size Δt that will yield correct, stable results. Because the same Δt must be used everywhere, it must be known prior to integration, and because it depends on the discrete state of the solution, there is a computation and reduction step that must occur before each timestep begins.

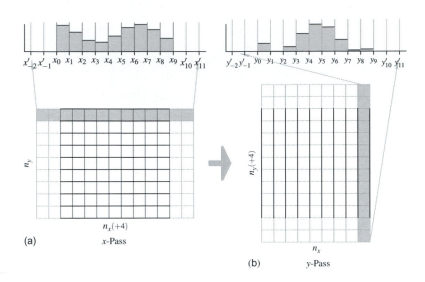

FIGURE 2.2

2D Godunov's scheme with dimensional splitting.

Dimensional splitting The classical formulation of Godunov's method is inherently one-dimensional, and the typical approach for two- and three-dimensional, problems is known as dimensional splitting, which is a special case of the more general approach of operator splitting, wherein the original equation is partitioned by operators into several equations, which are then solved sequentially with the previous result (Figure 2.2). The two spatial terms in Eq. (2.1) are split into separate timesteps; to advance a timestep from t_n to t_{n+1}, the solution is advanced (flux computation plus integration) from t_n using just the $\partial/\partial x$ terms to an intermediate state t_n^*, which is then advanced using just the $\partial/\partial y$ equation to t_{n+1}.

WHERE IT FITS

There are many families of PDEs and numerical techniques for discretization and integration; for a given problem, there may be many ways to achieve a solution, although some will naturally be better-suited—to problems and to architectures—than others.

Godunov's method fits in an interesting place because it is neither a stencil code (although it resembles one) nor is it characterized by a coupled linear system that might be solved with a Krylov subspace method. This means that preconceived notions about these other techniques will likely not apply.

Explicit stencil codes generally have very low arithmetic intensity—essentially, a multiply-add for every eight bytes read (in double precision). This makes them quickly memory bandwidth bound unless blocking/wavefront methods are used. As we shall see, the code required to compute fluxes and integrate a cell in Hydro2D has a greater number of operations to do for each unknown, and if we are careful, can be made compute bound.

Implicitly integrated problems usually produce large sparse matrices that must be solved using iterative techniques. It is the nature of these methods to have large working sets; from a intuitive standpoint, the mathematical "support" of the underlying operator is global. Every unknown is coupled to every other, and this translates into a computational need to use the entire system matrix, right-hand side, and unknowns (at a minimum) during each iteration. As a hyperbolic system, the fundamental operations in Hydro2D are almost all inherently local, which has profound implications on the working set size.

FEATURES OF MODERN ARCHITECTURES

To achieve performance on non-trivial codes, it is necessary to have a mental picture of how it should run in the computing environment. As we hope to show, this does not mean that each programmer must be an architect and compiler expert—a working model of the important, performance-critical aspects of the system should suffice.

PERFORMANCE-ORIENTED ARCHITECTURE

Performance and efficiency have always been a primary focus of the makers of computer hardware, and a great deal of the sophistication in modern computing architectures exists to address performance directly.

Memory subsystem Computer memory has been organized in a hierarchical fashion for decades now, with a stepped progression of containers that progressively trade diminished capacity for increased bandwidth and latency. In addition to main memory, nearly every contemporary computer has at least two levels of cache, with three becoming more common. The way the memory subsystem behaves within multicore and multisocket systems can also be significant.

The steadily widening gap between main memory bandwidth and compute capability is partially responsible for the deepening of the memory hierarchy, and the very real role the working set and cache capacity plays in achieving performance cannot be neglected.

Virtual memory is also very common on contemporary systems, which now supports a variety of page sizes. Hardware support for paging has reached the point where most codes need not worry about the capacity of the translation lookaside buffer (TLB), but there are situations where attention must be paid.

Thread-level parallelism For over a decade, nearly every mainstream processor has seen increasing numbers of cores, and multi-socket configurations made shared-memory parallelism available in workstations and servers before that.

By directly increasing the number of independent control paths and functional units, multicore and multisocket systems offer a relatively familiar mechanism for increasing performance. The introduction of hardware supporting simultaneous multithreading has sometimes been a source of confusion—these "hardware threads" supported by a single core are intended make it easier for code to use all of the resources on a core, but their use does not typically increase the facilities available on a core.

Data-level parallelism While it shares some similarities with the vector processors popular in 1980s, modern single instruction, multiple data (SIMD) instruction sets generally are built atop full-width functional units and benefit from many of the superscalar execution features present in hardware. SIMD generally performs best on "packed" input data, and by nature penalizes control divergences.

Instruction-level parallelism Contemporary hardware is highly superscalar, with many processors featuring out-of-order execution, multiple execution ports, and sophisticated prefetching, speculation, and branch prediction hardware. This sort of parallelism is often invisible to the programmer, although its absence (as measured by sustained instructions per cycle) carries a penalty and may indicate resource stalls.

PROGRAMMING TOOLS AND RUNTIMES

Fortunately for programmers, the tools we use—compilers, debuggers, and sampling profilers—have been increasing in power as hardware has grown in sophistication. OpenMP has recently matured to version 4.0 and is the tool of choice for thread programming.

We do not use any sophisticated OpenMP techniques in this chapter; we simply let the OpenMP runtime manage the number of threads and the details of their affinities. For scaling experiments, it is useful to set the environment variable `OMP_NUM_THREADS` to control the number of threads and `KMP_AFFINITY` scatter or compact to control how SMT (simultaneous multi-threading) is handled. Note that `KMP_AFFINITY` works with the Intel compiler; use `GOMP_CPU_AFFINITY` for gcc.

For vectorization, there are multiple approaches that are viable. The easiest is the autovectorization support that is present in many modern compilers; this aims to produce efficient SIMD code based on a handful of directives in the code. Writing code in such a way that the autovectorizer does the transformation and produces efficient code is something of an art, but it is the most satisfying approach.

Compiler intrinsics are the most reliable way to express vectorization in code; these are built-in data types and functions that directly translate to SIMD registers and instructions. However, They are vendor-specific and can be somewhat arcane.

A useful alternative to intrinsics, and what we use more than anything else in this chapter, are C++ classes that wrap built-in intrinsics. These classes are easy to write yourself or to find—the Intel compiler comes with a set of them—and they provide a convenient layer of abstraction to provide some flexibility across SIMD widths. It is even possible to overload the standard arithmetic operators for them, which makes code using them appear nearly identical to code using standard scalar C++ types.

OUR COMPUTING ENVIRONMENTS

Intel® Xeon® Processor E5-2680 A late-generation ×86-based multicore server architecture featuring super-scalar, out-of-order cores that support 2-way hyperthreading. In addition to scalar units, it has a 256 bit-wide SIMD unit that executes the AVX instruction set. Separate multiply and add ports allow for the execution of one multiply and one addition instruction (each 4-wide, double precision) in a single cycle. This chapter considers this in a 2-socket, 16-core configuration.

Intel® Xeon Phi™ Coprocessor This processor features many in-order cores on a single die; each core has 4-way multithreading support to help hide memory and multi-cycle instruction latency. The cores on the coprocessor are in-order, issue no more than one vector instruction per cycle, and run at a lower frequency than the processor. The cores have a special 512-bit wide vector instruction set with fused multiply-add (FMA) support, enabling them to execute an 8-wide

	Intel Xeon Processor E5-2680	Intel Xeon Phi coprocessor
Sockets×Cores×SMT	$2 \times 8 \times 2$	$1 \times 60 \times 4$
Clock (GHz)	2.7	1.09
Per-core sust. inst./cycle	2	2
Single precision GFLOP/s	691	2127
Double precision GFLOP/s	346	1063
L1 / L2 / L3 Cache (KB)	32 / 256 / 20,480	32 / 512 / -
DRAM	128 GB	4 GB GDDR
Bandwidth from STREAM	76 GB/s	150 GB/s

FIGURE 2.3

System configuration.

multiply-add operation in double precision every cycle per core. The specific variant of the coprocessor that we used is a preproduction model.

The coprocessor is physically mounted on a PCIe card with its own GDDR memory and Linux operating system. In this chapter, we run our experiments on the coprocessor "natively"—binaries and input are shared with the card and completely run there.

More can be found in Figure 2.3. The L1/L2 cache sizes for both the processor and the coprocessor are per core, while L3 cache size for the processor is per chip and shared among all cores on a chip.

PATHS TO PERFORMANCE

This section describes how we apply models of performance-centered features in our computing environments to speed up Hydro2D. We start with a brief tour of the reference code.

RUNNING HYDRO2D

Hydro2D is an implementation of Godunov's scheme for the 2D Euler equations; given a discrete initial boundary-value problem, it advances the solution from $t_{initial} = 0$ to some specified t_{final} through a series of timesteps.

The code comes with a number of parameter files that are read to describe the problem being solved and that specify how the program should behave during execution (about output, blocking, etc).

The number of threads is determined according to the OpenMP runtime; the following is an example of running the code with two threads using the default affinity (Figure 2.4).

The output of the command serves to inform the user of the parameters chosen and the solver's progress.

The .nml file does not contain a full discrete problem to solve; instead, the Hydro2D code has a number of procedurally generated test problems the user can specify, and the user need only specify dimensions and the number of the test problem (Figure 2.5).

HYDRO2D'S STRUCTURE

The Hydro2D reference code is nearly 5000 lines across 19 header/C file pairs, but the core computational routines are much more compact.

```
[user@localhost $] OMP_NUM_THREADS=2 ./hydro -i input_problem.nml
+-------------------+
|nx=250             |
|ny=125             |
|nxystep=125          |
|tend=200.000       |
|nstepmax=1000000   |
|noutput=0          |
|dtoutput=2.000     |
+-------------------+
Lower corner test case : 2 2
Hydro starts.
Hydro:     OpenMP mode ON
Hydro: OpenMP 2 max threads
Hydro: OpenMP 1 num threads
Hydro: OpenMP 4 num procs
Hydro: standard build
HydroC: Simple decomposition
HydroC: nx=1 ny=1
--> step=    1,   1.33631e-03,  1.33631e-03   {1034.06 Mflops 20307925 Ops} (0.020s)
--> step=    2,   2.67261e-03,  1.33631e-03   {1048.12 Mflops 19401667 Ops} (0.019s)
--> step=    3,   5.17799e-03,  2.50538e-03   {1241.47 Mflops 20307925 Ops} (0.016s)
--> step=    4,   7.68338e-03,  2.50538e-03   {1150.96 Mflops 19401667 Ops} (0.017s)
...
```

FIGURE 2.4

An example of running the reference Hydro2D code.

```
This namelist contains various input parameters for HYDRO runs

&RUN
tend=50
#noutput=10
nstepmax=1133
dtoutput=2.
/

&MESH
nx=256
ny=256
nxystep=125
prt=0
dx=0.05
boundary_left=1
boundary_right=1
boundary_down=1
boundary_up=1
testcase=1
/

&HYDRO
courant_factor=0.8
niter_riemann=10
/
```

FIGURE 2.5

An example input file for Hydro2D.

Computation scheme

The following is performed each time step to advance the solution to the next time level:

Update According to dimensional splitting, updates are done in alternating dimensions in a $x \rightarrow y / y \rightarrow x$ alternating pattern; each update consists of a **flux computation** where Riemann problems are constructed and solved at each cell interface normal to the update axis. All Riemann problems in an update are independent. When a flux for a cell has been computed, **integration** in time can proceed.

Timestep computation For integration to be stable, the *Courant number* of the solution must be computed based on the state in each cell and reduced. This is a reduction operation.

Data structures

Hydro2D has very simple data structures; the solution state is stored in a regular grid with a two-cell "halo" layer to simplify some boundary computations. The grid is ordered such that each of the $[\rho, \rho u, \rho v, E]^T$ variables is stored in its own "plane." We have assumed y-major ordering for spatial dimensions; due to the symmetry of the problem, x-major would be equally suitable.

Aside from the global problem state, the reference version of Hydro2D has a secondary data structure that is used for intermediate value storage.

The slab The Hydro2D reference code performs work in a separate, many-layered grid with smaller dimensions than the global state grid. This is called the *slab* and it allows out-of-place computation and serves as a work-sharing construct and blocking structure.

In each update step, a portion of the solution grid is copied to the slab. Then each part of the update procedure is done in the slab, which has separate storage for each intermediate value for each interface/cell in the subdomain. When the integration is complete, the results are written back to the solution grid and another subregion is copied to the slab, an so on, until the whole solution grid has been updated. See Figure 2.6 for a diagram of this procedure.

It is worth noting that the slab used in the reference code is used for both the x- and y-dimensional updates and that updates are always done in complete x "rows" and y "columns" to handle boundaries properly without further copies. Data copied to/from the slab from/to the global grid is transposed for the y-pass, and therefore the slab always must be wide enough to accommodate the larger of the x- and y-dimensions of the grid (the other dimension of the slab is a user-selectable parameter).

Key functions There are 11 functions responsible for the primary computation in the reference; several of them are trivial in implementation, and each is found it its own source file. A brief summary follows:

`compute_deltat()`: Computes largest eigenvalue among the local Riemann problems to compute the largest stable timestep size (`compute_deltat.c:159`).

`hydro_godunov()`: the toplevel routine for updates; it calls nearly all of the following functions to populate the slab, compute updates, and write them back. A parameter controls which dimensional pass is performed (`hydro_godunov.c:62`).

`gatherConservativeVars()`: transfers the stored solution from a subregion of the solution grid to the slab's conservative variable storage (`conservar.c:48`).

`constoprim()`: (partially) converts the conservative variables in the slab to the *primitive* form needed for flux computation (`constoprim.c:48`).

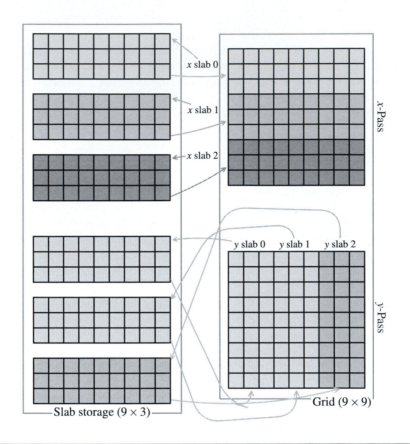

FIGURE 2.6

Slab-based Godunov scheme depicting the order of data movement and computation on the slab. Note that repetition in each column depicts a temporal sequence and not replication—there is one slab and one grid used in the computation.

equation_of_state(): uses the results of constoprim() plus the E term from the conservative variables to fill in the final primitive variable p; all done in dedicated storage in the slab (equation_of_state.c:48).

slope(): examines adjacent cells values (in primitive form) to compute (and limit) the slope to be used for flux computation. This code uses van Leer's MC limiter (slope.c:52).

trace(): applies the computed slope to the endpoints of each cell (trace.c:51).

qleftright(): copies the results of trace() to separate buffers in preparation for riemann() (qleftright.c:48).

riemann(): is the core of the flux computation; a scalar nonlinear system for intermediate pressure is formed and solved using Newton-Raphson. The remaining terms are derived from the computed pressure (riemann.c:80).

cmpflx(): differences the intermediate state computed in riemann() with the surrounding states and converted to conservative fluxes (cmpflx.c:51).

`updateConservativeVars()`: integrates cells with the neighboring fluxes and copies them back to the global solution grid (`conservar.c:122`).

The slab routines—`gatherConservativeVars()` through `updateConservative-Vars()`—operate successively in a "Bulk Synchronous Parallel" fashion. These routines have been organized (with input/output storage for each function) to have no data dependencies within them and so each exposes thread-level and data-level parallelism (through OpenMP and autovectorization). This is where the bulk of the computation occurs, and `hydro_godunov()` simply serves as a framework for these calls. Figure 2.7 shows the structure and dataflow for a 1D slice of this computation.

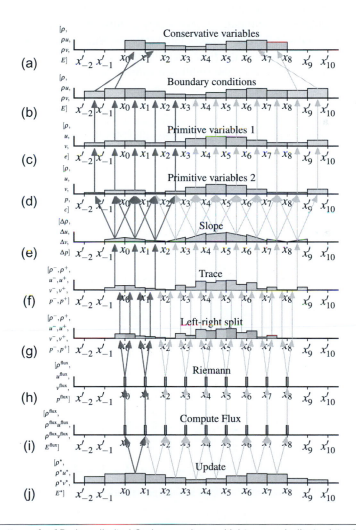

FIGURE 2.7

Steps and access patterns for 1D slope-limited Godunov scheme. Light arrows indicate data dependencies for cells across steps, and the heavy series of arrows indicate the dependencies for the first cells (between x_0 and x_1.)

`compute_deltat()` similarly uses the slab to compute a series of intermediate states (including `equation_of_state()`) that ultimately yield the maximum eigenvalues, which are reduced. These slab steps expose similar thread- and data-level parallelism as above.

Measuring performance

Of course, the objective of this chapter is to improve the performance of the Hydro2D code and not to perform novel scientific experiments. We are primarily interested in measuring performance in a manner that is representative of the way the code would be used in an experimental setting.

Fortunately, this is fairly simple: Hydro2D's performance is largely independent of the specific initial and boundary conditions specified, so we are free to choose any test problem. The Newton-Raphson iterations performed in the Riemann solver have control flow that may increase runtime for a flux computation depending on the input, but this is only significant for pathological cases.

To capture the sensitivity of the code to problem sizes, we will explore a variety of problem sizes and generally normalize our results to the time taken to process a single cell in a single timestep. The time covered in each step is dictated by the stability condition, which is a product of the solution state and the grid spacing. This means that two different initial conditions may take a differing number of steps to reach a given amount of time simulated.

Figure 2.8 shows the performance of the reference code in cell-steps/second. The coprocessor is less than 2 × the performance of the processor, and parallel efficiency is quite low.

OPTIMIZATIONS

The performance of the reference code is unsatisfactory despite having support for parallelism. As we shall show, this is partially due to inefficiencies in some of the high-level, conceptual constructs in the code, and partially due to inefficient translation into code. Just as adding an `#pragma omp parallel for` to a loop does not guarantee parallel efficiency, nor does `#pragma vector` necessarily mean productive vectorization.

We will describe how the reference falls short and how it may be improved upon.

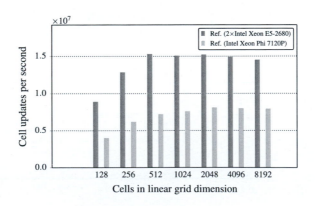

FIGURE 2.8

Performance of the reference Hydro2D code on all cores of the processor and the coprocessor in cell-steps/second.

General notes on the optimized code The optimized code we present here makes some structural and formatting departures from the original code. These changes do not affect the performance directly and serve only to improve clarity and maintainability:

- The file structure has been consolidated; the core routines are in `pcl-hydro-core.cpp` and `pcl-hydro-vcore.cpp` and utility routines have been moved to `pcl-hydro-util.cpp` and `pcl-hydro-params.cpp`. The top-level driver is in `run-tile.cpp`.
- Some identifiers have been renamed to improve their clarity (i.e., `constoprim()` has been renamed `conservative_to_primitive()`). `equation_of_state()` has been split into `equation_of_state()` and `speed_of_sound())` in recognition their distinct uses.
- `REAL_T` has been used as a drop-in replacement for `single` or `double` types.
- The reference Hydro2D used the `idim` parameter in most functions to make the control adjustments to the data access (in particular, ρu and ρv must be treated differently based on the current dimensional pass). In the optimized code, most such branches are superseded by directly passing each unknown's array (`rho`, `rhou`, `rhov`, `E`) to the callee in the correct order rather than the opaque multidimensional array `u`.
- The placeholder functions `my_sqrt()` and `rcp()` have replaced `sqrt()` and `1/<x>` to provide flexibility in choosing how those operations are carried out.
- Some constants like `Hgamma` from the original code have been replaced by `GAMMA`.
- Where possible, stack-allocated variables and function parameters are qualified with `const`.

MEMORY USAGE

The slab approach used in the reference code addresses GPU-like memory models and does not take full advantage of the memory hierarchies found in many modern systems.

The overhead of copying to and from the slab cannot be overlapped with other computation and has low arithmetic intensity. Worse still, the slab computation uses many intermediate variables, which increases occupancy dramatically. Some of this can be mitigated through reuse of intermediate storage, but the small region of dependence for each update suggests that a different approach be taken.

Consolidating `compute_deltat()` Performing a separate step for the stable timestep determination carries a potential penalty; additional synchronization is needed to safely enter and end the pass through the grid, and it requires that the entire grid be re-read and the speeds reduced; this can have a significant penalty.

In fact, it is evident that the timestep occurs at the very beginning of the computation and then only after x passes in odd-numbered steps. For all invocations after the first, the values that would be read by the `compute_deltat()` function are the same as those integrated in the last part of the x-pass in odd-numbered steps, and it should be possible to compute the maximum propagation speed that determines the stable timestep at each cell directly after integrating it.

The reduction that is done to find the maximum such speed across all cells can be made part of the work-sharing that is always done during the update step. Each thread privately computes and locally reduces the maximum speeds encountered during the pass, and the timestepping loop can coordinate a global reduction over these thread-specific values. It is possible to perform this reduction in a tree fashion, if communication costs begin to dominate.

By combining the `compute_deltat()` with the integration step, the overhead of a separate pass through the grid and extra synchronization is eliminated.

Rolling updates The vertical arrows in Figure 2.7 show the dependencies across steps of the flux computation and integration; for a one-dimensional row (or column) of the computational grid, we can see that there is reuse but also a "window" of dependency.

It is possible to promote complete reuse of intermediate computations and minimize intermediate storage by performing a "rolling" update along each strip of the grid:

- First, the whole-slab variants of the update step have been "shrunken"—namely, `constoprim()`/`conservative_to_primitive()`, `slope()`, `trace()`, `riemann()`, `cmpflx()`, and `updateConservativeVars()`/`update()`; `qleftright()` did no real work other than copy values, and has been eliminated. They now operate on single cells at a time: they take as parameters the minimum set of inputs for the subproblem and return their vector-valued results through output parameters.
- To begin a strip update, a *priming* stage applies boundary conditions (via `set_boundaries()`), loads the appropriate conservative variables, and computes all quantities necessary to determine the flux at the left boundary (i.e., the flux at x_0 in Figure 2.7i)—any intermediate values that are needed for a later cell update are kept in circular buffers, and all others are discarded. See `strip_prime()` (Figure 2.10) for the implementation of this code.
- Then, to perform the updates for all cells in the strip, a *stable* stage loads the circular buffers and the next conservative variable in the strip, then computes all intermediate values needed for the next flux. The flux from the previous step and the newly-computed one are combined in stage Figure 2.7j to update the current cell, and intermediate values that are needed for future stable steps placed into the circular buffers. See `strip_stable()` (Figure 2.11) for a figure of this code.

As is evident from Figure 2.7, the widest point of dependency for a single flux at x_i in step Figure 2.7i is the second round of primitive variable computation in step Figure 2.7d—four values are ultimately combined to produce the output. Thus, none of the circular buffers contain more than four values, keeping intermediate storage costs low.

```
1  struct strip_work
2  {
3      REAL_T flux        [4][2]; // flux at i-1/2, i+1/2
4      REAL_T left_flux   [4][2]; // left_flux at i, i+1
5      REAL_T prim        [5][3]; // prim for i, i+1, i+2
6  };
```

FIGURE 2.9

Rolling update data structure for `strip_prime()` and `strip_stable()`.

THREAD-LEVEL PARALLELISM

In the reference code, thread-level parallelism is only exposed across the *y*-dimension (or "height") of the slab (recall Figure 2.6), which effectively limits the amount of parallelism.

```
 1 void strip_prime(strip_work   *restrict sw,
 2                  const REAL_T *restrict rho,
 3                  const REAL_T *restrict rhou,
 4                  const REAL_T *restrict rhov,
 5                  const REAL_T *restrict E,
 6                  const hydro  *restrict h,
 7                  const int             stride,
 8                  const REAL_T          dtdx)
 9 {
10     REAL_T pre_prim[5][4]; // i-2, i-1, i, i+1
11     for(int i = 0; i < 4; ++i)
12     {
13         const int src_offs = (- 2 + i)*stride;
14         REAL_T E_internal;
15         conservative_to_primitive(pre_prim[0] +i, pre_prim[4] +i, pre_prim[1] +i,
16             pre_prim[2] +i, &E_internal,
                                      rho[src_offs],                 rhou[src_offs],
                                      rhov[src_offs], E[src_offs]);
17         pre_prim[3][i] = equation_of_state(pre_prim[0][i], E_internal);
18     }
19
20     REAL_T pre_dvar[4][2]; // i-1, i
21     if(h->iorder != 1)
22         for(int i = 0; i < 2; ++i)
23             for(int v = 0; v < 4; ++ v)
24                 pre_dvar[v][i] = slope(pre_prim[v][0+i], pre_prim[v][1+i],
                        pre_prim[v][2+i], h->slope_type, h->inv_slope_type);
25
26     REAL_T pre_left_flux [4][2]; // i-1, i
27     REAL_T pre_right_flux[4][2]; // i-1, i
28     for(int i = 0; i < 2; ++i)
29     {
30         const REAL_T prim_c = speed_of_sound(pre_prim[4][i + 1], pre_prim[3][i+1])
              ;
31         trace(pre_left_flux [0] + i,                 pre_left_flux [1] + i,
                  pre_left_flux [2] + i, pre_left_flux [3] + i,
32             pre_right_flux[0] + i,                   pre_right_flux[1] + i,
                  pre_right_flux[2] + i, pre_right_flux[3] + i,
33             pre_prim[0]      [i+1], pre_prim[4][i+1], pre_prim[1]      [i+1],
                  pre_prim[2]      [i+1], pre_prim[3]      [i+1],
34             pre_dvar[0]      [i],                    pre_dvar[1]      [i],
                  pre_dvar[2]      [i], pre_dvar[3]      [i],
35             prim_c, rcp(prim_c),
36             dtdx);
37     }
38
39     REAL_T gdnv_rho, gdnv_u, gdnv_v, gdnv_p;
40     riemann(&gdnv_rho,     &gdnv_u,         &gdnv_v,            &gdnv_p,
41         pre_left_flux [0][0], pre_left_flux [1][0], pre_left_flux [2][0],
                  pre_left_flux [3][0],
42         pre_right_flux[0][1], pre_right_flux[1][1], pre_right_flux[2][1],
                  pre_right_flux[3][1]);
43
44     cmpflx(sw->flux[0] + 0, sw->flux[1] + 0, sw->flux[2] + 0, sw->flux[3] + 0,
45         gdnv_rho,        gdnv_u,          gdnv_v,          gdnv_p);
46
47     for(int v = 0; v < 4; ++ v)
48         sw->left_flux[v][0] = pre_left_flux[v][1];
49
50     for(int v = 0; v < 5; ++ v)
51     {
52         sw->prim[v][0] = pre_prim[v][2];
53         sw->prim[v][1] = pre_prim[v][3];
54     }
55 }
```

FIGURE 2.10

Rolling update priming function; see Figure 2.9 for a description of `strip_work()`.

```
 1  REAL_T strip_stable(const hydro *restrict h,
 2                       REAL_T      *restrict rho,
 3                       REAL_T      *restrict rhou,
 4                       REAL_T      *restrict rhov,
 5                       REAL_T      *restrict E,
 6                       strip_work  *restrict sw,
 7                       const int             i,
 8                       const int             stride,
 9                       const REAL_T          dtdx,
10                       const bool            do_courant)
11  {
12      const int src_offs = (i + 2)*stride;
13
14      REAL_T E_internal;
15      conservative_to_primitive(sw->prim[0] + 2, sw->prim[4] + 2, sw->prim[1] + 2,
            sw->prim[2] + 2, &E_internal,
16                               rho[src_offs],                     rhou[src_offs],
                                rhov[src_offs], E[src_offs]);
17      sw->prim[3][2] = equation_of_state(sw->prim[0][2], E_internal);
18
19      REAL_T dvar[4];      // slope for i+1
20      if(h->iorder != 1)
21          for(int v = 0; v < 4; ++ v)
22              dvar[v] = slope(sw->prim[v][0], sw->prim[v][1], sw->prim[v][2], h->
                    slope_type, h->inv_slope_type);
23
24      REAL_T right_flux[4];
25      const REAL_T prim_c = speed_of_sound(sw->prim[4][1], sw->prim[3][1]);
26      trace(sw->left_flux [0] + 1,              sw->left_flux [1] + 1, sw->
            left_flux [2] + 1, sw->left_flux [3] + 1,
27          right_flux + 0,                    right_flux + 1,         right_flux
                + 2,             right_flux + 3,
28          sw->prim[0]        [1], sw->prim[4][1], sw->prim[1]        [1], sw->prim
                [2]      [1], sw->prim[3]        [1],
29          dvar[0],                                dvar[1],            dvar[2],
                                dvar[3],
30          prim_c, rcp(prim_c),
31          dtdx);
32
33      REAL_T gdnv_rho, gdnv_u, gdnv_v, gdnv_p;
34      riemann(&gdnv_rho,                &gdnv_u,                &gdnv_v,                &
            gdnv_p,
35          sw->left_flux [0][0], sw->left_flux [1][0], sw->left_flux [2][0], sw->
                left_flux [3][0],
36          right_flux[0],           right_flux[1],         right_flux[2],
                right_flux[3]);
37
38      cmpflx(sw->flux[0] + 1, sw->flux[1] + 1, sw->flux[2] + 1, sw->flux[3] + 1,
39          gdnv_rho,           gdnv_u,           gdnv_v,           gdnv_p);
40
41      const REAL_T new_rho  = update(rho [i*stride], sw->flux[0][0], sw->flux[0][1],
            dtdx);
42      const REAL_T new_rhou = update(rhou[i*stride], sw->flux[1][0], sw->flux[1][1],
            dtdx);
43      const REAL_T new_rhov = update(rhov[i*stride], sw->flux[2][0], sw->flux[2][1],
            dtdx);
44      const REAL_T new_E    = update(E   [i*stride], sw->flux[3][0], sw->flux[3][1],
            dtdx);
45
46      REAL_T courantv = (REAL_T) 0.0;
47      if(do_courant)
```

FIGURE 2.11

Rolling update stable-state function; see Figure 2.9 for a description of `strip_work()`.

```
48    {
49          REAL_T prim_rho, prim_inv_rho, prim_u, prim_v, E_internal;
50          conservative_to_primitive(&prim_rho, &prim_inv_rho, &prim_u, &prim_v, &
                E_internal,
51                                    new_rho,                new_rhou, new_rhov,
                                          new_E);
52          const REAL_T prim_p = equation_of_state(prim_rho,     E_internal);
53          const REAL_T prim_c = speed_of_sound   (prim_inv_rho, prim_p);
54          courant(&courantv, prim_u, prim_v, prim_c);
55    }
56
57    rho [i*stride] = new_rho;
58    rhou[i*stride] = new_rhou;
59    rhov[i*stride] = new_rhov;
60    E   [i*stride] = new_E;
61
62    for(int v = 0; v < 4; ++ v)
63    {
64          sw->flux      [v][0] = sw->flux      [v][1];
65          sw->left_flux[v][0] = sw->left_flux[v][1];
66    }
67    for(int v = 0; v < 5; ++ v)
68    {
69          sw->prim[v][0] = sw->prim[v][1];
70          sw->prim[v][1] = sw->prim[v][2];
71    }
72
73    return courantv;
74 }
```

Figure 2.11—Cont'd

The storage, communication, and load-balancing penalties incurred by the slab scheme suggest that an alternative should be found. We have transformed the reference code to use a domain-decomposition approach we refer to as "tiling." See Figure 2.12 for a visual depiction.

The simulation grid is diced into number of rectangular tiles through a series of cuts along the x- and y-dimensions; the tiles are then assigned to threads. This scheme does not necessarily require a one-to-one mapping of threads to tiles, but our current implementation only supports the one-to-one case. Each tile has an independently-allocated set of solution variables for its subdomain, as well as dimensions, strides, and other bookkeeping information (see Figure 2.13).

Halo regions Each tile maintains four (one for each cardinal direction in two dimensions) halo regions of width two that are used to effect communication between tiles and apply boundary conditions (to tiles sharing an exterior edge with the original grid). These are the {x,y}_{y,var}stride and {x,y}_edges fields in the tile structure.

Each tile behaves as its own grid (with smaller dimensions); the updates are applied in the same order and each tile computes their x- and y-passes independently. After a pass is completed, it is necessary for each tile to update some of its neighbor cells with the most recent integration data via the functions send_{low,high}_{x,y}_edge(). Before beginning an x-pass, the x halos must be exchanged, and before each y-pass, y halos are exchanged. The timestep calculation is done locally as part of x-passes in odd-numbered steps and the reduction is carried about among all tiles (Figures 2.14, 2.15 and 2.16).

Reducing communication To minimize communication overhead and the issue of false sharing between tiles, we allocate each halo region such that it shares no cache lines with the tile itself or any other halos; then, during each communication phase, each tile copies its own edge regions (of width two) to the appropriate neighbors.

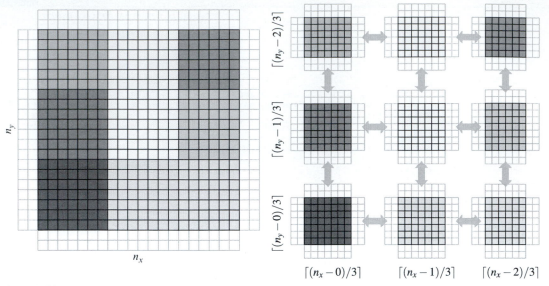

FIGURE 2.12

Tiling scheme: the domain is partitioned into a grid of subdomains. Each subdomain behaves exactly as the original except that the halo (or ghost) regions that form the interior of the decomposition are populated with the most recent updates from the neighboring tile in that direction.

```
1  struct hydro_decomp
2  {
3      struct tile
4      {
5          int    position[2];
6          tile *neighbors[4]; // w, e, s, n
7
8          int offset[2];
9          int n[2];
10
11         int ystride;
12         int varstride;
13
14         int     x_e_ystride;
15         int     x_e_varstride;
16         REAL_T *x_edges[2];
17         int     y_e_ystride;
18         int     y_e_varstride;
19         REAL_T *y_edges[2];
20
21         REAL_T *q;
22         REAL_T *rho;
23         REAL_T *rhou;
24         REAL_T *rhov;
25         REAL_T *E;
26     };
27
28     int    decomp[2];
29     int    ntiles;
30     tile *tiles;
31 };
```

FIGURE 2.13

Data structures for tiled Hydro computation.

```
1  REAL_T x_step(hydro_decomp *hd, const hydro *restrict h, const REAL_T dtdx, int
       tid, bool do_courant)
2  {
3      return tile_x_step(hd->tiles + tid, dtdx, h, 0, hd->tiles[tid].n[1],
           do_courant);
4  }
5
6  REAL_T tile_x_step(tile *restrict tl, const REAL_T dtdx, const hydro *restrict h,
       int jstart, int jend, bool do_courant)
7  {
8      static const REAL_T x_signs[4] = {1.0, -1.0, 1.0, 1.0};
9
10     REAL_T courantv      = 0.0;
11     for(int j = jstart; j < jend; ++j)
12     {
13         const int   ob = (j + 2) * tl->ystride + 0;
14         if(tl->neighbors[0])
15         {
16             for(int v = 0; v < 4; ++v)
17             {
18                 tl->q[v*tl->varstride + ob + 0] = tl->x_edges[0][v*tl->
                       x_e_varstride + j * tl->x_e_ystride + 0];
19                 tl->q[v*tl->varstride + ob + 1] = tl->x_edges[0][v*tl->
                       x_e_varstride + j * tl->x_e_ystride + 1];
20             }
21         }
22         else
23             set_boundaries(tl->q + ob,                x_signs, 2,  1, 4, tl->
                   varstride);
24
25         if(tl->neighbors[1])
26         {
27             for(int v = 0; v < 4; ++v)
28             {
29                 tl->q[v*tl->varstride + ob + tl->n[0] + 2 + 0] = tl->x_edges[1][v*
                       tl->x_e_varstride + j * tl->x_e_ystride + 0];
30                 tl->q[v*tl->varstride + ob + tl->n[0] + 2 + 1] = tl->x_edges[1][v*
                       tl->x_e_varstride + j * tl->x_e_ystride + 1];
31             }
32         }
33         else
34             set_boundaries(tl->q + ob + tl->n[0] + 3, x_signs, 2, -1, 4, tl->
                   varstride);
35
36         const int   o  = ob + 2;
37         strip_work sw;
38         strip_prime(&sw, tl->rho + o, tl->rhou + o, tl->rhov + o, tl->E + o, h,
                       1, dtdx);
39
40         for(int i = 0; i + 1 <= tl->n[0]; ++i)
41         {
42             const REAL_T cv = strip_stable(h,  tl->rho + o, tl->rhou + o, tl->rhov
                       + o, tl->E + o, &sw, i, 1, (REAL_T) dtdx, do_courant);
43             courantv        = std::max(courantv, cv);
44         }
45     }
46
47     return courantv;
48 }
```

FIGURE 2.14

x_step() and tile_x_step(); code for performing the *x*-pass for a given tile. Also contains code reducing/returning maximum encountered eigenvalue for timestep computation.

```
1  void    y_step(hydro_decomp *hd, const hydro *restrict h, const REAL_T dtdx, int
       tid)
2  {
3      tile_y_step(hd->tiles + tid, dtdx, h, 0, hd->tiles[tid].n[0]);
4  }
5
6  void tile_y_step(tile *restrict tl, const REAL_T dtdx, const hydro *restrict h,
       int istart, int iend)
7  {
8      static const REAL_T y_signs[4] = {1.0, 1.0, -1.0, 1.0};
9
10     for(int i = istart; i + 1 <= iend; ++i)
11     {
12         const int    ob = i + 2;
13         if(tl->neighbors[2])
14         {
15             for(int v = 0; v < 4; ++v)
16             {
17                 tl->q[v*tl->varstride +                ob ] = tl->y_edges[0][v*tl
                       ->y_e_varstride                + i];
18                 tl->q[v*tl->varstride + 1*tl->ystride + ob] = tl->y_edges[0][v*tl
                       ->y_e_varstride + 1*tl->y_e_ystride + i];
19             }
20         }
21         else
22             set_boundaries(tl->q + ob,                          y_signs, 2,  tl
                   ->ystride, 4, tl->varstride);
23
24         if(tl->neighbors[3])
25         {
26             for(int v = 0; v < 4; ++v)
27             {
28                 tl->q[v*tl->varstride + (2 + tl->n[1])*tl->ystride + ob] = tl->
                       y_edges[1][v*tl->y_e_varstride                + i];
29                 tl->q[v*tl->varstride + (3 + tl->n[1])*tl->ystride + ob] = tl->
                       y_edges[1][v*tl->y_e_varstride + 1*tl->y_e_ystride + i];
30             }
31         }
32         else
33             set_boundaries(tl->q + ob + (tl->n[1] + 3)*tl->ystride, y_signs, 2, -
                   tl->ystride, 4, tl->varstride);
34
35         const int    o = ob + 2 * tl->ystride;
36         strip_work    sw;
37         strip_prime(&sw, tl->rho + o, tl->rhov + o, tl->rhou + o, tl->E + o, h,
                   tl->ystride, dtdx);
38         for(int j = 0; j < tl->n[1]; ++j)
39             strip_stable(h,  tl->rho + o, tl->rhov + o, tl->rhou + o, tl->E + o, &
                   sw, j, tl->ystride, dtdx, false);
40     }
41 }
```

FIGURE 2.15

`y_step()` and `tile_y_step()`; code for performing the *y*-pass for a tile.

Threads must explicitly communicate to coordinate the halo region exchanges and compute the stable timestep; it is possible to avoid global synchronization between each pass by having threads working on a tile perform only point-to-point synchronization with those threads working on neighboring tiles. Even the stable timestep computation's global reduction can be implemented using a communication-avoiding tree reduction scheme.

```
1      hydro H;
2      load_hydro_params(&H, input_file, quiet);
3      const int nthreads = omp_get_max_threads();
4
5      init_hydro(&H);
6      hydro_decomp HD;
7      init_hydro_decomp(&HD, &H, nthreads, quiet);
8
9      REAL_T dt      = compute_timestep(&H) / (REAL_T) 2.0;
10     REAL_T dt_dx = dt/H.dx;
11     set_scheme(H.scheme, dt_dx);
12     // align and pad shared courantv array to avoid false sharing
13     REAL_T    *courantv     = (REAL_T*) _mm_malloc(64 * nthreads, 64);
14     const int   cache_stride = 64/sizeof(REAL_T);
15
16 #pragma omp parallel
17     {
18         const int tid = omp_get_thread_num();
19         barrier.init(tid);
20         send_low_x_edge (HD.tiles + tid);
21         send_high_x_edge(HD.tiles + tid);
22         send_low_y_edge (HD.tiles + tid);
23         send_high_y_edge(HD.tiles + tid);
24         barrier.wait(tid);
25         while(H.step < H.nstepmax && H.t < H.tend)
26         {
27             barrier.wait(tid);
28             if(tid == 0)
29                 H.t += dt;
30
31             if(H.step % 2 == 0)
32             {
33                 send_low_x_edge (HD.tiles + tid);
34                 send_high_x_edge(HD.tiles + tid);
35                 barrier.wait(tid);
36                 x_step(&HD, &H, dt_dx, tid, false);
37                 barrier.wait(tid);
38                 send_low_y_edge (HD.tiles + tid);
39                 send_high_y_edge(HD.tiles + tid);
40                 barrier.wait(tid);
41                 y_step(&HD, &H, dt_dx, tid);
42             }
43             else
44             {
45                 send_low_y_edge (HD.tiles + tid);
46                 send_high_y_edge(HD.tiles + tid);
47                 barrier.wait(tid);
48                 y_step(&HD, &H, dt_dx, tid);
49                 barrier.wait(tid);
50                 send_low_x_edge (HD.tiles + tid);
51                 send_high_x_edge(HD.tiles + tid);
52                 barrier.wait(tid);
53                 courantv[tid*cache_stride] = x_step(&HD, &H, dt_dx, tid, true);
54                 barrier.wait(tid);
55                 if(tid == 0)
56                 {
57                     // serial reduction among threads; tree scheme suitable for
                           large number of threads
58                     for(int i = 1; i < nthreads; ++i)
59                         courantv[0] = std::max(courantv[i*cache_stride], courantv
                               [0]);
60                     dt             = H.courant_number * H.dx / courantv[0];
61                     dt_dx          = dt/H.dx;
62                     set_scheme(H.scheme, dt_dx))
63                 }
64             }
65             barrier.wait(tid);
66         }
67     }
```

FIGURE 2.16

Timestepping loop for tiled Hydro2D code.

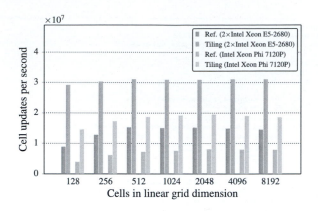

FIGURE 2.17

Performance in cell-steps/second for reference and thread/memory improvements.

Point-to-point synchronization and tree reductions are likely to have limited impact on systems with crossbars and small numbers of cores, but global barrier costs grow as $O(\log n)$ in the number of cores, and processors with increasing numbers of cores are more likely to experience expensive penalties related to non-uniform memory access (NUMA). The exchange buffers and halos do incur storage overhead, but it is negligible for large grids, even with 240 threads on the coprocessor, and is considerably less than the overhead of the large amounts of intermediate storage needed by the slab approach.

On the path to optimization The results of the just-presented optimizations—as compared to the reference code—are presented in Figure 2.17. This shows the performance of consolidated timestep calculations, rolling updates, and tiling for both the processor and the coprocessor, as compared to the reference code timings shown in Figure 2.8. So far, we have improved by **2.0–3.3** × on the processor and **2.3–3.6** × on the coprocessor. This demonstrates better use of the threading and memory subsystems in these computing environments, and notably, the same changes—in the same code path!—have benefited both architectures. As we shall soon see, there is more benefit to be had.

ARITHMETIC EFFICIENCY AND INSTRUCTION-LEVEL PARALLELISM

The microarchitecture of modern processors is quite sophisticated, but it is possible to reap a substantial benefit with a simple mental model of the underlying system.

Memorization Division and transcendental math functions are expensive—even when directly supported by the instruction set, they generally have latencies that are 1–2 orders of magnitude higher than multiplication and division. The reference Hydro2D uses many division and square root operations, which dominates the runtime of the code. The functional units in the hardware that perform these operations may have limited pipelining, which limits throughput and ultimately, instruction-level parallelism.

Since these are so expensive, and because some of these roots and divisions are recomputed several times, caching some frequently-used values can speed things up. In the original code,

```
1  int goon = 1;
2  int iter;
3  for (iter = 0; iter < Hniter_riemann ; iter++) {
4      if (goon) {
5          double wwl, wwr;
6          wwl = sqrt(cl_i * (one + gamma6 * (pstar_i - pl_i) / pl_i));
7          wwr = sqrt(cr_i * (one + gamma6 * (pstar_i - pr_i) / pr_i));
8          double ql = two * wwl * Square(wwl) / (Square(wwl) + cl_i);
9          double qr = two * wwr * Square(wwr) / (Square(wwr) + cr_i);
10         double usl = ul_i - (pstar_i - pl_i) / wwl;
11         double usr = ur_i + (pstar_i - pr_i) / wwr;
12         double delp_i = MAX((qr * ql / (qr + ql) * (usl - usr)), (-pstar_i));
13         pstar_i = pstar_i + delp_i;
14         // Convergence indicator
15         double uo_i = DABS(delp_i / (pstar_i + smallpp));
16         goon = uo_i > PRECISION;
17     }
18 }
```

FIGURE 2.18

Core Newton-Raphson loop of reference `riemann()`.

both `constoprim()`, `equation_of_state()` and `trace()` divide by ρ and c (the local speed of sound) several times. We can compute each of these reciprocals and store them for use throughout the flux computation. As an additional benefit, the use of reciprocal and multiply in place of direct division is strictly faster in many contemporary computing systems. Many compilers are unwilling to automatically do this transformation without user input because of precision concerns.

Factorization The innermost portion of the Hydro2D code—the Newton-Raphson iteration in `riemann.c`—has eight divisions; see Figure 2.18. With simple algebraic manipulation of the iterate, we can reduce the number of these operations. Examining the update to the iterate, Δp^*, we see the expression (from line 15 of Figure 2.18):

$$\Delta p^* = \frac{q_r q_l \left(u_l^* - u_r^*\right)}{\left(q_r + q_l\right)} \tag{2.3a}$$

with

$$q_l = \frac{2 w_l'^3}{w_l'^2 + c_l} \tag{2.3b}$$

$$c_l = \gamma p_l \rho_l \tag{2.3c}$$

$$u_l^* = u_l - \frac{p^* - p_l}{w_l'} \tag{2.3d}$$

$$q_r = \frac{2 w_r'^3}{w_r'^2 + c_r} \tag{2.3e}$$

$$c_r = \gamma p_r \rho_r \tag{2.3f}$$

$$u_r^* = u_r + \frac{p^* - p_r}{w_r'} \tag{2.3g}$$

(Recall that γ is the adiabatic ratio of the medium and a constant in this scheme.) Combining Eq. (2.3a) with Eqs. (2.3b)–(2.3g), we can reduce the overall number of divisions:

$$
\Delta p^* = \frac{\dfrac{2w_r'^3}{w_r'^2+c_r}\dfrac{2w_l'^3}{w_l'^2+c_l}\left(u_l-u_r-\dfrac{p^*-p_r}{w_r'}-\dfrac{p^*-p_l}{w_l'}\right)}{\dfrac{2w_r'^3}{w_r'^2+c_r}+\dfrac{2w_l'^3}{w_l'^2+c_l}}
$$

$$
= \frac{\dfrac{4w_r'^3 w_l'^3}{\left(w_r'^2+c_r\right)\left(w_l'^2+c_l\right)}\left(u_l-u_r-\dfrac{p^*-p_r}{w_r'}-\dfrac{p^*-p_l}{w_l'}\right)}{\dfrac{2w_r'^3\left(w_l'^2+c_l\right)+2w_l'^3\left(w_r'^2+c_r\right)}{\left(w_l'^2+c_l\right)\left(w_r'^2+c_r\right)}}
$$

$$
= \frac{2w_r'^3 w_l'^3\left(u_l-u_r-\dfrac{p^*-p_r}{w_r'}-\dfrac{p^*-p_l}{w_l'}\right)}{w_r'^3\left(w_l'^2+c_l\right)+w_l'^3\left(w_r'^2+c_r\right)}
$$

$$
= \frac{2w_r'^2 w_l'^2 Z}{w_r'^3\left(w_l'^2+c_l\right)+w_l'^3\left(w_r'^2+c_r\right)} \tag{2.4}
$$

with

$$
Z = w_r'w_l'\left(u_l-u_r\right)-w_l'\left(p^*-p_r\right)-w_r'\left(p^*-p_l\right)
$$

which eliminates the intermediate values $q_{l,r}$ and $u^*_{l,r}$ without introduce additional divisions. Finally, we can combine $w'_{l,r}$ with Eq. (2.3c) to avoid the division:

$$
w_l' = \sqrt{c_l\left(1+\frac{\gamma+1}{2\gamma}\frac{p^*-p_l}{p_l}\right)} \tag{2.5}
$$

$$
= \sqrt{c_l+\frac{\gamma+1}{2}\rho_l\left(p^*-p_l\right)}
$$

with a similar expression for w'_r; with our rewrite of Eqs. (2.4) and (2.5), we haved reduced the number of divisions/reciprocals in the Newton-Raphson iteration from eight to two. See Figure 2.19 for the optimized code.

Further on the path to performance The results of the combined thread-level/memory tiling approach with rolling updates, Courant/update combination (in Figure 2.17) with these arithmetic improvements are shown in Figure 2.20. Overall we see that our improvements to the specific instructions and arithmetic used have improved performance by **1.2–1.7×** on the processor and **1.4-1.6×** on the coprocessor. Once again, our improvements were guided by general principles of computer environments and identical code led to similar speedups on both of our target architectures.

DATA-LEVEL PARALLELISM

Data-level parallelism can dramatically improve performance, but its benefit is directly tied to the reduction in instructions brought about by vectorization—roughly speaking, we would like vector code to look as much like the serial code as possible.

```
 1  for(int i = 0; i < NITER_RIEMANN; ++i)
 2  {
 3      if(goon)
 4      {
 5          const REAL_T left_ww2  = left_rho  * ((REAL_T) 0.5) * ((GAMMA + (REAL_T)
                  1.0) * p_star + (GAMMA - (REAL_T) 1.0) * left_p);
 6          const REAL_T left_ww   = my_sqrt(left_ww2);
 7          const REAL_T right_ww2 = right_rho * ((REAL_T) 0.5) * ((GAMMA + (REAL_T)
                  1.0) * p_star + (GAMMA - (REAL_T) 1.0) * right_p);
 8          const REAL_T right_ww  = my_sqrt(right_ww2);
 9          const REAL_T tmp_num   = ((REAL_T)2.0) * left_ww2 * right_ww2 * (left_ww *
                  right_ww * (left_u - right_u) - left_ww * (p_star - right_p) -
                  right_ww * (p_star - left_p));
10          const REAL_T tmp_den   = right_ww2*right_ww * (left_ww2 + left_c) +
                  left_ww2*left_ww * (right_ww2 + right_c);
11          const REAL_T tmp       = tmp_num * rcp(tmp_den);
12          const REAL_T deleft_p  = std::max(tmp, -p_star);
13
14          p_star += deleft_p;
15
16          const REAL_T uo = std::abs(deleft_p * rcp(p_star + SMALLPP));
17          goon           = uo > PRECISION;
18      }
19  }
```

FIGURE 2.19

(Factored) Core Newton-Raphson loop of optimized code.

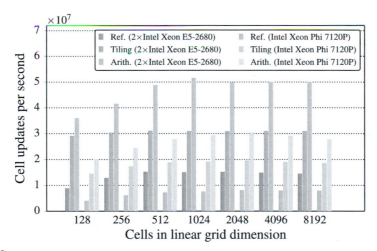

FIGURE 2.20

Performance in cell-steps/second for reference, thread/memory improvements, and arithmetic improvements.

The original code relies on compiler directives to achieve vectorization, but its anemic performance indicates that there is considerable instruction overhead, and the compiler is not always able to infer from code what the programmer knows.

We have vectorized the flux computation and integration code using the C++ SIMD classes, which represent a reasonable compromise between coding effort and performance; the manner of vectorization is clearly defined but the syntax hurdles and specifics of intrinsic or assembly coding are avoided.

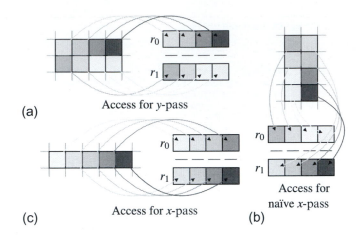

(a)   Access for y-pass

(c)   Access for x-pass

(b)   Access for naïve x-pass

FIGURE 2.21

Vectorization scheme: Strategies for moving grid data into SIMD registers (labeled r_0 and r_1). The y-pass (a) is simple because data is laid out the same as in the registers. A similar scheme for x-passes (b) requires extensive transposes, but a shifted scheme (c) can avoid the transpose and incur minimal overhead. The dark bars in each figure represent fluxes at cell interfaces being computed.

Our code uses the macro `SIMD_WIDTH` as a placeholder for the SIMD width of the underlying hardware (2 or 4 for the processor, 8 for the coprocessor).

SIMD two ways The slab approach used by the reference code ensured that all computation was performed on the same data layout (always in the slab's x-direction), our approach of updating the solution in-place with rolling updates requires that we access and compute data differently for the x- and y-passes. Figure 2.21 depicts various SIMD schemes for this method.

We achieve our implementation of these notions through the aforementioned C++ SIMD classes—the Intel compiler provides `<dvec.h>` for this. Each of the core update routines is made to accept the appropriate SIMD type (we use a `VREAL_T` macro to simplify this), and almost no change is needed to the core of the routine.

`vstrip_prime()` and `vstrip_stable()` functions that are practically identical to their serial counterparts are introduced. However, whereas `strip_prime()` and `strip_stable()` were used for both the x- and y-passes identically (save for strides and the order of the ρu and ρv variables), the fact that the x updates require that we move in the same direction as the data layout requires that we introduce an `hstrip_stable()` function that handles the circular buffers in a slightly different fashion. This is shown in Figure 2.21c; the alternative is to gather cells with the same y-coordinate as the naïve scheme shown in Figure 2.21b does.

Figure 2.22 shows this new x-pass update function; its main novelty is the use of the `rotate_left_wm1()`, `rotate_left_wm2()` functions, which shift the contents of the lanes of their first argument by one and two, respectively, and replace the newly "empty" lane with the leftmost lanes of the second argument. Figure 2.23 shows how the `tile_x_step()` function changes to accommodate SIMD. We have omitted the new `tile_y_step()` in the text for brevity's sake; it is predictably similar to the new `tile_x_step()` except for its initialization of boundaries and use of `vstrip_prime()` and `vstrip_stable()`.

```
1  VREAL_T hstrip_stable(const hydro    *restrict h,
2                        REAL_T         *restrict rho,
3                        REAL_T         *restrict rhou,
4                        REAL_T         *restrict rhov,
5                        REAL_T         *restrict E,
6                        vstrip_work    *restrict sw,
7                        const int                i,
8                        const int                stride,
9                        const VREAL_T            dtdx,
10                       const VMASK_T            write_mask,
11                       const bool               do_courant)
12 {
13     const int src_offs = (i + 2)*stride;
14
15     VREAL_T E_internal;
16     vconservative_to_primitive(sw->prim[0] + 2,       sw->prim[4] + 2, sw->prim[1]
           + 2,          sw->prim[2] + 2, &E_internal,
17                                loadu(rho + src_offs),                 loadu(rhou +
                                  src_offs), loadu(rhov + src_offs), loadu(E +
                                  src_offs));
18     sw->prim[3][2] = vequation_of_state(sw->prim[0][2], E_internal);
19
20     for(int v = 0; v < 5; ++v)
21     {
22         rotate_left_wm2(sw->prim[v] + 0, sw->prim[v][2]);
23         rotate_left_wm1(sw->prim[v] + 1, sw->prim[v][2]);
24     }
25
26     VREAL_T dvar[4];      // slope for i+1
27     if(h->iorder != 1)
28         for(int v = 0; v < 4; ++ v)
29             dvar[v] = vslope(sw->prim[v][0], sw->prim[v][1], sw->prim[v][2], (
                  VREAL_T) h->slope_type, (VREAL_T) h->inv_slope_type);
30
31     VREAL_T right_flux[4];
32     const VREAL_T prim_c = vspeed_of_sound(sw->prim[4][1], sw->prim[3][1]);
33     vtrace(sw->left_flux [0] + 1,                   sw->left_flux [1] + 1,
          sw->left_flux [2] + 1, sw->left_flux [3] + 1,
34         right_flux + 0,                          right_flux + 1,
              right_flux + 2,          right_flux + 3,
35         sw->prim[0]        [1], sw->prim[4][1], sw->prim[1]        [1], sw->prim
              [2]         [1], sw->prim[3]        [1],
36         dvar[0],                          dvar[1],                dvar[2],
                        dvar[3],
37         prim_c, rcp(prim_c),
38         dtdx);
39
40     for(int v = 0; v < 4; ++v)
41         rotate_left_wm1(sw->left_flux[v] + 0, sw->left_flux[v][1]);
42
43     VREAL_T gdnv_rho, gdnv_u, gdnv_v, gdnv_p;
44     vriemann(&gdnv_rho,              &gdnv_u,                  &gdnv_v,
          &gdnv_p,
45             sw->left_flux [0][0], sw->left_flux [1][0], sw->left_flux [2][0], sw
                  ->left_flux [3][0],
46             right_flux[0],          right_flux[1],          right_flux[2],
                  right_flux[3]);
47
48     vcmpflx(sw->flux[0] + 1, sw->flux[1] + 1, sw->flux[2] + 1, sw->flux[3] + 1,
49             gdnv_rho,          gdnv_u,          gdnv_v,          gdnv_p);
50
```

FIGURE 2.22

hstrip_stable(): a vector variant of strip_stable() for vectorized *x*-pass updates without gather/scatters

```
51      for(int v = 0; v < 4; ++v)
52          rotate_left_wm1(sw->flux[v] + 0, sw->flux[v][1]);
53
54      const VREAL_T new_rho  = vupdate(load(rho  + i*stride), sw->flux[0][0],
            sw->flux[0][1], VREAL_T(dtdx));
55      const VREAL_T new_rhou = vupdate(load(rhou + i*stride), sw->flux[1][0],
            sw->flux[1][1], VREAL_T(dtdx));
56      const VREAL_T new_rhov = vupdate(load(rhov + i*stride), sw->flux[2][0],
            sw->flux[2][1], VREAL_T(dtdx));
57      const VREAL_T new_E    = vupdate(load(E    + i*stride), sw->flux[3][0],
            sw->flux[3][1], VREAL_T(dtdx));
58
59      VREAL_T courantv = (VREAL_T) 0.0;
60      if(do_courant)
61      {
62          VREAL_T prim_rho, prim_inv_rho, prim_u, prim_v, E_internal;
63          vconservative_to_primitive(&prim_rho, &prim_inv_rho, &prim_u,  &prim_v,
                &E_internal,
64                                      new_rho,                    new_rhou, new_rhov,
                                       new_E);
65          const VREAL_T prim_p = vequation_of_state(prim_rho,      E_internal);
66          const VREAL_T prim_c = vspeed_of_sound  (prim_inv_rho, prim_p);
67          vcourant(&courantv, prim_u, prim_v, prim_c, write_mask);
68      }
69
70      maskstore(rho  + i*stride, new_rho,  write_mask);
71      maskstore(rhou + i*stride, new_rhou, write_mask);
72      maskstore(rhov + i*stride, new_rhov, write_mask);
73      maskstore(E    + i*stride, new_E,    write_mask);
74
75      for(int v = 0; v < 4; ++ v)
76      {
77          sw->flux      [v][0] = sw->flux      [v][1];
78          sw->left_flux[v][0] = sw->left_flux[v][1];
79      }
80      for(int v = 0; v < 5; ++ v)
81      {
82          sw->prim[v][0] = sw->prim[v][2];
83          sw->prim[v][1] = sw->prim[v][2];
84      }
85
86      return courantv;
87  }
```

Figure 2.22—Cont'd

Peeling and masking When considering SIMD on grids of arbitrary dimensions, we must consider how to handle "leftover" pieces of work (i.e., work at the end of a loop that does not fill a SIMD unit). Improperly handling these cases can result in both soft and hard errors in the execution; the general solution is to use *loop peeling*—the main loop advances by SIMD stride, and a separate, serial loop handles the remainder. Some overhead is incurred with this approach, particularly as the main loop length shrinks and the SIMD width grows, but for large grids, the benefit of SIMD is hardly diminished.

An alternative approach is available to instruction sets with support for write-masking, such as the Intel Xeon Phi coprocessor. Here, a bitmask determines which "lanes" of a vector register are written to memory and which are skipped. With this construction, it is possible to avoid loop peeling altogether. This same mechanism is also use to handle cases where different parts of a SIMD register must behave differently.

```
1  REAL_T tile_x_step(tile *restrict tl, const REAL_T dtdx, const hydro *restrict h,
       int jstart, int jend, bool do_courant)
2  {
3      static const REAL_T x_signs[4] = {1.0, -1.0, 1.0, 1.0};
4
5      VMASK_T alltrue;
6      mask_true(&alltrue);
7      VINT_T linear;
8      linear_offset(&linear);
9
10     VREAL_T courantv      = (VREAL_T) 0.0;
11     REAL_T  final_courantv = 0.0;
12     for(int j = jstart; j < jend; ++j)
13     {
14         const int   ob = (j + 2) * tl->ystride + 0;
15         if(tl->neighbors[0])
16         {
17             for(int v = 0; v < 4; ++v)
18             {
19                 tl->q[v*tl->varstride + ob + 0] = tl->x_edges[0][v*tl->
                       x_e_varstride + j * tl->x_e_ystride + 0];
20                 tl->q[v*tl->varstride + ob + 1] = tl->x_edges[0][v*tl->
                       x_e_varstride + j * tl->x_e_ystride + 1];
21             }
22         }
23         else
24             set_boundaries(tl->q + ob, x_signs, 2, 1, 4, tl-> varstride);
25
26         if(tl->neighbors[1])
27         {
28             for(int v = 0; v < 4; ++v)
29             {
30                 tl->q[v*tl->varstride + ob + tl->n[0] + 2 + 0] = tl->x_edges[1][v*
                       tl->x_e_varstride + j * tl->x_e_ystride + 0];
31                 tl->q[v*tl->varstride + ob + tl->n[0] + 2 + 1] = tl->x_edges[1][v*
                       tl->x_e_varstride + j * tl->x_e_ystride + 1];
32             }
33         }
34         else
35             set_boundaries(tl->q + ob + tl->n[0] + 3, x_signs, 2, -1, 4, tl->
                   varstride);
36
37         const int   o  = ob + 2;
38         strip_work sw;
39         strip_prime(&sw, tl->rho + o, tl->rhou + o, tl->rhov + o, tl->E + o, h,
                           1, dtdx);
40
41         vstrip_work vsw;
42         for(int v = 0; v < 4; ++ v)
43         {
44             vsw.flux      [v][0][SIMD_WIDTH-1] = sw.flux      [v][0];
45             vsw.left_flux [v][0][SIMD_WIDTH-1] = sw.left_flux [v][0];
46         }
47         for(int v = 0; v < 5; ++ v)
48         {
49             vsw.prim      [v][0][SIMD_WIDTH-2] = sw.prim      [v][0];
50             vsw.prim      [v][0][SIMD_WIDTH-1] = sw.prim      [v][1];
51             vsw.prim      [v][1][SIMD_WIDTH-1] = sw.prim      [v][1];
52         }
```

FIGURE 2.23

Vector version of `tile_x_step`; the differences from Figure 2.14 are: the SIMD_WIDTH stride of the update loops, the invocation of and mask generation for `hstrip_stable`, and the loop peeling cross-SIMD reduction of the Courant value.

```
53
54          int i = 0;
55          for(; i + SIMD_WIDTH <= tl->n[0]; i+=SIMD_WIDTH)
56          {
57              const VREAL_T cv = hstrip_stable(h,  tl->rho + o, tl->rhou + o, tl->
                    rhov + o, tl->E + o, &vsw, i, 1, (VREAL_T) dtdx, alltrue,
                    do_courant);
58              courantv          = std::max(courantv, cv);
59          }
60
61          for(; i < tl->n[0]; i+=SIMD_WIDTH)
62          {
63              const VMASK_T in_bounds = mask_lt(linear + (VINT_T) (double)i, (VINT_T
                    ) (double)tl->n[0]);
64              const VREAL_T cv        = hstrip_stable(h,  tl->rho + o, tl->rhou + o,
                    tl->rhov + o, tl->E + o, &vsw, i, 1, (VREAL_T) dtdx, in_bounds,
                    do_courant);
65              courantv                = std::max(courantv, cv);
66          }                                                                        29
67      }
68
69
70      for(int i = 0; i < SIMD_WIDTH; ++i)
71          final_courantv = std::max(final_courantv, courantv[i]);
72      return final_courantv;
73 }
```

Figure 2.23—Cont'd

The coprocessor has native support for per-lane masks; nearly every vector instruction accepts a mask argument, and there are dedicated mask registers for storing and manipulating these masks. The processor must achieve this effect through *blending* instructions, which can combine and interleave the contents of two registers. This can incur instruction overhead.

Control divergence One further challenge to effective vectorization is control divergence—the handling of branching code in SIMD. This occurs in data-dependent execution, and the solution in SIMD is usually to execute all branches and use blending/masking operations to ensure the results are correct. The instruction-reducing benefit of SIMD is diminished if more code must be executed.

Godunov's scheme is largely free of control divergence, with the exception of the Riemann solver; Newton-Raphson iterations do not necessarily converge uniformly. Some inputs may require more iterations than others, which can cause divergence issues for SIMD. See Figure 2.24 for the vectorized version of this loop.

Based on our observations, the Newton-Raphson iteration used in this Riemann solver exhibits very little control divergence; the reference code has a user-defined limit on iterations for the solver (usually 10), but 99% of all Riemann computations required a single iteration to converge.

Alignment Data alignment penalties vary based on architecture and their impact depends greatly on the proportion of loads to arithmetic SIMD operations. In our augmentation of the reference code, we found it a very simple matter to align the tile allocations; for some grid sizes, it was necessary to "pad" out rows to so that the zero-column of the grid preserved the alignment. See Figure 2.25 for the tile initialization code from our optimized implementation.

The last stop The arithmetic intensity revealed by our reduction of intermediate storage, tiling, and arithmetic optimizations is fully realized by our vectorization strategy. Figure 2.26 shows the performance of each incremental optimization, plus the reference code, and again, both architectures

```
1     for(int i = 0; i < NITER_RIEMANN && !all_zero(goon); ++i)
2     {
3         const VREAL_T left_ww2  = left_rho  * ((VREAL_T) 0.5) * (VREAL_T(GAMMA + (
              REAL_T) 1.0) * p_star + VREAL_T(GAMMA - (REAL_T) 1.0) * left_p);
4         const VREAL_T left_ww   = my_sqrt(left_ww2);
5         const VREAL_T right_ww2 = right_rho * ((VREAL_T) 0.5) * (VREAL_T(GAMMA + (
              REAL_T) 1.0) * p_star + VREAL_T(GAMMA - (REAL_T) 1.0) * right_p);
6         const VREAL_T right_ww  = my_sqrt(right_ww2);
7         const VREAL_T tmp_num   = ((VREAL_T)2.0) * left_ww2 * right_ww2 * (left_ww
              * right_ww * (left_u - right_u) - left_ww * (p_star - right_p) -
              right_ww * (p_star - left_p));
8         const VREAL_T tmp_den   = right_ww2*right_ww * (left_ww2 + left_c) +
              left_ww2*left_ww * (right_ww2 + right_c);
9         const VREAL_T tmp       = tmp_num * rcp(tmp_den);
10        const VREAL_T deleft_p  = std::max(tmp, -p_star);
11
12        p_star += select_true(goon, deleft_p, (VREAL_T) 0.0);
13
14        const VREAL_T uo = std::abs(deleft_p * rcp(p_star + SMALLPP));
15        goon             = mask_and(goon, mask_gt(uo, VREAL_T(PRECISION)));
16    }
```

FIGURE 2.24

Vectorized Newton-Raphson loop from `vriemann()`; note the `all_zero()` call, which causes all SIMD lanes to execute until they have all converged.

benefit—**1.4–1.5×** for the processor and **2.2-4.4×** for the coprocessor! At this point, thanks to its wide vector units, the coprocessor has pulled ahead for all but the smallest problem sizes. Given the higher peak throughput of the coprocessor, this is what we expect to see.

SUMMARY

Our augmented version of the Godunov scheme for the 2D Euler equations greatly improves upon the reference code's performance on both the coprocessor and the processor for a variety of problem sizes.

THE COPROCESSOR VS THE PROCESSOR

In the reference code, the coprocessor is nearly ½ the performance of the processor—contrary to expectations based on raw FLOP capability (e.g. see Figure 2.3). The optimized code reverses this, with the coprocessor outperforming the processor by a factor of 1.3-1.5. The high level of parallelism in the Intel Xeon Phi coprocessor means that it requires larger problems to reach peak performance, but given sufficient work, it outperforms the processor handily.

A RISING TIDE LIFTS ALL BOATS

Every optimization we have undertaken have yielded considerable benefit for both the processor and the coprocessor; for all problem sizes, performance is improved—by as much as **12×** for the coprocessor, and over **5×** for the processor. While the two architectures differ in many respects, they fundamentally achieve performance through similar routes, and optimizations that work on one generally carry through to the other.

```
1  inline unsigned long long round_to_alignment(unsigned long long x, int alignment)
2  {
3      if(x & (alignment-1))
4          x = (x & ~(alignment-1)) + alignment;
5      return x;
6  }
7
8  void init_tile(tile *tl, int xstart, int xend, int ystart, int yend)
9  {
10     static const int target_alignment = 64;
11     static const int arith_alignment  = target_alignment/sizeof(REAL_T);
12
13     tl->offset[0] = xstart;
14     tl->offset[1] = ystart;
15
16     tl->n[0] = xend - xstart;
17     tl->n[1] = yend - ystart;
18
19     const int min_stride = tl->n[0] + 2*2;
20     tl->ystride          = round_to_alignment(min_stride, arith_alignment);
21     tl->varstride        = tl->ystride * (tl->n[1] + 2*2);
22
23     const int alloc_offset = arith_alignment - 2;
24     tl->q     = ((REAL_T *)_mm_malloc( sizeof(REAL_T) * (4 * tl->varstride +
               arith_alignment), target_alignment)) + alloc_offset;
25     tl->rho   = tl->q + 0*tl->varstride;
26     tl->rhou  = tl->q + 1*tl->varstride;
27     tl->rhov  = tl->q + 2*tl->varstride;
28     tl->E     = tl->q + 3*tl->varstride;
29
30     const int min_x_e_varstride = tl->n[1] * 2;
31     tl->x_e_ystride = 2;
32     tl->x_e_varstride = round_to_alignment(min_x_e_varstride, arith_alignment);
33     tl->x_edges[0] = (REAL_T *) _mm_malloc( sizeof(REAL_T) * 4 * tl->x_e_varstride
               , target_alignment);
34     tl->x_edges[1] = (REAL_T *) _mm_malloc( sizeof(REAL_T) * 4 * tl->x_e_varstride
               , target_alignment);
35
36     const int min_y_e_varstride = tl->n[0] * 2;
37     tl->y_e_ystride   = tl->n[0];
38     tl->y_e_varstride = round_to_alignment(min_y_e_varstride, arith_alignment);
39     tl->y_edges[0] = (REAL_T *) _mm_malloc( sizeof(REAL_T) * 4 * tl->y_e_varstride
               , target_alignment);
40     tl->y_edges[1] = (REAL_T *) _mm_malloc( sizeof(REAL_T) * 4 * tl->y_e_varstride
               , target_alignment);
41 }
```

FIGURE 2.25

Tile initialization function `init_tile()` and helper function `round_to_alignment()`. `_mm_malloc()` is a compiler intrinsic for aligned allocations. Due to the halo regions, the desired SIMD access memory does not coincide where the allocation begins—this code will allocate the solution grid such that the starting non-halo cells in each row are aligned, which requires advancing the allocated pointer by `alloc_offset`.

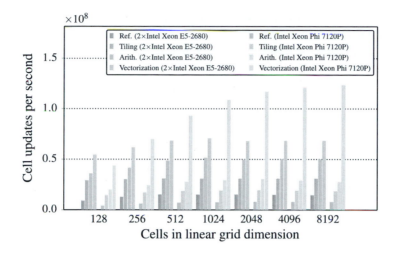

FIGURE 2.26

Performance in cell-steps/second for reference, thread/memory improvements, arithmetic improvements, and vectorization.

PERFORMANCE STRATEGIES

Scientists, and any author of performance-sensitive code, are keenly interested how to improve execution performance while minimizing programming effort and maintenance costs. This subject has no simple answers—there is no "silver bullet."

While we have performed in-depth analysis in this chapter, it is not our intention to assert that each programmer be a seasoned expert in microarchitecture, nor that they be intimately acquainted with the smallest details of each target processor. Instead, we hope that we have shown that by consciously ignoring or simplifying aspects of the hardware, significant improvements in efficiency are achievable, and that such reduced models are common to seemingly distinct processors.

- Pursuant to what we have described with our arithmetic optimizations, consider how different mathematically equivalent formulations perform on a given architecture. These changes often have localized code impact.
- Evaluate how "hot" loops' data accesses can be structured to take advantage of vector hardware, as we have with `vstrip_stable` and `hstrip_stable`. These modifications can often be limited to narrow code changes.
- Consider the potential ways work can be delivered among cores (and specifically, threads); this is related to how divergent tasks in the code are and their granularity. This may have ramifications for data access and storage as well—for example, see our material on tiling and alignment.
- Finally, consider the broader issues of memory/memory hierarchy usage and layout. This can often involve serious changes in code with commensurate gains; we have considered this with our "rolling updates" and tiling approaches.

The best general advice we can provide is to have a model of how the code should run on the hardware and utilize its resources, and the compiler tools, properly applied, can greatly simplify its realization.

Writing the simplest, most hardware-unaware code possible and applying *ex post facto* automatic optimization usually does not deliver high efficiency.

We hope we have shown the reader how these rough principles can be applied to a popular numerical technique, and while their generality to other codes will likely vary from what we have shown here, we believe that considering them will benefit a great deal of important computations, and hopefully help shoulder the burdens of the scientist-programmer.

FOR MORE INFORMATION

Godunov, S.K., 1959. A difference method for numerical calculation of discontinuous solutions of the equations of hydrodynamics. Matematicheskii Sbornik 89 (3), 271–306.

Lavallée, P., et al., 2012. Porting and optimizing HYDRO to new platforms and programming paradigms-lessons learn. Tech. rep, Parallel Programming Interfaces, France.

van Leer, B., 1977. Towards the ultimate conservative difference scheme. IV. A new approach to numerical convection. J. Comput. Phys. 23 (3), 276–299.

Leveque, R.J., 2002. Finite Volume Methods for Hyperbolic Problems. Cambgridge University Press ISBN: 978-0-521-00924-9.

Roe, P.L., 1981. Approximate Riemann solvers, parameter vectors, and difference schemes. J. comput. Phys. 43 (2), 357–372.

Satish, M., et al., 2012. Can traditional programming bridge the Ninja performance gap for parallel computing applications? In: Proceedings of the 39th Annual International Symposium on Computer Architecture, ISCA'12. IEEE Computer Society, Portland, Oregon, pp. 440–451. ISBN: 978-1-4503-1642-2. http://dl.acm.org/citation.cfm?id=2337159.2337210.

BETTER CONCURRENCY AND SIMD ON HBM

## 3

Jacob Weismann Poulsen[*], **Per Berg**[*], **Karthik Raman**[†]

Danish Meteorological Institute, Denmark, †Intel Corporation, USA

THE APPLICATION: HIROMB-BOOS-MODEL

The complete HIROMB-BOOS-Model (HBM) code features two-way dynamical nesting, with an arbitrary number of nesting levels, enabling high resolution in regional seas and very high resolution in narrow straits and channels, and has besides the basic physics components also a biogeochemical module that can optionally be activated. With its support for both distributed and shared memory parallelization, HBM has matured as an efficient and portable, high-quality ocean model code. HBM, by varying input setup specifications, is used for operational forecasting duties as well as for research, such as done for climate studies. This generalization of the model code makes it possible to apply the same code for very different applications in terms of geographical coverage, grid resolution, number of nested domains, simulation time span, and certain other model features, since these are considered as dynamical features which cannot be hard-coded.

User-specified input selected at runtime, specifically the selected number of time steps and the simulation period, is all that distinguishes an operational forecast application from a climate scenario run while running the same build of the source code. Because of this dynamic input, the number of MPI tasks and the number of OpenMP threads are selected at runtime for performance. It is important that the results are binary identical regardless of the choice of task and thread counts. It is this generalization, built into a portable model code with ability to run purely serial, with MPI, with OpenMP, or hybrid MPI-OpenMP at the choice of the user that distinguishes HBM from most other model codes available. The HBM code is also applied in numerous research and commercial projects with different focus areas ranging from forecasting to climate modeling. As an example, Danish Meteorological Institute (DMI) is currently developing a pan-European model that has two major scopes for future activities: (i) to provide homogenized forecasting on a pan-European scale and (ii) to address pan-European and regional aspects of climate change. With the latter, HBM must serve as a solid foundation for a coupled atmosphere-ocean model. Time to solution will be a vital factor for such a project to succeed. This pan-European setup has nine nested domains with high resolution (down to less than 185 m horizontally and 1 m vertically) in narrow straits and transient waters, and has a total of 18.6 million active wet-points, and thus the computational demands by far exceed any other single model ever run at DMI before. Nevertheless, sustained time consumption in the range 1.5-2.5 h for a 5-days forecast using a previous HBM release on available systems was demonstrated in a recent

PRACE (for URL see "For more information" at the end of this chapter) project, making operational forecasting a realistic goal (She et al., 2013). However, further speedup is needed if scenario modeling on climate time scales with this setup should be a realistic activity at DMI.

For more in-depth information on HBM, we see "For More Information" listed at the end of this chapter.

KEY USAGE: DMI

The DMI provides meteorological services, including forecasting, warnings and monitoring of weather, climate, and related environmental conditions in the atmosphere, on land and at sea, in the Commonwealth of the Realm of Denmark, the Faroe Islands, Greenland, and surrounding waters and airspace, with the purpose of safeguarding human life and property. As one of its duties, DMI carries the national responsibility for emergency preparedness and response to events such as storm surges affecting Danish coasts. At DMI, current versions of the ocean circulation model code have served as the operational storm surge model since 2001 as well as being extensively used in a number of EU-funded projects; it is the latest version of the HBM code that is used today to provide 5 days forecasts of water levels four times per day. This model must deliver the best quality water level predictions at Danish coastal stations and this is continuously being verified by comparison with *in situ* observations and with other predictions from forecasting centers around the North Sea and the Baltic Sea. Predictions of 3D fields of currents and water temperature from the same model run are also used to provide the basis for operational oil-spill modeling in Danish waters. In another model setup, using the exact same build of the source code, DMI operates the Baltic production component of MyOcean the focus of which is on the ocean state of the Baltic Sea including both physics and biogeochemical parameters. This model setup applies an increased resolution in the area of interest and provides a 2.5 days forecast two times per day. The quality of MyOcean products are continuously being monitored and validated. The interested reader should consult the MyOcean web pages mentioned at the end of this chapter.

DMI, as a governmental institute under the Ministry of Climate, Energy and Building, is challenged on its energy budget and has restricted means for energy consumption for computing. It is highly desirable to look into efficient usage, in terms of both elapsed run time and energy consumption, for a code like HBM. We are constantly working on improving the performance of HBM, and the work presented in this chapter has been implemented into the HBM source code repository as an integral part of improving overall HBM performance.

HBM EXECUTION PROFILE

As a guideline for development efforts toward more efficient execution of HBM, typical timings from the different parts inside the time loop of HBM for real applications are listed in table shown in Figure 3.1. Tracer advection is by far the most dominating part at 44%. The results shown in the table are obtained for a pure physics run with only two tracers: salinity and temperature. For an application such as the operational MyOcean run which has 12 additional passive tracers representing biogeochemical variables, the time consumption for tracer advection is approximately 2.5 times larger. In any case, it seems well justified that further optimization of HBM should look into the tracer advection part choosing one of two obvious choices: One could either implement and apply a simpler and less

Module	Time contribution
Tracer advection	44%
Turbulence mode	16%
Momentum equations	12%
Tracer diffusion	4%
Mass equation	2%
Remaining	<2% each

FIGURE 3.1

Relative time consumption for different code parts inside the time loop of typical HBM applications. The timings are for runs on one node (without MPI) and for model setups with only a single area; for model runs using more MPI tasks and/or more nested areas the percentages will change but the interrelation between the shown top-5 code parts will remain.

expensive scheme, or one could try to improve the performance of the existing more complex scheme. For the reasons explained below, we must refrain from the first of these options and thus improving the current implementation is the only way forward for a general model code like HBM.

The use of relatively coarse grids, with central difference or pure upwind schemes, for tracer advection gives false predictions of sharp fronts or may generate wiggles. The so-called total variation diminishing (TVD) scheme (Harten, 1997) enables prediction of sharper fronts and preserves monotonicity (absence of "overshoots") without spurious oscillations in the solution. These TVD properties are, however, often difficult or even impossible to prove for general multidimensional schemes and therefore in applications one-dimensional limiters are usually applied in each coordinate direction to ensure some sort of monotonicity. Needless to say, any physically appealing model must possess mass conservation and monotonicity. Even when applied for free-surface flows which might exhibit abrupt changes in space and time such as drying and wetting, this can indeed be achieved in some tracer advection schemes if two essential conditions can be fulfilled (Gross et al., 2002): The first one is the so-called consistency with continuity (CWC) concept which requires that the discretized tracer advection equation is consistent with the discretized, free-surface continuity equation. The other essential element is appropriate definition of flux heights at the faces of the grid cells.

The actual numerical scheme behind the tracer advection in HBM is attributed to Kleine (1993). The current implementation of that scheme with the required modifications for the CWC concept and appropriate flux face heights for dynamically two-way nested configurations with multiple tracers was done by the present authors who also adjusted all the data structures for the indirect addressing and added MPI and OpenMP support as well the improved concurrency and single instruction multiple data (SIMD) vectorization herein; it is that particular code which is treated in this chapter and the relevant code parts of the HBM (not the full code) have been made available for download and usage under BSD license.

OVERVIEW FOR THE OPTIMIZATION OF HBM

To make our points and not to complicate things more than necessary, we will not deal with nesting, meteo-forcing fields, and other forcing data in this chapter, which may even be restricted by proprietary rights, yet we would like to demonstrate our findings on realistically dimensioned data sets, not only on academic toy cases. Therefore, we have supplied with the source code relevant data from a Baffin Bay setup generated from the freely available ETOPO2 data set (for URL see "For more information" at the end of this chapter).

We start off in the next section by introducing the most important data structures that we use and which may be different from other circulation model codes. Then, we describe how thread parallelism is implemented in HBM. The steps toward SIMD vectorization of the code are described next; both some trivial obstacles and some not-so-obvious ones are treated. And finally, we wrap it all together and show comparison of performance results on Intel® Xeon® and Intel® Xeon Phi™. For this particular application we demonstrate a single node speedup of ~15% on an Intel Xeon Phi coprocessor compared to an Intel Xeon processor.

DATA STRUCTURES: LOCALITY DONE RIGHT

The authors believe that good SIMD and thread performance on modern hardware can only be obtained if the implementation puts focus on data proximity. *Location, location, location....* Yes, it is all about location and this section will describe the data-oriented design that is now used throughout the HBM model.

Figure 3.2 illustrates our classification of the grid points into active compute points termed wet-points (surface wet-points and subsurface wet-points, respectively) and inactive compute points (grid points on land or below the sea bottom) on a 3D grid. Figure 3.3 shows a typical shallow water domain. The reader should notice that the number of active compute points is considerably less than the total number of points within the 3D regular grid. As an example, only 11.1% of the points are active compute points in domain shown in Figure 3.3. All matrices used in the model computations are consequently rather sparse and this suggests that one uses a sparse representation for the data structures which should be intended both to save storage space and to increase proximity. We use a compact

FIGURE 3.2

Classification of points in the regular 3D grid with active compute points. On top is the surface layer where active compute points are shown with the lightest coloring. The column arrangement of the active subsurface compute points are shown in the medium coloring. The darkest coloring are using for inactive points.

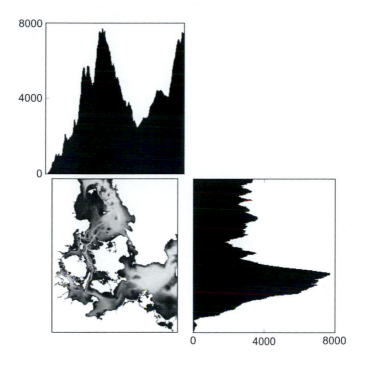

FIGURE 3.3

Illustration of a typical irregular computational domain. The figure shows the inner Danish water subdomain and the color coding shows the number of wet-points below each surface-points, white is on land, and the color scale runs from dark blue for 1 point to dark red for 75 points. The histogram to the right shows the distribution of number of wet-points along each zonal (i.e., constant latitude) grid line. The upper histogram shows the distribution of number of wet-points along each meridional (constant longitude) grid line.

representation that is described by three arrays `msrf(0:,0:)`, `mcol(0:)`, and `kh(0:)` holding the index for horizontal surface wet-points, the index for the first subsurface-point in the column, and finally the length of the column, respectively. The surface index array transforms a horizontal grid point `(i,j)` into its corresponding wet-point index and returns the value 0 if `(i,j)` is a point on land or a point below the sea bottom. The column index for a given surface index `iw` is defined by `mcol(iw)`, and `mcol(0)` naturally return 0. In the same way, the column length for a given surface index `iw` is defined by `kh(iw)`, again with `kh(0)` equal to 0. The code snippet shown in Figure 3.4 demonstrates how one can loop through all the wet-points with the 3D matrix represented by `u(:)`. Note that the opposite transformation of `msrf(0:,0:)`, i.e., from surface wet-point to grid location `(i,j)`, is given by `ind(1:2,:)`.

Figure 3.5 shows the three classes of points that we distinguish between in the 1D data structure. The code operates on a horizontally columnar grid. Indirect addressing is adopted in the horizontal only to map the permutation of columns given through `msrf(i,j)`. Note that this permutation is described as an unstructured arrangement of columns `(i,j)` but not of the data in each column; the data are nicely arranged for increased proximity with direct addressing applied through the surface-points and vertically through the subsurface-points.

```
do iw = 1,iw2
  i = ind(1,iw)
  j = ind(2,iw)

  ! Note that iw==msrf(ind(1,iw),ind(2,iw)) by
  ! definition of ind(1:2,:).
  ! All surface wet-points (i,j) reached with stride-1:
      ... u(iw) ...
enddo
do iw = 1,iw2
  kb = kh(iw)   ! bottom value at column iw
  if (kb < 2) cycle
  i = ind(1,iw)
  j = ind(2,iw)
  mi0 = mcol(iw) - 2
  do k = 2, kb
    ! all subsurface wet-points (i,j,k) are reached
    ! with stride-1:
    mi = mi0 + k
    ... u(mi) ...
  enddo
enddo
```

FIGURE 3.4

Code snippet demonstrating how to loop through the active wet-points.

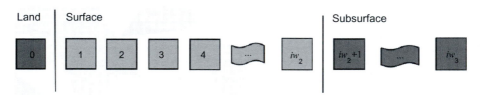

FIGURE 3.5

One-dimensional layout of the data structure for the 3D grid of Figure 3.2. The active surface-points are [1:iw2], the active subsurface-points are [iw2+1:iw3], and the inactive points are represented by [0].

From the code snippet in Figure 3.4 we see that data have been organized so that loops that deal with columns as independent quantities will have a perfect stride-1 access pattern. However, there are two additional aspects that we need to consider. Firstly, the HBM model computes on a 9-point stencil due to use of techniques like finite differencing. Therefore, some loops will need to address not only the actual point but also its neighbor's grid points to the East, West, North, South, North-East, South-East, North-West, and South-West. Therefore, when dealing with the column identified by position (i,j), we need to access these neighbor elements too and a suitable data layout would consequently attempt to preserve proximity in the 2D space to the 1D index space. Secondly, the HBM model will need to process the whole set of wet-points and not just a single column so the enumeration of the columns (or the outer loop order) is another important aspect.

Any enumeration of the surface-points may serve as the basis for the representation and the fact that *any* enumeration will work is an obvious tuning opportunity toward increased proximity. It is clear that a given enumeration imposes a unique cache pattern (D1, L2, L3, and TLB) and some are obviously better than others. Assuming we have the memory system of the target computer described by the sizes, the latencies and the type (exclusive/inclusive), and the data set described by the three index arrays, how can we tune the underlying enumeration for optimum proximity?

As an illustrative example, we will show the result of using two different enumeration heuristics, H1 and H2. Let H1 be the enumeration where we start in the upper North-West corner and then enumerate from North to South and once we reach the South-most coordinate, then move one grid line to the East and count onward from North to South again and so forth until we reach the point in the South-East corner. The result of using this strategy on a real case (the data set from the Baffin Bay setup in approximately 2 nautical miles horizontal resolution with 77,285 surface-points and 7,136,949 subsurface-points) is shown in the table in Figure 3.6 which illustrates how many of the eight geographically nearest-neighbor wet-points that can be classified as nearby neighbors in the index space, i.e., points there are within an index distance of 1-10 from a given point.

The scheme computes on a 9-point stencil so let heuristic H2 be an attempt to improve the D1 usage. For optimum proximity one would prefer to have neighboring cells as close as possible in the index enumeration and if we were to ensure this on a rectangle or a cube we could approach the task using space-filling curves (see Xu and Tirthapura, 2012). On an irregular set like the one shown in Figure 3.3 or in Figure 3.8 it becomes more challenging to come up with the right solution.

The table in Figure 3.6 clearly shows (row 1, 4) that H2 has managed to get a significantly larger portion of the stencil neighboring cells much closer in the index space. However, the permutation comes at a cost and the points that are not within a distances of 10 in the index space now have a significantly larger distance to the center of the stencil (row 2, 3). With H1, neighboring points that would not hit in D1 would maybe hit in L2 or L3 but with H2 they are likely to cause a TLB miss because the distances are so far. This example is meant to stress that it is hard to formulate optimum proximity

H1 distances to the eight neighbors

	NW	N	NE	E	SE	S	SW	W
DIST <10	3.32%	100.00%	3.18%	2.00%	3.18%	100.00%	3.32%	2.00%
MAX	400	1	398	399	400	1	398	399
MEAN	282.7	1	281.2	284.8	282.7	1	281.2	284.8
MEDIAN	318	1	318	320	318	1	318	320

H2 distances to the eight neighbors

	NW	N	NE	E	SE	S	SW	W
DIST <10	64.34%	76.23%	64.34%	83.80%	64.34%	76.23%	64.34%	64.34%
MAX	69326	69313	69326	69327	69326	69313	69326	69327
MEAN	395.1	281.9	432.5	210.9	395.1	281.9	432.5	210.9
MEDIAN	4	3	4	1	4	3	4	1

FIGURE 3.6

The table shows various statistics for distances for the eight neighbors using two different heuristics H1 and H2. The first row shows how large a percentage of the points that are neighbors in 2D are also close in the index space, where close is defined as an index number difference less than 10.

as a well-posed problem that takes the following into account: capacity of D1, L2, L3, and TLB, the latency for D1, L2, L3, and TLB, and finally the distances in the original 2D space and the distances in the 1D index space.

We consider it to be an *open problem* how one should formulate the question of optimum proximity as an optimization problem that will embrace all the relevant parameters and find the best suited enumeration. The solution must be sufficiently general to support any kind of realistic test case that users of the model code may come up with and any kind of caching system. Nevertheless, the formulation will lead to an optimization problem where finding the infimum will be NP-hard so we need to use heuristics or approximations. For the test cases used in this chapter, we will keep it simple and stick to heuristic H1 described above, and thus leave the problem as a possibility for future tuning.

THREAD PARALLELISM IN HBM

In the MPI parallelization and in the OpenMP parallelization of HBM, we assume that the enumeration of the surface-points and the columns below is fixed. Without this assumption we are facing an NP-hard problem but the simplification imposed by this new assumption implies that we are now facing a problem that is no longer NP-hard (i.e., the simplification that we now deal with subintervals instead of subsets makes the problem amenable). This allows us to treat the problem of balancing the threads (or tasks) both offline using an exact algorithm and online using various heuristics. Moreover, it allows us to evaluate different heuristics on different relevant test cases. It should be stressed that another enumeration of the points will impose another threaded layout of data no matter which approach we take to do the balancing. Below is a formal definition of the load-balancing problem and Figure 3.7 shows how the points are split among the threads.

Let $I = \{1, \ldots, m\}$ be the column index set and let $\{w_1, \ldots, w_m\}$ be the weights associated with the individual columns. Let n denote the number of threads/tasks used. A disjoint subinterval $I_i = \{[l_i : u_i]\}_{i=1,\ldots,n}$ covering of I induces a cost vector $(c_1, \ldots, c_n)$ with

$$c_i = \sum_{j=l_i}^{u_i} w_j$$

The cost of the covering is defined as $\max c_i$. The balance problem is to find a covering that minimizes the cost.

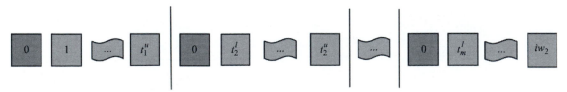

FIGURE 3.7

The figure shows how each thread deals with a subinterval of the set of surface-points and the subsurface columns corresponding to the surface-points. Moreover, note that each thread also has the notion of an inactive point.

The general NP-hard problem from the section on data structures has now been reduced to the well-known integer partitioning problem where exact algorithms exist with time complexity $O(nm^2)$, c.f., e.g., Chapter 8.5 in the book by Skiena (2008). Reasonable heuristics for moderate sizes for n and reasonable input sets would be a greedy approach where one would add columns to the current thread until the sum exceeds the average load per thread. Alternatively, one could try to account for the fact that this method is likely to overcommit, and instead only add the next column to the current thread pool if this brings the sum closer to an average load per thread. These two heuristics both have time complexity $O(n)$ and will serve as reasonable candidates for online experiments. It is the alternative fair-share version that is implemented as default in HBM.

The Baffin Bay test case is shown in Figure 3.8 and the challenges related to ensure a proper load balancing is shown in Figure 3.9.

We have split the columns into four subsets to figure out the length of a typical column and a rare column. The numbers above the intervals reflect the number of columns within the interval.

We have tried to quantify the differences between using the default heuristic for splitting the workload and the exact algorithm for the Baffin Bay test case in Figure 3.10. As shown in the figure, the two approaches (i.e., exact and heuristic) do give rise to solutions that are very close. It is actually difficult to pinpoint the differences from the pure load plots in both 2D and 3D but the difference plot does show that the solutions are not identical. A reasonable conjecture from glancing the 2D plots only is that

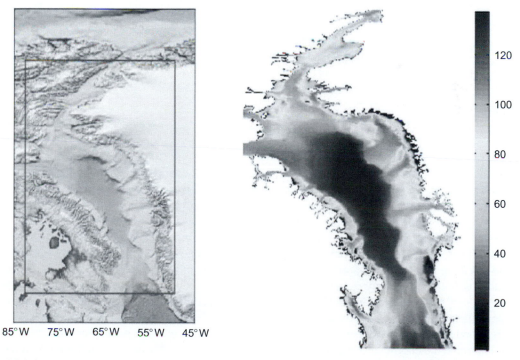

FIGURE 3.8

Map of the Baffin Bay test case (left) and the related gridded bathymetry (right) with depth scale in meters.

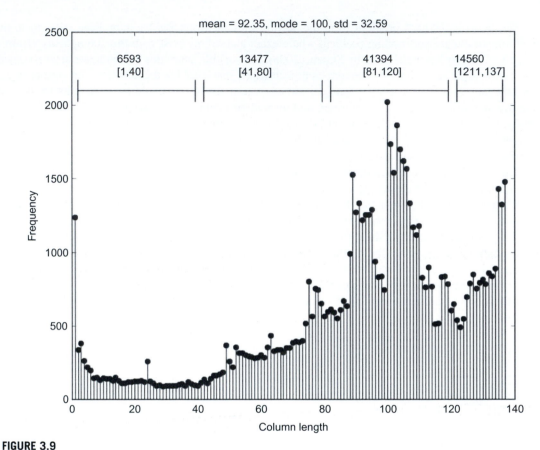

FIGURE 3.9

Distribution of column lengths in the Baffin Bay test case.

in this particular case it would be better to attack the balance challenge using the ideas from the data structures section than using an exact algorithm to split into the subintervals. As a corollary, we see no need for using the exact algorithm for distributions using fewer threads, e.g., for Intel Xeon processor runs using only 48 threads.

It deserves mentioning that the weights used in the definition of the balancing problem can be a sum of subweights while retaining problem complexity! That is, one definition could be to have the weight set to 1.0 if the point is a wet-point and to 0.0 elsewhere and this is the definition used in Figure 3.10. Another definition could try to account for the number of columns too, e.g., by setting the weight $w = \alpha * s_{wet} + \beta * ss_{wet}$ with s_{wet} being the number of wet surface-points and ss_{wet} being the amount of corresponding subsurface wet-points, and α and β being tunable parameters.

By conducting various experiments, one can try to find the relevant parameters for these weights and determine the coefficients that will lead to the best balancing. Please consult the HBM references for further details on this.

Once we have defined how we split the problem among the threads, we need to consider how the application should use the threads. In general, we believe that OpenMP parallelization of real applications

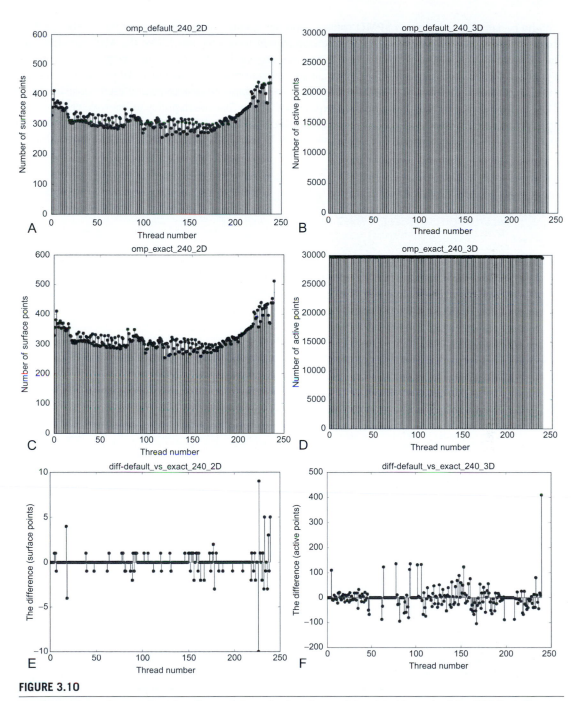

FIGURE 3.10

The figure shows the number of surface-points and subsurface-points related to each of the 240 threads. Note that the differences are rather insignificant when we confine ourselves to 240 threads. The 2D imbalance shown could be dealt with either using weights or by using another initial enumeration of the columns.

should be approached with an SPMD pattern approach and not along the lines of the celebrated loop-based approach. Thus, the OpenMP parallelization will look very much like the MPI parallelization and ideally one should only have OpenMP barriers surrounding the MPI halo swaps to minimize the synchronization between the threads. Such an approach implies that the OpenMP blocks will become rather huge and that loops and data structures used in all loops are structured and used consistently. On NUMA architectures we will need to deal explicitly with the first-touch policy to improve performance. Fortunately, it is relatively easy to ensure a proper NUMA layout (aka first touch) for all variables with our approach. This is illustrated in the code snippet in Figure 3.11. The subroutine `domp_get_domain`

```
!$OMP PARALLEL DEFAULT(SHARED)
call numa_ft(...); call foo( ... );call bar(...); ...
!$OMP BARRIER
call halo_update(...)
!$OMP BARRIER
call baz( ... );call quux(...); ...
!$OMP END PARALLEL
...
subroutine numa_ft(...)
  call domp_get_domain(kh, 1, iw2, nl, nu, idx)
  x(nl:nu) = 0.0_8  ! first touch of thread-local surface
  ...
  do n=nl,nu
    kb = kh(n)
    if (kb > 1) then
      ml = mcol(n)
      mu = ml + kb - 2
      x(ml:mu) = 0.0_8 ! first touch of thread-local subsurface
    endif
  enddo
end subroutine numa_ft

subroutine foo(...)
  call domp_get_domain(kh, 1, iw2, nl, nu, idx)
  do iw=nl,nu
    i = ind(1,iw)                    ! all threadlocal surface wet-points
    j = ind(2,iw)                    ! (i,j) reached with stride-1
    ... u(iw) ...
  enddo
  do iw=nl,nu
    kb = kh(iw)
    if (kb < 2) cycle
    i = ind(1,iw)
    j = ind(2,iw)
    mi0 = mcol(iw) - 2               ! mid-point in stencil
    mn0 = mcol(msrf(i-1,j)) - 2      ! north-point in stencil
    ub = min(kb,kh(msrf(i-1,j)))     ! upper bound on fat k-loop
    do k = 2, ub                     ! the fat stencil loop
      ! all threadlocal subsurface wet-points (k,i,j) and
      ! (k,i-1,j) are reached with stride-1
      mi = mi0 + k                   ! mid-point in stencil
      mn = mn0 + k                   ! north-point in stencil
      ... u(mi) ... u(mn)
    enddo
    do k = ub+1, ...                 ! remainder loops
    enddo
  enddo
end subroutine foo
```

FIGURE 3.11

Code snippet showing NUMA first touch.

will provide each thread with its lower and upper bounds (nl and nu, respectively) and its actual implementation can either read the decomposition in during initialization or generate it the first time it is called based on the specific model input, say kh and iw2. Then, after that any subsequent call of domp_get_domain will simply do a lookup in the idx array and pass the result of the decomposition (nl and nu) onto the caller. It should also be mentioned that this approach relieves one from the explicit thread-scoping burden. The scoping is handled by the Fortran language in the sense that all stack variables become thread private by construction.

DATA PARALLELISM: SIMD VECTORIZATION

In this section we describe what we have done to SIMD vectorize the HBM model. The code snippet in Figure 3.12 shows how loops have been structured throughout the HBM model.

The fact that we have already OpenMP parallelized the outermost loop implies that all data dependencies are gone in the loops. Thus, we could aim at SIMD vectorizing the outermost iw-loop too. However, the fact that we have stride-1 access within the k–loops and not necessarily within the iw–loops at the same time makes this idea less appealing. The SIMD hardware today does not truly support parallel reads/writes of nonunit stride access. For instance, the gather and scatter operations found in the VEX instruction set can be regarded as short-hand notation for a series of loads/stores when operating on elements from different cache lines. As investigated in Hofmann et al. (2014) using gather operations on vectors that straddle several cache lines is rather inefficient and consequently we will be better off by focusing only on the vertical loops where we can use ordinary vector load instructions due to the stride-1 pattern herein.

The aim is to ensure that all k-loops will SIMD vectorize well and this requires that the compiler does indeed recognize the k-loops as stride-1 loops.

TRIVIAL OBSTACLES

The trivial obstacles we faced with the original code was indirections, assumed-shape arguments, and branches inside the innermost k-loops. Before we turn our attention to tuning the SIMD-code generation, we will give a few examples of the more trivial transformation that eventually lead to code that we could tune. The steps shown in pseudo code snippets in Figures 3.13–3.15 provide an example of the initial rewrites required. The starting point of the original code is outlined in Figure 3.13.

```
do iw=        ! horizontal - mpi/openmp parallelization
  do k=       ! vertical    - vectorization
    ...
  enddo
enddo
```

FIGURE 3.12

Code snippet showing basic loop structure of HBM.

```
real(8), intent(in) :: u(0:)      ! OBSTACLE: assumed-shape
...
do iw=                            ! horizontal - mpi/openmp
                                  ! parallelization
  ...
  i  = ind(1,iw)
  jj = ind(2,iw)
  kb = kh(iw)
  do k=2,kb                       ! vertical    - vectorization
    mjj = mmk(i,jj,k)
    if (u(mjj) >= 0) then         ! OBSTACLES: indirect addressing
                                  !            and branching
      j = jj
    else
      j = jj + 1
    endif
    ...
  enddo
  ...
enddo
```

FIGURE 3.13

Original code layout.

```
real(8), intent(in), contiguous :: u(0:)
...
do iw=                          ! horizontal - mpi/openmp parallelization
  ...
  i   = ind(1,iw)
  jj  = ind(2,iw)
  mj0 = mcol(iw) - 2
  ub  = min(kh(iw),kh(msrf(i,jj+1)))
  j   = jj
  mi0 = mcol(msrf(i,j)) - 2
  do k=2,ub                ! main loop 1 - vectorization
    mjj = mj0 + k          ! mjj == mi
    mi  = mi0 + k
    t1(mjj) = ... * max(sign(one,u(mjj)),0)*foo(i,j,k)
  enddo
  j = jj+1
  mi0 = mcol(msrf(i,j)) - 2
  do k=2,ub                ! main loop 2 - vectorization
    mjj = mj0 + k          ! mjj /= mi
    mi  = mi0 + k
    t1(mjj) = ... * min(sign(one,u(mjj)),0)*foo(i,j+1,k)
  enddo
  do k=ub+1,kh(iw)         ! remainder loop
    t1(mjj) = 0
  enddo
enddo
```

FIGURE 3.14

Initial rewrite of the code, step 1.

```
do n=n2dl,n2dl
  i = ind(1,n)
  j = ind(2,n)
  mi0 = mcol(n) - 2
  do k=2,kh(n)
    mi = mi0 + k
    t4(mi) = foo(i,j,k)
  enddo
enddo
do n=n2dl,n2dl
  i = ind(1,n)
  j = ind(2,n)
  ub = min(kh(n),kh(msrf(i,jj+1)))
  mi0 = mcol(n) - 2
  me0 = mcol(msrf(i,jj+1)) - 2
  do k=2,ub
    mi = mi0 + k
    me = me0 + k
    uhx = hx(mi)*u(mi)
    t1(mi) = t4(mi)*max(uhx,0) + t4(me)*min(uhx,0)
  enddo
  do k=ub+1,kh(n)
    t1(mi) = 0
  enddo
enddo
```

FIGURE 3.15

Trivial rewrite, step 2.

We see that the indirect addressing in the original code comes from the three-dimensional index lookup table $mmk(i,jj,k)$. This array transforms the grid point index set (i,jj,k) into its corresponding wet-point index and returns the value 0 if (i,jj,k) is a point on land or below the sea bottom. As explained in the section on data structures, the same information can be obtained from the $msrf(i,j)$, $mcol(iw)$, and $kh(iw)$ arrays using much less storage and direct addressing can be utilized. The other two obstacles stemming from assumed-shape arguments and branches inside innermost loop can be dealt with by transforming the code into snippet (Figure 3.14) (the extra work introduced will be "removed" later in the process but we aim at conveying the individual steps that one needs to take to reach a tuned version).

In the pseudo code snippets, we use $foo(i,j,k)$ as a short-hand notation for a more complicated expression evaluated at grid point (i,j,k); thus foo here is not meant as an array lookup or a function call.

That is, $t1$ at point (i,jj,k) is either $t2$ terms from the same column (i,jj) or similar terms from the neighbor column $(i,jj+1)$ to the right. Note that while we in the code snippet in Figure 3.13 could run all the way to the bottom in the k-loop due to the indirect addressing, we must in the code snippet in Figure 3.14 have a remainder loop if we insist on having pure stride-1 in the two main k-loops. Then we found that we actually only used $t1$ in the combination with two other arrays hx and u as:

$$t1(mjj)*hx(mjj)*u(mjj)$$

such that we deduced that we might as well use factor

$$max/min(hx(mjj)*u(mjj),0)$$

as a discriminator instead of the `IF-ELSE` branch, but as a penalty we run through everything twice. The goal should now be to get rid of the double work. We first observe that we compute both `(i,jj)` and `(i,jj+1)` terms and then make the selection by:

```
uhx      = hx(mjj)*u(mjj)
t1(mjj)  = foo(i,jj,k)*max(uhx,0)
           + foo(i,jj+1,k)*min(uhx,0)
```

but when we get to the neighbor column on the right-hand side, `jj+1`, then we actually compute `foo` at point `(i,jj+1,k)` once more, but this time it will have weight `MAX()` instead of `MIN()`.

On the other hand, we should consider a two-step rocket where we run through everything only once, i.e., compute `foo` at `(i,j,k)` for all wet-points `(i,j,k)` and store it in a temporary array (say `t4`), and afterward fill it into `t1` using the max/min functions. The pseudo code for that looks like the snippet is shown in Figure 3.15.

The transformations shown above will allow the compiler to see that it can generate SIMD-code. However, these transformations are not sufficient to allow effective SIMD-code generation. The next step is to tune the code generated and roofline analysis will serve as guidance in the tuning process. We will have to ensure that the computational intensity is properly balanced and we also need to ensure that the pressure on caches is reasonable. The latter is analyzed by estimating how many loop trips it will take to flush caches. The former calls for a design choice. In this particular case where we work on a 9-point stencil we have two obvious choices. We can either try to maximize the length of the vector by splitting the loop into two subloops, namely, the loop handling the midpoint in the stencil, say `iw`, with the bounds 2 and `kh(iw)` and the loop taking the additional contributions from the eight neighbors. Actually, this neighbor loop can also be split into eight subloops in case that will pay off. Alternatively, we can try to make a fat loop handling the midpoint of the stencil and all its eight neighbors in one go but to ensure stride-1 access the trip count will then have to be the minimum, `kmin`, of the lengths of the nine columns. Afterward, up to eight remainder loops will take the remaining contributions from the columns that have a length exceeding `kmin`. Analyzing the loops within the tracer advection code one by one using simple roofline estimates we found that the latter design with one fat loop plus a number of (up to eight) remainder loops was much better than the alternative with (up to nine) slim loops with larger trip counts.

PREMATURE ABSTRACTION IS THE ROOT OF ALL EVIL

Actually, the tracer advection part of HBM is somewhat special in the sense that within the vertical loop we have another loop over the number of tracers. This innermost `nc`-loop is only present in the tracer related part of the HBM code. The code snippet in Figure 3.16 shows the tracer loop inside the vertical loop.

In this subsection we will show how the most simple hardware abstraction (a 2D-array) will result in more than 2× performance loss on an Intel Xeon Phi coprocessor and this hands-on finding confirms our hypothesis that hardware abstractions come at a cost.

The original design idea was to hold all tracers in one 2D-array and treat all tracers in a similar fashion in one go. A simplified illustration of this is shown in the code snippet in Figure 3.17.

Trying to build this snippet we find that:

> With dynamic `nc` the compiler vectorizes the `nc`-loop:
> `(4): (col. 7) remark: LOOP WAS VECTORIZED`
> With static `nc`, the compiler vectorizes the k-loop:
> `(1): (col 7) remark: LOOP WAS VECTORIZED`

```
do iw=      ! horizontal - mpi/openmp parallelization
  do k=      ! vertical   - vectorization
    ...
    do nc=   ! innermost loop (in advection) with
             ! number of tracers
      ...
    enddo
  enddo
enddo
```

FIGURE 3.16

Basic loop structure with tracer loop.

```
1 do k=2,kmax
2   k1 = k+off1
3   k2 = k+off2
4   t(1:nc,k) = t(1:nc,k) + A(k)*(B(1:nc,k1)-B(1:nc,k2))
5 enddo
```

FIGURE 3.17

Simplified illustration of code.

Alas, these are the codes generated:

AVX (essentially a software gather operation):

```
...
vmovsd (%r10,%rcx,2), %xmm6
vmovhpd 16(%r10,%rcx,2), %xmm6, %xmm6
vmovsd 32(%r10,%rcx,2), %xmm7
vmovhpd 48(%r10,%rcx,2), %xmm7, %xmm7
vinsertf128 $1, %xmm7, %ymm6, %ymm7
...
```

MIC (a hardware gather):

```
vgatherdpd (%r13,%zmm2,8), %zmm6{%k5}
...
```

Neither for the MIC target nor for the AVX (IVB) target we achieved what we aimed at. Admitted, there are known issues with 256-bit unaligned load/store on the SNB/IVB architecture so the software gather may not be as bad as it looks. Let us try to analyze why we did not get ordinary vector loads. A static nc implies unrolling and the unrolling implies that the optimizer sees the loop as a stride-nc-loop, c.f. code snippet in Figure 3.18 with nc=2.

We know better, so let us state what the compiler could have done; our suggestion is shown in Figure 3.19.

```
do k=1,kmax
    k1 = k+off1
    k2 = k+off2
    t(1,k) = t(1,k) + A(k)*(B(1,k1)-B(1,k2))
    t(2,k) = t(2,k) + A(k)*(B(2,k1)-B(2,k2))
enddo
```

FIGURE 3.18

Unrolled tracer loop.

Proper handling of a mix of 2D and 1D (load with nc=2):

		t(1,1)	t(2,1)	t(1,2)	t(2,2)	t(1,3)	t(2,3)	t(1,4)	t(2,4)
zmm1	=	t(1,1)	t(2,1)	t(1,2)	t(2,2)	t(1,3)	t(2,3)	t(1,4)	t(2,4)
zmm2	=	t(1,5)	t(2,5)	t(1,6)	t(2,6)	t(1,7)	t(2,7)	t(1,8)	t(2,8)
zmm3	=	B(1,1+k1)	B(2,1+k1)	B(1,2+k1)	B(2,2+k1)	B(1,3+k1)	B(2,3+k1)	B(1,4+k1)	B(2,4+k1)
zmm4	=	B(1,5+k1)	B(2,5+k1)	B(1,6+k1)	B(2,6+k1)	B(1,7+k1)	B(2,7+k1)	B(1,8+k1)	B(2,8+k1)
zmm5	=	B(1,1+k2)	B(2,1+k2)	B(1,2+k2)	B(2,2+k2)	B(1,3+k2)	B(2,3+k2)	B(1,4+k2)	B(2,4+k2)
zmm6	=	B(1,5+k2)	B(2,5+k2)	B(1,6+k2)	B(2,6+k2)	B(1,7+k2)	B(2,7+k2)	B(1,8+k2)	B(2,8+k2)
zmm7	=	A(1)	A(1)	A(2)	A(2)	A(3)	A(3)	A(4)	A(4)
zmm8	=	A(5)	A(5)	A(6)	A(6)	A(7)	A(7)	A(8)	A(8)

Proper handling of a mix of 2D and 1D (arithmetic):

zmm9	=	**zmm1**	+	**zmm7**	*	(**zmm3**	-	**zmm5**)	!k=1, 4; nc=1, 2
zmm10	=	**zmm2**	+	**zmm8**	*	(**zmm4**	-	**zmm6**)	!k=5, 8; nc=1, 2

FIGURE 3.19

Proper handling of mixed 2D and 1D data.

```
1 do k=2, kmax
2   k1 = k+off1
3   k2 = k+off2
4   t1(k) = t1(k) + A(k)*(B1(k1)-B1(k2))
5   t2(k) = t2(k) + A(k)*(B2(k1)-B2(k2))
6 enddo
```

FIGURE 3.20

Compiler friendly rewrite using only 1D arrays.

Thus, to optimize the generated code we have to bite the dust and change the code so that we use 1D arrays for the tracers too, i.e., use t1(:) and t2(:) instead of t(1:2,:) as shown in Figure 3.20.

Alternatively, we can try to interchange loops (with nc times the pressure on the memory bandwidth and with the vector length reduced by $1/nc$). The overall problem here is that the loop contains variables of mixed dimension. If all variables had the same dimension, the compiler would have collapsed the loops and generated proper code.

RESULTS

In this section, we will show the performance and some characteristics of the advection module from HBM. As mentioned before, the advection module was chosen for tuning since a single node run on both an Intel Xeon processor and an Intel Xeon Phi coprocessor showed that ~40% of the time was spent here. The time spent on the coprocessor was 3× the time on the processor prior to optimizing the code. With the aforementioned optimizations on data structures, SIMD and parallelization the pure OpenMP performance of the HBM advection module for the Baffin Bay test cases on the coprocessor alone in native mode is ~15% better than a dual-socket processor. However, our optimization work is still work in progress and we have identified some opportunities to improve cache usage which will further improve performance.

All the Baffin Bay cases are irregular and splitting an irregular grid into a load-balanced problem is significantly harder than the with ideal cube test cases. As regards to the performance, the aforementioned data locality, SIMD, and concurrency optimization efforts have significantly improved the performance on Xeon (E5-2697 v2) and more on the Intel Xeon Phi coprocessor (KNC) from where we had originally started. The performance currently on KNC 7120A in pure OpenMP case is ~15% better than the processors (E5-2697 v2) for the Baffin Bay cases as shown in the table in Figure 3.21.

The memory bandwidth measurements show that the application reaches ~90% of practical achievable bandwidth (POP) on the coprocessor and 100% of practical achievable bandwidth on the processor. The practical peak bandwidth is measured using Stream Triad where the coprocessor is 2.15× faster than the processor. The processor also uses 1.45 times more watt to attain its peak. The power measurement for the coprocessor is card-only power. Thus the inference from the bandwidth numbers are that there may be a slight potential on the Intel Xeon Phi coprocessor for further improving reuse of data which will make the time to solution go down and achieving 100% peak BW utilization.

Efficient vectorization is a key to performance (especially on Intel Xeon Phi coprocessors) as you would have read in the SIMD section of the chapter. Vectorization intensity (VI) is a metric that shows how well the loops were vectorized and how effectively it uses the VPUs (vector processing units). VI cannot exceed 8 for double precision code or 16 for single precision code due to the 512 bit-wide vector length. If the number is way smaller then it means that the loops were not well vectorized or the VPUs are not effectively used (low trip counts, masked instructions due to conditionals or vectorization was not possible). The advection module code uses double-precision data type, thus the VI metric (~7) shows that the loops are well vectorized and the VPUs were effectively used (82-96%) on the coprocessor.

Input	Xeon E5-2697 v2 Time (secs.)	KNC 7120A Time (secs.)	Xeon BW (GB/s)	POP Xeon (%)	KNC BW (GB/s)	POP KNC (%)	KNC VI	P/W
BaffinBay_2nm	81.581	70.662	89.23	100	161.55	89.75	7.04	1.63x
BaffinBay_1nm	320.81	273.095	88.56	100	160.69	89.27	6.87	1.62x

FIGURE 3.21

Advection module performance summary.

The Performance/Watt (P/W) improvement is basically the ratio of the processors (Xeon E5-2697 v2) and coprocessor (KNC 7120A) time to solution for the different test cases multiplied by the 1.45 factor. We use the 1.45 factor since the processors (Xeon E5-2697 v2) uses ~1.45 times more power (watts) compared to the coprocessor (KNC 7120A) to attain peak Triad bandwidth and also since the application achieves close to 90% of peak bandwidth.

PROFILING DETAILS

We used the Intel® VTune™ Amplifier XE 2013 for profiling. Although we used many performance metrics during the course of the optimization effort, we have highlighted only some of them in Figure 3.22 that we believe were more relevant.

VPU_INSTRUCTIONS_EXECUTED counts all the vector instructions and VPU_ELEMENTS_ACTIVE counts all active lanes of VPU for a vector operation (memory and arithmetic).

For the profile we have used, the hardware event-based sampling collector of the Intel® VTune™ Amplifier which profiles your application using the counter overflow feature of the Performance Monitoring Unit (PMU). The sample after value used for the above measurements is 10 million. As we are all aware sampling does not provide 100% accurate data. The average overhead of event-based sampling is about 2% on a 1 ms sampling interval.

SCALING ON PROCESSOR VS. COPROCESSOR

Figure 3.23 shows the OpenMP scaling of the BaffinBay_2nm test case on the Intel Xeon Phi coprocessor (KNC) where the *X*-axis represents the number of cores and *Y*-axis represents throughput (1/Time) normalized to 1.0. Time in the figure is elapsed time in seconds. All four threads in a core are utilized in the above case. As you can see we obtain an almost perfect core scaling for the advection module on KNC. Ideal core scaling and concurrency are really very keys for the Intel Xeon Phi coprocessor.

A similar scaling plot on an Intel Xeon dual-socket system in Figure 3.24 shows that the core scaling is not perfect. The main reason for that is memory bandwidth limitation. We have plotted the memory bandwidth usage in Figure 3.25 of each socket as a function of number of cores in Figure 3.24. The peak memory bandwidth per socket of a Xeon E5-2697 v2 is ~43 GB/s. Thus the peak memory bandwidth for the dual socket is in the range of ~84-88 GB/s. The application seems to hit a memory

Metric	Hardware Events Used
Bandwidth	UNC_F_CH0_NORMAL_READ,UNC_F_CH1_NORMAL_READ, UNC_F_CH0_NORMAL_WRITE, UNC_F_CH1_NORMAL_WRITE
Vectorization intensity	VPU_INSTRUCTIONS_EXECUTED, VPU_ELEMENTS_ACTIVE

FIGURE 3.22

PMU events used for bandwidth and vectorization efficiency calculations.

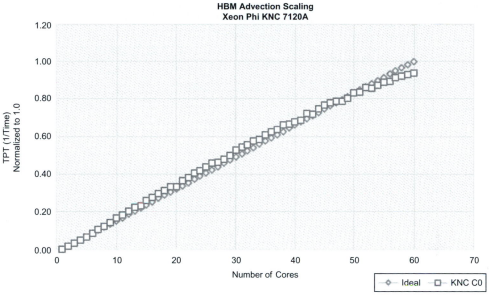

FIGURE 3.23

OpenMP thread scaling on Intel Xeon Phi coprocessor (KNC 7120A).

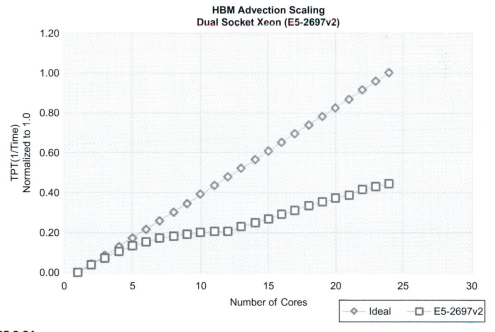

FIGURE 3.24

OpenMP thread scaling on dual-socket Intel Xeon processor (E5-2697 v2).

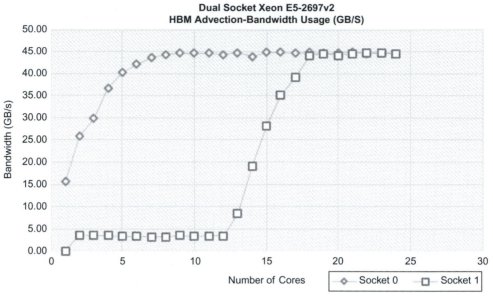

FIGURE 3.25

Bandwidth scaling with cores on dual-socket Intel Xeon processor.

bandwidth peak for socket 0 at ~6 cores (12 threads), and if you correlate with the scaling graph in Figure 3.24, you see that the scaling starts to flatten out at around that point. Then at around 13 cores when you had the second socket (socket 1), you start seeing some gains in scaling but again at around 17 cores you hit the peak bandwidth for socket 1 and thus the limit for the whole 2-socket system. Thus it proves that the processor performance and scaling are limited due to memory bandwidth limitations and that is where an Intel Xeon Phi coprocessor has an advantage and makes most of it for this application.

Figure 3.26 shows the importance of parallelism and good concurrency on the coprocessor. The X-axis again is the number of cores from 1 to 60 for the coprocessor and the Y-axis is the throughput (1/Time) for the advection module. As you can see the performance of the advection module on the Intel Xeon Phi coprocessor seems to match the Amdahl plot of 100% parallelism (no serial code). As an example even if you had 1%, 3%, or 5% of serial code in your application your time to solution will significantly increase and thus your throughput will significantly reduce as plotted in Figure 3.26. This validates Amdahl's law completely.

CONTIGUOUS ATTRIBUTE

The CONTIGUOUS attribute in FORTRAN 2008 explicitly indicates that an assumed-shape array is contiguous or that a pointer will only be associated with a contiguous object. There are a lot of conditions where an object can be CONTIGUOUS even if not specified (refer to Fortran Standard

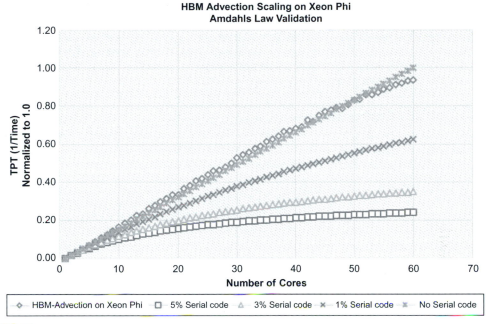

FIGURE 3.26

Amdahl's law validation and effects of serial code on Intel Xeon Phi coprocessor.

Specifications). But the CONTIGUOUS attribute makes it easier to enable compiler optimizations that rely on the memory layout of an object occupying contiguous blocks of memory.

The numbers in the table of Figure 3.27 clearly indicate that the CONTIGUOUS attribute improves performance on Intel Xeon (E5-2697 v2) in the range of 1-2% and more significantly on Intel Xeon Phi coprocessor (KNC 7120A) in the range of ~20%.

Input	With "Contiguous" Attribute		Without "Contiguous" Attribute		Performance Difference	
	2 Socket Xeon Time (seconds)	KNC 7120A Time (seconds)	2 Socket Xeon Time (seconds)	KNC 7120A Time (seconds)	2 Socket Xeon Time Speed-up	KNC 7120A Time Speed-up
BaffinBay_2nm	81.165	70.653	83.283	85.490	1.02x	1.21x
BaffinBay_1nm	320.97	273.158	323.401	333.252	1.01x	1.22x

FIGURE 3.27

Benefits of using CONTIGUOUS attribute in Fortran on Xeon and Xeon Phi.

SUMMARY

The thinking process and techniques used in this chapter have wide applicability: focus on data locality and then apply threading and vectorization techniques. This way of thinking should be on the mind of every programmer working to design a high-performance application. Such programming leads to improved performance on both Intel Xeon processors and Intel Xeon Phi coprocessors.

We have shown that good SIMD and thread performance on modern hardware is obtained when an implementation puts focus on data proximity. We described the data-oriented design used throughout the HBM model in order to get good performance. The key foundation is data structures for circulation model codes that are chosen to match the desire for parallelism. The steps toward SIMD vectorization of the code are described while pointing out both trivial and some not-so-obvious obstacles that had to be overcome. The techniques used apply both to Intel Xeon processors and Intel Xeon Phi coprocessors, but the superior aggregate memory bandwidth of the coprocessor allows it to scale more. For this particular application, we demonstrate a single node speedup of ~15% on the Intel Xeon Phi coprocessor compared to an Intel Xeon processor. The power efficiency of the Intel Xeon Phi coprocessor makes its use compelling even though we believe that the memory limitation of the coprocessor card is now the limiting factor in getting more speedup. The amount of this limitation should improve significantly in the next generation of Intel Xeon Phi coprocessors (Knights Landing).

REFERENCES

Gross, E.S., Rosatti, G., Bonaventura, L., 2002. Consistency with continuity in conservative advection schemes for free-surface models. Int. J. Numer. Methods Fluids 38 (4), 307–327.

Harten, A., 1997. High resolution schemes for hyperbolic conservation laws. J. Comput. Phys. 135 (2), 259–278. With an introduction by Peter Lax, Commemoration of the 30th anniversary of J. Comput. Phys.

Hofmann, J., Treibig, J., Hager, G., Wellein, G., Comparing the Performance of Different x86 SIMD Instruction Sets for a Medical Imaging Application on Modern Multi- and Manycore Chips, the Workshop on Programming Models for SIMD/Vector Processing at PPoPP 2014, Orlando, FL, Feb 16, 2014. Preprint: arXiv:1401.7494.

Kleine, E., 1993. Die konzeption eines numerischen verfahrens für die advektionsgleichung. Technical Report. Bundesant für Seeschifffahrt und Hydrographie, Hamburg.

Skiena, S., 2008. The Algorithm Design Manual, second ed. Springer, London.

Xu, P., Tirthapura, S., 2012. A lower bound on proximity preservation by space filling curves. In: IPDPS, pp. 1295–1305.

FOR MORE INFORMATION

- Readers interested in learning more about HBM are referred to (Berg and Poulsen, 2012) and (Poulsen and Berg, 2012a) for implementation details, design goals, and maintenance and testing criteria for the HBM code. Some performance studies and surveys of different applications are also given in these two technical reports while thread-scaling is treated in depth in a third report (Poulsen and Berg, 2012b).

- Berg, P., Poulsen, J.W., 2012. Implementation Details for HBM. DMI Technical Report No. 12-11. Technical Report, DMI, Copenhagen. http://beta.dmi.dk/fileadmin/Rapporter/TR/tr12-11.pdf
  - Poulsen, J.W., Berg, P., 2012a. More Details on HBM—General Modelling Theory and Survey of Recent Studies. DMI Technical Report No. 12-16. Technical Report, DMI, Copenhagen. http://beta.dmi.dk/fileadmin/Rapporter/TR/tr12-16.pdf.
  - Poulsen, J.W., Berg, P., 2012b. Thread Scaling with HBM. DMI Technical Report No. 12-20. Technical Report, DMI, Copenhagen. www.dmi.dk/fileadmin/user_upload/Rapporter/tr12-20.pdf.
- She, J., Poulsen, J.W., Berg, P., Jonasson, L., 2013. Next generation pan-European coupled Climate-Ocean Model—Phase 1 (ECOM-I). PRACE Final Report
- HIROMB: High Resolution Operational Model for the Baltic Sea, http://www.hiromb.org/
- BOOS: Baltic Operational Oceanographic System, http://www.boos.org/
- MyOcean is the main European project dedicated to the implementation of the GMES (Global Monitoring for Environment and Security) Marine Service for ocean monitoring and forecasting, http://www.myocean.eu/
- PRACE: Partnership for Advanced Computing in Europe, http://www.prace-ri.eu/
- ETOPO1 is a 1 arc-minute global relief model of Earth's surface that integrates land topography and ocean bathymetry, http://www.ngdc.noaa.gov/mgg/global/global.html
- Download the code from this, and other chapters, at http://lotsofcores.com
- Readers interested in learning more about space filling curves (SFCs) may be interested in:
  - Mitchison, G., Durbin, R., 1986. Optimal numberings of an $N \times N$ array. SIAM J. Algebr. Discrete Meth. 7 (4), 571–582.
  - Niedermeier, R., Reinhardt, K., Sanders, P., 1997. Towards optimal locality in mesh-indexings. In: Proceedings of the 11th International Symposium on Fundamentals of Computation Theory (FCT'97), Number 1279 in LNCS, Springer, pp. 364-375.
  - Niedermeier, R., Reinhardt, K., Sanders, P., 2002. Towards optimal locality in mesh-indexings. Discrete Appl. Math. 117 (1-3), 211–237

OPTIMIZING FOR REACTING NAVIER-STOKES EQUATIONS

4

Antonio Valles*, Weiqun Zhang†

*Intel, USA, †Lawrence Berkeley National Laboratory, USA

Intel® Xeon® processors and Intel® Xeon Phi™ coprocessors continue to increase the number of cores and total hardware threads per node. This provides new parallel opportunities at the node level which hybrid applications (MPI + OpenMP) can fully exploit. But, many applications are not properly optimized to take advantage of so many hardware threads per node. This chapter describes such analysis and parallel optimization work done by Lawrence Berkeley National Laboratories (LBNL) with Intel Corporation on an application called SMC.

GETTING STARTED

SMC is a combustion code that solves the multicomponent, reacting, compressible Navier-Stokes equations. It is developed at the Center for Computation Sciences and Engineering (CCSE) at LBNL. Minimalist versions of SMC are being used as a proxy application for architectural simulations and programming model exploration by high-performance computing system vendors and the Center for Exascale Simulation of Combustion in Turbulence of the US Department of Energy. Figure 4.1 shows output of SMC during combustion simulation. In this chapter, we use a minimalist version of SMC for analysis and optimization.

SMC is mainly written in Fortran with some parts in C. It is implemented within the BoxLib software framework, also developed at CCSE, with a hybrid MPI-OpenMP approach for parallelization. SMC uses a finite-difference method in which the numerical solution to the multicomponent Navier-Stokes equations is represented at Cartesian grid points in three dimensions. The data are stored as four-dimensional Fortran arrays with the dimensions corresponding to x, y, z, and component. Since column-major is used for arrays in Fortran, the data are contiguous in memory in x-direction. In SMC, the eighth-order stencils for spatial derivatives in each dimension use data from nine grid points in that dimension.

SMC version used in this chapter can be downloaded from GitHub (see "For more information" at the end of this chapter).

This chapter will explain four main optimizations done on SMC. These are releases 1-5 on GitHub. We will discuss these in detail in the sections to follow:

1. Version 1.0: Baseline
2. Version 2.0: Threadbox
3. Version 3.0: Stack memory

69

FIGURE 4.1

Temperature for a simulation of jet using a 39-species dimethyl ether chemistry mechanism.

4. Version 4.0: Blocking
5. Version 5.0: Vectorization

README file on GitHub discusses how to build and run. There are multiple build options (MPI, OpenMP, GNU compiler, Intel Compiler, etc.). Take some time to understand the different build options and the different run options in *inputs_SMC* file.

The performance is measured using the wall time for advancing five time steps excluding the time for initializing the computational model. The initialization time is also excluded in timing real runs because this initialization is done only once for a real run that can last for days or weeks.

SMC is a hybrid workload that can be executed with different number of MPI ranks and OpenMP threads. But, SMC has demonstrated excellent weak scaling behavior using up to 16,000 MPI ranks with an efficiency of more than 90%. Therefore, MPI is not the bottleneck. Thus, for the rest of the chapter we will focus on how to efficiently exploit concurrency using OpenMP threads and improve performance with vectorization. We will use only one box on one node with one MPI rank with $128 \times 128 \times 128$ grid points.

Two systems were used in this analysis:

1. Intel Xeon Phi Coprocessor 7120P (code-named Knights Corner):
   • 61 cores with 4 hardware threads per core for a total of $(61 \times 4 =)$ 244 hardware threads.
2. Intel® Xeon® Processor E5-2697 v2 (code-named IvyBridge-EP):
   • 2 sockets, each with 12 cores with Intel® Hyper-Threading Technology, for a total of (2 sockets $\times$ 12 cores $\times$ 2 hardware thread per core=) 48 hardware threads.

VERSION 1.0: BASELINE

We first present the baseline scaling results using SMC version 1.0. Figure 4.2 shows coprocessor OpenMP thread scaling and Figure 4.3 shows processor OpenMP thread scaling. Both graphs plot the inverse of SMC Advance time over the number of OpenMP threads; there are two *y*-axis: left *y*-axis is 1/Time; right *y*-axis is speedup over single-threaded result. We use the left *y*-axis to compare between platforms and versions (higher is better) and we use the right *y*-axis to understand how well each implementation scales vs. its single-threaded run.

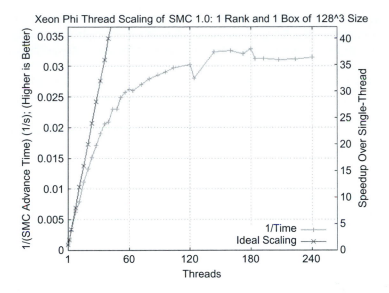

FIGURE 4.2

SMC version 1.0: coprocessor thread scaling.

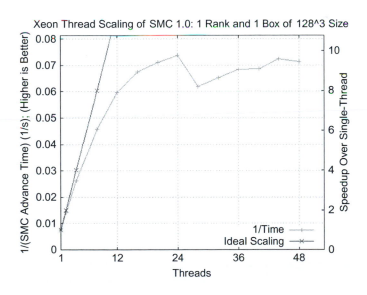

FIGURE 4.3

SMC version 1.0: processor thread scaling.

In both figures, we see that SMC version 1.0 does not scale well. We ran a coprocessor with 240 OpenMP threads but only see ~38x speedup over an Intel Xeon Phi coprocessor single-threaded result. Similarly, we ran a processor with 48 OpenMP threads but only see ~10x speedup over an Intel Xeon processor single-threaded result.

We use Intel® VTune™ Amplifier XE to help us understand OpenMP performance problems and potential opportunities. Figure 4.4 shows three screen shots from Intel VTune Amplifier XE 2015 version, containing OpenMP analysis capabilities, for SMC 1.0 Intel Xeon Phi coprocessor run. The first section, *OpenMP Analysis*, is used to show inefficiencies in the parallelization of the application. In particular, two items highlighted in pink: *Serial Time* and *Potential Gain* are very large in comparison to the *elapsed time* and *parallel region elapsed time*, respectively. *Serial Time* includes both SMC's initialization time and serial time while advancing the five time steps. For this reason, we will pay more attention to the *Potential Gain* metric instead as it encompasses only the parallel regions. The large *Potential Gain* vs. *parallel region elapsed time* ratio indicates we have some room to optimize. The middle section, *CPU Usage Histogram*, displays the percentage of wall time the specific numbers of CPUs were running simultaneously. In this case, we see that we are far away from our target concurrency of 240 Logical CPUs. The bottom section, *Over-Time View*, indicates what the CPUs were running over time. The first row of data is our application process, following rows are modules of that process. We see that *libiomp5.so* module was what was running the most and the actual work (labeled

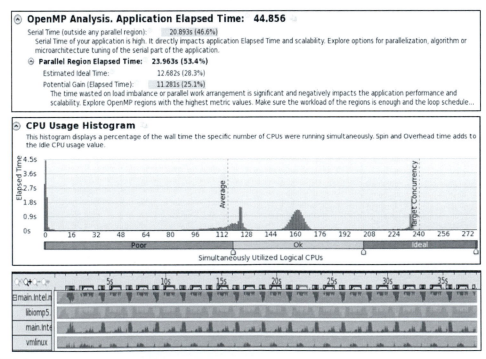

FIGURE 4.4

SMC version 1.0 (Intel Xeon Phi coprocessor): VTune Amplifier XE screen shots of three different analysis sections: OpenMP analysis, CPU Usage Histogram, over-time view.

as *main.intel…* module) was minimal. This indicates that either we have very small parallel regions or severe load imbalance. Whichever one is the case, VTune Amplifier shows that the main problem is most of our threads are waiting instead of running application code.

Investigating performance via hotspot analysis in VTune Amplifier, we see that the main hotspot is *diffterm_2* in source file *kernels.f90* (for our simplified example below, we will call this subroutine *diffterm*). This function computes the diffusive terms in the Navier-Stokes equations. Computing the diffusive terms involves many loops and many of the loops contain stencil operations in which data from neighboring cells are used. Looking at the source code, we see *diffterm* has a large parallel region (see Figure 4.5). Although, the parallel region is a good size, it contains more than one hundred small nested loops each with its own OMP DO. This is not optimal as it is too fine grain.

The fine-grain parallelism occurs due to how OpenMP works. An OpenMP-enabled application starts off with a single master thread and forks worker threads when it encounters a parallel region. At this point, all of the execution happens in parallel. When OpenMP encounters the OMP DO work-sharing construct, OpenMP splits up the loop iterations among the threads. The OpenMP Loop COLLAPSE(n) clause can also be added to collapse n nested loops into one iteration space and divide work among threads. The OpenMP work-sharing construct end point is marked with OMP END DO. There is an implicit barrier at OMP END DO unless the user adds a NOWAIT synchronization clause with the OMP END DO. The end of the parallel region is a barrier where all threads wait until all complete (the join). OpenMP continues with this fork-join behavior for all subsequent parallel regions.

Thus, the OMP DO work-sharing constructs denote the actual parallel work some of which may have implicit barriers at the end. These small parallel work-sharing regions will result in a lot of overhead and imbalance. A potential solution to investigate further is to take a coarse-grained approach for OpenMP.

VERSION 2.0: THREADBOX

In this version, we adopt a coarse-grain OpenMP approach that requires very little changes to the source code that computes the diffusive terms (*diffterm* subroutine). See Figure 4.5 for version 1 code and Figure 4.6 for version 2. The code in the figures has been simplified for brevity and to focus on main points.

In this approach, the computational domain is decomposed into subdomains. Each thread is responsible for one subdomain. The call to *get_threadbox* returns the lower and upper bounds of the assigned subdomain for each thread. The *diffterm* subroutine now contains no OpenMP directives. It now takes two new arguments specifying the work domain. This optimization works because the different thread subdomains are independent of each other in each of the hundred loops in *diffterm*.

We expected a performance improvement on both an Intel Xeon processor and Intel Xeon Phi coprocessor with this optimization due to much larger parallel section (i.e., parallel region without work-sharing constructs) and improved load balance. Indeed, we see a significant performance and scaling improvement on an Intel Xeon processor (now 16x, was 10x on version 1.0) as seen on Figure 4.7. But, this optimization actually caused performance degradation on an Intel Xeon Phi coprocessor as seen on Figure 4.8. We used VTune Amplifier to root cause this unexpected result on Intel Xeon Phi coprocessor. We found that *vmlinux* was now a major hotspot (see Figure 4.9). *Vmlinux* time ballooned due to multiple dynamic allocation calls in the code (for example, the *tmp* array in the example above is an allocatable

```
         call diffterm(U,dUdt,domlo,domhi)

         subroutine diffterm(U,dUdt,domlo,domhi)
           ! domlo, domhi: lower and upper bounds
           ! of the computational domain
           integer, intent(in) :: domlo(3), domhi(3)

           ! U and dUdt are four-dimensional arrays.
           ! The first three are for spatial dimensions,
           ! whereas the fourth for variable components such
           ! as density and velocity.
           ! U has four ghost cells on each side.
           real, intent(in) :: U(domlo(1)-4:domhi(1)+4,
                                  domlo(2)-4:domhi(2)+4,
                                  domlo(3)-4:domhi(3)+4,
                                  nU)
           real, intent(inout) :: dUdt(domlo(1):domhi(1),
                                        domlo(2):domhi(2),
                                        domlo(3):domhi(3),
                                        nU)

           ! tmp is a local array
           real, allocatable :: tmp(:,:,:)

           allocate(tmp (domlo(1)-4:domhi(1)+4,
                    domlo(2)-4:domhi(2)+4,
                    domlo(3)-4:domhi(3)+4)   )

         !$OMP PARALLEL PRIVATE(...)

         !$OMP DO COLLAPSE(2)
         do k = domlo(3)-4, domhi(3)+4
           do j = domlo(2)-4, domhi(2)+4
             do i = domlo(1)-4, domhi(1)+4
               tmp(i,j,k) = ......
             end do
           end do
         end do
         !$OMP END DO

         ! lots of nested loops threaded with OMP DO ...

         !$OMP DO COLLAPSE(2)
         do k = domlo(3), domhi(3)
           do j = domlo(2), domhi(2)
             do i = domlo(1), domhi(1)
               dUdt(i,j,k,1) = ......
             end do
           end do
         end do
         !$OMP END DO

         !$OMP END PARALLEL
         end subroutine diffterm
```

FIGURE 4.5

SMC 1.0, code showing fine-grain parallelism (not the actual code, code snippet simplified for brevity and to show main point).

```fortran
!$OMP PARALLEL PRIVATE(lo,hi)
call get_threadbox(lo,hi)
call diffterm(lo,hi,U,dUdt,domlo,domhi)
!$OMP END PARALLEL

subroutine diffterm(lo,hi,U,dUdt,domlo,domhi)
  ! lo, hi: lower and upper bounds of the assigned
  ! sub-domain for this thread
  ! domlo, domhi: lower and upper bounds of the
  ! computational domain
  integer, intent(in) :: lo(3), hi(3)
  integer, intent(in) :: domlo(3), domhi(3)

  ! U and dUdt are four-dimensional arrays.
  ! The first three are for spatial dimensions,
  ! whereas the fourth for variable components such
  ! as density and velocity.
  ! U has four ghost cells on each side.
  real, intent(in) :: U(domlo(1)-4:domhi(1)+4,
                        domlo(2)-4:domhi(2)+4,
                        domlo(3)-4:domhi(3)+4,
                        nU)
  real, intent(inout) :: dUdt(domlo(1):domhi(1),
                              domlo(2):domhi(2),
                              domlo(3):domhi(3),
                              nU)

  ! tmp is a local array
  real, allocatable :: tmp(:,:,:)

  allocate( tmp(lo(1)-4:hi(1)+4,
               lo(2)-4:hi(2)+4,
               lo(3)-4:hi(3)+4) )

  do k = lo(3)-4, hi(3)+4
    do j = lo(2)-4, hi(2)+4
      do i = lo(1)-4, hi(1)+4
        tmp(i,j,k) = ......
      end do
    end do
  end do

  ! lots of nested loops without any OMP directives

  do k = lo(3), hi(3)
    do j = lo(2), hi(2)
      do i = lo(1), hi(1)
        dUdt(i,j,k,1) = ......
      end do
    end do
  end do
end subroutine diffterm
```

FIGURE 4.6

SMC 2.0, code optimized for coarse-grain parallelism; OpenMP directives moved up from subroutine diffterm to where diffterm is called (not the actual code, code snippet simplified for brevity and to show main point).

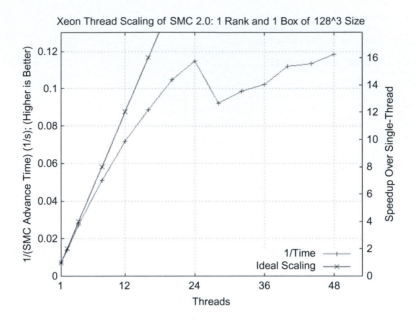

FIGURE 4.7

SMC version 2.0: processor OpenMP thread scaling, code optimized for coarse-grain parallelism; both performance and thread scaling improve.

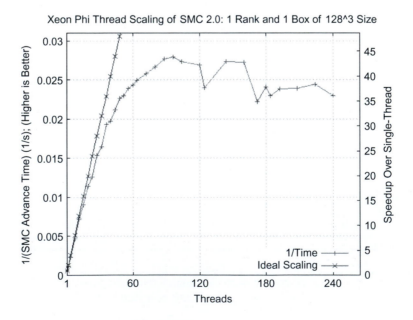

FIGURE 4.8

SMC version 2.0: coprocessor OpenMP thread scaling, code optimized for coarse-grain parallelism but coprocessor performance degrades vs. version 1.0.

FIGURE 4.9

SMC version 2.0 (Intel Xeon Phi coprocessor): VTune Amplifier XE screen shot of over-time view. Notice vmlinux (second row) has become a hotspot compared to over-time view in Figure 4.4.

array, the actual code has several allocatable arrays in the *diffterm* subroutine). In SMC version 1.0, the OMP PARALLEL directive was placed after the dynamic allocation calls. In version 2.0, the OMP PARALLEL directive was placed in the caller function and now each thread calls the *diffterm* subroutine with its own subdomain. Thus, in version 1.0 the heap allocations occur once per master thread, whereas in version 2.0 the heap allocations are per OpenMP thread. This affects Intel Xeon Phi coprocessors more than Intel Xeon processors primarily because of the number of threads (5x more threads). These dynamic memory allocation calls per thread cause *vmlinux* time to balloon inhibiting further thread scaling and preventing us from seeing any benefit from the ThreadBox optimization on coprocessors.

VERSION 3.0: STACK MEMORY

There are many local arrays in the *diffterm* subroutine. In Version 2, these arrays are dynamically allocated on the heap. These allocations are thread-safe but usually not scalable. In this version, we switch to use automatic instead of allocatable arrays for these local variables. For example, the *tmp* array in the example in last section becomes

```
real ::tmp( lo(1)-4:hi(1)+4,
             lo(2)-4:hi(2)+4,
             lo(3)-4:hi(3)+4 )
```

One caveat is that we need to make sure that each thread has a large enough stack memory space. This can be achieved by setting the "OMP_STACKSIZE" environment variable.

Figures 4.10 and 4.11 show the new SMC scaling for version 3.0. On Intel Xeon Phi coprocessors, we now see a dramatic improvement in performance and scaling (~70x vs. ~38x from version 1.0). Xeon performance and scaling also benefited slightly. But, we have traded one problem for another. Now, the OMP_STACKSIZE needs to be very large when running small number of threads. This is screaming for some type of blocking optimization.

VERSION 4.0: BLOCKING

Version 3 requires a large stack memory size for each thread especially when the number of threads used is small. To reduce the constraint on stack size, we can further divide the subdomain for each thread into even smaller blocks. The size of the block can be made into a runtime parameter via *inputs_SMC* file. The call to *diffterm* is now placed inside a loop over the blocks (see Figure 4.12). An additional advantage is that this can reduce the working set size resulting in better cache performance. Note that this has no effect for cases in which the subdomain before blocking is already smaller than the targeted block size.

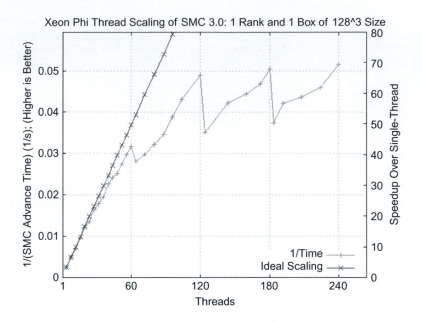

FIGURE 4.10

SMC version 3.0: Intel Xeon Phi coprocessor thread scaling, SMC scaling dramatically improved with threadbox optimization and replacing allocatable arrays with automatic arrays.

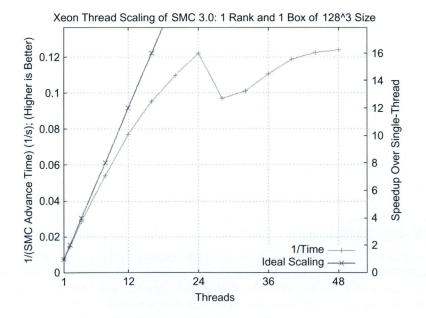

FIGURE 4.11

SMC version 3.0: processor thread scaling, only a slight benefit on an Intel Xeon processor vs. version 2.0.

```
Version 3.0:
!$OMP PARALLEL PRIVATE(lo,hi)
call get_threadbox(lo,hi)
call diffterm(lo,hi,U,dUdt,domlo,domhi)
!$OMP END PARALLEL

Version 4.0:
!$OMP PARALLEL PRIVATE(lo,hi,iblock,nblocks)
nblocks = tb_get_nblocks()
do iblock = 1, nblocks
    call get_threadbox(lo,hi,iblock)
    call diffterm(lo,hi,U,dUdt,domlo,domhi)
end do
!$OMP END PARALLEL
```

FIGURE 4.12

SMC version 4.0: partitioning subdomain from get_threadbox introduced in version 2.0 into smaller blocks

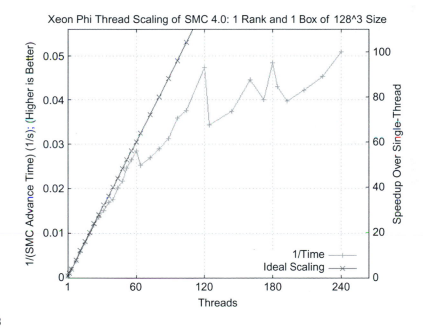

FIGURE 4.13

SMC version 4.0: coprocessor thread scaling after blocking (−1,4,5 used in inputs_SMC). Some of the points got slightly worse, but 240 thread performance similar to version 3.0.

Figures 4.13 and 4.14 show SMC scaling after the blocking optimization. Notice that there is not much of a difference. Some of the results are slightly worse, including the single-thread result which affected the scaling number (from 70x to 100x), but peak performance remains about the same. We still kept this change due to reducing the constraint on stack size especially for lower thread numbers or calculations using a large chemistry network.

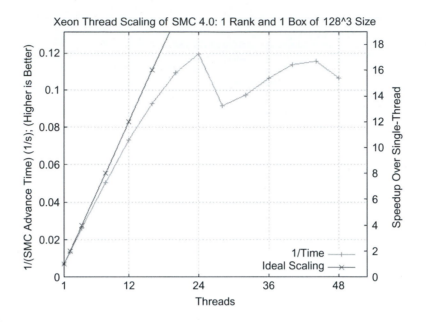

FIGURE 4.14

SMC version 4.0: processor thread scaling after blocking ($-1,16,16$ in inputs_SMC file). Notice 24 thread value similar to version 3.0, but 48 thread performance decreased.

VERSION 5.0: VECTORIZATION

A key ingredient for good performance on many-core architecture such as Intel Xeon Phi coprocessor is to take advantage of SIMD instructions. In this minimalist version of SMC, the computation of chemical reaction rates is relatively cheap because it uses a network with only nine species. However, for computations involving a large network with hundreds of species, the cost of computing reaction rates can be significant. This is because the cost of computing reaction rates grows with the number of species much more rapidly than that of computing diffusive terms. Here we present an approach to make the computation of reaction rates more vectorizable.

Figure 4.15 is the original computation of chemical reaction rates. Note that the inner loop involves a call to the *ckwyr* subroutine, which is very complicated and cannot be easily inlined. The *ckwyr* subroutine works on a single point, see Figure 4.16. It takes density, temperature, and mass fractions as inputs and returns the molar production rate of each species. The final results are stored in a four-dimensional array. This implementation cannot be vectorized due to the call in the inner loop that cannot be inlined and *ckwyr* subroutine only processing one cell at a time.

To get chemical reaction rates to vectorize, we first need to modify *ckwyr* subroutine to take vectors of density, temperature, and mass fractions. Figure 4.17 shows a new implementation that can now vectorize. To use this new implementation, the calling code was modified to generate the input vector, *Yt*, and use *ckwyr's* output vector, *wdot*, see Figure 4.18. This implementation gave a 4x speedup on the chemistry portion of the workload on the coprocessor.

In addition to vectorizing the chemical portion, the SIMD Fortran directive was added to multiple inner loops in *diffterm* where the compiler chose not to vectorize due to potential dependencies the compiler assumed to guarantee correctness.

```
Original computation of Chemical Reaction Rates:
do k=lo(3),hi(3)
      do j=lo(2),hi(2)
        do i=lo(1),hi(1)
          ! mass fraction
          Yt = q(i,j,k,qy1:qy1+nspecies-1)
          call ckwyr(q(i,j,k,qrho),
                     q(i,j,k,qtemp), Yt, wdot)
          up(i,j,k,iry1:iry1+nspecies-1) = wdot
                          * molecular_weight
        end do
      end do
    end do
```

FIGURE 4.15

SMC version 4.0: original chemical reaction rates computation, not vectorizable.

```
k_f[0] = 3.547e+15*exp(-0.406*T-
             8352.8934356925419706*invT);
k_f[1] = 50800.0*exp(2.67*T-
             3165.2328279116868543*invT);
k_f[2] = 2.16e+08*exp(1.51*T-
             1726.0331637101885462*invT);
// ......
k_f[5] = 6.165e+15*exp(-0.5*T);
// ......
k_f[9] = 1.66e+13*exp(-
             414.14731595728432012*invT);
// ......
k_f[11] = 3.25e+13;
// ......
k_f[20] = 5.8e+14*exp(-
             4809.2416750957054319*invT);
```

FIGURE 4.16

SMC version 4.0: code in original ckwyr C function. Processes one point at time.

```
for (int i=0; i<np; i++) {
    k_f[0][i] = 3.547e+15*exp(-0.406*T[i]-
                 8352.8934356925419706*invT[i]);
    k_f[1][i] = 50800.0*exp(2.67*T[i]-
                 3165.2328279116868543*invT[i]);
    k_f[2][i] = 2.16e+08*exp(1.51*T[i]-
                 1726.0331637101885462*invT[i]);
    // ......
    k_f[5][i] = 6.165e+15*exp(-0.5*T[i]);
    // ......
    k_f[9][i] = 1.66e+13*exp(-
                 414.14731595728432012*invT[i]);
    // ......
    k_f[11][i] = 3.25e+13;
    // ......
    k_f[20][i] = 5.8e+14*exp(-
                 4809.2416750957054319*invT[i]);
}
```

FIGURE 4.17

SMC version 5.0: chemical reaction rates computation modified to enable vectorization.

```
Optimized computation of Chemical Reaction Rates:
np = hi(1) - lo(1) + 1

do k=lo(3),hi(3)
   do j=lo(2),hi(2)

      do n=1, nspecies
         do i=lo(1),hi(1)
            Yt(i,n) = q(i,j,k,qy1+n-1)
         end do
      end do

      call ckwyr(np, q(lo(1):hi(1),j,k,qrho),
                     q(lo(1):hi(1),j,k,qtemp),
                     Yt, wdot)
      do n=1, nspecies
         do i=lo(1),hi(1)
            up(i,j,k,iry1+n-1) = wdot(i,n) *
                       molecular_weight(n)
         end do
      end do

   end do
end do
```

FIGURE 4.18

SMC version 5.0: chemical reaction rates computation modified to enable vectorization.

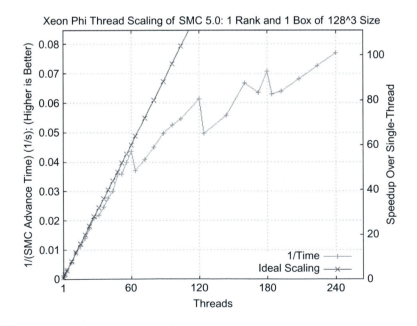

FIGURE 4.19

SMC version 5.0: coprocessor thread scaling after vectorization optimizations.

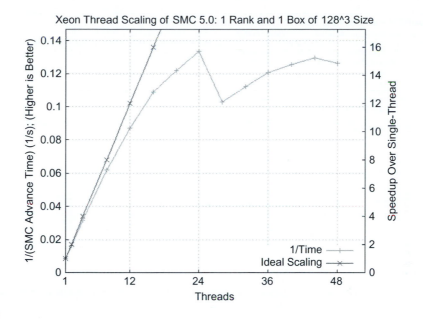

FIGURE 4.20

SMC version 5.0: processor thread scaling after vectorization optimizations.

For what we have covered in this chapter, Figures 4.19 and 4.20 show SMC performance and scaling after the current vectorization optimizations.

NOTE: The best performance shown on Figure 4.19 for the Intel Xeon Phi coprocessor is 12.99 seconds. We recently found that a few additional Fortran compiler options allow us to do better and achieve 9.11 seconds for the coprocessor (1.43x improvement *vs.* Figure 4.19) while keeping the processor performance the same. The compiler options for the improved performance are: -fno-alias -no-prec-div -no-prec-sqrt -fimf-precision=low -fimf-domain-exclusion=15 -align array64byte -opt-assume-safe-padding -opt-streaming-stores always -opt-streaming-cache-evict=0.

INTEL XEON PHI COPROCESSOR RESULTS

Optimizations benefited both Intel Xeon Phi coprocessor and Intel Xeon processors. Both performance and scaling improved as we applied the same programming techniques. Scaling on an Intel Xeon Phi coprocessor went from only a 38x scaling to 100x scaling over its single-thread result and performance more than doubled. The processor results also improved: 10x to 16x scaling and almost double the performance.

Figure 4.21 shows the final VTune Amplifier snapshots summarizing OpenMP performance. On the *OpenMP Analysis* portion, the potential *Gain time* and *Serial time* have significantly reduced. *Serial time* includes the initialization time which was not optimized and not part of SMC performance measurement. On the middle section, we see that the optimizations applied now enable us to hit the target concurrency on *CPU Usage Histogram*. And finally, the *libiomp5.so* module time in the *Over-Time view* has significantly reduced. This workload's concurrency has significantly improved.

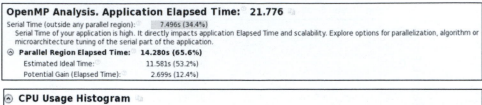

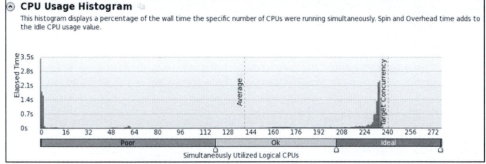

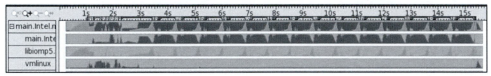

FIGURE 4.21

SMC version 5.0 (Intel Xeon Phi coprocessor): VTune Amplifier XE screenshots of three different analysis sections: OpenMP Analysis, CPU Usage Histogram, and over-time view. Shows significant improvement over SMC version 1.0 (Figure 4.4).

In absolute performance, the Intel Xeon processor outperforms the current Intel Xeon Phi coprocessor when both are optimized. Our optimization work yields significantly better performance on both processors and coprocessors when compared with the baseline. And, we did these optimizations with common programming techniques that will scale to multiple nodes.

We expect additional boosts when we move to the next generation Xeon Phi (code-named Knights Landing (KNL), available in the second half of 2015). The Intel approach for multicore and many-core sharing of programming models, languages, and tools benefits our work tremendously because our optimization work will carry forward for KNL both in coprocessor and KNL processor devices.

SUMMARY

Today's Intel processors and coprocessors have a large number of cores and hardware threads per node. The trend to increase cores and hardware threads in future processors does not appear to be slowing down. To fully exploit this parallel opportunity, cluster hybrid application developers need to analyze and optimize their parallel implementations. This case study discussed methods we used to improve concurrency. This included how we assessed and tracked performance and scaling, tools that help us analyze OpenMP performance, and OpenMP and vectorization optimization techniques.

For assessing and tracking performance we used an OpenMP thread scaling graph with two y-axis (one axis to describe performance and another axis to depict speedup over single thread). This single graph provided us with multiple capabilities: compare performance between versions and between platforms, clearly quantify thread scaling improvements, and enable us to do both at a per thread granularity.

For tools, we used VTune Amplifier XE 2015 with OpenMP analysis capabilities. The OpenMP analysis capability in VTune Amplifier provides an indication of potential gain from optimizations, illustrates how effectively the logical CPUs are being used, and illuminates what is actually running on the CPUs. These capabilities, combined with its traditional hotspot analysis capabilities, make VTune Amplifier instrumental in analyzing and optimizing parallel applications.

Four optimizations were done:

(1) *ThreadBox*: Created a coarse-grain parallel approach to optimize a previously fine-grained OpenMP parallelism approach at the loop level.
(2) *Stack allocation*: ThreadBox optimization had a side-effect we were not expecting. We fixed this by allocating data on the stack.
(3) *Blocking*: Stack allocation caused problems with smaller number of threads. This change enabled us to use smaller stack sizes especially for smaller thread numbers.
(4) *Vectorization*: Chemical reaction rates were transformed to enable vectorization and multiple *diffterm* loops now vectorize by using SIMD Fortran directive.

These optimizations significantly improved concurrency on both Intel Xeon Phi coprocessors and Intel Xeon processors. OpenMP thread scaling on the coprocessor with 240 threads vs. one thread is now 100x, was 38x in version 1.0. OpenMP thread scaling on the processor with 48 threads vs. one thread is now 16x, was 10x originally.

FOR MORE INFORMATION

Where did the name SMC originate? SMC is not an acronym. Someone who was trained as an astrophysicist chose the name. CCSE has a low Mach number combustion code called LMC. LMC can also stand for Large Magellanic Cloud, a satellite galaxy of the Milky Way. The LMC galaxy has a little brother called the Small Magellanic Cloud (SMC). Thus, SMC combustion code is also like a little brother of the LMC code.

Here are some additional reading materials we recommend related to this chapter:

- BoxLib software framework: https://ccse.lbl.gov/BoxLib/
- Emmetta, M., Zhang, W., Bell, J.B., 2014. High-order algorithms for compressible reacting flow with complex chemistry. Combust. Theor. Model. 18(3) (http://arxiv.org/abs/1309.7327)
- Minimalist SMC code used in chapter: https://github.com/WeiqunZhang/miniSMC
- Intel® Xeon Phi™ Coprocessor 7120P (code-named Knights Corner) details: http://ark.intel.com/products/75799/Intel-Xeon-Phi-Coprocessor-7120P-16GB-1_238-GHz-61-core
- Intel® Xeon® CPU E5-2697 v2 (code-named IvyBridge-EP) details: http://ark.intel.com/products/75283/Intel-Xeon-Processor-E5-2697-v2-30M-Cache-2_70-GHz?wapkw=e5-2697
- Intel VTune™ Amplifier XE: https://software.intel.com/en-us/intel-vtune-amplifier-xe
- Unat, D., Chan, C., Zhang, W., Bell, J., Shalf, J., 2013. Tiling as a durable abstraction for parallelism and data locality. In: Workshop on Domain-Specific Languages and High-Level Frameworks for HPC (http://sc13.supercomputing.org/sites/default/files/WorkshopsArchive/pdfs/wp118s1.pdf)

PLESIOCHRONOUS PHASING BARRIERS

5

Jim Dempsey

QuickThread Programming, LLC, USA

In telecommunications, a plesiochronous system is one where different parts of the system are almost, but not quite, perfectly synchronized. In any large-threaded application, synchronizing all threads via thread pool-wide barriers results in significant wasted processing time. When appropriate, adapting your application to use loosely synchronous (plesiochronous) barriers instead of strictly synchronous barriers can recover a substantial portion of previously lost thread barrier wait time. This chapter will apply these techniques to an example application that was presented from Chapter 4 of Intel® Xeon Phi™ Coprocessor High-Performance Programming, © 2013, Jim Jeffers and James Reinders, Morgan Kaufman Publications (HPP).

Before we get to the specifics of the plesiochronous phasing barrier usage, some preliminary code optimizations to the example application will be described. After these foundational improvements are discussed, the benefits and use of the plesiochronous phasing barrier will be presented bringing all the techniques together to demonstrate a significant improvement in application performance. The goal of this chapter is to deliver a full learning experience. The journey is most important, for the journey provides a means to the end, the end being becoming a better programmer.

Please take note that the programming enhancements presented in this chapter are equally applicable to programming processors. A discussion of the benefit to the host processor will be presented at the end of this chapter.

The system selected to produce the runtime data for this chapter is slightly different than the system used in the HPP book. The target host system is a workstation with one Intel® Xeon® E5-2620 processor in a motherboard with the x79 chipset. Two Intel Xeon Phi 5110P coprocessors are installed, but only one is used for the results presented. The HPP book showed runs on 61 core coprocessors, whereas we will show the revised code running on 60 cores coprocessors. Therefore, the tests run will use slightly different thread and core counts from those used in the HPP book examples.

The content of HPP Chapter 4 will not be duplicated here; rather the end of Chapter 4 is taken as a starting point. The program under investigation simulates diffusion of a solute through a volume of liquid over time within a 3D container such as a cube. Both the original and revised codes are available from http://www.lotsofcores.com. Though the text of this chapter is written assuming that you have a coprocessor, the referenced sample programs will compile and run on a processor as well.

We pick up where the other chapter ended with the results data (see Figure 5.1). This chart is an updated version of the chart from HPP using the new target test system with the 60 core coprocessor. The chart data represents the average of three runs of the program. This was done to smooth out any variations caused by the operating system.

Note, the numbers represent the ratio of the identified program version Mega-Flop/sec results versus the single-threaded "base" program Mega-Flop/sec results. Furthermore, the chart is not a scaling chart where the number of cores or threads change, but a comparison the performance benefits as we tune the implementation taking advantage of the full computational capability of the coprocessor.

Figure 5.1 illustrates the progress of the optimization process:

- Start with a functioning algorithm
  ```
  base        single thread version of the program
  ```
- Introduce parallel code
  ```
  omp         simplified conversion to parallel program
  ```
- Improve vectorization (interchangeable with adding parallel code)
  ```
  ompvect   adds simd vectorization directives
  ```
- Remove unnecessary code (improve efficiency)
  ```
  peel        removes unneeded code from the inner loop
  ```
- Improve cache hit ratios
  ```
  tiled       partitions work to improve cache hit ratios
  ```

After you finish the preceding optimization process, there is usually not much left to optimize. That is, unless you have overlooked something important.

In the aforementioned book, at the end of the chapter, the authors suggest that additional performance could be achieved with additional effort. Even an experienced parallel programmer might think that not much more could be squeezed out of the program with any addition tweaking.

Prior to listing the code changes, it is important to emphasize that given the highly parallel focus of the coprocessor; it would be unlikely to use a coprocessor to run a single-threaded application.

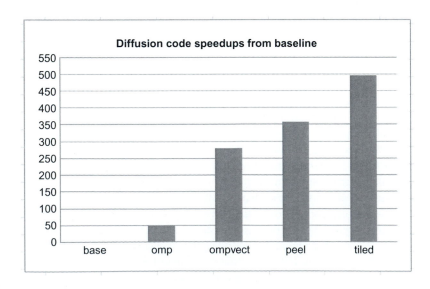

FIGURE 5.1

Xeon Phi™ 5110P relative performance improvement.

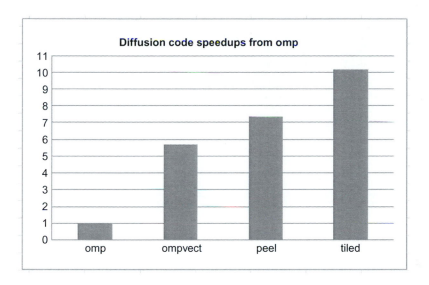

FIGURE 5.2

Performance relative to OpenMP.

Therefore, a better chart to use as a frame of reference is one that illustrates the speedup against the simple parallel OpenMP implementation, the column labeled omp in Figure 5.2.

The chart in Figure 5.2 clearly illustrates the benefits you get from following the advice in HPP Chapter 4. Now, let us get down to business to see where we can go from here!

First, minor edits to the original code were made to make it easier to run the described tests. None of the changes affects the intent or performance measurements of the code. The first change was to permit an optional -DNX=nnn on the C++ compiler command line to define the NX macro. This macro was used to specify the dimensions of a cube: nx=NX, ny=NX, nz=NX that sets the problem size. When the macro is not defined as a compiler command line option, the original value of 256 is used. Should the macro NX be defined on the command line, the command line value will be used. This was done to permit the Makefile to build a "small" model with arrays of $256\times256\times256$, and a large model with arrays of $512\times512\times512$ without having to edit the source code.

The compute section of the book's tiled code is shown in Figure 5.3.

WHAT CAN BE DONE TO IMPROVE THE CODE?

The compute intensive loop contains a single floating point expression with a handful of integer increments. The compiler optimization -O3 is going to unroll this loop and reduce the number of (x < nx-1) tests, as well as reduce the number of ++ operations through use of offsets. More importantly, the compiler will vectorize this loop.

This loop handles nx-2 indices of dimension x (254 in the small problem case). Whereas the expressions preceding and following the loop, handle the remaining 2 indices of x (x=0 and x=nx-1). With NX=256, the inner loop accounts for $254/256=99.22\%$ of the work.

```
#pragma omp parallel
{
  REAL *f1_t = f1;
  REAL *f2_t = f2;
  int mythread;
  for (int i = 0; i < count; ++i) {
#define YBF 16
#pragma omp for collapse(2)
for (int yy = 0; yy < ny; yy += YBF) {
  for (int z = 0; z < nz; z++) {
    int ymax = yy + YBF;
    if (ymax >= ny) ymax = ny;
    for (int y = yy; y < ymax; y++) {
      int x;
      int c, n, s, b, t;
      x = 0;
      c =  x + y * NXP + z * NXP * ny;
      n = (y == 0)    ? c : c - NXP;
      s = (y == ny-1) ? c : c + NXP;
      b = (z == 0)    ? c : c - NXP * ny;
      t = (z == nz-1) ? c : c + NXP * ny;
      f2_t[c] = cc * f1_t[c]
              + cw * f1_t[c]
              + ce * f1_t[c+1]
              + cs * f1_t[s]
              + cn * f1_t[n]
              + cb * f1_t[b]
              + ct * f1_t[t];
    #pragma simd
    for (x = 1; x < nx-1; x++) {
      ++c; ++n; ++s; ++b; ++t;
      f2_t[c] = cc * f1_t[c]
              + cw * f1_t[c-1]
              + ce * f1_t[c+1]
              + cs * f1_t[s]
              + cn * f1_t[n]
              + cb * f1_t[b]
              + ct * f1_t[t];
    }
    ++c; ++n; ++s; ++b; ++t;
    f2_t[c] = cc * f1_t[c]
            + cw * f1_t[c-1]
```

FIGURE 5.3

From tiled code in HPP Chapter 4.

```
                              + ce * f1_t[c]
                                       + cs * f1_t[s]
                                       + cn * f1_t[n]
                                       + cb * f1_t[b]
                                       + ct * f1_t[t];
                  } // tile ny
                } // tile nz
              } // block ny
              REAL *t = f1_t;
              f1_t = f2_t;
              f2_t = t;
            } // count
          } // parallel
```

FIGURE 5.3—Cont'd

The compiler does a good job of deciding where and when to insert prefetches. You can look at the disassembly code if you wish (via `-s compiler switch`). I experimented with different `#pragma prefetch` options all of which produce lower performance than using the compiler-generated prefetches. Curiously, I also noted that for this example using `#pragma no-prefetch`, produced marginally faster code (<1% faster). This is likely due to the fact that the loop is simple enough that the coprocessor's hardware prefetcher will perform the prefetching for you. Each unnecessary prefetch instruction that is eliminated from the loop often gains back at least one clock cycle.

The HPP book found the best performance was achieved using `KMP_AFFINITY=scatter` and `OMP_NUM_THREADS=183` (three threads from each core). On the test machine, with one fewer core, 180 threads were used. The tiling (`YBF=16`) was used to improve cache hit probability, and we assume the authors of the book tuned this factor to yield best performance.

WHAT MORE CAN BE DONE TO IMPROVE THE CODE?

Well, there are some problems with the code. These problems are not obvious when reading the code and relating it to the computational characteristics of the coprocessor, including its many in-order cores with four hardware threads each. The HPP book authors found that using three of the four hardware threads per core gave optimal performance (of this program) for use with the tiled algorithm. Test runs on the target system produced comparable numbers.

The first optimization beyond the HPP book relates to the L1 and L2 relationship of the threads within each core. The next subsection will describe how to take advantage of this relationship.

HYPER-THREAD PHALANX

The term phalanx is derived from a military formation used by the ancient Greeks and Romans. The formation generally involved soldiers lining up shoulder to shoulder, shield to shield multiple rows deep. The formation would advance in unison becoming "an irresistible force." I use the term

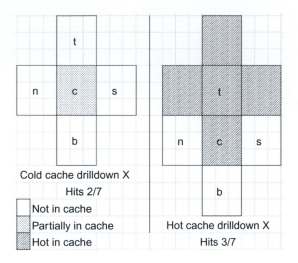

FIGURE 5.4

Single-thread cache likelihood.

Hyper-Thread Phalanx to refer to the Hyper-Thread siblings of a core being aligned shoulder-to-shoulder and advancing forward.

The HPP authors had a publishing deadline with additional programming examples to write, test, edit, and insert into the manuscript, and therefore did not explore this method. They noted that indeed additional optimizations were likely possible and hence we will explore these improvements.

The first optimization technique employed is to gang the hardware threads of each core into a cohesive working unit (phalanx) thus enhancing the L1 and/or L2 cache hit ratio. In the HPP book's code, each thread worked in a different section of the 3D problem space. Looking down the X direction (as viewed from Z/Y plane), each thread's L1 and/or L2 cache activity is illustrated in Figure 5.4 as it processes each column of X.

The left image of Figure 5.4 represents a view of the Z/Y plane, with X going into the page. Legends on the figure indicate probability of data residing in some cache. On the left image, only the center column c experiences a partial cache hit on the first traversal of X. As computation progresses toward x=nx-1, the c column has three reads (c+1, c, c-1). With the c+1 taking the memory hit, the c and c-1 reads will benefit from cache hits. At the end of the loop, all five columns c, n, s, t, b will be located in L1 and/or L2 cache (so will the f1_t[c+1] and f1_t[c-1] entries being in the same column as to f1_t[c]).

The right image illustrates each next traversal along x (++y, x=0:n-1). Note now that two of the five columns of x (c and t) are now "hot" in L1 and/or L2 cache, while three are "cold," meaning not in cache. Additionally, the [c-1] and [c+] references will be in cache. This same activity is progressing for all the threads, including the HT siblings of each core. Counting three hits for the center column we can estimate the cache hit ratio as 3/7 (42.86%). This hit ratio is estimated without prefetches, and assuming the x depth does not exceed the cache capacity.

The preceding was a simplistic description. Due to vectors along Z, into page, multiple cells will be processed at a time. The preceding narrative is used as a visualization aid.

WHAT IS NONOPTIMAL ABOUT THIS STRATEGY?

First, all the HT siblings of a core share the L1 and L2 cache of that core. Each core has separate L1 and L2 caches. Therefore, each of the three HT siblings of the original tiled code (which used three out of the four available HT siblings) could effectively only use one-third of the core's shared L1 and/or L2 cache. Additionally, depending on the start points, the HT siblings may experience false sharing and evict each other's hot cache lines. This is not an efficient situation.

Moving on from the best settings for the original tiled code, a different tactic to perform tiling is chosen and described here.

> **NOTE**
>
> Hardware threads (HT) vs. hyper-threads (HT). Technically, Intel has only called a Hardware thread a "hyper-thread" on the Intel Xeon processors where there are two hyper-threads available per core in some designs while other Intel Xeon processors remain single-threaded per core. On Intel Xeon Phi coprocessors, there are four threads per core but the cores are in order cores in the first product (codenamed Knights Corner, KNC). Intel is careful to point out that these are not hyper-threads because they are required to get top performance. Indeed, many HPC systems turn off hyper-threads to get top performance for some highly tuned workloads. Hyper-threads, it turns out, really shine for non-HPC users but have less to offer for HPC usage. Turning off hardware-threads, even if it were possible, on KNC would always lower performance. KNC threads are important for HPC usage. A key reason is that KNC is an in-order processor and needs the additional threads to hide memory latency and to access all the potential of the vector-processing unit. The next generation Intel Xeon Phi product (codenamed Knights Landing, KNL) will not be in order so it would be reasonable to guess it will have hyper-threads. Now you know. We wrestled with this wording, and then we realized that the techniques of this chapter work well with both HT capabilities. Therefore, we choose to carelessly say "hyper-threads" all the time and we end up saying HT much of the time. All this to say: HT works for us whatever it means, we know KNC does not have hyper-threads but we think KNL will. We like HT whatever you call it.

CODING THE HYPER-THREAD PHALANX

The Hyper-Thread Phalanx is introduced by changing the outer computation loop such that the HT threads within each core process neighboring z cells in the y direction and down x (vector by vector). The technique for doing so will be discussed later, but first let us examine the reasoning behind this choice of access pattern. For this specific computational loop, the Hyper-Thread Phalanx design permits higher L1/L2 cache hit ratios.

Expanding on Figure 5.4 of a single thread, we will look at illustrations of 2-wide and 4-wide Hyper-Thread Phalanxes. Note, the 2-wide Hyper-Thread Phalanx applies to host processors as well.

Of each image of Figure 5.5, the left c is the center of the X column being processed by HT(0) of the core, the right c is the center of the X column being processed by HT(1) of the core. The left image illustrates the cold cache penetration of X (into page), Z advances to right, Y down. The c's, lightly shaded, indicate one of the threads incurs a cache miss, while the adjacent thread accessing the same cell experience a cache hit. The right image illustrates the next drill down of X. Note now the estimated cache effect. The c's and t's of both threads experience cache hits. When using three threads per core and four threads per core, the image would widen to three c's and four c's. The cache hit ratio estimation: 10/14 (71.43%) for 2-wide, 16/21(76.19%) for 3-wide, and 22/18 (78.57%) for 4-wide Hyper-Thread Phalanxes. These sketches indicate a potential for significant improvements over the single-thread layout value of 3/7 (42.86%).

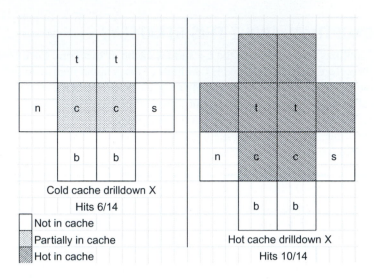

FIGURE 5.5

2-Wide Hyper-Thread Phalanx.

A second benefit is the HT siblings within a core now share all of the L1 and L2 cache space of that core. This effectively increases the thread's working set in these caches by 2-3 times over the prior technique of maintaining spatial separation of the work performed by each thread within a core.

A third benefit is eliminating intracore thread cache evictions due to false sharing.

The programming changes to implement the Hyper-Thread Phalanx are somewhat out of the ordinary for OpenMP programmers, yet are relatively easy to accomplish. To use the Hyper-Thread Phalanx you remove the `#pragma omp for collapse(2)` code structure, and insert hand partitioning of the iteration space by core and by HT sibling within core. This amounts to removing 5 lines of code and inserting 13 lines of code.

HOW TO DETERMINE THREAD BINDING TO CORE AND HT WITHIN CORE?

We could specify affinity and core placement using environment variables external to the program, but this may not be suitable or reliable. It is better to place the least constraints and requirements on the environment variables. While one set of affinity bindings may be best for this function, the overall application may benefit from a different arrangement of thread bindings. Therefore, this necessitates having the program determine the affinity bindings applied by the environment. The more effective route is for the program to perform thread to core-binding discovery.

The files HyperThreadPhalanx.h and HyperThreadPhalanx.c were used for the improved performance test programs.

The primary goal of the HyperThreadPhalanx.c utility function is to:

• Determine the number of OpenMP threads in the outer most region of the application
• Compute a logical core number (zero based and contiguous) for each thread
• Compute a logical HT number within the core (zero based and contiguous) for each thread
• Compute the number of logical cores
• Compute number of HTs per core as used in the working set

The application is free to choose almost any strategy that is reasonable for the non-HyperThreadPhalanx'ed parts. The only "reasonable" requirement is for each core used to have the same number of working threads. If they do not, the current code will choose the smallest number (though testing of adverse configurations has not been strenuously performed).

The header file must be included in the source files using HyperThreadPhalanx, and the object file from HyperThreadPhalanx must be linked with the application. These files are available at http://lotsofcores.com.

The header introduces into your namespace the `HyperThreadPhalanx` object and two Thread Local Storage variables `myCore` and `myHT`. The once-only initialization function, `HyperThreadPhalanxInit()`, must be called at program start.

Next we can integrate this function into the HPP book's code sample code.

THE HYPER-THREAD PHALANX HAND-PARTITIONING TECHNIQUE

Code for main computation function in diffusion_tiled_HT1 is shown in Figure 5.6.

```
diffusion_tiled(REAL *restrict f1, REAL *restrict f2,
  int nx, int ny, int nz,
  REAL ce, REAL cw, REAL cn, REAL cs, REAL ct,
  REAL cb, REAL cc, REAL dt, int count) {
#pragma omp parallel
{
  REAL *f1_t = f1;
  REAL *f2_t = f2;

  // number of Squads (singles/doublets/triplets/quadruples)
  // across z dimension
  int nSquadsZ = (nz + nHTs - 1) / nHTs;

  // number of full (and partial)
  // singles/doublets/triads/quads on z-y face
  int nSquadsZY = nSquadsZ * ny;
  int nSquadsZYPerCore = (nSquadsZY + nCores - 1) / nCores;

  // Determine this thread's triads/quads
  //(TLS init setup myCore and myHT)
  int SquadBegin = nSquadsZYPerCore * myCore;
  int SquadEnd = SquadBegin + nSquadsZYPerCore;
  if(SquadEnd > nSquadsZY)
    SquadEnd = nSquadsZY; // truncate if necessary

  // benchmark timing loop
  for (int i = 0; i < count; ++i) {
    // restrict current thread to its subset of Squads
    // on the Z/Y face.
    for(int iSquad=SquadBegin; iSquad<SquadEnd; ++iSquad) {
      // home z for 0'th team member for next Squad
      int z0 = (iSquad / ny) * nHTs;
      int z = z0 + myHT;  // z for this team member
      int y = iSquad % ny;

      // last Squad along z may be partially filled
      // assure we are within z
      if(z < nz)
      {
          // determine the center cells
          // and cells about the center
          int x = 0;
          int c, n, s, b, t;
          c =  x + y * nx + z * nx * ny;
```

FIGURE 5.6

diffusion_tiled_HT1 (edited for book layout).

```
n = (y == 0)    ? c : c - nx;
s = (y == ny-1) ? c : c + nx;
b = (z == 0)    ? c : c - nx * ny;
t = (z == nz-1) ? c : c + nx * ny;

// c runs through x, n and s through y,
// b and t through z
// x=0 special (no f1_t[c-1])
f2_t[c] = cc * f1_t[c]   + cw * f1_t[c]
        + ce * f1_t[c+1] + cs * f1_t[s]
        + cn * f1_t[n]   + cb * f1_t[b]
        + ct * f1_t[t];

// interior x's faster
#pragma noprefetch
#pragma simd
for (x = 1; x < nx-1; x++) {

    ++c; ++n; ++s; ++b; ++t;

    f2_t[c] = cc * f1_t[c]   + cw * f1_t[c-1]
            + ce * f1_t[c+1] + cs * f1_t[s]
            + cn * f1_t[n]   + cb * f1_t[b]
            + ct * f1_t[t];

} // for (x = 1; x < nx-1; x++)

// final x special (f1_t[c+1])
++c; ++n; ++s; ++b; ++t;

f2_t[c] = cc * f1_t[c] + cw * f1_t[c-1]
        + ce * f1_t[c] + cs * f1_t[s]
        + cn * f1_t[n] + cb * f1_t[b]
        + ct * f1_t[t];
    } // if(z < nz)

  } // for(int iSquad=SquadBegin;...)

// barrier required because we removed implicit barrier
// of #pragma omp for collapse(2)
#pragma omp barrier

REAL *t = f1_t;
f1_t = f2_t;
f2_t = t;
} // count
} // parallel
return;
}
```

Figure 5.6—Cont'd

Effectively we removed five lines of code relating to the OpenMP loop control and added thirteen lines for hand control (net eight lines of code difference). This tiledHT1 code also changed how the blocking factor was performed. Due to the data flow, blocking was removed in favor of data flow and hardware prefetching.

In making three runs of each problem size of the original tiled code and the newer tiled_HT1 code we find as shown in Figure 5.7.

The Hyper-Thread Phalanx strategy did show some improvement in the small model but not a similar improvement in the large model. Furthermore, the small model improvement was not as anticipated. The chart in Figure 5.8 includes the tiled_HT1 code.

The improvement to the small model looks good; however, something is not right with the large model. Let us discover what it is.

```
export KMP_AFFINITY=scatter
export OMP_NUM_THREADS=180

./diffusion_tiled_xphi
118771.945
123131.672
122726.906
Average: 121543.508

./diffusion_tiled_Large_xphi
114972.258
114524.977
116626.805
Average: 115374.680

export KMP_AFFINITY=compact
unset OMP_NUM_THREADS

./diffusion_tiled_HT1_xphi
134904.891
131310.906
133888.688
Average: 133368.162

./diffusion_tiled_HT1_Large_xphi
118476.734
118078.930
118157.188
Average: 118237.617
```

FIGURE 5.7

Run data for diffusion_tiled_HT1.

A LESSON LEARNED

An earlier study progressed making optimizations from here. However, discoveries made later caused a revisit to this code. At this point, let us take a slight divergence so that we can learn from that experience.

The test system is dual boot for the host with both CentOS Linux and Windows 7 installed on different hard drives. The question of whether there was any impact running the native coprocessor code based on which host operating system was running was pursued; with the expectation that there should be no noticeable difference.

The environment variables were configured to run the 3-wide phalanx and tests run on both CentOS and Windows 7 host (Figure 5.8 is for 4-wide phalanx). Surprisingly, running the same code (same binary file in fact) hosted on Windows and comparing the results run in the coprocessor on Linux, the relative performance figures were reversed! What was faster with a Linux host was slower with the Windows host, and vice versa. This did not make sense.

One of the thoughts that came to mind is there may be a memory alignment issue between the allocations of the arrays. This has been the author's experience on Intel64 and IA32 platforms. So, a printf() was added to display the address of the buffers. The two programs, tiled and tiled_HT, both had 16-byte alignment and approximately the same offset within the page, so data alignment differences could not be the cause. Curiously, by adding the printf of the addresses of the two buffers, the performance figures flipped again. The results of the runs were shown in Figure 5.9.

Clearly there is a shift of 5% in performance due to "code position shift."

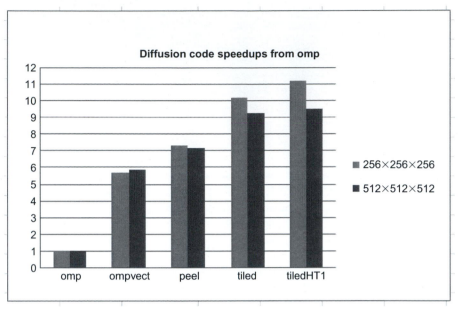

FIGURE 5.8

diffusion_tiled_HT1 relative to OpenMP.

```
[Jim@Thor-mic0 tmp]$ ./diffusion_tiled_xphi
f1 = 0x7fbbf3945010 f2 = 0x7fbbef944010  printf
FLOPS        : 122157.898 (MFlops) With printf
[Jim@Thor-mic0 tmp]$ ./diffusion_tiled_xphi
f1 = 0x7ffaf7c0b010 f2 = 0x7ffaf3c0a010  printf
FLOPS        : 123543.602 (MFlops) With printf
[Jim@Thor-mic0 tmp]$ ./diffusion_tiled_xphi
f1 = 0x7f3afa480010 f2 = 0x7f3af647f010  printf
FLOPS        : 123908.375 (MFlops) With printf
Average with printf: 123203.292 MFlops

[Jim@Thor-mic0 tmp]$ ./diffusion_tiled_xphi
FLOPS        : 114380.531 (MFlops) Without printf
[Jim@Thor-mic0 tmp]$ ./diffusion_tiled_xphi
FLOPS        : 121105.062 (MFlops) Without printf
[Jim@Thor-mic0 tmp]$ ./diffusion_tiled_xphi
FLOPS        : 116298.797 (MFlops) Without printf
Average without printf 117261.463 Mflops

With printf +5941.829 MFlops (+5.1% over without printf)
```

FIGURE 5.9

Code alignment effect on performance.

What this means then is that the relative performance difference measured in the original `tiled` code and the newer `tiled_HT` code (earlier versions) may be completely obscured by the fortuitous, or lack thereof, of placement of the code. One version might be +5%, and the other version −5%, yielding a comparative uncertainty of up to 10%. This difference is specific to this particular sample of code. Do not assume that all code exhibits this amount of performance difference due to code placement.

However, using this experience as an example, suggests that vigilance in the tuning process to look for code alignment issues is warranted.

BACK TO WORK

The expectation of the performance improvements has not yet been observed. We only achieved a 9.7% improvement for the small model and a 2.5% improvement for large model.

Applying Occam's razor: If we did not observe an increase in L1 hit ratio—it did not happen.

The estimated improvement in the L1 hit ratio was based on the amount of data we calculated should be in the L1 cache for the specified algorithm.

3-Wide, small data:

$$8 \times 256 \times 4 = 8 \text{ kB low side}, \quad 11 \times 256 \times 4 = 11 \text{ kB high side}$$

4-Wide, small data:

$$10 \times 256 \times 4 = 10 \text{ kB low side}, \quad 14 \times 256 \times 4 = 14 \text{ kB high side}$$

Both calculations indicate plenty of room in the 32 kB L1 cache. Something else must be going on and will need some future investigation (not addressed in this chapter).

Regardless of this discovery, the GFlop/sec is in the range of 133 GFlop/sec, far short of the capability of the Intel Xeon Phi Coprocessor.

Now I must ask myself: *What is nonoptimal about this strategy?* And: *What can be improved?*

There are two things, one is obvious, and the other is not so obvious.

DATA ALIGNMENT

A somewhat obvious thing is that vectorization improves with aligned data. Most compilers will examine the loop code and if beneficial, the compiler will insert preamble code that tests for alignment and executes up until an alignment is reached. This is called peeling. With peeling, the compiler inserts code that executes using the more efficient aligned data. Finally, postamble code is inserted to complete processing of any remaining unaligned data.

This sounds rather straightforward until you look at the inner loop (Figure 5.10).

In the Figure 5.10 code, the two terms: `f1_t[c-1]`, and `f1_t[c+1]` will muck up the vector alignment tests since `[c-1]`, `[c]`, and `[c+1]` can never all be aligned at the same time.

Are the compiler writers smart enough to offer some measure of optimization for such a loop? As it turns out, they are able to offer some measure of optimization for such a loop.

```
#pragma simd
for (x = 1; x < nx-1; x++) {
    ++c; ++n; ++s; ++b; ++t;
    f2_t[c] = cc * f1_t[c]   + cw * f1_t[c-1]
            + ce * f1_t[c+1] + cs * f1_t[s]
            + cn * f1_t[n]   + cb * f1_t[b]
            + ct * f1_t[t];
}
```

FIGURE 5.10

Inner loop of diffusion_... files.

Due to initial unknowns, the code has to do more work in the preamble and postamble sections, as well as, a reduced number of iterations in the interior body loop of code.

Take particular note that the input array f1_t is indexed in seven different ways. This means that the preamble code that determines alignment may have to work on minor permutations of the seven references in an attempt to narrow in on the time when the largest number of references are vector aligned. This is nontrivial for the compiler code generation, as well as a potential area for additional overhead.

USE ALIGNED DATA WHEN POSSIBLE

Data alignment is addressed in an additional improvement to the coding of the tiled_HT2 program.

First, the dimension NX as a multiple of REALs that fill a cache line is enforced. This is not an unreasonable requirement. The value 256 was used in the original example code. It is not too much of a restriction to require that NX must be a multiple of 16 for floats, or 8 for doubles.

To assure alignment, the malloc calls are changed to allocate the arrays using _mm_malloc with an alignment to cache line size (64). This is a relatively simple change. (This will be shown later after the next optimization which also affects allocation.)

Next, now that NX is always an even multiple of cache lines, and the arrays are cache line aligned, a function can be constructed to process the innermost loop with the foreknowledge that six of the array references are cache aligned and two are not (the extra reference is the output array). The two that are not aligned are the references to [c-1] and [c+1]. The compiler, knowing beforehand what is aligned and what is not aligned does not have to insert code to make this determination. This is to say: the compiler optimizer can reduce, or completely eliminate the preamble and postamble codes.

REDUNDANCY CAN BE GOOD FOR YOU

The second (nonobvious) improvement is that additional optimization can be achieved by redundantly processing x=0 and x=nx-1 as if these cells were at the interior of the parallel pipette being processed. This means that the preamble and postamble codes for unaligned loops can be bypassed, and that the elements x=1:15 could be directly processed as an aligned vector (as opposed to one-by-one computation or unaligned vector computation). The same is done for the 16 elements where the last element (x=nx-1) is computed differently than the other vector elements. This means that after calculating the incorrect values (for free) for x=0 and x=nx-1, we have to then perform a scalar calculation to insert the correct values into the X column. Essentially you are exchanging two scalar loops of 16 iterations for two of (one 16-wide vector operation + one scalar operation) where the scalar operations are in L1 cache.

Adding the redundancy necessitated allocating the array's two vectors worth of elements to be larger than the actual array requirement, and returning the second vector's array pointer address. Additionally, this requires zeroing one element preceding and one element following the working array size to perform a "first touch" write. The allocation then provides for two additional vectors of addressable memory (not used as valid data). Not performing the "first touch" write could result in a page fault depending on location and extent of allocation.

Change to allocations results in the code in Figure 5.11.

As an additional benefit, the compiler can now generate more code using Fused Multiply and Add instructions.

The tiled_HT2 code is shown in Figure 5.12.

```
// align the allocations to cache line
// increase allocation size by 2 cache lines
REAL *f1_padded = (REAL *)_mm_malloc(
  sizeof(REAL)*(nx*ny*nz + N_REALS_PER_CACHE_LINE*2),
  CACHE_LINE_SIZE);

// assure allocation succeeded
assert(f1_padded != NULL);

// advance one cache line into buffer
REAL *f1 = f1_padded + N_REALS_PER_CACHE_LINE;
f1[-1] = 0.0; // assure cell prior to array not SNaN
f1[nx*ny*nz] = 0.0; // assure cell following array not SNaN
// align the allocations to cache line
// increase allocation size by 2 cache lines
REAL *f2_padded = (REAL *)_mm_malloc(
  sizeof(REAL)*(nx*ny*nz + N_REALS_PER_CACHE_LINE*2),
  CACHE_LINE_SIZE);

// assure allocation succeeded
assert(f2_padded != NULL);

// advance one cache line into buffer
REAL *f2 = f2_padded + N_REALS_PER_CACHE_LINE;

f2[-1] = 0.0; // assure cell prior to array not SNaN
f2[nx*ny*nz] = 0.0; // assure cell following array not SNaN
```

FIGURE 5.11

Aligned and padded allocation.

```
void diffusion_tiled_aligned(
              REAL*restrict f2_t_c, // aligned
              REAL*restrict f1_t_c, // aligned
              REAL*restrict f1_t_w, // not aligned
              REAL*restrict f1_t_e, // not aligned
              REAL*restrict f1_t_s, // aligned
              REAL*restrict f1_t_n, // aligned
              REAL*restrict f1_t_b, // aligned
              REAL*restrict f1_t_t, // aligned
              REAL ce, REAL cw, REAL cn, REAL cs, REAL ct,
              REAL cb, REAL cc, int countX, int countY) {
  __assume_aligned(f2_t_c, CACHE_LINE_SIZE);
  __assume_aligned(f1_t_c, CACHE_LINE_SIZE);
  __assume_aligned(f1_t_s, CACHE_LINE_SIZE);
  __assume_aligned(f1_t_n, CACHE_LINE_SIZE);
  __assume_aligned(f1_t_b, CACHE_LINE_SIZE);
  __assume_aligned(f1_t_t, CACHE_LINE_SIZE);

  // countY is number of squads along Y axis
  for(int iY = 0; iY < countY; ++iY) {
    // perform the x=0:N_REALS_PER_CACHE_LINE-1
    // as one cache line operation.
    // On Phi, 16-wide vector with one iteration
    // On AVX 8-wide vector with two iterations
    // On SSE 4-wide vector withfour iterations
    #pragma noprefetch
    #pragma simd
    for (int i = 0; i < N_REALS_PER_CACHE_LINE; i++) {
      f2_t_c[i] = cc * f1_t_c[i] + cw * f1_t_w[i]
               + ce * f1_t_e[i] + cs * f1_t_s[i]
               + cn * f1_t_n[i] + cb * f1_t_b[i]
               + ct * f1_t_t[i];
    } // for (int i = 0; i < N_REALS_PER_CACHE_LINE; i++)
    // now overstrike x=0 with correct value
    // x=0 special (no f1_t[c-1])
    f2_t_c[0] = cc * f1_t_c[0] + cw * f1_t_w[1]
             + ce * f1_t_e[0] + cs * f1_t_s[0]
             + cn * f1_t_n[0] + cb * f1_t_b[0]
             + ct * f1_t_t[0];
```

FIGURE 5.12

diffusion_tiled_HT2.c excerpt.

```
                // Note, while we could overstrike x=[0] and [nx-1]
                // after processing the entire depth of nx doing so
                // will result in the x=0th cell being evicted from L1.
                // Do remainder of countX run including incorrect value
                // for i=nx-1 (countX-1)
                #pragma vector nontemporal
                #pragma noprefetch
                #pragma simd
                for (int i = N_REALS_PER_CACHE_LINE; i < countX; i++) {
                    f2_t_c[i] = cc * f1_t_c[i] + cw * f1_t_w[i]
                              + ce * f1_t_e[i] + cs * f1_t_s[i]
                              + cn * f1_t_n[i] + cb * f1_t_b[i]
                              + ct * f1_t_t[i];
                } // for (int i = 0; i < N_REALS_PER_CACHE_LINE; i++)
                // now overstrike x=nx-1 with correct value
                // x=nx-1 special (no f1_t[c+1])
                int i = countX-1;
                f2_t_c[i] = cc * f1_t_c[i] + cw * f1_t_w[i-1]
                          + ce * f1_t_e[i] + cs * f1_t_s[i]
                          + cn * f1_t_n[i] + cb * f1_t_b[i]
                          + ct * f1_t_t[i];
                // advance one step along Y
                f2_t_c += countX; f1_t_c += countX; f1_t_w += countX;
                f1_t_e += countX; f1_t_s += countX; f1_t_n += countX;
                f1_t_b += countX; f1_t_t += countX;
            } // for(int iY = 0; iY < countY; ++iY)
        } // void diffusion_tiled_aligned(

    diffusion_tiled(REAL *restrict f1, REAL *restrict f2,
      int nx, int ny, int nz,
      REAL ce, REAL cw, REAL cn, REAL cs, REAL ct,
      REAL cb, REAL cc, REAL dt, int count) {
      #pragma omp parallel
      {
        REAL *f1_t = f1;
        REAL *f2_t = f2;
        // place squads across z dimension
        int nSquadsZ = (nz + nHTs - 1) / nHTs;

        // number of full/partial squads on z-y face
        int nSquadsZY = nSquadsZ * ny;
        int nSquadsZYPerCore = (nSquadsZY + nCores - 1) / nCores;

        // Determine this thread's squads
        int SquadBegin = nSquadsZYPerCore * myCore;
        int SquadEnd = SquadBegin + nSquadsZYPerCore;
        if(SquadEnd > nSquadsZY)
          SquadEnd = nSquadsZY;

        for (int i = 0; i < count; ++i) {
          int nSquads;

          // restrict current thread to its subset of squads
          // on the Z/Y face.
          for(int iSquad = SquadBegin; iSquad < SquadEnd;
```

Figure 5.12—Cont'd

```
          iSquad += nSquads) {
            // determine nSquads for this pass
            if(iSquad % ny == 0)
              nSquads = 1; // at y==0 boundary
            else
            if(iSquad % ny == ny - 1)
              nSquads = 1;  // at y==ny-1 boundary
            else
            if(iSquad / ny == (SquadEnd - 1) / ny)
              nSquads = SquadEnd - iSquad;  // within 1:ny-1
            else
              nSquads = ny-(iSquad%ny)-1; // iSquad%ny:ny-1

            int z0 = (iSquad / ny) * nHTs; // home z for HT(0)
            int z = z0 + myHT;   // z for HT(myHT)
            int y = iSquad % ny;
            // last squad along z may be partially filled
            // assure we are within z
            if(z < nz) {
              int x = 0;
              int c, n, s, b, t;
              c =   x + y * nx + z * nx * ny;
              n = (y == 0)    ? c : c - nx;
              s = (y == ny-1) ? c : c + nx;
              b = (z == 0)    ? c : c - nx * ny;
              t = (z == nz-1) ? c : c + nx * ny;
              diffusion_tiled_aligned(
                  &f2_t[c], &f1_t[c], // aligned
                  &f1_t[c-1], &f1_t[c+1], // unaligned
                  &f1_t[s],&f1_t[n],&f1_t[b],&f1_t[t],// aligned
                  ce, cw, cn, cs, ct, cb, cc, nx, nSquads);
            } // if(z < nz)
          } // for(int iSquad = SquadBegin; ...
          // barrier required because we removed implicit
          // barrier of #pragma omp for collapse(2)
          #pragma omp barrier
          // swap buffer pointers
          REAL *t = f1_t;
          f1_t = f2_t;
          f2_t = t;
        } // count
      } // parallel
      return;
    } // diffusion_tiled
```

Figure 5.12—Cont'd

The performance chart in Figure 5.13 incorporates the two new programs, `diffusion_tiled_HT1` and `diffusion_tiled_HT2`.

The chart in Figure 5.13 clearly illustrates that the `diffusion_tiled_HT2` is starting to make some real progress, at least for the small model with another 9.5% improvement. Be mindful that code alignment may still be an issue. And the chart does not take this into consideration.

What else can be improved?

THE PLESIOCHRONOUS PHASING BARRIER

Now we can delve into our chapter title technique: the plesiochronous phasing barrier.

For this optimization, we needed to search for a descriptive term to match the "loosely synchronous" thread behavior and came across plesiochronous:

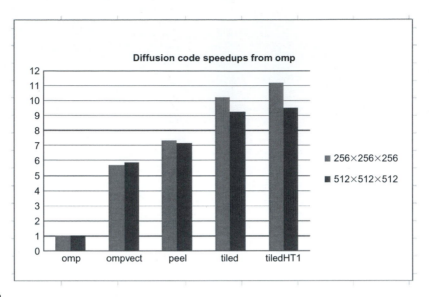

FIGURE 5.13

diffusion_tiled_HT2.

In telecommunications, a plesiochronous system is one where different parts of the system are almost, but not quite, perfectly synchronized.

In any large-threaded application, synchronizing all threads, with thread pool barriers, results in significant processing power waste. In the diffusion simulation program, and possibly your application, the simulation integrates multiple time intervals before doing something with the results. In the example program, it is the entire simulation run time. In a typical simulation program, the simulator would be configured to advance N intervals, then log or display the current state. And then proceed for another N intervals, etc.

In the `diffusion_tiled_HT2` code, small model ($256 \times 256 \times 256$), and 4 threads per phalanx, we have 64 squad slices across Z by 256 steps along Y. This represents 16,384 squad "drill holes" along X. Each core (60), partitions out: 16,384/60 (273.0666...) squad "drill holes" along X. Not being a whole number, all cores are not assigned the same number of "drill holes." 56 of the cores are scheduled 273 "drill holes" and 4 cores are scheduled 274 "drill holes." The work disparity is small, only 1/273. This is "the cost of doing business" so to say.

If only "the cost of doing business" were that simple. In practice, with 240 threads in 60 cores, you will not get all threads to start a parallel region at the same time, nor will all threads finish the region at the same time even if they are notionally performing the same amount of work. As mentioned earlier in this article, adding instrumentation to measure the total thread time in do-work section and at-barrier section, for the small problem ($256 \times 256 \times 256$) indicated approximately 25% of the computation time was spent at the barrier. As a conscientious programmer, "the cost of doing business" is too high.

Now then, what to do about lost time at barrier?

Constructing a simplified diagram for a two core, 4 threads/core, $16 \times 16 \times 16$ array (ignore vectors for the purpose of this illustration). In the `tiled_HT2` perfect world with zero skew at the start of a parallel region and identical compute times (resulting in zero time at the barrier), the time when the first thread reaches the barrier would look like Figure 5.14.

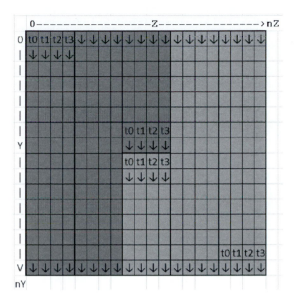

FIGURE 5.14

Synchronized termination.

The left zones are core 0 zones (HT threads 0:3 across width of each stripe) and right zones are core zones 1 (HT threads 0:3 across width of each stripe). Ideally with both cores starting at the same time and finishing at the same time.

The real picture is more like Figure 5.15.

Where, the white cells are the yet to be processed cells when the first of the threads' work is completed (t3 of second core).

In Figure 5.16, the first thread to reach the barrier (t3 lower right corner) waits for the remaining threads. The second thread reaching the barrier, additionally wastes time waiting for the other threads, and so on. The more out of synch the threads get, the longer the wasted burn time at the barrier.

In an extreme case, the situation can even look like Figure 5.16.

Where, one of the threads, t1 of first core, has yet to begin performing its work, when the first thread, t3 of second core, reaches the barrier. This situation is usually due to some other process running on that hardware thread. The O/S may be doing some housekeeping too.

In either the normal case, or unusual case, significant time is wasted at the barrier.

LET US DO SOMETHING TO RECOVER THIS WASTED TIME

The technique used is to assign the cores to a slice that is one count of Z (in phalanx-wide groupings of 4 in this case), and ny counts of Y (as well as nx of X).

The left and right zones represent the work area assigned for a first pass by each core (of the simplified 2-core 4-HT/core setup).

The first thread finishing work state may look like Figure 5.17.

Now, by using a core barrier, in place of a thread pool barrier, when the sibling threads of the core whose thread finishes first, finish, the state may look like Figure 5.18.

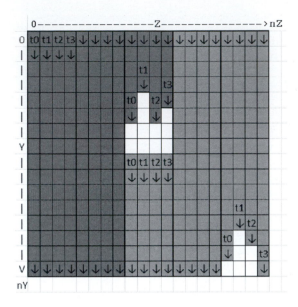

FIGURE 5.15

End of loop thread termination skew.

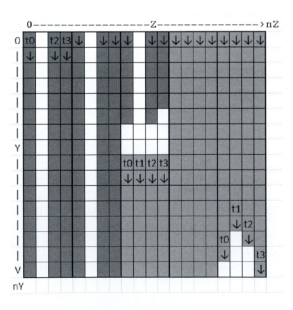

FIGURE 5.16

Preempted thread skew.

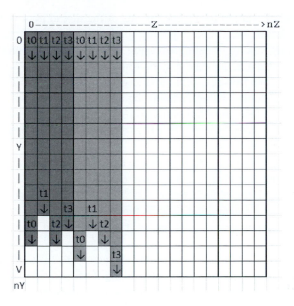

FIGURE 5.17

Phalanx run of Y.

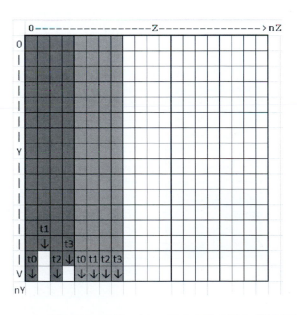

FIGURE 5.18

First core to finish run of Y.

At this point, instead of waiting for all the threads of the thread pool to reach the barrier (all four threads on the left side in this simplified diagram), the first core completing the core barrier can pick the next available Z group, and can begin processing *before* the other core(s) reach the barrier. When core 0 completes the core barrier, the state may be something like Figure 5.19.

The process of: as a core finishes, pick next Z group, continues in a modulus counter fashion (0 follows nz−1). The modulus counter contains the number of overflows.

The main benefit of the plesiochronous barrier is realized the moment when, and where in the code, the traditional thread pool barrier appears. This is at the end of the whole array iteration (often called a frame).

In the original OpenMP program, this was where the end of the #pragma omp parallel for implicit barrier was located and also in our revised diffusion_tiled_HT1 and diffusion_tiled_HT2 program where the explicit #pragma omp barrier was located.

The plesiochronous barrier technique permits the cores completing one frame, *to enter the next frame* provided that the dependencies for that next work area are satisfied. This is illustrated by Figure 5.20.

In Figure 5.20, unlabeled sections indicate dependencies are fulfilled (prior iteration completed from perspective of the picking thread). The next to right most stripe illustrates a core completing Frame n (no more unchosen stripes available in this pass of Z), the core not having an available Z group for his frame, passes through frame barrier *while* the last core has yet to reach the frame barrier. Upon reaching the first column of the next frame, the frame progress of the second column is consulted, and when greater than or equal to the next fram-1, core is permitted to enter the column.

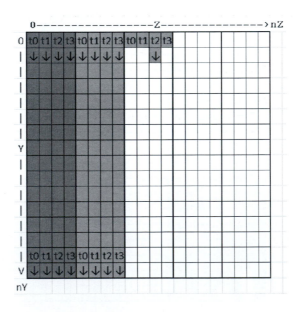

FIGURE 5.19

Time second core completes work.

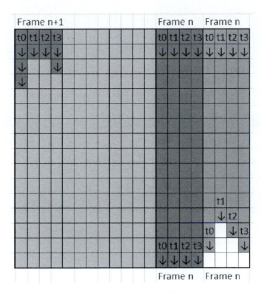

FIGURE 5.20

Plesiochronous frame crossing.

Caution: A caveat to this is a thread cannot progress unless the prior phase of the picked Z, *and its adjacent Z's (z-1, z, and z+1) is* at least at current phase-1. If (when) this is not true, then progressing might potentially use data that is not up-to-date. This is where the plesiochronous _barrier is placed.

Had the core processing the second column in the prior chart not finished, then the core processing the first column would have had to wait at the plesiochronous barrier.

The plesiochronous barrier technique should exhibit the best improvement when the number of core-columns (Hyper-Thread Phalanx columns) exceed the number of cores (Phalanx's) by a factor of two or more. In the large model, it does (512/4 = 128 phalanx columns/60 cores = 2.1333). This suggests that the large model will benefit more than the small model. In observations of test runs, substantial benefit is observed under all circumstances.

Here is the code exemplifying the plesiochronous barrier technique (Figure 5.21).

Now let us see what happened.

Figure 5.22 shows an additional 20% gained for small solution. For the large solution it recovered the expected gains missing from the HT1 and HT2 code changes.

At this point of optimization, we are now attaining 14x to 15x the performance of a simplified OpenMP approach to the problem. And 45% faster than that attained in the example from HPP Chapter 4. *What else can be done to improve performance?*

A FEW "LEFT TO THE READER" POSSIBILITIES

There are additional things, not covered in this chapter, which could be next phase of the programming enhancements. These include guided `prefetch` and `clevict` pragmas, as well as inserting compiler directives to hand align code. It might also be appropriate to consider what happens when the problem size is increased to the point where the memory capacity of a single coprocessor is insufficient. The plesiochronous barrier technique can equally apply to larger problems that do not fit within the memory constraints of a single coprocessor.

XEON HOST PERFORMANCE IMPROVEMENTS SIMILAR TO XEON PHI

It is important to point out that the effectiveness of the plesiochronous phasing barrier improves with core count. This said, it is effective on even a 1P, 6 core, 12 Hardware Thread system such as the Intel Xeon E5-2620 v2 processor charted in Figure 5.23.

Note: The chart in Figure 5.23 is presented differently for the host processor (E5-2620 v2) than for the earlier presented Intel Xeon Phi coprocessor charts. This is due principally to the fact that it is often the practice on the host processor to run with one thread per core. Whereas, on the coprocessor you always run with multiple threads per core. By making all runs relative to the respective threadness

```
#if defined(__MIC__)
#define WAIT_A_BIT _mm_delay_32(10)
#else
#define WAIT_A_BIT _mm_pause();
#endif
...
void diffusion_tiled_aligned(
   ... (same as for tiled_HT2)
}

diffusion_tiled(REAL *restrict f1, REAL *restrict f2,
  int nx, int ny, int nz,
  REAL ce, REAL cw, REAL cn, REAL cs, REAL ct,
  REAL cb, REAL cc, REAL dt, int count) {
  // zCountCompleted[nz] is a shared array indicating
  // the iteration counts completed for the z index.
  // Each thead processes all [x,y]'s for given z
  volatile int zCountCompleted[nz];
  for(int i = 0; i < nz; ++i)
    zCountCompleted[i]=-1; // "completed" one before first (0)

  // shared next Phalanx number
  volatile int NextPick = 0;

  // CorePick[nCores] NextPicked'd Phalanx number for core
  volatile int CorePick[nCores];
  for(int i = 0; i < nCores; ++i)
    CorePick[i] = -1;  // initialize to less than next pick

  #pragma omp parallel
  {
    REAL *f1_t;
    REAL *f2_t;
    int priorCount = -1;
    int myCount = -1;
    int myPick = -1; // (prior pick for 1st iteration of loop)
    // place squads across z dimension
    int nSquadsZ = (nz + nHTs - 1) / nHTs;
```

FIGURE 5.21

Plesiochronous barrier diffusion_tiled_HT3.c excerpt.

```
for(;;) {
  if(myHT == 0) {
    // team member 0 picks the next Squad
    CorePick[myCore] =
      myPick
        = __sync_fetch_and_add(&NextPick, 1);
  } else {
    // other team members wait until pick made by member 0
    while(CorePick[myCore] == myPick)
      WAIT_A_BIT;

    myPick = CorePick[myCore]; // pick up new pick
  } // myHT != 0

  myCount = myPick/nSquadsZ; // count interval for myPick

  // see if iteration count reached
  if(myCount >= count)
    break; // exit for(;;) loop

  // determine which buffers are in and out
  if(myCount & 1) {
    f1_t = f2;
    f2_t = f1;
  } else {
    f1_t = f1;
    f2_t = f2;
  }

  int z0 = (myPick % nSquadsZ) * nHTs;// home z for HT(0)
  int z = z0 + myHT;              // z for this team member
  int y = 0;

  // assure we are within z
  if(z < nz) {
    // perform plesiochronous barrier
    priorCount = myCount - 1;
    if(z) // then there is a z-1
      while(zCountCompleted[z-1] < priorCount)//wait z-1
        WAIT_A_BIT;

    while(zCountCompleted[z] < priorCount)    // wait z
      WAIT_A_BIT;

    if(z + 1 < nz) // then there is a z+1
      while(zCountCompleted[z+1] < priorCount) // wait z+1
        WAIT_A_BIT;

    int x = 0;
    int c, n, s, b, t;        // perform y==0
    y = 0;
    c =   x + y * nx + z * nx * ny;
    n = (y == 0)    ? c : c - nx;
    s = (y == ny-1) ? c : c + nx;
    b = (z == 0)    ? c : c - nx * ny;
    t = (z == nz-1) ? c : c + nx * ny;
    diffusion_tiled_aligned(
      &f2_t[c],      // aligned
      &f1_t[c],      // aligned
      &f1_t[c-1],    // unaligned
      &f1_t[c+1],    // unaligned
      &f1_t[s],      // aligned
      &f1_t[n],      // aligned
      &f1_t[b],      // aligned
      &f1_t[t],      // aligned
      ce, cw, cn, cs, ct, cb, cc, nx, 1);
```

Figure 5.21—Cont'd

```
// perform y==1:ny-2
y = 1;
c =   x + y * nx + z * nx * ny;
n = (y == 0)    ? c : c - nx;
s = (y == ny-1) ? c : c + nx;
b = (z == 0)    ? c : c - nx * ny;
t = (z == nz-1) ? c : c + nx * ny;
diffusion_tiled_aligned(
   &f2_t[c],      // aligned
   &f1_t[c],      // aligned
   &f1_t[c-1],    // unaligned
   &f1_t[c+1],    // unaligned
   &f1_t[s],      // aligned
   &f1_t[n],      // aligned
   &f1_t[b],      // aligned
   &f1_t[t],      // aligned
   ce, cw, cn, cs, ct, cb, cc, nx, ny-2);

// perform y==ny-1
y = ny-1;
c =   x + y * nx + z * nx * ny;
n = (y == 0)    ? c : c - nx;
s = (y == ny-1) ? c : c + nx;
b = (z == 0)    ? c : c - nx * ny;
t = (z == nz-1) ? c : c + nx * ny;
diffusion_tiled_aligned(
   &f2_t[c],      // aligned
   &f1_t[c],      // aligned
   &f1_t[c-1],    // unaligned
   &f1_t[c+1],    // unaligned
   &f1_t[s],      // aligned
   &f1_t[n],      // aligned
   &f1_t[b],      // aligned
   &f1_t[t],      // aligned
   ce, cw, cn, cs, ct, cb, cc, nx, 1);

// Inform other threads that [z] column is complete
zCountCompleted[z] = myCount;

// perform equivilent of Core barrier
int zEnd = (z0 + nHTs < nz) ? z0 + nHTs : nz;
for(int i = z0; i < zEnd; ++i)
   while(zCountCompleted[i] < myCount)
      WAIT_A_BIT;
   } // if(z < nz)
 } // for(;;)
} // parallel
return;
}
```

Figure 5.21—Cont'd

(1 or 2) of the OpenMP run, you would not see the comparative difference between the one and two threads per core runs. Therefore, the chart is presented in absolute form using Gflop/sec. Also, the `tiledHT3` code always ran using two threads per core as you cannot have a Hyper-Thread Phalanx of less than two threads per core.

Now then, in looking at Figure 5.23 you will note that in the "tiled" run (original best code) that the two threads per core runs showed less performance than the one thread per core run. This characteristic often happens and leads to the presumption by the programmer that two threads per core "generally" performs worse that one thread per core on floating point intensive programs. The relative performance

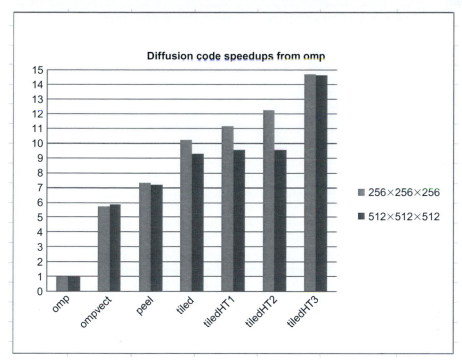

FIGURE 5.22

Intel Xeon Phi 5110P coprocessor.

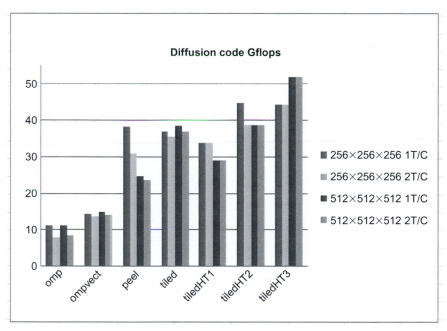

FIGURE 5.23

Intel Xeon E5-2620 v2 processor.

of the Plesiochronous Hyper-Thread Phalanx clearly disproves this presumption with the use of two threads per core.

$$256 \times 256 \times 256 \text{ tiledHT3}/\text{tiled} = 1:1.2 \quad (20\% \text{ faster})$$
$$512 \times 512 \times 512 \text{ tiledHT3}/\text{tiled} = 1:1.4 \quad (40\% \text{ faster})$$

Now let us look at a larger system "dual socket" system with Intel Xeon E5-2670 processors with a total of 16 cores and 32 threads.

In Figure 5.24 we see something completely unexpected. The large model of tiled with two threads per core has an unusual speedup. In all the other cases of running two threads per core for omp, omp-vect, peel, tiled, the two threads per core ran slower. Figure 5.24 illustrates for conventional optimization techniques that one cannot make a generalization that hyper-threads are not effective. You have to run the test. The `tiledHT3` run clearly shows the advantage of the combination of use of hyper-threads, in combination with the plesiochronous phasing barrier yields superior performance.

$$256 \times 256 \times 256 \text{ tiledHT3}/\text{tiled} = 1:1.23 \quad (23\% \text{ faster})$$
$$512 \times 512 \times 512 \text{ tiledHT3}/\text{tiled} = 1:1.086 \quad (8.6\% \text{ faster})$$

Had we used the one thread per core run as representative of the large tiled the ratio would have been:

$$512 \times 512 \times 512 \text{ tiledHT3}/\text{tiled} = 1:1.45 \quad (45\% \text{ faster})$$

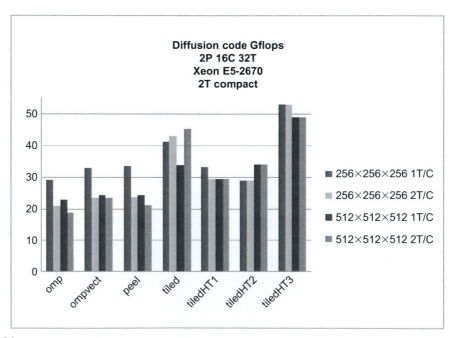

FIGURE 5.24

Dual socket system with Intel Xeon E5-2620 v2 processors.

SUMMARY

In this chapter, we presented a clear case for going to the extra step of using all your computational resources in an efficient manner. While at this time, the development of compiler optimizations and the use of `#pragma` directed programming do not permit the level of thread scheduling presented in this chapter, this does not preclude you from taking full advantage of the capabilities of your platform. *Time is money.*

FOR MORE INFORMATION

Here are some additional reading materials we recommend related to this chapter:

- http://en.wikipedia.org/wiki/Plesiochronous_system
- Download the code from this, and other chapters, at http://lotsofcores.com

PARALLEL EVALUATION OF FAULT TREE EXPRESSIONS

6

Jefferson Amstutz
SURVICE Engineering, USA

Hardware advances with Intel® Xeon® processors and Intel® Xeon Phi™ coprocessors enable complex scientific simulations to be visual and interactive. However, datasets in scientific and engineering simulations continue to increase in size, with the expectation that interactivity can be maintained. One of the key components to interactive simulation on processor and coprocessor hardware is exploiting SIMD parallelism. In this chapter, we explore how to find and use SIMD parallelism when evaluating large fault tree expressions on a large volume of input in an interactive application environment.

MOTIVATION AND BACKGROUND

EXPRESSIONS

Expressions embody the mathematical relationship between symbols according to some syntax grammar. In the context of this chapter, we focus on the need to evaluate large expressions that are easily modified at runtime. We also focus on the need for these modifiable expressions to scale well with expression size and instance count.

Expression evaluation forms the fundamental math that programmers encode to solve various computing problems. Scientific computing and engineering applications, by their very nature, rely heavily on evaluating mathematical expressions embedded in simulation codes. It is extremely common for these expressions to be large and complex while being applied to ever-growing datasets. Often, code flexibility is traded for increased performance, for example, when known simulation expressions are compiled directly into applications. However, parallel hardware enables applications to maintain interactivity while evaluating expressions over large datasets by exploiting parallelism. In certain applications, large expressions can be evaluated efficiently without hard coding.

EXPRESSION OF CHOICE: FAULT TREES

The phrase "evaluating large expressions" is nebulous and requires an appropriate scope, as well as a practical application, for meaningful discussion. Our example domain for this chapter is evaluating large fault trees for vulnerability assessment.

Vulnerability assessment is the process of identifying and quantifying vulnerabilities in a system of interest. A common environment for such studies is system engineering. Many systems are engineered to defend themselves against potential threats, expressed using a fault tree. Fault trees express failure relationships between systems using Boolean logic. Simulations use fault tree analysis (FTA) to evaluate the vulnerability of systems based on component reliability, system redundancy, physical protection, and other—potentially domain-specific—factors. After its introduction by Bell Laboratories in the 1960s, FTA has been adopted by the defense, aerospace, nuclear, chemical, and other high-hazard industries as the primary methodology for understanding system vulnerability.

AN APPLICATION FOR FAULT TREES: BALLISTIC SIMULATION

An example of vulnerability assessment is survivability analysis for military applications. Survivability analysis is a very broad field, so we discuss vehicle vulnerability to ballistic threats as the specific application. Ballistic simulation is widely used to assess how well vehicles can withstand impact from various ballistic threats.

Modern ballistic simulations require many different elements of computation to fully model an object's vulnerability to various threats. Ballistic events are chaotic and complex, which makes quantifiable assessment of outcomes for a target difficult. One common approach is to use probability of kill (P_k) as a metric. P_k defines the probability that an object or system of interest is no longer functional.

Vulnerability is measured at many levels using the P_k metric. Targets—in this case, vehicles—comprise thousands of components. Systems, in turns, comprise these individual components. High-level systems define vehicle functionality, and ultimately its ballistic survivability. Component P_k directly affects system P_k, according to engineering relationships. Fault trees express these system P_k relationships and adequately quantify vulnerability for ballistic events.

Understanding ballistic vulnerability requires sampling millions—even billions—of trajectories at which a threat may hit a vehicle. Every sample of a threat interacting with a target is a unique event that requires a unique instance of the fault tree. Recall that vehicle fault trees contain thousands of components with complex relationships. Thus, code scalability is critical for fault tree evaluation so that interactivity is maintained. Interactivity allows users to explore survivability outcomes on a target, which facilitates quick cognition rates and user feedback. To evaluate millions (or more!) of these large expressions at interactive rates, parallelism must be exploited effectively.

We use an approach for compiling fault trees to an in-memory encoding that is executed in parallel on each set of component P_k values. Our approach in this chapter focuses on SIMD parallelism because application threading/MPI architecture varies by domain and implementation.

It is important to note that our implementation is not limited to fault tree syntax and evaluation. Any mathematical expression can follow the principles we discuss in this chapter to maximize SIMD efficiency. Ballistic simulation gives us a compelling reason to evaluate such a high volume of an expression. Any Monte Carlo simulation that applies a large volume of inputs to a uniform expression will benefit from insights in this chapter.

EXAMPLE IMPLEMENTATION

Our example implementation, as illustrated in Figure 6.1, parses a fault tree from an input file, compiles an instruction array, and finally uses the instruction array to evaluate N sets of component values.

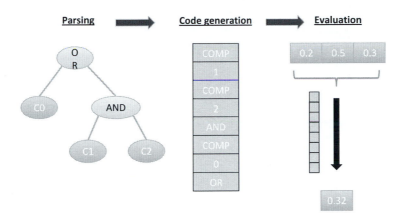

FIGURE 6.1

End-to-end process used to evaluate fault trees.

Syntax and parsing results

The input file syntax of our fault tree implementation is a list of system definitions. Systems are defined as an expression containing AND/OR operators, constants, components, and sub-systems. The grammar we parse is as follows:

Expression = ([OR_Operand] | [OR_Operand])+
OR_Operand = ([AND_Operand] & [AND_Operand])+
AND_Operand = [Name, Constant, Expression]

Parsing input is straightforward, especially with available tools such as yacc and lex. However, details of our input parsing code are out of scope for this chapter and are not relevant to efficient evaluation. Interested readers can examine the input parser portion of our example.

The result of parsing input data is a parse tree. The tree contains nodes of various types. We define an enumeration of each node type (Figure 6.2).

Name nodes are identifiers that the input file contains. Name pools, a collection of names, of components and systems are maintained during input parsing. Names are assumed to be components (tree leaves) unless they are assigned an expression. The tree is traversed after it is constructed to change name nodes into component or system nodes by using the contents of the component and system name pools. After the name conversion operation completes, the tree is traversed to assign components indices into evaluation input state values. Once component indices have been assigned, the tree is ready to be used for evaluation array construction.

Creating evaluation arrays

The goal of creating an evaluation array, or code array, is to build a set of instructions, which calculate a given system's value given a set of input component values. Our example implementation uses Reverse Polish Notation (RPN) to encode system evaluation operations. We chose to use RPN because the algorithm to evaluate instructions in RPN form is straightforward. Figure 6.3 illustrates a simple example.

Building the code array requires traversal of the parse tree. We use the Visitor Pattern to traverse each tree node and progressively append the evaluation array. A requirement of evaluating RPN expressions is

```
struct ftNode
{
    NodeType type; // Enum representing type
                   //(ex: 'op', 'comp', 'end', etc)
    std::string text;
    union {
        struct {
            int index;
        } name;
        struct {
            float value;
        } constant;
        struct {
            ftNode *lhs;
            ftNode *rhs;
        } op;
    };
};
```

FIGURE 6.2

The node class contains information about the type of node, parsed text from the file, and a union of node-type-specific information.

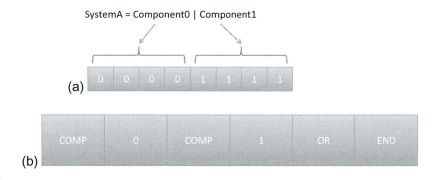

FIGURE 6.3

(a) Input component states of four trees: numbers in each element indicate which component index.
(b) Example RPN code array for "SystemA."

to have stack memory available for each evaluation. During the evaluation code generation, a maximum stack size is maintained to appropriately size the memory used for evaluation stacks. Details can be found in the chapter's downloadable code at http://lotsofcores.com.

It is also important to note that this step is relatively low overhead. In a visual and interactive system, the code array could be very quickly modified or recreated, allowing flexibility in the application to give immediate feedback from a newly selected expression.

Evaluating the expression array

System evaluation is the section of computation that we focus on optimizing because it is the computation that is embedded within a parent simulation code. Recall that our goal is to evaluate N trees, all sharing the same system to be evaluated. Therefore, the constructed code array is shared among all evaluation instances. System evaluation assumes that $M \times N$-component values have been calculated according to the parent simulation, where M is the number of components in the system to be evaluated and N is the number of instances of the tree to be evaluated. The function in Figure 6.4 is called for each instance of the fault tree, looping over each entry in the code array and handling the operations according to each instruction.

The code in Figure 6.4 implements AND $(P(A) * P(B))$ and OR $(P(A) + P(B) - P(A) * P(B))$ operations on input components values. A status value for each evaluation of the tree is held in an array to do error checking. After the code array has been executed, the final system values are on the top of each evaluation's stack.

USING ISPC FOR VECTORIZATION

The system evaluation implementation is straightforward to understand but does not take advantage of SIMD execution units. Because evaluating fault trees of the same system is a data parallel operation; it is a perfect candidate for SIMD hardware. One approach for writing explicit SIMD code is to use intrinsic functions. While this may seem straightforward in our small example, in production code it presents a larger maintenance burden on developers to maintain the implementations for SSE4.x, AVX/ AVX2, IMCI (on the coprocessor), AVX-512, and beyond. In addition to higher maintenance cost, intrinsic-based code is less readable and thus harder to understand. To alleviate these issues, we use the open-source Intel SPMD Program Compiler (ispc) to do vectorization for us. The code shown in Figure 6.5 implements the same code in the previous C++ implementation, but now done with ispc.

The ispc implementation of evaluateCode() is almost identical to the C++ implementation. The only difference is the introduction of ispc-specific qualifiers to specify which variables are uniform across ispc gangs. Additionally, the evaluate function that calls evaluateCode() is defined in ispc to take advantage of the ispc "foreach" construct. Using "foreach" in place of the regular C/C++ "for" helps the compiler better map loop iterations to SIMD lanes for execution in parallel. With this ispc version of the code, we only see a 1.57× speedup from the regular C++ implementation. While there is a performance gain, it indicates poor SIMD utilization. In this case, ispc is unable to do a good job at vectorizing the implementation, likely because it cannot make good assumptions about the switch statement always being traversed coherently in gangs.

The previous two implementations iterate over all the instructions per evaluation. Rearranging the computation to iterate over each evaluation per instruction helps scope how the code should be vectorized. The version in Figure 6.6 implements iterations over all evaluations per instruction.

Notice that the general form in Figure 6.6 is to use an ispc "foreach" over each evaluation for every instruction in the code array (e.g., the cases in the switch statement). This requires a local buffer of lvalues and rvalues instead of using a single varying lvalue and rvalue. The buffers are sized by the section size, which minimizes the local array footprint while enabling the call to the evaluate() function to be thread safe. Because the "foreach" loops are much tighter, ispc is able to better figure out how to vectorize the code.

```
void ftEvaluator::evaluateCode(int *code, const int
    numEvaluations, int evaluation, float *compVals,
    float *stack, ftStatus *status)
{
    int sp;          // stack position
    int index;       // system/component index
    float lvalue;    // cache for left value (stack[sp])
    float rvalue;    // cache for right value (stack[sp+1])

    *status = GoodStatus;
    sp = -1;
    int pc = 0;
    for (;;) {
        switch (code[pc++]) {
        case CompType:
            index = code[pc++];
            stack[++sp] = compVals[(numEvaluations *
                                     index) + evaluation];
            break;
        case ConstType:
            // push constant value in next code word on
            // stack as float
            stack[++sp] = *((float *)&code[pc++]);

            break;
        case AndType:
            rvalue = stack[sp--];
            lvalue = stack[sp];
            if (lvalue != 0.0f) {
                stack[sp] = lvalue * rvalue;
            }
            break;
        case OrType:   // assumes statistical independence
            rvalue = stack[sp--];
            lvalue = stack[sp];
            stack[sp] = lvalue + rvalue -
                          (lvalue * rvalue);
            break;
        case EndType:
            // end of code, check stack pointer
            // and return
            if (sp != 0) {
                *status = StackErrStatus;
            }
            return;   // exit for loop
        default:
            *status = BadCodeStatus;
            return;   // exit for loop
        }
    }
}
```

FIGURE 6.4

C++ implementation of code execution: this version is called for every evaluation instance of the system to be evaluated.

```
inline void evaluateCode(uniform int    *uniform code,
                         uniform int     numEvaluations,
                         varying int     evaluation,
                         uniform float *compVals,
                         uniform float *stack,
                         uniform int8  *status)
{
    uniform int sp;        // stack position
    uniform int index;     // system/component index
    varying float lvalue;  // cache for left value
    varying float rvalue;  // cache for right value

    *status = GoodStatus;
    sp = -1;
    uniform int pc = 0;
    while (true) {
        switch (code[pc++]) {
        case CompType:
            index = code[pc++];
            stack[++sp] = compVals[(numEvaluations *
                                    index) + evaluation];
            break;
        case ConstType:
            // push constant value in next code word
            // on stack as float
            stack[++sp] = *((float *)&code[pc++]);
            break;
        case AndType:
            rvalue = stack[sp--];
            lvalue = stack[sp];
            if (lvalue != 0.0f) {
                stack[sp] = lvalue * rvalue;
            }
            break;
        case OrType:  // assumes statistical independence
            rvalue = stack[sp--];
            lvalue = stack[sp];
            stack[sp] = lvalue + rvalue -
                        (lvalue * rvalue);

            break;
        case EndType:
            // end of code, check sp and return
            if (sp != 0) {
                *status = StackErrStatus;
            }
            return;  // exit for loop
        default:
            *status = BadCodeStatus;
            return;  // exit for loop
        }
    }
}

export void evaluate(const uniform int sectionStart,
                     const uniform int sectionEnd,
                     uniform int numEvals,
                     uniform int compCount,
                     uniform int *uniform code,
```

FIGURE 6.5

Nonoptimized ispc evaluation: naïve version is a direct translation of the C++ version into ispc.

```
                            uniform float *uniform compVals,
                            uniform float *uniform stack,
                            const uniform int stackSize,
                            uniform float *uniform results,
                            uniform int8  *uniform status)
    {
        const uniform int end = sectionEnd < numEvals ?
                                    sectionEnd : numEvals;
        foreach (i = sectionStart ... end) {
            evaluateCode(code, numEvals, i, compVals,
                         stack + i * stackSize),
                         status + i);

            if (status[i] == GoodStatus) {
                results[i] = stack[i*stackSize];
            }
        }
    }
```

Figure 6.5—Cont'd

```
    inline void evaluateCode(const uniform size_t secStart,
                             const uniform size_t secEnd,
                             const uniform size_t numEvals,
                             const uniform size_t numComps,
                             const uniform int code[],
                             const uniform int stackSize,
                             uniform float *stack,
                             uniform float *uniform compVals,
                             uniform float *uniform results,
                             uniform int8  *uniform status)
    {
        uniform int sp;       // stack position
        uniform int index;    // system/component index
        uniform int pc = 0;   // program counter (code index)
        uniform bool stop;    // flag to break out of eval loop

        uniform float lvalues[SECTION_SIZE];
        uniform float rvalues[SECTION_SIZE];

        sp = -1;
        pc = 0;
        stop = false;

        // Initialize evaluation status
        foreach (i = sectionStart ... sectionEnd) {
            status[i] = GoodStatus;
        }

        cwhile (true) {
            switch (code[pc++]) {
            case CompType:
                index = code[pc++];
                ++sp;
```

FIGURE 6.6

Optimized ispc evaluation.

```
            foreach (i = sectionStart ... sectionEnd) {
                stack[(stackSize*sp)+i] =
                    compVals[(numEvaluations*index)+i];
            }
            break;
        case ConstType:
            ++sp;
            foreach (i = sectionStart ... sectionEnd) {
                stack[(stackSize*sp)+i] = *((float *)
                                        &code[pc]);
            }
            pc++;
            break;
        case AndType:
            foreach (i = sectionStart ... sectionEnd) {
                rvalues[i-sectionStart] =
                    stack[(stackSize*sp)+i];
                lvalues[i-sectionStart] =
                    stack[(stackSize*(sp-1))+i];
                cif (lvalues[i-sectionStart] != 0.0f) {
                    stack[(stackSize*(sp-1))+i] =
                            lvalues[i-sectionStart] *
                            rvalues[i-sectionStart];
                }
            }
            sp--;
            break;
        case OrType:  // assumes statistical independence
            foreach (i = sectionStart ... sectionEnd) {
                rvalues[i-sectionStart] =
                    stack[(stackSize*sp)+i];
                lvalues[i-sectionStart] =
                    stack[(stackSize*(sp-1))+i];
                stack[sp-1] = lvalues[i-sectionStart] +
                            rvalues[i-sectionStart] -
                            lvalues[i-sectionStart] *
                            rvalues[i-sectionStart];
            }
            sp--;
            break;
        case EndType:
            foreach (i = sectionStart ... sectionEnd) {
                cif (sp != 0) {
                    status[i] = StackErrStatus;
                } else {
                    results[i] = stack[0+i];
                }
            }
            stop = true; // exit while loop
            break;
        default:
                foreach (i = sectionStart ... sectionEnd) {
                    status[i] = BadCodeStatus;
                }
                stop = true; // exit while loop
                break;
            }
            cif (stop) break;
        }
    }
```

Figure 6.6—Cont'd

```
export void evaluate(const uniform size_t sectionStart,
                     const uniform size_t sectionEnd,
                     const uniform size_t numEvals,
                     const uniform size_t compCount,
                     const uniform int code[],
                     uniform float *uniform compVals,
                     uniform float *uniform stack,
                     const uniform int stackSize,
                     uniform float *uniform results,
                     uniform int8  *uniform status)
{
    const uniform int end = sectionEnd < numEvals ?
        sectionEnd : numEvals;
    evaluateCode(sectionStart, end, numEvals, compCount,
            code, stackSize, stack, compVals,
            results, status);
}
```

Figure 6.6—Cont'd

In addition to better vector code generation by ispc, we use a coalesced memory layout of initial component values instead of a strided layout. This is particularly important in preventing scatter/gather memory transactions. Processor and coprocessor vector read/write instructions are most efficient when an entire vector can be directly fetched or written. This layout is best achieved through two code characteristics. First, we use arrays of individual data components instead of an array of structures (AOS) containing one of each data component. Imagine all of the argument arrays into evaluate() and evaluateCode() residing in a structure: this follows the general suggestion to use a structure of arrays (SOA) instead of an AOS. In addition to using an SOA layout, we coalesce component state elements by grouping each element by component index instead of by evaluation index. When evaluating batches of evaluations that share the same code array, all of a single-component index is accessed at once. Consecutive component index values in memory prevent vector gathers from occurring, which is illustrated in Figure 6.7.

The second ispc version of the implementation runs at 7.9× faster than the first ispc implementation and 12.7× faster than the C++ implementation. We measured the performance of using only one thread to isolate the performance gains from using SIMD hardware. Thus, the speedup is a direct result of much better SIMD scaling (and even some caching benefits too). Evaluating trees is an embarrassingly parallel operation; thus, implementing a multithreaded solution is very straightforward.

OTHER CONSIDERATIONS

Science and engineering applications vary by architecture and design; some applications can be adjusted to further maximize performance. In the case of ballistic simulation, the entire fault tree is not always used for evaluation. In practice, an input file contains all of the system and component relationships for a vehicle, but often the user does not choose a system that contains every component. By using a compressed set of components, a nontrivial amount of memory can be saved when evaluating

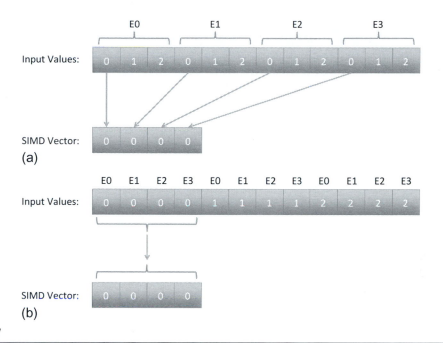

FIGURE 6.7

Memory layout: (a) *Strided*: elements are grouped by evaluation, causing a "gather" operation requiring four memory fetches. (b) *Coalesced*: elements are grouped by component index, allowing a single-vector memory fetch.

fault trees. This is done by a translation from global component index (all components) to compressed component index (selected system relevant components) when populating initial component values. Doing this translation before evaluation saves the overhead of translating between indices for each component lookup during evaluation. Applications that operate on a subset of the input expression will benefit from this memory compression optimization. The sample code for this chapter follows this optimization.

Another optimization is to form packets of computation in a large, multithreaded application. Multicore processors and manycore coprocessors are flexible enough to allow multithreaded applications to work on different stages of computation independently of each other. However, each thread ought to work on a subset of data at least as wide as SIMD instruction width. Thus a "packet" of evaluations for the Intel Xeon Phi coprocessor's 16-wide float vectors should contain at least 16 evaluations, while maintaining the data layout as discussed in the previous section. Threads that execute evaluations based on packets can independently arrive at the system evaluation stage of computation and maintain maximum SIMD efficiency.

It is also noteworthy to mention that the SIMD utilization techniques discussed in this chapter apply to any SIMD hardware architecture, such as GPUs and ARM NEON CPUs. The production ballistic simulation code that inspired this chapter was first implemented using NVIDIA's CUDA GPU computing environment within the open-source Visual Simulation Laboratory (VSL) framework.

SUMMARY

Developments in SIMD hardware found in processors and coprocessors enable many scientific and engineering applications to run at interactive rates. Large expressions are found in such applications and require adequate SIMD parallelization. Monte Carlo simulations are a family of simulations that benefit from wide SIMD hardware parallelism. We looked at fault tree evaluation as a large expression found in ballistic simulations that can be evaluated in SIMD well by using ispc.

Our example implementation parses input fault trees, creates an array of evaluation instructions, then executes them using SIMD parallelism. We looked at two characteristics of the final evaluation code that dramatically improve the evaluation performance. First, arranging the ispc code to use smaller loops helps the ispc compiler better generate vectorized code. Second, using a coalesced SOA data layout minimizes expensive vector scatter/gather memory transactions.

FOR MORE INFORMATION

Here are some additional reading materials we recommend related to this chapter:

- General Fault Tree Analysis Information: http://en.wikipedia.org/wiki/Fault_tree_analysis.
- Complex fault tree analysis with GPUs: Aghassi, H., Aghassi, F., 2013. Fault tree analysis speedup with gpu parallel computing. Int. J. Comput. Inf. Syst. Indust. Manag. Appl. 5, 106–114.
- More information on the ispc language can be found at: http://ispc.github.io/.
- VSL was developed by the U.S. Army Research Laboratory. More information on the project and code is available at http://vissimlab.org/.
- Download the code from this, and other chapters, http://lotsofcores.com.

DEEP-LEARNING NUMERICAL OPTIMIZATION

Rob Farber

TechEnablement.com, USA

Deep-learning numerical optimization algorithms have experienced a resurgence of interest due to the general availability of massively parallel coprocessors in combination with the abundance of video, audio, and social media data that are now available. Enabling new and more powerful Internet search capabilities or utilizing the ability of these algorithms to perform complex real-time pattern recognition for self-driving cars and augmented reality workflows are but a few examples of the many financially compelling reasons driving the use of these algorithms. With the right parallel mapping, a single Intel® Xeon Phi™ coprocessor can exceed a TeraFLOP per second (TF/s) of sustained hybrid single and double precision performance on real machine-learning and numerical optimization problems in a production environment. It is interesting to note that this performance can be achieved entirely in user-developed code without relying on the performance of optimized libraries such as the Intel Math Kernel Library, demonstrating that "normal" programmers outside of Intel can write very high-performance applications in compiled code. Near-linear scaling and petascale performance can be achieved through the use of Message Passing Interface to coordinate the computations of several thousand Intel coprocessors. For example, the massively parallel mapping and code discussed in this chapter delivered 2.2 PetaFLOP per second (PF/s) of average sustained hybrid precision training performance on 3000 Intel Xeon Phi coprocessors in the TACC (Texas Advanced Computing Center) Stampede supercomputer. Both high performance and large memory make the Intel Xeon Phi coprocessor family an ideal platform for training on the large datasets that are required to solve complex and high-dimensional pattern recognition problems.

FITTING AN OBJECTIVE FUNCTION

Mathematical modeling is a branch of applied mathematics that creates an abstraction of reality that can be used for analysis and prediction. Data-driven numerical models are generally amenable to computer implementation making them useful analytic and embedded system tools. In particular, functions inferred by neural networks have predictive power, meaning they can correctly forecast future values in a time series, perform classification tasks, signal processing, plus respond and adapt to complex and unforeseen stimuli in robotics and real-time systems. See the references to Duda and Hart, as well as, Farber and Lapedes in the additional information section at the end of this Chapter.

Data-driven model fitting can be phrased as a form of function optimization where a set of model parameters are adjusted to fit some dataset with a minimum error. The error is determined by an objective function, sometimes called a cost function, which evaluates how well a model fits the data for a given set of model parameters (Figure 7.1).

The LMS (least means squares) objective function is commonly utilized to fit a model to a set of N-observed data points that represent a curve or surface. The LMS error defined in Figure 7.2 is always positive, which means a perfect fit will result in a zero error. Due to numerical precision issues, noisy data, and other challenges, parameterized models rarely achieve a zero error. Generally, the numerical optimization techniques utilized to determine the model parameters find a local minima, or a low point in the cost function from which the optimization algorithm cannot escape. There is no guarantee that the best overall fit, or global minimum, will be found, but the error value reported by the LMS objective function can be used to get a sense of how well the model represents the data.

The widespread adoption of machine-learning and numerical optimization techniques for research and throughout industry demonstrates that models based on empirically determined parameters (e.g., linear regression, nonlinear regression, neural networks, etcetera) often provide solutions that are "good enough" or are the only practical approach due to data size, complexity, noise, and other issues even with the challenges of local minima.

Training artificial neural networks (ANNs) can be expressed as a function optimization problem that seeks to determine the best network parameters (e.g., the model parameters or internal network weights and biases) which will minimize the error on a training dataset. This fitting or training process is computationally expensive as it requires repeatedly evaluating an objective function with different parameter sets. The runtime of each objective function evaluation is $O(N_{param} * N_{data})$ since the error must be calculated for each example in the training data. In most cases, the number of parameters, N_{param}, is small relative to the size of the training data, N_{data}, which means the overall runtime is dominated by the size of the dataset. In fact, the over-specification of data relative to the number of parameters is important so the ANN does not memorize the training dataset. This is why cross-validation datasets (e.g., datasets containing unique examples of the data that are not presented to the ANN during training) are so important, because cross-validation detects cases where the ANN fits the training data well but generalizes poorly.

Parallelization of a data-parallel objective function can result in significant runtime speedups on massively parallel computers as indicated by Figure 7.3, which shows that the runtime decreases as a

$$Error = func(P_0, P_1, ..., P_n)$$

FIGURE 7.1

An objective function.

$$Error = \sum_{i}^{N} (Known_i - Predicted_i)^2$$

FIGURE 7.2

Sum of squares of differences error.

$$O\left(\frac{N_{\text{data}} * N_{\text{param}}}{N_{\text{processors}}}\right)$$

FIGURE 7.3

An ideal runtime for a data-parallel objective function.

function of the number of processors. This is referred to as *strong scaling* as the runtime for a given dataset (or problem size) can be reduced by a factor of the number of processing elements.

Most data-parallel objective functions are also floating-point intensive and amenable to vectorization, which makes them ideal candidates to run efficiently on all the cores and each of the per-core vector units of the coprocessors. The combination of scalable parallelism and efficient vectorization indicates that data-intensive machine-learning and numerical optimization problems fit nicely in the high-performance regime of the Intel Xeon Phi coprocessor family (e.g., the bottom right quadrant of Figure 7.4).

The neural network training code in this chapter will utilize the massively parallel mapping that I developed, in the 1980s, at Los Alamos National Laboratory and the Santa Fe Institute. Thearling surveyed various parallel neural network mappings including my "Farber" mapping. (The link to this survey is in Section "For more information.")

- *Naïve implementation*: Each node in the neural network was mapped to a processor. While massively parallel, this approach is both memory bandwidth and network communications limited.

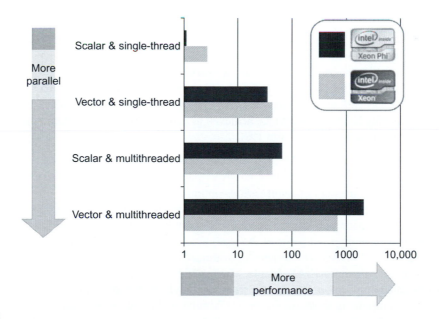

FIGURE 7.4

Intel® Xeon Phi™ coprocessor performance envelope.

Courtesy: James Reinders Intel Corp.

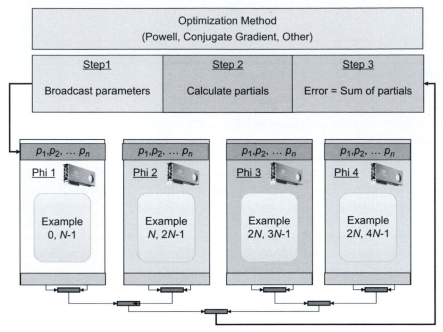

FIGURE 7.5

A general mapping: Energy=func($P1$, $P2$, … Pn).

- *An improved method*: Zhang proposed an improved method where he and his colleagues carefully mapped multiple network nodes to the same processor. This allowed for reduced communication cost and more efficient computation of the network node outputs.
- The Farber mapping, shown in Figure 7.5, is able to run efficiently on individual and collections of coprocessors as well as other massively parallel systems. According to Thearling, this approach was "the fastest performance achieved to date." It has been in continuous use on machines around the world since the 1990s.

The box labeled "Optimization Method" indicates that many generic, library-based numerical optimization libraries can be utilized with this massively parallel mapping. The book *Numerical Recipes* is an excellent source of information about various optimization algorithms.

All results in this chapter utilized the popular and freely available open-source *nlopt* optimization library written by Johnson and can be downloaded from http://ab-initio.mit.edu/nlopt. However, the reader is free to replace *nlopt* with one of the many free and licensed numerical toolkits that are available including SLATEC, NAG (Numerical Algorithms Group), MINPACK, the GNU scientific library, Matlab, Octave, scipy, gnuplot, SAS, Maple, Mathematica, and a plethora of others.

The Farber mapping demonstrating near-linear scaling behavior to 3000 coprocessors on the TACC Stampede supercomputer is shown in Figure 7.6. Similar scaling plots—essentially plots that also look linear to the eye—have been achieved using 60,000 processor cores on the TACC Ranger supercomputer, 16,384 GPUs on the ORNL (Oak Ridge National Laboratory) Titan supercomputer, and 64,000 processing cores on the Thinking Machines CM-2 along with numerous other supercomputers and compute clusters since the 1980s.

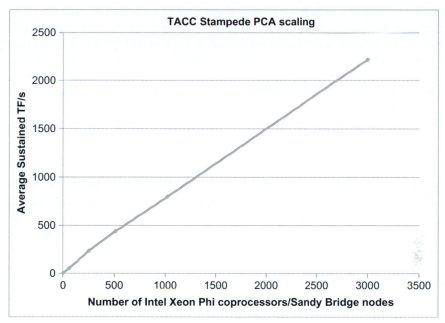

FIGURE 7.6

Scaling to 3000 Intel Xeon Phi on the TACC Stampede Supercomputer.

The near-linear scaling of this mapping is the result of the aggregate runtime of steps 1-3:

- *Step 1*: Parameters are broadcast to all the processor(s). In general, the MPI global broadcast is extremely efficient and has a constant runtime. The time spent on broadcasting data is usually limited by the bandwidth of the network interconnect hardware.
- *Step 2*: Each MPI node independently calculates a partial error for the data subset contained in local memory, which means the runtime exhibits strong scaling according to the number of processing nodes. The runtime of this step is determined by the amount of data per MPI node and the computational speed of the node. (*Note*: The per node MPI data load of the partial datasets occurs once at the beginning of the calculation and generally scales according to the available network bandwidth.)
- *Step 3*: The scalability of this mapping is mainly affected by the runtime behavior of the reduction operation on very large systems. Most MPI reduction operations require $O(\log_2(N_{nodes}))$ runtime, where N_{nodes} is the number of MPI nodes. In practice, the latency of the network interconnect limits the performance of the reduction as the number of bytes in the partial sum is small, generally 8 bytes for each 64-bit partial sum.

Experience has shown that even the largest problems can utilize single precision (32-bit) floating-point storage for the parameters and data, but the accumulation of the partial errors in steps 2 and 3 should utilize double precision (64-bit) arithmetic. Otherwise, information loss may cause the optimization algorithm to get trapped in local minima purely from the precision losses that occur when summing millions of partial errors using single precision arithmetic. The runtime impact of the use of a 64-bit, double precision accumulator to perform the hybrid precision reduction is minimal.

Near-linear scalability can only be achieved when using an optimization technique based on an objective function that returns a single error value rather than an error vector. Some optimization algorithms utilize an error vector to determine the next set of parameters to evaluate during the optimization process. Unfortunately, the size of the error vector scales according to the size of the data. The all-to-one communication pattern of even small error vectors can quickly saturate the network interconnect, or the memory subsystem and processor(s) of the MPI node running the optimization algorithm. Thus, only error-vector-based optimization algorithms that have been designed to run in parallel and eliminate the issues associated with using error vectors at scale can be used with this mapping.

OBJECTIVE FUNCTIONS AND PRINCIPLE COMPONENTS ANALYSIS

Neural networks are *computationally universal*, meaning that they can, in theory, learn any computable function. The argument supporting this claim is the simple observation that a neural network can implement all the logic gates (e.g., *or*, *xor*, *and*, *not,* etc.) that are used to build other computationally universal devices like a general-purpose computer.

Recently, neural networks have become a popular way to perform *deep-learning* by training individual layers of a multilayer neural network. It is this ability to define hidden layers that gives ANNs the ability to simulate other computational devices and create internal representations of complex data or perform *feature extraction*. Feature extraction refers to the identification of the salient aspects or properties of data to facilitate its use in a subsequent task such as regression or classification. Lapedes and I showed that only two hidden layers are required to perform modeling and prediction tasks as well as symbolic learning. However, clever human-aided design can create smaller networks that utilize fewer parameters, albeit with more than two hidden layers, or be fine-tuned to perform better on complex deep-learning tasks as reported by Hinton.

The discussion in this chapter will focus on using multi-layer ANNs to perform PCA (principle components analysis) and NLPCA (nonlinear principle components analysis).

PCA is extensively used in data mining and data analysis to (1) reduce the dimensionality of a dataset and (2) extract features from a dataset. PCA analysis accounts for the maximum amount of variance in a dataset using a set of orthogonal straight lines where each line is defined by a weighted linear combination of the observed variables. Similarly, NLPCA can utilize continuous open or closed curves to account for variance in data. A circle is one example of a *closed curve* that joins itself where there are no end points.

The ANN architecture shown in Figure 7.7 can be used to find the principle components of a dataset through the use of a restricted number of linear hidden neurons, or bottleneck neurons. Similarly, the ANN in Figure 7.7 can be used to perform an NLPCA when a nonlinear operator is used for the bottleneck neurons (labeled B in Figure 7.7). These nonlinear operators can be either open or closed curves.

NLPCA has wide applicability to numerous challenging problems including pattern recognition, biological modeling, climate modeling, and chemistry. There are also numerous Web sites, tutorials, and books published about NLPCA. A search on "nlpca" will provide a good starting point.

During training, the multilayer ANN shown in Figure 7.7 is presented with each training vector in the training set via the input, or *I* neurons at the bottom of the image. The ANN essentially teaches itself find the linear or nonlinear principle components because it is forced to pass the input vector information through the lower half of the network (thus transforming each input vector from a high- to low-dimensional space, or from two dimensions to one in Figure 7.7) so that the error is minimized when the upper half of the network reconstructs the original high-dimensional input vector at the output

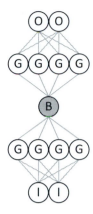

FIGURE 7.7

A multilayer PCA or NLPCA neural network.

neurons. This is an example of *unsupervised learning* where the objective function is able to calculate the error based only on inputs from the training set. (Specifically, the LMS error can be calculated by subtracting and squaring the difference between the input and output neurons.) Alternatively, *supervised learning* occurs when a teacher provides values for the output neurons that reflect a desired or known outcome for each training example, which means the LMS error can be calculated by subtracting and squaring the difference between the known values and predicted output neurons.

SOFTWARE AND EXAMPLE DATA

Complete working code and build scripts for the PCA and NLPCA examples in this chapter can be found in the *farbopt* repository on github (see URL in Section "For more information").

The code snippet in Figure 7.8 illustrates the simplicity of an OpenMP implementation of *func()*, the LMS objective function used to train a neural network on a single device as well as across all the

```
{
    {
        err=0.; // initialize error here for offload
#pragma omp parallel for reduction(+ : err)
        for(int i=0; i < nDeviceExamples; i++) {
        float d=myFunc(i, param, deviceExample,
                            nDeviceExamples, NULL);
            err += d*d;
        }
    }
}
```

FIGURE 7.8

An OpenMP version of an LMS data-parallel objective function.

nodes in an MPI environment. Regardless of environment (e.g., a single coprocessor or MPI implementation), the following loop performs the majority of the computationally intensive work.

The user-provided inline function *myFunc()* calculates the error of the model for a specified example in the dataset being fit. The OpenMP compiler is responsible for correctly parallelizing the reduction loop across the processor cores. The programmer is responsible for expressing *myFunc()* so the compiler can correctly vectorize the parallel *myFunc()* instances to make full use of the per core vector units on the coprocessor.

Note that the call to both *func()* and *myFunc()* is generic, which means the *farbopt* example code can be used to optimize arbitrary parallelizable objective functions such as support vector machines, independent component analysis, expectation maximization, and many others.

The example code used in this chapter implements a C language version of ANN shown in Figure 7.7, which will be trained via LMS. Conditional compilation allows specification of the type of transform for the bottleneck B and G neurons at compile time. Choices include a linear operator for a PCA analysis plus several implementations of a sigmoid for the NLPCA analysis. The use of conditional compilation (1) simplifies testing and benchmarking and (2) frees the compiler to optimize the inline *myFunc()* code to best run on the coprocessor vector units.

The LMS objective function is called via the *nlopt* optimization library during the optimization of the ANN parameters (e.g., the weights and neuron biases). The actual *nlopt* call is shown in the following code snippet. The *getTime()* function returns the wall-clock time for the overall optimization process. Similar instrumentation in *func()* records the amount of time spent in the objective function so the user can verify that the runtime of the LMS objective function does indeed dominate the overall application runtime.

The MPI code utilizes a master/slave paradigm where the optimization method runs on the master node and work is portioned out to all the slave nodes. For efficiency, the master node can also act as a slave node during the evaluation of the objective function.

The MPI slave nodes, those nodes with an MPI rank greater than zero, call the *startClient()* method after the *MPI_Init()* call. The code for startClient is shown in Figure 7.9.

The optimization method (an NLOPT example is shown in Figure 7.10) is passed the mpiObjFunc() that (1) runs on the master, (2) performs the MPI communications, and (3) also runs part of the objective function. The code is shown in Figure 7.11.

TRAINING DATA

The scaling behavior and runtime for the PCA version of the ANN (compiled using a linear operator) are evaluated for a dataset containing 30 million observations of a cigar-shaped distribution of noisy data with a mean of 0 and variance of 0.1 around a straight line. A small sample of this distribution is shown in Figure 7.12.

Similarly, the runtime behavior of the NLPCA ANN was evaluated using 30 million points taken from the nonlinear relationship between $z1$ and $z2$ as defined in Figure 7.13. Noise with a mean of 0 and a variance of 0.1 was again introduced to make the training process more difficult for the ANN.

A simple sigmoid, $x/(1+|x|)$, shown in the code snippet in Figure 7.14 was used to implement the nonlinear transform for the G and B neurons in the ANN shown in Figure 7.7. The principle advantage of this sigmoid is that we know the exact number floating-point operations. While useful for

```
void startClient(void * restrict my_func_data)
{
  int op;

  double xFromMPI[N_PARAM];
  double partialError,sum;

  for(;;) {
    // loop until the master says I am done - then exit
    MPI_Bcast(&op, 1, MPI_INT, 0, MPI_COMM_WORLD);
    // receive the op code
    if(op==0) { // we are done, normal exit
      break;
    }
    // receive the parameters
    MPI_Bcast(xFromMPI, N_PARAM, MPI_DOUBLE, 0,
                            MPI_COMM_WORLD);
    partialError =
      objFunc(N_PARAM,  xFromMPI, NULL, my_func_data);
    MPI_Reduce(&partialError, &sum, 1, MPI_DOUBLE,
                      MPI_SUM, 0, MPI_COMM_WORLD);
  }
}
```

FIGURE 7.9

MPI slave code.

```
double startTime=getTime();
// initialize error here for offload
int ret=nlopt_optimize(opt, x, &minf);
printf("Optimization Time %g\n",getTime()-startTime);
```

FIGURE 7.10

The NLOPT call to start the optimization process.

benchmarking purposes, better formed sigmoidal functions like *tanh()* and the logistic function are generally used in real-world applications because the parameter optimization during training tends to converge more quickly to a solution.

A plot of the NLPCA data (represented by the triangles) and resulting ANN predicted model (represented by the line) is shown in Figure 7.15.

```
double mpiObjFunc(unsigned n,  const double * restrict x,
double * restrict grad,
                void * restrict my_func_data)
{
  int op;
  double partialError, totalError=0.;
  // Send the master op code

  MPI Bcast(&masterOP, 1, MPI INT, 0, MPI COMM WORLD);

  MPI Bcast((void*) x, N PARAM, MPI DOUBLE, 0,
            MPI COMM WORLD); // Send the parameters

  partialError = objFunc(N PARAM,  x, NULL,
                                    my func data);
  MPI Reduce(&partialError, &totalError, 1, MPI DOUBLE,
        MPI SUM, 0, MPI COMM WORLD); // get the totalError

  return(totalError);
}
```

FIGURE 7.11

The MPI master for the objective function.

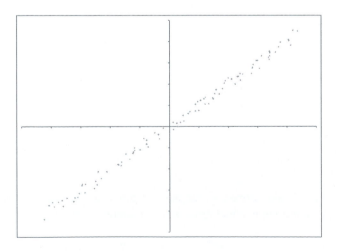

FIGURE 7.12

Example of a linear dataset for PCA.

$$z1 = t + e1$$
$$z2 = t^3 + e2$$

FIGURE 7.13

A nonlinear relationship.

```
char *desc="Eliott activation: x/(1+fabsf(x))";
inline float G(float x) { return( x/(1.f+fabsf(x)) ) ;}
```

FIGURE 7.14

A simple sigmoid.

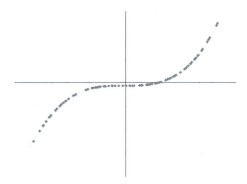

FIGURE 7.15

Example NLPCA data and ANN prediction.

RUNTIME RESULTS

Output from the example code confirms that the application runtime is indeed dominated by the time spent in the LMS objective function (Figure 7.16).

The performance results reported in Figure 7.17 demonstrate that a single coprocessor was able to exceed a TF/s when running in native execution mode and that the average performance is quite close to the maximum observed GigaFLOP per second (GF/s) performance even with a substantial variation between the minimum and maximum reported floating-point rate.

	Mode	Data Size	Nparam	%time in func()
PCA	Native	30M	83	99.1324
NLPCA	Native	30M	83	99.7844
PCA	Offload	30M	83	99.9998
NLPCA	Offload	30M	83	99.9992

FIGURE 7.16

Time in func() for Native and Offload PCA and NLPCA Runs.

	Mode	Min (GF/s)	Ave (GF/s)	Max (GF/s)
PCA	Native	15.1494	1012.8	1037.03
NLPCA	Native	22.0354	369.315	374.58
PCA	Offload	14.2368	946.761	973.886
NLPCA	Offload	20.5346	359.672	363.216

FIGURE 7.17

GF/s performance for a two input PCA and NLPCA ANN.

Floating-point performance in offload execution mode is quite good even with the overhead of moving the parameters to the coprocessor and retrieving the partial error(s) on each call to *func()*. This offload floating-point performance is indicative of the expected performance—including communications overhead—when running on more than one coprocessor in a node or when running across a compute cluster or leadership class supercomputer using MPI. The communications overhead is unavoidable when running across multiple devices whether the coprocessor is natively running the MPI code or if it is being indirectly utilized by the host via offload mode. The TACC Stampede results shown in Figure 7.4 show the performance when a single coprocessor is accessed via offload mode from a host-based MPI code.

The *farbopt* github repository also includes a python-based neural network generator called *genFunc.py* that can be used to investigate the performance impact of different ANN architectures. For example, a neural network that has four input neurons will have to load four floating-point data values from memory to calculate an error as opposed to the length two vectors loaded by the architecture shown in Figure 7.7. The impact of the additional data loads can be seen by comparing the performance results reported in Figures 7.17 and 7.18.

In particular, note that the PCA performance decreased due to memory bandwidth limitations caused by fetching four values instead of two. In contrast, the NLPCA calculation is more compute intensive, which means it spends more time processing vector registers than waiting for data to be retrieved from memory. As a result, the NLPCA performance benefitted from the additional parameters in the larger four input neuron ANN as both offload and native mode performance increased compared to the smaller two input neuron ANN.

	Mode	Min (GF/s)	Ave (GF/s)	Max (GF/s)
PCA	Native	23.8488	822.883	855.79
NLPCA	Native	31.0903	430.143	437.162
PCA	Offload	22.2739	821.65	850.331
NLPCA	Offload	27.3932	427.277	434.41

FIGURE 7.18

GF/s performance for a four input PCA and NLPCA ANN.

SCALING RESULTS

Scaling according to dataset size on a single coprocessor is shown in Figure 7.7 and demonstrates that the native PCA code exceeds a TF/s for several of the larger datasets. In addition, the performance of the processor (a 12-core 3.3 GHz Intel® Xeon® X5680 processor) quickly plateaus at a significantly lower GF/s rate than the coprocessor. The flat line indicates that the processor is hitting a resource limitation. The asymptotic behavior as the coprocessor approaches a TF/s also indicates a resource limitation. The highest performance on this graph corresponds roughly to 50% of the peak processor single-precision performance. These results indicate that memory bandwidth is the likely culprit that is limiting the performance of both devices (Figure 7.19).

As previously discussed, near-linear scaling and PF/s performance was observed when training a single ANN using MPI and up to 3000 coprocessors on the TACC Stampede supercomputer (see Figure 7.3). It is expected that future systems containing tens of thousands of coprocessors will also exhibit the same near-linear scaling behavior to deliver exascale performance.

SUMMARY

From individual TF/s devices to observed petascale performance and expected exascale capability, the Intel Xeon Phi product family opens broad new vistas for research and commercial applications at a new price/performance and performance-per-watt levels. The key to such high performance on both ×86 processors and Intel Xeon Phi coprocessors is the near-linear scaling across processors and heavy vector-processing load within each device created by the massively parallel mapping. For instance,

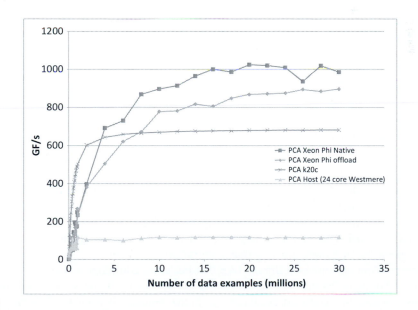

FIGURE 7.19

Scaling by dataset size.

these same examples scaled to 60,000 processing cores—and achieved a true peak four single-precision operations per clock—on the ×86-based TACC Ranger supercomputer.

While the training process is computationally expensive, this chapter demonstrates that the training process maps nicely to massively parallel systems plus the resulting parameterized models can run very quickly on a variety of low power and small memory devices ranging from CPUs to DSPs, FPGAs, and even ASIC hardware. This characteristic, along with their ability to learn to perform complex pattern recognition, signal processing, and classification tasks, explains in part why ANNs are so heavily utilized across a broad range of applications from large-scale Internet search engines to time critical robotics and real-time vision applications.

Through the use of the concepts and example code discussed in this chapter, the reader can begin to explore the capabilities of both the feed forward neural networks as well as *recurrent* neural networks. Recurrent neural networks are ANNs that utilize both forward and reverse connections in the network architecture. The addition of directed cycles in the ANN architecture means that recurrent networks are able to create and use internal memory to solve problems and process arbitrary sequences of inputs. Recursive ANNs provide a remarkably high computation to data ratio (meaning that the coprocessor has to perform a large number of floating-point arithmetic operations per byte of data transferred) because they must be iterated to transport information both forward and backwards in the ANN. Thus, recursive neural networks are ideally suited to coprocessor acceleration.

In addition, researchers can address the computational challenges of optimizing multiterm objective functions. Such objective functions are common in science, engineering, and every-day life but are extremely difficult to solve. For example, most purchase decisions require making a cost versus benefit decision. Similarly, engineers are always confronted with weight versus strength design challenges. Balancing the conflicting objectives of a multi-term objective function means that many possible solutions must be investigated as the weighted importance of each term relative to the others is varied (i.e., to emphasize strength rather than weight or vice versa). Such optimizations are time consuming and subject to local minima. However, the teraflops to exascale computational resources provided by Intel Xeon Phi coprocessors and other massively parallel devices means that researchers now have the computational horsepower required to investigate these valuable and common yet computationally expensive optimization problems.

FOR MORE INFORMATION

- Duda, R., Hart, P. E., Stork, D.G., 2001. Pattern Classification, second ed. Wiley.
- Farber, R., 2011. CUDA Application Design and Development. Morgan Kaufmann.
- Lapedes, A.S., Farber, R., 1987. How neural networks work. Proceeding of IEEE Denver Conference on Neural Netorks. Denver: IEEE.
- NLPCA: www.cs.toronto.edu/~hinton/ and http://nlpca.org.
- Johnson, S.G., 2014. The NLopt nonlinear-optimization package. http://ab-initio.mit.edu/nlopt.
- farbopt repository on github, https://github.com/rmfarber/farbopt.
- Open-source nlopt optimization library, http://ab-initio.mit.edu/nlopt.
- Thearling, Massively Parallel Architectures and Algorithms for Time Series Analysis, available at http://www.thearling.com/text/csss93.htm or in the Addison-Wesley *1993 Lectures in Complex Systems*.

OPTIMIZING GATHER/ SCATTER PATTERNS

8

Simon J. Pennycook*, Christopher J. Hughes†, Mikhail Smelyanskiy†

*Intel Corporation, UK, †Intel Corporation, USA

Many modern microarchitectures rely on single-instruction multiple-data (SIMD) execution to provide high compute capabilities in an energy efficient manner. Such microarchitectures, including those employed by the most recent Intel® Xeon® processors and Intel® Xeon Phi™ coprocessors, are typically optimized for data laid out contiguously in memory. However, they support SIMD execution even when data are non-contiguous in memory, through *gather* and *scatter* operations.

Exactly how these operations are performed is platform-specific, sometimes taking place in software and other times making use of dedicated hardware instructions. However, their function is always the same: a gather operation reads individually addressed elements from memory and packs them into a single SIMD register, and a scatter operation unpacks elements from a SIMD register and writes them to individual memory locations. The memory addresses involved in gather/scatter operations do not need to be known until run-time, and can represent any access pattern (including contiguous access), allowing programmers (and compilers) to vectorize even the most irregular of loops.

Figure 8.1 shows an example loop that contains both an indirect read and an indirect write which require gather/scatter operations to vectorize. When we vectorize the loop, a single SIMD iteration will read a group of `A[B[i]]` and write a group of `D[E[i]]`. In general, the `A[B[i]]` (and the `D[E[i]]`) are in memory locations unknown until run-time, and may be stored at non-contiguous addresses. Thus, normal SIMD load and store instructions, which grab a set of contiguous elements, will not suffice. Instead, we need a gather operation to read the individually addressed `A[B[i]]` elements, and a scatter operation for the writes to `D[E[i]]`.

Gathers and scatters require the hardware to do more work than contiguous SIMD loads and stores—they typically have higher instruction overheads, are less predictable, and are likely to access more cache lines/pages (depending on the specific access pattern). Programmers should therefore aim to minimize their use, by avoiding indirection and non-contiguous accesses whenever possible.

However, indirection may be an inherent part of an algorithm. For instance, data elements may be accessed in an input-dependent order, or computation may be performed on a subset of data elements to reduce computational complexity. Such algorithms are common, particularly in domains where relationships between data elements are not known *a priori* (e.g., graph problems, unstructured mesh), and alternative algorithms may not necessarily perform as well—even if their SIMD efficiency is higher.

```
for (i = 0; i < N; i++) {
  C[i] = A[B[i]];                  // indirect read
  D[E[i]] = C[i] + some_constant;  // indirect write
}
```

FIGURE 8.1

Example of a loop that leads to gathers and scatters.

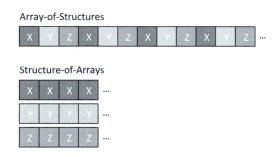

FIGURE 8.2

Two of the most common data layouts in high-performance computing applications.

Non-contiguous accesses are also commonly introduced by a programmer's choice of data layout, a good example being storing data as an Array-of-Structures (AoS) rather than a Structure-of-Arrays (SoA). Figure 8.2 shows how an array of four elements, each consisting of three struct members {x, y, z}, would be arranged in the two layouts.

AoS enables programmers to write applications in terms of data types that are meaningful to their domain (e.g., particles), but often does not lend itself well to SIMD execution—any access to a single struct member for multiple array elements will not be contiguous. SoA can lead to contiguous accesses in some, but not all situations—it only guarantees contiguous loads/stores if the array itself is not accessed via indirection. Further, with SoA, the distance between struct members for a single element can lead to poor cache behavior. Even hybrid approaches (e.g., Array-of-Structure-of-Arrays) cannot hope to be the best layout for all situations. To complicate matters further still, different layouts may be optimal for different areas of the same code, and external libraries often require data to be supplied in a particular form (outside of an application developer's control). In short, choosing the best data layout for an application depends on several factors, among which SIMD usage is just one.

When gathers and scatters must be used, or when they are too convenient to avoid, it is important to help the hardware make them as fast as possible—their performance depends in part on several things under the programmer's control. The remainder of this chapter details a number of methods for optimizing gather/scatter patterns on both processors and coprocessors: specifically, using domain knowledge to improve temporal and spatial locality; choosing an appropriate data layout; performing on-the-fly transposition between AoS and SoA layouts; and amortizing gather/scatter costs over multiple loop iterations.

We focus on the application of these methods to the gather/scatter patterns present in the miniMD benchmark from Sandia National Laboratories' Mantevo Suite, using the Lennard-Jones inter-atomic potential. However, the optimizations that we discuss apply to a wide set of applications.

GATHER/SCATTER INSTRUCTIONS IN INTEL® ARCHITECTURE

Complete understanding of our optimizations requires some knowledge of Intel's instruction sets. Of particular importance is the support for gather and scatter operations. See Section "For more information" for links to the instruction set documentation.

For programs using Intel® Streaming SIMD Extensions (SSE) and Intel® Advanced Vector Extensions (AVX), gather and scatter operations both need to be performed with scalar loads/stores and shuffle instructions. The scalar loads/stores read or write the individual data elements, and the shuffles (e.g., `pinsrd`, `extractps`, `vinsertf128`) insert or extract individual elements/groups of elements into or out of vector registers.

AVX2 includes several flavors of gather instructions. These take the base address, a set of 32-bit or 64-bit signed integer indices packed into a SIMD register, and a completion mask stored in the sign bits of a SIMD register—elements whose mask bits are set are gathered; other elements are not gathered, and the corresponding destination element is unmodified. The instructions clear the mask on completion.

The Intel® Initial Many-Core Instructions (IMCI) used on the current generation of Intel Xeon Phi coprocessors include both a gather instruction and a scatter instruction. The gather instruction is similar to the AVX2 gather, but uses a mask register to hold the completion mask. Further, the gather instruction only reads the elements on a single (typically, 64 bytes wide) cache line. Since data being gathered may be spread across multiple cache lines, software typically tests the completion mask to see if all elements have been read, and if not, loops back and re-executes the instruction. Thus, performance of a gather operation decreases as the distance (in memory) between data being gathered increases. The scatter instruction is analogous; however, instead of reading elements from memory, it writes values contained in a source SIMD register to elements in memory.

Finally, AVX-512 contains gather and scatter instructions very similar to the IMCI instructions but, like the AVX2 gather instruction, they read or write all elements in one instruction execution, regardless of how many cache lines they need to touch. AVX-512 instructions will be supported by the next generation of Intel Xeon Phi coprocessors, and processors, codenamed by Intel as "Knights Landing."

NOTE

SSE introduced floating-point SIMD capabilities to Intel architectures, with instructions operating on 128-bit vector registers. New instructions were introduced in SSE2, SSE3, and SSE4, but SIMD width remained fixed until the introduction of 256-bit instructions in AVX. Similarly, AVX2 introduced new instructions without altering SIMD width. IMCI increased SIMD width to 512-bit, but has instructions unique to the current generation of coprocessors; AVX-512 also increases SIMD width to 512-bit, but will additionally support SSE and AVX instructions.

GATHER/SCATTER PATTERNS IN MOLECULAR DYNAMICS

Molecular dynamics is an example of an *N*-body simulation, with applications simulating the movement of a potentially very large number of atoms and/or molecules (i.e., bodies) through space in a relatively simple manner—each atom has a total force exerted on it by other atoms, which in turn affects its velocity and position.

Profiling miniMD, our chosen molecular dynamics code, (e.g., with Intel® VTune™ Amplifier) highlights two key hotspots. The first of these, accounting for almost 80% of runtime, is the force calculation kernel, which computes the force acting upon each atom. Naively computing this force scales as $O(N^2)$, since every atom exerts some force on every other atom. This is prohibitively expensive for a large number of atoms. Therefore, molecular dynamics packages typically separate the force on each atom into two components: a short-range force, computed for all pairs of atoms separated by some "cut-off" distance R_c; and a long-range force, approximated for all pairs of atoms without the need for direct computation (e.g., through a fast Fourier transform). This separation allows the force computation to scale as $O(Nk)$, where k is the expected number of "neighbors" for each atom (itself a function of simulation parameters like density and R_c). As a benchmark code, miniMD does not include a long-range force estimation kernel—we focus on short-range forces henceforth. The second hotspot, accounting for 10% of runtime, is the neighbor list build kernel, which constructs a list of all atom pairs that are separated by less than the cut-off plus some "skin" distance R_s. This skin distance allows the list to be reused for a number of time-steps, at the expense of considering more atom pairs than are strictly necessary.

Figure 8.3 shows the neighborhood of a single atom in two dimensions—in three dimensions, the neighborhood is a sphere, and the simulation volume is a cube. The simulation space is also divided into "cells" or "bins," which are used to accelerate the neighbor list build. By carefully discretizing

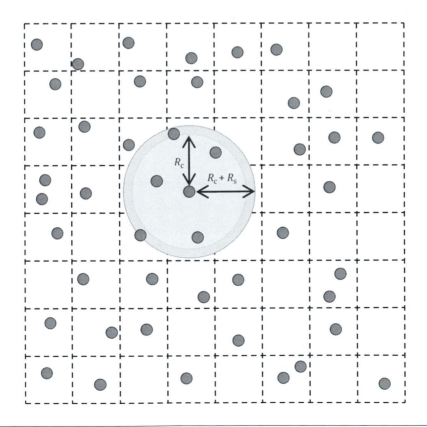

FIGURE 8.3

The neighborhood of a particle in 2D, as defined by some cut-off distance (R_c), and skin distance (R_s).

space in this way, and by precomputing a list of the atoms in each bin, the neighbor list build can also avoid $O(N^2)$ complexity—for each atom, it is only necessary to check a predetermined set of nearby bins for neighbors, rather than the entire simulation volume.

The original miniMD source code for these two hotspots is given in Figures 8.4 and 8.5 for the short-range force computation and neighbor list build kernels, respectively. As shown in these figures, for each kernel there are two reasons that gather/scatter operations are necessary; the relevant lines are emphasized in bold. First, for each atom index (i), the indices of the neighboring atoms (j) are stored in look-up arrays (neighs and loc_bin). The result is that neighbor positions must be gathered (from x) and that the computed contribution to neighbor forces must be accumulated into the force array (f) by performing a gather, a subtraction, and finally, a scatter. Removing this indirection from the code is only possible by introducing redundant computation and/or storage—since the neighbor-hoods of different atoms will partially and unpredictably overlap, it is impossible to order atoms such that all (minimal) neighborhoods are runs of contiguous indices. Second, the position and force arrays are stored in AoS, with the size of the struct controlled by a variable (PAD) defined at compile time. However, converting these arrays to SoA would not affect the number of gather/scatter operations in the code, since the atom indices themselves are not contiguous.

```
for (int i = 0; i < nlocal; i++) {
    neighs = &neighbor.neighbors[i*neighbor.maxneighs];
    const int numneighs = neighbor.numneigh[i];
    const float xtmp = x[i*PAD+0];
    const float ytmp = x[i*PAD+1];
    const float ztmp = x[i*PAD+2];
    float fix = 0.0; float fiy = 0.0; float fiz = 0.0;
    #pragma simd reduction(+:fix, fiy, fiz)
    for (int k = 0; k < numneighs; k++) {
        const int j = neighs[k];
        const float delx = xtmp - x[j*PAD+0];
        const float dely = ytmp - x[j*PAD+1];
        const float delz = ztmp - x[j*PAD+2];
        const float rsq = delx*delx + dely*dely + delz*delz;
        if (rsq < cutforcesq) {
            const float sr2 = 1.0 / rsq;
            const float sr6 = sr2 * sr2 * sr2 * sigma6;
            const float force = 48.0*sr6*(sr6-0.5)*sr2*epsilon;
            fix += delx * force;
            fiy += dely * force;
            fiz += delz * force;
            if (GHOST_NEWTON || j < nlocal) {
                f[j*PAD+0] -= delx * force;
                f[j*PAD+1] -= dely * force;
                f[j*PAD+2] -= delz * force;
            }
            if (EVFLAG) {
                // compute contribution to energy/virial
            }
        }
    }
    f[i*PAD+0] += fix;
    f[i*PAD+1] += fiy;
    f[i*PAD+2] += fiz;
}
```

FIGURE 8.4

The original short-range force compute loop in miniMD (energy/virial computation omitted to save space).

```
for (int i = 0; i < nlocal; i++) {
  int* neighptr = &neighbors[i * maxneighs];
  int n = 0;
  const float xtmp = x[i*PAD+0];
  const float ytmp = x[i*PAD+1];
  const float ztmp = x[i*PAD+2];
  const int ibin = coord2bin(xtmp, ytmp, ztmp);
  for (int k = 0; k < nstencil; k++) {
    const int jbin = ibin + stencil[k];
    int* loc_bin = &bins[jbin * atoms_per_bin];
    if (ibin == jbin)
      // check for neighbors in own bin
    else {
      for (int m = 0; m < bincount[jbin]; m++) {
        const int j = loc_bin[m];
        if (halfneigh && !ghost_newton && (j < i))
          continue;
        const float delx = xtmp - x[j*PAD+0];
        const float dely = ytmp - x[j*PAD+1];
        const float delz = ztmp - x[j*PAD+2];
        const float rsq =
          delx*delx + dely*dely + delz*delz;
        if((rsq <= cutneighsq)) neighptr[n++] = j;
      }
    }
  }
  numneigh[i] = n;
}
```

FIGURE 8.5

The original neighbor list build loop in miniMD (check for neighbors in own bin omitted to save space).

Other molecular dynamics codes (such as LAMMPS, also developed at Sandia National Laboratories) may have additional gather/scatter operations present inside both of these loops. In simulations featuring different atom types (e.g., hydrogen and oxygen), some of the constants (e.g., the cut-off distance) in the code-snippets shown would in fact differ based on the combination of atom types being considered. Other, more complex, inter-atomic potentials (e.g., the embedded atom method) may introduce additional table look-ups based on the calculated distance between the two atoms (because the cost of computing the force values directly would be too expensive).

Given that such a high percentage of time in molecular dynamics simulations is spent computing forces, and that computing forces requires many gather/scatter operations, reducing the overheads of gather/scatter operations can significantly improve the performance of the application as a whole.

OPTIMIZING GATHER/SCATTER PATTERNS
IMPROVING TEMPORAL AND SPATIAL LOCALITY

The memory system's response to the individual reads and writes that make up a gather or scatter operation can have a large effect on the operation's performance. Write latency can be hidden by useful work, whereas instructions that use the result of a read cannot execute until the read completes—consequently, gathers are more sensitive to latency than scatters. Gathers and scatters will additionally be slower to complete if any of the elements are not in cache (i.e., there is little reuse/temporal locality) and/or if the elements are spread across many cache lines (i.e., there is little spatial locality). For our molecular dynamics example, one way to increase both temporal and spatial locality for the gathers and scatters is sorting. The sorts, as we will describe below, do not need to be exact; even a partial sort will increase temporal or spatial locality, and therefore have a good chance of improving performance.

To increase temporal locality, we can sort the atoms by their spatial position. Atoms close together in space are likely to have common neighbors. Thus, the effect of this sort is that adjacent iterations of the outermost loop (over the atoms) will use gathers and scatters that touch many of the same neighbors. For a given neighbor that we access via a gather or scatter, there is a high probability of a cache hit, since it was probably accessed recently as a neighbor of a different atom.

To increase the spatial locality of each individual gather/scatter operation, we can sort the indices in each atom's neighbor list. This will minimize the number of cache lines that a given gather/scatter operation touches.

Sorting may not be the best approach for all applications to improve spatial or temporal locality, but the principles of maximizing the amount of reuse for each piece of data and minimizing the number of cache lines touched by each gather/scatter operation are generally applicable.

The graph in Figure 8.6 compares the execution times when atoms are: (1) ordered randomly and (2) sorted by spatial position. The sort uses a simple scan-line ordering, based on the atom's bin index—this is the default sort in the most recent version of miniMD, and mimics the sort available in LAMMPS. Both platforms are significantly impacted by the random ordering: on the processor, sorting improves performance by 1.48×; on the coprocessor, sorting improves performance by 1.36×.

In previous work, we have demonstrated that a spatial decomposition across threads (followed by spatial sorting within each thread's local domain) can provide even higher levels of temporal and spatial locality, and hence greater performance improvements. We are still discussing with the original developers of miniMD the best way to integrate such a decomposition within the original benchmark—all results in this chapter use a so-called "atom decomposition," where each thread is simply assigned an

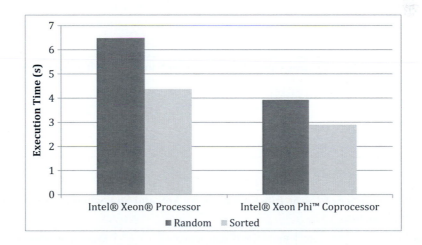

FIGURE 8.6

Comparison of execution times when atoms are ordered randomly and when atoms are sorted by spatial position (scan-line ordering).

equal number of atoms. Using the atom decomposition provides better load balancing, but the probability that a thread will have to access an atom belonging to another thread increases with the number of threads.

CHOOSING AN APPROPRIATE DATA LAYOUT: AOS VERSUS SOA

As discussed previously, the choice of whether to lay out data in AoS or SoA should be made based on access pattern—as a rule of thumb: if the data is accessed via indirection and multiple elements are accessed from each struct, use AoS; otherwise, use SoA.

To understand this rule of thumb better, consider the memory access patterns of the best- and worst-case gather/scatter operations for both data structures, assuming a SIMD width of N, a struct of M elements, and a cache line size (in elements) of C, as shown in Tables 8.1 and 8.2. The best case for both layouts is when the indices of the elements being gathered/scattered are contiguous; the worst case for both layouts is when the indices of the elements being gathered/scattered are non-contiguous. Note that the factor of two in the worst case accounts for the fact that, without proper attention to alignment, the data being accessed may be spread across two cache lines.

To apply these equations to miniMD, running in single precision on the coprocessor, we have $N=16$, $M=3$, and $C=16$ (since a 64-byte cache line can hold 16 4-byte floating-point numbers). Since we access all three components of an atom's position and force, we are concerned with the second set of equations. Since the neighbors of each atom are non-contiguous, we expect to touch three times more cache lines per gather/scatter if we use SoA instead of AoS. By setting $M=4$ (i.e., padding the struct with one extra element), we can guarantee alignment and reduce the worst-case number of cache lines by a factor of two.

miniMD already uses AoS, and so converting to SoA should not be expected to improve performance. Indeed, in our experiments we observed a slight (<5%) slowdown on both platforms. That the performance difference is so low reflects that miniMD (with sorting) is not memory bound—rather, the instruction overhead of the gather/scatter operations is the performance bottleneck. As explained previously, loading {x, y, z} data from AoS or SoA are both gather operations, and therefore the instruction

Table 8.1   The Number of Cache Lines Accessed by AoS and SoA when Loading 1 Element from an M-Wide struct

Data Layout	Best Case (Contiguous)	Worst Case (Non-contiguous)
AoS	$\text{ceil}(N \times M/C)$	N
SoA	1	N

Table 8.2   The Number of Cache Lines Accessed by AoS and SoA when Loading M Elements from an M-Wide struct

Data Layout	Best Case (Contiguous)	Worst Case (Non-contiguous)
AoS	$\text{ceil}(N \times M/C)$	$2 \times N \times \text{ceil}(M/C)$
SoA	M	$2 \times N \times M$

sequence generated by the compiler is the same in both cases (the most significant difference being the effect that layout has on address calculations).

ON-THE-FLY TRANSPOSITION BETWEEN AOS AND SOA

The results in the previous section should not be taken to mean that AoS and SoA are generally interchangeable without any performance impact. In fact, as a result of the differences in memory access pattern, different optimization techniques are applicable to the two layouts. Gathering the $\{x, y, z\}$ data for positions and forces in miniMD from SoA will always require three gather operations: one for the x values, one for the y values and one for the z values. Gathering from AoS, on the other hand, can be thought of as a single gather of structs, followed by transposition between the two layouts.

When viewed as a transpose operation, it is clear that some implementations may introduce redundancy. For instance, the hardware may load one element of the struct from the cache at a time, and thus need three accesses to read out each struct. If we instead read an entire struct with one memory access, we may reduce the number of memory accesses and the number of instructions required. The trade-off is that we must use a sequence of additional "shuffle" instructions to reorder the x, y, and z values.

Figure 8.7 illustrates part of the AoS-to-SoA transpose process for the miniMD position array using SSE. We first load one entire neighbor at a time (i.e., four consecutive 32-bit values, including padding) into SIMD registers. In our example, we load neighbors with indices i, j, k, and l. We can then use a series of seven shuffle and/or permute instructions (one to construct each of the four intermediate registers shown, and one to construct each of the final x/y/z registers) to perform the transpose. To extend this sequence to instruction sets with wider SIMD, more than one atom must be loaded into each of the vector registers. Effectively, we must treat a 256-bit AVX register as two 128-bit lanes, and a 512-bit IMCI register as four 128-bit lanes.

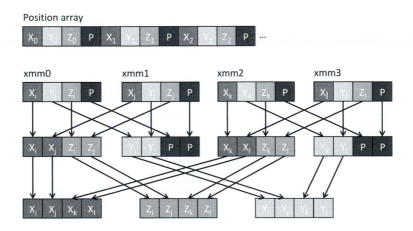

FIGURE 8.7

Register and memory contents during an AoS-to-SoA transpose. The red elements are padding, to guarantee data alignment.

The SoA-to-AoS transpose process is simply the reverse of the AoS-to-SoA process, using the same sequence of shuffles. In addition to the vector registers containing the x, y, and z values in SoA format, we must also fill a register with our padding value (typically 0).

Figures 8.8 and 8.9 give excerpts from the intrinsics code used for these transposes in AVX-512. The full transpose intrinsics for the single precision case, along with intrinsics for other instruction sets, are provided as part of the source code made available for download from the book's website (lotsofcores.com).

NOTE

Readers unfamiliar with compiler intrinsics and the Intel® instruction sets may find the Intel® Intrinsics Guide and Instruction Set Reference manuals helpful in understanding the code excerpts shown here. Links to these resources can be found at the end of the chapter.

```
#define _MM_BCAST4_PS(a) _mm512_extload_ps(a,
_MM_UPCONV_PS_NONE, _MM_BROADCAST_4X16, _MM_HINT_NONE)
#define _MM_MASK_BCAST4_PS(v, m, a)
_mm512_mask_extload_ps(v, m, a, _MM_UPCONV_PS_NONE,
_MM_BROADCAST_4X16, _MM_HINT_NONE)

__m512 tmp0 = _MM_BCAST4_PS(&data[indices[0]]);
tmp0 = _MM_MASK_BCAST4_PS(tmp0, mask_00F0,
&data[indices[4]]);
tmp0 = _MM_MASK_BCAST4_PS(tmp0, mask_0F00,
&data[indices[8]]);
tmp0 = _MM_MASK_BCAST4_PS(tmp0, mask_F000,
&data[indices[12]]);

// repeat loads for tmp1 with indices[1,5,9,13]
// repeat loads for tmp2 with indices[2,6,10,14]
// repeat loads for tmp3 with indices[3,7,11,15]

__m512 xz01 = _mm512_mask_swizzle_ps(tmp0, mask_0xAAAA,
tmp1, _MM_SWIZ_REG_CDAB);
__m512 yw01 = _mm512_mask_swizzle_ps(tmp1, mask_0x5555,
tmp0, _MM_SWIZ_REG_CDAB);
__m512 xz23 = _mm512_mask_swizzle_ps(tmp2, mask_0xAAAA,
tmp3, _MM_SWIZ_REG_CDAB);
__m512 yw23 = _mm512_mask_swizzle_ps(tmp3, mask_0x5555,
tmp2, _MM_SWIZ_REG_CDAB);

x = _mm512_mask_swizzle_ps(xz01, mask_0xCCCC), xz23,
_MM_SWIZ_REG_BADC);
y = _mm512_mask_swizzle_ps(yw01, mask_0xCCCC), yw23,
_MM_SWIZ_REG_BADC);
z = _mm512_mask_swizzle_ps(xz23, mask_0x3333), xz01,
_MM_SWIZ_REG_BADC);
```

FIGURE 8.8

An excerpt from an AoS-to-SoA transpose for single precision data, expressed using IMCI intrinsics.

```
#define _MM_PACKSTORE4_PS(a, m, v)
_mm512_mask_extpackstorelo_ps(a, m, v,
_MM_DOWNCONV_PS_NONE, _MM_HINT_NONE)

__m512 p = zeroes;

__m512 xz01 = _mm512_mask_swizzle_ps(x, mask_0xCCCC, z,
_MM_SWIZ_REG_BADC);
__m512 yw01 = _mm512_mask_swizzle_ps(y, mask_0xCCCC, p,
_MM_SWIZ_REG_BADC);
__m512 xz23 = _mm512_mask_swizzle_ps(z, mask_0x3333, x,
_MM_SWIZ_REG_BADC);
__m512 yw23 = _mm512_mask_swizzle_ps(p, mask_0x3333, y,
_MM_SWIZ_REG_BADC);

__m512 tmp0 = _mm512_mask_swizzle_ps(xz01, mask_0xAAAA,
yw01, _MM_SWIZ_REG_CDAB);
__m512 tmp1 = _mm512_mask_swizzle_ps(yw01, mask_0x5555,
xz01, _MM_SWIZ_REG_CDAB);
__m512 tmp2 = _mm512_mask_swizzle_ps(xz23, mask_0xAAAA,
yw23, _MM_SWIZ_REG_CDAB);
__m512 tmp3 = _mm512_mask_swizzle_ps(yw23, mask_0x5555,
xz23, _MM_SWIZ_REG_CDAB);

_MM_PACKSTORE4_PS(&data[indices[0]], mask_000F, tmp0);
_MM_PACKSTORE4_PS(&data[indices[4]], mask_00F0, tmp0);
_MM_PACKSTORE4_PS(&data[indices[8]], mask_0F00, tmp0);
_MM_PACKSTORE4_PS(&data[indices[12]], mask_F000, tmp0);

// repeat stores for tmp1 with indices[1,5,9,13]
// repeat stores for tmp2 with indices[2,6,10,14]
// repeat stores for tmp3 with indices[3,7,11,15]
```

FIGURE 8.9

An excerpt from an SoA-to-AoS transpose for single precision data, expressed using IMCI intrinsics.

Table 8.3   Instruction Counts for the Default Gather/Scatter Sequence

	Scalar	**128-Bit**	**256-Bit**	**512-Bit**
# Elements	1	4	8	16
Load Indices	1	4	8	16
Gather	1	12	27	144

Tables 8.3 and 8.4 compare the instruction counts for a default compiler-generated gather/scatter operation, and the optimized approach we have described. Note that the 512-bit number of instructions is for the worst case, assuming that the 3 gathers each touch 16 cache lines and require 3 instructions (vgatherps, cmp, jmp) per cache line. On upcoming generations of processors and coprocessors, which will have support for AVX-512 instructions, this number is expected to fall to three instructions. Only a single call to vgatherps will be required for each gather operation using AVX-512, regardless of how many cache lines it accesses.

The number of instructions required for our optimized gather/scatter routines scales with the number of elements gathered. This is not unexpected. What is important is the relative difference in cost

Table 8.4   Instruction Counts for the Optimized Gather/Scatter Sequence

	Scalar	128-Bit	256-Bit	512-Bit
# Elements	1	4	8	16
Load Indices	1	4	8	16
Load Data	1	4	8	16
Shuffle	0	7	7	7

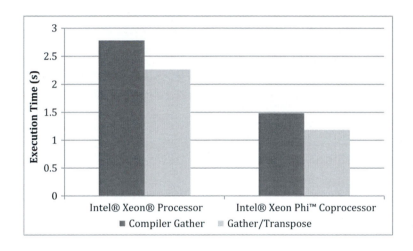

FIGURE 8.10

Comparison of short-range force compute execution times when using the default compiler gather and our gather/transpose intrinsics routines.

between the original and optimized sequences, and the impact that this can have upon performance, as shown in Figure 8.10.

The speed-up we see from this optimization is 1.23× on the processor and 1.25× on the coprocessor. Both of these speed-ups are less than the reduction in the number of instructions shown in Tables 8.3 and 8.4, but we should not expect the numbers to match up exactly due to the superscalar and pipelined nature of modern architectures. Additionally, with regards to the coprocessor specifically, the number of instructions required for a compiler-generated gather are not likely to be as high as the worst-case number (due to our previous sorting optimizations), and a large number of additional mov instructions that we do not account for may be introduced due to the finite number of general-purpose and mask registers.

AMORTIZING GATHER/SCATTER AND TRANSPOSITION COSTS

Performing a transpose between AoS and SoA layouts on the fly can reduce the instruction overhead of gather/scatter operations significantly, but the process of transposition quickly becomes a bottleneck for kernels that perform very little compute upon the gathered data. The neighbor build kernel in miniMD is a good example of such a function: for each potential neighboring atom, only a few arithmetic operations and a compare are required to determine whether the atom should be added to the neighbor list.

However, unlike the force compute kernel (where the probability of two atoms having identical neighbor lists is very small), the neighbor list build compares several atoms (those in the same bin) to a fixed set of potential neighbors. It is therefore possible to perform the gather and transpose this fixed set of potential neighbors only once, before reusing the SoA data multiple times. This is demonstrated in Figure 8.11.

We use a pre-allocated array (scache) of a fixed size to cache the transposed stencil for a given bin. In order to keep the loop over atoms intact, as required by the use of atom decomposition, we detect whether to perform the gather and transpose step (emphasized in bold) based upon a change in

```
int cached_bin = -1;
int ncache = 0;
for (int i = 0; i < nlocal; i++) {
  int* neighptr = &neighbors[i * maxneighs];
  int n = 0;
  const float xtmp = x[i*PAD+0];
  const float ytmp = x[i*PAD+1];
  const float ztmp = x[i*PAD+2];
  const int ibin = coord2bin(xtmp, ytmp, ztmp);

  if (ibin != cached_bin) {
    ncache = 0;
    for (int k = 0; k < nstencil; k++) {
      int jbin = ibin + stencil[k];
      int* loc_bin = &bins[jbin * atoms_per_bin];
      for (int m = 0; m < bincount[jbin]; m++) {
        const int j = loc_bin[m];
        scache[0*CACHE_SIZE+ncache] = j;
        scache[1*CACHE_SIZE+ncache] = x[j*PAD+0];
        scache[2*CACHE_SIZE+ncache] = x[j*PAD+1];
        scache[3*CACHE_SIZE+ncache] = x[j*PAD+2];
        ncache++;
      }
    }
    cached_bin = ibin;
  }

  for (int c = 0; c < ncache; c++) {
    const int j = scache[0*CACHE_SIZE+c];
    if (halfneigh && !ghost_newton && (j < i))
      continue;
    const float delx = xtmp - scache[1*CACHE_SIZE+c];
    const float dely = ytmp - scache[2*CACHE_SIZE+c];
    const float delz = ztmp - scache[3*CACHE_SIZE+c];
    const float rsq = delx*delx + dely*dely + delz*delz;
    if((rsq <= cutneighsq)) neighptr[n++] = j;
  }

  numneigh[i] = n;

}
```

FIGURE 8.11

The optimized neighbor list build loop in miniMD. We show the scalar code (without intrinsics) to improve readability.

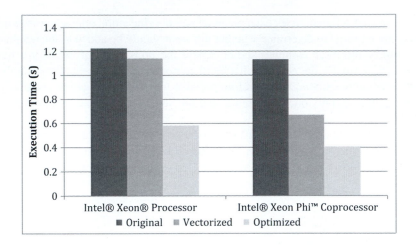

FIGURE 8.12

Comparison of neighbor list build execution times for the original scalar code, a vectorized implementation performing an on-the-fly transpose, and the optimized implementation that caches the result of the transpose.

bin index—re-use of the stencil is ensured by the fact that particles are sorted by bin index. The second loop appends atoms to the neighbor list in exactly the same way as done previously, but loads SoA data directly from `scache` instead of AoS data from the position array (`x`).

In addition to the ability to reuse the transposed neighbor data, this approach to building the neighbor list has a number of other benefits. First, it improves cache behavior—rather than being spread out in memory, the potential set of neighbors is stored contiguously in one location, and may be small enough to remain in a level of cache close to the compute units (i.e., L1 or L2). Second, it makes the code easier to vectorize—the nested loop over stencil index and bin contents in the original code is collapsed into a single loop over the contents of `scache` in the optimized code, simplifying the process of completely filling a vector register. The performance impact of this optimization is shown in Figure 8.12.

SUMMARY

In this chapter, we have described gather and scatter operations and explained why they are needed to vectorize certain loops. Due to their high cost relative to contiguous SIMD loads and stores, and since they cannot always be avoided, we demonstrated four optimization techniques for improving the performance of gather and scatter operations: using domain knowledge and sorting to improve temporal and spatial locality; choosing an appropriate data layout for hot compute loops, based on their access patterns; minimizing the number of instructions for each individual gather/scatter operation, through on-the-fly transposition between AoS and SoA layouts; and amortizing gather/scatter and transposition costs over multiple loop iterations (where possible).

For a representative molecular dynamics application, we see a performance gap of approximately 2× between the un-optimized and optimized versions of the code on both current-generation processors and coprocessors. The optimizations employed are not only the same for both processing platforms, but are also generally applicable and not specific to current-generation Intel® microarchitectures. We expect them to apply to future products and to other processor designs, and therefore optimizing gather/scatter patterns in applications today will ensure that they continue to exhibit good levels of performance in the future.

FOR MORE INFORMATION

Here are some additional reading materials we recommend related to this chapter:
- Exploring SIMD for Molecular Dynamics, Using Intel® Xeon® Processors and Intel® Xeon Phi™ Coprocessors, http://dl.acm.org/citation.cfm?id=2511458.
- Fast Parallel Algorithms for Short-Range Molecular Dynamics, http://dl.acm.org/citation.cfm?id=201628.
- Intel Intrinsics Guide, http://software.intel.com/sites/landingpage/IntrinsicsGuide/.
- Intel® 64 and IA-32 architectures Software Developer's Manual, Volume 2: Instruction Set Reference, A-Z, http://www.intel.com/content/dam/www/public/us/en/documents/manuals/64-ia-32-architectures-software-developer-instruction-set-reference-manual-325383.pdf.
- Intel® Xeon Phi™ Coprocessor Instruction Set Architecture Reference Manual, https://software.intel.com/sites/default/files/forum/278102/327364001en.pdf.
- Intel® Architecture Instruction Set Extensions Programming Reference, https://software.intel.com/sites/default/files/managed/68/8b/319433-019.pdf.
- Download the code from this and other chapters, http://lotsofcores.com.
- Download the newest version of miniMD, http://mantevo.org.

A MANY-CORE IMPLEMENTATION OF THE DIRECT N-BODY PROBLEM

9

Alejandro Duran[*], Larry Meadows[†]
Intel Corporation, Spain, †Intel Corporation, USA

N-BODY SIMULATIONS

N-Body simulations are a common astrophysics problem that computes the movement of gravitationally interacting particles through space. At each time step of the simulation, the force that each particle exacts upon each other is computed using the following equation:

$$F_{ij} = K \frac{m_1 m_2 (\vec{r_i} - \vec{r_j})}{|\vec{r_i} - \vec{r_j}|^3}$$

Based on this, the velocity and position of each particle are updated. The process is iterative and finishes after simulation of the desired number of time steps.

While the direct N-body kernel is generally not practical by itself because of its $O(n^2)$ complexity, it is still used to compute the interaction of particles of the same domain in more complex N-body algorithms which have smaller computational complexity, like Barnes-Hut that has an $O(n \log n)$ complexity, and in some scenarios where the numerical approximations of other methods are not desirable such as the study of the evolution of star clusters.

In this chapter, we explain the optimization process we followed to get such a kernel optimized for a many-core architecture such as the Intel® Xeon Phi™ coprocessor which features up to 61 cores with 4 hardware threads per core. The optimization work, to get high scaling for many-core architecture, also yields performance improvements for multicore processors in general.

INITIAL SOLUTION

Vladimirov and Karpusenko developed an initial study of the Intel Xeon Phi coprocessor using a simplified direct N-body kernel and applying some optimizations. We expand their work by introducing in the kernel the softening factor, typically a constant commonly used to correct the interaction of close range particles, and also considering particles to have different masses.

We also explore the performance difference between doing the computation in single precision (SP) and double precision (DP) across a wide range of number of elements configurations.

Our initial solution to the kernel is shown in Figure 9.1. It applies the two optimizations described by Vladimirov and Karpusenko:

- Convert the code from array of structures to structure of arrays. This change allows the vectorization to be effective as the elements of the same field will now be consecutive in memory.
- Instruct the compiler to generate code without maintaining IEEE precision by using the `-fp-model fast=2` compiler flag. This flag allows the compiler to generate shorter code sequences, but they come at the expense of having lower precision. To improve the performance in DP, we explicitly requested to use the SP `sqrt` version. For the DP version, the compiler generates a longer code sequence even with the `-fp-model fast=2` compiler flag.

The OpenMP loop schedule type is dynamic. Empirically, we found that this was the best choice. This is probably because of load imbalance introduced by memory accesses that miss in the L2 cache. Also note that for the expression `1.0f/sqrtf`, the compiler automatically will use the inverse square root primitive available in the Intel Xeon Phi coprocessor.

Figure 9.2 shows the time step of the N-body simulation where on each time step the above kernel is called and then the positions of the different particles are updated.

The hardware used for the evaluation described in this chapter was an Intel Xeon Phi coprocessor 7120P (with turbo disabled unless otherwise noted). It features 61 cores at 1.23 GHz for a total of 244

```
template <class T>
void computeForces(ParticleSystem<T> p, const T dt)
{
  int n = p.nParticles;
  #pragma omp parallel for schedule(dynamic)
  for (int i = 0; i < n; i++) {
    T Fx = static_cast<T>(0.0);
    T Fy = static_cast<T>(0.0);
    T Fz = static_cast<T>(0.0);

    for (int j = 0; j < n; j++) {
        const T dx = p.x[j] - p.x[i];
        const T dy = p.y[j] - p.y[i];
        const T dz = p.z[j] - p.z[i];

        const T drSquared = dx*dx + dy*dy + dz*dz
                            + p.softening;
        const T drPowerN12 = 1.0f / sqrtf(drSquared);
        const T drPowerN32 = drPowerN12 * drPowerN12 *
                             drPowerN12;
        const T s = p.m[j] * drPowerN32;

        Fx += dx * s; Fy += dy * s; Fz += dz * s;
    }
    p.vx[i] += dt*Fx; p.vy[i] += dt*Fy; p.vz[i] += dt*Fz;
  }
}
```

FIGURE 9.1

Initial N-body kernel.

```
for (int iter = 0; iter < nIters; iter++)    {
    computeForces(p,dt);
    for (int i = 0; i < p.nParticles; i++) {
        p.x[i] += p.vx[i] * dt;
        p.y[i] += p.vy[i] * dt;
        p.z[i] += p.vz[i] * dt;
    }
}
```

FIGURE 9.2

Time step loop.

threads for a peak performance of 2.4 TFLOPS in SP and 1.2 TFLOPS in DP. The coprocessor has 16 GB of GDDR5 memory. Each core features a 32 kB L1 and 512 kB L2 caches.

The compiler was the Intel C/C++ compiler version 14.0.2. The compiler flags that were used are `-openmp -mmic -fp-model fast=2 -O3`. When measuring the performance, we performed a single untimed iteration before the real computation for warm-up. All performance numbers are reported in Giga Interactions per second (i.e., how many billions of pairs of elements are processed each second). In order to compute the number of GFLOPS, this number can be multiplied by 20 since each interaction consists of 20 floating point operations.

Figure 9.3 shows the performance obtained for our initial solution for SP and DP. In SP, while the performance is reasonable for numbers of particles between 10k and 60k, the performance degrades beyond that. For DP, we also observe that the performance degrades after 40k particles but the degradation is smoother.

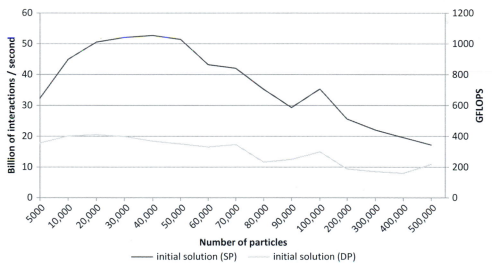

FIGURE 9.3

Performance of our kernel for single and double precision.

THEORETICAL LIMIT

A common problem when optimizing applications lies in understanding the goal (i.e., how do we know when should we stop?). We can construct a theoretical model of the application to determine how many operations are required, and use that to determine the maximum possible performance (often called the "speed of light" for a given application).

Let us apply this idea to our problem. The N-body kernel is dominated by the computation of the force interaction of the particles which has an $O(n^2)$ complexity. The update of the positions has only $O(n)$ complexity. The force interaction computation is dominated by the computations in the inner *j*-loop (the updates at the end of the *i*-loop are again of $O(n)$). If we consider the code from Figure 9.1 and we map it to the Knights Corner Instruction Set (KNCi) that uses our Intel Xeon Phi coprocessor, there are:

- three substractions (vsub),
- three multiplications and additions (vfmadd),
- one reverse square root (vrsqrt),
- three multiplications (vmul), and
- three multiplications and additions (vfmadd).

This could result in the code from Figure 9.4 for SP which is a direct translation of the above sequence with the addition of a broadcast for the softening value. Due to the destructive nature of the *vfmadd* instruction, the value is lost and needs to be restored after each iteration.

Assuming all memory accesses hit the L1 cache, the latency for each of those instructions is 4 cycles so it will take 52 cycles to compute the interaction of 16 particles (16 is the width of the SP vector registers in the coprocessor) for one thread. Luckily, the other three threads of the core can overlap perfectly to fill the empty cycles. So with 4 threads per core, it will take 56 cycles to compute the interaction of 64 particles (except for the last iteration where it will take 3 more cycles for all the threads to complete that are not overlapped; we can ignore this for a large number of particles). This gives 1.142 particle interactions computed on average per core per cycle in SP.

```
vsubrps     (%r14,%r10,4), %zmm7, %zmm12
vbroadcastss .L_2il0floatpacket.2(%rip), %zmm8
vsubrps     (%r9,%r10,4), %zmm6, %zmm13
vfmadd231ps %zmm12, %zmm12, %zmm8
vsubrps     (%rbx,%r10,4), %zmm5, %zmm15
vfmadd231ps %zmm13, %zmm13, %zmm8
vfmadd231ps %zmm15, %zmm15, %zmm8
vrsqrt23ps %zmm8, %zmm10
vmulps      (%r15,%r10,4), %zmm10, %zmm9
vmulps      %zmm9, %zmm10, %zmm11
vmulps      %zmm11, %zmm10, %zmm14
vfmadd231ps %zmm12, %zmm14, %zmm2
vfmadd231ps %zmm13, %zmm14, %zmm1
vfmadd231ps %zmm15, %zmm14, %zmm3
```

FIGURE 9.4

Single precision code for the inner *j*-loop of compute forces without prefetching nor loop counting.

```
vcvtpd2ps {rn}, %zmm5, %zmm14
vcvtpd2ps {rn}, %zmm3, %zmm4
vblendmps %zmm4, %zmm6, %zmm15{%k3}
vpermf32x4 $68, %zmm14, %zmm15{%k1}
vrsqrt23ps %zmm15, %zmm16
nop
vpermf32x4 $238, %zmm16, %zmm17
vcvtps2pd %zmm16, %zmm20
vcvtps2pd %zmm17, %zmm22
```

FIGURE 9.5

Using vrsqrt for double precision (with restricted precision).

For DP, we can use the same code sequence on packed DP vectors, which have a width of eight elements, except for the computation of the reciprocal square root. The first generation Intel Xeon Phi coprocessor only supports SP *vrsqrt,* which means the DP vectors need to be converted to SP. If we unroll the loop by a factor or two, we can pack 16 elements from two DP vectors into one SP vector for the reciprocal sqrt. The code sequence that computes the reciprocal square root with the conversions and the marshalling/unmarshalling of the DP vectors is outlined in Figure 9.5. This sequence takes 36 cycles. Using the unrolled loop, the other operations take 104 cycles bringing the total to 140 cycles to compute 64 elements by each core using all 4 threads. This gives 0.457 particle interactions computed on average per core per cycle in DP.

The next generation of the Intel Xeon Phi coprocessor codenamed Knights Landing will support the AVX-512 instruction set which includes a DP reverse square root instruction. This will improve the number of interactions in DP to 0.571 interactions per core per cycle and eliminates precision losses due to the conversion to SP.

Combining this cost model with the number of cores and the clock frequency of each of the different Intel Xeon Phi coprocessors models, we obtain the maximum number of interactions per second that can be achieved for each model. The results are listed in the table of Figure 9.6.

This optimistic upper bound shown in Figure 9.6 combined with the performance obtained with our initial versions shows that there is still room for improvement. The SP performance was

Model	Cores	Frequency (GHz)	Max GigaInteractions/s (Single Precision)	Max GigaInteractions/s (Double Precision)
7120×	61	1.238	85.7	34.3
7120× (with turbo)	61	1.333	92.9	37.2
5110×	60	1.053	72.2	28.9
3120×	57	1.1	71.7	28.7

FIGURE 9.6

Upper bound of GigaInteractions per second for the different Intel Xeon Phi coprocessors.

52.7 billion interactions per second out of 85.7 (61%). The DP performance was 20.5 billion interactions per second out of 34.3 (59%).

REDUCE THE OVERHEADS, ALIGN YOUR DATA

The next optimization addresses two issues that result from visual inspection of our initial code:

- The OpenMP *parallel* construct is located inside the computeForces routine. This has two implications. First, the update of the position vectors is done serially. For a large number of particles, this is not as important, since the complexity of computeForces dominates, but it can have an effect for a small number of particles. Second, the parallel region is created on every time step. While the Intel OpenMP runtime keeps the underlying threads alive and are reused there is still an overhead that can be non-negligible for a small number of particles.
- The data are neither aligned nor has the compiler been instructed to issue aligned instructions. Data alignment is critical for the compiler to be able to generate aligned loads/stores and to use memory operands on vector operations. Without data alignment, we will not be using the optimal instruction sequences described in the previous section.

Figure 9.7 shows how the initialization and time step code changes in this version. The data are allocated using _mm_malloc which ensures proper alignment. The OpenMP parallel construct has been modified to enclose the entire time step loop and an OpenMP *for* worksharing loop has been used to update the particles positions. Note that the implicit barrier after the worksharing loop keeps the iterations synchronized between the threads (every thread seems the same value for iter and iterates the same number of times).

Figure 9.8 shows the changes to the computeForces kernel. Instead of a *parallel* construct, the code now uses an OpenMP *for* construct. The *vector aligned* directive was also introduced to instruct the compiler to emit only code for aligned data. Forcing the compiler to emit aligned code now means that the data must be aligned or the application will experience hardware exceptions.

Figures 9.9 and 9.10 show how these changes affect performance for SP and DP, respectively. The dotted lines mark the performance upper bound that we computed in the previous section. We can see

```
... = (T *) _mm_malloc(bytes, 64);
...
#pragma omp parallel
for (int iter = 0; iter < nIters; iter++)     {
    computeForces(p,dt);
    #pragma omp for
    for (int i = 0; i < p.nParticles; i++) {
        p.x[i] += p.vx[i] * dt;
        p.y[i] += p.vy[i] * dt;
        p.z[i] += p.vz[i] * dt;
    }
}
```

FIGURE 9.7

Initialization and time step loop for our second version.

```
template <class T>
void computeForces(ParticleSystem<T> p, const T dt)
{
  int n = p.nParticles;
  #pragma omp for schedule(dynamic)
  for (int i = 0; i < n; i++) {
    ...
    #pragma vector aligned
    for (int j = 0; j < n; j++) {
      ...
    }
    ...
  }
}
```

FIGURE 9.8

N-Body kernel for our second version.

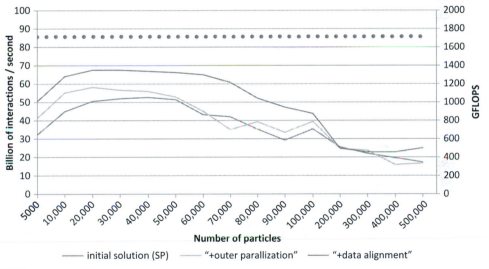

FIGURE 9.9

Single precision performance of our second version.

how moving the parallel construct to the time step loop helps when the number of particles is small particularly in SP. Using aligned instructions significantly increases the performance both in SP (up to 67.5) and DP (up to 26.9).

Even with the previous optimizations, performance still begins to degrade at roughly the same number of particles as before. What is the limiting factor?

Analyzing the application with the Intel® VTune™ Amplifier shows a significant number of L2-to-L2 transfers. Figure 9.11 shows the number of L2-to-L2 transfers as the percentage of the total number of requests (left y-axis) as well how much of the L2 capacity is used from each core by the four

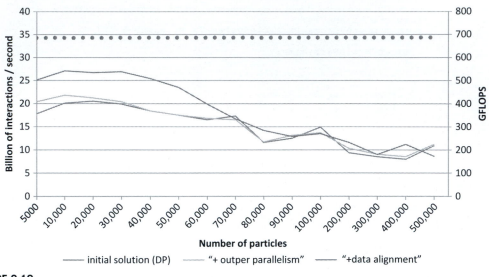

FIGURE 9.10

Double precision performance of our second version.

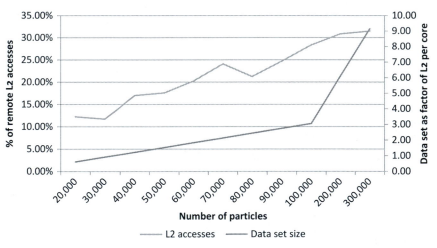

FIGURE 9.11

L2 pressure for our second version.

arrays used in the inner *j*-loop (right *y*-axis). Figure 9.11 shows that even for numbers of particles as small as 40k, the L2 cache is already too small. The increase in L2-to-L2 transfers occurs because the required data are often available in another core's L2 cache. Transferring data from another L2 is faster than fetching data from main memory. Still, the number of transfers increases as the number of particles increases and the overall application performance decreases.

OPTIMIZE THE MEMORY HIERARCHY

To improve locality and reuse particles more efficiently for every *i*-loop iteration, we utilize a well-known technique called loop tiling. Specifically, we tiled the *i*- and *j*-loops with square tiles of particles of size *BF*. Each tile is assigned to a thread and if the tile size is chosen appropriately, the elements of the *j*-tile will be reused across all the elements in the *i*-tile without being evicted from cache. This will improve data locality.

The code changes in the kernel and the computation of the tiling factor are shown in Figure 9.12. The OpenMP *collapse* clause was used on the *for* construct to distribute the tiles among the threads. The OpenMP atomic construct was used because multiple threads might need to update the velocity arrays at the same time. We do not expect the use of an atomic update to have a large impact because it is in the *i*-loop.

Note that the *schedule(dynamic)* clause was removed because better performance is achieved with the default *static* scheduling. We believe this is because the improved memory behavior removes the imbalance caused by threads accessing the core interconnect so that dynamic scheduling is no longer required to load balance the work between the threads.

Choosing the right tiling factor, *BF*, is a tricky issue. At each *j* iteration, we need to fit three tiles: the *i*-tile, the current *j*-tile, and the prefetch of the *j*-tile for the next iteration. Each of the four threads of the core uses a tile that contains four vectors: *x*, *y*, *z*, and *m*. A straightforward computation would give us

$$BF = \frac{L2\ size}{\#\ of\ vectors * threads\ per\ core * size\ of\ type * \#\ tiles}$$

```
int align = CACHELINE_SIZE/sizeof(T);
BF = nParticles / sqrt(omp_get_max_threads()) / 4;
BF = (BF+align-1)/align * align;
if ( BF > max_block<T>::value ) BF = max_block<T>::value;
...
int n = p.nParticles;
#pragma omp for collapse(2)
for ( int ii = 0; ii < n ; ii += BF )
for ( int jj = 0; jj < n; jj += BF ) {
    int imax = min(ii+BF,n);
    int jmax = min(jj+BF,n);
    for (int i = ii; i < imax ; i++ ) {
        ...
        #pragma vector aligned
        for (int j = jj; j < jmax; j++) {
            ..
        }
        #pragma omp atomic
        p.vx[i] += dt*Fx;
        #pragma omp atomic
        p.vy[i] += dt*Fy;
        #pragma omp atomic
        p.vz[i] += dt*Fz;
    }
}
```

FIGURE 9.12

2D tiled N-body kernel.

Thus, a 512-kB L2 cache means that a maximum SP tile size of 2730 elements, or half that number when using larger DP tiles.

Another requirement for the tiling factor is that *BF* must be a multiple of the alignment of the data type. Otherwise, a few elements of each tile will be executed in the prologue and epilog surrounding the main vectorized part of the tile. This can add a significant amount of overhead if the tile size is not a multiple of the alignment. With all this in mind, we need to choose a maximum tiling factor of 2688 for *B* in SP, or half of that in DP.

Collapsing and parallelizing both of the tiled loops also mean that the total number of iterations available to distribute among the threads is reduced by the tiling factor, which can be a problem for runs with small number of particles. A run with 30,000 particles that uses the maximum tiling factor, for example, reduces the number of iterations to distribute across the threads to 144, which is not enough to occupy all the threads on the Intel Xeon Phi coprocessor.

To avoid this issue, we compute a tile size where each thread is guaranteed to perform more than one iteration of work with the following formula:

$$BF = \min\left(\max BF, \frac{n\text{Particles}}{\sqrt{\# \text{ of thread} * \text{slack factor}}} \right)$$

The slack factor in the formula is used to ensure more than one iteration per thread and reduce the possible effect of load imbalance. We used a value 4 for the slack factor.

One further optimization is to take advantage of the fact that the L2 cache is shared by the different threads of the same core. We can do this by distributing the same tile to all threads of the core (instead of distributing one tile to each thread). Sharing tiles means there will be space in the L2 cache for larger tiles and reduces the amount of parallel work required to feed the full coprocessor by a factor of four as work is now distributed to cores and not threads. With this in mind, we used a max*BF* value of 4096 in SP, or half of that in DP, and a slack factor of 2.

```
core = omp_get_thread_num() / core;
// compute thread number inside core
cid = omp_get_thread_num() % 4;
// compute core_start and core_end as in schedule(static)
...
for ( l = core_start; l < core_end ; l++ ) {
    int ii = (l/nb) * BF;
    int jj = (l%nb) * BF;

    int imax = min(ii+BF,n);
    int jmax = min(jj+BF,n);
    for ( int i = ii+cid; i < imax ; i+= 4 ) {
        ...
        #pragma vector aligned
        for (int j = jj; j < jmax; j++) {
            ...
        }
        ...
    }
}
```

FIGURE 9.13

N-Body kernel using multiple threads per tile.

Unfortunately, OpenMP provides very little support for the shared tile approach without resorting to the use of nested parallelism. The overhead of nested parallelism in the current implementation of OpenMP is too high. Therefore, we developed a version, outlined in Figure 9.13, where the loop collapsing and work distribution are done manually. The key aspects are that the distribution of the outer loop is performed using the core identifier, so threads of the same core will get the same iterations and

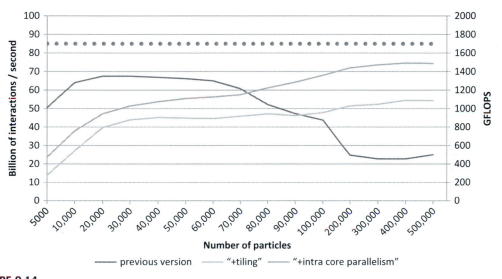

FIGURE 9.14

Single precision performance of our tiled versions.

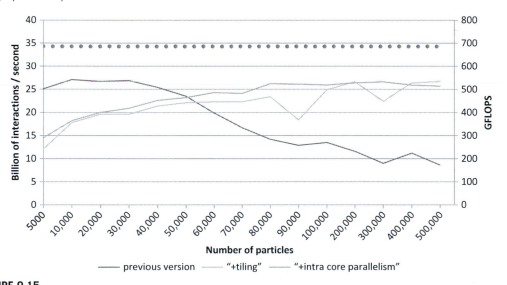

FIGURE 9.15

Double precision performance of our tiled versions.

that in the inner i-loop threads on the same core start on different iterations, by using their core id, and then advance using a step of four. Note that this version of the optimized code assumes that OpenMP threads are placed consecutively on the hardware threads of the coprocessor which we achieve by using the KMP_AFFINITY environment variable.

Figures 9.14 and 9.15 show the results for both tiling approaches (with intracore parallelism and without it) for SP and DP, respectively. Note that both versions improve performance as the number of particles increases. The caveat is that a significant number of particles are required to outperform the previous versions. To achieve the best overall application performance, two version of the code would be required to best support both small and large numbers of particles. Also note that the version using intracore parallelism performs significantly better for SP while the DP exhibits slower but more stable performance.

IMPROVING OUR TILING

An alternative approach is to use two different tiling factors: *BFI* for the i-loop and *BFJ* for the j-loop. Utilizing two tiling factors means the i-loop factor can be chosen to provide enough parallelism to avoid the use of the OpenMP collapse clause while also providing the flexibility to choose the tiling factor for the j-loop that allows optimizing accesses to the L2 cache.

Figure 9.16 illustrates the changes to the N-body kernel to implement this idea. The atomic construct can also be removed because only one thread will work on each i iteration.

Figure 9.17 shows how the *BFI* and *BFJ* tiling factors are computed. *BFI* is computed such as that all threads have only one iteration in the ii-loop, and to be cache line aligned which improves performance as previously discussed. An unfortunate side effect of cache line alignment is that some threads may not have any iterations to run. Thus, there is a trade-off here between cache aligned tile sizes and the imbalance they may create. Aligned cache sizes that cause up to 2% imbalance were observed to deliver the best performance. Otherwise, the unaligned tile size was chosen to maximize the load balance.

A *BFJ* value of 4096 was chosen for SP runs, or 2048 for DP runs. The following observation suggested an additional optimization: at various points in time threads in the same core may be using the same data as they traverse the j-loop. The chance of data sharing within the core increases as the

```
#pragma omp for
for ( int ii = 0; ii < n ; ii += BFI ) {
    imax = min(n,ii+BFI);
    for ( int jj = 0; jj < n; jj += BFJ ) {
        jmax = min(n,jj+BFJ);
        for (int i = ii; i < imax ; i++ ) {
            ...
            #pragma vector aligned
            for (int j = jj; j < jmax; j++) {
            }..
        }
    }
}
```

FIGURE 9.16

Tiled N-body kernel with two tiling factors.

```
int nthreads = omp_get_max_threads();
BFI_unaligned = (nParticles+nthreads-1)/nthreads;

int align = CACHELINE_SIZE/sizeof(T);
BFI = (BFI_unaligned+align-1)/align*align;

int iters = nParticles / BFI;
if ( nParticles % BFI != 0 ) iters++;
float balance = ((float) iters) / nthreads;
if ( balance < 0.98 ) BFI = BFI_unaligned;

BFJ = bf<T>::max_value;
float
l2_ocupancy=((float)nParticles)*sizeof(T)*4)/(512*1024);
if ( l2_ocupancy < 4 ) BFJ *= 2;
if ( l2_ocupancy < 2 ) BFJ *= 2;
```

FIGURE 9.17

N-Body kernel improved tiling factor computation.

number of particles in the simulation decreases. In particular, at least two threads share particles when the total number of particles in the working set is not four times the L2 size. When the working set is less than twice the size of the L2 then chances are that four threads are working on shared particles. When this is the case, the tile size is increased by a factor of two or four.

Figures 9.18 and 9.19 show the performance results when the *BFI* and *BFJ* tiling factors are adjusted as described in the preceding paragraphs. In particular, simulations utilizing small numbers of particles show significant improvement plus there is a slight improvement when the number of particles is large. The nontiled version performs better only when using particle set sizes not exceeding 5000 particles.

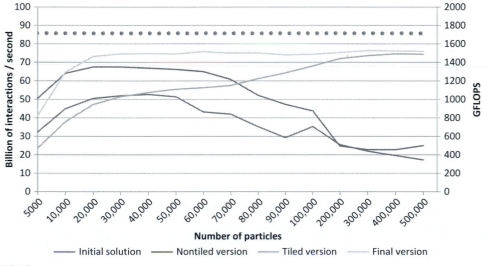

FIGURE 9.18

Single precision performance of the different optimization steps.

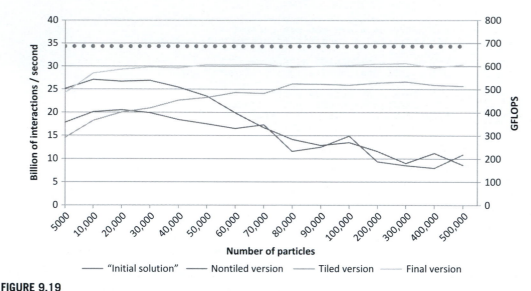

FIGURE 9.19

Double precision performance of the different optimization steps.

As a result of the optimizations discussed in this chapter, both SP and DP implementations achieved 89% of the upper bound predicted by the performance model. Specifically, the SP performance achieved 76.3 billion interactions per second, while the DP implementation achieved 30.6 billion of interactions per second.

In absolute terms, the SP version reaches 1.53 TFLOPS, which represent a 63.72% of the coprocessor peak performance. In DP, it reaches 612 GFLOPS, which represent a 50.90% of the coprocessor peak performance.

WHAT DOES ALL THIS MEAN TO THE HOST VERSION?

Our initial solution presented in Figures 9.1 and 9.2 was largely architecture agnostic. One can wonder how all the optimizations that we have presented in the previous sections affect the performance of the N-body kernel in an Intel Xeon® processor.

Figures 9.20 and 9.21 show a comparison of the performance of the initial version of the N-Body problem compared to the performance of the final version described in Figures 9.16 and 9.17 on a dual socket E5-2697v2 Intel Xeon processor based system with a total of 24 cores with two threads per core. The code was run without any modification and the only compilation change was to change the -mmic flag with the -xHost flag. All the 48 threads of the system were used as that produced the best performance.

We can see in Figures 9.20 and 9.21 that there is a rough 10% increase in the performance for both SP and DP executions. This increase was obtained when aligning the data and using aligned vector instructions. If we look at the initial version performance, there is no drop in the performance for large numbers of particles as it happened in the coprocessor. This hints that when running on the Xeon

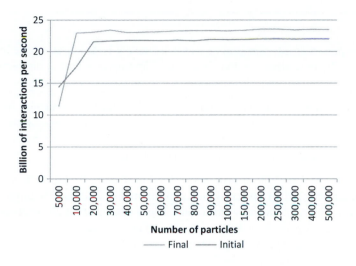

FIGURE 9.20

Double precision performance of the different optimization steps.

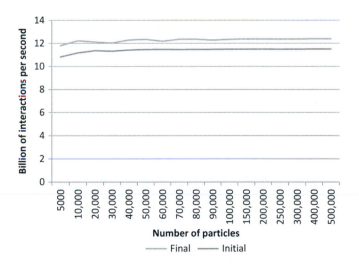

FIGURE 9.21

Double precision performance of the different optimization steps.

processor there is less difficulty in providing the cores with the data needed for the computation (this is partly explained because the memory pressure is lower and because the uncore architecture with a last-level cache seems to behave better) and it explains why loop tiling did not affect performance (it improved the *hit ratio* in the L1 and L2 caches but this did not translate into an increase in the performance). The other optimizations also did not boost performance but as importantly they did not hinder it either, so we still have a single version of the kernel that is able to run efficiently on both the host and the coprocessor.

SUMMARY

In this chapter, we presented an optimized version of a direct N-body kernel for the Intel Many Integrated Core architecture. The optimized version also showed an improvement in the performance on regular processors. Important optimizations for the Intel Xeon Phi coprocessor were discussed including:

- Effective vectorization, proper data alignment, use of vector transcendental functions, and data layout.
- Providing enough parallelism, reducing overhead, and avoiding load imbalance.
- Effective use of the memory hierarchy by using loop tiling.

These optimizations increased the maximum performance of 52.7 and 20.5 billion interactions per second in SP and DP, respectively, to maximum performance of 76.3 (a 44% improvement) and 30.6 (a 66% improvement) billion interactions per second. These optimization also increased the performance on an Intel Xeon processor by about 10% using the identical source code.

This chapter also discussed how to quickly get a target for the optimization process. The final optimized version of the code obtained an 89% of the upper bound performance which seems a satisfactory stopping point for our optimization efforts.

We also showed that overall our efforts to optimize for the Intel Xeon Phi coprocessor also had a positive effect on our performance on an Intel Xeon processor.

FOR MORE INFORMATION

Following is a list of additional reading materials that are related to the concepts discussed in this chapter:

- Vladimirov, A., Karpusenko, V., 2013. Test-driving Intel® Xeon Phi™ coprocessors with a basic N-body simulation. http://research.colfaxinternational.com/post/2013/01/07/Nbody-Xeon-Phi.aspx.
- N-Body problem, http://en.wikipedia.org/wiki/N-body_problem.
- Arora, N., Shringarpure, A., Vuduc, R.W., 2009. Direct N-body kernels for multicore platforms. In the International Conference on Parallel Processing ICPP'09.
- Rodionov, S.A., Sotnikova, N.Ya., 2005. Optimal choice of the softening length and time step in N-body simulations. Astronomy Reports 49 (6), 470–476.
- Loop tiling, http://en.wikipedia.org/wiki/Loop_tiling.
- Download the code from this and other chapters: http://lotsofcores.com.

N-BODY METHODS

10

Rio Yokota, Mustafa AbdulJabbar
King Abdullah University of Science and Technology, Saudi Arabia

Optimization techniques discussed in this chapter include the use of compiler options and directives to increase the performance with minimum modifications to the code. We show that fused multiply-add and reciprocal square root operations are generated by the compiler without explicitly rewriting the code. We also show that the outer loop of a double loop can be vectorized with the use of a simple directive. We compare this directive-based code with a hand-tuned code using intrinsics. We also compare the same code on the Intel® Xeon® processor and Intel® Xeon Phi™ coprocessor. We were able to achieve 1.5 TFlop/s single precision performance on the coprocessor without rewriting our original C code. We use a direct N-body method to demonstrate the effect of the above-mentioned optimizations. N-Body methods have traditionally been used in particle-based simulations such as astrophysical and molecular simulations. They have recently been extended to solve more general forms of partial differential equations as well. You will find reference material for these uses in Section "For More Information". The inner kernel of the N-body method has high arithmetic intensity since it performs $20N^2$ operations for every $4N$ floating point numbers it loads. If we compare this with a matrix-matrix multiplication, which performs $2N^3$ operations for every $2N^2$ numbers loaded, we can see that the flop/Byte ratio of the N-body kernel is higher. This high arithmetic intensity allows N-body methods to remain compute-bound on architectures of the future. In this chapter, we focus on the optimization of the N-body method on the Intel Xeon Phi coprocessor and show the effect of these optimizations on an Intel Xeon processor as well.

FAST N-BODY METHODS AND DIRECT N-BODY KERNELS

The direct N-body kernel calculates the all-pairs interaction of N--bodies against N-bodies, which results in an operation count of $O(N^2)$. Fast approximation methods that use hierarchical domain decomposition of the bodies, along with truncated series expansions of the kernel can drive the operation count lower to $O(N \log N)$ or even $O(N)$ as described by Barnes et al. (see Section "For more information"). The $O(N)$ method is often referred to as the fast multipole method (FMM). The rationale behind these fast N-body methods is that bodies in the far-field need not be considered individually, but can be grouped into multipoles. However, bodies in the near-field must still be calculated accurately by using the direct N-body kernel. Therefore, the performance of the direct N-body kernel is critical for these fast N-body methods.

The arithmetic complexity refers to the asymptotic amount of arithmetic operations performed as the problem size increases. The arithmetic intensity refers to the amount of arithmetic operations performed per amount of data loaded. The combination of the $O(N)$ optimal complexity of the FMM and the high arithmetic intensity of the direct *N*-body kernel inside it makes the FMM an interesting alternative to many algorithms on architectures of the future. This is because conventional algorithms with high arithmetic intensity like dense linear algebra tend to have high arithmetic complexity as well. They are compute-bound and can utilize most of arithmetic units, but are computationally very expensive to begin with. On the other hand, methods with low arithmetic complexity like fast Fourier transform (FFT) and sparse linear algebra have low arithmetic intensity. They are very efficient, but are not able to achieve a high percentage of the peak arithmetic performance of modern processors. FMMs have an exceptional combination of $O(N)$ complexity and an arithmetic intensity that is higher than matrix-matrix multiplication. This means that *N*-body methods provide a very efficient algorithm that scales favorably with problem size, but should also remain compute bound on future architectures for the next few decades.

The direct *N*-body kernel is easy to isolate from the FMM, since it is usually being called as a function inside the neighbor finding routine. This function call takes up a majority of the execution time of the FMM. Therefore, if we can optimize the direct *N*-body kernel it will automatically optimize the hotspot of the FMM. The direct *N*-body kernel is only a few tens of lines of code, so even optimizing at the assembly level is not so much work. In this chapter, we will show a very specific example of how far we can go with just compiler options, and then introduce intrinsics to squeeze even more performance out of the direct *N*-body kernel.

APPLICATIONS OF *N*-BODY METHODS

N-Body methods can be naturally applied to problems where the physics itself is described by a collection of discrete points, even before numerical discretization. A many-body problem under gravitational or electrostatic forces is a typical example, where stars and atoms can be represented as point sources of mass and electrostatic charge, respectively. *N*-Body methods can be extended from discrete fields to continuum fields through discretization. This makes it possible to use these methods for solving problems in structural mechanics, fluid mechanics, electromagnetics, acoustics, and even quantum mechanics. However, just because it is applicable does not mean that it is the optimal method to solve that particular problem.

Fast *N*-body methods have been favored in applications where the geometry information changes dynamically. If the geometry is stationary, it makes much more sense to store this information in the form of a matrix, and to perform sparse/dense linear algebra operations on this same matrix over and over again. *N*-Body methods could be thought of as "matrix-free" methods, where a matrix is formed on-the-fly before being multiplied to a vector of source points. It is obvious that such methods become advantageous only when the matrix/geometry changes frequently, since storing them would not save any computation in such cases. This is precisely the case for particle-based methods where each particle advances its location every time step. Adaptive mesh refinement may also result in a similar amount of geometry updates if the system is very dynamic.

There are many factors that could influence the comparative advantage of the *N*-body approach over other elliptic Partial Differential Equation (PDE) solvers like FFT and multigrid. The asymptotic constant plays a critical role in determining the relative performance of these different $O(N)/O(N \log N)$ algorithms. The FFT is known to have as few as $2N \log N$ operations and multigrid could have as few as $5N$ operations. The FMM on the other hand would typically have a much larger asymptotic constant. However, the use of translational and rotational symmetry while prescribing the position of points can reduce this constant significantly.

Comparing FFT against FMM is difficult because FFT has a higher spatial resolution per unknown, so comparing for the same N is not fair. However, for fields that have local features or discontinuities, the homogenous spatial resolution of FFT certainly becomes a disadvantage. Furthermore, when translational and rotational symmetry is utilized in the FMM by prescribing the position of points, it can use BLAS 3 operations much more efficiently than multigrid. Therefore, FMM becomes faster than multigrid to solve the same problem up to the same accuracy in such cases.

The FMM in the traditional sense requires a Green's function solution; so, the type of scientific applications that it can handle is limited to those that have a Green's function. Generalization of the FMM to hierarchical low-rank approximations of matrices enables the same framework to be applied to a much wider range of applications. These methods use low-rank approximation methods such as rank-revealing QR, truncated SVD, or adaptive cross approximation instead of multipole expansions. This frees the FMM from its dependence on the existence of Green's functions and can be applied to problems like variable coefficient Poisson equations or covariance matrices, which were not solvable with the original FMM.

When predicting the performance of FFT, FMM, and multigrid on future architectures, a useful indicator is communication complexity since the bottleneck of any algorithm becomes the communication as it approaches its limit of parallel scalability. FFT has a communication complexity of $O(P^{1/d})$ for a d-dimensional decomposition. Multigrid has a communication complexity of $O(\log P)$. We have recently been able to prove that FMM also has a communication complexity of $O(\log P)$. Therefore, we see that both FMM and multigrid are communication optimal. This proof for $O(\log P)$ of FMM can be extended to its algebraic variants as well.

DIRECT *N*-BODY CODE

We will now show an example of a direct *N*-body kernel, first in plain C language and then using SIMD intrinsics. The plain *N*-body kernel is shown in Figure 10.1. We define eight arrays that describe the properties of the body. The arrays *x, y, z* are the coordinates, *m* is the mass/charge, *p* is the potential, and *ax, ay, az* are the acceleration in each direction. The equation we calculate is the smoothed Laplace potential

$$\phi_i = \sum_{j=1}^{N} \frac{m_j}{r_{ij}}$$

and acceleration

$$a_i = \nabla \phi_i = -\sum_{j=1}^{N} \frac{m_j r_{ij}}{r_{ij}^3}$$

where

$$r_{ij} = \sqrt{\left(x_i - x_j\right)^2 + \left(y_i - y_j\right)^2 + \left(z_i - z_j\right)^2 + \varepsilon^2}$$

is the distance between the bodies at i and j, and ε is the smoothing factor.

```
#pragma simd
#pragma omp for
for (i=0; i<N; i++) {
  float pi = 0;
  float axi = 0;
  float ayi = 0;
  float azi = 0;
  float xi = x[i];
  float yi = y[i];
  float zi = z[i];
  for (j=0; j<N; j++) {
    float dx = x[j] - xi;
    float dy = y[j] - yi;
    float dz = z[j] - zi;
    float R2 = dx * dx + dy * dy + dz * dz + EPS2;
    float invR = 1.0f / sqrtf(R2);
    float invR3 = m[j] * invR * invR * invR;
    pi += m[j] * invR;
    axi += dx * invR3;
    ayi += dy * invR3;
    azi += dz * invR3;
  }
  p[i] = pi;
  ax[i] = axi;
  ay[i] = ayi;
  az[i] = azi;
}
```

FIGURE 10.1

Code listing—Direct *N*-body kernel. Targets (outer loop) are vectorized.

The arrays *x, y, z, m* are the given prescribed values—in the present example, a random number between 0 and 1. These values are used to calculate the potential and acceleration on all *N* bodies, which is induced by all *N* bodies. This results in a double loop from 0 to $N-1$ as shown in Figure 10.1. The loop for *i* goes over the target bodies, while the loop for *j* goes over the source bodies.

We will use the code in Figure 10.1 as a base case to see how much performance we can achieve on the coprocessor without changing the code. The combination of the two pragmas for SIMD and OpenMP makes it possible to parallelize the outer loop both over threads and SIMD vectors. The performance results when using different compiler options are shown in the following section. This same code runs on both the processor and the coprocessor.

The coprocessor has 512-bit wide SIMD intrinsics, which are similar to SSE and AVX. Since these intrinsic instructions directly map to assembly instructions, it leaves less ambiguity in what the compiler is doing to the code. To be more specific, it tells the compiler to explicitly perform *load, store, fmadd*, and *rsqrt* operations, and also the loop to be vectorized is also explicitly specified.

The direct *N*-body kernel has an outer loop for the targets and an inner loop for the sources. With the use of SIMD intrinsics, it is possible to specify that the outer loop should be vectorized by putting 16 array elements into the SIMD registers and using a stride of 16 for the loop, as shown in Figure 10.2. The general structure of the direct *N*-body code has not changed, but all the operations are now written in *_mm512* intrinsics, and all intermediate values are declared as *__m512* registers. When possible the *fmadd* instruction is explicitly specified.

An alternative form of vectorizing the inner loop is shown in Figure 10.3. The code is almost identical to the one in Figure 10.2, except the stride of 16 is now in the *j* loop, and a *reduce-add* operation must be performed at the end instead of a simple *store*.

```
#pragma omp for
for (i=0; i<N; i+=16) {
    __m512 pi = _mm512_setzero_ps();
    __m512 axi = _mm512_setzero_ps();
    __m512 ayi = _mm512_setzero_ps();
    __m512 azi = _mm512_setzero_ps();
    __m512 xi = _mm512_load_ps(x+i);
    __m512 yi = _mm512_load_ps(y+i);
    __m512 zi = _mm512_load_ps(z+i);
    for (j=0; j<N; j++) {
        __m512 xj = _mm512_set1_ps(x[j]);
        xj = _mm512_sub_ps(xj, xi);
        __m512 yj = _mm512_set1_ps(y[j]);
        yj = _mm512_sub_ps(yj, yi);
        __m512 zj = _mm512_set1_ps(z[j]);
        zj = _mm512_sub_ps(zj, zi);
        __m512 R2 = _mm512_set1_ps(EPS2);
        R2 = _mm512_fmadd_ps(xj, xj, R2);
        R2 = _mm512_fmadd_ps(yj, yj, R2);
        R2 = _mm512_fmadd_ps(zj, zj, R2);
        __m512 mj = _mm512_set1_ps(m[j]);
        __m512 invR = _mm512_rsqrt23_ps(R2);
        mj = _mm512_mul_ps(mj, invR);
        pi = _mm512_add_ps(pi, mj);
        invR = _mm512_mul_ps(invR, invR);
        invR = _mm512_mul_ps(invR, mj);
        axi = _mm512_fmadd_ps(xj, invR, axi);
        ayi = _mm512_fmadd_ps(yj, invR, ayi);
        azi = _mm512_fmadd_ps(zj, invR, azi);
    }
    _mm512_store_ps(p+i, pi);
    _mm512_store_ps(ax+i, axi);
    _mm512_store_ps(ay+i, ayi);
    _mm512_store_ps(az+i, azi);
}
```

FIGURE 10.2

Code listing—Direct N-body kernel with intrinsics. Targets (outer loop) are vectorized.

The code for AVX intrinsics is very similar to the ones shown in Figures 10.2 and 10.3 except the "fmadd" are changed to separate "mul" and "add" operations and the "reduce:add" operation in Figure 10.3 becomes a combination of "permute2f128", "add," and "hadd" operations.

PERFORMANCE RESULTS

In this section, we report the performance of the direct N-body kernel shown in Figures 10.1 and 10.2 on an Intel Xeon E5 v2 processor and an Intel Xeon Phi coprocessor. The tests are performed on a Intel Xeon Phi 7120P coprocessor with Intel® MPSS 3.2.1 and Intel® C++ Composer XE version 14.0.1 in native mode, and two Intel Xeon E5-2680 v2 (Ivy Bridge) processors with Intel® C++ Composer XE version 13.0.1. The runs were performed with $N=65,536$, and we counted 20 Flop/s per pair of bodies. The compiler options "−mavx −openmp −O3" were used on the processor and "−mmic −openmp −fimf-domain-exclusion=15 −O3" were used on the coprocessor. Figure 10.1 shows the comparison against the processor and coprocessor with directives and with intrinsics.

```
#pragma omp for
for (i=0; i<N; i++) {
   __m512 pi = _mm512_setzero_ps();
   __m512 axi = _mm512_setzero_ps();

   __m512 ayi = _mm512_setzero_ps();
   __m512 azi = _mm512_setzero_ps();
   __m512 xi = _mm512_set1_ps(x[i]);
   __m512 yi = _mm512_set1_ps(y[i]);
   __m512 zi = _mm512_set1_ps(z[i]);
   for (j=0; j<N; j+=16) {
      __m512 xj = _mm512_load_ps(x+j);
      xj = _mm512_sub_ps(xj, xi);
      __m512 yj = _mm512_load_ps(y+j);
      yj = _mm512_sub_ps(yj, yi);
      __m512 zj = _mm512_load_ps(z+j);
      zj = _mm512_sub_ps(zj, zi);
      __m512 R2 = _mm512_set1_ps(EPS2);
      R2 = _mm512_fmadd_ps(xj, xj, R2);
      R2 = _mm512_fmadd_ps(yj, yj, R2);
      R2 = _mm512_fmadd_ps(zj, zj, R2);
      __m512 mj = _mm512_load_ps(m+j);
      __m512 invR = _mm512_rsqrt23_ps(R2);
      mj = _mm512_mul_ps(mj, invR);
      pi = _mm512_add_ps(pi, mj);
      invR = _mm512_mul_ps(invR, invR);
      invR = _mm512_mul_ps(invR, mj);
      axi = _mm512_fmadd_ps(xj, invR, axi);
      ayi = _mm512_fmadd_ps(yj, invR, ayi);
      azi = _mm512_fmadd_ps(zj, invR, azi);
   }
   p[i] = _mm512_reduce_add_ps(pi);
   ax[i] = _mm512_reduce_add_ps(axi);
   ay[i] = _mm512_reduce_add_ps(ayi);
   az[i] = _mm512_reduce_add_ps(azi);
}
```

FIGURE 10.3

Code listing—Direct *N*-body kernel with intrinsics. Sources (inner loop) are vectorized.

We use all 40 threads on the two processor socket hosts and all 244 threads on the coprocessor. The thread scalability on the coprocessor is very good, as we will show in more detail in Figure 10.5. The legends "−mavx + pragma," "_mm256," "−mmic + pragma," "_mm512" stand for host processor with directives, the processor with intrinsics, the coprocessor with directives, and the coprocessor with intrinsics, respectively. On the processor, the intrinsics-based version outperforms the directive-based version, but on the coprocessor, the directive-based version is faster. Both our directive-based and intrinsics-based code outperform the previous direct *N*-body work on the coprocessor.

In Figure 10.5, we show the strong scalability of the direct *N*-body kernel when different numbers of threads are used. The Intel Xeon Phi 7120P coprocessor has 61 cores running 4 threads each, so the thread count goes up to 244. We test the effect of the thread affinity by changing "KMP_AFFINITY" to *compact*, *balanced*, and *scatter*. Both the *scatter* and *balanced* options show ideal scalability up to 61 cores, while there is one thread running per core. The *compact* option scales ideally when all four threads are running on a core. This means that the scalability of the core count is very good, while the scalability among the four threads within a core is not as good. In the end, when all 244 threads are utilized the different "KMP_AFFINITY" options do not make any difference.

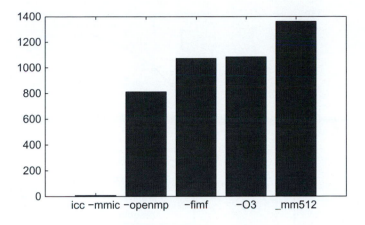

FIGURE 10.4

Single precision gigaFlop/s for the direct N-body kernel using directives and intrinsics on an Ivy Bridge processor (avx/mm256) and an Intel Xeon Phi coprocessor (mic/mm512).

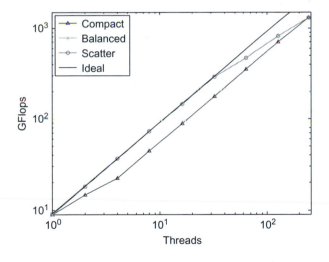

FIGURE 10.5

Single precision GFlops of the direct N-body kernel on Intel Xeon Phi coprocessor without intrinsics on different number of cores.

So far the experiments shown in Figures 10.4 and 10.5 were for a specific problem size $N=65,536$. Figure 10.6 shows the single precision gigaFlop/s of the direct N-body kernel for different problem sizes. In the legend, "I intrinsics," "J intrinsics," "I pragma," "J pragma," represent the target loop vectorization with intrinsics, source loop vectorization with intrinsics, target loop vectorization with directives, and source loop vectorization with directives, respectively. The error bars show the standard deviation in the gigaFlop/s among the 256 runs that we performed for each case. We show these error bars because we noticed that some cases had very large variation in the runtime. First, we see that the

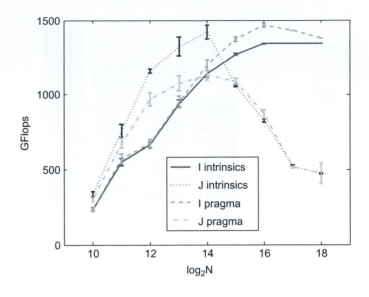

FIGURE 10.6

Single precision gigaFlop/s, on an Intel Xeon Phi coprocessor, for the direct *N*-body kernel with intrinsics and without intrinsics with vectorization of the outer loop for *i* or inner loop for *j* for different problem sizes.

source vectorized versions peak at $N = 2^{14} = 16{,}384$. With the use of SIMD intrinsics and the directive *#pragma simd*, we are able to explicitly tell the compiler to vectorize the outer loop, and this results in higher performance for $N > 16{,}384$. The use of SIMD intrinsics is faster for the source vectorization, but the directive-based version is faster for the target vectorized case. The optimal choice between vectorizing the outer loop or inner loop is dependent on the problem size.

SUMMARY

In this chapter, we described how to optimize a direct *N*-body kernel on the coprocessor. We were able to achieve about 1.5 TFlop/s single precision performance by simply using the compiler option "icc -mmic -openmp -fimf-domain-exclusion=15" and adding a "#pragma simd" to the original C code for CPUs. The use of OpenMP and simd directive benefit processor. The strong scalability of the execution was close to ideal, while the scalability of the intra-core threading was less efficient. The choice of "KMP_AFFINITY" did not have any effect when all 244 threads were utilized.

By using the *_mm512* intrinsics, we were able to increase the performance to about 1.4 TFlop/s even at smaller problem sizes. We found a strong dependence of the performance on the problem size and the relation was not monotonic. Up to a certain problem size, vectorizing the inner loop gave better performance, but after $N > 16{,}384$, vectorizing the outer loop gave better performance. The vectorization of the outer loop was made possible by the use of a portable and general *#pragma simd* directive or the more specific *_mm512* intrinsics.

FOR MORE INFORMATION

Here is some additional reading materials we recommend related to this chapter.

- Mini *N*-body kernels, https://github.com/harrism/mini-nbody.
- Test-driving Intel Xeon Phi Coprocessors with Basic *N*-body Simulation.
- http://research.colfaxinternational.com/post/2013/01/07/Nbody-Xeon-Phi.aspx.
- Download the code from this and other chapters, http://lotsofcores.com.
- Aarseth, S., 1963. Dynamical evolution of clusters of galaxies. Mon. Not. R. Astron. Soc. 126, 223–255.
- Alder, B.J., 1957. Phase transition for a hard sphere system. J. Chem. Phys. 27, 1208–1209.
- Sambavaram, S.R., Sarin, V., Sameh, A., Grama, A., 2003. Multipole-based preconditioners for large sparse linear systems. Parallel Comput. 29, 1261–1273.
- Barnes, J., Hut, P., 1986. O(NlogN) force-calculation algorithm. Nature 324, 446–449.
- Greengard, L., Rokhlin, V., 1987. A fast algorithm for particle simulations. J. Comput. Phys. 73, 325–348.
- Johnson, S., Frigo, M., 2007. A modified split-radix FFT with fewer arithmetic operations. IEEE Trans. Signal Process. 55, 111–119.
- Gholami, D., Malhotra, H., Sundar, G. Biros, FFT, FMM, or multigrid? A comparative study of state-of-the-art Poisson solvers. SIAM J. Scient. Comput., submitted, http://users.ices.utexas.edu/~hari/files/pubs/sisc14.pdf.
- Greengard, L., Gueyffier, D., Martinsson, P.G., Rokhlin, V., 2009. Fast direct solvers for integral equations in complex three-dimensional domains. Acta Numerica 18, 243–275.
- Gu, M., Eisenstat, S.C., 1996. Efficient algorithms for computing a strong rank-revealing QR factorization. SIAM J. Scient. Comput. 17, 848–869.
- Grasedyck, L., Hackbusch, W., 2003. Construction and arithmetics of H-matrices. Computing 70, 295–334.
- Rjasanow, S., 2002. Adaptive cross approximation of dense matrices. In International Association for Boundary Element Methods, UT Austin, TX, USA, May 28–30, 2002.
- Yokota, R., Turkiyyah, G., Keyes, D., 2014. Communication complexity of the FMM and its algebraic variants, *arXiv:1406.1974*.
- Vladimirov, V., Karpusenko, Test-driving Intel Xeon Phi Coprocessors with Basic *N*-body Simulation, Colfax International, 2013, http://research.colfaxinternational.com/post/2013/01/07/Nbody-Xeon-Phi.aspx.

DYNAMIC LOAD BALANCING USING OPENMP 4.0

11

Gilles Civario, Michael Lysaght
ICHEC, Ireland

For many years, OpenMP has been the model of choice for programming on shared memory multiprocessors within the high-performance computing community. Although OpenMP is promoted as being easy to use and allows incremental parallelization of codes, naive implementations frequently yield poor performance. In practice, as with other models such as MPI, the same care and attention should be exercised over algorithm and hardware details when programming with OpenMP.

This is even more so the case now that the newly released OpenMP 4.0 standard, supporting an offload mode, can take advantage of emerging many-core coprocessors such as the Intel® Xeon Phi™ Coprocessor. In many cases, employing OpenMP on a given processor (e.g., a multicore processor such as an Intel® Xeon® processor) can be relatively straightforward. However, taking advantage of all of the resources available on a heterogeneous system, such as those found on a "Stampede" or "Tianhe-2" node which uses both Intel Xeon processors and Intel Xeon Phi coprocessors, can be far less so. For example, determining the optimal approach for managing data transfers between a "host" processor and a coprocessor "device" (or indeed multiple devices) in parallel can, in itself, pose several challenges. On top of this, an extra layer of complexity is added in ensuring that the balance of workload between what is offloaded to each device and what remains on the host is optimal. In this chapter, by means of a simple N-Body sample algorithm, we guide the reader from a serial version to a fully parallelized version of the algorithm, where all processing elements available on a heterogeneous processor/coprocessor platform are exploited and where each device is automatically assigned the optimal amount of work on a dynamic basis so that the achieved speedup is maximized. Our dynamic load-balancing method is entirely written in fully standard OpenMP 4.0, which makes it perfectly portable, and is generic enough to be easily adapted to a wide range of computing problems such as those found in astrophysics and molecular dynamics. This makes it particularly interesting not only for code developers but also for software vendors eager to distribute binary versions of their codes, without obfuscating the sources or sacrificing efficiency.

MAXIMIZING HARDWARE USAGE

In the rest of this chapter, we use the traditional terminology in the field of many-core accelerators. By CPU, processor, or host system, we generally mean the Intel Xeon processor (CPU) based computing system. By coprocessor, device, or accelerator, we mean the Intel Xeon Phi coprocessor. We will also use the term "compute device" in contexts where the term applies to both the coprocessor and CPU.

The Intel Xeon Phi coprocessor can today be approached using three main programming paradigms: "native," "symmetric," and "offload" modes. The native mode is a fast way to get existing software running with minimal code changes. Unlike general-purpose graphics processing units, Intel Xeon Phi coprocessors are able to execute native applications where the application runs in the coprocessor's operating system and does not require a host process executing on the CPU. In this way, each coprocessor can be seen as a standalone many-core symmetric multiprocessing compute device. Of course, to run a code in native mode on the coprocessor, the code needs to be ported, but the commonality between the Intel processor and coprocessor devices and software stacks makes this porting phase relatively trivial. Exploiting the larger number of cores (as well as wider vector units) on the coprocessor might require more work compared to using a standard multicore processor, but with the advantage that the same programming models can be used for both. This is why this native approach is the natural first step that users are likely to take when approaching the Intel Xeon Phi architecture. However, approaching the coprocessor in native mode limits access to only one Intel Xeon Phi coprocessor and ignores the resources available on the CPU host.

The symmetric mode is of interest for codes already able to run in parallel on distributed memory systems (e.g., MPI-based codes). It is called symmetric because it allows the code to exploit both the processor and the coprocessor resources available on a given cluster simultaneously. In this case, all compute devices can be accessed in parallel. While the steps needed for a basic porting to coprocessor-based clusters in symmetric mode is generally as trivial as those taken to enable the code in native mode, the complexity of load balancing over such a heterogeneous system of compute devices can in reality be very challenging.

With the offload mode, the application is launched on the host system (i.e., using the CPU) and initialization of data also takes place on the host. The code subsequently uses the PCIe bus to push (offload) a part of the data and specialized executable code to the device for processing. After processing, results are pulled back to the host. In the case of the Intel Xeon Phi coprocessor, the programmer can use compiler directives to initiate offload. The offload mode can be used on standalone machines, as well as in clusters, where on each machine, one or several MPI processes are launched, each performing offload.

Although offload mode is often the mode that requires the most programming effort, it is often the mode in which the potential reward is the highest. In particular,

- it allows a single code to exploit both the host, and the device;
- it avoids the complexity of load balancing at the MPI level, which can be particularly challenging for large-scale codes; and
- it prepares the codes for any foreseeable future evolution of products with the Intel Xeon® and Intel Xeon Phi™ brands.

However, exploiting the advantages of the offload mode in an efficient manner can present its own challenges. For example, exploiting the host and device concurrently, so as to avail of their *combined* computing potential rather than alternating between the two compute devices, can often be nontrivial (Figure 11.1). In addition, achieving an optimal balance of workload over each compute device so that there is no time lost in waiting for a particular compute device to reach synchronization points can also be challenging.

In this chapter, we demonstrate how to achieve an optimal balance of workload between Intel Xeon processors and any number of Intel Xeon Phi coprocessors. Moreover, to take full advantage of the unified programming model of the both, we will use the newly released OpenMP 4.0 standard. This standard

FIGURE 11.1

The difficulty of adapting workloads to individual parts of a collaborative work becomes apparent if equal workloads are given while the ability to do the work is unequal.

will allow us, by virtue of a few compiler directives, to use the exact same code base to exploit the full potential of a heterogeneous platform in a fully portable and elegant way. The only OpenMP 4.0 specific features we need for achieving this are the new SIMD directives, for full-code performance, and the offload directives, for piloting the Intel Xeon Phi coprocessors from the Intel Xeon processor.

In order to demonstrate the overall method, we will use a classical N-Body algorithm such those commonly used in astrophysics codes. Similar algorithms can also be found in molecular dynamics codes, where the force of gravity is replaced by Coulombic forces. Indeed, it should be emphasized that the load-balancing method demonstrated here is independent of the actual computing kernel, and can therefore be adapted to many other iterative algorithms.

THE N-BODY KERNEL

To help illustrate the method, let's assume we want to simulate the free evolution of nonrelativistic particles in space, for example, satellites, planets, stars, galaxies, etc. For such objects, Newton's second law of motion states that the sum of all forces applied on each particle (body) is equal to the product of its mass by its acceleration. Moreover, Newton's law of universal gravitation states that each pair of particles attracts each other following a force proportional to their masses, and inversely proportional to the square of the distance between them. For our collection of N bodies, Newton's second law can be described by the following equation:

$$\forall i \in \{1,\ldots,N\} \, m_i . \vec{a}_i = G \sum_{i \neq j} \frac{m_i . m_j}{d_{ij}^2} \vec{u}_{ji},$$

(11.1)

where m_i is the mass of particle i, $\bar{a}_i$ is its acceleration, G is the gravitational constant, d_{ij} is the distance between particles i and j, and $\bar{u}_{ji}$ is the unitary vector between particles i and j. Equation (11.1) can be rewritten as

$$\forall i \in \{1,\ldots,N\}\frac{d\bar{v}_i}{dt} = G\sum_{i\neq j}\frac{\bar{x}_j-\bar{x}_i}{d_{ij}^3}m_j, \tag{11.2}$$

where $\bar{v}_i$ is the particle's velocity, $\bar{x}_i$ is its position, and t is the time.

Working from Eq. (11.2), it is straightforward to write our N-Body gravitational kernel, which is shown in Figure 11.2. In addition, since we also want to evaluate the influence of floating-point precision in performance, let's also introduce a generic "real" type, which will either be `float` or `double` depending on a preprocessor macro.

To make sure that our performance comparisons are not biased because of a suboptimal initial kernel, we will parallelize and optimize our `Newton` function using OpenMP directives:

```
#ifdef DOUBLE
  typedef double real;
  #define Sqrt sqrt
#else
  typedef float real;
  #define Sqrt sqrtf
#endif

real *x, *y, *z, *vx, *vy, *vz, *m;
const real G = 6.67384e-11;

void Newton( size_t n, real dt ) {
  const real dtG = dt * G;
  for ( size_t i = 0; i < n; ++i ) {
    real dvx = 0, dvy = 0, dvz = 0;
    for ( size_t j = 0; j < n; ++j ) {
      if ( j != i ) {
        real dx = x[j] - x[i], dy = y[j] - y[i],
          dz = z[j] - z[i];
        real dist2 = dx*dx + dy*dy + dz*dz;
        real mjOverDist3 = m[j] /
          (dist2 * Sqrt( dist2 ));

        dvx += mjOverDist3 * dx;
        dvy += mjOverDist3 * dy;
        dvz += mjOverDist3 * dz;
      }
    }
    vx[i] += dvx * dtG;
    vy[i] += dvy * dtG;
    vz[i] += dvz * dtG;
  }
  for ( size_t i = 0; i < n; ++i ) {
    x[i] += vx[i] * dt;
    y[i] += vy[i] * dt;
    z[i] += vz[i] * dt;
  }
}
```

FIGURE 11.2

Our initial N-Body gravitational kernel.

1. we enclose the whole body of the function in an OpenMP "`parallel`" construct;
2. we add two OpenMP `for` directives—one before each of the two `for` loops over i—to distribute them across multiple OpenMP threads;
3. we add a "`schedule(auto)`" directive to the `for` constructs, to delegate the decision regarding scheduling to the compiler so we don't have to focus on this;
4. we also add two OpenMP "`simd`" directives to force the compiler to vectorize the loop over j and the second loop over i; and
5. to avoid the cost of the test over equality between i and j, likely to impede the vectorization of the enclosing loop over j, we split it into two: first iterating from 0 to i and subsequently from i+1 to n.

With these modifications, our kernel function's body can be seen in Figure 11.3.

```
void Newton( size_t n, real dt ) {
  const real dtG = dt * G;
  #pragma omp parallel
  {
    #pragma omp for schedule( auto )
    for ( size_t i = 0; i < n; ++i ) {
      real dvx = 0, dvy = 0, dvz = 0;
      #pragma omp simd
      for ( size_t j = 0; j < i; ++j ) {
        real dx = x[j] - x[i], dy = y[j] - y[i],
             dz = z[j] - z[i];
        real dist2 = dx*dx + dy*dy + dz*dz;
        real mjOverDist3 = m[j] /
             (dist2 * Sqrt( dist2 ));
        dvx += mjOverDist3 * dx;
        dvy += mjOverDist3 * dy;
        dvz += mjOverDist3 * dz;
      }
      #pragma omp simd
      for ( size_t j = i+1; j < n; ++j ) {
        real dx = x[j] - x[i], dy = y[j] - y[i],
             dz = z[j] - z[i];
        real dist2 = dx*dx + dy*dy + dz*dz;
        real mjOverDist3 = m[j] /
             (dist2 * Sqrt( dist2 ));
        dvx += mjOverDist3 * dx;
        dvy += mjOverDist3 * dy;
        dvz += mjOverDist3 * dz;
      }
      vx[i] += dvx * dtG;
      vy[i] += dvy * dtG;
      vz[i] += dvz * dtG;
    }
    #pragma omp for simd schedule( auto )
    for ( size_t i = 0; i < n; ++i ) {
      x[i] += vx[i] * dt;
      y[i] += vy[i] * dt;
      z[i] += vz[i] * dt;
    }
  }
}
```

FIGURE 11.3

Our optimized N-Body gravitational kernel.

We can now test our N-Body kernel, both on an Intel Xeon processor and also on an Intel Xeon Phi coprocessor running in native mode (Figure 11.4). In order to do so, we write a program, which allocates and fills the position and velocity arrays with random initial conditions, and subsequently calls the `Newton` kernel function for a given number of iterations. For the simulations we discuss here, we choose n=50,000 particles, a time step, dt=0.01 and allow the system to evolve over 1 s of "simulated" time, which in this case represents 100 iterations. Using the Intel compiler, we compile the code for both the processor and native mode on the coprocessor and run it on our development platform.[1] Figure 11.5 shows strong scaling of the code over OpenMP threads for separate runs on the Intel

FIGURE 11.4

Unequal work distribution is inefficient. We could easily give the processor or coprocessor all the work while the other sits idle. These wasteful scenarios are the motivation for the load-balancing techniques described in this chapter.

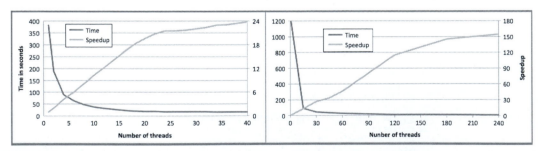

FIGURE 11.5

Strong scaling of our kernel over OpenMP threads running on two processors (left) and on coprocessor (right).

---

[1]Compute node with two 10 cores Intel Xeon E5-2660 v2 processors and two 60 cores Intel Xeon Phi 5110P coprocessors.

Xeon processor and Intel Xeon Phi coprocessor, respectively, where good scalability is demonstrated on both. It is worth noting that the code exploits the hardware threading capability not only on the coprocessor (which is to be expected) but also on the processor, where we gain an extra 21% from the use of hardware threads on the processor (also called hyper-threads). Ultimately, the minimum times are obtained with the number of threads corresponding to the ones used by default by the Intel runtime library, which means that in our case, not setting OMP_NUM_THREADS at all leads to optimal performance. These are the conditions which we will continue to use throughout the rest of this chapter.

The absolute performance (in both single and double precision) on both the host and device, respectively, can be seen in Figure 11.6. There it can be seen that we achieve a 2.17× and 3.19× speedup on the Intel Xeon Phi coprocessor relative to our two 10-core Ivy Bridge Intel Xeon processors, in single and double precision, respectively. If we consider our square root to be a normal floating-point operation, this corresponds to a performance (in single precision) of approximately 125 GFLOPs on the Intel Xeon processor and 540 GFLOPs on an Intel Xeon Phi coprocessor. This means that our simple N-Body kernel (in single precision) can exploit 36% of the processor's peak performance and 27% of the coprocessor's peak performance, which is a respectable achievement, considering the small amount of effort we put into optimizing the kernel.

From this solid ground (Figure 11.7), we can now confidently start our journey to a fully integrated code.

THE OFFLOADED VERSION

Our goal here will be to simply enable the offload mode in our code, running the program on the host processor and pushing the computation and data to a coprocessor (Figure 11.7). To do this, we only need to add three extra OpenMP directives:

- A "#pragma omp declare target" and its corresponding "#pragma omp end declare target" surrounding all variable and function definitions to be used on the coprocessor. This will force the compiler to generate two versions of these, one for the processor and the other for the coprocessor, and to link both into our binary.

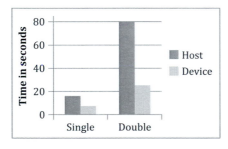

FIGURE 11.6

Time to completion in seconds for our code on two (host) processors and one (device) coprocessor (lower is better).

FIGURE 11.7

Now that they are aware of each other, the host and device are in a position to cooperate on sharing the workload.

- A "#pragma omp target" immediately before the "#pragma omp parallel" inside our Newton function. This will instruct the compiler to offload the computation onto the first available Intel Xeon Phi coprocessor device on the machine.
- And finally, a "#pragma omp target data" immediately before the main loop where our Newton function is called, as shown in Figure 11.8. This directive will instruct the compiler to allocate on the device the memory required for the various arrays listed, to copy their initial value from host to the device before proceeding any further, and finally to also retrieve the value of the ones listed as "map(tofrom:)" from the device upon exit of the for loop.

We can now run our new offloaded version of the code and compare its performance to the native processor and native coprocessor versions, results for which can be seen in Figure 11.9.

So, at this point we now have a code that we run as usual (without the need of directly logging into an Intel Xeon Phi coprocessor) and which incurs only a small performance penalty relative to its native counterpart. It is now time to use the processor and coprocessor resources available on our development system in a combined manner, so as to exploit the system to its full potential.

```
#pragma omp target data \
        map( tofrom: x[0:n], y[0:n], z[0:n] ) \
        map( to: vx[0:n], vy[0:n], vz[0:n], m[0:n] )
for ( int it = 0; it < 100; ++it ) {
    Newton( n, 0.01 );
}
```

FIGURE 11.8

The data offloading OpenMP directive for our N-Body kernel call.

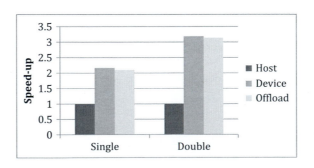

FIGURE 11.9

Speedup of the code (in single and double precision) compared to two Intel Xeon E5-2660 v2 Ivy Bridge processors (higher is better) for three versions of the code: native on host processor, native on coprocessor, and offloaded to the coprocessor.

A FIRST PROCESSOR COMBINED WITH COPROCESSOR VERSION

Our goal now is to find a way of:

1. offloading only a partial amount of the workload to the Intel Xeon Phi coprocessor, while retaining the rest of the workload for computing on the Intel Xeon processor (host) and
2. making sure that only the right amount of work is delegated to the device, so that both host and device can run in parallel for the same duration of time. This point is the key to ensure that no time is wasted while one compute device is waiting for the other one to finish its share of the work (Figure 11.10).

Of course, since at every single time step of the computation, the system needs to have a full up-to-date view of the particles' positions and velocities, this host-device distribution of work also implies some data transfers during each time step. These extra data transfers will not only have to be managed carefully to ensure code correctness, but may also have a significant impact on the performance.

So, how can we address these points? The first stage will be, for allowing the host and device parts to run concurrently, to create two threads, each managing one part. This can easily be achieved by enclosing our time loop with a "`#pragma omp parallel num_threads(2)`" directive. However, this has some consequences for the host part of our code:

- To allow for the computation to continue to run in parallel on the host, we need to allow nested OpenMP parallelism. Fortunately, this only requires the additional call to "`omp_set_nested(true)`" in the initialization section of our code.

FIGURE 11.10

Workloads can be tailored to match individual capabilities. This can help minimize idle time on the processor and coprocessor by matching the time each takes to complete.

- Managing our device will require one dedicated OpenMP thread on the host, and will therefore reduce by one the number of threads available for computation on the host side. This will have a limited impact for hosts with a large number of cores like our testing machine, but could become noticeable otherwise.

Once this first step has been addressed, the next step is to distribute the work over the host and device. Here again, the principle is quite simple and consists in slightly modifying our Newton function so that it accepts two extra input parameters, corresponding to the "start" and "end" indices of the i loop. Inside the Newton function, we simply use these extra parameters to limit the scope of the loop over i to the allocated amount of work. In addition, to selectively offload the computation to the device, we can add an extra "if (n0 == 0)" clause to our initial "#pragma omp target," where n0 is our "start" index input parameter. In this way, only the first set of iterations of the entire loop over i will be offloaded to our device, while the rest will remain on the host.

At this stage we need to ensure that the data on the host and device are synchronized at the end of each time step. For this, we will use an OpenMP directive "#pragma omp target update" followed by the list of data to send to or retrieve from the device. To ensure data consistency, we also need to put a barrier before and after the update. Moreover, since these exchanges must only be made by one thread, we can enclose them in a "#pragma omp single" directive, which also includes an implicit barrier at its end, sparing the corresponding explicit call. Once this is done, almost everything is in place for permitting us to run our code, but the computation of the ratio of work to offload to the device relative to the amount to be retained on the host. Let's now see how to proceed.

We first assume that both the host and the device have a given "speed" for computing, which we don't know initially, but which we assume is fixed. The speed of each compute device can be expressed in iterations per second for the outer i loop over particles inside our Newton function. In order to balance workload over the compute device, we dynamically adjust the number of iterations according to the measured speed at each time step so that the times for completing the Newton function on the host and device are identical. This leads to the following equation:

$$r' = \frac{t_h r}{t_h r + t_d (1 - r)} \tag{11.3}$$

where r is the ratio of work done on the device at the previous iteration, r' is the new ratio to be used in the next iteration, t_h is the time spent on computation on the host, and t_d is the time spend on computation of the device.

Using the above formula, we can now compute the optimal amount of work to offload to the device at each time step, provided we measure the time taken for computing on both compute devices at the previous iteration. For initial conditions, we simply set our ratio to an arbitrary value of 0.5 and we let the system adjust it automatically.

Our main function will now look as in Figure 11.11. The absolute performance of the code in Figure 11.11 can be seen in Figure 11.12.

In Figure 11.13, we show the computed workload ratio at each time step, where it can be seen that, once passed a short warming-up phase, its value stabilizes to approximately 0.7 (single precision) and 0.76 (double precision), which is consistent with the timings we measured previously.

One last remark about this version of the code is, at the moment, the data updates are carried out sequentially by one single thread. It would be relatively straightforward to update the data in parallel with, for example, the first thread managing the updates to x[], y[], and z[], and the second thread

```
omp_set_nested( true );
double ratio = 0.5;
double tth[2];
#pragma omp target data \
        map( to: x[0:n], y[0:n], z[0:n], \
                 vx[0:n], vy[0:n], vz[0:n], m[0:n] )
{
  #pragma omp parallel num_threads( 2 )
  {
    const int tid = omp_get_thread_num();
    for ( int it = 0; it < 100; ++it ) {
      size_t lim = n * ratio;
      size_t l = n - lim;
      double tt = omp_get_wtime();
      Newton( lim*tid, lim + l*tid, n, 0.01 );
      tth[tid] = omp_get_wtime() - tt;
      #pragma omp barrier
      #pragma omp single
      {
        #pragma omp target update \
                from( x[0:lim], y[0:lim], z[0:lim], \
                      vx[0:lim], vy[0:lim], vz[0:lim] )
        #pragma omp target update \
                to( x[lim:l], y[lim:l], z[lim:l], \
                    vx[lim:l], vy[lim:l], vz[lim:l] )
        ratio = ratio*tth[1] /
                (ratio*tth[1] + (1- ratio)*tth[0]);
      }
    }
  }
}
```

FIGURE 11.11

Balanced host plus one device N-Body kernel call.

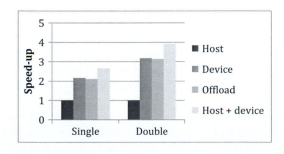

FIGURE 11.12

Speedup (in single and double precision) of several versions of our N-Body code relative to two Intel Xeon E5-2660 v2 Ivy Bridge processors (higher is better).

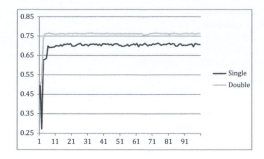

FIGURE 11.13

Evolution of the ratio of work offloaded to the Intel Xeon Phi coprocessor.

doing the same for vx[], vy[], and vz[]. This would have the interesting consequence of taking full advantage of the bidirectional capability of the PCI express bus connecting the Intel Xeon Phi co-processor to the host. However, in our case, the negligible measured performance improvement does not justify the increased complexity in the code. A version of it including this refinement is nonetheless provided in the downloadable code bundle.

VERSION FOR PROCESSOR WITH MULTIPLE COPROCESSORS

Until now, we assumed the existence of at least one Intel Xeon Phi coprocessor device on our machine. However, if several such devices are available, our code is only able to take advantage of a single co-processor. Let's now see how to address the case of an arbitrary number of devices in our code, where we continue to exploit the coprocessors as transparently and effectively as possible (Figure 11.14). To achieve this, we will make use of two extra features that OpenMP 4.0 offers us:

- A runtime library function "omp_get_num_devices()" allowing for the retrieval of the number of usable devices on the current system.
- An extra "device(*dev*)" statement applicable to the various "#pragma omp target" directives we have in the code, defining the index of the device the statement applies to.

These two features are all that we need to allow us to reach our goal of full-code versatility: we can discover the number of usable devices and access each of them individually, depending on some conditional statement we define. But we still need to figure out how to modify our code so that we can allocate and transfer arrays to an arbitrary number of devices. Indeed, at the moment, if we were simply to adapt our previous version to an arbitrary number of devices, our main code would be as shown in Figure 11.15.

As we can see from Figure 11.15, it seems difficult, maybe even impossible, to enclose our parallel construct into an arbitrary number of "target data" directives—one per device. However, by simply realizing that we can swap the "target data" and the "parallel" directives, the issue gets solved quite easily. Indeed, instead of trying to have all our devices managed by our master thread for the data allocation, we simply delegate this to as many threads as are needed, each managing at most one single device. The previous code snippet therefore becomes as shown in Figure 11.16.

FIGURE 11.14

More muscle can join to help accomplish even more; once we have load balancing we can envision adding more processors or coprocessors to share the burden.

```
const int dev = omp_get_num_devices();
#pragma omp target data device( ?? ) \
        map( to: x[0:n], y[0:n], z[0:n], m[0:n], \
                 vx[0:n], vy[0:n], vz[0:n] )
{
  #pragma omp parallel num_threads( dev + 1 )
  {
    const int tid = omp_get_thread_num();
    for ( int it = 0; it < 100; ++it ) {
      ...
```

FIGURE 11.15

A nonworking approach for the multidevice version.

```
const int dev = omp_get_num_devices();
#pragma omp parallel num_threads( dev + 1 )
{
  int tid = omp_get_thread_num();
  #pragma omp target data device( tid ) if( tid < dev ) \
          map( to: x[0:n], y[0:n], z[0:n], m[0:n], \
                   vx[0:n], vy[0:n], vz[0:n] )
  {
    for ( int it = 0; it < 100; ++it ) {
      ...
```

FIGURE 11.16

A working approach for the multidevice version.

To complete our code, we now only need to compute the balance of workload over each of the compute devices available to us, and to adjust the data updates after each time step. The principle for computing the ratios is the same as that used previously, and relies on the assumption that each compute device runs at its own fixed speed. The desired goal that all of them compute their share of the work in the same amount of time leads to the following formula:

$$\forall i,j \in \{0,\dots, \text{dev}\} \frac{r'_i}{r_i} t_i = \frac{r'_j}{r_j} t_j, \tag{11.4}$$

where r and t are the ratio and time, respectively, i and j are device indices, and r' is the ratio for the next iteration. As we also know that

$$\sum_{i=0}^{\text{dev}} r'_i = 1, \tag{11.5}$$

we can subsequently deduce that

$$\forall j \in \{0,\dots, \text{dev}\} r'_j = \frac{r_j}{t_j \sum \frac{r_i}{t_i}}. \tag{11.6}$$

Since what we actually want to compute are starting indices (or displacements within the arrays) for the loop over i, we can use the function computeDisplacements in Figure 11.17 for doing so. Regarding the data updates after each time step, there are two points we must pay attention to.

• Since potentially several devices will have to update the host side with data they computed, it is far better for performance reasons (although not mandatory) to make the updates one at a time for a given array. This is why we will enclose our "update from" directives inside a "critical" section. Moreover, we will add a barrier after it to make sure that the host data have been fully updated before sending the updated arrays back to the devices. As for the previous version of the code, we certainly could take advantage of the multiple arrays we have to update to still keep a level of parallelism in this phase, but the complexity it would introduce compared to the expected gain makes it counterproductive here.

```
void computeDisplacements( size_t *displ,
        const double *tth, int dev ) {
  double sumLengthOverT = 0;
  size_t length[dev+1];
  for ( int i = 0; i < dev+1; ++i )
    length[i] = displ[i+1] - displ[i];
  for ( int i = 0; i < dev+1; ++i )
    sumLengthOverT += length[i] / tth[i];
  for ( int i = 0; i < dev; ++i )
    displ[i+1] = displ[i] + round( (displ[dev+1] * length[i]) /
                            (tth[i] *sumLengthOverT) );
}
```

FIGURE 11.17

Function computing new displacements after each time step where we assumed that we initialize displ[0] to 0 and displ[dev+1] to n.

- Since each device already has its previous chunk of data up-to-date, only the complement needs to be sent from the host. This can be done using at most two array segments. Moreover, since here we have no risk of data inconsistency, data send to all devices can be done in parallel.

Our final loop can be seen in Figure 11.18. We can now run our code on our machine containing two Intel Xeon Phi coprocessor devices, where absolute performance results for the latest version of the code relative to previous versions can be seen in Figure 11.19.

Figure 11.20 shows how the workload (ratio of number of particles) is dynamically balanced over the Intel Xeon processor and the two Intel Xeon Phi coprocessors available on our development platform, where it can be clearly seen that, after a warming-up phase for the first few iterations, the balance of workload evolves to a steady state. In this way, we can see that, although the second device performs slightly better than the first one,[2] the method adapts transparently to deliver nearly optimal performance.

At this stage, we can consider that the code is ready to dynamically adapt itself to its run-time environment in order to efficiently exploit all available resources. However, we can think of some extra refinements which would make it even more resilient to other possible situations.

- The transfers could be timed individually to evaluate their impact.
- In the case where some compute device on the platform is so slow compared to other devices, due to its intrinsic performance or due to the transfer times it incurs, we could allow for the option of completely disregarding it.

```
for ( int it = 0; it < 100; ++it ) {
    size_t s = displ[tid], l = displ[tid+1] - displ[tid];
    double tt = omp_get_wtime();
    Newton( n, s, l, 0.01, tid, dev );
    tth[tid] = omp_get_wtime() - tt;
    #pragma omp critical
    {
      #pragma omp target update device( tid ) \
              if( tid < dev ) \
              from( x[s:l], y[s:l], z[s:l], \
                    vx[s:l], vy[s:l], vz[s:l] )
    }
    #pragma omp barrier
    #pragma omp target update device( tid ) \
            if( tid < dev ) \
            to( x[0:s], y[0:s], z[0:s], \
                vx[0:s], vy[0:s], vz[0:s] )
    size_t s1 = s+l, l1 = n-s-l;
    #pragma omp target update device( tid ) \
            if( tid < dev ) \
            to( x[s1:l1], y[s1:l1], z[s1:l1], \
                vx[s1:l1], vy[s1:l1], vz[s1:l1] )
    #pragma omp single
    computeDisplacements( displ, tth, dev );
}
```

FIGURE 11.18

Our final main time loop.

[2]We verified this difference in performance by a separate mean.

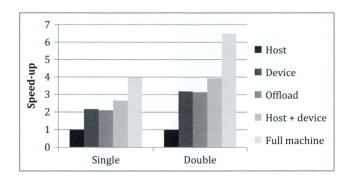

FIGURE 11.19

Speedup of the latest version of the code in single and double precision relative to two Intel Xeon E5-2660 v2 Ivy Bridge processors (higher is better).

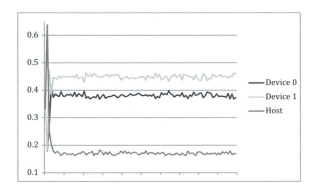

FIGURE 11.20

Evolution of the ratios of workload for all devices, including the host processors on our development platform.

Both refinements are worth exploring and should be considered by developers interested in releasing optimal code. However, they fall beyond the scope of this chapter and would make the example code we provide far less concise and readable.

FOR MORE INFORMATION

Here are some additional reading materials we recommend related to this chapter:

- Newton's law of motion, http://en.wikipedia.org/wiki/Newton%27s_laws.
- Newton's law of universal gravitation, http://wikipedia.org/wiki/Newton%27s_law_of_universal_gravitation.
- OpenMP 4.0 standard specifications, http://www.openmp.org/mp-documents/OpenMP4.0.0.pdf.
- Download the code from this and other chapters, http://lotsofcores.com.

CONCURRENT KERNEL OFFLOADING

12

Florian Wende[*], **Michael Klemm**[†], **Thomas Steinke**[*], **and Alexander Reinefeld**[*]

[*]*Zuse Institute Berlin, Germany,* [†]*Intel, Germany*

The Intel® Xeon Phi™ product family offers powerful devices for workloads that can take advantage of parallelism at different levels of granularity. All of the computational resources available on Intel Xeon Phi coprocessors can be utilized when large data sets need to be processed.

> *But is the coprocessor attractive for small-scale workloads that cannot exploit the provided resources on their own?*

In this chapter, we show how to leverage the potential of the Intel Xeon Phi coprocessor for workloads that process small data sets, but many of them. This is important since an increasing number of innovative algorithms support execution flows with multiple levels of parallelism. When work is placed on Intel Xeon Phi coprocessors from within parallel instances of the host program, a sufficient load on the coprocessor can be generated.

NOTE

Our ultimate optimization target in this chapter is to improve the computational throughput of multiple small-scale workloads on the Intel Xeon Phi coprocessor by concurrent kernel offloading.

SETTING THE CONTEXT

Concurrent kernel offloading to the Intel Xeon Phi coprocessor is the ultimate means for certain classes of workloads and production environments to improve both computational throughput and resource utilization. Potential usage scenarios in this respect, using a single coprocessor device for simplicity, are summarized in Figure 12.1.

- **Single host process or thread offloads to a dedicated coprocessor:** These setups are typical for today's HPC production environments where only a single user job is allocated per compute node.
  - *Single offloads* with huge data sets can effectively utilize the coprocessor resources (Figure 12.1a).
  - *Multiple sequential offloads* with varying computational intensity may result in underutilization of the coprocessor (Figure 12.1b).
  - *Multiple concurrent (small-scale) offloads* can improve device utilization (Figure 12.1c).

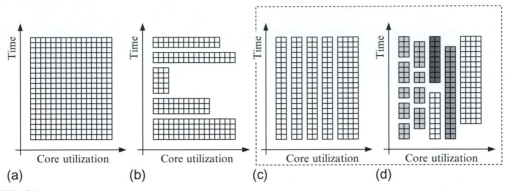

FIGURE 12.1

Scenarios for kernel offloading to the Intel Xeon Phi coprocessor: a single host process or thread (a) utilizes the entire coprocessor device, (b) sequentially offloads multiple kernels with varying computational intensity and hence varying core utilization, and (c) offloads multiple concurrent kernels to the coprocessor. (d) Multiple host processes or threads offload (multiple) kernels to a shared coprocessor each.

- **Multiple host processes or threads offload to a shared coprocessor:** A typical example is a throughput-oriented single-user production environment with complex workflows or concurrent execution steps (Figure 12.1d).
- **Offloading to a shared remote coprocessor:** If the coprocessor is virtualized, multiple workloads from remote nodes can be executed on it (Figure 12.1d). However, additional scheduling policies should be considered to avoid resource oversubscription. This is a typical scenario for cloud environments where not all nodes are equipped with coprocessors.

This chapter focuses on concurrent offloading from applications that use either MPI or OpenMP to achieve parallelism on the host, as shown in Figure 12.1c and d. There are many real-world use cases with potential for concurrent offloading. They range from simple batch processing of small-scale loads to sophisticated (parallel) applications with cooperating offloads. Beside presenting generic representatives, we will also cover useful techniques regarding the host and coprocessor setup in these cases.

MOTIVATING EXAMPLE: PARTICLE DYNAMICS

A core part in particle dynamics (PD) simulations is to evaluate for each of N particles the force $\mathbf{F}_i = \sum_{j \neq i} \mathbf{F}_{ij}$ exerted by all other particles $j \neq i$ on particle i, and to use these forces to evolve the entire system over time via numerical integration of the equations of motion. Symmetries in the forces can help reduce the effort for the force computation by a factor of two by using Newton's 3rd law: $\mathbf{F}_{ij} = -\mathbf{F}_{ji}$. While evaluating the forces sequentially is straight forward, doing the same in parallel poses difficulties with memory constraints and synchronization. The problem is that forces $\mathbf{F}_i$ now have contributions $\mathbf{F}_{ij}$ from different threads. A simple approach is to allocate for each thread a separate buffer to hold all its force contributions, and to merge the buffers afterwards. However, the memory consumption then increases with the number of threads.

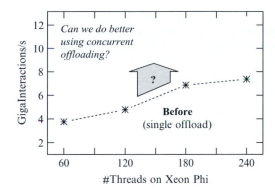

FIGURE 12.2

Performance of a PD simulation with 16k particles using Newton's 3rd law for the force computation. The performance metric is billion particle-particle interactions per second: "GigaInteractions/s" for short (larger values are better).

We can do better with just one additional buffer, unfortunately, at the cost of explicit barrier synchronization (see Section "Force computation in PD using concurrent kernel offloading"). Figure 12.2 shows the performance of a PD simulation using this approach. For the data points, a single offload kernel is placed on an Intel Xeon Phi coprocessor, and the number of threads used for the force computation is increased from 60 to 240.

The performance obviously does not scale with the number of threads. In fact, we found acceptable scaling behavior in the 16k-particle case just for up to about 30 threads. Hence, the question is:

Can we improve the performance by using 8 concurrent offloads solving 1/8-th of the entire problem using 30 threads each, instead of making 240 threads do the whole job within one large offload?

The answer to this question is yes, but there are a few technicalities that we need to consider. We will now go through these technicalities and then come back to the PD application.

ORGANIZATION OF THIS CHAPTER

When offloading multiple concurrent kernels to the Intel Xeon Phi coprocessor, the partitioning of the device is most important. Placing work on the coprocessor without setting up the stage appropriately may result in degraded performance, because groups of threads may interfere with each other in an unfortunate way. In Section "Coprocessor device partitioning and thread affinity," we show how to achieve a particular thread-to-core mapping on the coprocessor in the concurrent case. We study the impact of different affinities on the performance of multiple small-scale `dgemm` computations, using the Intel Math Kernel Library (MKL), to emphasize the significance of well-conceived thread placements.

Apart from the kernel execution, data transfers between the host and the coprocessor also affect the performance. They are needed at least at the beginning and at the end of the host execution. Frequent data transfers between successive kernel offloads—as is the case for iterative algorithms—can slow down an application significantly in the concurrent case, even though they seem to have minor impact when only a single host thread or process offloads to the coprocessor. In Section "Concurrent data transfers," we investigate the impact of data transfers between host and coprocessor on the program performance using the concurrent MKL `dgemm` computation as representative. In particular, we show important differences when offloading from MPI and OpenMP in a concurrent setup.

Finally, in Section "Force computation in PD using concurrent kernel offloading," we apply concurrent kernel offloading to a PD simulation, and demonstrate how multiple small-scale offloads can outperform a single large-scale offload solving the same problem. Our investigations in this respect address the use case of cooperating concurrent kernel offloading.

NOTE: HARDWARE AND SOFTWARE SETUP

For coprocessor benchmarks, we use a dual-socket Intel® Xeon® X5680 processor-based system with 24 GB main memory and two Intel Xeon Phi 7120P coprocessors installed in PCIe x16 slots. Each coprocessor provides 61 physical CPU cores with 4-way hardware multi-threading, and 16 GB main memory. For benchmarking, we use just 60 of the physical cores, as it is best to leave one core for the operating system on the coprocessor when using offload. The host runs a CentOS 6.3 Linux with kernel 2.6.32-279 and with Intel MPSS 3.1.4 installed. Codes are compiled using the Intel C++ compiler 14.0.3 and Intel MPI 4.1.1.036. We use compile flags `-O3 -xHost -openmp -fno-alias -opt-assume-safe-padding -std=c++11`.

For processor benchmarks, we use a dual-socket Intel Xeon E5 2670 compute node with 32 logical CPU cores (Hyper-Threading enabled). The system is equipped with 64 GB main memory, runs a CentOS 6.3 Linux with kernel 2.6.32-279, and provides a software stack that is comparable to that of our coprocessor benchmarking system.

Throughout this chapter, we use Intel's Language Extension for Offload (LEO) for code samples. Codes can be translated to OpenMP 4.0, using the new "target" directive, with minor modifications. We have done so and we are supplying versions using OpenMP 4.0 with the downloads. However, for consistency, we give all code snippets using LEO in this chapter. Complete source codes are downloadable from http://lotsofcores.com with versions using LEO and versions using OpenMP 4.0 target directives.

CONCURRENT KERNELS ON THE COPROCESSOR

The offload model is the standard means to involve the Intel Xeon Phi coprocessor into a host program that is not entirely parallel, and hence, not a candidate for native execution. As an autonomous coprocessor to the host, the simultaneous execution of multiple offloaded program sections is natively supported on Intel Xeon Phi. However, placing work on it without giving thought about the appropriate thread-to-core mapping, may cause interference between multiple concurrent offloads.

COPROCESSOR DEVICE PARTITIONING AND THREAD AFFINITY

The Intel Xeon Phi coprocessor runs a Linux operating system which, besides providing services to the user, is responsible for scheduling work to the coprocessor's CPU cores. To achieve parallelism on the coprocessor, both the OpenMP and MPI programming models are natively supported, however in offloaded code sections, OpenMP is the usual means. Similar to executing OpenMP programs on the host system, specific thread placements are accessible via environment variables like `KMP_AFFINITY` and `OMP_PLACES`. The effect of setting these environment variables in the non-concurrent case is well known. When multiple host threads or processes offload work to the coprocessors concurrently, however, it is not. In order to figure out the effect of the different placement schemes, we use the code from

```
#pragma omp parallel num_threads(m)   // m threads on the host
{
  int hostId=omp_get_thread_num();
  #pragma offload target(mic:0)
  {
    #pragma omp parallel num_threads(n)   // n threads per offload
    {
      int phiId=omp_get_thread_num();
      cpu_set_t cpuMask;
      sched_getaffinity(0,sizeof(cpu_set_t),&cpuMask);
      printf("thread(hostId=%d,phiId=%d): ",hostId,phiId);
      for(int i=0;i<256;i++)
        if(CPU_ISSET(i,&cpuMask))
          printf("%d ",i);
      printf("\n");
    }
  }
}
```

FIGURE 12.3

Determining the thread-to-core mapping.

Figure 12.3. The CPU mask of a particular thread can be obtained via sched_getaffinity() (see listing). The CPU cores on which this thread can execute on can then be extracted from the bits of its CPU mask.

To establish particular parameters of environment variables on the coprocessor—maybe different from those used on the host—we set the host environment variable MIC_ENV_PREFIX to MIC. The offload runtime then is triggered on the coprocessor to override parameters assigned to XXX by those assigned to MIC_XXX.

MIC_KMP_AFFINITY can be assigned parameters, for example, compact, scatter and balanced. MIC_OMP_PLACES can be set to, for example, threads, cores and sockets. We found the "balanced" scheme does not work as expected in the concurrent case. The "sockets" placement on the Intel Xeon Phi coprocessor does not make sense, as it has just one socket. For the other placement schemes, we will investigate the resulting thread-core assignment in the concurrent case when offloading from OpenMP and MPI.

Offloading from OpenMP host program

Setting the MIC_KMP_AFFINITY environment variable to scatter or compact results in each thread on the coprocessor being assigned exactly one logical CPU core. When using scatter, all threads are distributed across the entire system with non-unit stride regarding the logical core IDs, whereas with compact, the threads are placed as close as possible, filling up the physical cores one after another. When offloading concurrently to the coprocessor, parallel regions within offloaded sections are created concurrently, too. As a result of this, it is not guaranteed that threads within the same offload region are assigned contiguous (logical) core IDs. For the scatter scheme this should be immaterial, since none of the coprocessor cores is distinguished over the others. However, for the "compact" scheme, threads within the same offload region might be mapped to different physical cores even if they would fit on a single physical core.

MIC_OMP_PLACES=threads and MIC_KMP_AFFINITY=compact have the same effect. With MIC_OMP_PLACES=cores, threads are assigned entire physical cores. If the total number of threads spawned on the coprocessor is larger than its physical core count, logical cores will be

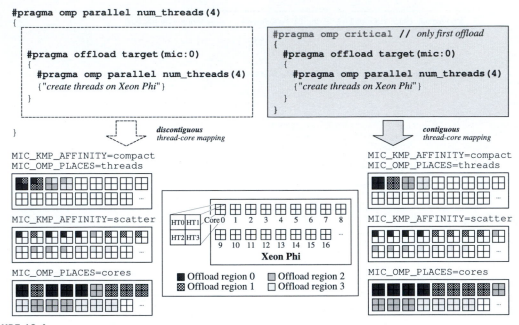

FIGURE 12.4

Thread-core assignment for environment variables `MIC_KMP_AFFINITY` and `MIC_OMP_PLACES` with their particular parameters. The schematic is for $m = 4$ host threads offloading to the coprocessor and spawning $n = 4$ threads within the offloaded region each. Coprocessor cores are represented by squares that consist of four tiles—one tile per hardware thread (HT0..3). Different box types highlight the thread-core assignment within concurrent offloads. The left-hand side mappings are discontiguous: threads within the same offload region are not assigned contiguous (logical) cores (see the "compact" scheme). This behavior is fixed on the right-hand side, by offloading to the coprocessor mutually exclusively at program start.

multi-allocated. Threads belonging to different offload regions then can reside on the same physical core. These threads then potentially interfere with each other in an unfortunate way.

The effect of the different thread placement schemes is illustrated in Figure 12.4 for $m = 4$ host threads offloading to the coprocessor, and with $n = 4$ threads within each offload region. The discontiguous thread-core mapping becomes obvious on the left-hand side of Figure 12.4 (e.g., for the "compact" scheme). Offload programs with cache-optimization may see performance degradation in this case.

To remove the discontiguous thread-to-core mapping in the concurrent offloading case, a simple workaround (or "fix") is to mutually exclusively offload to the coprocessor right at the beginning of the program, and to spawn all needed threads within that offload region before the actual offload computation. In Figure 12.3 we need to place a `critical` region around the first offload, as is shown on the right-hand side of Figure 12.4.

However, executing the respective program twice does not guarantee the same thread-core assignments. To overcome the last issue, threads can be explicitly assigned cores via the Linux scheduler interface, e. g., using `sched_setaffinity()`, as illustrated in Figure 12.5.

```
#pragma offload target(mic:0)
{
    #pragma omp parallel num_threads(4)  // four threads on Xeon Phi
    {
        int threadId=omp_get_thread_num();
        cpu_set_t cpuMask;
        CPU_ZERO(&cpuMask);  // clear cpuset
        CPU_SET(1+2*4+threadId,&cpuMask);  // use 3rd physical core
        sched_setaffinity(0,sizeof(cpu_set_t),&cpuMask);
    }
}
```

FIGURE 12.5

Explicit thread-to-core mapping on the coprocessor using the Linux scheduler interface. In this example, we consider a single offloaded region with $n = 4$ threads, and we want all four threads to reside on the third physical core.

NOTE

When offloading to the coprocessor concurrently from multi-threaded applications, it is meaningful in a first step to offload to the coprocessor mutually exclusively and to spawn coprocessor-side threads before the actual offload computation. In this way, thread affinities within the offloaded regions meet the parameters assigned to MIC_KMP_AFFINITY and MIC_OMP_PLACES.

Offloading from MPI host program

Concurrent offloading from within different MPI processes poses the difficulty that principally each process assumes the coprocessor is used exclusively without interfering with other processes.

Setting environment variables like MIC_KMP_AFFINITY or MIC_OMP_PLACES affects only the individual processes, but does not address the partitioning of the coprocessor together with thread placement. Particularly, the per-process offload runtimes do not coordinate their offloading and hence will map threads that are spawned on the coprocessor on the same execution units, resulting in over-subscription of coprocessor cores.

An obvious solution to this issue is to implement an explicit thread pinning scheme, for example, using sched_setaffinity(), together with some logic to partition the device across multiple processes. However, it is possible to achieve the same effect by means of the MIC_KMP_PLACE_THREADS=XXc,YYt,ZZO environment variable which can allow the coprocessor to be partitioned into multiple chunks. In particular, the partition (XXc,YYt,ZZO) is a set of XX successive coprocessor cores starting from core ZZ, where the first YY $\in \{1,2,3,4\}$ hardware threads per core are available for computation. Environment variables MIC_KMP_AFFINITY and MIC_OMP_PLACES then determine the thread-core assignment within the partition(s) when offloading.

For example, if we want $m = 2$ MPI processes to offload computations to a single Intel Xeon Phi coprocessor 7xxx device, using $n = 60$ threads per offload each, we can do as follows:

```
$> mpirun -genv MIC_OMP_NUM_THREADS=60
-np 1 -env MIC_KMP_PLACE_THREADS=30c,2t,0O ./prog.x :
-np 1 -env MIC_KMP_PLACE_THREADS=30c,2t,30O ./prog.x
```

NOTE

Establishing a particular thread pinning scheme within offloaded regions from MPI applications requires either explicit thread-core assignment on the coprocessor, or device partitioning and thread placement, e.g., via `MIC_KMP_PLACE_THREADS` together with `MIC_KMP_AFFINITY` or `MIC_OMP_PLACES`.

Case study: concurrent Intel MKL dgemm offloading

BLAS (basic linear algebra subprograms) is essential to many scientific codes. Parallel applications that throughout their thread or process execution paths make intensive use of matrix-matrix multiplication might benefit from placing this portion of the work on the coprocessor for a faster execution.

We consider multiple concurrent OpenMP threads and MPI processes that progressively offload the execution of MKL `dgemm` to the coprocessor. `dgemm` is a particularly suited example to assess the impact of different thread-core assignment schemes on the overall program performance for at least two reasons: first, MKL `dgemm` is cache-optimized, so that unfortunate thread placements should have negative impact on the overall performance, and second, it is not memory bound. The second point allows us to actually study the placement aspect without being affected by all concurrent offloads sharing the coprocessor's main memory bandwidth.

The core of our benchmark program is given in Figure 12.6. Additional data transfers between host and coprocessor will be considered in Section "Concurrent data transfers." For now, we will focus on the offload computation.

NOTE: TIMING CONCURRENT KERNELS

To assess the performance of multiple concurrent computations on the coprocessor, we note the start and stop time for each of multiple offloads per thread or process, and afterwards determine the time frame (or "concurrency window") in which all threads or processes have overlapping offloads. The concurrency window is then given by the latest start time of the first offload and the earliest stop time of the last offload across all threads or processes. Within that time frame, we assume 100% concurrency. By counting the number of offloads that fall in the concurrency window, we can derive our performance metric.

In the case of `dgemm`, we multiply the number of offloads in the concurrency window by the number of floating point operations per matrix-matrix multiplication, and divide this value by the window length. This way, we obtain floating point operations per second (Flops/s) for a particular run. In all cases our approach tends to underestimate the actual compute performance, but it never overestimates it. This is important as otherwise our results would be too optimistic.

The floating point performance for up to $m = 15$ concurrent offloads with $n = 16$ OpenMP threads on an Intel Xeon Phi coprocessor is illustrated in Figure 12.7. Performance values are for 2048×2048 matrices and for different thread-core assignments. Each host thread or process offloads 100 `dgemm` computations to the coprocessor. We compare the performance obtained by offloading from OpenMP and MPI host, respectively. For MPI runs, we use the `MIC_KMP_PLACE_THREADS` environment variable to achieve the desired device partitioning.

The left-hand side sub-plot illustrates the performance gap between explicit thread pinning on the coprocessor via `sched_setaffinity()`, and using environment variables without our "fix." Our explicit thread pinning resembles the "compact" scheme. In this case, threads involved into the same matrix-matrix multiplication can share the same physical core's L1 cache. Hence, the negative effect of

```
..
double start[15][numOffloads],stop[15][numOffloads];
#pragma omp parallel num_threads(15)
{
   double *a=_mm_malloc(N*N*sizeof(double),64),*b=..,*c=..;
   // #pragma omp critical // our "fix"
   // {
   // initialize a[], b[] and create persistent buffers on Xeon Phi for a[], b[] and c[]
   #pragma offload target(mic:0)\
     in(a:length(N*N) align(64) alloc_if(1) free_if(0))\
     in(b:length(N*N) align(64) alloc_if(1) free_if(0))\
     nocopy(c:length(N*N) align(64) alloc_if(1) free_if(0))
   {
     mkl_set_num_threads(16); // use 16 threads on Xeon Phi
     #pragma omp parallel num_threads(16)
     {
       ; // just create threads! MKL uses OpenMP.
     }
   }
   // }
   #pragma omp barrier
   for(int i=0;i<numOffloads;i++){ // now start the offload computations
     start[omp_get_thread_num()][i]=get_time_stamp();
     #pragma offload target(mic:0)\
       in(a:length(0) alloc_if(0) free_if(0))\
       in(b:length(0) alloc_if(0) free_if(0))\
       out(c:length(0) alloc_if(0) free_if(0))
     {
       cblas_dgemm(..); // matrix-matrix multiplication: c=a*b
     }
     stop[omp_get_thread_num()][i]=get_time_stamp();
   }
   // release memory a[], b[] and c[] on host and Xeon Phi
}
// determine concurrent performance: extract concurrency window from start[][],stop[][]
..
```

FIGURE 12.6

Core of the MKL dgemm benchmark for $N \times N$-matrices with $m = 15$ host threads and $n = 16$ threads on the coprocessor per offload—for a total of 240 threads, matching the logical core count on the Intel Xeon Phi coprocessor. Persistent buffers are managed on the coprocessor via alloc_if and free_if. No data transfers between coprocessor and host take place.

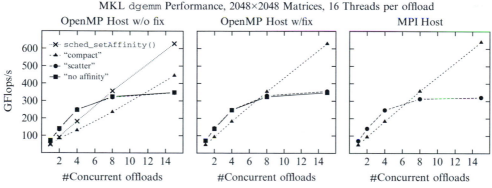

FIGURE 12.7

Performance of MKL dgemm on Intel Xeon Phi 7120P coprocessor. Up to 15 concurrent offloads execute dgemm on the coprocessor, using 16 OpenMP threads each. The plots illustrate the impact of different thread-core assignments on the overall performance. The middle and right-hand side sub-plot do not contain data points for explicit thread pinning on the coprocessor via sched_setaffinity() as they fall on the same points of the "compact" scheme. For executions with MPI on the host, the "compact" and "scatter" scheme is used only.

the discontiguous thread-to-core mapping becomes obvious, when using environment variables without our "fix." Using it, the "compact" scheme approximates explicit thread pinning—we, therefore, display just the data points for the "compact" scheme. Further, it can be seen that for the "scatter" scheme the actual thread-core assignment is immaterial, as none of the physical cores on the coprocessor is distinguished over the others.

The right-hand side sub-plot (MPI) contains data points for "scatter" and "compact" only. Both schemes were established via `MIC_KMP_AFFINITY=[scatter|compact]` after having partitioned the coprocessor appropriately. The performance is almost on par with the executions using threading on the host. However, the data also shows up that the MPI setup introduces overhead which causes a small performance decrease.

Persistent thread groups and affinities on the coprocessor

Both LEO and OpenMP 4.0 use the Coprocessor Offload Infrastructure (COI) API to create coprocessor-side processes and thread(s) (group(s)) together with memory buffers and communication channels between the coprocessor and the host. In particular for each host process that offloads work to the coprocessor, there is a corresponding process on the coprocessor. Within the context of that process, at least as many threads exist as there are host threads that have offload pragmas along their execution paths. Host threads and corresponding coprocessor-side threads are linked by a so-called COIPipeline (see Newburn et al., 2013). The COIPipeline data type implements a FIFO command queue for kernel invocation on the coprocessor and data transfers to and from it up to a few kilobytes—larger amounts of data are transferred using COIBuffers, typically triggered by kernel invocations via the COIPipeline. The important point is that via the COIPipelines persistent per-thread connections between the coprocessor and the host are established that preserve the threads within OpenMP parallel regions on the coprocessor as well as their affinities.

NOTE

Successive (concurrent) offloads inherit thread configurations of the previous offloads unless the shapes of the parallel regions change. Applying a particular thread pinning scheme right at the beginning of an application thus can persist throughout the entire execution.

CONCURRENT DATA TRANSFERS

When offloading computations to the coprocessor, data transfers between the coprocessor and the host take place at least at the beginning and at the end of the computation, but usually also in-between, for example, separating successive offloads. Although in the concurrent offloading case each host thread has a separate COIPipeline for kernel invocation, in the current COI implementation all data transfers within the same process context use a shared data channel to the coprocessor. When using multiple OpenMP threads on the host, data transfers can suffer from implicit serialization and contention for shared COI resources, potentially causing kernel serialization, too.

Offload data transfers with MPI on the host can use multiple data channels to the coprocessor. Applications with frequent data transfers between host and coprocessor thus should see better performance with MPI on the host instead of threading. However, this applies only if messages are small. For larger messages even a single data transfer can saturate the PCIe bandwidth and concurrent data transfers are effectively serialized.

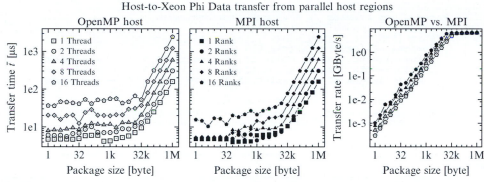

FIGURE 12.8

Transfer times $\bar{t}$ and transfer rates for moving different sized data packages from host to coprocessor. The plots illustrate the performance impact of an increasing number of concurrent data transfers from either an OpenMP or MPI host application. We use a dual-socket Intel Xeon X5680 host with Intel Xeon Phi 7120P coprocessor devices placed in PCIe ×16 slots.

Figure 12.8 shows the transfer times $\bar{t}$ for different sized data packages (messages) and different numbers of concurrent data transfers, either from an OpenMP or MPI parallel host application. All transfer times $\bar{t}$ have been estimated using the "concurrency window" method described previously for the MKL performance evaluation.

Data points in Figure 12.8 are the minimum transfer times obtained from 25 independent program runs. For each run, the concurrency window, and hence $\bar{t}$, has been determined for 5000 data transfers per thread or process for each package size.

Transfer times in the left-hand side sub-plot increase almost proportional to the number of host threads for data packages up to about 16 kB. Although transferring data packages smaller than 16 kB does not saturate the PCIe bandwidth, at most one such package is on the line at any time due to serialization on the single per-process data channel. In case of using MPI, for each MPI rank such a data channel exists. For packages up to 64 bytes transfer times are almost equivalent, independent of the number of MPI ranks used. At 64 bytes, the Symmetric Communications InterFace (SCIF) implementation, which is the communication back-end used by COI, switches from non-DMA to DMA data transfers—small data transfers to/from the coprocessor are managed by the CPU itself. Packages larger than 16 kB already saturate the PCIe bandwidth, so that the performance of data transfers from OpenMP and MPI converges.

NOTE

If small amounts of data are frequently transferred between host and the coprocessor, and if kernel execution times are of the same order as data transfer times, concurrent offloading might work best with MPI parallelism on the host.

Case study: concurrent MKL dgemm offloading with data transfers

So far we did not study the impact of concurrent data transfers on kernel executions in-between. For that purpose, we extend our MKL `dgemm` benchmark to additionally perform data transfers before and

```
..  // See Figure 12.6
#pragma omp barrier  // now start the offload computations
for(int i=0;i<numOffloads;i++){
  start[omp_get_thread_num()][i]=get_time_stamp();
  #pragma offload target(mic:0)\
    in(a:length(xA*N*N) alloc_if(0) free_if(0))\  // ← data transfer
    in(b:length(xB*N*N) alloc_if(0) free_if(0))\  // ← data transfer
    out(c:length(xC*N*N) alloc_if(0) free_if(0))  // ← data transfer
  {
    cblas_dgemm(..);  // matrix-matrix multiplication: c = a*b
  }
  stop[omp_get_thread_num()][i]=get_time_stamp();
}
..
```

FIGURE 12.9

Modifications applied to Figure 12.6. Now, each offload computation is surrounded by data transfers to and from the coprocessor. The fraction of the total array sizes to be transferred is given by $xA, xB, xC \in [0,1]$.

after the offload computation. The modifications applied to Figure 12.6 are summarized in Figure 12.9. The fraction of the matrix elements to be transferred is determined by xA, xB, and xC, respectively.

In the case of ($xA = 1.0$, $xB = 0.0$, $xC = 1.0$), a constant matrix b, for example, the matrix representation of an operator in quantum mechanics, is repeatedly applied to matrix a, and the result of the computation c is copied back to the host. For ($xA = 1.0$, $xB = 1.0$, $xC = 1.0$) the entire problem is transferred between coprocessor and host. Figure 12.10 illustrates the overall performance in these two cases when offloading from OpenMP and MPI, respectively. We use the "compact" pinning scheme on the coprocessor.

With OpenMP on the host, serialization of data transfers is inherent due to the single per-process data channel. Multiple MPI processes, in contrast, have separate channels. However, the matrices considered have size 32 MB each, and a single thread can saturate the PCIe bandwidth by copying its matrices to/from the coprocessor. Serialization of data transfers thus should have no effect on the

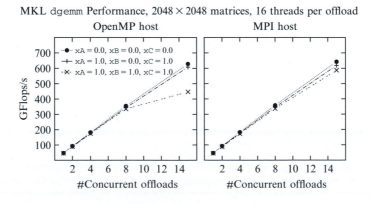

FIGURE 12.10

MKL dgemm performance on Intel Xeon Phi 7120P coprocessor placed in a PCIe x16 slot. Up to 15 concurrent offloads use 16 OpenMP threads on the coprocessor each. The plots illustrate the impact of data transfers between consecutive offload computations on the overall performance.

overall performance. Moreover, there should be almost no difference to using MPI, as data transfers over multiple channels share the PCIe bandwidth, and hence experience no gain over the serialized transfers.

However, with an increasing number of concurrent offloads from OpenMP, we observe a significant performance loss due to data transfers. For 2048×2048 matrices the compute time (380 ms for 16 threads at 45 GFlops/s) and data transfer time (15 ms for three matrices at 6.8 GB/s) differ by a factor ≈ 25. In this case, it should be possible to overlap up to 25 threads' or processes' data transfers with computation. Basically, this is supported by our executions using MPI.

NOTE

Multi-threaded concurrent offloading seems to suffer from contention on COI-internal data structures, which are duplicated in case of using MPI. Since there is no workaround for these internals, it appears best, when exchanging data with the Intel Xeon Phi coprocessor, to either use only a moderate number of concurrent offloading threads, or to switch to MPI or hybrid MPI + OpenMP.

FORCE COMPUTATION IN PD USING CONCURRENT KERNEL OFFLOADING

We now come back to the PD example that initially served as the motivation for concurrent kernel offloading to the coprocessor. Remember, we argued to make use of symmetries in the forces, but found that our implementation of the force computation does not scale with an increasing number of threads. Subsequently, we will describe our parallel algorithm to evaluate the forces, and detail the relevant parts of a possible implementation using C++ and Intel LEO.

PARALLEL FORCE EVALUATION USING NEWTON'S 3RD LAW

According to Newton's 3rd law, it holds that $\mathbf{F}_{ij} = -\mathbf{F}_{ji}$, where $\mathbf{F}_{ij}$ is the force exerted by particle j on particle i. By making use of this symmetry, we can save a constant factor of two when evaluating the per-particle forces $\mathbf{F}_i = \sum_{j \neq i} \mathbf{F}_{ij}$ for each of N particles: we need to compute $\mathbf{F}_i = \sum_{j < i} \mathbf{F}_{ij}$, and add the contributions $\mathbf{F}_{ji} = -\mathbf{F}_{ij}$ to $\mathbf{F}_j$ throughout the summation. For reasons of simplicity, we evaluate the forces $\mathbf{F}_i$ directly, which results in an algorithm with computational complexity $O(N^2)$. Further, we consider pairwise contributions $\mathbf{F}_{ij}$ that depend on the spatial separation $x_{ij} = |\mathbf{x}_i - \mathbf{x}_j|$ of the particles i and j and their electric charges q_i and q_j only. For instance,

$$\mathbf{F}_{ij} = \left(a \frac{b^6}{x_{ij}^8} \left(\frac{2b^6}{x_{ij}^6} - 1 \right) + \frac{q_i q_j}{x_{ij}^3} \right)(\mathbf{x}_i - \mathbf{x}_j)$$

is derived from a combination of the Lennard-Jones and the Coulomb potential (see Thijssen, 2013).

What makes the parallel implementation of the $O(N^2)$ algorithm on the coprocessor difficult? First, there is the "threading requirement" on the coprocessor (see Jeffers and Reinders, 2013), that is, at least two hardware threads need to be instantiated per physical core. Second, the force computation using the symmetries must be thread safe, which sounds expensive with hundreds of threads.

The thread-safety requirement follows from the fact that $\mathbf{F}_i$ receives contributions $\mathbf{F}_{ij}$ from different threads in the parallel case. An obvious approach to tackle this issue is for each of P threads to allocate an additional buffer to hold the force components $\mathbf{F}_{ji} = -\mathbf{F}_{ij}$, and afterwards to accumulate these buffers into $\mathbf{F}_i$. The memory consumption, however, then is in $O(P \cdot N)$, and it is going to "explode" with an increasing number of threads. A better approach with space complexity $O(N)$ is as follows:

Parallel Algorithm (non-concurrent): (0a) Create two buffers $\mathbf{F}$ and $\mathbf{F}^*$ of length N each, and set $\mathbf{F}$ $\equiv \mathbf{0}$ and $\mathbf{F}^* \equiv \mathbf{0}$. **(0b)** Distribute computations of forces $\mathbf{F}_i$ evenly among P threads. Now perform the following iteration, starting at $k = 0$:

(1) Thread $p \in [0, P - 1]$ performs computation:
    for i **in** "my i-values" **do**
        for $j = \mathrm{mod}(p + k, P)$ **to** $i - 1$ **increment by** P **do**
            $\mathbf{f} =$ "compute $\mathbf{F}_{ij}$", $\mathbf{F}[i] = \mathbf{F}[i] + \mathbf{f}$, $\mathbf{F}^*[j] = \mathbf{F}^*[j] - \mathbf{f}$
        end for
    end for
(2) Increment $k = k + 1$: **if** k equals P **then** merge buffers, that is, $\mathbf{F} = \mathbf{F} + \mathbf{F}^*$ and EXIT, **else** SYNCHRONIZE threads and go to step **(1)**.

Step **(1)** is executed P times. In each iteration, threads access disjoint elements of buffer $\mathbf{F}^*$ by computing contributions $\mathbf{F}_{ij}$ for j-values that are apart by value P and have an offset from $j = 0$ that is unique across all threads—see "$\mathrm{mod}(p + k, P)$" in the second loop. Thread safety together with space complexity $O(N)$ hence is achieved at the expense of thread synchronization between consecutive iterations.

The performance of this algorithm using up to 240 OpenMP threads executing on an Intel Xeon Phi coprocessor is illustrated in Figure 12.2 (using a SIMD optimized code base) for $16\,\mathrm{k}$ particles. The scaling is acceptable for up to 30 threads only.

Parallel Algorithm (concurrent): Instead of just one thread group of size P, we use m groups of size $P^\dagger = P/m$ each. The threads now have a group identifier $g^\dagger \in [0, m - 1]$, a per-group thread identifier $p^\dagger \in [0, P^\dagger - 1]$, and a global thread identifier $g^\dagger m + p^\dagger$ that is used to distribute the i-values among all P threads.

By **(0a)** † allocating the buffers $\mathbf{F}^\dagger$ and $\mathbf{F}^{*\dagger}$ per group, and **(0b)** † initializing them to zero, we can use our non-concurrent algorithm within the groups (we start at $k = 0$):

(1) † Execute step **(1)** with substitution $p \to p^\dagger$, $P \to P^\dagger$, $\mathbf{F} \to \mathbf{F}^\dagger$, $\mathbf{F}^* \to \mathbf{F}^{*\dagger}$.
(2) † Increment $k = k + 1$: **if** k equals $P^\dagger$ **then** merge buffers, that is, $\mathbf{F}^\dagger = \mathbf{F}^\dagger + \mathbf{F}^{*\dagger}$ and EXIT, **else** SYNCHRONIZE threads in the same group and go to step **(1)** †.

The number of iterations in the concurrent case is $P^\dagger < P$, and the number of threads participating in the per-group synchronizations is reduced to $P^\dagger$. To get the final values of $\mathbf{F}_i$, it is necessary **(3)** † to accumulate the force contributions of the m groups.

Figure 12.11 illustrates the parallel algorithm using concurrent offloading to the coprocessor from within a multi-threaded host region of size $m = 8$. Step **(0a)**† is implicit and therefore not shown. Steps **(0b)**†, **(1)**† and **(2)**† are placed on the Intel Xeon Phi coprocessor, where $P^\dagger = 30$ threads are used per offload. To distinguish the buffers $\mathbf{F}^\dagger$ and $\mathbf{F}^{*\dagger}$, we introduce the subscripts "$(g^\dagger + 1)$." For threading and offloading elements we draw on OpenMP and LEO pragmas. Before step **(3)**†, all host threads synchronize, and then offload to the coprocessor for the force accumulation.

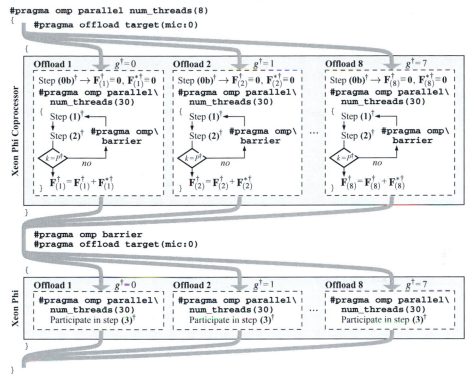

FIGURE 12.11

Schematic of the concurrent offloading of the force computation and force accumulation to the Intel Xeon Phi coprocessor: 8 host threads place 1/8th of the entire problem on the coprocessor, and use 30 threads on it to solve their sub-problems each.

IMPLEMENTATION OF THE CONCURRENT FORCE COMPUTATION

We will now go through a possible implementation of our parallel force computation algorithm using concurrent offloading (the full source code, including SIMD optimizations via loop unrolling and tiling, is downloadable from http://lotsofcores.com). Before actually going into the details, we need to figure out a way to share data across the concurrent offloads, as might be beneficial in the force accumulation in step $(3)^\dagger$.

NOTE: SHARING COPROCESSOR DATA ACROSS CONCURRENT OFFLOADS FROM OPENMP

Offload computations from within the same host process also share the corresponding coprocessor-side process. Memory allocated on the coprocessor throughout any of the host thread executions thus can be used within offload regions of other host threads in the same process context as long as the associated host pointer is shared among them.

The listing below illustrates using shared memory to fill up the elements of the array pointed to by `ptr` with the array index values using 8 concurrent offloads. The correct functioning of this approach, when offloading work to the Intel Xeon Phi coprocessor, results from the fact that both Intel's LEO and OpenMP 4.0 implementation use COI, and COI works as described above and is not expected to undergo changes in this respect.

```
int *ptr=_mm_malloc(512*sizeof(double),64);
#pragma offload_transfer target(mic:0)\
  in(ptr:length(512) align(64) alloc_if(1) free_if(0))

#pragma omp parallel num_threads(8)  // 8 threads on host
{
  int id=omp_get_thread_num();
  #pragma offload target(mic:0)\
    in(ptr:length(0) alloc_if(0) free_if(0))  // ← shared memory
  {
    for(int i=id; i<512; i+=8)
      ptr[i]=i;  // concurrent offloads can use the shared memory pointed to by ptr
  }
}

#pragma offload_transfer target(mic:0)\
  out(ptr:length(512) alloc_if(0) free_if(1))
// the content of the memory pointed to by ptr now is: 0 1 2 3 .. 511
```

The force computation is the core part of a PD simulation, for which the basic functionality is implemented in the C++ class named pd. Figure 12.12 contains the class declaration. The constants CONCURRENT_OFFLOADS and THREADS_PER_OFFLOAD determine the number of concurrent offloads m respectively the number of threads $P^{\dagger}$ to be used in the offloaded regions each.

Constructor (Figure 12.13): Memory for the particle positions and charges as well as the buffers force_i and force_j[0..(CONCURRENT_OFFLOADS-1)] for the force computation (corresponding to the per-group buffers $\mathbf{F}^{\dagger}$ and $\mathbf{F}^{*\dagger}$) are allocated on the host and the coprocessor. Attributes to be used within the offloaded regions have to be placed on the stack of the constructor. If we would not do this, for example, for the attribute position, the compiler would translate each occurrence of position into this->position, which on the coprocessor is not valid as the pd object does not exist on it. The consequence would be a segmentation fault when accessing the pointer on the coprocessor. To work around, we create a local copy of the attribute. For the local copy the offload runtime then can create its counterpart on the coprocessor.

```
#define ALLOC align(64) alloc_if(1) free_if(0)
#define REUSE alloc_if(0) free_if(0)
#define FREE alloc_if(0) free_if(1)

#define CONCURRENT_OFFLOADS (8)    // corresponds to m
#define THREADS_PER_OFFLOAD (30)   // corresponds to P†

// Class pd: provides the basic functionality for a PD simulation.
class pd{
  public:
    pd(double *position,double *charge,..,int numParticles);
    ~pd();
    void computeForce();
    .. // see source code downloadable from http://lotsofcores.com.
  private:
    int numParticles,deviceId=0;
    double *position,*charge,*force_i,*force_j[CONCURRENT_OFFLOADS];
    ..
};
```

FIGURE 12.12

Declaration of C++ class pd. Only the relevant sections are listed.

```
// Constructor: particle positions have format (x₁,...,xₙ),(y₁,...,yₙ),(z₁,...,zₙ). Factor "3."
pd::pd(double *position,double *charge,..,int numParticles){
   int sizeBytes=numParticles*sizeof(double);
   this->numParticles=numParticles;
   this->positon=_mm_malloc(3*sizeBytes,64);
   this->charge=_mm_malloc(sizeBytes,64);
   memcpy(this->positon,positon,3*sizeBytes);
   memcpy(this->charge,charge,sizeBytes);
   // create buffers force_i and force_j[]
   this->force_i=_mm_malloc(3*sizeBytes*CONCURRENT_OFFLOADS,64);
   for(int c=0;c<CONCURRENT_OFFLOADS;c++)
     this->force_j[c]=_mm_malloc(3*sizeBytes,64);
   // allocate and set up position, charge, force_i and force_j[] on the coprocessor
   double *pos=this->position,*chg=this->charge,*f_i=this->force_i;
#pragma offload_transfer target(mic:deviceId)\
   in(pos:length(3*numParticles) ALLOC)\
   in(chg:length(numParticles) ALLOC)\
   nocopy(f_i:length(3*numParticles*CONCURRENT_OFFLOADS) ALLOC)
#pragma omp parallel num_threads(CONCURRENT_OFFLOADS)
   {
      double *f_j=this->force_j[omp_get_thread_num()];
      #pragma omp critical
      {
        #pragma offload target(mic:deviceId)\
          nocopy(f_j:length(3*numParticles) ALLOC)
        {
          #pragma omp parallel num_threads(THREADS_PER_OFFLOAD)
          {
            ;  // just create threads
          }
        }
      }
   }
}
```

FIGURE 12.13

Constructor of class `pd`. Attributes `force_i` and `force_j[]` need to be converted to local variables on the constructor's stack. Why is this necessary? `force_i` actually refers to `this->force_i` which is not valid on the coprocessor as the `pd` object does not exist on it. Accessing `this->force_i` would give a segmentation fault on the coprocessor.

`force_i` points to a memory area of size "CONCURRENT_OFFLOADS · *N*," holding the force contributions $\mathbf{F}_i = \sum_{j<i} \mathbf{F}_{ij}$ of all concurrent offloads in disjoint sub-arrays of size "*N*" each. In contrast, `force_j[]` contains "CONCURRENT_OFFLOADS" pointers, each of which pointing to a memory area of size "*N*." Unlike `force_j[]`, which are per-offload buffers for contributions $\mathbf{F}_{ji} = -\mathbf{F}_{ij}$, `force_i` is used as a shared memory across concurrent offloads in the force-reduction step—so we want it be contiguous.

We further create all OpenMP threads on the coprocessor using our "fix" from Section "Coprocessor device partitioning and thread affinity"—we will use `MIC_KMP_AFFINITY=compact` with all threads within the same offload region being assigned contiguous logical cores on the coprocessor.

Destructor (Figure 12.14): Pointer-valued attributes are placed on the destructor's stack, and the respective memory areas are freed, first on the coprocessor and then on the host.

Method `computeForce()` (Figure 12.15): Host part of the force computation. Again, all relevant attributes are placed on the method's stack in order to access them in the offloaded region(s). Within that method, we create "CONCURRENT_OFFLOADS" host threads, each of which offloading first the force computation `__computeForce()` to the coprocessor, and afterwards the force accumulation `__accumulateForce()`. The two offloads are separated by a barrier synchronization on the host.

```
// Destructor: release coprocessor and host memory
pd::~pd(){
  double *pos=this->position,*chg=this->charge,*f_i=this->force_i;
  #pragma offload target(mic:deviceId)\
    in(pos,chg,f_i:length(0) FREE)
  {
    ; // just release memory
  }
  _mm_free(this->position);
  _mm_free(this->charge);
  _mm_free(this->force_i);
  for(int c=0;c<CONCURRENT_OFFLOADS;c++){
    double *f_j=this->force_j[c];
    #pragma offload target(mic:deviceId)\
      in(f_j:length(0) FREE)
    {
      ; // just release memory
    }
    _mm_free(this->force_j[c]);
  }
}
```

FIGURE 12.14

Destructor of class `pd`.

```
// Concurrent force computation: host part of the force computation.
void pd::computeForce(){
  int n=this->numParticles;
  double *pos=this->position,*chg=this->charge,*f_i=this->force_i;
  #pragma omp parallel num_threads(CONCURRENT_OFFLOADS)
  {
    int offloadId=omp_get_thread_num();
    double *f_j=this->force_j[offloadId];
    #pragma offload target(mic:deviceId)\
      in(pos,chg,f_i,f_j:length(0) REUSE)
    {
      __computeForce(pos,chg,&f_i[3*n*offloadId],f_j,n,offloadId);
    }
    #pragma omp barrier
    #pragma offload target(mic:deviceId)\
      in(f_i:length(0) REUSE)
    {
      __accumulateForce(f_i,n,offloadId);
    }
  }
}
```

FIGURE 12.15

`pd`-method implementing the host part of the concurrent force computation.

Each host thread gives (local) pointers `pos` and `chg` to the positions and charges of the particles, and `f_i` and `f_j` to the buffers for the force computation as input to `__computeForce()`. Further, the number of particles n, and the host thread identifier `offloadId` are passed to the compute kernel. For the force accumulations, only the buffer `f_i` together with the particle count n and the host thread identifier `offloadId` is necessary. Note, that for the force accumulation, all force contributions by the different offloads are accessible via `f_i` (shared memory). The implementation of `__accumulateForce()` can be found on http://lotsofcores.com.

```
// Compute kernel: implements O(N²) force computation using Newton's 3rd law.
__attribute__((target(mic))) void __computeForce(const double *pos,
  double *chg,double *f_i,double *f_j,int n,int offloadId){
  memset(f_i,0,3*n*sizeof(double));  // step (0b)† of algorithm above
  memset(f_j,0,3*n*sizeof(double));  // step (0b)† of algorithm above
  double *pos_x=&pos[0*n],*pos_y=&pos[1*n],*pos_z=&pos[2*n];
  double *f_i_x=&f_i[0*n],*f_i_y=&f_i[1*n],*f_i_z=&f_i[2*n];
  double *f_j_x=&f_j[0*n],*f_j_y=&f_j[1*n],*f_j_z=&f_j[2*n];
  #pragma omp parallel num_threads(THREADS_PER_OFFLOAD)
  {
    int id=offloadId*THREADS_PER_OFFLOAD+omp_get_thread_num();
    double r_ij_x,r_ij_y,r_ij_z,f;
    for(int k=0;k<THREADS_PER_OFFLOAD;k++){
      int jStart=(k+omp_get_thread_num())%THREADS_PER_OFFLOAD;
      int jIncrement=THREADS_PER_OFFLOAD;
      // Step (1) of algorithm above: distribute i-values evenly among threads
      for(int i=id;i<n;i+=CONCURRENT_OFFLOADS*THREADS_PER_OFFLOAD){
        int jStop=i;
        for(int j=jStart;j<jStop;j+=jIncrement){  // disjount j-values
          r_ij_x=pos_x[i]-pos_x[j];
          r_ij_y=pos_y[i]-pos_y[j];
          r_ij_z=pos_z[i]-pos_z[j];
          f=f_ij(r_ij_x,r_ij_y,r_ij_z,chg,..);  // magnitude of force
          f_i_x[i]+=f*r_ij_x; f_j_x[j]-=f*r_ij_x;  // Newton's
          f_i_y[i]+=f*r_ij_y; f_j_y[j]-=f*r_ij_y;  // 3rd law
          f_i_z[i]+=f*r_ij_z; f_j_z[j]-=f*r_ij_z;  // Fᵢⱼ = −Fⱼᵢ
        }
      }
      #pragma omp barrier  // step (2)† of algorihm above: else-clause
    }
    // step (2)† of algorihm above: if-clause → accumulate forces f_i and f_j into f_i
    int chunkSize=(int)ceil((double)(n)/THREADS_PER_OFFLOAD);
    int start=omp_get_thread_num()*chunkSize;
    int stop=start+chunkSize; stop=(stop<n?stop:n);
    for(int i=start;i<stop;i++){
      f_i_x[i]+=f_j_x[i];
      f_i_y[i]+=f_j_y[i];
      f_i_z[i]+=f_j_z[i];
    }
  }
}
```

FIGURE 12.16

Kernel implementing the force computation using Newton's 3rd law.

Compute kernel `__computeForce()` (Figure 12.16): Implements our parallel algorithm for the force computation (within a thread group). The individual steps **(0b)†**, **(1)†** and **(2)†** are highlighted in the source code. The host thread identifier `offloadId` together with the thread identifier within the kernel (obtained via `omp_get_thread_num()`) determines the global thread identifier `id` across all concurrent offloads. `id` then is used to achieve an even distribution of the *i*-values for the evaluation of the contributions $\mathbf{F}_i = \sum_{j<i} \mathbf{F}_{ij}$ across all threads. The implementation of the evaluation of the magnitude of the force is encapsulated in `f_ij()`.

Additional functionalities of class pd (Figure 12.12): ...like updating positions and velocities throughout a PD simulation, or taking measurements, are not listed here (see the dots "..." in the listings), as discussing them does not contribute to the understanding of our concurrent offloading approach. However, they can be found in the code that is downloadable from http://lotsofcores.com (the code incorporates SIMD optimizations, and is used for our benchmarks).

PERFORMANCE EVALUATION: BEFORE AND AFTER

At the beginning of this chapter we motivated concurrent kernel offloading with the unfavorable scaling behavior of the above algorithm for the force computation in case of using a single offload (with up to 240 threads on the coprocessor) only. Instead of using a single offload, we now switch to the approach presented in this section, that is, we use multiple concurrent offloads, each of which using 30 threads on the coprocessor.

Figure 12.17 illustrates the performance increase for different numbers of concurrent offloads compared to a single offload using the same overall number of threads.

NOTE

In all cases we compared the simulation results of the underlying PD simulation and found almost exact agreement throughout 1000 PD update steps. Perfect agreement is not to be expected because of different summation orders and non-associativity of floating point operations.

Our performance metric is the number of billion particle-particle interactions per second, or "GigaInteractions/s" for short (larger values are better).

For different numbers of interacting particles, the concurrent offloading approach is superior to its non-concurrent counterpart. The concurrent execution scales almost linearly with the number of cooperating thread groups, and hence threads. For 64 k particles, **we achieve a speedup of 1.25 over the non-concurrent case**. Our initial motivation for making use of symmetries in the force calculation together with concurrent offloading to the coprocessor hence is supported. We have shown that multiple small-scale offload computations can outperform a single large-scale offload computation solving the same problem.

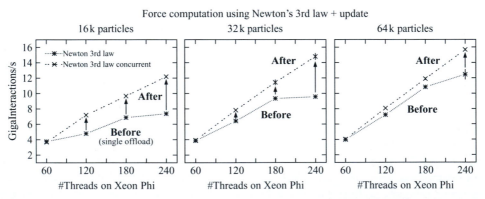

FIGURE 12.17

Performance of a PD simulation using Newton's 3rd law for the force computation with and without concurrent offloading. In the concurrent case up to eight host threads offload the same force computation kernel as in the non-concurrent case, but with 30 threads per offload: for the "120 threads" data points, 4 concurrent host threads offload to the coprocessor. All values are for 1000 PD update steps using an Intel Xeon Phi coprocessor for offload computation.

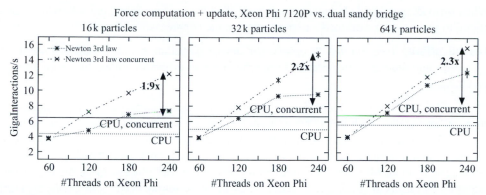

FIGURE 12.18

Performance of a PD simulation using Newton's 3rd law for the force computation with and without concurrent offloading. The meaning of the sub-plots is the same as in Figure 12.17. The performance is additionally compared against a dual-socket Intel Xeon processor (Sandy Bridge) execution using 32 threads. The dotted horizontal line is for the non-concurrent case. The solid line is for the execution using two thread groups of size 16, residing on separate CPU sockets.

Comparison against CPU: Our implementation of the force computation scheme using Newton's 3rd law (together with concurrent offloading) is at no point specific to the coprocessor, except for the offload pragmas. Hence, the same code base can be used for execution on a standard CPU, for example, if no coprocessor is present.

For the CPU benchmarks, we use the compute node described at the beginning of this chapter. The two CPU sockets of this system span two separate NUMA domains connected by the Intel QuickPath Interconnect (QPI) link. Communication over QPI, for example, for synchronization, potentially can slow down an application compared to on-socket communication. Using two concurrent thread groups of size 16, with each group residing on a single CPU socket, may help gain the overall compute performance on the host.

Figure 12.18 compares the performance for executing the same code on an Intel Xeon Phi 7120P coprocessor and the host. The host processor execution with two concurrent thread groups of size 16 each, is ahead to the non-concurrent processor execution with 32 threads by a factor 1.5 for 16k particles, and by a factor 1.2 in case of 64k particles. With respect to the coprocessor execution up to a factor of 2.3 can be noted in favor of the coprocessor.

With a measurable performance increase by using the concurrent kernel execution approach, our PD example supports the point that optimizing codes for execution on the coprocessor is of double advantage when brought back to the CPU.

THE BOTTOM LINE

If offload regions do not expose enough parallelism to satisfy the threading requirements of a coprocessor, concurrent kernel offloading may be a good choice to gain its overall utilization.

When offloading multiple kernels concurrently from the host we found the following measures are beneficial to improve the workload's performance on the coprocessor:

Thread affinity (see Section "Coprocessor device partitioning and thread affinity"): OpenMP thread groups and their affinities persist during the program execution unless the shape of the parallel region changes.

- When offloading from an OpenMP host program, an initial mutually exclusive offload to the coprocessor together with thread creation on the coprocessor should be performed before the actual computation(s). In this way, thread placements within the offload regions meet the parameter assignments to `MIC_KMP_AFFINITY` and `MIC_OMP_PLACES`.
- Offloading from an MPI host program requires explicit thread placement on the coprocessor, for example, by means of `sched_setaffinity()` or by setting `MIC_KMP_PLACE_THREADS` to apply an appropriate logical partitioning of the coprocessor. Within the partitions the parameters assigned to `MIC_KMP_AFFINITY` and `MIC_OMP_PLACES` are effective.

Data transfers (see Section "Concurrent data transfers"): The current COI implementation provides thread exclusive communication channels between the coprocessor and the host (for kernel invocation in the offload model), but uses a single data transfer channel only.

- Concurrent data transfers from within an OpenMP host application can suffer from serialization because of the single data channel, and additionally from contention on COI internal data structures. The effect becomes obvious when data packages are small.
- With MPI on the host, each MPI process has its own data channel. Contention effects are not present unless the application uses hybrid MPI + OpenMP parallelism.
- If frequent transfers of small messages take place, use a moderate number of OpenMP threads or switch to MPI or hybrid MPI + OpenMP.

We applied the concurrent kernel offloading approach to two real-world use cases: MKL `dgemm` computation and a PD simulation, namely.

For `dgemm` (see Sections "Coprocessor device partitioning and thread affinity" and "Concurrent data transfers") the observation is, that the overall compute performance on the coprocessor increases almost linearly with the number of concurrent offloads as long as the coprocessor can handle the total thread count. Data transfers between successive `dgemm` offloads can break down the performance significantly when using OpenMP on the host. However, switching to MPI, almost no performance loss compared to no data transfers can be noted. For workloads that execute several `dgemm`-like operations, programmers may use our MKL examples as a recipe on how to easily partition a coprocessor for multiplication of small or medium-sized matrices.

Our PD example shows how the MKL recipe can be applied to more complex workloads and how to avoid some of the peculiarities associated with concurrent offloading. Our code uses concurrent kernel offloading in a way which at first sight seems strange, but after a short time of thinking makes sense: we split up a computation with P threads into m concurrent computations with P/m threads each. Within each of the concurrent offloads the threads solve $1/m$-th of the entire problem each, and afterwards combine their results. Since our PD compute kernel does not scale to thread counts that meet the coprocessor threading requirements the concurrent approach can help increase the program performance. With 8 concurrent offloads using 30 threads each, we observe about 25% gain over using 240 threads within a single offload.

Applications that display a similar scaling behavior like our PD example, can use our approach to potentially increase their overall performance. For example, the integration of concurrent kernel offloading into a thermodynamical simulation code is described in a paper on Concurrent Kernel Execution (see Wende et al., 2014).

FOR MORE INFORMATION

Jeffers, J., Reinders, J., 2013. Intel Xeon Phi Coprocessor High Performance Programming, first ed. Morgan Kaufmann Publishers Inc., San Francisco, CA, USA.

Newburn, C.J., Deodhar, R., Dmitriev, S., Murty, R., Narayanaswamy, R., Wiegert, J., Chinchilla, F., McGuire, R., 2013. Offload compiler runtime for the Intel Xeon Phi coprocessor. In: Supercomputing. Springer, Berlin, Heidelberg.

Thijssen, J., 2013. Computational Physics, second ed Cambridge University Press.

Wende, F., Cordes, F., Steinke, T., 2014. Concurrent kernel execution on Xeon Phi within parallel heterogeneous workloads. In: Silva, F., et al. (Eds.), Euro-Par 2014 Parallel Processing – 20th International Conference, Porto, Portugal, August 25–29, 2014, Proceedings, LNCS vol. 8632. Springer, pp. 788–799.

Codes from this and other chapters are available on http://lotsofcores.com.

HETEROGENEOUS COMPUTING WITH MPI

13

Jerome Vienne, Carlos Rosales, Kent Milfeld
TACC, USA

MPI IN THE MODERN CLUSTERS

To many users, message passing interface (MPI) is a black box that "just works" behind the scenes to transfer data from one MPI task (process) to another. The beauty of MPI for the program developer is that the algorithmic coding is independent of the hardware layer below the programming paradigm. Nevertheless, over the last decade the hardware has become layered and more complex, more so than when MPI-1 became a standard in 1993.

Figure 13.1 illustrates a typical system at the time of the first MPI-1 standard. Each node in a rack contains a single processor, connected to a NIC (network interface card), and each NIC is connected to a single port on a switch. The system is uniform in its connectivity, and the location of a set of an application's tasks has no effect on the communication performance.

Figure 13.2 illustrates a typical configuration of a heterogeneous high-performance computing (HPC) system of today, in the era of MPI-3. Multiple processors are in each node. And each node is connected in a hierarchy (here a "fat tree" topology) of switches. Within the node each processor has multiple cores and an Intel® Xeon Phi™ coprocessor (or GPU) with many-cores. The coprocessor is connected to the NIC (actually a host channel adapter, HCA), as are the processors, through a PCI-e "bus."

The configuration of a many-core coprocessor introduces a concern to the application developer and user. With 60+ cores on a single coprocessor and 10–40 cores within multiple processors, an application running with a MPI task on each core may certainly create communication storms within the node and across nodes (out through the NIC). Compared to a single-node, single-task MPI execution as envisioned in Figure 13.1, the number of communication channels within a modern node, and out through the NIC, is about two orders greater.

To mitigate communication bottlenecks, applications often use hybrid techniques, employing a few MPI tasks and many OpenMP threads using the symmetric mode of computing (MPI tasks on both the processors and the coprocessors). When the characteristics of an application are amenable to offloading, MPI tasks on the host direct threaded computational work to be executed on the coprocessor. The latter approach avoids using tasks on the coprocessor, thereby reducing the number of MPI tasks on the node; but it is still necessary to thread an application with OpenMP, pthreads, Intel Cilk Plus, etc. for offloading—effectively hybridizing the MPI code.

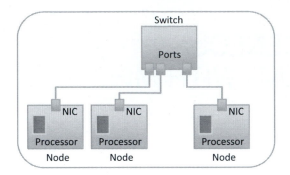

FIGURE 13.1

Single processor nodes in early days of MPI computing.

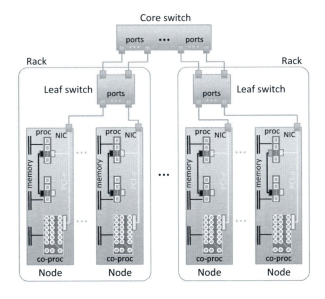

FIGURE 13.2

Multiprocessor, many-core accelerated nodes, connected through a switch hierarchy, in a modern HPC cluster.

With this in mind, high performance of HPC applications now requires selecting an optimal number of MPI tasks (and threads) to use, positioning the tasks, and balancing the workload.

MPI TASK LOCATION

In the early days of MPI, the compute nodes, as depicted in Figure 13.1, were simple and there was no concern about positioning MPI tasks. The mpirun launcher read a file with hostnames, and initiated a single MPI process (task) on each host (node). Each MPI process was assigned a rank ordinally, according to the position in the list. By rearranging the list, a different mapping between the ranks and the hardware processors could be achieved, though there was no need to do that here because the communication interconnects were symmetric, down to the (single-core) processors.

The nodes in modern HPC systems have multiple processors, coprocessors, and graphics accelerators. Each coprocessor and graphics device have its own memory, while the processors share memory. Hence, devices like the Intel Xeon Phi coprocessor have a uniform memory access (UMA), and the processors have a nonuniform memory access (NUMA) to memory. Also, not all of the processors and devices may be connected directly to the network interface.

On multicore systems, launching an MPI task on every core is a common practice, and a node may have 10s of tasks. When all cores are occupied by an MPI task for a generic program, a random mapping is often as good as any. However, for applications in scientific domains that communicate between neighbors, or aggregate communication between nodes through a single on-node task, mapping may enhance communication performance, as explained below.

In systems with a coprocessor, it is more likely that MPI hybrid programs will drive several MPI tasks on the host and a few more or less on the coprocessor, the OpenMP parallel regions will employ a different number of threads for host and device parallel regions. So, with hybrid programs running across heterogeneous architectures, asymmetric interfaces and NUMA architectures, it is understandable that positioning tasks and threads will be more important on the modern HPC systems.

Unless you have an architecture diagram of a node there isn't much you can do to determine the hardware location of the cpu-ids and the intra-device connections. Fortunately, since about 2010 the Portable Hardware Locality software package, called hwloc, has been available to detect and list NUMA memory nodes (processor + local memory) and I/O devices such as Infiniband HCAs, PCI bridges, etc. hwloc does not require root access, so users can download, install and run hwloc in their own directories.

Figure 13.3 shows the architectural features of a node on the Stampede system. An inspection of this diagram will disclose configuration details needed in making task and thread assignments on the host. First, the two containers labeled Socket P#0 and P#1 are the two 8-core processors of the compute node. In numa parlance, a NUMA "node" is a processor and its memory. Note the "(16 GB)" memory designation for the NUMA node is the local memory for the processor. The processors and their memory hierarchy on the die are labeled NUMANode P#0 and P#1. (Socket is the usual name in HPC circles for the packaged processor die and the mechanical support mechanism of the motherboard.) We will use NUMA node and socket interchangeably.

Within a socket the cores are labeled as PU (Processing Units) P#0 … P#7, and PU P#8 … P#15 for Sockets 0 and 1, respectively. If HyperThreading is turned on, each dark gray box has two processing units. These PU numbers are the physical index as set by the BIOS/OS. They are also recorded in the /proc/cpuinfo file as the "processor" number and used when mapping tasks (ranks) and threads (thread ids) to processors.

On the right-hand side in each NUMA node are the device interconnects. The lines are PCI express lanes and the small clear boxes are bridges. In NUMA node #0, the PCI bus of the processor in Socket #0 is connected to Ethernet (eth0/1) and a disk (sda). In NUMA node #1, Socket #1 is connected to the InfiniBand HCA (mlx4_0) and the Intel Xeon Phi coprocessor (mic0) is attached to the PCI 8086:225c controller.

Once you have the architecture layout, you are in a position to make intelligent decisions about placing MPI tasks and threads.

Figure 13.4 categorizes and illustrates ways that tasks (white discs as possible hybrid threads) might be distributed across the processors and coprocessors on the Stampede system. As mentioned earlier, the Pure MPI approach is impractical, unless there is only a trivial amount of communication, and the communication storage per task is small on the coprocessor. Also, the host-only MPI (+offload)

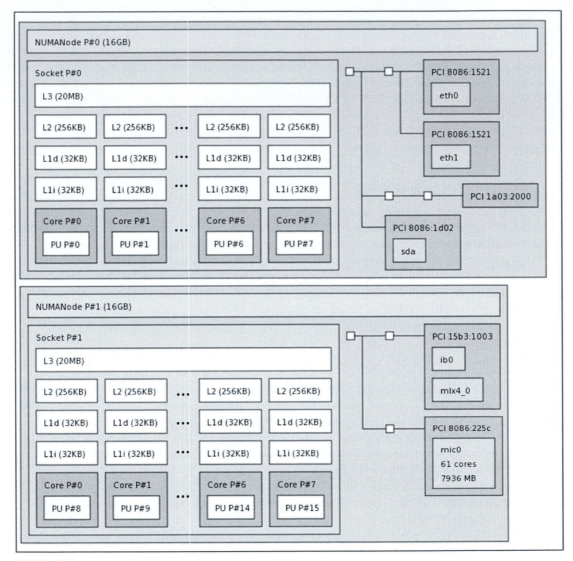

FIGURE 13.3

Hardware Locality (hwloc) output for Stampede node.

requires no tasking on the coprocessor, and will not be covered here (although some aspects of the hybrid approaches apply to the MPI tasks on the host doing offloading).

The Hybrid distributions in Figure 13.4 are all reasonable and common approaches in HPC applications for single-node and multi-node computing. Fortunately, Intel® MPI makes intelligent decisions about placing tasks and threads on the processors and the coprocessor. Nevertheless, it is good to have a strategy, and know the relative cost of inefficient task distributions for working around an MPI implementation's nonoptimal defaults.

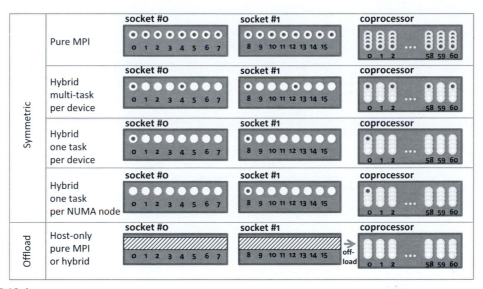

FIGURE 13.4

Common task distributions across Host and coprocessor for MPI applications (Stampede node).

SINGLE-TASK HYBRID PROGRAMS

The Hybrid case with one task per NUMA node (single task on the host, and a single task on the coprocessor) has the fewest concerns. On the coprocessor, the single task can be positioned on any core since all cores are symmetric (except possibly core 60 which deals specifically with some daemon operations). The three modes of distributing the threads across the cores are compact, balanced, and scatter. The meaning of the different affinity types is best explained with an example. Imagine that we have a system with four cores and four hardware threads per core. In Figure 13.5, we have placed eight threads on the system with the assignments for compact, scatter, and balanced types. A *scatter* distribution spreads threads 1–4 across the cores and then begins anew on the first core in round robin fashion. A *balanced* distribution distributes the threads the same way, but numbers them sequentially. A *compact* distribution leaves cores idle in this case. For this reason, the *scatter* or *balanced* (coprocessor only) distributions are often recommended when using fewer than all cores.

For the single-task case, the KMP_AFFINITY environment variable is used to hand the OpenMP runtime the distribution (or affinity) settings for the coprocessor or host processor when the threads are created in a parallel region. The syntax is

export KMP_AFFINITY=[<modifier>,] type

where the three general types of distribution are compact, balance, and scatter; and there is an explicit type which uses a proclist in the modifier to pin threads explicitly to specific cores. Apart from the proclist for explicitly binding threads, on the coprocessor, the fine and core modifiers are used with the distributions to allow the affinitized thread to be pinned to a single hardware thread of a core, or allow the thread on the core to "float" among all of the hardware threads.

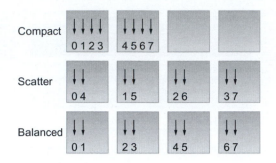

FIGURE 13.5

KMP affinity-type distributions. For the host scatter and compact work in a similar manner across the sockets.

For the coprocessor, it makes sense to use one of the three general distribution patterns. When experimenting with affinity settings a good starting point is to try

KMP_AFFINITY="granularity=core,balanced".

On the processors (the host side) the same KMP_AFFINITY settings can be applied for a single-task execution. The position of the task can be set (thread 0) through an offset. For example, setting KMP_AFFINITY=compact,0,8 will position the first thread, also the MPI task, on core 8 (the 0 is the default permute option—not used here).

On the host, Intel MPI is smart about assigning the first task of a node to a core of the processor that is directly connected to the HCA. For applications that run a single task on the host, this will ensure the best communication performance.

As illustrated in Figure 13.5, the PCI bus of PU #1 is directly connect to the HCA (not an uncommon configuration). Hence, the first rank assigned on the host is put on PU #1 by Intel MPI. Point-2-point communication between nodes that use PU #0 for MPI tasks is subpar relative to the performance observed for communication between PU #1 sockets. Performance can decrease as much as 40% with messages below 4 kbyte, and 20% to 1% for messages ranging from 8 kbytes to 16 Mbytes, respectively.

When more than a single task is used on the host or coprocessor, it is more challenging to set the location of the tasks and provide a range of cores or hardware threads that can be used for each task. The Intel MPI defaults are reasonable. For instance, if two tasks are launched on a Stampede host, each is assigned to different processors, and the threads are forked only on the cores of the task's processor. Intel MPI has quite a few mechanisms to tailor MPI task and OpenMP thread placement and distributions. For Hybrid applications, the KMP_AFFINITY is used to describe the distribution of a task's threads, while the I_MPI_PIN_DOMAIN is used to describe (assign) a range of cores (domain) that each task will use to launch its threads. For instance, for launching a task on each of the NUMA memory nodes (there are 2 on the Stampede node) setting I_MPI_PIN_DOMAIN=socket will insure that tasks will be assigned on different processors.

For applications that require detailed selection of each domain, I_MPI_PIN_DOMAIN can be set to a mask list, with each mask element of the list corresponding to the cores of a domain. Tasks are assigned to each element, ordinally. That is, on a node, the lowest rank is assigned to the first domain, the next rank to the second domain, etc. For example if OMP_NUM_THREADS = 3, and two tasks are requested on a node, and the user wants rank 0 to run its three threads on cores 8, 9, 10 and rank 1 to run its threads on 0, 1 and 3. The mask should look like this:

Mask element 1: 0000 0111 0000 0000
Mask element 2: 0000 0000 0000 0111

To make life "simpler," the hexadecimal number of the mask is used in the variable assignment. A mask list is designated with brackets, and the two masks for rank 0 and 1 above would be set with
export I_MPI_PIN_DOMAIN="[1500,15]"
Experts often avoid using vendor-specific methods to set the affinity—which are usually passed to the runtime through environment variables. On Unix systems, `sched_setaffinity` and `sched_getaffinity` utilities are used within a code to bind a task's thread (each thread has a unique id) to a particular core.

SELECTION OF THE DAPL PROVIDERS

Selecting the correct list of providers can help improve the performance of your communication. In this section we will look at the performance of providers and show how to designate providers through an I_MPI environment variable.

Intel MPI can select automatically the list of providers, but the selection does not necessarily provide the best performance. The provider selection can be controlled directly through the environment variable **I_MPI_DAPL_PROVIDER_LIST**. This variable takes a comma separated list of up to three providers with the following syntax:

I_MPI_DAPL_PROVIDER_LIST = \
<Provider1,Provider2,Provider3>

Each of the providers in the list has a different role:

- Provider1: for small messages. This provider should have the lowest latency performance.
- Provider2: for large on-node messages. Applicable to MPI runs involving the coprocessor, or when using DAPL for intra-node communications.
- Provider3: for large messages between nodes.

On Stampede the values for the providers are:

I_MPI_DAPL_PROVIDER_LIST = \
ofa-v2-mlx4_0-1u, ofa-v2-scif0, ofa-v2-mcm-1

THE FIRST PROVIDER *OFA-V2-MLX4_0-1U*

Provider 1 is automatically set by Intel MPI and doesn't require any manipulation on the user side. On Stampede, it directly uses the low latency of the InfiniBand card available on the node to exchange messages.

THE SECOND PROVIDER ofa-v2-scif0 AND THE IMPACT OF THE INTRA-NODE FABRIC

The second provider ofa-v2-scif0, called scif, has a strong impact on large message performance inside the node. Also the choice of fabric that is used has an important influence on scif's effect. The fabric can be selected by using the following environmental variable:

I_MPI_FABRICS=
<fabric>|<intra-node fabric>:<inter-nodes fabric>

On InfiniBand clusters, the recommended fabric for internode communication is DAPL, and Intel MPI uses Shared Memory by default for intra-node communication. However, the MPI performance can be increased if DAPL is chosen for both intra-node and internode communications for some codes. This means that there are two possible fabric options that might be chosen through the I_MPI_FABRICS environment variable:

I_MPI_FABRICS=dapl

or

I_MPI_FABRICS=shm:dapl

Which one is optimal depends on the application, as mentioned, and the size of the messages at a particular scale of the MPI execution.

To illustrate these effects, Figure 13.6a provides a performance comparison of DAPL (with and without using the scif provider) versus shm:dapl, for internode communication using two CPUs, Intel MPI 5.0. Similar results can be observed inside the coprocessor in Figure 13.6b and between the CPU and the coprocessor in Figure 13.6c. These results were obtained with the Pingpong test of the Intel MPI Benchmarks (IMB) 4.0.

As you can see, shm:dapl provides the best performance at low message sizes, while dapl+scif is the optimal for applications that use messages larger than 256 kB. We also found that scif isn't used automatically by Intel MPI for CPU to CPU or coprocessor to coprocessor communications. The best performance in these cases is obtained by explicitly specifying the optimal combination. This is probably an issue that will be fixed in a future release of Intel MPI.

In all cases, the second provider doesn't have an impact on performance when the shm:dapl option is selected for the fabric.

THE LAST PROVIDER, ALSO CALLED THE PROXY

When using the InfiniBand network interface, the limited P2P local read bandwidth provided by the Intel® Xeon® E5 processor architecture significantly impacts the performance of communication from Intel Xeon Phi coprocessor. As shown in Figure 13.7, the low bandwidth of the point-to-point local read operation is a bottleneck for the MPI library.

To overcome this problem, Intel MPI has introduced an enhanced design to work around this limitation and provide better performance for MPI messaging across hosts and coprocessors on the Stampede system and similar clusters.

The Intel Xeon E5 processor family can now deliver a read bandwidth up to 7 GB/s between the CPU and a PCI device, and a similar bandwidth for a write. Also, the internode host-host communication bandwidth can reach 6 GB/s for a single-port InfiniBand FDR HCA.

For large message internode exchanges between a coprocessor and another node, the mechanism used by the provider is to employ a host-based approach called a proxy that takes advantage of these

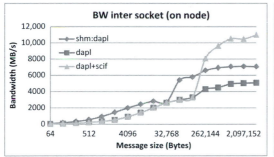
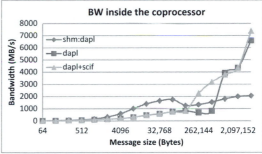
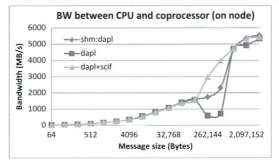

FIGURE 13.6

MPI provider performance for (a) CPU-to-CPU communication, (b) coprocessor-to-coprocessor communication, and (c) CPU-to-coprocessor communication.

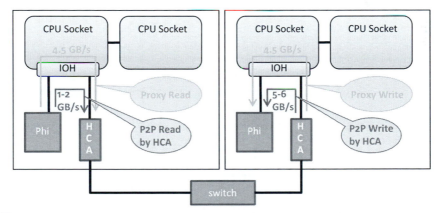

FIGURE 13.7

Local MPI read/write performance.

two channels (coprocessor-host and host-HCA) and works around the limited P2P local read bandwidth. The limitation, low bandwidth, for local P2P reads is shown in Figure 13.7.

The proxy is enabled by default, for internode communication that involves a coprocessor. But to demonstrate how important this proxy is, we tested the coprocessor to coprocessor internode communications with Intel MPI 5.0, with and without the proxy. The IMB 4.0 Pingpong was used to

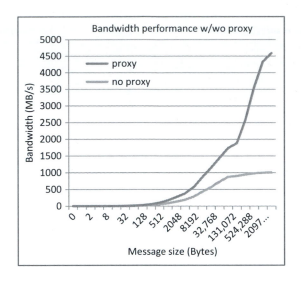

FIGURE 13.8

Intel MPI with and without InfiniBand proxy.

measure the performance. While the problem with the low read performance is overcome with the proxy (Figure 13.8), the 4.5 GB/s proxy bandwidth is lower than what could be obtained if the local read performance were as fast as the local write performance.

HYBRID APPLICATION SCALABILITY

It is important to see how the results obtained in microbenchmarks translate into measurable effects when using a scientific application. We have chosen a multiphase lattice Boltzmann method (LBM) as the application for this study. The particular implementation used corresponds to lbs3d-mpi, an open-source code available via the mplabs package. See Section "For more information" for details and code download.

The LBM is a mesoscopic technique used to investigate fluid dynamics at a high level of detail. LBM differs from traditional Computational Fluid Dynamics techniques in that a linear solver is not used. A regular Cartesian grid and fully explicit time evolution allow for relatively simple parallelization and optimization of the code. The dynamic evolution of the problem occurs via a series of local calculations performed at every computational grid point, followed by several memory moves of the results to the neighboring grid points. This is known as the collision-stream implementation of LBM. The book by Sauro Succi referenced in Section "For more information" contains a complete description of the technique.

The lbs3d-mpi code is based on a Free-Energy implementation by Zheng, Shu, and Chew. It uses an underlying model based on a D3Q19 decomposition for the velocity and a D3Q7 decomposition for the fluid phase, which leads to communication with neighboring MPI tasks across the six faces and twelve edges of each MPI task subdomain at every time step. Figure 13.9 shows the velocity discretization for D3Q7 and D3Q19. For clarity only the links corresponding to D3Q7 have been numbered.

In order to accommodate the MPI exchanges a single ghost layer is used around every task computational domain. In its current implementation lbs3d-mpi does not overlap communication and computation, so it should be a good example of the impact that the Intel MPI proxy can have in overall application performance on a worst case scenario.

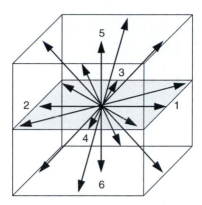

FIGURE 13.9

Velocity discretization directions for D3Q19 model. Notice that data must be exchanged across all faces and edges of the domain.

The implementation used here is based on an MPI domain decomposition and OpenMP parallelization of the main code loops. This hybrid implementation is necessary to obtain high performance on the coprocessor. The OpenMP parallelization is performed in the outermost loop for the calculations in order to maximize the amount of work for each thread. The computational domain is distributed equally among MPI tasks, and the partitioning can be controlled by the user. The examples presented here favor partitioning along the Y direction so that the loops in the X and Z directions can take advantage of vectorization and OMP parallelization, respectively. No MPI calls are made within OMP parallel regions.

Because of the nature of the algorithm, LBM simulations tend to use fairly large computational grid sizes, and MPI communication time is typically dominated by the large message data exchange across subdomain faces. This effect is even more evident when using hybrid implementations due to the larger message size per task. Since the proxy is most effective for large data exchanges, a significant difference in scalability is expected when enabling Intel's proxy-based communication in both native coprocessor only and symmetric (host and coprocessor) execution modes of this code.

Figure 13.10 shows the effect of enabling the proxy on the overall performance of the lbs3d-mpi code from mplabs, with performance reported in terms of Millions of Lattice Updates Per Second:

$$MLUPS = (Grid\ Volume \times Time\ Steps)/(Execution\ Time \times 10^6)$$

Native execution was performed using 240 OMP threads with a compact affinity setting, and a single MPI task per node. The computational domain is kept to $240 \times 240 \times 240$ grid points per node. In this example, MPI communication is dominated by messages over 1 MB in size. Measurements with the proxy enabled were taken with the environmental variable setting:

I_MPI_DAPL_PROVIDER_LIST = ofa-v2-mlx4_0-1u,ofa-v2-mcm-1

The results in Figure 13.10 clearly show the benefit of using the proxy for any communications involving the coprocessor. The line with square symbols shows the scalability for the CPU native execution, which does not change with the use of the proxy. The lines with crosses and triangles correspond to coprocessor native executions with and without the proxy respectively. The performance improvements are as high as 22% for the native coprocessor execution when running on 64 nodes.

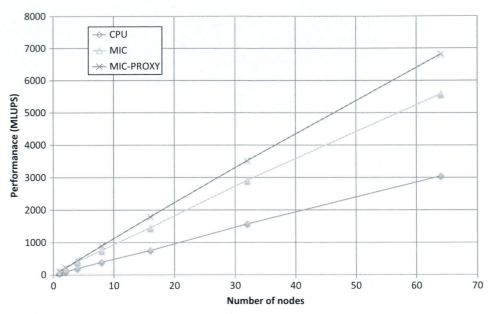

FIGURE 13.10

Scalability of LBM code with and without proxy enabled for native CPU and native coprocessor execution.

Notice that this corresponds, proportionally, to a much higher reduction in communication time, since MPI communication is only a fraction of the total runtime.

A similar effect for the proxy on the overall performance of the lbs3d-mpi code is observed when using a symmetric execution model, where the effect of the proxy is even more pronounced, providing a 31% improvement in performance when executing the code on 64 nodes. Because the code runs approximately twice as fast on the coprocessor than on the host processors, three MPI tasks are used per node, two assigned to the coprocessor and one to the host processors. This achieves a reasonable static workload balance, but also triples the number of MPI tasks per node and increases communication.

LOAD BALANCE

As mentioned above, since this code uses domain decomposition, and the execution on a single coprocessor is approximately twice as fast as the host execution on two sockets (comparing 16 threads on the CPU host with 240 threads on the coprocessor), twice as many MPI tasks were assigned to the coprocessor as to the host. This is a simple way to adjust static load balance between the two. Notice that not doing this will lead to reduced performance, as illustrated in Figure 13.11.

TASK AND THREAD MAPPING

It is important to note that for all the presented cases, the MPI task mapping was performed using the following settings:

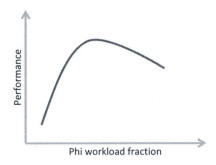

FIGURE 13.11

Performance model for coprocessor workload fraction. Notice degradation in the performance if too much or too little work is assigned to the coprocessor.

```
I_MPI_PIN_MODE=omp:compact
KMP_AFFINITY=compact,granularity=fine
```

One can manually set up the MPI task and OMP thread mapping and affinity, but care must be taken to avoid binding multiple logical threads to the same core on the host or the same hardware thread on the coprocessor. In the worst-case scenario, all threads could be executed on the same core or hardware thread, leading to a tremendous slowdown in execution due to the serialization of the multiple thread execution. As an example, binding all threads to host core 0 leads to a performance of only 4 MLUPS, more than an order of magnitude slower than the correct binding provided (~50 MLUPS). The effect is even more pronounced on the coprocessor, where the performance of the example test case drops to 1.4 MLUPS, which is two orders of magnitude slower than the performance obtained for optimally placed threads (~112 MLUPS).

While the bindings selected by the Intel MPI library use hardware information and sensible distribution mechanisms for thread placements, and generally provide the highest overall performance, it is important to keep in mind the hardware configuration and distribution patterns when working with other MPI implementations and analyzing performance of hybrid codes.

SUMMARY

MPI implementations have adapted over the years to accommodate more complicated nodes with hierarchical NUMA architectures, asymmetric connectivity, and heterogeneous microprocessors (processors and coprocessors). When there are fewer tasks than cores, assignment of tasks and threads to cores can make a significant difference in performance.

In order to achieve good performance across a wide range of message sizes it is necessary to designate appropriate MPI providers. Using the Intel MPI provided proxy is critical to obtaining optimal communication performance across multiple coprocessors, as illustrated by the application showcased in this chapter.

Acknowledgments

Stampede is funded by the National Science Foundation (NSF) through award ACI-1134872. XSEDE (Extreme Science and Engineering Discovery Environment) support is funded through the NSF award ACI-1053575.

FOR MORE INFORMATION

- Goglin, Brice Managing the Topology of Heterogeneous Cluster Nodes with Hardware Locality (hwloc). In Proceedings of 2014 International Conference on High Performance Computing & Simulation (HPCS 2014), Bologna, Italy, July 2014. hwloc, http://www.open-mpi.org/projects/hwloc/.
- https://software.intel.com/en-us/articles/intel-mpi-benchmarks.
- mplabs code, https://github.com/carlosrosales/mplabs.
- Ramachandran, Vienne, J., Van Der Wijngaart, R., Koesterke, L., Sharapov, I., 2013. Performance evaluation of NAS parallel benchmarks on Intel Xeon Phi. In 6th International Workshop on Parallel Programming Models and Systems Software for High-End Computing (P2S2), in conjunction with ICPP, Lyon, October 2013.
- Rosales, Porting to the Intel Xeon Phi: Opportunities and Challenges, XSCALE13, Boulder, CO, USA.
- https://www.xsede.org/documents/271087/586927/CRosales_TACC_porting_mic.pdf.
- Succi, S, 2001. The Lattice Boltzmann Equation for Fluid Dynamics and Beyond. Oxford University Press, Oxford, UK.
- Zheng, H.W., Shu, C., Chew, Y.T., 2006. A lattice Boltzmann model for multiphase flows with large density ratio. J. Comput. Phys. 218, 353–371.
- The TACC Stampede system is a cluster of 6400 nodes, each containing two 8-core Intel E5-2680 Xeon processors and an Intel Xeon Phi 61-core SE10P coprocessor. The nodes are connected through an FDR InfiniBand network. Additional details at: https://www.tacc.utexas.edu.
- All measurements presented in this chapter were performed using MPSS version 2.1.6720, the Intel compiler version 14.0.1.106, and Intel MPI version 4.1.3.049.

POWER ANALYSIS ON THE INTEL® XEON PHI™ COPROCESSOR

14

Claude J. Wright

Intel Corporation, USA

POWER ANALYSIS 101

In this chapter, we present a methodology and tools for Intel Xeon Phi Coprocessor Power Analysis while running High Performance Computing (HPC) workloads.

Power is defined as the amount of energy consumed per unit time, where the unit of time is joule per second (J/s) or more commonly, watt. We will use watt as our standard unit of measurement for power going forward.

The formula for instantaneous power is based on Ohm's Law: Power=Current multiplied by Voltage. Current is the flow of electrons through a conductor and amperes (amps) is its standard unit of measurement. Voltage is equal to the work done per unit charge against a static electric field, and Volt is its standard unit of measurement.

We can compute power (watts) by multiplying the amperage by the voltage. There are various ways we can measure power. For example, we can measure the instantaneous raw power, average power, peak power, minimum power, root mean square power, or a moving average applied to the raw power data. For this chapter, we use a standard called the "1-second moving average." This form of power analysis is chosen because it is thermally relevant. This averaging provides correlation to real-world measureable thermal events. For example, if we only measure instantaneous power, we may see spikes in power levels for very short durations that will not have measureable impacts to the silicon temperature on the heat sink or other thermal solution. In fact, the Intel MPSS control panel uses the 1-s moving average when displaying the power being consumed in watts.

Another common power term used for electronics is thermal design power (TDP) rating which is typically specified in watts. The TDP rating refers to the maximum amount of heat generated by the device which the cooling system is required to dissipate in typical operation. For example, TDP is 300 W for some coprocessor models and 245 W for other models. The TDP specification is also a good baseline number of the wattage power budget needed to run the coprocessor for full performance. This does not mean that the coprocessor power is strictly limited to the TDP rating. The TDP rating is not the same as "peak possible power" but more like a power rating when running typical applications. A carefully crafted program (like power virus) could exceed the TDP rating, but this would not be a typical HPC workload by any means.

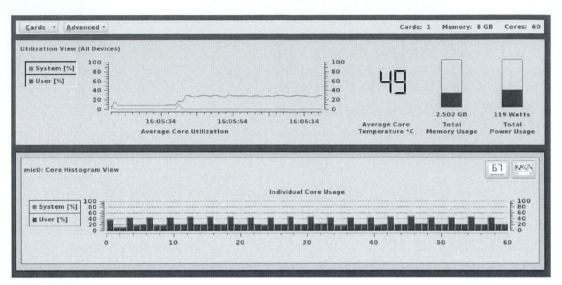

FIGURE 14.1

The Intel® MPSS micsmc tool showing power and temperature.

One of the most common methods for measuring direct current (DC) power involves using what is known as a sense resistor. This resistor has a very low resistance (measured in ohms). When electrical current flows through a sense resistor, it produces a small voltage that is proportional to the amount of current that is flowing through the sense resistor. This provides the amps we need to multiply by the voltage to compute the power level. We measure voltage by attaching instrument probes to the positive and negative terminals of the power source to be measured. We then multiply the current (or amps) by the voltage to get the raw instantaneous power. This work is typically performed by some data acquisition hardware like an oscilloscope, Data Acquisition (DAQ) unit, or even a simple microcontroller. In fact, the coprocessor comes with a simple built-in power analyzer accessible with the standard Intel MPSS tools as shown in Figure 14.1.

The coprocessor utilizes a microcontroller on the circuit board called the system management controller (SMC), and one of its jobs is to monitor the incoming DC power to the coprocessor, the coprocessor silicon die temperature sensor and the other various thermal sensors as indicated in Figure 14.2. The location of the supplemental 2×3 and 2×4 12 V power connectors is also shown in Figure 14.2 (these two power connectors are required for normal operation). The SMC also manages the fan speed on coprocessors that have an active fan. In the context of a software-based power analyzer, we will exploit this SMC feature as a means to get the coprocessor power and coprocessor silicon temperature. As shown below, there are other thermal sensors beside the coprocessor CPU temperature that we may query, such as the memory, intake, and exhaust temperatures. These extra thermal sensors will be of interest to those who are also doing the server or compute node thermal tuning when running some high-power HPC workloads, such as dialing in the minimum server fan speed or even adjusting the data center ambient temperature for ideal cooling conditions.

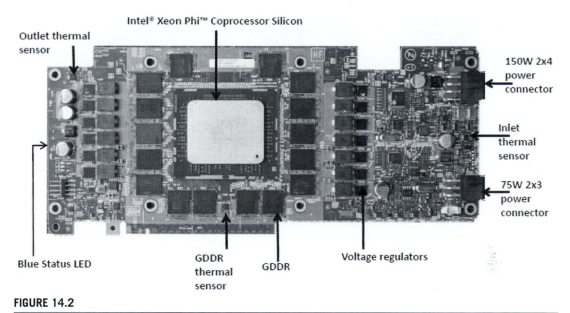

FIGURE 14.2

Thermal sensor locations on the coprocessor card.

MEASURING POWER AND TEMPERATURE WITH SOFTWARE

As seen in Figure 14.1, there is support in the standard Intel MPSS control panel to monitor both total power and coprocessor silicon temperature. This is the micsmc utility and should also already be in your path if Intel MPSS was installed per the default user guide instructions. For the usage discussions in this chapter, we assume a Linux-based default Intel MPSS installation. Now, go ahead and execute the control panel tool by executing:

    $ micsmc

The Intel MPSS control panel will pop up and will present continuously monitored coprocessor power, thermals, coprocessor core utilization, and memory utilization. A parameter-driven command line interface is also available to support power analysis with micsmc as needed. If we enter the following command:

    $ micsmc –a

The terminal will show all the coprocessor power, thermal, and utilization indicators in a command line environment. To get a list of all the useful micsmc commands:

    $ micsmc --help

The micsmc tool is very useful for monitoring the coprocessor power and temperature. To only see the power that is being consumed by the coprocessor, we can use micsmc with the –f flag:

    $ micsmc –f

As seen in Figure 14.3, micsmc gives us the total power that is being consumed on the coprocessor at any given time. Also notice that the coprocessor silicon core frequency is also reported at the same

```
mic0 (freq):
    Core Frequency: ........... 1.24 GHz
    Total Power: ............. 115.00 Watts
    Low Power Limit: ......... 315.00 Watts
    High Power Limit: ........ 375.00 Watts


mic1 (freq):
    Core Frequency: ........... 1.24 GHz
    Total Power: ............. 109.00 Watts
    Low Power Limit: ......... 315.00 Watts
    High Power Limit: ........ 375.00 Watts
```

FIGURE 14.3

Total power of the coprocessor from the micsmc tool.

time. Another great feature of the micsmc utility is that it can report measurements for all the coprocessors in the system simultaneously. This feature enables retrieving a snapshot of the instantaneous power for all coprocessors in the system at the requested time. We can also query micsmc for the coprocessor temperatures readings with the –t option:

    $ micsmc –t

As seen in Figure 14.4, we can use the micsmc utility to also show us the temperature profile for the coprocessor. Notice that we get much more information than just the coprocessor CPU silicon temperature. We can see the memory and intake/exhaust thermal readings. Figure 14.2 shows the location of these sensors on the coprocessor. This feature may be useful when performing platform tuning and ideal minimum fan speed settings for the host server or compute node to minimize the total fan power being

```
mic0 (temp):
    Cpu Temp: ................ 66.00 C
    Memory Temp: ............. 46.00 C
    Fan-In Temp: ............. 39.00 C
    Fan-Out Temp: ............ 46.00 C
    Core Rail Temp: .......... 46.00 C
    Uncore Rail Temp: ........ 47.00 C
    Memory Rail Temp: ........ 47.00 C

mic1 (temp):
    Cpu Temp: ................ 64.00 C
    Memory Temp: ............. 44.00 C
    Fan-In Temp: ............. 35.00 C
    Fan-Out Temp: ............ 44.00 C
    Core Rail Temp: .......... 43.00 C
    Uncore Rail Temp: ........ 44.00 C
    Memory Rail Temp: ........ 44.00 C
```

FIGURE 14.4

Temperature profile of the coprocessor from the micsmc tool.

consumed. The micsmc tool displays the power and thermal data for all the coprocessors installed in a system or a node of a cluster.

CREATING A POWER AND TEMPERATURE MONITOR SCRIPT

We saw in the previous section that we can use the Intel MPSS micsmc utility to display the power and temperature profile of a coprocessor. This is very handy when we need to see the power and thermal indictors while running key HPC applications, as well as performing thermal tuning of a platform under load. Because micsmc is running on the host server or compute node, we can use standard scripting to create a very simple but useful power and thermal monitor based around the Intel MPSS micsmc utility.

A handy script would be the one that would monitor only the coprocessor power and coprocessor CPU temperature including a timestamp, but not other available temperature readings. In the previous micsmc examples, we saw that the output was much more than just the coprocessor's total power and CPU temperature. We may sometimes want to display only power and thermal information. Such a power and thermal monitor shell script might output information as shown in Figure 14.5. Figure 14.6 shows the code to produce this power and temperature logger.

The code in Figure 14.6 can be found in the shell script called power_monitor.sh (download with other code from this book at lotsofcores.com). When run you should see a display similar to what is shown in Figure 14.5. This is a handy little script that can run in the background to monitor the coprocessor power and silicon temperature. It would be straightforward to log or echo that same information to a text file.

NOTE

One thing to note about using the Intel MPSS micsmc tool for power measurements is that the Intel Xeon Phi Coprocessor supports various modes of low-power idle states; however, the act of querying the power with micsmc will bring the coprocessor out of the current idle state immediately. This means we cannot use the micsmc utility to measure the true idle power of the coprocessor.

CREATING A POWER AND TEMPERATURE LOGGER WITH THE micsmc TOOL

In the previous section, we showed an example of a script to monitor the coprocessor power and CPU silicon temperature. This is useful as a simple power monitor or power meter when doing HPC workload power/performance tuning or platform thermal tuning.

```
Timestamp: 11:00:18.576

mic0 Power:        101.00 Watts
mic1 Power:        107.00 Watts

mic0 Temp:         37.00 C
mic1 Temp:         39.00 C
```

FIGURE 14.5

Sample power and temperature logger output.

```bash
#!/bin/bash

while : ; do

    # Build the Timestamp string
    STR=`echo $(date +%N) | sed 's/^0*//'`
    STR=`printf "%03d" $(($STR/1000000))`
    STR=`echo $(date +%H:%M:%S)"."$STR`
    TIME="Timestamp: $STR"

    # Format the power and thermal data string as desired
    DATA="$({ micsmc -f; micsmc -t; sleep .1; } | grep -e Cpu -e temp -e
Total -e freq | paste -d ' ' - - | awk '{print $1,$4,"\t",$6,$7 }')"

    # Display our power and thermal data strings
    clear

    echo "$TIME"
    echo "$DATA"

done
```

FIGURE 14.6

Coprocessor power and temperature monitor bash shell script [power_monitor.sh].

However, one desirable capability is logging the power and thermal data into some standard format like .cvs for better postprocessing of the raw power data using other power profiles or plots. We may also want to timestamp the power/thermal log data for temporal alignment with the HPC application compute phase to determine the flops-per-watt.

We also likely may need a more advanced scripting language than bash for more sophisticated data manipulation. We use Python for our next code example, leveraging its support for various data types. Our improved power and thermal logger script might output a log file that looks something like shown in Figure 14.7.

The output in Figure 14.7 imports directly into Microsoft® Excel allowing the production of a variety of plots and charts. Because we now have power data with exact timestamps, we can later overlay this information with statistics from the compute phase of our HPC workload in order to compute real

Time	Mic0 Power	Mic0 Temp
35:24.8	106	44
35:25.0	104	44
35:25.1	141	47
35:25.3	148	48
35:25.5	239	49
35:25.7	244	51
35:25.8	246	52

FIGURE 14.7

Sample power and temperature logger output using Python.

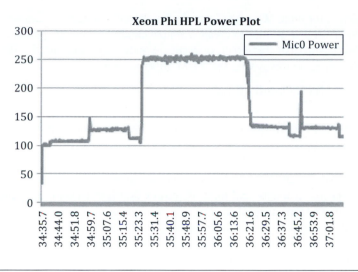

FIGURE 14.8

The Xeon Phi HPL power plot from the power logger script.

flops-per-watt data. We should not include the HPC code initialization phase and memory cleanup phase power data when computing the efficiency, and we would use the timestamps as a way to align the power data with the HPC program parallel compute phase. In this example, we will use the high-performance LINPACK (HPL) native workload that is supplied with the Intel MPSS RPMs (micperf RPM) and can be executed by the micprun application. Figure 14.8 shows an example of what the power profile looks like when we plot the data.

The power plot above shows the entire power profile while running HPL on the coprocessor. A typical HPC workload may include phases for initialization, computation, and memory cleanup work. In order to compute the true flops-per-watt number, we need to align the compute phase of HPL with the various power samples in our log file taken during the parallel compute phase. There are a number of ways to accomplish this, for example, one may use timestamps in the HPC program log when the compute phase starts and ends. Our power log data would need to be filtered to throw away the power samples that fell outside of the parallel compute phase, so that we can then filter to compute the average of all the valid power samples. We have found that most of the time, the compute phase of an HPC program correlates to the highest power envelope in our power plot. This is an easy way to also find the compute phase preamble and postamble without having to overlay the HPC compute phase start and end times. The power plot in Figure 14.8 shows clearly when we are doing the heavy floating-point computation on the sparse matrix, and this is clear also in the raw power log file as well.

Our improved power and temperature logger for HPC flops-per-watt analysis will now use standard imported Python modules and an improved program structure with flexible logging features. You may download this code sample from lotofcores.com.

POWER ANALYSIS USING IPMI

There is a neat method to measure the host server or compute node power consumption by utilizing the common intelligent platform management interface (IPMI). Most Intel servers support this feature that queries the server for total AC power from the baseboard management controller. We will use the open-source IPMI driver and utilities to create a simple compute node AC power analyzer.

We need to first ensure that the server, or compute node, is set up with the IPMI driver and IPMI utilities. One easy way to do this is with the YUM utility shown below:

```
$ yum install OpenIPMI OpenIPMI-tools
$ service ipmi start
```

We can confirm all is working by querying the entire server or compute node sensor data records (SDR) with the following command:

```
$ ipmitool sdr
```

Figure 14.9 shows the output and we can see that we have access to many sensors like host CPU temperatures, fan speeds, voltages, and total AC power. Not just server power and thermals but total server health. This can be very handy!

That is a lot of sensor data to sort through! In our application for power analysis, we really just need the server total power (one might add the host server CPU thermal sensors):

```
$ ipmitool sensor get 'PS1 Input Power' 'PS2 Input Power'
```

This will now give us only the AC power being consumed on the two main power supplies (PS1 and PS2) in the server as shown in Figure 14.10.

You may have noticed that one of the power supplies in the target server is showing 0 W. This is normal since this is a dual power supply based server, and only one of the power supply units is needed to power this server under the current load condition.

We could use a simple script at this point to issue the IPMI command to query the power supply units and proceed to timestamp and log this info into a log file for later processing of the average power during the compute phase of the HPC workload. The bash script we used for the simple power and thermal monitor could be used also for this IPMI tool to gather the server or compute node total AC power.

HARDWARE-BASED POWER ANALYSIS METHODS

We have shown some examples in this chapter on how to use Intel MPSS tools, as well as, industry-standard tools like IPMI to create a simple power analyzer that can be used for flops-per-watt analysis

Pwr Unit Status	0x00	ok
Pwr Unit Redund	0x0a	ok
IPMI Watchdog	0x00	ok
Physical Scrty	0x00	ok
FP NMI Diag Int	0x00	ok
SMI Timeout	0x00	ok
System Event Log	0x20	ok
System Event	0x00	ok
Button	0x00	ok
VR Watchdog	0x00	ok
Fan Redundancy	0x01	ok

FIGURE 14.9

A typical server sensor data record with the power consumption information highlighted.

SSB Therm Trip	0x00	ok
IO Mod Presence	0x00	ok
SAS Mod Presence	0x00	ok
BMC FW Health	0x00	ok
System Airflow	80 CFM	ok
BB P1 VR Temp	15 degrees C	ok
Front Panel Temp	17 degrees C	ok
SSB Temp	43 degrees C	ok
BB P2 VR Temp	16 degrees C	ok
BB Vtt 2 Temp	20 degrees C	ok
BB Vtt 1 Temp	17 degrees C	ok
HSBP 1 Temp	16 degrees C	ok
Exit Air Temp	24 degrees C	ok
LAN NIC Temp	33 degrees C	ok
System Fan 1	7987 RPM	ok
System Fan 2	7987 RPM	ok
System Fan 3	8085 RPM	ok
System Fan 4	7987 RPM	ok
System Fan 5	7987 RPM	ok
PS1 Status	0x01	ok
PS2 Status	0x09	ok
PS1 Input Power	332 Watts	ok
PS2 Input Power	0 Watts	ok
PS1 Curr Out %	40 unspecified	ok
PS2 Curr Out %	0 unspecified	ok
PS1 Temperature	19 degrees C	ok
PS2 Temperature	18 degrees C	ok
P1 Status	0x80	ok
P2 Status	0x80	ok
P1 Therm Margin	-80 degrees C	ok
P2 Therm Margin	-79 degrees C	ok
P1 Therm Ctrl %	0 unspecified	ok
P2 Therm Ctrl %	0 unspecified	ok
P1 ERR2	0x00	ok
P2 ERR2	0x00	ok
CATERR	0x00	ok
P1 MSID Mismatch	0x00	ok
CPU Missing	0x00	ok
P1 DTS Therm Mgn	-80 degrees C	ok
P2 DTS Therm Mgn	-78 degrees C	ok
DIMM Thrm Mrgn 1	-77 degrees C	ok
DIMM Thrm Mrgn 2	-73 degrees C	ok
DIMM Thrm Mrgn 3	-76 degrees C	ok
DIMM Thrm Mrgn 4	-74 degrees C	ok
Mem P1 Thrm Trip	0x00	ok
Mem P2 Thrm Trip	0x00	ok
Agg Therm Mgn 1	-36 degrees C	ok
BB +12.0V	11.83 Volts	ok
BB +5.0V	4.96 Volts	ok
BB +3.3V	3.24 Volts	ok
BB +5.0V STBY	4.94 Volts	ok
BB +3.3V AUX	3.24 Volts	ok
BB +1.05Vccp P1	0.83 Volts	ok
BB +1.05Vccp P2	0.85 Volts	ok
BB +1.5 P1MEM AB	1.50 Volts	ok
BB +1.5 P1MEM CD	1.50 Volts	ok
BB +1.5 P2MEM AB	1.50 Volts	ok
BB +1.5 P2MEM CD	1.48 Volts	ok
BB +1.8V AUX	1.77 Volts	ok
BB +1.1V STBY	1.08 Volts	ok
BB +3.3V Vbat	3.21 Volts	ok
BB +3.3 RSR1 PGD	3.23 Volts	ok
BB +3.3 RSR2 PGD	3.03 Volts	ok

Figure 14.9—Cont'd

Sensor ID	PS1 Input Power (0x54)
Entity ID	10.1
Sensor Type (Analog)	Other
Sensor Reading	332 (+/- 0) Watts
Status	ok
Upper Non-Critical	868.000
Upper Critical	920.000
Sensor ID	PS2 Input Power (0x55)
Entity ID	10.2
Sensor Type (Analog)	Other
Sensor Reading	0 (+/- 0) Watts
Status	ok
Upper Non-Critical	868.000
Upper Critical	920.000

FIGURE 14.10

Server input power sensors and limits.

and estimates. This is very useful for the software developer who is writing an HPC workload to see quickly how well the system is doing for compute energy efficiency.

However, to measure power in a nonintrusive manner (i.e., no software load on the unit under measurement), we need to employ some kind of hardware-based power analysis methodology. There are several methods one could employ here, but we will cover a couple common methods used today for the Green 500 tuning and measurement, plus methods used for specific tasks for hardware-based power analysis.

One method to measure the total power of an HPC cluster is to use a power distribution unit (PDU). These are useful devices that look much like an AC power strip but have built-in power measurement capability. In fact, many of these include a built-in Web server that allows the administrator or user to remotely monitor the instantaneous power that is being consumed while the HPC cluster is under load. These smart PDUs can be used in conjunction with SNMP (simple network management protocol) and Python scripts to create a power logger at the cluster level. One advantage to the PDU as a power analyzer is that all of the rack device power are captured, including the fabric (switches). We would otherwise not have an easy means to query the total AC power of that particular device. All the hardware that a data center rack may contain are typically all pulling power from these PDUs, so we can simply ask these smart PDUs what power is at any instance in time. Figure 14.11 shows an example of a typical PDU.

Another technique for hardware-based power analysis at the compute node level is to use an AC power analyzer. These are devices that connect between the AC power socket (source of power) and the load (the server or compute node). These AC power analyzers will also give us a nonintrusive power measurement which will not affect any of the software threads on the system under test. For example, we do not want to have the compute node spending compute resources logging its own power consumption data. By utilizing nonintrusive power measurement techniques, we can offload the measurement and logging burden to another system that issues SNMP or GPIB commands to retrieve and log the power data for later postprocessing.

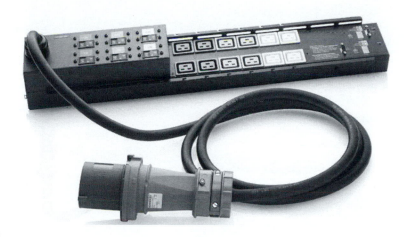

FIGURE 14.11

A typical power distribution unit (PDU) for the data center.

A HARDWARE-BASED COPROCESSOR POWER ANALYZER

The last topic to cover is a hardware-based coprocessor power analyzer that can perform advanced analysis nonintrusively on the HPC system under test. This methodology uses PCIe interposers and sense resistors along with the National Instruments LabVIEW Signal Express software package to sample and perform real-time analysis of the coprocessor power.

Figure 14.12 shows my hardware-based power analyzer. I developed it using standard off the shelf components (PCIe interposer from Adex Electronics) and National Instruments LabVIEW software. This setup can sample power data at very high sample rates (25,000 samples per second), as well as with high accuracy (24-bit ADC). It is based around a PCIe interposer to read the PCI express power (from the PCIe 3.3 V and PCIe 12 V) plus sense resistors for the external 2×3 and 2×4 12 V supplemental power rails. We simply feed the raw voltage and current signals into a data acquisition unit that is then sampled by LabVIEW to compute the instantaneous power of the coprocessor. Figure 14.13 shows an example of the power being measured and logged with LabVIEW.

The power scope shot above was taken while I increased the number of coprocessor cores to use for an HPC workload to see how linear the power was in relation to active core scaling. The horizontal axis is time and the vertical axis is power in watts. The raw power data are sampled at about 5 kHz and LabVIEW is used to compute the 1-s moving average in real time (using a finite impulse response filter in software) to produce this scope shot while running the HPC workload. One major advantage here is that I can now perform advanced power analysis without asking the processor or coprocessor for any computation or logging. This has the effect of keeping all the hardware threads free for the HPC workload we need to run.

There are four power rails (adding up to the 300 W TDP) we need to consider getting all the incoming power to the Intel Xeon Phi Coprocessor as shown in Figure 14.14.

The PCIe 3.3 V and PCIe 12 V we can sample from a PCIe interposer and the 2×3 and 2×4 supplemental power can be sampled from standard sense resistors in series with the incoming power to the coprocessor. In this example, I used a 10 mΩ sense resistor for the PCIe interposer and I used

FIGURE 14.12

A Xeon Phi Coprocessor hardware power analyzer.

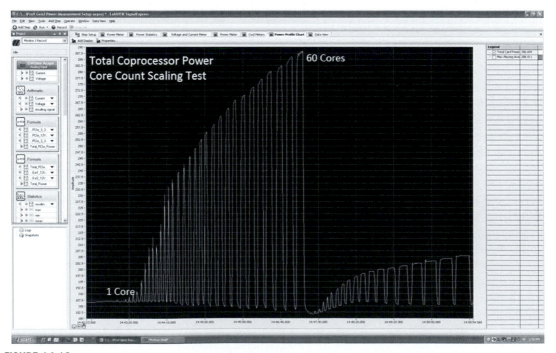

FIGURE 14.13

Total coprocessor power measured with LabVIEW.

Coprocessor Power Rail (V)	Power Rail Spec (W)
PCI Express 3.3	10
PCI Express 12	65
2x3 Supplemental	75
2x4 Supplemental	150

FIGURE 14.14

Total input power rails for coprocessor.

heavy-duty 25 mΩ sense resistors for the 2×3 and 2×4 supplemental 12 V power. The raw power data for these four power rails might look something like the one shown in Figure 14.15.

Figure 14.15 shows the real-time instantaneous power of the coprocessor with thousands of samples per second. I combined the PCIe 3.3 V and PCIe 12 V into a single label called total PCIe power, and just added this with the 2×3 and 2×4 supplemental 12 V power to get the total power shown at the top of the scope shot. This same data may be recorded and logged by LabVIEW for further postprocessing of the raw power data. We can also have LabVIEW give the power data with statistics applied in text format if needed as shown in Figure 14.16.

Figure 14.16 shows what LabVIEW can do for us with respect to statistics, which include min, max, and average. Notice that the PCIe 3.3 V auxiliary power shows no real power, as the coprocessor does not pull any power from the PCIe 3.3 V aux power that is typically reserved for network cards that need standby power to wake on an event.

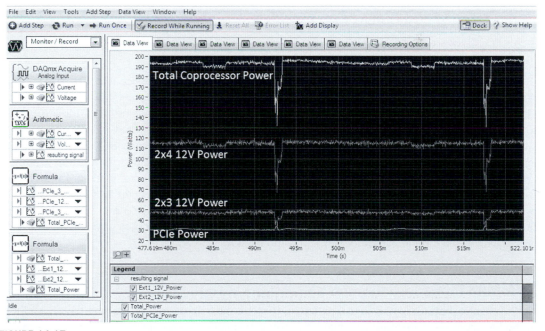

FIGURE 14.15

The raw instantaneous power of the coprocessor.

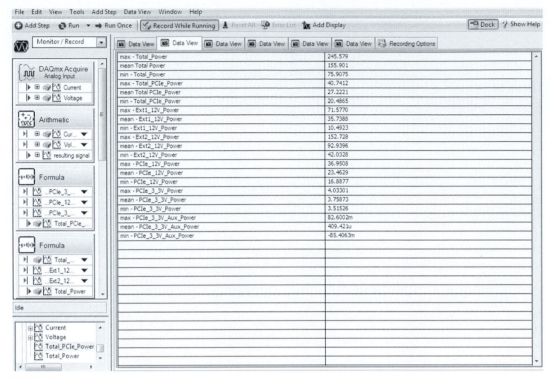

FIGURE 14.16

Real-time power rail statistics on the coprocessor.

I used a hardware-based power analyzer like this to give some confidence that the software-based power analyzer we created in the beginning of this chapter is within an acceptable range or tolerance. One thing we need to consider when doing this correlation test with software-based tools is we want to ensure we are using the same method to compute the total power. The Intel MPSS micsmc utility gathers power data from the on-board SMC that internally calculates power using the 1-s moving average method. In LabVIEW Signal Express, I also use a 1-s moving in some instrumentation windows to compare apples-to-apples. In my lab setup, I typically observe slightly higher total card power (about 4-6 W) with my hardware-based power analyzer, and this is primarily due to the fact that the SMC does not monitor the PCIe 3.3 V power rail, only the 12 V rails (PCIe 12 V, 2×3 and 2×4). The logging feature of LabVIEW Signal Express can give us very accurate raw power data using either raw text or power data in scientific notation for further postprocessing.

SUMMARY

In this chapter, because power consumption has become such an important limiting factor, we looked at the key methods to measure and analyze power consumption on a coprocessor using software-only tools and simple scripts.

I also showed how I've done nonintrusive power measurement methods that offload the power analysis and logging to another dedicated server and keep all the threads frec on the compute node for the real HPC workload. This method has helped validate that the software-only method, which is easier and cheaper, can be used as a reliable and accurate method for understanding power while performing a workload but not idle power.

We are fortunate that useful power and thermal measurements are available and accurate for active HPC systems using software-only methods. We can have confidence on them. This is, in no small part, because of the hardware-based power analysis we've done in my lab at Intel.

FOR MORE INFORMATION

Here are some additional reading materials we recommend related to this chapter:

- Intel Xeon Phi™ coprocessor: Datasheet. http://www.intel.com/content/www/us/en/processors/xeon/xeon-phi-coprocessor-datasheet.html.
- Intel® Xeon Phi™ System Software Developer's Guide. http://www.intel.com/content/dam/www/public/us/en/documents/product-briefs/xeon-phi-coprocessor-system-software-developers-guide.pdf.
- Green 500 Methodology. http://www.green500.org/docs/pubs/RunRules_Ver1.0.pdf.
- Intel IPMI Site. http://www.intel.com/content/www/us/en/servers/ipmi/ipmi-home.html.
- Download the code from this and other chapters, at http://lotsofcores.com.

INTEGRATING INTEL XEON PHI COPROCESSORS INTO A CLUSTER ENVIRONMENT

15

Paul Peltz*, **Troy Baer***, **Ryan Braby***, **Vince Betro***, **Glenn Brook***, **Karl Schulz**†

University of Tennessee, Knoxville—NICS, USA, †Intel Corporation, USA

EARLY EXPLORATIONS

The University of Tennessee and the Oak Ridge National Laboratory jointly operate the Joint Institute for Computational Sciences (JICS). In 2007 JICS, through the National Science Foundation (NSF) award for the Kraken project, established National Institute of Computational Sciences (NICS). In early 2011, NICS and Intel embarked on a multiyear strategic engagement to pursue the development of next-generation, high-performance computing (HPC) solutions based on the Intel® Many Integrated Core (Intel® MIC) architecture, now branded as the Intel® Xeon Phi™ product family. NICS received early access to Intel MIC technologies in return for application testing, performance results, and expert feedback to help guide ongoing development efforts at Intel. The resulting collaboration allowed the Application Acceleration Center of Excellence within JICS to explore software performance using several preproduction codename Knights Ferry (KNF) software development platforms that were networked together to produce one of the first clusters equipped with Intel MIC technology outside of Intel. Shortly thereafter, NICS and Intel joined with Cray to deploy a two-node Cray CX1 "cluster-in-a-box" supercomputer equipped with one KNF coprocessor per node and Appro, a computer systems manufacturer, to deploy a four-node conventional cluster with two KNF coprocessors per node.

At the 2011 International Conference for High Performance Computing, Networking, Storage, and Analysis (SC11), NICS and Intel announced their strategic engagement, and NICS presented early results for scientific applications that it had successfully ported to the Intel MIC architecture. The presented results included porting status and selected performance results for major scientific application codes such as NWChem and Enzo, along with the electronic structure code Elk and an in-house Boltzmann computational fluid dynamics solver. The announcements and videos on these results can be found in Section "For more information."

The initial work conducted at JICS with the KNF coprocessors led to the development and subsequent expansion to the Beacon project, which is currently funded by the NSF and the University of Tennessee to explore the impact of the Intel Xeon Phi coprocessor on computational science and engineering applications.

BEACON SYSTEM HISTORY

The initial strategic partnership expanded into Beacon, which began as an Strategic Technologies for CyberInfrastructure grant from the NSF, Award #1137097 in 2012. The proposed system was a 16-node cluster where each node contained dual preproduction KNF coprocessors interconnected with a single FDR Infiniband switch. This was a small cluster and expected to be very simple to deploy and manage. However, the operating software for the KNF cards was not yet designed to work with diskless NFS root installations. Therefore, methods other than the NICS preferred method of cluster management based on a diskless NFS root had to be used.

Early users (including those external to the University of Tennessee) were able to make significant progress in porting codes to the coprocessor. The Beacon project included a planned upgrade from KNF to the production generation of coprocessors codenamed Knights Corner (KNC). However, the Beacon project was successful enough that the University of Tennessee decided to invest beyond the original plan, allowing a larger and highly power efficient cluster to be deployed.

This new, upgraded Beacon supercomputer, comprised 48 Cray CS300-AC (Appro Greenblade nodes at the time, subsequently Cray acquired Appro) nodes with dual Intel® Xeon® E5 processors and four Intel Xeon Phi coprocessors per node, was rapidly deployed. Working with many teams spread around the world, including teams from Intel, Appro, and NICS, a major effort was undertaken to complete the cluster build and system-wide tuning and perform high-performance Linpack runs in time for a submission to the Green500 list. As a result, Beacon took the #1 spot on the Green500 list at SC12. Following the conference, Pradeep Dubey, an Intel Fellow who worked on the project stated that "this is the most remarkable collaboration story that I can think of in my Intel career so far" (Figure 15.1).

NSF researchers are currently using Beacon to optimize and modernize applications for the highly parallel capability of the Intel Xeon Phi coprocessors and future highly parallel architectures. Please see "For More Information," at the end of this Chapter, to learn more about the Green500 and Pradeep Dubey's blog in which he is quoted.

BEACON SYSTEM ARCHITECTURE
HARDWARE

Beacon is a Cray CS300-AC™ Cluster comprised 48 compute nodes and 6 I/O nodes with an FDR Infiniband interconnect. Each compute node contains two 8-core Intel Xeon E5-2670 processors, 256GB Memory, 960GB SSD Storage, and four Intel Xeon Phi 5110P coprocessors. Overall, Beacon provides 768 conventional cores and 11,520 coprocessor cores that provide over 210TFLOP/s of combined computational performance, 12TB of system memory, 1.5TB of coprocessor memory, and over 73TB of SSD storage, in aggregate. Beacon also supports two Ethernet networks; one is the private internal network and the other is for out of band system management.

SOFTWARE ENVIRONMENT

As of this writing, the deployed Intel® Many-core Platform Software Stack (Intel® MPSS) on Beacon is version 3.2.3. The Intel MPSS documentation and associated tools that Intel provides support installation in workstations and "vanilla" cluster environments, but there are unique challenges when

FIGURE 15.1

Green500 Award.

extending and customizing coprocessors installations within a diverse multipurpose user HPC cluster environment like Beacon's. This chapter highlights one approach for completing the key steps necessary for such integration on an existing cluster. Note that the authors assume that the reader has familiarity with the readme and user guide that Intel provides, as the authors will reference the tools and configurations referenced therein. Links to Intel MPSS downloads and reference guide can be found in Section "For more information."

There are a few system administration tools that the authors deem necessary in order to properly deploy and maintain a cluster. One of the most important of these tools is the adoption of a configuration manager such as Puppet, Chef, Salt, or Ansible. Any of these should work, but the configuration manager of choice at NICS is Puppet. There are many reasons why using a configuration manager is beneficial, but the primary reason is to restore configuration files after the Intel MPSS `micctrl` utility is invoked. The configuration manager will also be used to distribute the Intel MPSS configuration files to all of the compute nodes in the cluster. The authors also recommend setting up a resource and workload manager for the cluster in order to manage user job scheduling. Most general-purpose clusters utilize a job scheduler, and Beacon relies on a combination of TORQUE and Moab. TORQUE or a similar resource manager will be an important tool to use to stage (i.e., prepare) the Intel Xeon Phi coprocessors' environment for each individual job. More information will be discussed in detail in Section "Setting up the resource and workload managers". It will also be necessary to have a tool to manage the users' environment. Either `modules` or `Lmod` can be used. One last tool that the authors will reference in this chapter is `pdsh`, which is a multithreaded remote shell client that executes commands on remote hosts in parallel. Links to the tools mentioned in this section can be found in Section "For more information."

INTEL MPSS INSTALLATION PROCEDURE

Beacon utilizes a "diskful" installation of the operating system, so information on installing the Intel MPSS stack will be focused on this type of environment. A "diskful" installation is where the node has the operating system installed onto a physical drive on the node. This can be a challenge to systems administrators because, on occasion, configurations and software packages can get out of sync with other nodes in the cluster if, for instance, one of the nodes has to be taken offline for hardware work and changes are made to the rest of the nodes. If the changes are not done using a configuration manager and done by hand, then that node's configuration may end up varying slightly. A "diskless," NFS root file system solves this problem by booting every node from a single system image every time the nodes are rebooted. This way all of the nodes have the exact same operating system image. There was some initial work done on Beacon to deploy with a read-only NFS root file system for the OS image on the compute nodes, but because of time constraints and technical limitations of the previous Intel MPSS versions, there was not enough time to implement a "diskless" root on the Beacon cluster. The compute nodes are also provisioned with static IP addresses to simplify the administration of the configuration files for the coprocessors.

PREPARING THE SYSTEM

Section 19 of the Intel *MPSS Users Guide* provided with Intel MPSS 3.2.3 provides some recommendations on how to install the Intel MPSS stack on a cluster, but it lacks some of the specifics needed for an HPC cluster. Acquiring the Intel MPSS software and documentation can be done by following the link provided in Section "For more information." Some preparation will need to be done on the cluster in order to use the scripts and tools that will be provided in this chapter. Even if the reader is using the dynamic host configuration protocol on their cluster, they can enable static provisioning of IP addresses instead of a dynamic pool to ensure that each host and coprocessor has a fixed IP address associated with it. Having a structured `/etc/hosts` file, as shown below, is a necessity for the Intel MPI library and the provided scripts to work. In this theoretical example, we choose a sequential range of IP addresses in a private subnet with one IP address per host corresponding to the *eth0* interface, and two additional IP addresses mapping to the two theoretical coprocessors installed on each compute host. On Beacon, there would be four IP addresses associated with the four coprocessors that are in each Beacon compute node. Note that the scripts could easily be modified to reference a different file instead of `/etc/hosts` if desired. It would also be desirable to have the same `/etc/hosts` file on the coprocessors as well. If the hosts file is placed in `/var/mpss/common/etc/hosts`, the

```
10.0.0.12      node001           node001-eth0
10.0.0.13      node001-mic0
10.0.0.14      node001-mic1
10.0.0.15      node002           node002-eth0
10.0.0.16      node002-mic0
10.0.0.17      node002-mic1
```

FIGURE 15.2

Sample /etc/hosts file.

coprocessors will boot and overlay the file to `/etc/hosts` on the coprocessor's filesystem. Please see the *MPSS User Guide* for more information on how the coprocessor's `/var/mpss` configuration directory works (Figure 15.2).

The coprocessors require ssh keys to permit direct ssh access. Please refer to section 19.2, *RSA/DSA Key Creation* of the *MPSS Users Guide* for information on how to generate these files as they will need to be generated so that they can be distributed to the coprocessors later.

If the cluster is using an Infiniband fabric for its high-speed interconnect, the OpenFabrics Enterprise Distribution (OFED) software stack will need to be installed on the cluster. As of this writing, Intel provides two versions that can be used for OFED, version 1.5.4.1 and 3.5-1-MIC. Version 1.5.4.1 is from February of 2012, so it is a very old branch of the OFED stack. This is also the version that the Intel MPSS stack has supported from its initial public release. Intel provides drivers and libraries in the MPSS stack that provide support for the 1.5.4.1 version still, but with the release of the 3.2 version, the Intel MPSS stack added support for the newer 3.5-1-MIC version. This is a branch off of the official OFED 3.5 release that contains host-side extensions for the Intel MIC Architecture. Depending on which version is being installed, there are different install instructions. See section 2 of the *MPSS Users Guide* for more information.

NOTE

For version 1.5.4.1, the OFED stack will need to be installed and the RPMs from the $MPSS_LOCATION/ofed/ directory. If the newer 3.5-1-MIC version is being installed then only the OFED stack is needed, and the files from the $MPSS_STACK/ofed/ directory should not be installed.

INSTALLATION OF THE INTEL MPSS STACK

To install the Intel MPSS stack on the Beacon system, we first begin by downloading and untarring the Intel MPSS file into a shared directory, such as an NFS share, that is readable by all of the compute nodes. As of this writing, version 3.2.3 is the latest build available, so instructions for installation and configuration will be referencing this version, but future 3.x versions should be similar. By default, the Intel MPSS assumes you are using the stock kernels from each Red Hat Enterprise Linux (RHEL)/ CentOS release. For instance, if the RHEL/CentOS 6.2 version of the Intel MPSS 3.2.3 package is downloaded from Intel, then it contains the Intel MPSS drivers built against the original kernel for that RHEL/CentOS release. Note that future versions of Intel MPSS will combine all OS release versions into one package. The kernel provided in the RHEL/CentOS 6.2 release would be version 2.6.32-220. There are security vulnerabilities that this kernel has and administrators will want to use a patched

```
1) Ensure the prerequisites are installed:
   > sudo yum install kernel-headers kernel-devel

2) Regenerate the Intel(R) MPSS driver module package:
   > cd $MPSS_LOCATION/src/
   > rpmbuild --rebuild \ mpss-modules-*.el6.src.rpm

3) Copy the mpss-modules binary RPM from the
   $HOME/rpmbuild/RPMS/x86_64 directory to $MPSS_LOCATION
   (overwriting the mpss-modules binary RPM that was
   provided with the precompiled driver).
```

FIGURE 15.3

Kernel rebuild instructions.

kernel to keep the cluster secure. Fortunately, Intel MPSS provides source RPMs for the host driver (and OFED kernel modules) that can be used to rebuild against newer kernel releases. The following highlights example steps to build the host coprocessor driver from source (Figure 15.3).

Once all of the prerequisites have been completed, the pdsh tool is used to install Intel MPSS packages on all of the compute nodes by issuing command shown in Figure 15.4.

Note that as an alternative to direct yum installation, and depending on the underlying configuration management strategy adopted, the Intel MPSS RPMs can also be integrated into a compute appliance and distributed directly under the auspices of the configuration management system.

In order to support "symmetric" MPI communication between distributed coprocessors on a cluster, the associated Intel MPSS OFED packages are also required. If the OFED-1.5.4.1 packages have been installed on the compute nodes, it will be necessary to install the Intel MPSS OFED RPMs via pdsh or the configuration manager as well. Note that similar to the host Intel MPSS coprocessor driver, the OFED kernel module will also have to be rebuilt if using a different kernel than the one supported by the Intel MPSS version. This rebuild can be accomplished by doing the command in the $MPSS_LOCATION/src/ directory (Figure 15.5).

The RPM can then be copied from the $HOME/rpmbuild/RPMS/x86_64/ directory and copied to $MPSS_LOCATION/ofed/ directory. The older OFED kernel module RPM should be moved

```
sudo pdsh -w cluster\[xxx-xxx\] yum -y install \
--nogpgcheck -noplugins -disablerepo=* \
$MPSS_LOCATION/*.rpm
```

FIGURE 15.4

Intel MPSS installation command.

```
rpmbuild --rebuild ofed-driver-*.src.rpm
```

FIGURE 15.5

OFED RPM rebuild command.

to another location so that both versions are not installed. As noted earlier rebuilding the OFED driver is not necessary if using the OFED 3.5 branch.

The last step will be to check if the Intel Xeon Phi coprocessor's firmware needs to be updated. The *MPSS Users Guide* documents the firmware update process via the use of the provided `micflash` utility.

GENERATING AND CUSTOMIZING CONFIGURATION FILES

Intel provides the `micctrl` command to do many things in order to create configuration files and manage the coprocessors. As mentioned previously, this command provides default configurations that allow quick setup in a single host or workstation environment. For clustered environments, however, a combination of `micctrl`, local script-based customizations, and a configuration management system is frequently adopted to complete the integration and deployment process. The steps that follow document this particular approach as implemented on Beacon.

If the reader is performing a first time install or starting with a new Intel MPSS release, the Intel MPSS configuration files will need to be generated initially on a representative compute node using the commands provided in Figure 15.6.

The `micctrl` utility in Intel MPSS 3.2.3 will automatically scan for any users available locally on the host in order to set up ssh key access for the coprocessor. However, many HPC sites will want to manage ssh access to the coprocessor in coordination with the chosen resource manager, and the default configuration can be customized to only provide the bare minimum of administrative users on the coprocessor via the additional command given in Figure 15.7.

The files generated by the above commands will then be used as templates for each node-specific MPSS configuration files as they will each have slightly different network configurations. To begin, copy the `/etc/mpss/default.conf` and `/etc/mpss/mic0.conf` file to a location such as `/etc`, where the `mic-create-conf.sh` script provided in Figure 15.8 will run to generate the host specific configuration files.

In a cluster environment, it is desirable for the coprocessors to be part of the network topology and utilize direct communication from coprocessor to coprocessor via TCP/IP. This can be achieved by using

```
sudo micctrl --cleanconfig
sudo micctrl --initdefaults
```

FIGURE 15.6

micctrl commands.

```
sudo micctrl --userupdate=none
```

FIGURE 15.7

micctrl command.

```
#!/bin/bash
### Script to create /etc/mpss/mic*.conf
### Currently setup for MPSS 3.2

if [ -d /sys/class/mic ]
then
  for MICN in $( cd /sys/class/mic ; echo mic* )
  do
    MICIPADDR=$(grep ${HOSTNAME}-${MICN} /etc/hosts | awk
'{print $1}')
    HOSTIPADDR=$(grep ${HOSTNAME}-eth0 /etc/hosts | awk
'{print $1}')
    if [ -n "$MICN" -a -n "$MICIPADDR" -a -n
"$HOSTIPADDR" ]
    then
# generate /etc/mpss/default.conf files
      cat /etc/default.conf.template | sed
"s/HOSTIPADDR/$HOSTIPADDR/g" > /tmp/default.conf
      delta=$(diff -u /tmp/default.conf
/etc/mpss/default.conf | wc -l)
      if [ -n "$delta" -a $delta -gt 0 ]
      then
        cp /etc/mpss/default.conf /tmp/default.conf.bak
        cp /tmp/default.conf /etc/mpss/default.conf
      fi
# generate /etc/mpss/micN.conf files
      cat /etc/micN.conf.template | sed
"s/NODE/$HOSTNAME/g" | sed "s/HOSTIPADDR/$HOSTIPADDR/g" |
sed "s/MICN/$MICN/g" | sed "s/MICIPADDR/$MICIPADDR/g" >
/tmp/${MICN}.conf
      delta=$(diff -u /tmp/${MICN}.conf
/etc/mpss/${MICN}.conf | wc -l)
      if [ -n "$delta" -a $delta -gt 0 ]
      then
        cp /etc/mpss/${MICN}.conf /tmp/${MICN}.conf.bak
        cp /tmp/${MICN}.conf /etc/mpss/${MICN}.conf
      fi
    fi
  done
fi
```

FIGURE 15.8

mic-create-conf.sh script.

external bridging. See the `Bridge` line in the sample `default.conf` template file in Figure 15.9 for the syntax necessary (the HOSTIPADDR variable will be replaced by the node-specific IP address).

It will also be necessary to add an option to the `Network` line in the `micN.conf.template` file as shown in Figure 15.10.

The `mic-create-conf.sh` script assumes there is a `/etc/hosts` file that is in the same syntax as referenced in Figure 15.2. Once the configuration file templates and script have been customized as needed, the `mic-create-conf.sh` script should be executed to generate the configuration files. It will also be necessary to have custom `ifcfg-ethX` and `ifcfg-micbr0` files for the external bridging to function. These files are located in `/etc/sysconfig/network-scripts/`. Sample ifcfg files are shown in Figures 15.11 and 15.12.

In this case, `eth0` is the internal private TCP/IP Ethernet network. Replace `eth0` with the appropriate interface as needed. The `ifcfg-micbr0` file calls `grep` which gets the appropriate IP address from

```
# Source for base of embedded Linux file system
Base CPIO /usr/share/mpss/boot/initramfs-
knightscorner.cpio.gz

# MIC card unique overlay files such as etc, etc.
CommonDir /var/mpss/common

# Additional command line parameters.  Caution should be
used in changing these.
ExtraCommandLine "highres=off"

# MIC Console
Console "hvc0"

ShutdownTimeout 300

# Storage location and size for MIC kernel crash dumps
CrashDump /var/crash/mic/ 16

Bridge micbr0 External HOSTIPADDR 24 9000

PowerManagement "cpufreq_on;corec6_off;pc3_off;pc6_off"
```

FIGURE 15.9

default.conf.template.

```
Version 1 1

# Include configuration common to all MIC cards
Include default.conf

# Include all additional functionality configuration
files by default
Include "conf.d/*.conf"

# Unique per card files for embedded Linux file system

MicDir /var/mpss/MICN

# Hostname to assign to MIC card
Hostname "NODE-MICN"

# MAC address configuration
MacAddrs "Serial"

Network class=StaticBridge bridge=micbr0 micip=MICIPADDR
mtu=64512 modhost=no modcard=no

# MIC OS Verbose messages to console
VerboseLogging Disabled

# MIC OS image
OSimage /usr/share/mpss/boot/bzImage-knightscorner
/usr/share/mpss/boot/System.map-knightscorner

# Boot MIC card when MPSS stack is started
BootOnStart Enabled

# Root device for MIC card
RootDevice ramfs /var/mpss/MICN.image.gz

Cgroup memory=disabled
```

FIGURE 15.10

micN.conf.template.

```
DEVICE=eth0
BOOTPROTO=static
IPV6INIT=no
MTU=9000
NM_CONTROLLED=no
ONBOOT=yes
TYPE=Ethernet
BRIDGE=micbr0
USERCTL=no
```

FIGURE 15.11

ifcfg-eth0 file.

```
DEVICE=micbr0
TYPE=Bridge
BOOTPROTO=static
IPV6INIT=no
MTU=9000
NM_CONTROLLED=no
ONBOOT=yes
TYPE=Ethernet
IPADDR=$(grep `hostname -s`-eth0 /etc/hosts | \
awk '{print $1}')
NETMASK=255.255.254.0
USERCTL=no
```

FIGURE 15.12

ifcfg-micbr0.

```
DEVICE=mic0
ONBOOT=yes
NM_CONTROLLED="no"
BRIDGE=micbr0
```

FIGURE 15.13

ifcfg-mic0.

```
sudo micctrl --resetconfig
```

FIGURE 15.14

micctrl command to update the coprocessors.

/etc/hosts. This approach allows the same ifcfg-micbr0 file to be used on the entire cluster. The coprocessors also need to have their respective ifcfg-micX files configured as shown in Figure 15.13.

For each coprocessor in the system, a corresponding ifcfg-micX file will need to be created. The template files, ifcfg files, and script should be placed under configuration manager control in order to deploy across the entire cluster. After the configuration files have been distributed to the entire cluster, it will be necessary to run the mic-create-conf.sh script and then run the command in Figure 15.14 via pdsh.

```
sudo micctrl --initdefaults
```

FIGURE 15.15

ifcfg-mic0.

The `micctrl` command will update the configuration files in the coprocessor with the configuration files that were generated on the host. Use the `chkconfig` command to enable the `mpss` and `ofed-mic` services to start at the desired run level. The entire cluster can be rebooted at this point and each host and coprocessor should be accessible on the internal private network.

MPSS UPGRADE PROCEDURE

As of this writing, no direct upgrade path is provided for Intel MPSS versions. In order to update the stack, it is necessary to remove the previous installation and then install the new version. A good practice to follow before deploying a new version of Intel MPSS is to do a test install and configure the new version on a single compute node. It has been the authors' experience that this process is never as simple as just removing the prior stack and then installing the new one. New options in the configuration files will need to be put in place or there may be changes to the existing syntax. We expect that such configuration file changes between versions become less frequent with future releases.

In the Intel MPSS, an `uninstall.sh` script is provided that will remove the current running stack. On the test node, turn off the configuration manager, install the new MPSS stack, and run the command given in Figure 15.15.

Compare the syntax of the previous configuration files with the newly generated ones for any differences. Adjust the template files as necessary and reboot the node to test the validity of the configuration files. If everything is working as expected, update the configuration files in the configuration manager. The configuration manager can then be restarted on the test node.

Check if there are any firmware updates as mentioned in Section "Installation of the MPSS stack" and update the coprocessors as necessary. Once all of this has been done, use `pdsh` again to remove the Intel MPSS and install the new one on each compute node.

SETTING UP THE RESOURCE AND WORKLOAD MANAGERS
TORQUE

The resource manager is the most important application for staging the coprocessor. This chapter gives examples for TORQUE, but the general concepts discussed should be easily transferable to other resource managers such as SLURM. The TORQUE prologue will have the primary responsibility for setting up the user environment, mounting external filesystems, and checking the health of the coprocessors. The epilogue will be responsible for removing temporary files, killing stray processes, unmounting filesystems, and returning the node(s) to a clean state for the next job. The full TORQUE prologue and epilogue can be found with the other examples at http://lotsofcores.com.

PROLOGUE

It is recommended to create a temporary directory for the users to place the previously generated ssh keys, user data, and some Intel MPI binaries that are necessary for the Intel MPI library to work (Figure 15.16).

The user environment will need to be created on the coprocessor and this can be accomplished by creating a `.profile` based on the user's loaded module. Note that this example references environment variables that are provided via the modules deployed on Beacon, but these variables can be set statically as well. The $IMPI is the path to the Intel MPI install location and $INTEL_COMPILERS is the path to the Intel compilers install location (Figure 15.17).

The Intel Xeon Phi coprocessor occasionally does not get initialized properly, or can be left in a bad state from previous usage. Consequently, best practice suggests doing some basic health checking before attempting to stage them for use. If the health check fails, the prologue should then attempt to restart the coprocessors. If that fails, the resource manager should alert the cluster administrators and take the node offline so that it is no longer allocable by the resource manager. A representative example of this type of prologue check is shown in Figure 15.18 in pseudocode.

```
tmp=/tmp/pbstmp.$jobid
mkdir -m 700 $tmp && chown $user.$group $tmp
cp ssh-id_rsa.key $tmp/.micssh/
```

FIGURE 15.16

$tmp in TORQUE prologue.

```
cat <<EOF > $tmp/profile
export TMPDIR=$tmp
export PATH=$TMPDIR/bin
export LD_LIBRARY_PATH=$TMPDIR/lib:$IMPI:$INTEL_COMPILERS
EOF
```

FIGURE 15.17

Building the .profile in TORQUE prologue.

```
if [mpss status is stopped]
    service mpss restart
    service ofed-mic start
fi
if [(micctrl -s | grep -c online) < #coprocessors]
    service ofed-mic stop
    micctrl -Rw
    service mpss start
    service ofed-mic start
fi
if [(micctrl -s | grep -c online) < #coprocessors]
    mail -s "Coprocessor boot failure" admin@org.com
    disable node from resource manager and exit
fi
```

FIGURE 15.18

Coprocessor health check in TORQUE prologue.

The coprocessor allows the mounting of NFS shares, and there are a few of these shares that need to be mounted. It is recommended to share the Intel Parallel Studio compiler suite to the coprocessors so that users will not have to copy over every library. For example on Beacon, the `/global/opt` filesystem is exported to the coprocessors and contains the Intel compilers, various debuggers, applications, and other libraries that have been built specifically for the coprocessor. More information will be provided in Section "User software environment" on how the user libraries are built and managed. Another useful filesystem to export from the host are any high-performance filesystems that may be provided for the system and/or the users NFS home area. This is necessary because if the user's application generates output that is written to the coprocessor's filesystem, the output data will be lost. This is because the coprocessor's filesystem is volatile (i.e., memory based) and will be reset once the coprocessor is rebooted when the job is complete. When reexporting a networked filesystem to a coprocessor, it is important to pay attention to the export options. To avoid adding a potential layer of noncoherent cache, the authors recommend using the `sync` export option whenever reexporting a networked file system through NFS.

The coprocessor has a few different methods for user management. The default way is to use a "micuser" account for all users, which unfortunately does not scale well in a multiuser environment. Intel MPSS version 3.2 and above provides the ability to leverage the `micctrl` command directly to dynamically add and delete users to the locally attached coprocessor(s). Syntax for using this option is highlighted in Figure 15.19.

Prior to Intel MPSS version 3.2, a common way to handle user management was to do something similar to the following in the prologue script to enable user access for the duration of a job (Figure 15.20).

On Beacon, the host-side credentialing is accommodated via LDAP, so both approaches above require an LDAP query to be executed and parsed before either running the `micctrl` command or piping directly to `/etc/passwd`. If using the `micctrl` approach, a default `.profile` will be created for the user. However, because we previously generated a profile that was based on the user's current environment, we prefer to use the original version instead.

```
micctrl --useradd=<name> --uid=<uid> --gid=<gid> \
[--home=<dir>] [--comment=<string>] [--app=<exec>] \
[--sshkeys=<keydir>] [--nocreate] \
•[--non-unique] [mic card list]
```

FIGURE 15.19

micctrl --useradd command.

```
getent passwd $user | sed "s:/.*/$user:/User:" | \
sed 's:/bin/.*sh:/bin/sh:' | ssh ${node}-$mic \
"cat >> /etc/passwd"
getent group $group | ssh ${node}-$mic "cat >> /etc/group
scp $SSH_KEY_LOCATION/id_rsa* to micX:/$user/.ssh
```

FIGURE 15.20

TORQUE prologue, cont.

```
scp $tmp/profile micX:/etc/profile
ssh micX "mount nfs shares exported from host"
scp $IMPI/mic/bin/{mpiexec.hydra,mpi_proxy} \
micX:$tmp/bin/
scp $SSH_KEY_LOCATION/id_rsa* to micX:/$user/.ssh
```

FIGURE 15.21

TORQUE prologue, cont.

Continuing through the prologue steps on Beacon, the next step is to mount exported NFS filesystems on the coprocessor. Intel MPI also requires two binaries to be present on the coprocessor, so those will need to be copied over as well and placed in the user's tmp directory. Finally, the ssh keys previously generated will need to be copied over to the coprocessor. These steps are highlighted in Figure 15.21.

EPILOGUE

After the user's job concludes, the epilogue is responsible for clearing the user's processes on the system and then setting it back to a clean state for the next user. First, the NFS filesystems are unmounted which is intended to keep the NFS servers in a clean state. The Intel Xeon Phi coprocessors are then rebooted to ensure they are in a clean state for the next user. This adds approximately 60 s to the epilogue, but it is a convenient way to verify that the coprocessor is in a clean state for the next job. Finally, the epilogue script cleans up the user created directories on the host and exits. The entire process is outlined in Figure 15.22.

TORQUE/COPROCESSOR INTEGRATION

Versions 4.2.0 and newer of TORQUE can be configured to integrate with the Intel Coprocessor Offload Infrastructure library. When enabled, the pbs_mom daemon automatically detects the coprocessors and periodically queries them for metrics such as number of cores and threads, maximum clock frequency, total and available memory, and load average. This information is then made available through the PBS scheduler API. Users can also explicitly request nodes with coprocessors (e.g., "qsub -l nodes=2:mics=4 ...") when this functionality is enabled. This functionality is being explored on Beacon, but it is not currently being used in production. This functionality is useful if the number of coprocessors in the nodes differs within the cluster, or if only a subset of the nodes have coprocessors in them.

```
kill all $user processes
umount NFS_shares
service ofed-mic stop
micctrl -Rw
service ofed-mic start
rm /tmp/$user_stuff
```

FIGURE 15.22

TORQUE epilogue.

```
# Node sets
# group jobs first within cages, then within racks
# then within the whole system
NODESETPOLICY                ONEOF
NODESETATTRIBUTE             FEATURE
NODESETLIST                  r1c1,r1c2,r1c3,r1c4,r2c1,\
                             r2c2,r2c3,r2c4,r4c1,r4c2,\
                             r4c3,r4c4,r1,r2,r4,beacon2
NODESETISOPTIONAL            FALSE
```

FIGURE 15.23

Moab node sets.

MOAB

TORQUE is designed to support external schedulers, and one of the most commonly used schedulers is Adaptive Computing's Moab workload manager. Moab does not necessarily need to be aware of the presence of Intel Xeon Phi coprocessors in hosts in the way that TORQUE's job prologue and epilogue do, so long as the desired scheduling policies are such that nodes are allocated on a whole-node basis (i.e., no node sharing between jobs), as is typical on accelerator/coprocessor-based systems.

IMPROVING NETWORK LOCALITY

MPI applications typically perform best in configurations where communications go through as few intermediate hops as possible; on InfiniBand-based systems, this usually means placing jobs within the same leaf switch or module when possible. Moab can accomplish this through the use of node sets. Assigning features to nodes indicating their location in the system, and then configuring Moab to treat those features as node sets accomplishes this task. It is also possible to assign a node to multiple node sets, allowing for several placement options if the optimal placement is not available. For instance, the following Moab configuration will attempt to pack nodes for a job into a cage/subrack, then into a rack, and finally across the whole machine (Figure 15.23).

MOAB/COPROCESSOR INTEGRATION

Moab 7.2.0 and later versions support low-level Intel Xeon Phi integration through TORQUE. If the TORQUE coprocessor integration is present, Moab can make scheduling decisions based on the presence or absence of the coprocessors and record the coprocessor metrics in its node event logs.

HEALTH CHECKING AND MONITORING

Intel provides RPMs and documentation for deploying Ganglia on the Intel Xeon Phi coprocessors. Ganglia is a useful tool for gathering statistics and monitoring the overall usage of the cluster. The authors have been using Ganglia to perform cluster monitoring and health checking on Beacon. A link to the Ganglia project page can be found in Section "For more information."

There are currently a couple of methods to install and run Ganglia on the coprocessors. The first, outlined in the *MPSS Users Guide,* is to install the Intel provided prebuilt RPMs using a script when the coprocessor boots. The coprocessor's host runs a python `SimpleHTTPServer` to distribute the packages to the coprocessor via `zypper`. While this works nicely in a workstation environment, it does not scale well in a cluster environment when using python as the HTTP server to provide the RPMs. Indeed, the python process may frequently hang and stop distributing files when there are too many requests. The authors instead recommend using a stripped down and restricted web server such as Apache to handle distributing the RPMs through the user created zypper repo. The httpd process is also much easier to manage with the configuration manager.

One other issue encountered is that when the Ganglia RPMs are installed, they overwrite the `gmond.conf` file that is placed in `/var/mpss/etc/ganglia/gmond.conf`. It is recommended that the configuration file be renamed to something else, such as `ganglia.conf`, and that file be specified to gmond when that daemon is started. The documentation also recommends using `ssh` to log into the coprocessor and start the gmond process manually. Instead, we prefer to modify the `install-service` script outlined in the *MPSS Users Guide* documentation as shown below and then move this `install-service` script to `/var/mpss/common/etc/init.d/install-service`. The appropriate soft link should be made in `/etc/rc3.d/` directory so that the coprocessor automatically launches it at boot. In the example given in Figure 15.24, the `$HOST` should be replaced with the host in which the Webserver is located.

Another option that is provided in Intel MPSS is the ability to customize the coprocessor's filesystem via the overlay capabilities provided with `micctrl --overlay`. More information on the overlay method can be found in the *MPSS Users Guide*. Using the overlay option is a more permanent method to install Ganglia on the coprocessor, but not as explicitly documented as the previous method discussed.

Once an install method has been selected, all of the install steps are completed, and Ganglia is properly configured, the Web front end will show the current usage of each coprocessor and host. However, the host needs to be configured to use Ganglia as well. Please visit Ganglia's project page link in Section "For more information" to see how to install Ganglia on the host and how the monitoring system works.

Another useful ability of Ganglia is to measure the CPU metrics of the coprocessor. Note that this ability is not enabled by default in the `ganglia.conf` file because some applications will see a slight performance penalty. For this reason, Intel does not recommend running Ganglia with the CPU metrics enabled. Internal testing on Beacon has not shown any negative impact with the CPU metrics enabled, but there has been one case reported where gathering the CPU metrics has caused an issue. Therefore, it is recommended an option be provided to the user to disable Ganglia in the resource and workload manager during job submission.

Future work being developed on Beacon is to tie the metrics recorded by Ganglia into the accounting database so that systems administrators can monitor usage of the Intel Xeon Phi coprocessor for

```
zypper ar http://$HOST:8000 k1om-mpss-3.2.3
zypper --gpg-auto-import-keys -n --no-gpg-checks \
install ganglia
zypper --gpg-auto-import-keys -n --no-gpg-checks \
install mpss-ganglia
/usr/sbin/gmond -c /etc/ganglia/ganglia.conf
```

FIGURE 15.24

Ganglia install-service.

reporting purposes and determine to what extent the CPUs are used versus the coprocessor per job. These usage statistics can also be given to the computational scientists to help them monitor the efficiency of user applications and determine if tuning is required to increase performance. The computational scientists can then proactively reach out to users with efficiency issues and offer support. Some users are not aware that their applications are inefficient and wasting CPU hours. The intention is to help users get results faster in fewer CPU hours, which will also free up the system to allow more jobs to run. The Keeneland project deployed a similar system on GPU-based accelerators and is the inspiration for this work. More information on the Keeneland project can be found in Section "For more information."

SCRIPTING COMMON COMMANDS

On Beacon, a few additional scripts have been created to wrap common commands such as `ssh` and `mpiexec` to make the user environment more friendly. For example, it is important to wrap the `ssh` command to prevent the user from having to add `-i $TMPDIR/.micssh/micssh-id_rsa` every time the `ssh` command is invoked. The added text on such a common command becomes extremely cumbersome to the user. Figure 15.25 shows the `micssh` script that wraps the ssh command.

Simply by changing the last line, the `micssh` script can be converted to a `micscp` script by replacing `ssh $SSH_ARGS $*` with `scp $SSH_ARGS $*`. The `micscp` script works on a small scale to move files across nodes and coprocessors, but will not work when distributing files to a large number of nodes. The `allmicput` included with the examples lets users easily copy files to every coprocessor that was allocated by the scheduler for their job.

Another possibility for ssh is to place the lines shown in Figure 15.26 in to the users `~/.ssh/config` file. For example on Beacon, it would look like the one in Figure 15.26.

The `micmpiexec` script (shown in Figure 15.27) performs important tasks such as sending the users `$LD_LIBRARY_PATH` along with other environment variables such as `$IMICROOT`, which is the location of the Intel Xeon Phi coprocessor compiler libraries. The `$I_MPI_ROOT` variable contains the path to the Intel MPI root install directory and `$MKLMICROOT` contains the location of the

```
#!/bin/sh
if [ -n "$PBS_JOBID" -a -n "$TMPDIR" ]
then
  if [ -r $TMPDIR/.micssh/micssh-id_rsa ]
  then
    SSH_ARGS="-i $TMPDIR/.micssh/micssh-id_rsa"
  fi
fi
isroot=$(echo $* | grep -c root)
if [ $isroot -gt 0 ]
then
  echo This program may not be used as root
  exit -1
fi
export SSH_ARGS
ssh $SSH_ARGS $*
```

FIGURE 15.25

micssh script.

```
Host beacon0??-mic?
       IdentityFile ~/.micssh/micssh-id_rsa
```

FIGURE 15.26

~/.ssh/config file.

```
AcceptEnv MIC_LD_LIBRARY_PATH MIC_ENV_PREFIX
```

FIGURE 15.27

/etc/ssh/sshd_config setting.

coprocessor Math Kernel Library files. It is important that these paths are sent to the coprocessor so that the MPI jobs get the full environment that the user has currently loaded. These paths could change when the user invokes the `module` command to change their environment. For example, they should not be statically set in the coprocessor's `/etc/profile`. Instead, the coprocessor's `/etc/ssh/ sshd_config` file should have the line shown in Figure 15.27 in it so that the ssh daemon accepts the environment variables.

There is also a section in the `micmpiexec` script that handles passing the debugger syntax that is necessary to launch `mpiexec` with the proper command line arguments. Figure 15.28 shows the `micmpiexec` script that will accomplish this task.

```
#!/bin/sh
if [ -n "$PBS_JOBID" -a -n "$TMPDIR" ]
then
    if [ -r $TMPDIR/.micssh/micssh-id_rsa ]
    then
      MPI_ARGS="-bootstrap ssh -bootstrap-exec mics\
      micssh -genv LD_LIBRARY_PATH $TMPDIR/lib:\
      $IMICROOT:$I_MPI_ROOT/mic/lib:$MKLMICROOT:\
      $LD_LIBRARY_PATH"
fi fi
export MPI_ARGS
export EXEC=""
if [ $1 = "-ddt" ]
then
    shift
    EXEC="ddt-client $DEBUGGER_OPTIONS"
elif [ $1 = "-tv" ]
then
shift
    EXEC="totalview -mmic -args"
fi
if [ -e $TMPDIR/bin/mpiexec.hydra ]
then
    $EXEC $TMPDIR/bin/mpiexec.hydra $MPI_ARGS $*
else
    $EXEC mpiexec.hydra $MPI_ARGS $*
fi
```

FIGURE 15.28

micmpiexec script.

USER SOFTWARE ENVIRONMENT

The heterogeneous environment on Beacon provides for a special set of challenges when installing software for the user. Fortunately, over the course of development of the Beacon system, both local workarounds and Intel engineering fixes have largely mitigated these challenges. In this section, the issues discovered and their solutions are discussed; additionally, the current user software environment on Beacon is illuminated in detail.

The Beacon software stack structure is generated using `swtools`, a software installation management package maintained by the Oak Ridge Leadership Computing Facility, and the previously mentioned `module` system. This allows those maintaining the software to have an automated system for rebuilding the application or libraries, generating Web-based documentation and software lists automatically, and testing the libraries or applications to make sure they work correctly on all platforms. It also allows for assuring that the most stable version is set as default and that other versions can be listed as "beta" or "deprecated." Finally, it allows for documentation on what the software does and who supports it, as well as an automated process to check for newer versions.

The first conundrum that must be addressed when creating a software stack using the above construct for a heterogeneous system is that the software must be compiled for both the Intel Xeon processor and the Intel Xeon Phi coprocessor separately. When Beacon was first put into production, the software tree was bifurcated into a `MIC` branch and a `XEON` branch, to make this distinction more evident to users. While a bifurcated tree simplifies the user's process of choosing the correct module for native mode or offload mode applications, it also complicates the process of compiling and running in symmetric mode, where a version is compiled for the coprocessor and the processor and then each is run on the appropriate pieces of hardware in a common MPI communicator, as these modules cannot be loaded simultaneously.

After conducting testing, the Scientific Computing group at NICS determined that the compiler is capable of skipping the libraries in the incorrect format when compiling for one mode or the other. Experiments on Beacon determined that the module files could be combined into one mixed-mode tree. Thus, the command in Figure 15.29 loads the paths to both sets of libraries/binaries into the `LD_LIBRARY_PATH` and `PATH` environment variables, respectively.

Additionally, the existence of the `MIC_LD_LIBRARY_PATH` environment variable, which contains coprocessor version paths to module libraries, is quite helpful in keeping the Xeon and Xeon Phi libraries separate, while also allowing one path to be appended to the other in the case where all libraries are needed but order is important. This is crucial in allowing the user to load only one module file and run on processors, coprocessors, or both seamlessly.

When compiling in the mixed library environment, warnings will appear that libraries of the wrong type are being skipped, but the correct ones are always found at compile and run time. Then, if a user desires to run the code in symmetric mode, both sets of libraries are available at compilation and runtime, often for multiple compilers.

```
module load example-lib
```

FIGURE 15.29

module command example.

At present, there is no native Intel compiler, however, MPSS does provide the GNU toolchain for use natively on the Intel Xeon Phi. This GNU toolchain is only provided to build tools, not applications, for the coprocessor because it is not optimized for the coprocessor's available instruction sets. To accommodate software builds using the Intel toolchain for native execution on the coprocessor, the code is cross-compiled with the `-mmic` flag on the host. Successful cross-compilation of complex codes requires that all cross-compilation options have to be set properly so the coprocessor-targeted compilation of the code does not try to execute on the host as an intermediate step and thus cause the install or configuration to fail. Cross-compilation can still fall short in circumstances where the software must compile and run a program to obtain values to complete the installation. The aforementioned scenario requires a very tedious process of compiling to a point for both the processor and coprocessor, running the processor executable on the host (or the proper targeted version on the coprocessor, which involves sending and receiving code and data), passing the generated file back into to the coprocessor compilation, editing the outcome file to be sure it is set up for coprocessor execution or further compilation, then resuming the coprocessor compilation only on the host.

The software stack on Beacon contains 30 pieces of preinstalled software available to all users including libraries and applications such as OpenFOAM, and R, as well as frequently used development libraries like Boost, GlobalArrays, MAGMA, HDF5, NETCDF, Metis, and more. Also, performance analysis tools beyond those that come with the Intel Parallel Studio XE are available, such as FPMPI and MPInside. The systems administrator sets each module to a default version, though the user may choose any version they wish.

In addition to the Intel, GNU, and CAPS compilers (which allow for the conversion of OpenACC code into OpenCL code that can be compiled to run on the coprocessor), Beacon utilizes both Rogue Wave's TotalView debugger and Allinea's DDT debugger and MAP profiler. Recently, the ability to submit a job asking for a different MPI implementation was added, to allow for use of Intel's IMPI 5.0, OpenMPI, and eventually MVAPICH.

FUTURE DIRECTIONS

Going forward, a major issue with cluster deployments using Intel Xeon Phi coprocessors is expected to be the scalability of software deployment and management. The installation and configuration of early Intel MPSS releases were focused on more of a workstation-style environment that was difficult to install and automate on tens or hundreds of nodes at once. Fortunately, through community feedback and direct collaboration as part of the Beacon project and other HPC deployments, Intel has made a number of improvements in MPSS to move to a model that is friendlier to either automated installation through a configuration management system, or stateless operating system deployment (such as NFS root). Additional work to support clustered HPC environments and provide configuration file transparency is on the Intel MPSS roadmap and should help to reduce administrator overhead for future deployments. Also, as Intel MPSS matures, its APIs and configuration file formats should change less and less over time, which will reduce the difficulty and risk associated with upgrading to newer versions.

The authors expect that many of the software management issues associated with currently available Intel Xeon Phi coprocessors will improve greatly after the release of the codenamed "Knights Landing" (KNL) next generation of the Intel Xeon Phi hardware. The socketed KNL will be able to boot an off the shelf Linux operating system distribution, such as RHEL. Having the Intel Xeon Phi processor as a standard bootable platform will likely alleviate many of the current difficulties and complexities with resource management systems, monitoring, and general administration and automation due to managing both the host and coprocessor within the same node.

SUMMARY

The Intel MIC architecture, as represented by the current generation of Intel Xeon Phi coprocessors, offers performance advantages over conventional CPUs for highly parallel applications, along with improvements in usability over competing accelerators and coprocessing devices; but these advantages come with increased burdens related to system administration, particularly in cluster environments. Based on the experiences gained through working with Intel over several years to deploy and operate several supercomputing platforms equipped with developmental and production versions of coprocessors, NICS has developed approaches and best practices to address most of the operational challenges associated with the architecture, easing the deployment and operation of the devices and providing a more friendly operating environment for users. These approaches and practices are expected to lower the barrier for entry for the broader computing community and to increase user productivity. As new Intel MPSS stacks and new generations of the Intel MIC architecture become available, these cluster administration techniques will be continually refined and improved to ensure continuing relevancy for the general supercomputing community.

Acknowledgments

The authors would like to thank George Butler and Jesse Hanley from NICS. Their insight, experience, and efforts greatly contributed toward this work.

This material is based upon work supported by the National Science Foundation under Grant Number 1137097 and by the University of Tennessee through the Beacon Project. Any opinions, findings, and conclusions or recommendations expressed in this material are those of the author(s) and do not necessarily reflect the views of the National Science Foundation or the University of Tennessee.

FOR MORE INFORMATION

- NICS announces strategic engagement with Intel, http://www.nics.tennessee.edu/intelpartnership.
- Video: Intel's Knights Corner Does 1 Teraflop on a Single Chip at SC11, http://insidehpc.com/2011/11/16/video-intels-knights-corner-does-1-teraflop-on-a-single-chip-at-sc11/.
- Scientific Applications for Intel MIC Architecture, https://www.youtube.com/watch?v=TOVokMClr5g.
- nfsroot—Linux Cluster NFS root support, https://code.google.com/p/nfsroot/.
- The Green500 List—November 2012, http://www.green500.org/news/green500-list-november-2012.

- Collaborating to create the most energy-efficient supercomputer, http://blogs.intel.com/intellabs/2012/11/14/green500-sc12/.
- Intel Many-core Platform Software Stack (MPSS), http://software.intel.com/en-us/articles/intel-many-core-platform-software-stack-mpss/.
- TORQUE Resource Manager—Adaptive Computing, http://www.adaptivecomputing.com/products/open-source/torque/.
- Moab HPC Suite Basic Edition—Adaptive Computing, http://www.adaptivecomputing.com/products/hpc-products/moab-hpc-basic-edition/.
- Modules—Software Environment Management, http://modules.sourceforge.net/.
- Lmod: Environmental Modules System, https://www.tacc.utexas.edu/tacc-projects/lmod/.
- pdsh—Parallel Distributed Shell, https://code.google.com/p/pdsh/.
- MPSS Users Guide, http://registrationcenter.intel.com/irc_nas/4245/MPSS_Users_Guide.pdf.
- Ganglia Monitoring System, http://ganglia.sourceforge.net/.
- Vetter, J.S., Glassbrook, R., Dongarra, J., Schwan, K., Loftis, B., McNally, S., Meredith, J., Rogers, J., Roth, P., Spafford, K., Yalamanchili, S., 2011. Keeneland: bringing heterogeneous GPU computing to the computational science community. IEEE Comput. Sci. Eng. 13, 90–95.
- SWTools, https://www.olcf.ornl.gov/center-projects/swtools/.
- NICS Beacon Resource Page, https://www.nics.tennessee.edu/beacon.
- TACC Stampede User Guide, https://www.tacc.utexas.edu/user-services/user-guides/stampede-user-guide.
- Scripts and configuration files mentioned in this chapter, http://lotsofcores.com/.

SUPPORTING CLUSTER FILE SYSTEMS ON INTEL® XEON PHI™ COPROCESSORS

16

Michael Hebenstreit
Intel Corporation, USA

If users want to access the Intel Xeon Phi coprocessor as a compute node in a cluster rather than using offload techniques alone, some special configuration becomes necessary: (1) the network layout needs to be addressed and (2) the file systems available within the cluster need to be mounted on the Intel Xeon Phi coprocessor. With a proper configuration enabled, a user will be able to *ssh* from any other node in the cluster directly to a coprocessor, and find an environment (like cluster file systems) similar or identical to a standard node. In this chapter, we will discuss how the coprocessors can be configured to allow this cluster-wide view of coprocessors at compute nodes. In particular, this will enable applications to run MPI codes in all possible use modes including (1) on the host processor while using the coprocessor in offload mode, (2) as native coprocessor only MPI codes, and (3) both host processor and coprocessor cooperating MPI codes.

To illustrate our goal, let's show an example of running an MPI code on a cluster configured with host nodes and coprocessor 'nodes' using the Intel® MPI Library. The MPI cluster run model allows a straightforward addition of a coprocessor run MPI application. As shown below, the steps can be as easy as

- Set the Intel MPI library and Intel C/C++ compiler environments:

```
$ . /opt/intel/impi/latest/bin64/mpivars.sh
$ . /opt/intel/compiler/latest/bin/iccvars.sh intel64
```

- Compile an MPI binary for the host processor

```
$ mpiicc -o mpitest test.c
```

- Compile the SAME code for coprocessor

```
$ mpiicc -mmic -o mpitest.mic test.c
```

- Create a node file listing of the host and coprocessor nodenames

```
$ echo test1-mic0 > hostfile
$ echo test2-mic0 >> hostfile
```

```
$ echo test1 >> hostfile
$ echo test2 >> hostfile
```

- Set a few coprocessor enabling options and run the code:

```
$ export I_MPI_MIC=enable
$ export I_MPI_MIC_POSTFIX=.mic
$ mpirun -bootstrap ssh -perhost 1 -f hostfile -n 4 ~/mpitest
```

This chapter will describe necessary coprocessor and cluster configuration steps to make this conceptual simplicity possible.

NETWORK CONFIGURATION CONCEPTS AND GOALS

Configuring coprocessors for network use requires more thought than for coprocessors utilized by a single user in a workstation. In particular, the impact on multiple users and user expectations for connectivity must be considered. The flexibility to utilize an Intel Xeon Phi coprocessor as an offload processor, as a standalone native SMP system, or as a cluster of compute nodes requires important configuration decisions based on the needs of the system users.

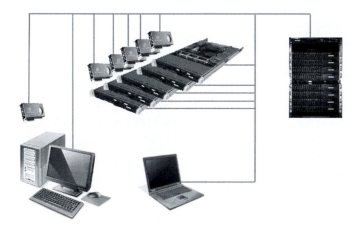

For example, users in a network expect to be able to connect directly to all other systems from their workstation or laptop. Even more so in a cluster, they expect to connect via *ssh* to every compute node *without* entering a password. This is a necessary prerequisite for MPI-based programs and allows easier scripting.

A LOOK AT NETWORKING OPTIONS

Starting at the interface level, we note that a coprocessor installation on a Linux server creates two additional network interfaces for every coprocessor present as shown in the figure below.

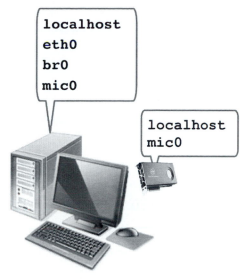

These interfaces are used by the Intel® Many-core Platform Software Stack (Intel® MPSS) to allow IP communication with each coprocessor. Unfortunately, both the host and coprocessor card interfaces are called `mic0`. This chapter use the names host.mic0 and card.mic0 to differentiate between the host and coprocessor interfaces.

There are basically three network configuration options:

1. Create a private network between host and coprocessor. For example, the following illustrative configuration will allow communication between the host and coprocessor card without anyone else on the network being able to reach the coprocessor.
   ```
   host.mic0 192.168.0.1 netmask 255.255.255.0
   card.mic0 192.168.0.2 netmask 255.255.255.0
   ```
2. Configure all cards to listen to unique addresses. This configuration will allow remote systems to reach coprocessors **if** you add explicit routings on every system for every coprocessor—or install a routing demon that discovers and broadcasts the required information. This author strictly advises against the latter installation, as size and complexity of routing tables grows by the (number of systems) squared. On a large system, this will impact network performance.

3. Deploy a network bridge on the host-system to provide network accessibility to the coprocessor(s). In this configuration, the host.mic0 interface as well as the host.eth0 interface are connected via the host.br0 device. In addition, the card.mic0 interface is now able to automatically listen to network traffic for information sent to the coprocessor address.

To avoid problems, the host.mic0 and the card.mic0 interfaces require unique MAC addresses that are stable across reboots. For example, a switch will see five MAC addresses for a server containing two coprocessors running in a bridged configuration. This is not a problem *per se* unless the MAC addresses change after each reboot of the coprocessors. Should this happen—especially on a cluster—the buffers on switches, or file servers, could get overrun. Generally, this should not be a problem as coprocessors can utilize their serial number to determine a unique and correct MAC address.

STEPS TO SET UP A CLUSTER ENABLED COPROCESSOR

1. Ensure that the various symbolic hostnames are known to all systems in the cluster. This includes names and IP addresses for the Ethernet and IP over InfiniBand interfaces of the host and a similar pair for every coprocessor present.
2. InfiniBand support requires a suitable OFED version be installed. At the time of writing, this is either OFED 1.5.4.1 or OFA-3.5.2-mic. Please use the download link listed in the "For More Information" section for the current Intel MPSS versions and compatible OFED versions and updated installation information.
3. Ensure a recent Intel MPSS and coprocessor card firmware version is installed.
4. Recompile and install the Intel MPSS kernel modules for the current Linux kernel version according to the instructions accompanying the Intel MPSS package. Intel provides packages for standard Redhat and SuSE* Enterprise Linux releases, but does not compile/test kernel modules against distribution updates. NOTE: it is likely that the Intel MPSS kernel modules will need to be updated after a distribution update of the Linux kernel.
5. Recompile and install the MIC-OFED kernel modules. *Note*: it is likely that these modules will need to be rebuilt after a Linux kernel distribution update. Be aware that the Intel MPSS-kernel-module DEVELOPMENT files must be installed to recompile the MIC-OFED kernel modules.
6. Configure the host system to use the bridged networking configuration (previously described as option three). The following is an example Redhat* Enterprise Linux version 6 system configuration for bridge br0:

```
# cat /etc/sysconfig/network-scripts/ifcfg-br0
DEVICE=br0
TYPE=Bridge
ONBOOT=yes
DELAY=0
NM_CONTROLLED="no"
MTU=9000
BOOTPROTO=dhcp
NOZEROCONF=yes
```

Modify the file /etc/sysconfig/network-scripts/ifcfg-eth0 to use the br0 bridge:

```
# cat /etc/sysconfig/network-scripts/ifcfg-eth0
DEVICE=eth0
ONBOOT=yes
BRIDGE=br0
MTU=9000
```

Ensure that the old address advertised by eth0 is now assigned to br0.

7. Create a basic configuration for the coprocessors with the command:
   ```
   micctrl --initdefaults
   ```
8. Configure network and bridged networking for the coprocessor either via *micctrl* or via the host operating system. The following is an example for a Redhat* Enterprise Linux version 6 system:
   ```
   # cat /etc/sysconfig/network-scripts/ifcfg-mic0
   DEVICE=eth0
   ONBOOT=yes
   BRIDGE=br0
   MTU=9000
   ```
9. The network configuration of the coprocessor system supports both static IP addresses as well as DHCP. Configuration is along standard Linux principles. On Intel MPSS 3.x, each coprocessors' network configuration file is located in:
   ```
   /var/mpss/mic[012…]/etc/networking/interfaces
   ```
   Beware: on older Intel MPSS 2.x the files were located in /opt/intel/mic/filesystem/mic[012…]/etc/sysconfig/network and followed a different syntax.
10. Start the coprocessor with the typical sequence of micctrl commands (−r reset coprocessor; −w wait till operation is completed; −b boot the coprocessor)
    ```
    # micctrl -r
    # micctrl -w
    # micctrl -b
    ```
11. Test you have access to the coprocessor as root. If access fails, your /root/.ssh directory might not be set up correctly.
    ```
    # ssh `hostname`-mic0 pwd
    /root
    ```

COPROCESSOR FILE SYSTEMS SUPPORT

If users want to program the coprocessor to act as a compute node in a cluster rather than just using offload techniques, some additional configuration is necessary. Now that we have addressed the network layout considerations, the file systems available within the cluster will need to be mounted on the coprocessor.

The following discussion details how to configure the coprocessors for NFS, Lustre®, BeeGFS®, and Panasas® PanFS® file systems.

Once these changes are complete, a user can run MPI applications directly on the coprocessor.

SUPPORT FOR NFS

NFS version 3 is provided with Intel MPSS for the coprocessor. The principle challenge with NFS lies in correctly configuring the network. Once a coprocessor can ping successfully and directly to the NFS server, then the mount command used is no different from a standard Linux system.

```
test-mic0# mkdir -p /mnt
test-mic0# mount -o rw,nolock 10.101.235.1:/scratch1 /mnt
test-mic0# mount | grep /mnt
10.101.235.1:/scratch1 on /mnt type nfs
(rw,relatime,vers=3,rsize=1048576,wsize=1048576,namlen=25
5,hard,proto=tcp,port=65535,timeo=70,retrans=3,sec=sys,lo
cal_lock=none,addr=36.101.235.1)
```

Support for NFS v4 is disabled in the kernel. Administrators interested in version 4 could recompile the coprocessor Linux OS Kernel with NFS4 activated.

SUPPORT FOR LUSTRE® FILE SYSTEM

Coprocessors can support the Lustre parallel file system. Compiling the Lustre client modules for the coprocessor is very similar to building a client module for the host side. The Intel MPSS installation provides a cross compiler capable of building kernel modules.

For Intel MPSS 2.1.x releases, the coprocessor OS kernel sources are in */opt/intel/mic/src/card/ kernel* and the build instructions use these commands:

```
$ export PATH=/usr/linux-k1om-4.7/bin:$PATH
$ test -e ./autogen.sh && sh ./autogen.sh
$ ./configure --with-linux=/opt/intel/mic/src/card/kernel \
  --disable-server --without-o2ib \
  --host=x86_64-k1om-linux --build=x86_64-pc-linux
$ make
$ make rpms
```

Note that Intel MPSS version 3.1.2 and greater have connected mode RDMA available, which means Lustre can therefore be compiled with direct InfiniBand support for those versions. Attention must be paid to architecture changes. With Intel MPSS 3.x versions, the microarchitecture changed names to *k1om-mpss-linux* from *x86_64-k1om-linux*.

This can become a problem if no *autogen.sh* file is present. A workaround is to modify all *config. sub* files:

```
$ find . -name config.sub -exec \
    sed -e 's,x86_64-\* |,x86_64-* | k1om-*|,' -i {} \;
```

For Intel MPSS 3.x, these are the compilation commands:

```
$ . /opt/mpss/3.x/environment-setup-k1om-mpss-linux
$ test -e ./autogen.sh && sh ./autogen.sh
```

```
$ ./configure --with-linux=/SOMEPATH/linux-2.6.38+mpss3.x \
  --with-o2ib=/usr/src/ofed-driver \
  --host=k1om-mpss-linux --build=x86_64-pc-linux
$ make
$ make rpms
```

As of Intel MPSS 3.2.3, the path *--with-o2ib=/usr/src/ofed-driver* actually relates to the host side *mpss-ofed-dev-*.x86_64.rpm* package. This is possible as both the host side OS and the coprocessor OS are using the same OFED version and API.

The modules must be loaded into the kernel running on the Intel Xeon Phi coprocessor. For simplicity, mount an NFS file system to provide the same path for both the host and coprocessor(s). Once the RPMs have been created, change to the rpm directory and use rpm2cpio to extract the files.

On the host:

```
$ cd /NFSPATH
$ rpm2cpio ~/rpmbuild/RPMS/x86_64/lustre-client-mic-2.5.0-
2.6.38.8_gefd324e.x86_64.rpm | cpio -idm
$ rpm2cpio ~/rpmbuild/RPMS/x86_64/lustre-client-mic-modules-
2.5.0-2.6.38.8_gefd324e.x86_64.rpm | cpio -idm
```

Without InfiniBand support execute on the coprocessor as `root`:

```
# INSTALLPATH=/NFSPATH/opt/lustre/2.5.0/ARCHITECTURE
# LIBPATH=/lib/modules/`uname -r`
# for I in $INSTALLPATH/$LIBPATH/updates/kernel/*/lustre/*.ko \
    do cp $I $LIBPATH \
  done
# depmod -a
# modprobe lustre
# lsmod
# mkdir /mnt
# $INSTALLPATH/sbin/mount.lustre 12.12.11.1@tcp:/lfs08 /mnt
```

Systems using MPSS 3.x with InfiniBand must configure the *ipoib* interface. You can either use the methods provided in the Intel MPSS documentation, or if desired, directly load the driver and configure the interface:

```
# /sbin/modprobe ib_ipoib
# /sbin/ifconfig ib0 12.12.12.100 netmask 255.255.0.0
# /sbin/modprobe ibp_sa_client
# /sbin/modprobe ibp_cm_client
```

To mount Lustre file systems then execute the following on the coprocessor as `root`:

```
# INSTALLPATH=/NFSPATH/opt/lustre/2.5.0/k1om-mpss-linux/
# LIBPATH=/lib/modules/`uname -r`/updates/kernel
# mkdir -p $LIBPATH/net/lustre
# mkdir -p $LIBPATH/fs/lustre
```

```
# FILES=`cd $INSTALLPATH/$LIBPATH; ls */lustre/*.ko`
# for I in $FILES
  do
    ln -s $INSTALLPATH/$LIBPATH/$I $LIBPATH/$I
  done
# echo 'options lnet networks="o2ib0(ib0)"' \
    > /etc/modprobe.d/lustre.conf
# /sbin/depmod -a
# /sbin/modprobe lustre
# /sbin/lsmod
# mkdir /mnt
# $INSTALLPATH/sbin/mount.lustre 12.12.12.1@o2ib:/lfs08 /mnt
```

Note: At the time of this writing rdma_cm support is still considered experimental. Some of these steps may not be necessary in future Intel MPSS versions.

SUPPORT FOR FRAUNHOFER BEEGFS® (FORMERLY FHGFS) FILE SYSTEM

The BeeGFS (formerly known as FHGFS) file system developed by the Fraunhofer ITWM institute provides native Intel Xeon Phi coprocessor support along with InfiniBand support.

InfiniBand support requires the rdma_cm kernel module, which requires Intel MPSS version 3.1.2 or later. Once OFED and Intel MPSS are installed and running, the BeeGFS kernel modules can be compiled for the coprocessor.

The BeeGFS sources can be downloaded from http://www.fhgfs.com/cms/download. The default install location is */opt/fhgfs/src/client*, though you can easily copy/move the directory to a different location. Change to the */opt/fhgs)/src/client/fhgfs_client_module/build* directory (or the user specified build directory).

The following make command assumes the default directory:

```
$ make KDIR=/PATHTO/linux-2.6.38+mpss.../
  STRIP=/usr/linux-k1om-4.7/bin/x86_64-k1om-linux-strip
  CC=/usr/linux-k1om-4.7/bin/x86_64-k1om-linux-gcc
  LD=/usr/linux-k1om-4.7/bin/x86_64-k1om-linux-ld
  LDFLAGS="-m elf_k1om"
  FHGFS_OPENTK_IBVERBS=1
  OFED_INCLUDE_PATH=/PATHTO/mpss-ofed/src/kernel/include/
```

This creates modules

```
.../src/client/fhgfs_client_opentk_module/build/fhgfs-client-
opentk.ko
```

and

```
.../src/client/fhgfs_client_module/build/fhgfs.ko.
```

Transfer these kernel modules to each coprocessor's file system and load them with the usual Linux commands. For instance,

```
$ insmod fhgfs-client-opentk.ko
$ insmod fhgfs.ko
```

Now the BeeGFS volumes can be natively mounted in the usual way on the coprocessor.

SUPPORT FOR PANASAS® PANFS® FILE SYSTEM

As of Panasas PanFS version 5.0.1.e, Panasas customers can download driver and native utilities for Intel Xeon Phi coprocessors from the Panasas Web site http://www.panasas.com.

As Panasas also licenses the client source code, one might wish to compile it directly for Intel Xeon Phi coprocessor environments. This is possible, but somewhat complicated. The porting effort requires (1) the creation of a native build environment including Perl tools and (2) the removal of small number lines of PanFS source code that utilizes Intel® MMX assembler instructions.

CHOOSING A CLUSTER FILE SYSTEM

In many cases, Intel Xeon Phi coprocessors will be integrated into an existing cluster, and the choice for a cluster file system (CFS) will already be made. If the main CFS in the cluster is not among the ones listed, one can either use an intermediate server to mount and re-export, or try to port the client software. Based on the author's experiences, such a task sounds more daunting then it really is.

Between the four file systems mentioned, the author would in an ideal cluster use all four of them because they offer different advantages:

NFS is easily and natively supported everywhere (even Windows); uses Ethernet; has low single thread performance; has low scalability; use for administrative file system; use for data file systems on small clusters (<500 nodes)

Lustre uses Ethernet and InfiniBand; moderate single thread performance; provides high scalability; use for fast scratch file system

BeeGFS uses Ethernet and InfiniBand; has high single thread performance; provides high scalability; use for fast scratch file systems

PanFS uses Ethernet; has low single thread performance; provides high scalability; is highly reliable and therefore high data security; use for data file systems

These are by no means fixed boundaries. One can improve, for instance, single thread performance of PanFS by using a router-box translating between 10GE and InfiniBand, or dramatically increase reliability of Lustre using appropriate hardware and software.

SUMMARY

This chapter provided the necessary information to create a cluster where Intel Xeon Phi coprocessors can be addressed as standard independent nodes in the network topology. Both network configuration and cluster file systems need to be addressed. With those components in place, utilizing distributed MPI programs running on the coprocessor can be as easy as recompiling them using the steps provided in this chapters' introduction—though optimizing the programs to account for the specific computational capabilities and differences between processors and coprocessors in the cluster will still be another step.

FOR MORE INFORMATION

Intel MPSS software download:

- https://software.intel.com/en-us/articles/intel-manycore-platform-software-stack-mpss.

NFS:

- http://en.wikipedia.org/wiki/Network_File_System.

Lustre:

- http://wiki.lustre.org/index.php/Main_Page.
- http://www.intel.com/content/www/us/en/software/intel-solutions-for-lustre-software.html.

Panasas:

- http://www.panasas.com/.

BeeGFS:

- http://www.fhgfs.com/cms/.

Introduction to Clustering:

- http://www.hpcgeeks.com/index.php/hpc-hardware/hpc-clusters/5-build-your-own-cluster.
- http://www.admin-magazine.com/HPC/Articles/real_world_hpc_setting_up_an_hpc_cluster.
- http://www.wikihow.com/Build-a-Supercomputer.

MPI:

- http://www.mpi-forum.org/docs/.

Linux network bridges:

- http://www.linuxfoundation.org/collaborate/workgroups/networking/bridge.

NWCHEM

QUANTUM CHEMISTRY SIMULATIONS AT SCALE

17

Edoardo Aprà*, **Karol Kowalski***, **Jeff R. Hammond**†, **Michael Klemm**‡

Pacific Northwest National Laboratory, USA, †Intel USA, ‡Intel, Germany

INTRODUCTION

Methods based on quantum mechanics equations have been developed since the 1930s with the purpose of accurately studying the electronic structure of molecules. However, it is only during the past two decades that an intense development of new computational algorithms has opened the possibility of performing accurate simulations of challenging molecular processes with high-order many-body methods. A wealth of evidence indicates that the proper inclusion of instantaneous interactions between electrons (or the so-called electron correlation effects) is indispensable for the accurate characterization of chemical reactivity, molecular properties, and interactions of light with matter. The availability of reliable methods for benchmarking of medium-size molecular systems provides also a unique chance to propagate high-level accuracy across spatial scales through multiscale methodologies. Some of these methods have the potential to utilize computational resources in an efficient way since they are characterized by high numerical complexity and appropriate level of data granularity, which can be efficiently distributed over multiprocessor architectures. The broad spectrum of coupled cluster (CC) methods falls into this class of methodologies. Several recent CC implementations clearly demonstrated the scalability of CC formalisms on architectures composed of hundreds thousand computational cores. In this context, NWChem provides a collection of Tensor Contraction Engine (TCE) generated parallel implementations of various CC methods capable of taking advantage of many thousand of cores on leadership class parallel architectures.

The emergence of hybrid architectures based on GPUs or the Intel Many Integrated Core architecture offers yet another means of reducing the time to solution of high-order CC methods. A very good illustration of the progress is provided by recent implementations of the CCSD(T) approach for the Intel® Xeon Phi™ coprocessor. CCSD is considered by many to be the "gold standard" of high-accuracy computational chemistry.

For the domain expert, bringing these simulation tools to the hardware at high productivity is a key requirement for success in addition to obtaining high performance. At the time of its launch, the Intel Xeon Phi coprocessor made the promise of being a more productive compute device than traditional accelerator solutions and porting code to the coprocessor would be much easier than before. In our experience with the NWChem chemistry package, we rely on this promise by making use of the tool chain that consists of the MIC Platform Software Stack, Intel Composer XE for Fortran, and Intel VTune Amplifier XE. It is our desire to not rewrite the existing Fortran code in a way that renders it unusable for the Intel® Xeon® platform; instead we wish to continue the development of Fortran code and optimizations that we apply should both be beneficial (or at least not harmful) for both the Intel Xeon processor and the Intel Xeon Phi coprocessor.

In this chapter, we will show how we achieved the goal of high-productivity development of a high-performance offload solution that exposes excellent scale-out with high parallel efficiency across a system ranked top 20 in the recent Top500 list. For our work, we have defined a new methodology to provide an engineering process that developers can follow to decide on offload candidates and to receive guidance on the steps they need to make to bring their solution to the Intel coprocessor. Our process provided us with the necessary input to make informed decisions on optimizations for both the placement of offload directives as well as the tuning of the compute kernels. Let us start with a quick introduction into the theoretical background and its fundamental architecture for NWChem.

OVERVIEW OF SINGLE-REFERENCE CC FORMALISM

Let us begin with a short overview of single-reference CC formalism. We will also stress the connections between the algebraic form of the equations and parallelization strategies. The CC theory is predicated on the assumption that there exists a judicious choice of a single Slater determinant $|\Phi\rangle$ referred further to as the reference function, which is capable of providing a reasonable zeroth-order description of the exact ground-state electronic state described by the wavefunction $|\Psi\rangle$. Usually, reference wavefunctions are chosen as Hartree-Fock (HF) determinants although other choices are possible. The wavefunction in the CC parametrization takes the form of the exponential Ansatz

$$|\Psi\rangle = e^{T}|\Phi\rangle, \tag{17.1}$$

where cluster operator T is represented by connected diagrams only. A typical way of introducing CC equations for cluster operator is to introduce (17.1) into the Schrödinger equation, i.e.,

$$He^{T}|\Phi\rangle = Ee^{T}|\Phi\rangle, \tag{17.2}$$

and premultiply both sides of Eq. (17.2) by e^{-T}

$$e^{-T}He^{T}|\Phi\rangle = E|\Phi\rangle. \tag{17.3}$$

Using well-known Baker-Campbell-Hausdorff lemma

$$e^{-B}Ae^{B} = A + [A,B] + \frac{1}{2!}[[A,B],B] + \frac{1}{3!}[[[A,B],B],B] + \cdots, \tag{17.4}$$

one can show that Eq. (17.2) can be cast into the following form:

$$(He^{T})_{C}|\Phi\rangle = E|\Phi\rangle, \tag{17.5}$$

where the subscript "C" designates connected diagrams of a given operator expression. By projecting Eq. (17.5) onto all possible excited configurations $|\Phi^{a_1 \cdots a_n}_{i_1 \cdots i_n}\rangle$ with respect to the reference determinant $|\Phi\rangle$, one can decouple the equations for the cluster amplitudes

$$\langle \Phi^{a_1 \cdots a_n}_{i_1 \cdots i_n} | (He^{T})_{C} | \Phi \rangle = 0 \tag{17.6}$$

from the equation for the energy, obtained by projecting (17.5) onto the reference function

$$E = \langle \Phi | (He^{T})_{C} | \Phi \rangle. \tag{17.7}$$

The above equations are used in determining cluster amplitudes and corresponding energies. One should notice that in the first step nonlinear equations for T operator need to be solved iteratively, then the energy can be calculated using known cluster amplitudes.

In practical applications, the cluster operator is approximated by many-body expansion truncated at a certain excitation level m_A ($m_A \ll N$, where N designates number of correlated electrons in the system)

$$T = \sum_{m_A}^{n=1} T_n, \tag{17.8}$$

where T_n is a part of cluster operator T which produces N-tuple excitations when acting onto the reference function. The most common approximation used in routine calculations is the CCSD method (CC with singles and doubles), where the cluster operator is defined by singly (T_1) and doubly excited (T_2) many-body components. This leads to the following representation of the CCSD wavefunction:

$$| \Psi_{CCSD} \rangle = e^{T_1 + T_2} | \Phi \rangle, \tag{17.9}$$

where T_1 and T_2 are represented by singly (t_a^i) and doubly excited (t_{ab}^{ij}) cluster amplitudes and corresponding strings of creation/annihilation operators (X_p^+/X_p)

$$T_1 = \sum_{i,a} t_a^i X_a^+ X_i, \tag{17.10}$$

$$T_2 = \frac{1}{4} \sum_{i,j,a,b} t_{ab}^{ij} X_a^+ X_b^+ X_j X_i. \tag{17.11}$$

As always, the $i,j,\ldots$ ($a,b,\ldots$) indices refer to occupied (unoccupied) spin-orbital indices in the reference function $|\Phi\rangle$. Standard CCSD equations for the cluster amplitudes are obtained from the connected form of the Schrödinger equation defined by projections on singly ($|\Phi_i^a\rangle$, $|\Phi_i^a\rangle = X_a^+ X_i |\Phi\rangle$)) and doubly ($|\Phi_{ij}^{ab}\rangle$, $|\Phi_{ij}^{ab}\rangle = X_a^+ X_b^+ X_j X_i |\Phi\rangle$)) excited configurations

$$\langle \Phi_i^a | (He^{T_1+T_2})_C | \Phi \rangle = 0 \; \forall i,a, \tag{17.12}$$

$$\langle \Phi_{ij}^{ab} | (He^{T_1+T_2})_C | \Phi \rangle = 0 \; \forall i,j,a,b \tag{17.13}$$

where H designates electronic Hamiltonian operator. Once the cluster amplitudes are determined from Eqs. (17.12) and (17.13), the CCSD energy is calculated from the expression

$$E = \langle \Phi | (He^{T_1+T_2})_C | \Phi \rangle. \tag{17.14}$$

Using diagrammatic techniques one can easily determine the algebraic structure of Eqs. (17.12) and (17.13) and the corresponding numerical complexity of the equations which is proportional to $n_o^2 n_u^4$ (n_o and n_u stand for number of occupied and unoccupied spin-orbitals, respectively). Unfortunately, the accuracy obtained with the CCSD formalism in many cases is not sufficient to provide the so-called chemical accuracy, which is typically defined as an error below 1 kcal/mol. To achieve chemical accuracy, the inclusion of triple excitations (represented by the T_3 operator) is necessary.

The direct inclusion of the three-body effects (T_3) in the cluster operator results in high numerical scaling ($\simeq n_o^3 n_u^5$) and huge memory demands ($\simeq n_o^3 n_u^3$) which prohibits the CCSDT (CC with singles, doubles, and triples) calculations even for relatively small molecular systems. In order to reduce the scaling of the CCSDT method without significant loss of accuracy, several methods have been introduced in the past, where T_3 amplitudes are estimated perturbatively (see Section "For more information"; Bomble et al., 2005; Crawford and Stanton, 1998; Gwaltney and Head-Gordon, 2000; Gwaltney et al., 2000, 2002; Hirata et al., 2001; Kallày and Gauss, 2005; Kowalski and Fan, 2009; Kowalski and Piecuch, 2000; Kowalski and Valiev, 2009; Kucharski and Bartlett, 1998; Piecuch and Wloch, 2005; Piecuch et al., 2006; Raghavachari et al., 1989; Stanton, 1997; Taube and Bartlett, 2008a,b; Urban et al., 1985 at the end of the chapter). The most popular method in this class of formalisms is the CCSD(T) method in which the ground-state energy is represented as a sum of the CCSD energy (E^{CCSD}) and noniterative CCSD(T) correction, which combines elements of fourth- and fifth-order of the standard many-body perturbation theory expansion containing triply excited intermediate states:

$$E^{\text{CCSD(T)}} = E^{\text{CCSD}} + \langle \Phi \,|\, (T_2^+ V_{\text{N}}) R_3^{(0)} V T_2 \,|\, \Phi \rangle \tag{17.15}$$
$$+ \langle \Phi \,|\, (T_1^+ V_{\text{N}}) R_3^{(0)} V T_2 \,|\, \Phi \rangle,$$

where V_{N} is two-body part of electronic Hamiltonian in normal product form. Currently, the CCSD(T) method is the most frequently employed CC approach especially in studies of spectroscopic properties, geometry optimization, and chemical reactions.

Using the definition of the three-body resolvent $R_3^{(0)}$, the CCSD(T) energy can be rewritten

$$E^{\text{CCSD(T)}} = E^{\text{CCSD}} \tag{17.16}$$

$$+ \sum_{\substack{i<j<k \\ a<b<c}} \frac{\langle \Phi \,|\, (T_2^+ V_{\text{N}}) \,|\, \Phi_{ijk}^{abc} \rangle \langle \Phi_{ijk}^{abc} \,|\, V T_2 \,|\, \Phi \rangle}{\epsilon_i + \epsilon_j + \epsilon_k - \epsilon_a - \epsilon_b - \epsilon_c}$$

$$+ \sum_{\substack{i<j<k \\ a<b<c}} \frac{\langle \Phi \,|\, (T_1^+ V_{\text{N}}) \,|\, \Phi_{ijk}^{abc} \rangle \langle \Phi_{ijk}^{abc} \,|\, V T_2 \,|\, \Phi \rangle}{\epsilon_i + \epsilon_j + \epsilon_k - \epsilon_a - \epsilon_b - \epsilon_c}$$

where ϵ's are the orbital energies. The most expensive part of the CCSD(T) correction (scaling as $n_o^3 n_u^4$) is associated with the presence of the $\langle \Phi_{ijk}^{abc} | V T_2 | \Phi \rangle$ term, which is defined by the expression:

$$\langle \Phi_{ijk}^{abc} \,|\, V_{\text{N}} T_2 \,|\, \Phi \rangle = v_{ma}^{ij} t_{bc}^{mk} - v_{mb}^{ij} t_{ac}^{mk} + v_{mc}^{ij} t_{ab}^{mk} \tag{17.17}$$
$$- v_{ma}^{ik} t_{bc}^{mj} + v_{mb}^{ik} t_{ac}^{mj} - v_{mc}^{ik} t_{ab}^{mj}$$
$$+ v_{ma}^{jk} t_{bc}^{mi} - v_{mb}^{jk} t_{ac}^{mi} + v_{mc}^{jk} t_{ab}^{mi}$$
$$- v_{ab}^{ei} t_{ec}^{jk} + v_{ac}^{ei} t_{eb}^{jk} - v_{bc}^{ei} t_{ea}^{jk}$$
$$+ v_{ab}^{ej} t_{ec}^{ik} - v_{ac}^{ej} t_{eb}^{ik} + v_{bc}^{ej} t_{ea}^{ik}$$
$$- v_{ab}^{ek} t_{ec}^{ij} + v_{ac}^{ek} t_{eb}^{ij} - v_{bc}^{ek} t_{ea}^{ij},$$
$$(i < j < k, a < b < c)$$

where v_{rs}^{pq} is the tensor of two-electron integrals. Equation (17.17) can be separated into terms defined by contractions over occupied indices (A_{ijk}^{abc}; first nine terms on the right-hand side (r.h.s.) of Eq. (17.17)) and terms corresponding to contraction over unoccupied indices (B_{ijk}^{abc}; remaining nine terms on the r.h.s. of Eq. (17.17)), i.e.,

$$\langle \Phi_{ijk}^{abc} \,|\, V_{\text{N}} T_2 \,|\, \Phi \rangle = A_{ijk}^{abc} + B_{ijk}^{abc}. \tag{17.18}$$

The TCE CCSD(T) implementation uses the spin-orbital representation of all tensors defining cluster and Hamiltonian operators. This fact enables the TCE CCSD(T) approach to employ various types of reference functions including Restricted Hartree-Fock determinants for closed-shell systems as well as Restricted Open-Shell and Unrestricted HF Slater determinants for open-shell molecules. However, compared to other CCSD(T) implementations geared toward the description of closed-shell systems only (such as the CCSD(T) implementation based on the orbital nonorthogonally spin-adapted formalism NOSA-CCSD(T)), this approach involves a larger number of cluster amplitudes.

The general CCSD(T) spin-orbital formulations is expected to be several times slower than the NOSA-CCSD(T) formalism because of two factors: (1) in the spin-orbital formulation there are four types of (T) terms as far as the spin structure of intermediate triple excitations is concerned: $|\Phi^{\alpha\alpha\alpha}_{\alpha\alpha\alpha}\rangle$, $|\Phi^{\alpha\alpha\beta}_{\alpha\alpha\beta}\rangle$, $|\Phi^{\alpha\beta\beta}_{\alpha\beta\beta}\rangle$, and $|\Phi^{\beta\beta\beta}_{\beta\beta\beta}\rangle$, and (2) the internal contractions are performed over spin-orbital indices (which is twice as expensive compared to the orbital contraction in the NOSA-CCSD(T) method). In fact the antisymmetrization of triply excited amplitudes in the spin-orbital representation introduces another factor, which leads to increase of numerical complexity of the spin-orbital CCSD(T) expressions. However, all these factors must be related to the algebraic structure of underlying theory and not to the efficiency (or its lack) of a given implementation.

NWCHEM SOFTWARE ARCHITECTURE

Two main concepts influenced the original design of NWChem conceived in 1993:

- scalability to large number of processing elements on massively parallel computers
- modular structure as the foundation to implement new theoretical methods, n

These two defining features distinguish the NWChem development from more traditional development techniques widely used in several successful computational chemistry packages.

The modular structure of the code architecture is achieved by using an object-oriented approach within the realm of the Fortran programming language. For a more detailed description of this topic, we refer the reader to publications that have already described in details the various components of the NWChem architecture.

GLOBAL ARRAYS

In order to achieve parallel scalability, the NWChem software development adopts, for the bulk of its communication, the Global Arrays (GA) toolkit (see Figure 17.1). The GA toolkit is a library that was designed for parallelizing codes whose main quantities are large and dense arrays. GA forms an abstraction layer for the scientific programmer by distributing the arrays among the memory of the processing elements of the parallel computer and providing a set of operations for easily manipulating the elements of the arrays. While a more traditional message-passing approach would require synchronization of sender and receiver to perform tasks such as array transformation, the NWChem code uses one-sided GA operations for this purpose. GA operations can be classified in two categories: collective and local. Collective calls require all processes to participate, while local operations may be called by each process independently. Fetching (`ga_get`) or updating (`ga_put`) are the most common local operations. Commonly used linear algebra operations belong to the collective category (e.g., matrix multiply, eigensolvers, etc.) GA provides language bindings for Fortran and C/C++. The library is meant to be compatible with MPI, while using MPI itself for some of its functionality (e.g., process creations, some collective calls).

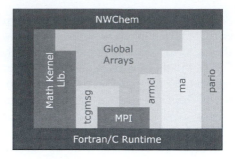

FIGURE 17.1

The components of the NWChem software stack.

Efficiency of GA on a given computer architecture relies heavily on the performance of the Aggregate Remote Memory Copy Interface (ARMCI) library. ARMCI fulfills the role of GA's primary communications layer by mapping to many different communication channels such as MPI, OpenIB, Portals, etc.

TENSOR CONTRACTION ENGINE

The TCE automates the derivation and parallelization of quantum many-body methods such as CC using a multistep approach. First, operator expressions are transformed into multidimensional array expressions; second, these array expressions are transformed into an optimized operation tree using performance heuristics; finally, parallel code that implements the optimized operation tree is generated using a source template. Because of TCE, the first parallel implementations of numerous methods were created and applied to larger scientific problems than previously possible. The initial TCE implementation in NWChem was general (i.e., lacked optimizations for known special cases) and required significant tuning to scale CC to more than 1000 processes in NWChem. The tuning applied to the TCE addressed essentially all aspects of the code, including more compact data representations (spin-free integrals are antisymmetrized on the fly in the standard case), reduction in communication by applying additional fusion that the TCE compiler was not capable of applying.

For a term such as

$$Z(i,j,a,b) + = \sum_{d,e} X(i,j,c,d) * Y(c,d,a,b), \qquad (17.19)$$

which is a bottleneck in the solution of the CCSD equations, the data are tiled over all the dimensions for each array and distributed across the machine in a 1-dimensional GA. Multidimensional GA are not used here because this cannot exploit block sparsity or index permutation symmetries. Remote access is implemented by using a lookup table for each tile and a `ga_get` operation. The global data layout is not always appropriate for the local computation, however; therefore, immediately after the `ga_get` operation completes, the data are rearranged into the appropriate layout for the computation. For compactness of notation, we use the `Fetch` operation to represent the just mentioned action of copying data from global memory to local memory followed by data reorganization. The `Symm` function is a condensation of a number of logical tests in the code that determine whether a particular tile will be nonzero. These tests consider the indices of the tile but ignore indices within the tile because each tile is

```
Tiled Global Arrays: X, Y, Z
Local Buffers: x, y, z
for all i, j ∈ Otiles do
    for all a,b ∈ Vtiles do
        if Symm(i, j, a, b) == True then
            Allocate z for Z(i, j, a, b) tile
            for all c, d ∈ Vtiles do
                if Symm(i, j, c, d) == True then
                    if Symm(a, b, c, d) == True then
                        Fetch X(i, j, c, d) into x
                        Fetch Y(c, d, a, b) into y
                        Contract z(i, j, a, b) += x(i, j, c, d)*y(c, d, a, b)
                    end if
                end if
            end for
            Accumulate z into Z(i, j, a, b)
        end if
    end for
end for
```

FIGURE 17.2

Pseudocode for the default TCE implementation of Eq. (17.19).

grouped such that the symmetry properties of all its constitutive elements are identical. Each tile index represents a set of contiguous indices so the contraction is between multidimensional arrays, not single elements. However, one can think of the local operation as the dot product of two tiles.

The template for the (T) evaluation (Figure 17.3) is quite similar. The inner loop where the local 6D triples intermediate is computed requires fetching the V, T_1, and T_2 contributions in a manner similar to the algorithm shown in Figure 17.2.

ENGINEERING AN OFFLOAD SOLUTION

One key design decision when porting new software to the Intel Xeon Phi coprocessor is what mode of operation and which programming model to use. With the native or symmetric mode, the coprocessors are autonomous compute nodes that participate in the computation by executing MPI or GA ranks with or without participation of their respective hosts. In the offload model, some computation remains on the host, while some kernels along with their input data are transferred to the coprocessor devices for execution.

From our domain knowledge, we understand that the structure of the TCE CCSD(T) algorithm exhibits excellent opportunities to use the offload model. It contains several floating-point intensive and highly parallel kernels. There are also opportunities for data reuse, so that communication between host and coprocessor can largely be avoided. In addition, some of the computation in preliminary steps of the algorithm (e.g., evaluation of two-electron repulsion integrals) require a substantial tuning effort if a native approach is used, whereas in the offload model we can keep these computations on the host. Finally, we also expect that GA achieves a higher message rate and communication bandwidth on the host than it would on coprocessor.

Tiled 4D Global Arrays: V, D
Local Scalar: es, ed
Local 4D Buffers: v, d
for all $i, j, l \in Otiles$ **do**
   for all $a, b, c \in Vtiles$ **do**
      if $\mathrm{Symm}(i, j, k, a, b, c) ==$ True **then**
         Allocate ts, td (local 6D buffers)
         Compute ts ($\langle \Phi_{ijk}^{abc} | V_N T_1 | \Phi \rangle$)
         Compute td ($\langle \Phi_{ijk}^{abc} | V_N T_2 | \Phi \rangle$)
         Compute es (term 2 in Eq. 16)
         Compute ed (term 3 in Eq. 16)
      end if
     end for
   end for
   Reduce es, ed

FIGURE 17.3

Pseudocode for the default TCE implementation of Eq. (17.16). The computation of ts and td include fetching of the tiles of V (i.e., V_2) and D (i.e., T_2) and perform all of the local contractions associated with the permutations shown in Eq. (17.17).

Because we prefer the offload solution over native execution and symmetric MPI across host and coprocessors, potential offload candidates have to be identified. In complex applications such as NWChem it is a major effort, if not virtually impossible, without a proper methodology in place that guides developers through the process of evaluating the potential of an offload solution versus the native mode and of finding offload candidates. The methodology also helps implement the offload solution and apply optimizations to it. Our methodology is inspired by the iterative top-down methodology of software optimization (Yasin, 2014), in which a hotspot analysis is combined with optimizations of the most intriguing bottlenecks in the application code.

Figure 17.4 gives a graphical summary of the analysis methodology. All starts with the selection of the benchmark that mimics the application behavior as closely as possible, but on a smaller, more manageable scale. An ideal benchmark runs from a few up to 15 min and triggers the same code regions as the production data. With the benchmark, we execute the application and collect information to produce a hotspots profile. The hotspots in the profile are potential offload candidates that we then select for a call-tree analysis, which will give us information about (potentially) existing common functions that can be used as a common anchor points for offloading. As the next step, one needs to determine whether an offload candidate is suitable for execution on the coprocessor. The next data point (potentially augmented with additional performance data such as memory bandwidth, vectorization potential, etc.) comes from the loop analysis. Here we take a closer look at a hotspot and locate any loops, their minimum, maximum, and average trip counts. We also add information from the compiler's vectorization report for more complex loops to gain insight into a loop's suitability for both vectorization and parallelization.

The last three steps then deal with actual implementation work. After the analysis has been completed, we have all necessary data available to introduce appropriate offload pragmas (Intel Language Extensions for Offload), offload keywords (Intel Cilk Plus), or OpenMP target directives to the code. It is very likely that simply adding a offload for a single candidate leads to a suboptimal solution that will

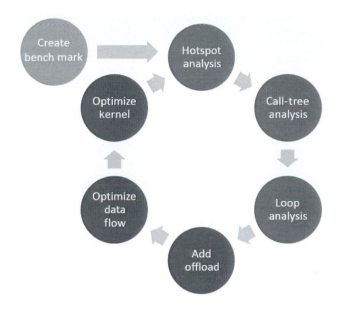

FIGURE 17.4

Iterative analysis methodology applied to NWChem.

issue too many data transfers over the PCIe bus. Here, we take the call-tree analysis into account and use that information to hoist offloads and data transfers up in the call tree so that data transfers can be minimized. Finally, we work to optimize the individual offload regions to improve their performance on the target device.

We have applied the above methodology to the NWChem CCSD(T) method. As a benchmark, we use the uracil dimer benchmark as the input for the analysis. VTune Amplifier XE is our tool of choice to collect the hotpot profile for NWChem.

Figure 17.5 shows a screenshot of the GUI and various application hotspots. As can be seen, there is one big contribution (58%) to compute time by the comex_make_progress function that handles communication between NWChem processes and that consumes many cycles while waiting for incoming messages from other processes. In total, there are 38% of compute time that are attributed to a total 18 functions of the form $sd\_t\_dX\_Y$ ($sd\_t\_d1\_1$ to $sd\_t\_d1\_9$ and $sd\_t\_d2\_1$ to $sd\_t\_d2\_9$). All of them are called from the same anchor function ($ccsd\_d\_doubles\_l\_2$ in $ccsd\_t\_doubles\_l.F$). Because of their exposure in the hotspot profile, these functions might be potential offload candidates.

As our next step, we analyze the call tree that contains the $sd\_t\_dX\_Y$ functions. Figure 17.6 shows the corresponding screenshot of VTune Amplifier XE. The call-tree analysis reveals that all of the $sd\_t\_dX\_Y$ are called from a single function $ccsd\_d\_doubles\_l\_2$. As we will see in Section "Offload architecture," this function will be the main focus of the optimization work to avoid unnecessary data transfers to and from the coprocessor devices.

Taking the process further, we are now going to have a closer look at each individual $sd\_t\_dX\_Y$ kernel and make a final judgment about the suitability for offloading. As we know, the coprocessor requires both multithreading and SIMD vectorization to deliver optimal performance. Hence, we need

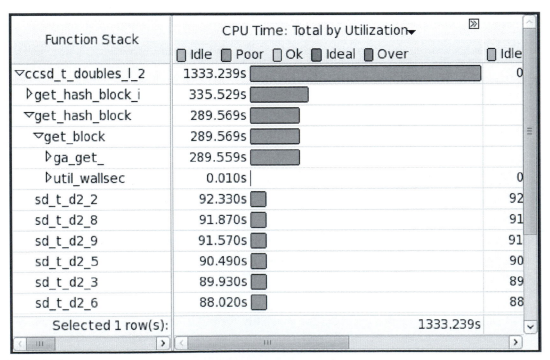

Basic Hotspots   Hotspots by CPU Usage viewpoint (change) ❷

◁ | ⊕ Analysis Target | 🅰 Analysis Type | ▦ Collection Log | 🗟 Summary | ⚙ Bottom-up | ⚙ Caller/Callee | ⚙

Grouping: | Function / Call Stack

Function / Call Stack	CPU Time by Utili...▾ ☆ ⊠ ☐ Idle ☐ Poor ☐ Ok ☐ Ide	Overhead and ⊠ Spin Time	Module	Start Address
▷comex_make_progress	52.0%	0.250s	nwchem	0x295658
▷sd_t_d2_2	4.2%	0s	nwchem	0x16a0d7
▷sd_t_d2_8	4.2%	0s	nwchem	0x16a272
▷sd_t_d2_9	4.2%	0s	nwchem	0x16a2e3
▷sd_t_d2_5	4.2%	0s	nwchem	0x16a1a4
▷sd_t_d2_3	4.1%	0s	nwchem	0x16a3aa
▷sd_t_d2_6	4.1%	0s	nwchem	0x16a345
▷sd_t_d2_1	3.1%	0s	nwchem	0x16a40b
▷sd_t_d2_4	3.0%	0s	nwchem	0x16a142
▷sd_t_d2_7	1.4%	0s	nwchem	0x16a211
▷_mq_test	1.2%	0.030s	nwchem	0x29565a
▷ Selected 18 row(s):	38.0%	0s		

FIGURE 17.5

Result of the VTune Amplifier XE Hotspot analysis for NWChem's CCSD(T) method.

Function Stack	CPU Time: Total by Utilization▾ ⊠ ☐ Idle ☐ Poor ☐ Ok ☐ Ideal ☐ Over	☐ Idle
▽ccsd_t_doubles_l_2	1333.239s	0
▷get_hash_block_i	335.529s	
▽get_hash_block	289.569s	
▽get_block	289.569s	
▷ga_get_	289.559s	
▷util_wallsec	0.010s	0
sd_t_d2_2	92.330s	92
sd_t_d2_8	91.870s	91
sd_t_d2_9	91.570s	91
sd_t_d2_5	90.490s	90
sd_t_d2_3	89.930s	89
sd_t_d2_6	88.020s	88
Selected 1 row(s):	1333.239s	

FIGURE 17.6

Call-tree analysis of the hotspots in Figure 17.5.

```
subroutine sd_t_d1_1(h3d,h2d,h1d,p6d,p5d,p4d,
1                    h7d,triplesx,t2sub,v2sub)
 integer h3d,h2d,h1d,p6d,p5d,p4d,h7d,h3,h2,h1,p6,p5,p4,h7
 double precision triplesx(h3d,h2d,h1d,p6d,p5d,p4d)
 double precision t2sub(h7d,p4d,p5d,h1d), v2sub(h3d,h2d,p6d,h7d)
 do p4=1,p4d
 do p5=1,p5d
 do p6=1,p6d
 do h1=1,h1d
 do h7=1,h7d
 do h2=1,h2d
 do h3=1,h3d
    triplesx(h3,h2,h1,p6,p5,p4) = triplesx(h3,h2,h1,p6,p5,p4)
c       - t2sub(h7,p4,p5,h1)*v2sub(h3,h2,p6,h7)
    ...
 enddo
 end
```

FIGURE 17.7

Example kernel (`sd_t_d1_1`) of NWChem.

to assess the kernels under these two metrics and determine which of the kernels will be a good offload candidate. Figure 17.7 shows the code of the `sd_t_d1_1` kernel as a stand-in for all 18 kernels, which have the same basic code structure. Each kernel consists of seven perfectly nested loops that compute a very tight inner-most loop body. The trip counts of each of the loops are on the order of 20-30, which is not enough for trivial parallelization with OpenMP. Trivial (auto-)vectorization will also lead to a too low vectorization potential of about 80% only. However, the loops do not contain any loop-carried dependencies that would inhibit parallelization and vectorization, and are thus perfect candidates for offloading. Section "Kernel optimizations" will later present the optimizations applied to overcome the limited vectorization and parallelization potential.

With the outcome of the analysis methodology we now have a plan on how to bring NWChem's CCSD(T) method to the Intel Xeon Phi coprocessor. The offload candidates identified are the kernels `sd_t_dX_Y` that are computationally very intensive fragments of code. The `ccsd_d_doubles_1_2` function is the common anchor point of all the kernel invocations and we will introduce offload directives to the Fortran code to bring the kernels to execution and optimize the data transfers in the anchor point.

OFFLOAD ARCHITECTURE

While the Intel Xeon Phi coprocessor supports several offload programming models each with unique properties, only the Intel Language Extensions for Offloading (LEO)—albeit a proprietary offload language that preceded the availability of the `target` constructs in OpenMP 4.0—provide the needed flexibility of transfer of data and control, and required incremental changes to the existing Fortran source code.

The most important LEO directive we have adopted for moving data between host and coprocessor is shown in Figure 17.8.

```
#define ALLOC alloc_if(.true.)  free_if(.false.)
#define FREE  alloc_if(.false.) free_if(.true.)
#define REUSE alloc_if(.false.) free_if(.false.)

cdir$ offload target(mic:mic_device)
     N      in(triplesx:length(0) REUSE)
     I      in(h3d,h2d,h1d)
     I      in(p6d,p5d,p4d,h7d)
     I      in(t2sub:length(l_t2sub) REUSE)
     R      in(v2sub:length(l_v2sub) REUSE)
```

FIGURE 17.8

Offload directive used to transfer data and control from the host to the coprocessor.

The main steps of the algorithm and of our offloading solution are the following:

1. The `triplesx` 6-dimensional array ($\langle\Phi_{ijk}^{abc}|V_N T_2|\Phi\rangle$ in Eq. (17.18)) is first created and initialized to zero on the coprocessor (therefore requiring no data movement up to this point).
2. Next, the offload directive of Figure 17.8 is issued before the call of each `sd_t_dX_Y` kernel that multiplies together the 4-dimensional array, `v2sub` and `2sub`. As far as the `triplesx` array is concerned, once again no data movement is necessary at this stage. During the offload phase, we are accumulating directly on the coprocessor the contributions resulting from multiplying together the `v2sub` and `t2sub` quantities. The only data movement that occurs in this phase concerns these two 4-dimensional arrays. They are first computed on the host and then copied to the coprocessor (requires less than a microsecond to complete given the size of the arrays). We use synchronous offloading, that is, the host thread and the core it is running on stay idle until control returns to the host from the coprocessor.
3. While the host core is idle and waits for the offload to return, we use the idle core to execute a second thread from another GA process on the same node. Using this approach, we can reuse the existing load-balancing infrastructure of GA. This ensures that a potential load imbalance between the processing on the coprocessor and the host CPUs is automatically compensated. Asynchronous offloading would require to extend the existing load-balancing facilities to a two-stage algorithm that also takes asynchronous load balancing into account. Please see Section "Performance evaluation" for more information on the setup.
4. Once all the required contributions are computed, the large 6-dimensional `triplesx` array is copied back from the coprocessor to the host once at end of each task. In each task the number of executions of a particular kernels is proportional to the total number of occupied tiles `noab` (A term in Eq. (17.18)) or to the total number of unoccupied tiles `nvab` (B term in Eq. (17.18)).

Figure 17.9 summarizes the above data managements and offload steps. For brevity, we only show the structure of the code as pseudocode and use `sd_t_dX_Y` as a champion for the 18 compute kernels.

KERNEL OPTIMIZATIONS

As our loop analysis in Section "Engineering an offload solution" has shown, the `sd_t_dX_Y` kernels do not make optimal use of the coprocessor if naive threading and vectorization are applied to

```
cdir$ offload_transfer target(mic:dev) nocopy(triplesx:length(tsx_l) ALLOC)
cdir$ offload_transfer target(mic:dev) nocopy(t2sub:length(t2sub_l) ALLOC)
cdir$ offload_transfer target(mic:dev) nocopy(v2sub:length(v2sub_l) ALLOC)
cdir$ offload target(mic:dev) nocopy(triplesx:length(0) REUSE)
        call zero_triplesx(triplesx)
        do ...
          if (...)
cdir$ offload target(mic:dev)
      N      in(triplesx:length(0) REUSE)
      I      in(h3d,h2d,h1d)
      I      in(p6d,p5d,p4d,h7d)
      I      in(t2sub:length(l_t2sub) REUSE)
      R      in(v2sub:length(l_v2sub) REUSE)
           call sd_t_dX_Y(h3d,h2d,h1d,p6d,p5d,p4d,h7,triplesx,t2sub,v2sub)
         endif
       enddo

cdir$ offload_transfer target(mic:dev) out(triplesx:length(tsx_l) REUSE)
```

FIGURE 17.9

Pseudocode of the `ccsd_d_doubles_1_2` function with offload directive for data management and transfer of control using `sd_t_dX_Y` as one example of 18 kernel invoked.

the kernels. Hence, there are some code changes necessary. In this section, we will show the simple code transformations that we be applied to the Fortran code to improve both threading and vectorization for each of the compute kernel. We restrict the discussion to some example kernels, because the same ideas and transformations have been applied to the remaining kernels. As mentioned earlier, our goal is to keep the Fortran unmodified where possible and if we do modify the code, the optimization needs to not only improve situation for the coprocessor but also boost performance for the host execution.

The code transformations allow for highly productive optimization work, without any need to codify the kernels in low-level programming models such as C/C++ intrinsic code. Other than transforming the Fortran code, we completely rely on the auto-vectorization capabilities of Intel Composer XE 2013 for Fortran and its implementation of OpenMP.

Figure 17.10 shows the OpenMP directive that was added to the kernel of Figure 17.7. Because of the low trip count of the outer-most loop (on the order 20-30, depending on the tile size of the input data), it does not *per se* provide enough parallelism for the Intel Xeon Phi coprocessor. We use the `collapse` clause to instruct the OpenMP compiler to collapse some of the outer loops into a single product loop that exposes at least two orders of magnitude more iterations than the original outer-most loop. The `OMPCOLLAPSE` parameter can be used to fine-tune the loop collapsing at compilation time of NWChem; our experiments have shown that the sweet spot for most of the input sets we have evaluated is 3, effectively collapsing the `p4`-`p6` loops into a single, long-running product loop.

The inner-most loop is perfectly suited for auto-vectorization by Intel Composer XE. It neither contains loop-carried dependencies that would inhibit vectorization nor does it have nonunited stride accesses. Although being a perfect candidate from a correctness perspective, the vectorization potential of the inner-most loop is too low for optimal performance. The vectorization potential is a measure

```
        subroutine sd_t_d1_1(h3d,h2d,h1d,p6d,p5d,p4d,
    1                         h7d,triplesx,t2sub,v2sub)
        integer h3d,h2d,h1d,p6d,p5d,p4d,h7d,h3,h2,h1,p6,p5,p4,h7
        double precision triplesx(h3d*h2d,h1d,p6d,p5d,p4d)
        double precision t2sub(h7d,p4d,p5d,h1d), v2sub(h3d*h2d,p6d,h7d)
!$omp parallel do private(p4,p5,p6,h2,h1,h3,h7) collapse(OMPCOLLAPSE)
        do p4=1,p4d
        do p5=1,p5d
        do p6=1,p6d
        do h1=1,h1d
        do h7=1,h7d
!dec$ loop count max=1000, min=20
        do h3h2=1,h2d*h3d
           triplesx(h3h2,h1,p6,p5,p4) = triplesx(h3h2,h1,p6,p5,p4)
              - t2sub(h7,p4,p5,h1)*v2sub(h3h2,p6,h7)
        ...
        enddo
!$omp end parallel do
        end
```

FIGURE 17.10

Example kernel of Figure 17.7 with OpenMP and manual loop collapsing.

for the average filling degree of a vector register and the efficiency of vectorization. The higher the vectorization potential is, the more vector lanes in the register are used for computation. In the optimal case, it is close to 100%, which indicates that the vector instructions work on a full vector register all the time.

In our example, the vectorization potential is around 83% for a tile size of 20. Because the tile size is typically not a multiple of the vector width, the compiler needs to emit a remainder loop that takes care of the excess loop iterations. For a vector width of 8 double precision elements and a tile size of 20, the vectorized loop will process 16 elements (2 trips with 1 full vector width) and the remainder loop executes 4 iterations. On average, this leads to a vectorization potential for both the vector and remainder loop of 6.6 elements per vector or 83% utilization.

The situation can be improved by manually collapsing the two inner-most loop (h3 and h2 into an h3h2 loop. This transformation increases the trip count by at least an order of magnitude and pushes the vectorization potential close to 100%. For the above tile size of 20, the vectorization potential even becomes optimal. The h3h2 loop runs for 20×20 iterations (400), which is a multiple of eight and this gives the optimal vectorization potential. Collapsing the inner-most loops also gives some additional performance gain, because some of the loop overhead associated with the two (short) nested loops now is effectively avoided and the product loop imposes much less overhead.

In addition to the code transformations, we make use of compiler directives of the Intel Composer XE for Fortran. The directive in Figure 17.10 informs the compiler about the expected minimum and maximum trip counts of the loop nest. We determined that information through the loop analysis in Section "Engineering an offload solution." Without the directives, the compiler does not have a clear picture about the trip counts and overestimates the actual number of iterations executed. For some of the kernels this triggered counterproductive compiler optimizations

```
      subroutine sd_t_d1_1(h3d,h2d,h1d,p6d,p5d,p4d,
    1                      h7d,triplesx,t2sub,v2sub)
      integer h3d,h2d,h1d,p6d,p5d,p4d,h7d,h3,h2,h1,p6,p5,p4,h7
      double precision triplesx(h3d*h2d,h1d,p6d,p5d,p4d)
      double precision t2sub(h7d,p4d,p5d,h1d), v2sub(h3d*h2d,p6d,h7d)
!$omp parallel do private(p4,p5,p6,h2,h1,h3,h7) collapse(OMPCOLLAPSE)
      do p4=1,p4d
      do p5=1,p5d
      do p6=1,p6d
      do h2=1,h2d
      do h3=1,h3d
      do h7=1,h7d
      do h1=1,h1d
        triplesx(h1,h3,h2,p6,p5,p4) =  triplesx(h1,h3,h2,p6,p5,p4)
    c       - t2sub(h7,p4,p5,h1)*v2sub(h3,h2,p6,h7)
      ...
      enddo
!$omp end parallel do
      end
```

FIGURE 17.11

Kernel `sd_t_d1_1` of NWChem with nonunit stride memory access.

(e.g., loop blocking and loop unrolling) that inhibit optimal vectorization for the coprocessor. Avoiding these automatic compiler transformations by adding the compiler directives improved performance by a rough 10%.

In our set of 18 `sd_t_dX_Y` functions, there are several kernels that are problematic with respect to vectorization. Figure 17.11 shows one of them. If this kernel is compiled as it is, the compiler will emit, gather, and scatter instructions for the accesses to `t2sub`. A closer look at the loop nest reveals that this situation cannot be improved easily. Any permutation of the loops h2, h7, h3, and h2 will introduce gather/scatter instructions for at least one of the arrays. However, if `t2sub` was transposed, then we can find a loop nest that does not require gather/scatter instruction and that can be vectorized with unit-stride load/store operations. While the transformation improves the situation for kernels that are similar to Figure 17.11, it does not harm the other kernels. Either the transformation is beneficial, or the access to `t2sub` is invariant for the inner-most loops and thus transposing `t2sub` does not make any difference to the kernel. The transposition operation is performed on the host process after it received the data from another process and its overhead negligible compared to the kernel runtime on the target device. In fact, it is completely hidden in the measurement noise of the system.

PERFORMANCE EVALUATION

With our NWChem implementation, we have been able to show scale-out with high parallel efficiency on a cluster of up to 460 nodes that consist of dual-socket Intel Xeon E5-2670 processors with 8 cores at 2.6 GHz and 128 GB of main memory. Each node is equipped with two Intel Xeon Phi 5110P coprocessors with 60 cores at 1.053 MHz and 8 GB of on-card GDDR5 memory. This corresponds to a total of 7360 Xeon processor cores and a total 62560 cores for the heterogeneous runs with offloading enabled. As a benchmark we use a NWChem input that computes the correction to the CCSD(T) correlation energy of the closed-shell pentacene molecule ($C_{22}H_{14}$). The benchmarks uses a tile size of 24, which is well within the limit of 8 GB available on-card memory.

In more chemical terms the input data adopts a cc-pVDZ basis set for a total of 378 basis functions, with 51 correlated occupied orbitals (in frozen-core approximation) and 305 unoccupied correlated orbitals. No symmetry has been used in the test calculations.

The best heterogeneous setup for the cluster at hand is to run eight GA ranks per node. Four of these eight ranks execute on the host and spawn four threads, to utilize all 16 host cores. The other four ranks perform concurrent offloads to the coprocessor devices. Because all offloads are synchronous operations, that is, the host rank waits for the offload while it executing on the target, the other (host-only) ranks can utilize the idle core with their OpenMP threads. This is why we can oversubscribe the host system with a total of 16 OpenMP threads.

In the spirit of Chapter 12 we concurrently offload from multiple host ranks to the same device. The first rank is assigned the first partition of the first target device (cores 0-28), while the second rank targets the second partition on the first coprocessor (cores 29-57). Each executes on all four hyperthreads of the physical cores, which corresponds to 116 OpenMP threads per partition. As usual, we leave two cores free for the operating system and the handling of data transfers. Correspondingly, the third and fourth offload rank execute on the first and second partition of the second coprocessor, respectively.

The total amount of memory allocated on the coprocessor per offload rank is about 1.5 GB for the `triplesx` array and about 2.7 MB for the each of the `t2sub` and `v2sub` arrays. We can achieve a significant reduction of data-transfer times (about 30%) by using large pages on the coprocessor to effectively avoid a large number of page faults during transfer and computation. We also reduce additional penalties that incur through misses in the Translation Lookaside Buffer in the coprocessor. For each of the offload ranks, we use the `MIC_USE_2MB_BUFFERS` environment variable set to `16K`. This value allocates all data transfers larger than 16 kB in large pages, which in our case is sufficient to direct all transfers into the memory arena of large pages.

As Figure 17.12 shows, our offload solution achieves a speedup of about 2.5× of the heterogeneous offload code ("Xeon & Xeon Phi") over the pure host execution ("Xeon only"). Our implementation is able to keep that performance advantage of the coprocessor across the full cluster of 460 nodes. We also have tested how a coprocessor-only configuration would perform. We now neglect the compute power of the host and only use the host ranks as communication stubs that only perform message passing and then immediately transfer control to the coprocessor. Thus, the performance is about 1.1× to 1.3× lower than for the heterogeneous case. This proves that true heterogeneous computing can effectively utilize the compute power of both the Xeon world and Xeon Phi world.

A similar observation can be made for the second scale-out benchmark, a 1,3,4,5-tetrasily-limidazol-2-ylidene molecule (formula $Si_4C_3N_2H_{12}$) in its triplet state. The benchmark was setup such that it uses a aug-cc-pVTZ basis set for a total of 706 basis functions, with 26 correlated α-occupied orbitals (24 correlated β-occupied orbitals) in frozen-core approximation and 655 unoccupied α (657 unoccupied β) orbitals. Again we do not use symmetry in the test calculations (Figure 17.13).

This second benchmark has higher floating-point requirements, and thus the coprocessor excels at speeding up the offloaded computation. This results in a slightly higher performance advantage of 2.7× of the heterogeneous system over the host-only TCE code.

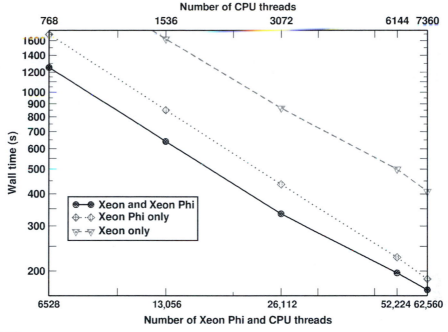

FIGURE 17.12

Wall time to solution (in s) for the perturbative triples correction to the CCSD(T) correlation energy of the pentacene molecule ($C_{22}H_{12}$). A logarithmic scale is used on all the axis.

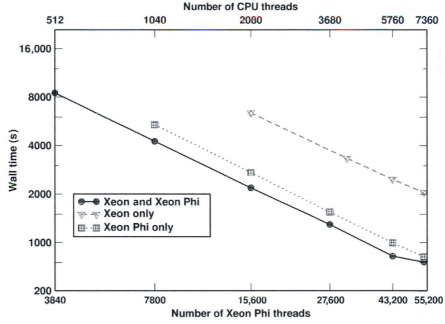

FIGURE 17.13

Wall time to solution (in s) for the perturbative triples correction to the CCSD(T) correlation energy of the 1,3,4,5-tetrasilylimidazol-2-ylidene molecule (formula $Si_4C_3N_2H_{12}$) in its triplet state. A logarithmic scale is used on all the axis.

SUMMARY

Heterogeneous computing on both the Intel Xeon processor and Intel Xeon Phi coprocessor can lead to a faster time to solution for scientific applications. The NWChem chemical package is another good example of how this principle can be applied in reality. The promise of the Intel Xeon Phi coprocessor of being a more productive compute device than traditional accelerator solutions and porting simplified through the ability to use the same tools and programming models held true, and we made strong use of it to offload key kernels.

Our heterogeneous offload solution implemented for the NWChem CCSD(T) method shows that obtaining outstanding performance across a large-scale cluster is not only possible but also feasible by relying on well-known standard programming languages (Fortran) and parallel programming models (OpenMP). These building blocks are well suited to bring compute kernels to the coprocessor device at maximum speed without losing the productivity of the established tool chains. Using the same programming models for the host and the coprocessor also facilitates the optimization process, because all improvements made for the coprocessor also immediately improved the performance on the host.

Our analysis methodology to determine offload candidates leads to a straightforward porting process. The analysis steps to find hotspots, find common a anchor point for offloads, and the loop analysis provides valuable insights into the code. All implementation work then can use these insights to make informed design decisions about where to place offload directives, how to hoist them up in the call tree to find the best location for data and offload transfers. It also helps understand the structure of the compute kernels and their potential for vectorization and parallelization.

With the added compute power of the Intel Xeon Phi coprocessor and the speed-up it yields for the NWChem's highly accurate CCSD(T) method, more accurate simulations can be carried out (see also Aprà et al., 2014 for an in-depth discussion). Instead of narrowing the algorithm simpler simulations of less accurate system (e.g., the Kobayashi-Rendell approach for closed-shell molecular systems), the CCSD(T) method can be applied to a broader category of molecular systems (open-shell with unpaired electrons). Because of the higher computational intensity of the more accurate simulation, only smaller molecular systems could be simulated or time to solution would be unacceptable. The rough threefold performance gain of the offloaded NWChem CCSD(T) method closes this gap and allows for highly accurate simulations or reduces the time to solution.

The work done for the first Intel Xeon Phi coprocessor should transfer well to the next-generation Intel Xeon Phi products (code-named *Knights Landing* (KNL)) which are expected to be available as a socket-based solution that no longer requires to offload to a coprocessor and offers some high-bandwidth on-package memory. The single-thread performance of KNL is projected to be three times higher than today's Intel Xeon Phi coprocessor. Additional parts of NWChem's CCSD(T) method can execute on the many-core chip than before in the coprocessor scenario. The OpenMP-parallel kernels that we have implemented to enable the coprocessor can serve a starting point to increase the amount of code that is multithreaded. We anticipate that a true hybrid GA/OpenMP implementation will be required to fully exploit performance available on the KNL processor. There will also be work to be done to improve the vectorization potential of the remaining code base. The on-package memory should be an interesting optimization target for memory locality of key NWChem data structures.

ACKNOWLEDGMENTS

The research described here was performed using EMSL, a DOE Office of Science User Facility sponsored by the Office of Biological and Environmental Research and located at Pacific Northwest National Laboratory.

FOR MORE INFORMATION

The code for this gem, NWChem version 6.5, and additional information can be obtained from http://lotsofcores.com/NWChem.

Aprà, E., Klemm, M., Kowalski, K., November 2014. Efficient implementation of many-body quantum chemical methods on the Intel Xeon Phi coprocessor. In: Proceedings of the International Conference on High Performance Computing, Networking, Storage and Analysis, New Orleans, LA.

Bomble, Y.J., Stanton, J.F., Kallày, M., Gauss, J., 2005. Coupled-cluster methods including noniterative corrections for quadruple excitations. J. Chem. Phys. 123 (5), 054101.

Crawford, T.D., Stanton, J.F., 1998. Investigation of an asymmetric triple-excitation correction for coupled-cluster energies. Int. J. Quantum Chem 70 (4–5), 601–611. International Symposium on Atomic, Molecular, and Condensed Matter Theory at the 38th Annual Sanibel Symposium, St. Augustine, FL, February 21–27, 1998.

Gwaltney, S.R., Byrd, E.F.C., Van Voorhis, T., Head-Gordon, M., 2002. A perturbative correction to the quadratic coupled-cluster doubles method for higher excitations. Chem. Phys. Lett. 353 (5–6), 359–367.

Gwaltney, S.R., Head-Gordon, M., 2000. A second-order correction to singles and doubles coupled-cluster methods based on a perturbative expansion of a similarity-transformed Hamiltonian. Chem. Phys. Lett. 323 (1–2), 21–28.

Gwaltney, S.R., Sherrill, C.D., Head-Gordon, M., Krylov, A.I., 2000. Second-order perturbation corrections to singles and doubles coupled-cluster methods: General theory and application to the valence optimized doubles model. J. Chem. Phys. 113 (9), 3548–3560.

Hirata, S., Nooijen, M., Grabowski, I., Bartlett, R.J., 2001. Perturbative corrections to coupled-cluster and equation-of-motion coupled-cluster energies: a determinantal analysis. J. Chem. Phys. 114 (9), 3919–3928.

Kucharski, S.A., Bartlett, R.J., 1998. Noniterative energy corrections through fifth-order to the coupled cluster singles and doubles method. J. Chem. Phys. 108 (13), 5243–5254.

Kowalski, K., Fan, P.-D., 2009. Generating functionals based formulation of the method of moments of coupled cluster equations. J. Chem. Phys. 130 (8), 084112.

Kallày, M., Gauss, J., 2005. Approximate treatment of higher excitations in coupled-cluster theory. J. Chem. Phys. 123 (21), 214105.

Kowalski, K., Piecuch, P., 2000. The method of moments of coupled-cluster equations and the renormalized CCSD[T], CCSD(T), CCSD(TQ), and CCSDT(Q) approaches. J. Chem. Phys. 113 (1), 18–35.

Kowalski, K., Valiev, M., 2009. Extensive regularization of the coupled cluster methods based on the generating functional formalism: application to gas-phase benchmarks and to the S(N)2 reaction of CHCl3 and OH− in water. J. Chem. Phys. 131 (23), 234107.

Piecuch, P., Wloch, M., 2005. Renormalized coupled-cluster methods exploiting left eigenstates of the similarity-transformed Hamiltonian. J. Chem. Phys. 123 (22).

Piecuch, P., Wloch, M., Gour, J.R., Kinal, A., 2006. Single-reference, size-extensive, non-iterative coupled-cluster approaches to bond breaking and biradicals. Chem. Phys. Lett. 418 (4–6), 467–474.

Raghavachari, K., Trucks, G.W., Pople, J.A., Head-Gordon, M., 1989. A 5th-order perturbation comparison of electron correlation theories. Chem. Phys. Lett. 157 (6), 479–483.

Stanton, J.F., 1997. Why CCSD(T) works: a different perspective. Chem. Phys. Lett. 281 (1–3), 130–134.

Taube, A.G., Bartlett, R.J., 2008a. Improving upon CCSD(T): Lambda CCSD(T). I. Potential energy surfaces. J. Chem. Phys. 128 (4), 044110.

Taube, A.G., Bartlett, R.J., 2008b. Improving upon CCSD(T): Lambda CCSD(T). II. Stationary formulation and derivatives. J. Chem. Phys. 128 (4), 044111.

Urban, M., Noga, J., Cole, S.J., Bartlett, R.J., 1985. Towards a full CCSDT model for electron correlation. J. Chem. Phys. 83 (8), 4041–4046.

Yasin, A., 2014. A top-down method for performance analysis and counters architecture. In: Proceedings of the 2014 IEEE International Symposium on Performance Analysis of Systems and Software. Monterey, CA, pp. 35–44.

EFFICIENT NESTED PARALLELISM ON LARGE-SCALE SYSTEMS

18

Evgeny Fiksman*, **Anton Malakhov**†

Intel Corporation, USA, †Intel Corporation, Russian Federation

In this chapter, we present an approach for nested parallelism on Intel® Xeon Phi™ coprocessors and Intel® Xeon® processors that contain a large number of cores and utilize nonuniform memory access (NUMA). The presented solution is based on the Intel® Threading Building Blocks (Intel® TBB) task arenas.

MOTIVATION

Recent increases in the number of cores in Intel Xeon processor and Intel Xeon Phi coprocessor leads us to review the approaches taken in parallel libraries. In general, we have observed that scalability tends to be an issue because the overhead spent by a threading library tends to increase if there are more threads to synchronize when the total amount of data to be processed remains the same. As a result, scalability across processing cores suffers. Some applications are driven by *task parallelism*, or the ability to run multiple tasks in parallel, as well as, *data parallelism* (the ability to run a single task in parallel across a data set). The combination of task and data parallelism provides an opportunity to minimize threading library overheads.

NUMA motivates an approach to localize execution of a data parallel task to a specific node while minimizing intra-node memory transfers—along with other approaches discussed in this chapter. Modern Intel Xeon processor based server systems typically have two or more NUMA nodes (CPU sockets). Each node has its own set of memory banks and consists of several processors (cores). Individual processors in a node can access a memory bank of another node through Intel® QuickPath Interconnect (Intel® QPI) bus; however, such accesses incur communications latencies. Unfortunately, threading libraries, as Intel® TBB, do not help to match the user data layout to NUMA topologies in the most efficient way. Tasks can be spread across an entire system to exploit parallelism, while mapping them to stay within boundaries of a NUMA node makes them more efficient.

This approach was applied in STAC™ A2 benchmark and provided significant performance improvement over a simplistic use of a threading or tasking library.

THE BENCHMARK

An artificial benchmark was created for the purposes of this chapter to expose threading library overheads and physical memory limitations as observed on Intel Xeon Phi coprocessor, and NUMA effects on multisocket Intel Xeon platforms. The *kernel* task of the benchmark computes a square root of a double precision floating point array. The size of the array is chosen to be large enough to exceed the last level cache (LLC) of a processor thereby forcing DRAM memory accesses and magnifying the NUMA overheads. Each kernel task instance, executed by a worker thread, is configured to prolong enough time to simulate real workload timings. OpenMP® 4.0 *simd* directives are used to generate vector instructions available on modern processors. Figure 18.1 lists a benchmark main loop. The full benchmark source is available separately on http://lotsofcores.com.

In addition to parallel loops executing data parallelism within a kernel task, multiple instances of a kernel task are executed simultaneously, thus presenting additional task (or functional) parallelism. This execution scheme creates a multilevel parallelism, which is also called nested parallelism since parallel loops are nested into plurality of tasks running in parallel.

```
#define DATA_SIZE  (32*1024*1024)
#define BLOCK_SIZE (4*1024)
typedef std::vector<double,
                    tbb::cache_aligned_allocator<double> >
                    data_vector_t;
void compute_sqrt_block(const double* src, double* dst,
                           int begin, int end)
{
    #pragma omp simd aligned(src, dst: 64)
    for(int i=begin; i<end; ++i){
        dst[i] = sqrt(src[i]);
    }
}
void kernel_task() {
    data_vector_t src(DATA_SIZE);
    data_vector_t dst(DATA_SIZE);
    // Generate input data
    tbb::parallel_for(0, DATA_SIZE, BLOCK_SIZE,
        [&](int i) {
            auto rand_val = std::bind(distribution, generator);
            int begin = i,
                end = std::min(i+BLOCK_SIZE, DATA_SIZE);
                for( int j=begin;j<end;++j)
                    src[i] = rand_val();
    });
    // Perform multiple iterations on the same data block
    tbb::affinity_partitioner partitioner;
    for(int t=0; t<ITERATIONS; ++t) {
        tbb::parallel_for(0, DATA_SIZE, BLOCK_SIZE,
            [&](int i) {
                int begin = i,
                    end = std::min(i+BLOCK_SIZE, DATA_SIZE);
                #pragma noinline
                compute_sqrt_block(&src[0], &dst[0], begin, end);
            }, partitioner);
    }
}
```

FIGURE 18.1

Benchmark kernel task routine, based on Intel® TBB model.

BASELINE BENCHMARKING

Performance evaluation of the abovementioned benchmark was performed using the latest available platforms from Intel. The system consisted of dual-socket Intel Xeon E5-2695 v2 processor and Intel® Xeon Phi™ 7120A coprocessor. Intel® Composer XE 2013 SP1 update 3 compiler was used to compile for both Intel Xeon processors and Intel Xeon Phi coprocessors. Three different threading libraries were used for evaluation: Intel TBB 4.2, OpenMP 4.0, and Intel® Cilk™ Plus. GCC 4.7 or greater was available on a testing machine for C++11 features support.

The benchmark goal is to execute a pool of data parallel tasks as fast as possible. Since each task requires a significant amount of memory for its execution, the number of simultaneously running tasks is bounded by available physical memory which is limited on Intel Xeon Phi coprocessors.

Figure 18.2 depicts the threading library efficiency as a function of number of processed tasks, as measured on Intel Xeon Phi 7120A coprocessor. The efficiency, which optimal value is 1, defined as

$$E = \frac{T_{Based}^{Normalized}}{T_{Measured}^{Normalized}} = \frac{T_{Task}^{Serail}/N_{cores}}{T_{Measured}/M_{tasks}},$$

where $T_{Task}^{Serail}/N_{cores}$ represents the optimal time to executed a task on a machine with N cores. $T_{Measured}$ is a time required to execute M tasks on the same machine; therefore, $T_{Measured}/M_{tasks}$ represents effective execution time for a task. The measured time excludes threading library initialization time.

Both Intel® TBB and Intel Cilk Plus achieve efficiency which is close to 1. However it appears after certain point, when memory resources become critical. Each one of the threading libraries has different behaviors, which depend on its scheduler internals. The Intel TBB efficiency significantly

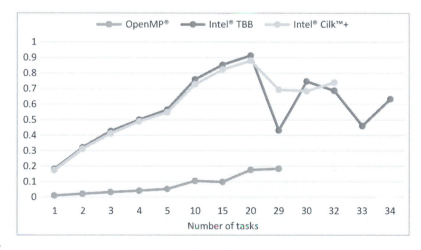

FIGURE 18.2

Benchmark performance as a function of number of kernel tasks.

drops after $M_{tasks} = 20$, but it is capable of processing a maximum of 34 tasks on Intel Xeon Phi 7120A coprocessor, while OpenMP® and Intel® Cilk™ Plus were able to process 29 and 32 tasks, respectively. The OpenMP efficiency is very low for this benchmark, and it's relates to the way OpenMP handles nested parallelism.

Neither of threading libraries is capable to handle more than specific maximum number of tasks. The solution for overcoming Intel Xeon Phi coprocessor memory limitations and the absence of swap space is to limit the number of simultaneously executed parallel kernel tasks. Two approaches that are presented in the next section help to facilitate the deployment of memory hungry applications on these devices through the use of Intel TBB capabilities, specifically the parallel pipeline and the user-managed task arena features. These are a few of the rich set of C++ classes and multitask application support provided by the Intel TBB library.

PIPELINE APPROACH—FLAT_ARENA CLASS

As shown in the previous section, threading libraries have a certain number of simultaneously executed tasks that are executed efficiently. The immediate implementation of such a requirement is a well-known synchronization primitive, the *semaphore*. However, using a semaphore within a worker thread will stall this thread and effectively reduce an amount of compute resources. Therefore, synchronization primitives cannot be used to limit the number of running tasks. Intel® TBB library has parallel pipeline constructs, which can be used to limit the number of running tasks.

Pipeline features are provided by a class tbb::pipeline or by the function tbb::parallel_pipeline that enables type-safety and lambda expressions. The tbb::parallel_pipeline is used to create a pipeline consisting of a series of filters (pipeline stages) which are applied to a stream of items. Each filter operates in one of three modes:

- Parallel—processes multiple instance of a filter in parallel without any order.
- Serial in-order—process a single instance of a filter at a time in the same order.
- Serial out of order—process a single instance of a filter at a time, without any order.

One of the parameters to the pipeline interface is a maximum number of live tokens, which control the number of pipeline items at any given time.

Figure 18.3 shows the usage of tbb::parallel_pipeline for task dispatching within a task arena.

The given implementation of the parallel_pipeline approach requires the task list to be constructed in advance. Though, it is possible to enhance the initial implementation to handle dynamic task submission by using tbb::concurrent_queue, for example.

However, transforming the program structure for pipelined execution might not be quite convenient. On the outermost level, the program can be organized with parallel_for, flow::graph, or other high-level TBB algorithms, which might not be practical to split back into separate tasks and feed them to the pipeline manually, since the program will lose the benefits of using these constructs.

An alternative approach that is based on multihierarchy task arenas is presented in the following sections and fits well with any type of high-level TBB algorithm.

```
parallel_pipeline( /*max_number_of_live_token=*/16,
    make_filter<void, std::function<void(void)> >(
        filter::serial,
        [&](flow_control& fc)->auto{
            if( !list.empty() ) {
                std::function<void(void)> f = list.front();
                list.pop_front();
                return f;
            } else {
                fc.stop();
                return std::function<void(void)>([]{});
            }
    }) &
    make_filter< std::function<void(void)>,void>(
        filter::parallel,
        [](std::function<void(void)> f)->float
            { f(); }
));
```

FIGURE 18.3

Task dispatching by tbb::parallel_pipeline within an arena.

INTEL® TBB USER-MANAGED TASK ARENAS

In Intel® TBB terminology, a *task arena* is a place for worker threads to share and steal tasks. Each application thread, or *master thread,* maintains its own *implicit* task arena which can be assisted by *worker threads* that are created by the Intel® TBB library. Succinctly, worker threads initially reside in a global thread pool (aka Market) while waiting for a work. Later when work arrives, worker threads join a task arena and participate in work execution.

Figure 18.4 depicts multiple task arenas in an application and illustrates worker threads created by Intel® TBB library plus master threads created by an application.

Intel® TBB version 4.1 introduces a community preview feature for *user-managed* (or *explicit*) task arenas following requests for concurrency control and work isolation to not be tied solely to application threads. The interface to user-managed task arenas is provided by class tbb::task_arena. When creating a task_arena, a user may specify a desired concurrency and how much of this concurrency should be reserved for application threads.

Until Intel® TBB version 4.3, the task_arena, being an Intel® TBB library preview feature, requires the TBB_PREVIEW_TASK_ARENA macro to be defined during compilation; for versions up to 4.2.1, linkage with preview binaries is also required. However, since Intel® TBB version 4.2.1 all the necessary functionality exists in the regular library binaries and does not require linking with a special library.

Example of user-managed task arena declaration is depicted in Figure 18.5. In this example, the task arena is created with four thread slots, while one slot is reserved for a master thread.

There are two methods for submitting tasks to a task_arena:

- task_arena::enqueue()—asynchronous method, fire-and-forget style, performed by a submitting thread that doesn't join the arena and returns immediately.

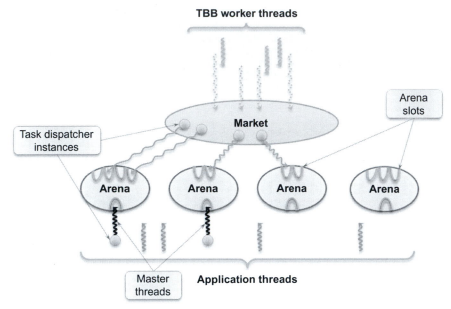

FIGURE 18.4

Task arenas within application.

```
#define TBB_PREVIEW_TASK_ARENA 1 // for TBB < 4.3
#include <tbb/task_arena.h>
tbb::task_arena user_arena(4,1);
...
```

FIGURE 18.5

User-managed task arena declaration.

- task_arena::execute()—synchronous method, which does not return until the submitted task is completed. If possible, the caller thread joins the arena and participates in task execution there, if the thread cannot join the arena, it is blocked for the time necessary to complete arena's tasks.

An instance of a functor class or a C++11 lambda expression could be used as work descriptor argument for the above functions. Figure 18.6 provides an example for task_arena usage.

Although it's possible to submit asynchronous jobs into a task_arena, there is no explicit method to determine when that asynchronous task completes. This functionality is achieved by using of tbb::task_group interface. Figure 18.7 demonstrates how to utilize tbb::task_group interface for task execution waiting.

```
user_arena.execute([&]()
   {
        // Some parallel work
        tbb::parallel_for(0,N,[&](int i) {
            // Parallel kernel code
            ...
        });
    });
```

FIGURE 18.6

Execution of parallelized loop within an arena.

```
tbb::task_group waiting_group;

// Submit 1st asyncronious task
user_arena.enqueue([&]{
    waiting_group.run([&]{
        // Some code section #1
    });
});
// Submit 2nd asyncronious task
user_arena.enqueue([&]{
    waiting_group.run([&]{
        // Some code section #2
    });
});
// Do some other work
...
// Join calling thread to arena and wait for completion
user_arena.execute([&]{
    waiting_group.wait();
});
```

FIGURE 18.7

Asynchronous task and waiting for completion with task_arena.

HIERARCHICAL APPROACH—HIERARCHICAL_ARENA CLASS

A nice feature of the user-managed task arena interface is that it provides an ability to configure arena concurrency by controlling the number of simultaneously running tasks After task is submitted to an arena, it is assigned only when a free worker thread is available that can join the arena. This property is used within a hierarchical approach implemented in hierarchical_arena class. The class allocates an outermost task_arena in order to control concurrency of the outermost tasks. The task is then rescheduled to the second level task_arena of the hierarchy, where it runs in a data parallel fashion. The second level arenas concurrency is bounded so the multiplicative concurrency of the both levels will match the number of available threads.

The default behavior of Intel® TBB doesn't imply any thread management, e.g., thread affinity. In order to improve data locality, hierarchical_arena class implementation affinitizes worker threads to the closest logical cores, in a way that threads entering second level arena will reside on the same or

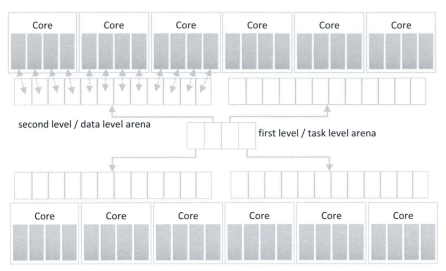

FIGURE 18.8

Two-level hierarchical arena (4 slots on first level, 12 slot on second level, total 48).

physically close cores. In this way, nearest indexes within data array will processed by hardware threads sharing same caches which reduces QPI latencies, and other limited core resources, such as TLB, which reduce DRAM memory access latencies as well. Complete implementation of the hierarchical_arena class, including affinity and other optimizations, is accessible in arenas.h referenced in Section "For more information".

Figure 18.8 depicts schematic assignment between processor threads and arenas. This diagram presents an arena hierarchy, which has 4-way concurrency on the first task level and 12-way concurrency on the second level, while creating 48-way concurrency in total.

As opposed to the pipeline based implementation, the hierarchical arena approach supports dynamic task submission without additional effort and is compatible with any TBB algorithm used on the first level; however, since a processor is partitioned into equal groups, the number of partitions is limited by the number of processor cores divided by desired group size.

PERFORMANCE EVALUATION

Figure 18.9 depicts performance evaluation of the modified benchmark that is based on the pipeline and hierarchical arena approaches. The graph expresses threading library efficiency, measured on an Intel Xeon Phi 7120A coprocessor, as a function of simultaneously executed tasks, when the total amount of running tasks is 120. For the hierarchical arena approach, the best efficiency is achieved when a number of simultaneously running tasks is 20 and for the pipeline approach it is achieved for 25 tasks.

These results match previous threading library analysis presented in Figure 18.2, wherein the maximum efficiency was achieved for 20 simultaneous running tasks but dropped for 29 tasks due to memory limitations.

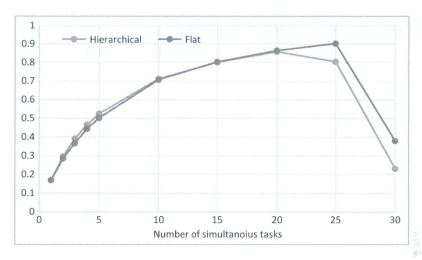

FIGURE 18.9

Threading model efficiency as a function of simulations tasks.

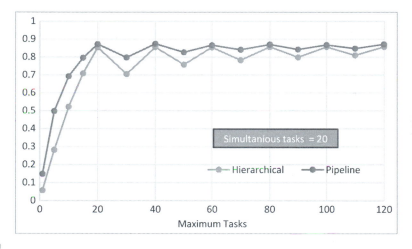

FIGURE 18.10

Threading model efficiency as a function of total tasks.

In further evaluation of the execution efficiency for the maximum number of tasks, the benchmark will be configured for 20 tasks, or on an Intel Xeon Phi 7120A coprocessor, each task will utilize three cores or 12 hardware threads. Figure 18.10 expresses the efficiency of the pipeline and hierarchical arena approaches as a function of maximum number of executed tasks. The maximum value of 120 tasks is evaluated, but this value is not limited.

As in the evaluation of a number of simultaneously running tasks, the maximum efficiency is achieved for 20 tasks. For the larger numbers, the pipeline approach provides more stable results than the hierarchical arenas one. This is because in the first case sub-tasks are distributed across a single task_arena. While in the second case, sub-tasks execution is limited only to the second level arenas.

IMPLICATION ON NUMA ARCHITECTURES

As presented in the previous sections, hierarchical arenas approach helps to resolve memory constraints on the Intel Xeon Phi coprocessor by a restriction of the simultaneously running tasks. Additionally, this approach provides an ability to localize execution of a task to a set of predefined cores, controlled by a thread affinity. When number of groups is equal to a number of NUMA nodes and second level arena workers are affinitized to the same NUMA node, this approach helps to eliminate latencies caused by unnecessary Intel® QPI transfers, and in addition, provides deterministic task execution time, which is critical for near real-time applications.

Figure 18.11 shows execution results on a dual-socket Intel Xeon E5-2697v2 processor based system. The "Total time" represents benchmark wall-clock execution time, the "Min Exec. Time" represents the shortest execution time of a single task and the "Max Exec. Time" represents the longest execution time of a single task.

Although, the wall-clock time of the hierarchical approach is 30% slower than the baseline threading libraries, OpenMP, Intel TBB, and Intel Cilk Plus, the hierarchical approach provides significantly shorter and deterministic task execution time. Execution with the pipeline (flat arena) approach provides less stable task execution times and the wall-clock time is significantly higher. Therefore, the last is not a viable solution.

In order to understand the memory sub-system implications, Intel® VTune™ Amplifier XE was used to approximate the amount internode accesses occurred during execution of the benchmark. The following events were acquired: MEM_LOAD_UOPS_MISS_RETIRED.REMOTE_DRAM – counts

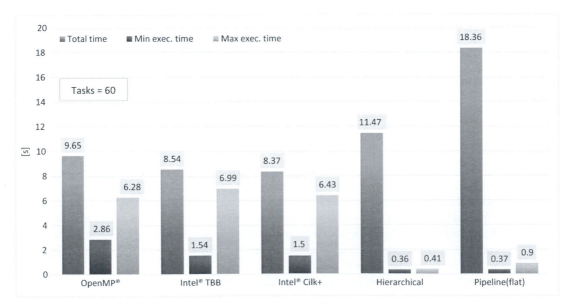

FIGURE 18.11

Benchmark execution on a dual-socket Intel Xeon® E5-2697 v2.

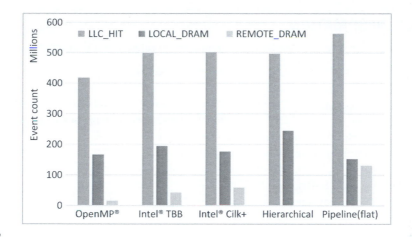

FIGURE 18.12

Memory sub-system counters (LOAD) as measured by the benchmark.

events related to the internode accesses through Intel® QPI, higher values of the counter indicate higher intersocket communication rate and as a result increased memory access latencies; MEM_LOAD_ UOPS_MISS_RETIRED.LOCAL_DRAM—counts events related to loads from a local DRAM and MEM_LOAD_UOPS_RETIRED.LLC_HIT—counts loads from the processor LLC, which does not require DRAM accesses. Figure 18.12 presents values of the counters as were measured during benchmark execution. The majority of the events occurs in the main compute function—compute_sqrt_block().

As expected, the remote DRAM accesses were eliminated by the hierarchical arena approach. It is important to mention that Intel® VTune Amplifier XE is a statistical tool. Therefore, measured results depend on other events occurring during execution of the benchmark, this accounts for the relatively low amount of events during measuring of the OpenMP® baseline.

SUMMARY

In this chapter, we explore the benefits of nested parallelism. Because of the high degree of compatibility in programming methods shared by Intel Xeon Phi coprocessors and Intel Xeon processors, our approaches have value for both processors and coprocessors.

We presented a case study of an artificial "memory hungry" benchmark that is limited by physical memory size on an Intel Xeon Phi coprocessor.

We showed two approaches based on the Intel TBB library, which offer some relief on the physical memory limitations on a coprocessor. Each approach has different characteristics and might be chosen for different scenarios. Properties to be taken into account: type of the outermost algorithm, machine topology, and number of tasks to be executed.

Finally, we showed that the same hierarchical arena approach is applicable on multisocket Intel Xeon processor based systems and helping to achieve deterministic execution times and minimize latencies related to intersocket communication.

FOR MORE INFORMATION

Here are some additional reading materials we recommend related to this chapter:

- STAC™ A2 benchmark specifications and Intel audited results:
  https://stacresearch.com/a2.
  https://stacresearch.com/news/2013/06/23/stac-reports-stac-a2-intel-xeon-and-intel-xeon-phi.
- Kukanov, A., Polin, V., Voss, M.J., 2014. Flow Graphs, Speculative Locks and Task Arenas in Intel® Threading Building Blocks, The Parallel Universe, Issue 18.
  https://software.intel.com/sites/default/files/managed/6a/78/parallel_mag_issue18.pdf.
- Voss, M., Wilmarth, T., 2009. Intel® threading building blocks: ready for nonuniform memory access platforms. Intel Softw. Insight Mag. (20).
- Download the code from this and other chapters, http://lotsofcores.com.
- Intel® threading building blocks TBB,
  https://www.threadingbuildingblocks.org/.
- OpenMP, http://openmp.org/wp/.
- Intel® Cilk™ Plus, http://www.cilkplus.org.

PERFORMANCE OPTIMIZATION OF BLACK-SCHOLES PRICING

19

Iosif Meyerov[*], **Alexander Sysoyev**[*], **Nikita Astafiev**[†], **Ilya Burylov**[†]

Lobachevsky State University of Nizhni Novgorod, Russia, †Intel, Russia

High-performance computing—although a dynamic and expanding area of computer science, as an industry, tends toward being conservative when it comes to investing in new optimizations—even if they promise a disruptive speedup potential. The emergence of the Intel® Xeon Phi™ coprocessor family, combining many processing cores with a traditional x86 processing architecture, offers the speeds of massively parallel architecture but requires effort in application transformation to extract all of the provided parallelism. The need to transform the application poses questions such as: What data structures and algorithms apply? How to best scale applications? What optimization techniques bring benefits? What applications fit well with new highly parallel architectures? Is it possible to optimize programs simultaneously for host Intel® Xeon® processors and for Intel Xeon Phi coprocessors?

This chapter presents our experiences optimizing the calculation of fair prices for a set of European options with Intel Xeon processors and Intel Xeon Phi coprocessors.

We have chosen this topic for the following reasons: First, European option pricing is traditionally used as a benchmark for verifying the capabilities of new architectures. Second, it is one of the basic elements of financial market analysis, and requires HPC systems computational power and, therefore, has great practical interest. Third, the implementation methodology is quite simple to understand. The option pricing algorithm is based on the prevalent Black-Scholes formula which is well described in financial mathematics textbooks and does not require any special implementation knowledge. Finally, this algorithm takes only a few lines of code, which while implying simplicity, still leaves room for experimentation!

Looking at the description of the Black-Scholes algorithm, it may be difficult to imagine that pitfalls and mysteries still are contained in its implementation and that it provides great opportunities to demonstrate optimization techniques.

In this case study, we will walk step by step through various methods of application optimization, which can, in our opinion, be useful for the development of other software for both host processors and coprocessors. We report both our progress and temporary failures, including promising optimizations that did not have a positive effect. We include these optimization steps in our discussion to stress that implementation of similar methods in other applications can lead to successful improvements. Who would have thought that a mere two hundred lines of code would provide so many learning opportunities!

The chapter is organized as follows: First, a short description of a financial market model is given, the basic concepts are discussed to ensure an understanding of the key elements of the algorithm. The baseline implementation is then described, performance analysis is done, then step-by-step optimizations are applied including the elimination of unnecessary type conversion, loop-invariant code hoisting, equivalent conversions replacing "heavy" mathematical functions by "lighter" ones, vectorization of calculations, parallelization, "warming up" of thread creation to avoid skewing the results with one-time overhead, reduction of the accuracy of floating-point calculations, memory optimization (via the use of streaming stores), and finally, the optimization effects are shown for both the processor and coprocessor. In other words, we start our optimizations with the most generic ones that help any parallel program and illustrate their effect showing the processor run times. Only toward the end of the chapter the difference between coprocessor and processor comes out. This way we illustrate a fruitful optimization methodology: first, extract general parallelism and then focus on architecture-specific fine-tuning.

FINANCIAL MARKET MODEL BASICS AND THE BLACK-SCHOLES FORMULA
FINANCIAL MARKET MATHEMATICAL MODEL

Let us consider a financial market evolving in continuous time and consisting of two types of assets—shares (risk-based assets, S) and bonds (risk-free assets, B). For market modeling, we take the widely used Black-Scholes model. This model, after a number of transformations, is represented by a system of stochastic differential equations that looks as follows:

$$dB_t = rB_t\,dt, \quad B_0 > 0 \tag{19.1}$$

$$dS_t = S_t\big((r-\delta)dt + \sigma dW_t\big), \quad S_0 > 0 \tag{19.2}$$

Equation (19.1)—an ordinary differential equation, describes the behavior of the price of a bond B_t, which is influenced by r—*interest rate*. Equation (19.2)—a stochastic differential equation describing the evolution of the price of a share S_t. Along with the interest rate r, the equation contains a *dividend rate* δ, *volatility* σ, and *Wiener stochastic process* (WSP) $W=(W_t)_{\{t\geq 0\}}$. The initial share and bond prices (S_0 and B_0, respectively) are predefined constants.

Let us briefly explain the economic logic of the considered model. The first equation shows capabilities for investment in *risk-free assets*—bonds. Imagine that we come to a bank and deposit money at an interest rate determined by the bank depending on inflation, its unique state of affairs and the market as a whole. The second equation shows the influence of two groups of factors on the price of a share (*a risk asset*)—determinate and random. The first part—$S_t(r-\delta)dt$—is similar to the right part in Eq. (19.1) with the sole difference that on shares, unlike bonds, dividends can be paid, which is reflected in the dividend rate δ.

The term $S_t\sigma dW_t$ is of the greatest interest here. It is included into the equation additively and is used to model the influence of random, hard-to-predict factors in the market.

Volatility σ represents the randomness of processes in the market: $\sigma=0$ means everything is determined, that is, there is no risk. The bigger σ is, the higher the risk (both possible profit and possible losses). Multiplier dW_t—the WSP differential—describes random factors influencing changes in the price of a share at a given point in time t.

The WSP is a mathematical model of Brownian motion in continuous time with these definitions:

1. $W_0 = 0$ with probability 1.
2. W_t—process with independent increments.
3. $W_t - W_s \sim N(0, t-s)$, where $s < t$, and $N(0, t-s)$ is Gaussian distribution with zero mean and variance $t - s$.
4. Process trajectories $W_t(\omega)$—continuous functions of time with probability 1.

For the resulting implementation, here are some key assumptions:

- In the formulas and calculations below as well as for the purpose of simplification, we assume $\delta = 0$ (model without dividends).
- If time is measured in years, then all the interest rates in the equations are numbers from 0.0 to 1.0—annual interest, expressed in fractions.
- We assume that interest rate and volatility are constant—they do not depend on time.

Given the assumption of constant interest rates and volatility, the system of the differential equations (19.1) and (19.2) has an analytical solution. Otherwise, the system has to be solved numerically using one of the known methods (Euler, Runge-Kutta, etc.). When constructing a difference scheme, the only difference from an ODE is that each WSP (Wiener stochastic process) increment is modeled by a random number obtained from $N(0, t-s)$. The solution to Eq. (19.2) looks as follows:

$$S_t = S_0 e^{\left(r - \frac{\sigma^2}{2}\right)t + \sigma W_t} \tag{19.3}$$

EUROPEAN OPTION AND FAIR PRICE CONCEPTS

An *option* is a derivative financial instrument or a contract between parties P_1 and P_2, which gives the right to P_2 at some point of time t in the future to buy from or to sell to P_1 a share at price K fixed in the contract. In return for this right, P_2 shall pay the fixed amount (fee) C to P_1. K is called the *strike price*, and C—*the option price*.

In this study, the simplest variant of an option—the *European share call option* is considered. The main idea of the contract is a game of two parties, P_1 and P_2. The second party pays an amount C and at some point of time T (*maturity*, fixed in the contract) makes a decision: to buy shares at price K from the first party or not. The decision is made depending on the ratio of price S_T and K. If $S_T < K$, it is not profitable to buy the shares, the first received profit C, and the second incurred losses C. If $S_T > K$, the second party buys from the first party shares at K, in some cases getting a profit (depending on the ratio between C and $S_T - K$).

The main problem is the calculation of a *fair price* of such an option contract, it occurs when there is a balance of gains and losses for each of the parties. It is logical to define such a price as an average gain of party P_2:

$$C = E\left(e^{-rT} \cdot \max\left(S_T - K, 0\right)\right) \tag{19.4}$$

In Formula (19.4), the fair price of the call option C is obtained as the mathematical expectation E of the *cash flow* function $\max(S_T - K, 0)$ multiplied by a *discounting* factor e^{-rT} which accounts for inflation with interest rate r over the time period $(0, T)$.

BLACK-SCHOLES FORMULA

Under the assumptions made earlier, Eq. (19.4) has an analytical solution known as the Black-Scholes formula for European call option price:

$$C = S_0 F(d_1) - Ke^{-rT} F(d_2)$$

$$d_1 = \ln\frac{S_0}{K} + \frac{\left(r + \dfrac{\sigma^2}{2}\right)T}{\sigma\sqrt{T}}$$

$$d_2 = \ln\frac{S_0}{K} + \frac{\left(r - \dfrac{\sigma^2}{2}\right)T}{\sigma\sqrt{T}}$$

(19.5)

where F is the cumulative normal distribution function.

We will use this formula in further calculations. "What is there to calculate?" you might ask. At first glance everything looks elementary. In practice, everything is not that simple, which will be shown.

OPTIONS PRICING

Certainly, for pricing a single option, one does not need a high-performance computer. In practice, organizations operating in financial markets calculate prices for huge quantities of different options, which may be issued in specific market conditions. Timing of financial calculations significantly influences decision-making speed, so every second counts. Therefore, reducing valuation time for a set of options is a very important factor.

Let us construct a diagram of data dependencies for one option (Figure 19.1).

Generally, when constructing a set of options, it is possible to vary all five parameters (initial price of a share, strike price, interest rate, volatility, maturity). Nevertheless, be cognizant of the fact that

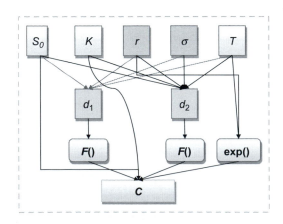

FIGURE 19.1

Data dependence diagram.

CPU	2 x Intel Xeon E5-2690 processors (8 cores, 2.9 GHz)
Coprocessor	Intel Xeon Phi 7110X coprocessor (61 cores)
RAM	64 GB
Operating system	Linux CentOS 6.2
Software	Intel Parallel Studio XE 2013 SP1

FIGURE 19.2

Test infrastructure.

market parameters (interest rate and volatility) at a specific time are identical for all options. Therefore, in the calculations below, we will assume that different options differ only by the initial price of a share, strike price, and maturity.

TEST INFRASTRUCTURE

The computational experiments were performed on the following test infrastructure (Figure 19.2).

CASE STUDY
PRELIMINARY VERSION—CHECKING CORRECTNESS

We set the following parameters (Figure 19.3).

We start our software implementation with the function **GetOptionPrice()** that prices one option using the Black-Scholes formula (19.5). It is noteworthy, that here, and in all other functions, we use single precision. Double precision is not required for the nature of the problem (for example, input data usually comes as single precision, type "float"). Later we will see that precision can be decreased further (Figure 19.23).

The nontrivial part of Formula (19.5) is a cumulative normal distribution function F. For its evaluation, the **cdfnormf()** function is used.

Let us build the code (Figure 19.4) and see if it works. The result of function execution must equal 20.924.

REFERENCE VERSION—CHOOSE APPROPRIATE DATA STRUCTURES

After ensuring the application is functionally correct, we now proceed to our main goal—estimating a set of options. Let us introduce the following variables (Figure 19.5).

```
const float sig = 0.2f;    // Volatility (0.2 -> 20%)
const float r   = 0.05f;   // Interest rate (0.05 -> 5%)
const float T   = 3.0f;    // Maturity (3 -> 3 years)
const float S0  = 100.0f;  // Initial stock price
const float K   = 100.0f;  // Strike price
```

FIGURE 19.3

Constants.

```
float GetOptionPrice()
{
  float C;
  float d1, d2, p1, p2;

  d1 = (logf(S0 / K) + (r + sig * sig * 0.5f) * T) /
       (sig * sqrtf(T));
  d2 = (logf(S0 / K) + (r - sig * sig * 0.5f) * T) /
       (sig * sqrtf(T));
       p1 = cdfnormf(d1);
       p2 = cdfnormf(d2);
       C  = S0 * p1 - K * expf((-1.0f) * r * T) * p2;

  return C;
}
```

FIGURE 19.4

Preliminary version.

```
int numThreads = 1;        // The number of threads
                           // (will be useful later)
int N;                     // The number of options
```

FIGURE 19.5

Variables.

First, we will discuss the data storage requirements of our program. It appears to be trivial. We need four arrays (three to hold input data and one for the results). We also need a few scalar variables.

Data layout in memory can significantly impact software performance. So, in many applications similar to ours, a dilemma arises: whether to use the SoA pattern (structure of arrays) or the AoS pattern (array of structures).

- In the SoA case, data will be organized in memory as follows: the first array comes as a whole block, then the second array, etc.
- In the AoS case: all data related to the first subject domain object comes first, then all data related to the second subject domain object, etc.

Generally, the question of which data layout is better has no predefined answer. However, in certain cases it is possible to make recommendations. The AoS pattern allows localization of memory access and potentially maximal reuse of processor cache, but at the price of more complicated addressing for accessing individual structure members. With the SoA data layout, cache memory can be utilized effectively for several arrays simultaneously in smaller tasks with independent iterations and straightforward memory access requirements. This arrangement simplifies addressing and reduces the total number of machine instructions. Our code belongs to the second type of application, and the SoA pattern helps achieve significant gains in performance(~3×) as will be shown in the second version of **GetOptionPrices()** function. Therefore, we choose to use SoA data pattern.

A **GetOptionPrices()** function utilizing an SoA data layout is shown in the following example (Figure 19.6).

```
void GetOptionPrices(float *pT, float *pK, float *pS0,
  float *pC)
{
  int i;
  float d1, d2, p1, p2;
  for (i = 0; i < N; i++)
  {
    d1 = (log(pS0[i] / pK[i]) + (r + sig * sig * 0.5) *
          pT[i]) / (sig * sqrt(pT[i]));
    d2 = (log(pS0[i] / pK[i]) + (r - sig * sig * 0.5) *
          pT[i]) / (sig * sqrt(pT[i]));
    p1 = cdfnormf(d1);
    p2 = cdfnormf(d2);
    pC[i] = pS0[i] * p1 - pK[i] *
            exp((-1.0) * r * pT[i]) * p2;
  }
}
```

FIGURE 19.6

Reference version 1.

N	60 000 000	120 000 000	180 000 000	240 000 000
Reference version	17.002	34.004	51.008	67.970

FIGURE 19.7

Reference version. Time in seconds.

We compile the code using the Intel C ++ Compiler with a **-O2** key and launch it on the Intel Xeon host processor. Execution time depends on the number of options, N, shown in Figure 19.7.

REFERENCE VERSION—DO NOT MIX DATA TYPES

A typical mistake made by many C programmers (and not just beginners) is to mix "float" and "double" types when working with floating-point numbers. Let us consider how precision influences performance. Specifically, we consider the performance impact when data are represented in "float" (32-bit single precision) type and "double" (64-bit double precision) type when calling mathematical functions to perform calculations. Notice that in Figure 19.8 code for the **GetOptionPrice()** function, the single precision function **logf()** is called. Should the programmer call the **log()** function instead, the compiler will have to perform precision conversions as follows: function **log()** in the C language is passed a "double" argument and returns a "double" result, so the element of **pT[i]** array will first be converted from "float" type to "double" after which all calculations will be carried out using the "double" type. Only at the very end of the expression evaluation, during the result assignment to d1, is a backward conversion to "float" type performed. Taking into account that "float" numbers in many cases are processed faster than "doubles" (in particular, the difference becomes noticeable when using vectorization), such unexpected conversions can have an adverse effect on overall performance. We will check the difference in our case.

For this purpose, we modify the code by calling functions **logf()**, **sqrtf()**, and **expf()** and by properly specifying constants (meaning that constant 1.0 that does not have a suffix "f" will be stored as double). The changes are indicated in boldface.

```
void GetOptionPrices(float *pT, float *pK, float *pS0,
  float *pC)
{
  int i;
  float d1, d2, p1, p2;
  for (i = 0; i < N; i++)
  {
    d1 = (logf(pS0[i] / pK[i]) + (r + sig * sig * 0.5f) *
          pT[i]) / (sig * sqrtf(pT[i]));
    d2 = (logf(pS0[i] / pK[i]) + (r - sig * sig * 0.5f) *
          pT[i]) / (sig * sqrtf(pT[i]));
    p1 = cdfnormf(d1);
    p2 = cdfnormf(d2);
    pC[i] = pS0[i] * p1 - pK[i] *
            expf((-1.0f) * r * pT[i]) * p2;
  }
}
```

FIGURE 19.8

Reference version 2.

N	60 000 000	120 000 000	180 000 000	240 000 000
Reference version	17.002	34.004	51.008	67.970
Do not mix data types	16.776	33.549	50.337	66.989

FIGURE 19.9

Do not mix data types. Time in seconds.

Using the abovementioned infrastructure, the authors obtained the following execution times (Figure 19.9). As Figure 19.9 shows, the execution time was slightly reduced if compared to reference version in all data sizes. Let us look at the **GetOptionPrice()** function profile collected with Intel VTune Amplifier XE (Figure 19.10) to better understand the reasons.

The VTune *Basic Hotspots* analysis shows that most of the time is spent in the **cdfnormf()** function that hides the overhead of the double precision **exp()**, **log()**, **sqrt()** computations. Nevertheless, the technique is generally applicable and we have used it previously to improve performance by several times in certain cases. The conclusion: Do not mix data types if possible!

VECTORIZE LOOPS

Vectorization of performance-critical code is one of the most important and very effective optimization techniques. We can ask the compiler to use a set of AVX instructions by adding the **-mavx** switch into the compilation line (the **-O2** switch by default assumes only SSE2 instructions). However, our experiments show that the use of this flag did not change the execution time.

To understand the reasons, we add a request for a vectorization report from the compiler with the **-vec-report3** switch. The digit "3" corresponds to the level of detail of the report (the range is 1-6). Note the sixth report type (**-vec-report6**) offers additional recommendations concerning vectorization.

The vectorization report when compiling the code in Figure 19.8 is shown in Figure 19.11. The compiler reports a possible dependency between arrays in our key loop. Our experience is that diagnostics

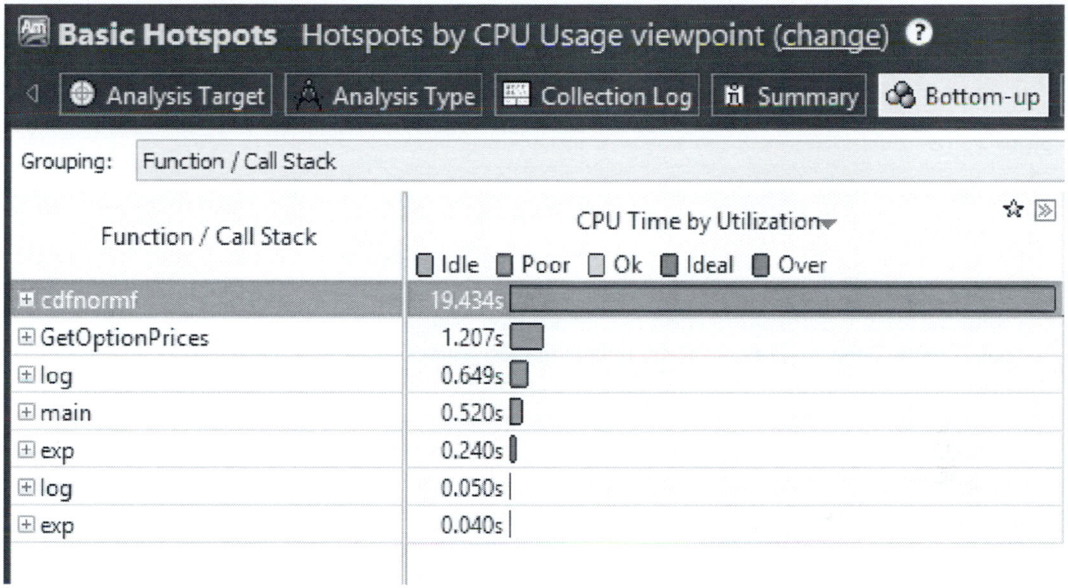

FIGURE 19.10

GetOptionPrice() function reference version profile, cdfnormf() is used.

```
sh-4.1$ icc -O2 -openmp -mavx -vec-report3 main.cpp -o option_prices
main.cpp(279): (col. 3) remark: loop was not vectorized: nonstandard loop is not
 a vectorization candidate
main.cpp(99): (col. 3) remark: loop was not vectorized: nonstandard loop is not
a vectorization candidate
main.cpp(115): (col. 3) remark: loop was not vectorized: nonstandard loop is not
 a vectorization candidate
main.cpp(131): (col. 3) remark: loop was not vectorized: nonstandard loop is not
 a vectorization candidate
sh-4.1$
```

FIGURE 19.11

Vectorization report.

from the Intel C/C ++ compilers very often helps the programmer identify exactly what hampers vectorization. In this case, we have a bit more work to do to identify the root issue.

Based on the vectorization report, let us "persuade" the compiler to vectorize the loop (Figure 19.12). Different ways can be used to "explain" to the compiler that there are no dependencies between arrays. Let us consider these ways in more detail.

1. Using the keyword **restrict** in declaration of the formal parameters of function (**restrict** is a keyword in the C99 standard). It will tell the compiler it is safe to vectorize the loop because there are no overlapping memory references.
2. Using the directive **#pragma ivdep** before the loop telling the compiler to ignore possible data dependencies. This directive will be ignored if the compiler can "prove" the existence of

```
for (i = 0; i < N; i++)
{
    ...
}
```

FIGURE 19.12

Main computational loop.

a dependency. Caution should be exercised when using **ivdep** as it can cause code with subtle, undetected "real" dependencies to produce incorrect results when vectorized.

3. Using the directive **#pragma simd** before the loop. This directive requests the compiler to vectorize the code regardless of any dependencies. Therefore, the programmer is responsible to "guarantee" against any issues preventing vectorization. This directive is the most aggressive compiler optimization, but responsibility for results is assumed by the programmer. Use this method only when you are sure no data dependencies exist.

4. Apart from the abovementioned methods, it is possible to specify a special option –**ansi-alias,** indicating to the compiler that there are no overlapping (in memory) arrays in the program. However, this option affects the **whole** source file and can unexpectedly "break" the code, if used without caution.

We can successfully vectorize the code in Figure 19.8 using any of the presented techniques. The results are provided in Figure 19.13.

It should be noted that the execution time of the vectorized version is about 8% lower than the scalar version on an Intel Xeon processor. The Intel Xeon E5-2690 processor used in our experiments supports AVX instructions allowing eight single precision floating-point elements to be processed at the same time. Why was not the code accelerated by 8x? We infer that in this example, the overhead of data packing into vector registers and unpacking the results must be negligible because of the use of the SoA pattern which keeps the data contiguously in memory.

To understand the lower than expected performance increase, we profile the application using Intel VTune Amplifier XE both before and after vectorization (see Figures 19.10 and 19.14).

Inspecting the profile, we notice that **logf()** and **expf()** functions were replaced by their respective vector analogs from the SVML (short vector math library) runtime library from the Intel Compiler. VTune also reports that the time-consuming **cdfnormf()** function remained scalar. This explains the lack of significant speedup from vectorization as **cdfnormf()** is responsible for the 90% of the runtime. *Note*: future versions of the compiler could improve the vectorization of **cdfnormf( ).**

N	60 000 000	120 000 000	180 000 000	240 000 000
Reference version	17.002	34.004	51.008	67.970
Do not mix data types	16.776	33.549	50.337	66.989
Vectorize loops	15.445	30.977	46.608	62.141

FIGURE 19.13

Vectorize loops. Time in seconds.

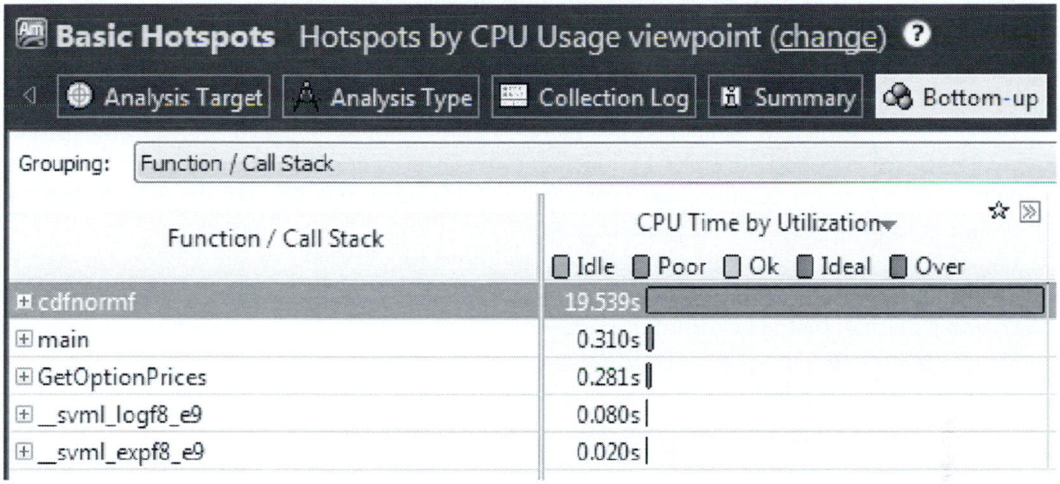

FIGURE 19.14

GetOptionPrice() function profile, cdfnormf() is used, after vectorization.

The lack of a vectorized math function analog is quite illustrative. We cannot expect further improvements without achieving full vectorization of the hot spots, especially on the coprocessor which can process 16 single precision floating-point elements per vector. However, we are able to get past this problem with the help of basic arithmetic and the profiler.

USE FAST MATH FUNCTIONS: ERFF() VS. CDFNORMF()

It is common that some math functions in a compiler may be better optimized than others. In our example, the calculations performed with the help of **cdfnormf**() function can be achieved using the **erff()** function (Figure 19.15).

```
void GetOptionPrices(float *pT, float *pK, float *pS0,
    float *pC)
{
  int i;
  float d1, d2, erf1, erf2;
  for (i = 0; i < N; i++)
  {
    d1 = (logf(pS0[i] / pK[i]) + (r + sig * sig * 0.5f) *
        pT[i]) / (sig * sqrtf(pT[i]));
    d2 = (logf(pS0[i] / pK[i]) + (r - sig * sig * 0.5f) *
        pT[i]) / (sig * sqrtf(pT[i]));
    erf1 = 0.5f + 0.5f * erff(d1 / sqrtf(2.0f));
    erf2 = 0.5f + 0.5f * erff(d2 / sqrtf(2.0f));
    pC[i] = pS0[i] * erf1 - pK[i] * expf((-1.0f) * r *
        pT[i]) * erf2;
  }
}
```

FIGURE 19.15

erff version.

The next example recodes the GetOptionPrices() using the following formula:

$$\mathbf{cdfnorm}(x) = 0.5 + 0.5\mathrm{erf}\left(\frac{x}{\sqrt{2}}\right) \tag{19.6}$$

Using the infrastructure mentioned in Figure 19.2, the authors obtained the run times shown in Figure 19.16. We expected the **erff()** function to be faster than **cdfnormf()** given its numerical properties allow simpler floating-point approximation. However, that was not the only reason for the speedup. Let us inspect the VTune profile again.

Figure 19.17 shows that the compiler has employed an SVML vector analog for **erff()**, which provided a significant speedup resulting in 29× improvement versus the scalar code with **cdfnormf()**. Not bad! This result also shows a potential for further improvement with a coprocessor given its even wider vector instructions.

N	60 000 000	120 000 000	180 000 000	240 000 000
Reference version	17,002	34,004	51,008	67,970
Do not mix data types	16,776	33,549	50,337	66,989
Vectorize loops	15.445	30.977	46.608	62.141
Use fast math functions + improved vectorization	0.522	1.049	1.583	2.091

FIGURE 19.16

Use fast math functions. Time in seconds.

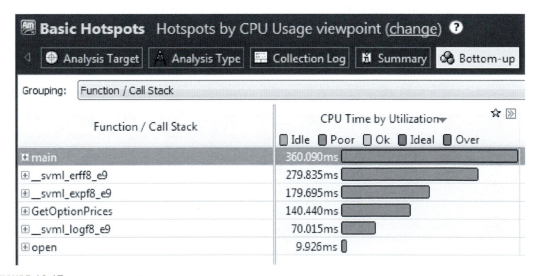

FIGURE 19.17

GetOptionPrice() function profile, erff() is used, after vectorization.

EQUIVALENT TRANSFORMATIONS OF CODE

The program can be optimized a little bit more by lifting "invariant" one-time calculations out of the loop. In this case, `1.0f / sqrtf(2.0f)`.

We can evaluate this expression separately by introducing the following constant (Figure 19.18):

There is also the noteworthy method of replacing division by multiplication. In some situations, this optimization leads to a considerable execution time reduction. In this example, we can replace `1/sqrtf()` expression by the `invsqrtf()` function. We can check, whether the compiler performed these substitutions automatically.

As is shown in Figure 19.19, the execution time of the new code version almost equals the time obtained earlier. Most likely, the compiler had performed the necessary substitutions in the code without our help. That can be confirmed by inspecting the compiler's assembler listing (e.g., add **-Fa** switch to the command line).

Despite the fact that the execution time hardly changed, the loop invariants hoisting and replacement of division by multiplication optimizations we performed are generally useful and in the case of a less "intelligent" compiler, they often provide a benefit. Retaining these optimizations may help when porting to a different architecture so we will take this version (Figure 19.20) as the new base line, plus we will include them in our upcoming coprocessor experiments.

ALIGN ARRAYS

Another potentially useful software optimization deals with data alignment. SIMD register-size aligned data accesses are performed much faster by the processor than unaligned ones. In some cases, the compiler and/or hardware can minimize the performance impact, but often significant performance increases—especially for vector codes—can be achieved by ensuring alignment. For this reason, it is worthwhile to check memory address alignment. To guarantee alignment, we replace **new/delete** operators with calls to the **memalign()/free()** functions. The rest of the code does not change (Figure 19.21).

```
const float invsqrt2 = 0.707106781f;
```

FIGURE 19.18

"1.0f / sqrtf(2)" constant.

N	60 000 000	120 000 000	180 000 000	240 000 000
Reference version	17.002	34.004	51.008	67.970
Do not mix data types	16.776	33.549	50.337	66.989
Vectorize loops	15.445	30.977	46.608	62.141
Use fast math functions + improved vectorization	0.522	1.049	1.583	2.091
Equivalent transformations	0.538	1.071	1.614	2.133

FIGURE 19.19

Equivalent transformations of code. Time in seconds.

```
void GetOptionPrices(float *pT, float *pK, float *pS0,
  float *pC)
{
    int i;
    float d1, d2, erf1, erf2, invf;
    float sig2 = sig * sig;

 #pragma simd
    for (i = 0; i < N; i++)
    {
      invf = invsqrtf(sig2 * pT[i]);
      d1 = (logf(pS0[i] / pK[i]) + (r + sig2 * 0.5f) *
          pT[i]) * invf;
      d2 = (logf(pS0[i] / pK[i]) + (r - sig2 * 0.5f) *
          pT[i]) * invf;
      erf1 = 0.5f + 0.5f * erff(d1 * invsqrt2);
      erf2 = 0.5f + 0.5f * erff(d2 * invsqrt2);
      pC[i] = pS0[i] * erf1 - pK[i] * expf((-1.0f) * r *
            pT[i]) * erf2;
    }
}
```

FIGURE 19.20

New base line version.

```
int main(int argc, char *argv[])
{
  pT = (float *)memalign(32, 4 * N * sizeof(float));
//  pT  = new float[4 * N];

    ...

  free(pT);
//  delete [] pT;
  return 0;
}
```

FIGURE 19.21

Data alignment.

The recommended value of alignment (the first parameter in **memalign()** function) depends on the width of the SIMD registers in use. For SSE instructions, use 16 bytes, for AVX instructions—32 bytes, and for the coprocessor instruction set—64 bytes.

It is also useful to add one more directive into the code before the loop:

#pragma vector aligned

This directive will inform the compiler that the arrays in the loop are aligned and corresponding aligned memory read/write instructions can be used. It should be noted that if we "deceive" the compiler, the software could crash in an attempt to use aligned access on misaligned data.

In this case, the compiler had already coped with the alignment: Figure 19.22 shows no difference between the last two experiments, but it does not mean that it will always be like this, and for all compilers. Our experience indicates you should align your data whenever possible!

N	60 000 000	120 000 000	180 000 000	240 000 000
Reference version	17.002	34.004	51.008	67.970
Do not mix data types	16.776	33.549	50.337	66.989
Vectorize loops	15.445	30.977	46.608	62.141
Use fast math functions + improved vectorization	0.522	1.049	1.583	2.091
Equivalent transformations	0.538	1.071	1.614	2.133
Align arrays	0.539	1.072	1.617	2.135

FIGURE 19.22

Align data. Time in seconds.

REDUCE PRECISION IF POSSIBLE

Earlier we said that there is no need to use **double** type in the solution of this particular problem. Now, we go further. Here **float** type single precision is also excessive (as not more than four decimal digits are used in a subject domain). Precision decrease provides potential for further optimization of calculations.

The following Intel compiler command-line options influence the precision of calculation of mathematical functions.

    icc … -fimf-precision=low -fimf-domain-exclusion=31

The **-fimf-precision=low** option tells the compiler to use implementations of mathematical functions with 11 accurate bits in mantissa (out of 24 bits available in single precision), which more closely corresponds to the precision of the input parameters. The **-fimf-domain-exclusion** option allows special values in mathematical functions (such as infinity, NaN, and extreme values of arguments) to be excluded from processing. This command-line option can be used when it is safe to assume that the program does not have to deal with such extreme values.

Figure 19.23 shows that the use of the lower precision command-line options reduced the application runtime by approximately 23%. Note that the reduced precision also impacted the numeric result

N	60 000 000	120 000 000	180 000 000	240 000 000
Reference version	17.002	34.004	51.008	67.970
Do not mix data types	16.776	33.549	50.337	66.989
Vectorize loops	15.445	30.977	46.608	62.141
Use fast math functions + improved vectorization	0.522	1.049	1.583	2.091
Equivalent transformations	0.538	1.071	1.614	2.133
Align arrays	0.539	1.072	1.617	2.135
Reduce precision	0.438	0.871	1.314	1.724

FIGURE 19.23

Reduce precision if possible. Time in seconds.

of the **GetOptionPrices()** function: we got 20.920 instead of a reference 20.924, but the difference does not occur until the 5th decimal digit. It has to be specially mentioned though that proper accuracy analysis should always be carried out in order to safely use the precision controls.

WORK IN PARALLEL

Just like vectorization helps saturate the core resources available to the single-threaded application, thread-level parallelization helps to distribute the work across the multiple cores and single-core resources available in SMT architectures. Parallelization of the computational loop across processing units (e.g., threads and cores) is rather simple due to the absence of any dependencies between iterations. It is simply enough to add **omp parallel for** pragma before the loop (as noted in boldface in Figure 19.24 below) and to localize all writable variables via the **private** list.

Note that **-openmp** compiler command-line switch was added earlier, so additional command line changes are not required.

As Figure 19.25 shows, scaling improves with the growth of data volume, from 7.59x to 11.27x for 240 million samples.

USE WARM-UP

The times of execution in the last experiment became rather short; therefore the overhead costs for thread creation may include a significant contribution to the parallel region execution time. Let us try and remove that overhead. The approach uses the fact that the majority of OpenMP implementations do not destroy the threads created for the first parallel section of code but put them into a sleep state, so they can be resumed much more quickly on subsequent use. This is known as creating a "thread pool."

```
void GetOptionPrices(float *pT, float *pK, float *pS0,
  float *pC)
{
  int i;
  float d1, d2, erf1, erf2, invf;
  float sig2 = sig * sig;
#pragma simd
#pragma omp parallel for private(d1, d2, erf1, erf2,
invf)
  for (i = 0; i < N; i++)
  {
    invf = invsqrtf(sig2 * pT[i]);
    d1 = (logf(pS0[i] / pK[i]) + (r + sig2 * 0.5f) *
        pT[i]) * invf;
    d2 = (logf(pS0[i] / pK[i]) + (r - sig2 * 0.5f) *
        pT[i]) * invf;
    erf1 = 0.5f + 0.5f * erff(d1 * invsqrt2);
    erf2 = 0.5f + 0.5f * erff(d2 * invsqrt2);
    pC[i] = pS0[i] * erf1 - pK[i] * expf((-1.0f) * r *
        pT[i]) * erf2;
  }
}
```

FIGURE 19.24

OpenMP version.

N	60 000 000	120 000 000	180 000 000	240 000 000
Reference version	17.002	34.004	51.008	67.970
Do not mix data types	16.776	33.549	50.337	66.989
Vectorize loops	15.445	30.977	46.608	62.141
Use fast math functions + improved vectorization	0.522	1.049	1.583	2.091
Equivalent transformations	0.538	1.071	1.614	2.133
Align arrays	0.539	1.072	1.617	2.135
Reduce precision	0.438	0.871	1.314	1.724
Work in parallel (16 cores)	0.058	0.084	0.126	0.153

FIGURE 19.25

Work in parallel. Time in seconds, 16 cores are used.

Accordingly, if **GetOptionPrices()** is called two times in a row in **main()** function, then the second call overhead costs will be minimized. This approach is called "warm-up."

Is warm-up fair for benchmarking? The authors' experience is that real production programs always create threads long before formula computations are executed, so thread creation overhead is reasonable to exclude for benchmarking measurements. However, additional savings may also come from the data cache warm-up: two subsequent calls of the same function using the same data may result in different execution times due to the fact that the first call will suffer from cache misses, while the second one will likely benefit from cache hits due to the data remaining in high-speed cache.

Is this good or bad? On one hand, it is not completely fair: there is a well-known benchmarking mistake—carrying out single-threaded and multi-threaded experiments (operating on the same dataset) within a single process. The resulting super-linear speedup immediately disappears when experiments are done correctly—each in its own process. On the other hand, in real programs, other setup computations are typically carried out around the hot-spot function gradually loading target calculation data into the cache.

Generally, we recommend the following:

1. In case of long execution times, e.g., seconds, warm-up is not needed.
2. If execution times are small (fractions of a second), and the number of threads is large, it makes sense to apply the warm-up, otherwise the real world algorithm execution time will be hidden by the overheads.
3. If it is suspected that preloading the cache is distorting the performance timing results, the programmer can introduce a special dummy parallel section outside and prior to the measured region for the sole purpose of thread creation. This approach only removes the thread startup overhead without touching the caches.

The difference between "Reduce precision" and "Reduce precision+warm cache" results in Figure 19.26 illustrates the benefits of operating in "warm" cache. Warm-up also allowed us to exclude the thread creation overhead from the measurements in parallel versions (last row in Figure 19.26), and see that the computational part indeed scaled by 13x on 16 cores.

N	60 000 000	120 000 000	180 000 000	240 000 000
Reference version	17.002	34.004	51.008	67.970
Do not mix data types	16.776	33.549	50.337	66.989
Vectorize loops	15.445	30.977	46.608	62.141
Use fast math functions + improved vectorization	0.522	1.049	1.583	2.091
Equivalent transformations	0.538	1.071	1.614	2.133
Align arrays	0.539	1.072	1.617	2.135
Reduce precision	0.438	0.871	1.314	1.724
Reduce precision + warm cache	0.409	0.812	1.226	1.603
Work in parallel (16 cores)	0.058	0.084	0.126	0.153
Parallel, warm cache, threads creation overhead excluded	0.033	0.062	0.091	0.118

FIGURE 19.26

Use warm-up. Time in seconds.

USING THE INTEL XEON PHI COPROCESSOR—"NO EFFORT" PORT

The coprocessor is showcased best through its effective use of a large number of threads (from 120 to 240), provided that the code also vectorizes well. Let us see what a simple recompilation based "no effort port" could give us. Furthermore, we will analyze the influence of optimizations applied on the processor. We start experiments from the "Equivalent transformations" version, taking it as a baseline.

To build our program for a coprocessor, we simply add **-mmic** switch to the compilation line. In addition, we should not forget to increase the alignment factor in **memalign()** call from 32 to 64 for the coprocessor architecture.

Figure 19.27 contains the timings of the sequential version on the coprocessor compared to the best sequential version on the processor. It should be noted that for the coprocessor transition to calculations

N	60 000 000	120 000 000	180 000 000	240 000 000
The best sequential CPU version	0.409	0.812	1.226	1.603
Equivalent transformations	1.544	3.089	4.633	6.174
Align arrays	1.545	3.091	4.634	6.179
Reduce precision	0.676	1.352	2.027	2.703
Reduce precision + warm cache	0.422	0.845	1.269	1.690

FIGURE 19.27

Using Intel Xeon Phi coprocessor. Time in seconds, serial version.

with reduced precision allows 2.3x gains versus 23% on the CPU. It is also shown that warm cache gives a more considerable gain (about 60%). Finally, it is noteworthy that the execution times of the sequential versions on the coprocessor and processor are almost equal.

USE INTEL XEON PHI COPROCESSOR: WORK IN PARALLEL

Naturally, the potential of the coprocessor is clearly seen when using all its sources of parallelism: both SIMD and its many-cores with SMT. Now we look at parallel versions on the coprocessor. It should be noted that, so far, we have not applied any optimization specific to the coprocessor. We just recompiled the same source version of the code we used for the processor and ran it on the coprocessor in native mode.

As Figure 19.28 shows, the version without warm-up is hardly accelerated, which supports the assumption that the thread creation overheads are comparable to the execution time of the program.

Adding the warm-up, we exclude the one-time overheads from the measurements and are now able to see how the computational part scales: speedup varies from 50.5 to 60.4. Note that there is good scaling until the thread count reaches the number of cores. Adding more threads to fully utilize the execution pipelines on each core somewhat improves the situation in the 120 threads case (i.e., two threads per core), but things get worse when we fully subscribe the machine with 240 threads (i.e., four threads per core) as shown in Figure 19.28. It is clear that, what worked well for 16 threads on the processor does not scale well to 240 threads. Let us see, if there is anything we can do to improve this for the coprocessor.

N	60 000 000	120 000 000	180 000 000	240 000 000
Work in parallel, 60 threads	0.134	0.149	0.164	0.175
Speedup	5.0336	9.050	12.331	15.437
60 threads, no overhead	0.008	0.017	0.025	0.033
Speedup	50.585	51.178	51.783	51.546

N	60 000 000	120 000 000	180 000 000	240 000 000
Work in parallel, 120 threads	0.234	0.255	0.257	0.255
Speedup	2.885	5.303	7.883	10.590
120 threads, no overhead	0.007	0.014	0.021	0.028
Speedup	59.422	59.587	60.389	59.839

N	60 000 000	120 000 000	180 000 000	240 000 000
Work in parallel, 240 threads	0.532	0.527	0.533	0.558
Speedup	1.269	2.564	3.800	4.842
240 threads, no overhead	0.008	0.016	0.024	0.031
Speedup	53.286	54.248	53.969	53.964

FIGURE 19.28

Use Intel Xeon Phi Coprocessor. Time in seconds, 60, 120, 240 threads are used.

USE INTEL XEON PHI COPROCESSOR AND STREAMING STORES

`GetOptionPrices()` function works with four arrays (**pT**, **pK**, **PS0**, **pC**). Three of the arrays are used as read-only inputs, and one (**pC**) is written to as the output. Please note that with the current benchmark data organization, the lengthy **pC** array is only accessed once in the loop. Thus, the **pC** array data does not need to be cached and may be tagged nontemporal. In other words, we now come to the conclusion that our example has hit the memory bandwidth wall which prevents it from scaling with increased thread count.

Streaming store instructions on the coprocessor should help us to save bandwidth by eliminating cache coherency traffic (known as "RFO—read-for-ownership" (traffic)). Computing X options requires 3X reads and X writes, plus X RFO requests to maintain cache coherency upon writes, total 5X. The use of streaming stores eliminates the RFO requests and reduces the traffic to 4X. If our benchmark is memory bandwidth limited, then we would expect 5X/4X = 1.25 speedup from this optimization. We got close to that in case of the largest data set: 0.031/0.026 = 1.19, see Figure 19.29 (Figure 19.30).

As a result, evaluation of 240,000,000 options using the coprocessor version is approximately 4.5 times faster than the host processor version, but we hit the memory bandwidth wall which prevents efficient scaling of the program beyond 65.4x.

SUMMARY

The Black-Scholes formula for pricing European options is a *de facto* standard financial benchmark. Despite the fact that several assumptions in the model invented by Black and Scholes are rarely satisfied in real life, the Black-Scholes formula is still widely used in practice. A typical problem being solved is pricing of millions of options simultaneously. Such a problem is time consuming, requiring significant compute power and, therefore, is relevant to the HPC field. This raises the challenge of a high-performance implementation of Black-Scholes formula on modern multicore and many-core hardware.

N	60 000 000	120 000 000	180 000 000	240 000 000
The best parallel CPU version	0.033	0.062	0.091	0.118
Work in parallel + Warm-up, 120 threads	0.007	0.014	0.021	0.028
Work in parallel + Warm-up, 240 threads	0.008	0.016	0.024	0.031
Work in parallel + Warm-up, streaming stores, 120 threads	0.007	0.013	0.019	0.026
Work in parallel + Warm-up, streaming stores, 240 threads	0.007	0.013	0.019	0.026

FIGURE 19.29

Use Intel Xeon Phi coprocessor and streaming stores. Time in seconds.

```
void GetOptionPrices(float *pT, float *pK, float *pS0,
  float *pC)
{
  int i;
  float d1, d2, erf1, erf2, invf;
  float sig2 = sig * sig;
#pragma simd
#pragma vector nontemporal
#pragma omp parallel for private(invf, d1, d2, erf1,
erf2)
  for (i = 0; i < N; i++)
  {
    invf = invsqrtf(sig2 * pT[i]);
    d1 = (logf(pS0[i] / pK[i]) + (r + sig2 * 0.5f) *
        pT[i]) * invf;
    d2 = (logf(pS0[i] / pK[i]) + (r - sig2 * 0.5f) *
        pT[i]) * invf;
    erf1 = 0.5f + 0.5f * erff(d1 * invsqrt2);
    erf2 = 0.5f + 0.5f * erff(d2 * invsqrt2);
    pC[i] = pS0[i] * erf1 - pK[i] * expf((-1.0f) * r *
        pT[i]) * erf2;
  }
}
```

FIGURE 19.30

Streaming stores version.

This chapter presented a study of performance optimization of Black-Scholes formula computation on Intel Xeon processors and Intel Xeon Phi coprocessors from a very basic to a heavily tuned implementation. Step-by-step analysis of typical optimization techniques showed performance improvements on both processor and coprocessor. The final optimized version computes 2067 million options per second on the processor and 9231 million options per second on the coprocessor in single precision floating point. We illustrated how the performance limiting factors changed with application optimizations—namely the processor application is compute bound while the coprocessor memory bandwidth appears to be the limiting factor after the compute intensive mathematical calculations are tuned.

The study with the source codes has been published as a part of "Programming on Intel Xeon Phi coprocessors" tutorial in Russian (http://hpc-education.unn.ru/ru/obuchenie/courses/xeon-phi) and the code is also available at: http://lotsofcores.com. Work was prepared in UNN HPC Center in collaboration with Intel Numerics engineers.

FOR MORE INFORMATION

- Knuth, D., 1997. The Art of Computer Programming, Seminumerical Algorithms, vol. 2, third ed. Addison-Wesley Professional, 784 p.
- Li, S. Achieving Superior Performance on Black-Scholes Valuation Computing using Intel® Xeon Phi™ Coprocessors. https://software.intel.com/en-us/articles/case-study-achieving-superior-performance-on-black-scholes-valuation-computing-using.
- Jeffers, J., Reinders, J., 2013. Intel® Xeon Phi™ Coprocessor High Performance Programming. Copyright, Morgan Kaufman.

- Smelyanskiy, M., Sewall, J., Kalamkar, D.D., et al., 2012. Analysis and optimization of financial analytics benchmark on modern multi- and many-core IA-based architectures. In: High Performance Computing, Networking, Storage and Analysis (SCC), 2012 SC Companion, pp. 1154-1162.
- Bastrakov, S., Meyerov, I., Gergel, V., et al., 2013. High performance computing in biomedical applications. Procedia Comput. Sci. 18, 10-19.
- Black, F., Scholes, M.S., 1973. The pricing of options and corporate liabilities. J. Polit. Econ. 81(3), 637-654.

DATA TRANSFER USING THE INTEL COI LIBRARY

20

Louis Feng
Intel Corporation, USA

There are many ways we can take advantage of the compute power on the Intel® Xeon Phi™ coprocessor. For example, one may use the offload model where the compiler automatically generates sections of code to run on the coprocessor. Data transfers in this model are managed automatically and how they are processed can be opaque to the programmer. For many types of applications, especially compute kernels in legacy applications and tightly coupled computations with hotspot kernels, the offload model is easy to adapt code and works fairly well to gain performance. On the other side of the spectrum, one may write and compile a standalone program (i.e., native) for the coprocessor, particularly if the whole program is highly parallel, and run the program wholly on the coprocessor. For applications that fit into a client-server or other forms of loosely coupled computation, it makes sense to divide the computations and run them on the architectures where they perform best.

When computations can be divided into separate processes to target the host processor and the coprocessor, and there are fine-grained communications between these processes, the Intel® Coprocessor Offload Infrastructure (Intel® COI) API and library is a good way to handle the data transfer. The COI library is built on top of the Symmetric Communications InterFace which provides low level and optimized process and coprocessor communications within the Intel® Many-core Platform Software Stack (Intel® MPSS). In contrast to the compiler-assisted offload mechanism (which also uses the COI library), using the COI library directly allows the programmer to manually control how data are explicitly transferred onto and off of the coprocessor. In this chapter, we will introduce how to use COI buffers to transfer data, evaluate the effectiveness of the COI library in real world applications, and discuss characteristics of the different types of COI buffers through benchmarks.

FIRST STEPS WITH THE INTEL COI LIBRARY

The COI library is designed for communication between the processes on the host and the coprocessor. In COI lingo, one process is a *source*, and the other process is a *sink*. The communication channel between them is a *pipeline* initiated from the source to the sink. Source and sink are two binary executables compiled and built for their respective architectures. The source process is responsible for launching the coprocessor process through the COI API calls. Figure 20.1 shows code for initializing the source process.

```
uint32_t engineCount = 0;
COIEngineGetCount(COI_ISA_MIC, &engineCount);
if (engineCount < 1) {
  return -1;
}
COIENGINE engine = NULL;
COIEngineGetHandle(COI_ISA_MIC, 0, &engine);
COIPROCESS proc = NULL;
const char* sinkName = "sink_mic";
COIProcessCreateFromFile(engine, sinkName, 0, NULL,
    false, NULL, true, NULL, 0, NULL, &proc);
const char* funcName = "receiveData";
COIFUNCTION func[1];
COIPIPELINE pipeline;
COIPipelineCreate(proc, NULL, 0,&pipeline);
COIProcessGetFunctionHandles(proc, 1, &funcName, func);
```

FIGURE 20.1

Initialization code for COI on the source side (host).

The host enumerates the coprocessor (COIENGINE), initializes and spawns the coprocessor process (COIPROCESS), then sets up corresponding function pointers (COIFUNCTION) to be used in a COI pipeline. Once these steps are completed, we can start to use a COI buffer to send data between the processes.

On the coprocessor side, in the main function of the sink, there are only two COI API calls we need to make, as shown in the code in Figure 20.2. The sink process needs to use the COINATIVELIBEXPORT macro to export functions which the source process can call from the host side through a pipeline "run function." The exported COI run function parameters must match the COI API specified run function prototype.

NOTE

The COI library is released as part of the Intel Many-core Platform Software Stack (Intel MPSS). Once installed, you can find the API documentation and tutorials source code under the directory /usr/share/doc/intel-coi-<version> on Linux.

COI BUFFER TYPES AND TRANSFER PERFORMANCE

COI source and sink code use pipelines to communicate and transfer data. Pipeline commands are executed in order and can be either synchronous or asynchronous. Synchronization points can be made by using the COI completion event mechanism to block execution until a pipeline event has occurred. It is important to point out that there are actually two places where data can be sent through pipeline run function calls. One is using the buffer pointer parameter; the other is using the miscellaneous data parameter. The miscellaneous data is limited in the amount of data which can be transferred (32 kB

```
int main(int , char**)
{
  COIPipelineStartExecutingRunFunctions();
  COIProcessWaitForShutdown();
  return 0;
}
COINATIVELIBEXPORT
void receiveData(uint32_t bufferCount,
                void** bufferPointers,
                uint64_t* bufferLengths,
                void* miscData,
                uint16_t miscDataLength,
                void* returnValue,
                uint16_t returnValueLength)
{
  // Process data buffers...
}
```

FIGURE 20.2

Initialization code for COI on the sink side (coprocessor).

by default), but is the most efficient way to send small chunks of data such as command parameters without allocating COI buffers.

There are four buffer types in the COI library for data transfer; each one is slightly different from others in both their usage and performance.

- Streaming (deprecated since Intel MPSS 3.2)
- Normal
- Pinned
- OpenCL

We will focus on the first three types of buffers. The OpenCL buffer is similar to the normal buffer, but is used by the Intel OpenCL SDK. All COI buffers are created using the `COIBufferCreate` function. When a buffer is no longer needed, use `COIBufferDestroy` to clean up resources. An example of using COI streaming buffer is shown in Figure 20.3. The direction of data transfer is from source to sink.

As described in the COI reference manual, a streaming buffer is consumed by a pipeline run function. Although `COIBufferMap` can be used to map the streaming buffer for write operations, a new buffer is created under the hood. So, there is an overhead to reuse a streaming buffer through `COIBufferMap` (see Figure 20.4). In contrast, a buffer created using the other three buffer types can be reused for data transfer until it is destroyed manually. The COI buffer benchmarks in this chapter are collected on a system with two Intel® Xeon® E5-2697 v2 2.7 GHz processors and an Intel® Xeon Phi™ 7120A coprocessor using Intel MPSS 3.2.1.

```
COIBUFFER buffer;
COIBufferCreate(bytes, COI_BUFFER_STREAMING_TO_SINK,
                0, data, 1, &proc, &buffer));
COIEVENT completion_event;
COI_ACCESS_FLAGS flag = COI_SINK_READ;
COIPipelineRunFunction(pipeline, func[0], 1, &buffer,
    &flag, 0, NULL, misc_data, strlength, return_value,
    strlength, &completion_event);
// do something else.
COIEventWait(1, &completion_event, -1, true, NULL, NULL);
COIBufferDestroy(buffer);
```

FIGURE 20.3

COI streaming buffer creation and data transfer. The `data` parameter in the `COIBufferCreate` function is a pointer to the user data from where the buffer should copy. The buffer size is specified with the `bytes` parameter. The pipeline run function can be called asynchronously by passing in a `COIEVENT` object.

Data Size (MB)	Buffer Create		Buffer Transfer		Buffer Map	
1	1.03 ms	970 MB/s	0.34 ms	2941 MB/s	0.48 ms	2096 MB/s
4	6.36 ms	629 MB/s	0.90 ms	4469 MB/s	2.98 ms	1340 MB/s
16	22.31 ms	717 MB/s	2.83 ms	5662 MB/s	9.73 ms	1644 MB/s
64	112.77 ms	568 MB/s	10.26 ms	6237 MB/s	40.04 ms	1598 MB/s
256	448.88 ms	570 MB/s	39.78 ms	6436 MB/s	158.78 ms	1612 MB/s
1024	1804.06 ms	568 MB/s	158.50 ms	6461 MB/s	641.45 ms	1596 MB/s

FIGURE 20.4

COI streaming buffer performance.

When there are large amounts of data to be transferred, reusing a non-streaming buffer is more efficient than creating a new buffer for each data transfer. Normal buffers can be created in a similar fashion as streaming buffers but their usages are different. Although `COIBufferMap` can be used to access the buffer data, if we just want to copy a new block of data to the buffer, we could use `COIBufferWrite`, as shown in Figure 20.5.

Normal buffers and pinned buffers differ in how the buffers are allocated as well as how data are transferred from source to sink. For a normal buffer, when the buffer is created on the source side, memory is allocated just on the host and virtual memory is reserved on the co-processor. So, writing to this buffer on the source side is a local operation. The first time the `COIPipelineRunFunction` is called, a corresponding memory cache is allocated on the co-processor to store the actual transferred data. This memory cache will be reused in subsequent run function calls (Figure 20.6).

```
COIBUFFER buffer;
COIBufferCreate(bytes, COI_BUFFER_NORMAL,
                0, data, 1, &proc, &buffer));
COIBufferWrite(buffer, 0, data, bytes, COI_COPY_USE_DMA,
                0, NULL, NULL);
COI_ACCESS_FLAGS flag = COI_SINK_READ;
COIEVENT completion_event;
COIPipelineRunFunction(pipeline, func[0], 1, &buffer,
        &flag, 0, NULL, misc_data, strlength, return_value,
        strlength, &completion_event);
// do something else.
COIEventWait(1, &completion_event, -1, true, NULL, NULL);
COIBufferDestroy(buffer);
```

FIGURE 20.5

COI normal buffer create, write, and transfer.

Data Size (MB)	Buffer Create		Buffer Write		Buffer Transfer	
1	0.74 ms	1353 MB/s	0.20 ms	5128 MB/s	0.41 ms	2427 MB/s
4	2.19 ms	1830 MB/s	1.18 ms	3396 MB/s	0.88 ms	4555 MB/s
16	10.09 ms	1585 MB/s	5.16 ms	3098 MB/s	2.74 ms	5833 MB/s
64	54.11 ms	1183 MB/s	23.78 ms	2691 MB/s	10.24 ms	6249 MB/s
256	217.96 ms	1175 MB/s	95.03 ms	2694 MB/s	39.78 ms	6435 MB/s
1024	872.55 ms	1174 MB/s	377.83 ms	2710 MB/s	158.53 ms	6460 MB/s

The results are measured on subsequent pipeline run function calls after the initial warm up call.

FIGURE 20.6

COI normal buffer performance.

A pinned buffer can be created and used similarly to the normal buffer implementation as shown in Figure 20.5. To create a pinned buffer, simply replace the buffer-type parameter of the COIBufferCreate function from COI_BUFFER_NORMAL to COI_BUFFER_PINNED. The rest of the code in Figure 20.5 can remain the same. When a pinned buffer is used, as the name suggests, all memory allocations are upfront, both on the host and on the coprocessor. It differs from the normal buffer in how the sink accesses the transferred data. Instead of copy and caching the whole buffer from source to sink during pipeline run function call, the sink can access the pinned buffer data through a paging mechanism. That is, data are transferred on access at the page level. The results in Figure 20.7 can confirm that the buffer transfer time remains fairly constant regardless of the amount of data being transferred.

Since the pinned buffer data is not accessed on the sink side in the benchmark, there is actually no buffer data transfer and the bandwidth is not measured. This unique model can be useful when only

Data Size (MB)	Buffer Create		Buffer Write		Buffer Transfer	
1	0.62 ms	1618 MB/s	0.32 ms	3144 MB/s	0.22 ms	N/A
4	2.18 ms	1838 MB/s	1.06 ms	3780 MB/s	0.23 ms	N/A
16	10.40 ms	1539 MB/s	5.05 ms	3169 MB/s	0.25 ms	N/A
64	52.29 ms	1224 MB/s	24.57 ms	2605 MB/s	0.28 ms	N/A
256	231.40 ms	1106 MB/s	98.04 ms	2611 MB/s	0.31 ms	N/A
1024	947.81 ms	1080 MB/s	391.85 ms	2613 MB/s	0.36 ms	N/A

Note that buffer transfer bandwidth column does not show how much data are transferred per second because the buffer data is actually not transferred during the COI run function call for the pinned buffer.

FIGURE 20.7

COI pinned buffer create, write, and transfer performance.

a small fraction of the pinned buffer data needs to be accessed by the sink and there is no good way to figure out beforehand what these data might be. One caution for using pinned buffers is that since memory address spaces are pinned on both the host and the coprocessor, the total pinned buffer size is restricted to the physical amount of memory on the coprocessor. If not managed carefully, the coprocessor memory can be exhausted quickly.

APPLICATIONS

When we separate the computations by targeting the different host processor and coprocessor architectures, we realize several benefits:

- *Ease of maintenance*: Usually each process has a very clear role in the system and the different components have to communicate through a set of APIs, which enforces encapsulation.
- *Flexible*: By decoupling the program, we can run different components on different architectures.
- *Performance*: Some components will perform much better on the host system with processors, while others can take more advantage of the highly parallel and wide SIMD architecture of the coprocessors.

One example of such application is the open source Intel Embree renderer and high-performance ray tracing library (see Chapter 21). The rendering computation is essentially a type of physical simulation. It tries to compute how light propagates in a virtual 3D world. The computation is based on the particle model of how light travels in the physical world. Ray tracing is a highly parallel algorithm since each ray computation is independent of the other rays and can scale well with the large number of threads on the coprocessor.

The Embree ray tracing kernels are a set of acceleration data structures and have been further optimized to take advantage of the vector processing power of the coprocessor. Other parts of the renderer are written using the Intel ISPC open source compiler to take advantage of threading and

SIMD vector processing. Overall, the Embree renderer and kernel library run very well on the coprocessor architecture. The renderer provides a GUI for visualization purpose. This renderer is also used at DreamWorks Animation, where it provides an interactive light transport simulation for lighting a 3D scene. There are cameras, lights, and geometry objects that need to be processed and sent over to the coprocessor for the rendering task. In a complex scene, that could range from tens of thousands to millions of scene objects.

Compared to the Intel Xeon Phi coprocessor, the host processor is much faster at single thread operations. This is also true for disk IO operations since the coprocessor does not have direct access to the storage subsystem. So it is logical to load a large amount of scene data on the host side, and after processing these data, we only transfer what is required to the coprocessor for parallel rendering. The rendered image is then sent back to the host for either writing as a file to disk or for display in the GUI. An execution flow diagram of the renderer is shown in Figure 20.8.

In Embree, command parameters which are generally small chunks of data, are sent using the miscellaneous data parameters of the COI pipeline run function. It is up to the programmer to define, serialize, and deserialize these data to use them properly once the data are transferred to their destination.

In addition to the transfer bandwidth, another important metric we need to keep an eye on is the COI run function latency, which is about 0.3 ms even without any buffer data transfer. When handling a large number of geometries, if we were to transfer geometry objects one at a time, for one million objects, it will take at least 300 s. For large number of data transfers, such as geometries, it is more efficient to reuse the normal buffer to send large chunks of data. From the results in Figure 20.6, we can observe that `COIBufferWrite` function slows down as the amount of data increases. This is due to the benchmark code being single threaded and nonuniform memory access limiting the memory bandwidth available to a single core. But as the amount of data increases, the transfer bandwidth improves. If our goal is to minimize the total amount of time (buffer write and transfer) to send D amount of data, we need to solve a minimization problem. Let the buffer write bandwidth width be x, and transfer bandwidth be y, then the total time T of sending D amount of data is:

$$T = \frac{D(x+y)}{xy}$$

Based on the measurements in Figure 20.6, a normal buffer size of 16 MB provides the optimal performance to transfer data. This is only based on a single test system configuration and will likely differ on different systems. The key is to properly evaluate these metrics and their impact on transfer speed to find what is optimal for your application.

FIGURE 20.8

Embree renderer execution flow. The load, convert and write boxes are computations run on the host processor, and the build and render boxes are computations run on the coprocessor. The arrow into build and out of render are where data transfers occur.

SUMMARY

In this chapter, we described how to use the COI library to transfer data between the host and the coprocessor; we discussed the pros and cons of different buffer types and analyzed their bandwidth and latency performance. Any nontrivial application that takes advantage of the coprocessor will have data communications with the host. While the compiler-assisted offload model provides convenience, the COI library offers control. It is an important tool for any developers targeting their applications for the coprocessor where optimal performance is critical. This chapter only covered the tip of the iceberg of the COI library. Readers who are interested in more advanced usages of the library should consult the COI API documentation for all the options.

Using Embree as a real world application of the COI library, we demonstrated how to efficiently transfer different types of data between the host and the coprocessor. While each COI run function call has a reasonably low latency, if not properly managed and optimized, data transfer can dramatically slow down the application.

I would like to especially thank COI tech lead Russell McGuire for his helpful insights and clarification on the COI library.

FOR MORE INFORMATION

Here are some additional reading materials we recommend related to this chapter:
- Intel® Manycore Platform Software Stack (MPSS), https://software.intel.com/en-us/articles/intel-manycore-platform-software-stack-mpss
- Embree, http://embree.github.io
- Code for this and other chapters is available for download at http://lotsofcores.com

HIGH-PERFORMANCE RAY TRACING

21

Gregory S. Johnson*, Ingo Wald*, Sven Woop†, Carsten Benthin†, Manfred Ernst*,[1]

*Intel Corporation, USA, †Intel Corporation, Germany

Ray tracing is a technique for generating images of synthetic scenes. Because ray tracing simulates the physics of light transport in the real world, it can be used to achieve high quality and even photorealistic results (Figure 21.1). For this reason, ray tracing is commonly found in professional rendering applications such as film production, architectural rendering, and automotive previsualization.

Unfortunately, ray tracing is computationally intensive. Millions of rays may be traced in the course of producing a single image. Moreover, the computation of high-quality illumination effects such as specular reflection and refraction limits the value of cache-based optimizations when tracing neighboring rays.

That said, ray tracing is a highly parallel workload. Rays originating from different pixels in the same image can be traced independently of one another, and even some of the operations on any single ray can be performed in parallel. In principle, ray tracing is well suited to modern multicore vector parallel chip architectures. In practice, a key challenge for the programmer is to efficiently map the parallelism intrinsic to ray tracing onto the functional units on the chip.

In this chapter, we describe an open source ray tracing framework called Embree. Embree is designed to achieve very high performance in professional rendering applications where geometrically complex scenes and high-quality illumination effects are common. Embree consists of a set of low-level compute kernels for accelerating several fundamental ray tracing operations. These kernels maximize utilization of modern x86 architectures using a combination of multithreading and instruction set architecture (ISA)-specific vectorization. A high-level API enables the kernels to be used in existing rendering applications (renderers) with minimal coding effort. In this chapter, we present an overview of ray tracing, introduce the parallelization approach employed in Embree to achieve high performance on Intel® Xeon® processors and Intel® Xeon Phi™ coprocessors, and illustrate the use of the Embree kernels in a full rendering application via sample code.

BACKGROUND

A fundamental operation in ray tracing is to identify the objects in the scene visible from a given point along a given direction (i.e., a ray). This operation can be used to render an image as shown in Figure 21.2. One or more rays are emitted from the camera through each pixel in the image plane.

---

[1] Current affiliation: Google Incorporated, USA.

FIGURE 21.1

An image generated with a ray tracer built on the Embree kernels. The surface of the dragon uses a physically based reflection model that simulates the look of copper.

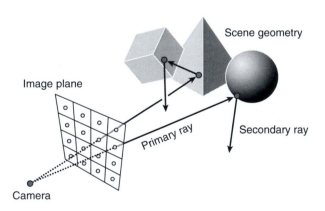

FIGURE 21.2

A fundamental operation in ray tracing is to identify the objects which intersect a ray. One or more primary rays may be traced per pixel in the image plane. At each hit point a secondary ray may be issued.

At each hit point, a secondary ray may be produced if the surface is reflective or translucent. This process continues recursively until a cutoff is reached (e.g., the length of the ray path) or a ray fails to intersect an object. The color of a given pixel is determined from the illumination carried along the ray path, averaged over the rays issued from the pixel.

A naïve implementation of this operation would test each ray for intersection with each geometric primitive in the scene. However, the computation required is impractical in scenes containing millions of primitives, when rendered with millions of rays. For this reason, scene geometry is typically stored

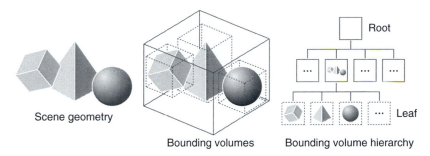

Scene geometry **Bounding volumes** **Bounding volume hierarchy**

Root

... Leaf

FIGURE 21.3

A bounding volume hierarchy (BVH) can be used to reduce the number of ray-geometry intersection tests. Each node in the BVH stores the union of the spatial bounds of its children, and scene geometry is stored at the leaf nodes. Objects which are nearby in the scene are stored in neighboring nodes in the BVH.

within a hierarchical spatial data structure, such as a bounding volume hierarchy (BVH) (Figure 21.3). Each ray is tested for intersection with the root node of the data structure (i.e., the global scene bounds), and then only with the children of nodes bounding subregions of the scene traversed by the ray. The actual scene geometry is stored at the leaf nodes, and it is here that ray-geometry intersection is performed. The use of such a data structure substantially reduces the total number of intersection tests required to generate an image, at the cost of increased complexity when parallelizing the code.

VECTORIZING RAY TRAVERSAL

At the task level, ray tracing is trivially parallel. Rays associated with different pixels in an image can be traced independent of one another. Tiles of pixels are commonly rendered on different threads, with the tile size and thread assignment chosen to maximize load balancing while preserving spatial coherence between neighboring rays in the same tile.

Unfortunately, efficiently exploiting the vector units of modern CPUs for ray tracing is much more challenging. For example, stepping a ray through a hierarchical spatial data structure requires fine-grained data-dependent branching and irregular memory access patterns, inhibiting auto-vectorization. Worse, the optimal mapping of such a kernel to a specific ISA is not always obvious, even for an experienced programmer.

It is possible to vectorize ray traversal through a BVH by assigning different rays to vector lanes, and tracing the ray "packet" through the BVH. Since packet tracing is independent of the vector unit width or ISA, it is broadly applicable and can achieve high vector utilization for spatially coherent rays (i.e., rays with similar origins and directions). However, packet tracing performs less well for spatially incoherent rays (lower vector unit utilization), and the renderer must be parallelized so that multiple rays are available to be traced together.

Alternatively, spatial data structure traversal can be vectorized for individual rays (referred to as "single-ray vectorization"). For example, multibranching BVH structures enable multiple nodes or primitives to be tested for intersection against the same ray in parallel. BVH data structures with four children per node perform well with 4-wide and 16-wide vector units, but higher branching factors offer diminishing returns.

Generally speaking, single-ray vectorization is faster than packet tracing for incoherent rays and can be used within a scalar renderer, but is slower for coherent rays. For this reason, hybrid techniques have been developed that dynamically switch between packet tracing where rays are coherent, and single-ray vectorization where not.

THE EMBREE RAY TRACING KERNELS

The development of Embree is motivated by four observations. First, full-featured renderers can be built from a small set of common ray tracing operations (e.g., BVH build and traversal). Second, while CPU architectures are in principle suited to compute intensive workloads with abundant fine-grained data-dependent branching (e.g., hierarchical data structure traversal), achieving high throughput in practice is challenging. Third, ray tracing is widely used in professional rendering, and there is a need to achieve high performance in these applications. Fourth, much recent work in accelerating ray tracing has not found its way into actual use due to the complexity of integrating these techniques into existing renderers, or because the methods are specialized.

Following from these observations, Embree implements a set of low-level kernels for high-performance BVH construction, ray traversal, and ray-triangle intersection on x86 architectures. These kernels exploit parallelism at multiple levels, with an emphasis on efficient vectorization and state-of-the-art optimizations. High performance is achieved over a range of workloads and ISAs by providing several versions of each kernel.

On Intel Xeon Phi coprocessors, both packet tracing (for spatially coherent rays) and single-ray traversal (for incoherent rays) are supported, as well as logic for dynamically switching between these methods at runtime, based on the number of rays that are currently active in a packet. When packet tracing, 16 rays are traced at a time. In contrast, during single-ray traversal of the BVH, four bounding boxes are tested against the ray in parallel, and each axis of the intersection test (i.e., x, y, z) is computed in parallel. Similarly, during single-ray intersection at the BVH leaf nodes, four triangles are tested against the ray in parallel, with the three axes of each intersection test computed at the same time.

The Embree kernels can be accessed from within an application using a high-level API that hides implementation details such as data structure memory layout and ISA-specific optimizations. The kernels are in turn built over a common set of components which include cross-platform wrappers for atomic and vector parallel operations, synchronization, and threading. Through this layer, all current x86 architectures, operating systems (Linux, Microsoft Windows, Apple Mac OS), and compilers (Intel C++ Compiler, GCC, Clang, and Microsoft Visual Studio) are supported.

USING EMBREE IN AN APPLICATION

The Embree kernels are designed to be used in existing renderers with minimal effort. However (as in many applications), there exists a tradeoff between performance and degree of parallelization in the renderer. The Embree single-ray SIMD kernels can be used within a renderer that is otherwise scalar, and often achieve good utilization for a vector width of 4. However, single-ray methods are less effective on 16-wide vector units (e.g., Intel Xeon Phi coprocessors). Hybrid packet/single-ray techniques are necessary to achieve high utilization, and require a renderer capable of generating multiple rays in parallel.

There are several ways to implement a parallel renderer for use with Intel Xeon processors and Intel Xeon Phi coprocessors. The Intel SPMD Program Compiler (ispc) is one option and Figure 21.4

```
/* Render a tile of pixels in the image. */
task void renderTile(uniform int* uniform pixels,
                     const uniform int imageWidth,
                     const uniform int imageHeight,
                     const uniform Camera& camera)
{

  /* Tile indices. */
  uniform int tileCountX = (imageWidth + TILE_WIDTH - 1) / TILE_WIDTH;
  uniform int tileIndexY = taskIndex / tileCountX;
  uniform int tileIndexX = taskIndex - tileIndexY * tileCountX;

  /* Tile extents in image coordinates. */
  uniform int x0 = tileIndexX * TILE_WIDTH;
  uniform int y0 = tileIndexY * TILE_HEIGHT;
  uniform int x1 = min(x0 + TILE_WIDTH, imageWidth);
  uniform int y1 = min(y0 + TILE_HEIGHT, imageHeight);

  /* Render pixels across SIMD lanes. */
  foreach (y = y0 ... y1, x = x0 ... x1) {

    Vec3f color = renderPixel(x, y, camera);
    unsigned int r = (unsigned int) (255.0f * clamp(color.x, 0.0f, 1.0f));
    unsigned int g = (unsigned int) (255.0f * clamp(color.y, 0.0f, 1.0f));
    unsigned int b = (unsigned int) (255.0f * clamp(color.z, 0.0f, 1.0f));
    pixels[y * imageWidth + x] = (b << 16) + (g << 8) + r;

  }

}

/* Called by the C++ code to render an image. */
export void renderImage(uniform int* uniform pixels,
                        const uniform int imageWidth,
                        const uniform int imageHeight,
                        const uniform Camera& camera)
{

  /* Image dimensions in tiles. */
  uniform int tileCountX = (imageWidth + TILE_WIDTH - 1) / TILE_WIDTH;
  uniform int tileCountY = (imageHeight + TILE_HEIGHT - 1) / TILE_HEIGHT;
  uniform int tileCount  = tileCountX * tileCountY;

  /* Render tiles of pixels on different threads. */
  launch[tileCount] renderTile(pixels, imageWidth, imageHeight, camera);

  /* Wait until all tiles have been rendered. */
  sync;

}
```

FIGURE 21.4

ispc code for a simple renderer that can be used with the Embree ray tracing kernels. The computation is multithreaded and vectorized.

FIGURE 21.5

The output from a sample application which uses the Embree ray tracing kernels. Code for the renderer portion of this application is shown in Figures 21.4 and 21.6.

illustrates the ispc code for a simple renderer capable of issuing multiple rays in parallel (Figure 21.5). ispc incorporates a large subset of the C89 language specification, several features from C99 and C++, language support for task parallelism, and several keywords related to data parallelism. A key advantage of the SPMD programming model is that the code need not be rewritten for different ISAs or vector widths.

ispc code for tracing a given ray using the Embree API is illustrated in Figure 21.6. The Embree API includes functions for defining geometry and building a BVH over this geometry (not shown here), and issuing intersection and occlusion queries. Though use of the API is not required, it can simplify application development. Importantly, the API hides technical details such as which combination of kernels and data layout in memory give the best performance for the given geometry and ISA. The API assumes the kernels and application are in the same address space.

PERFORMANCE

Ray traversal rates for direct and indirect illumination for three renderers on an Intel Xeon Phi 7120 coprocessor (61 cores, 1.28GHz), for the four scenes shown in Figure 21.7 are reported in Figure 21.8. Results are reported for a scalar renderer written in C++ with scalar ray traversal, a scalar renderer using the Embree single-ray SIMD kernels, and a parallel renderer written in ispc using the Embree hybrid packet/single-ray SIMD kernels. The scalar renderer contains no explicit vectorization code, but does use several convenience classes from Embree including high-level tuple types (e.g., points, colors) and associated operations which are automatically mapped to low-level SIMD types and instructions. Version 2.2 of the Embree kernel library is used, as built with Intel Composer XE 14.0.1 and Intel ispc

```
/* Compute a color at the hit point of the ray. */
Vec3f shadePixel(const RTCRay& ray) {

    /* Look up the color associated with the hit primitive. */
    Vec3f color = colorLookupTable[ray.primID] * 0.5f;

    /* A vector in the direction of the simulated light source. */
    Vec3f lightVector = normalize(Vec3f(-1.0f, -1.0f, -1.0f));

    /* Cosine of the light vector and surface normal for diffuse shading.  */
    float weight = clamp(-dot(lightVector, normalize(ray.Ng)), 0.0f, 1.0f) ;

    /* Initialize a shadow ray. */
    RTCRay shadowRay;
    shadowRay.org = ray.org + ray.tfar * ray.dir;
    shadowRay.dir = neg(lightVector);
    shadowRay.tnear = 0.001f;
    shadowRay.tfar = inf;
    shadowRay.geomID = RTC_INVALID_GEOMETRY_ID;
    shadowRay.primID = RTC_INVALID_GEOMETRY_ID;

    /* Determine if the original hit point is occluded. */
    rtcOccluded(sceneID, shadowRay);

    /* Add a diffuse component if the hit point is not in shadow. */
    return((shadowRay.geomID >= 0) ? color : color + color * weight);

}

/* Render a pixel in the image. */
Vec3f renderPixel(float x, float y, const uniform Camera& camera) {

    /* Initialize a primary ray. */
    RTCRay ray;
    ray.org = camera.position;
    ray.dir = normalize(x * camera.vx + y * camera.vy + camera.vz);
    ray.tnear = 0.0f;
    ray.tfar = inf;
    ray.geomID = RTC_INVALID_GEOMETRY_ID;
    ray.primID = RTC_INVALID_GEOMETRY_ID;

    /* Find the nearest object in the scene hit by the ray. */
    rtcIntersect(sceneID, ray);

    /* Compute shading if an object in the scene was hit by the ray. */
    return((ray.geomID >= 0) ? shadePixel(ray) : Vec3f(0.0f, 0.0f, 0.0f));

}
```

FIGURE 21.6

ispc code for rendering a single pixel with simple shading using the Embree kernels through the Embree API.

FIGURE 21.7

The models used in our performance evaluation: Headlight (800 K triangles), Bentley from TurboSquid (2.3 M triangles), the Imperial Crown of Austria by Martin Lubich (4.8 M triangles), and Dragon from the Stanford Computer Graphics Laboratory (7.4 M triangles).

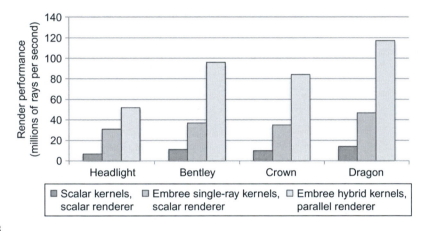

FIGURE 21.8

Performance (higher is better) for three renderers with different levels of vectorization. Results are given as the total rays traced divided by total frame time, including sampling (16 samples per pixel) and shading (typically 30-50% of the total frame time).

1.6.0. While these results are indicative of the performance achievable with the Embree kernel library in a complete renderer, your mileage may vary based on the application and workload.

Vectorization in the renderer often improves the performance of both shading and sampling code, and enables the use of the Embree packet and hybrid traversal kernels. These results illustrate both benefits and indicate that a fully vectorized renderer is important to exploiting the compute capability of architectures with wide vector widths. In some cases, design limits or the level of effort required may make it infeasible to vectorize a renderer. Here, the Embree single-ray SIMD kernels can still be used to improve ray traversal performance.

But how does the performance of Embree compare to ray tracing on a state-of-the-art graphics processing unit (GPU)? Figure 21.9 compares the performance of a parallel renderer written in ispc using the Embree hybrid packet/single-ray SIMD kernels, with a GPU-based renderer built using the OptiX framework from NVIDIA. OptiX simplifies development of high-performance renderers for NVIDIA GPUs, and incorporates low-level kernels, a programmable ray tracing pipeline, a domain-specific

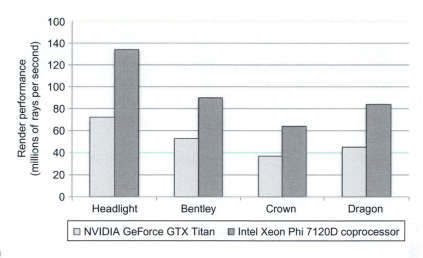

FIGURE 21.9

Performance (higher is better) for a parallel GPU-based renderer built in the NVIDIA OptiX system, and a parallel renderer written in ispc with the Embree hybrid packet/single-ray SIMD kernels.

programming model and compiler, and a scene graph specification (OptiX 3.5.1 with CUDA 5.5 is used here). Both renderers compute diffuse-only shading to minimize the impact of this application-specific computation on render time. In all cases, the Embree renderer on an Intel Xeon Phi 7120 coprocessor performs favorably compared to the OptiX renderer on a NVIDIA GeForce GTX Titan.

SUMMARY

Ray tracing is an important and widely used method for rendering high-quality images of computer-generated scenes. Though ray tracing is computationally intensive, it is also a highly parallel workload. As such, ray tracing benefits from modern chip architectures which rely on functional unit parallelism (e.g., multiple cores) to achieve high throughput. Rays associated with different pixels in an image can be traced independently of one another, and the operations per ray can often be performed in parallel. This abundant parallelism may be mapped to multicore vector processors and coprocessors in a variety of ways. Unfortunately, the mapping which yields the best performance is not always obvious to the programmer. For example, straightforward vectorization strategies such as packet tracing have reduced benefit in cases where the rays diverge (common in the case of secondary rays).

Embree addresses this challenge by providing a set of kernels for commonly used ray tracing operations, individually tuned for different vector widths, workloads (e.g., coherent and incoherent ray distributions, static and dynamic scenes), and application-specific needs (e.g., maximal performance or minimal memory usage). Renderers built on these kernels can achieve BVH build and ray traversal performance on Intel Xeon Phi coprocessors comparable to (and often higher than) existing methods on any current CPU or GPU.

Moreover, the Embree kernel approach is broadly applicable and avoids placing design or target platform restrictions on the renderer. For example, the Embree kernels enable maximal performance in renderers capable of tracing multiple rays in parallel, but there is no requirement that the renderer be parallelized. The Embree single-ray SIMD kernels can be used in a scalar renderer, through the same API. By seamlessly supporting both types of renderers across multiple ISAs, Embree enables developers to incrementally move from scalar to fully parallel rendering, and to migrate between Intel processors and coprocessors.

FOR MORE INFORMATION

The following are additional reading materials we recommend related to high-performance ray tracing on Intel processors and coprocessors:

- Complete source code for the example seen in this chapter: https://github.com/embree/embree/tree/master/tutorials/tutorial00
- Embree technical overview: http://embree.github.io
- Embree kernel library source code: https://github.com/embree
- Embree—a kernel framework for efficient CPU ray tracing. ACM Transactions on Graphics (Proceedings of ACM SIGGRAPH), 2014
- Intel SPMD Program Compiler: https://ispc.github.io

PORTABLE PERFORMANCE WITH OPENCL

22

Simon McIntosh-Smith[*] **Tim Mattson**[†]

University of Bristol, United Kingdom, †Intel, USA

A modern multicore processor can be observed to be a heterogeneous platform with multiple cores programmed with a multithreading programming model and the vector units associated with each core. This view applies to the Intel® Xeon® processor, but even more so for the Intel® Xeon Phi™ coprocessor. The OpenCL standard is motivated by a world that has embraced a view of a computer as a heterogeneous system. In this world, one programming model is used for the CPU while a different programming model is used for the GPU.

In an ideal world, a compiler would vectorize our programs automatically by unrolling loops and restructuring them so the innermost blocks of instructions map onto the vector instruction set of the processor. In practice, automatic compiler vectorization on its own is often not very effective. Programmers are forced to coerce code into a form the compiler can vectorize, or in some cases vectorize the code themselves by hand using explicit vector constructs within a programming language or even the assembly code-like vector intrinsic functions. The resulting code can be sensitive to the width of the vector instructions and hence highly nonportable.

We explore the following hypothesis in this chapter: If we view the multiprocessor system as a heterogeneous platform, programming it in much the same way one would write code for a GPU, a single programming model can be used for the multiple cores and the vector units. Furthermore, the resulting code should also run well on a GPU giving the programmer the higher degrees of portability they need to amortize programming costs as broadly as possible.

The programming model used in this chapter is OpenCL. We will introduce the key concepts by walking the reader though a matrix multiplication program resulting in an optimized version of the code that achieves a significant fraction of the peak performance available from an Intel Xeon Phi coprocessor. We will then go on to look at a real case study, based on the BUDE molecular docking code. BUDE uses OpenCL to sustain 32% of peak performance on an Intel Xeon Phi coprocessor, while also delivering high fractions of peak across a wide range of parallel hardware, including processors and GPUs from multiple vendors.

THE DILEMMA

Increasingly, parallel computing can mean running applications in a heterogeneous environment containing different processing elements. Programmers seek to map their applications onto scalar instructions within a CPU thread, specialized instructions for vector units, blocks of work offloaded to a coprocessor, and even GPUs. Each of these platforms is actively evolving and presents a moving target that may incorporate fundamental changes between generations.

The days when a developer could write a simple sequential program that covers the full range of target platforms are gone forever. Not only must a programmer write their programs to run efficiently on the full range of today's hardware platforms, but they must also write programs to run on future hardware since application software generally lives longer than any particular hardware platform. A programmer may not be able to afford to pick a single hardware target and disregard the rest.

The end result is a dilemma. Programmers are faced with seemingly opposing tensions. On one hand, they need to specialize to the specific processing elements in their parallel and heterogeneous platform. On the other hand, they need to manage the complexity of their software with, in the ideal case, a single code-base supporting all relevant systems.

OpenCL was created to address the many-core programmer's dilemma. This chapter will not address arguments about whether OpenCL is the best solution. Programmers are free to choose whatever approach fits their needs and there is no benefit to the artificial expectation that all programmers will adopt a single approach. OpenCL is the first broadly deployed standard that specifically seeks to encompass FPGAs, CPUs, coprocessors, GPUs, and other accelerators within a single programming system. For programmers needing to support such a diversity of platforms, OpenCL offers what is easily the most supported solution today aimed at tackling this dilemma. Therefore, it is valuable to understand the OpenCL standard and how to use it.

A BRIEF INTRODUCTION TO OPENCL

OpenCL is an industry standard designed to address the dilemma posed in targeting heterogeneous systems. With OpenCL, you can write a single program to run on a wide range of heterogeneous systems.

OpenCL 1.0 was released in late 2008 and support by multiple CPU and GPU vendors appeared by mid-2009. Since its initial release, OpenCL has evolved rapidly through two minor releases (OpenCL 1.1 in 2010 and 1.2 in 2011) and a major OpenCL 2.0 release in 2013. The rapid pace of evolution in the OpenCL standard is challenging for programmers to track and absorb. These modifications to the standard have been required, due to the rapid pace of evolution in computer hardware.

This section will now focus on the core features of OpenCL; those that have not changed much since the introduction of the first standard. We explain OpenCL in terms of a few key models.

- Platform model
- Execution model
- Memory model

The platform model is presented in Figure 22.1 and consists of a host and one or more devices. The *host* is a familiar CPU-based computer supporting file I/O, user interaction, and other functions expected of a typical laptop or server. The *devices* are where the bulk of the computing takes place in an OpenCL program. Example devices include GPUs, many-core coprocessors, and other devices specialized to carry out the OpenCL computations. A device consists of one or more compute units each of which presents the programmer with one or more processing elements. These processing elements are the finest grained units of computation within an OpenCL program.

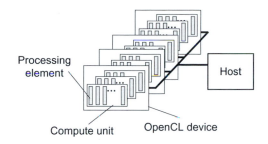

Processing element

Host

Compute unit OpenCL device

FIGURE 22.1

The OpenCL platform model with a single host and multiple devices. Each device has one or more compute units each of which has one or more processing elements.

The platform model gives programmers a view of the hardware they can use when optimizing their OpenCL programs. Then by understanding how the platform model maps onto different target platforms, programmers can optimize their software without sacrificing portability.

OpenCL programs execute as a fine-grained SPMD (single program multiple data) model. Consider the sequential matrix multiplication program in Figure 22.2a that contains a triply nested loop where element $C(i,j)$ of the product matrix is the dot product of row i of the matrix A with column j of the matrix B.

The central ideal behind OpenCL is to define an index space of 1, 2, or 3 dimensions. Programmers map their problem onto the indices of this space and define a block of code, called a *kernel*, an instance of which runs at each point in the index space.

For our matrix multiplication program, for example, we map the outermost two loops onto a two-dimensional (2D) index space and run the innermost loop (over k) within a kernel function. We then run an instance of this kernel function, called a *work-item* in OpenCL terminology, for each point in the index space. The resulting code can be found in Figure 22.2a and b. Comparing the two examples, notice that the two outermost loops in the serial code are replaced by a query to find the coordinates for a work-item within the index space. We then execute an instance of the kernel at each point in the index space to solve the problem.

A more detailed view of how an OpenCL program executes is provided in Figure 22.3 that summarizes the OpenCL execution model. The global index space, in this case two dimensions each of size 16, implies a set of work-items that execute a kernel instance at each point. These work-items are grouped together into blocks with the same shape as the global index space. Blocks of work-items, called *work-groups*, cover the full index space.

Logically the work-items in a single work-group run together. Hence, they can synchronize their execution and share memory in the course of their computation. This is not the case, however, for the work-groups. There are no ordering constraints between the work-groups of a single kernel instance, hence, there are no synchronization constructs between work-groups. This limitation has important implications for sharing data, which we will cover as part of the memory hierarchy discussion.

To a programmer used to the flexibility of programming with threads (e.g., pthreads, java threads, etc.), these restrictions on synchronization may seem onerous. They were included in the OpenCL execution model, however, for a good reason. OpenCL is designed for high-throughput parallel computing typically associated with highly data parallel algorithms. High performance is achieved by creating

```
void mat_mul(const unsigned int Order,
                  const float *A,
                  const float *B,
                        float *C)
{
   int i, j, k;
   for (i=0; i < Order; i++)
      for (j=0; j < Order; j++)
         for (k = 0; k < Order; k++)
            C[i*Order+j] += A[i*Order+k] * B[k*Order+j];
}
```

(a)

```
__kernel void mat_mul(const unsigned int Order,
                        __global const float *A,
                        __global const float *B,
                        __global       float *C)
{
   int i, j, k;
   i = get_global_id(0);
   j = get_global_id(1);
   for (k = 0; k < Order; k++)
     C[i*Order+j] += A[i*Order+k] * B[k*Order+j];
}
```

(b)

FIGURE 22.2

(a) Serial matrix multiplication function. (b) Parallel matrix multiplication function as an OpenCL kernel.

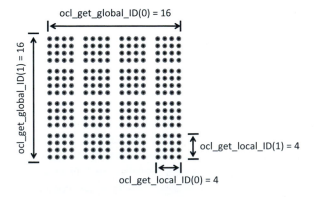

FIGURE 22.3

A problem is decomposed onto the points of an *N* dimensional index space (*N*=1, 2, or 3) known in OpenCL as an NDRange. A kernel instance runs at each point in the NDRange to define a work-item. Work-items are grouped together into work-groups which evenly tile the full index space.

a large internal work-pool of work-groups that are ready to execute. A scheduler can then stream these runnable work-groups through the compute units of a device to keep them fully occupied.

Because compute devices such as GPUs and FPGAs may have their own discrete on-board memories, a heterogeneous platform often cannot provide a single coherent address space. The memory model in OpenCL, therefore, takes this into account by defining how the memory in OpenCL is decomposed into different address spaces aligned with the platform model. We present this concept in Figure 22.4.

Starting at the bottom of the figure, consider the host memory. As the name implies, *host memory* is defined by the host and only directly visible to the host (although this is relaxed in OpenCL 2.0). The next layer in the memory hierarchy is the *global memory*, which includes a read-only memory segment called the *constant memory*. Global and constant memories hold OpenCL memory objects and are visible to all the OpenCL devices involved in a computation (i.e., within the context defined by the programmer). The on-board DRAM of a discrete GPU or FPGA will typically be mapped as global memory. It is worth noting that, for discrete devices, moving data between host memory and global memory usually requires transferring data across a bus, such as PCI Express, which can be relatively slow.

Within an OpenCL device, each compute unit has a region of memory local to the compute unit called *local memory*. This local memory is visible only to the processing elements within the compute

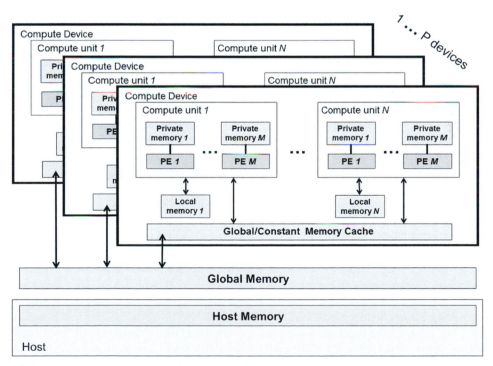

FIGURE 22.4

The memory model in OpenCL 1.X and its relationship to the platform model. P devices exist in a single context and therefore have visibility into the global/constant memory.

unit, which maps nicely onto the OpenCL execution model, with one or more work-groups running on a compute unit and one or more work-items running on a processing element. The local memory within a compute unit corresponds to data that can be shared inside a work-group. The final part of the OpenCL memory hierarchy is *private memory*, which defines a small amount of per work-item memory visible only within a work-item.

Data movement between the layers in the memory hierarchy in OpenCL is explicit. That is, the user is responsible for the transfer of data from host memory to global memory and so on. Commands in the OpenCL API and kernel programming language must be used to move data from host memory to global memory, and from global memory to either local or private memory.

A MATRIX MULTIPLY EXAMPLE IN OPENCL

To understand these address spaces, we need a more complex example. Consider the matric multiplication kernel in Figure 22.5a. This program may seem complex at first, but the basic idea behind this kernel is simple. We use a well-known restructuring of the problem by taking each loop (three of them) and turning them into a pair of loops; i.e., a loop over blocks and a second loop over the elements within each block. This approach allows us to choose the sizes of the blocks so that the working space needed for the computation fits in faster memories (i.e., local or private memory), potentially yielding dramatically faster programs.

To implement this approach, we replace a work-item as a single vector dot product (Figure 22.2a and b) with a more complex work-item that computes a "matrix dot product" of a row-block from the A matrix and a column-block from the B matrix. A simple graphical view of this algorithm is shown at the top of Figure 22.5b. Each step in this computation is a serial matrix multiplication, which performs a relatively greater amount of work per data transfer to better amortize the cost of moving data from global memory into faster memory closer to the processing elements.

Let us consider this kernel in more detail. At the top of the kernel we establish the block size that defines the size (blksz) for the square A, B, and C blocks. The block size is selected so the resulting trio of blocks fit in a faster level of the OpenCL memory hierarchy, such as local memory. We then begin the definition of the kernel itself. The function is marked as a kernel so the system knows to prepare it for the multiple device types in the context. The arguments to the kernel are labeled according to the address space from which they are coming from. The original matrices are marked "__global" to indicate, of course, that they reside in global memory. Two additional arguments are marked as "__local" to indicate they come from the shared memory local to a compute unit (and thus are shared only between the work-items within a work-group).

Recall that each work-item will run the same kernel. This is an instance of the SPMD pattern. Each work-item will determine its unique global ID and (unique only within a work-group) local ID, and then, based on those IDs, perform its part of the overall computation. One can see the necessary code for discovering a work-item's global and local IDs at the beginning of the example kernel, with calls to the ocl_get_global_ID() functions to find the coordinates of the work-item in the index space. These coordinates define which element of the result matrix this work-item is responsible for. The following calls to ocl_get_group_ID() find the coordinates of the work-group the work-item resides within. This will define the coordinates of the submatrix blocks each work-item will process. Finally, we call the function ocl_get_local_ID() to find the coordinates of the work-item within the work-group. See Figure 22.3 for an example where the global dimensions are (16,16) and local dimensions are (4,4).

```
#define blksz 16                        // upper-left-corner and inc for A and B
__kernel void mmul(                        int Abase = Iblk*N*blksz;
        const unsigned int N,              int Ainc  = blksz;
        __global float* A,                 int Bbase = Jblk*blksz;
        __global float* B,                 int Binc  = blksz*N;
        __global float* C,
        __local  float* Awrk,           // C(Iblk,Jblk) = sum over Kblk of
        __local  float* Bwrk)           //          A(Iblk,Kblk)*B(Kblk,Jblk)
{                                          for (Kblk = 0;  Kblk<Num_BLK;  Kblk++)
    int kloc, Kblk;                        {
    float Ctmp=0.0f;                         //Load (Iblk,Kblk) and B(Kblk,Jblk).
                                             //Each work-item loads single
    // compute element C(i,j)                //elements of the two shared blocks
    int i = get_global_id(0);                  Awrk[jloc*blksz+iloc]            =
    int j = get_global_id(1);                          A[Abase+jloc*N+iloc];
                                               Bwrk[jloc*blksz+iloc]            =
    // element C(i,j) is in                            B[Bbase+jloc*N+iloc];
    // block C(Iblk,Jblk)                       barrier(CLK_LOCAL_MEM_FENCE);
    int Iblk = get_group_id(0);
    int Jblk = get_group_id(1);
                                               #pragma unroll
                                               for(kloc=0;   kloc<blksz;   kloc++)
    // C(i,j) is element                         Ctmp += Awrk[jloc*blksz+kloc]
    // C(iloc, jloc) inside                              * Bwrk[kloc*blksz+iloc];
    // the block                               barrier(CLK_LOCAL_MEM_FENCE);
    int iloc = get_local_id(0);                Abase += Ainc; Bbase += Binc;
    int jloc = get_local_id(1);            }
    int Num_BLK = N/blksz;                 C[j*N+i] = Ctmp;
  (a)                                   }
```

FIGURE 22.5

(a) OpenCL kernel for blocked matrix multiplication. The algorithm computes a product of the row-blocks of *A* with the column-blocks of *B* within a work-group. Blocks are copied into local memory shared between work-items so the cost of moving data from global memory is paid only once. (b) A pictorial representation of the blocked matrix multiplication algorithms where a row-block from *A* is multiplied by a column-block from matrix *B* to compute a block of *C*. The index computations for the offsets (Abase and Bbase) into global memory objects for matrices *A* and *B* plus the increments for subsequent matrix blocks (Ainc and Binc) is shown for the case of order 16 matrices using the decomposition of the NDrange from Figure 22.3.

Any one work-item can therefore have a global ID ranging from (0,0) to (15,15) and a local ID ranging from (0,0) to (3,3).

At the top of the second column in Figure 22.5a, we carry out index computations for the offset and increments for the blocks of the matrices in global memory. In Figure 22.5b we show an example of these index computations for the NDRange from Figure 22.3 for the multiplication of matrices of order 16.

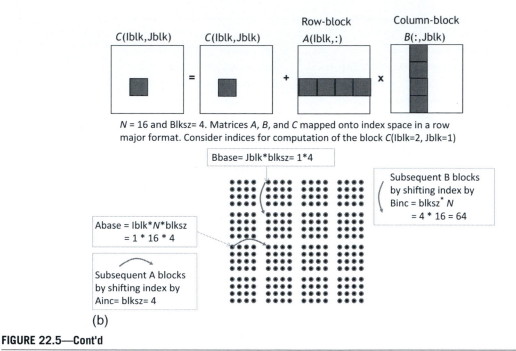

N = 16 and Blksz = 4. Matrices *A*, *B*, and *C* mapped onto index space in a row major format. Consider indices for computation of the block *C*(Iblk=2, Jblk=1)

(b)

FIGURE 22.5—Cont'd

The major loop driving the work of the kernel follows the index computations. This is the loop (Kblk) over row-blocks of the *A* matrix and the column-blocks of the *B* matrix. At the beginning of the loop, the work-items, in parallel, load the matrix blocks from global memory and copy them into local memory. Subsequent statements later in the loop will work with these blocks so the programmer must follow these copy operations with a barrier. This barrier uses a local memory fence to assure that after the barrier, all the work-items in the work-group will have a consistent view of the local memory. Without the barrier, some work-items might try to start reading from the local memory copy before other work-items have finished their writes. The barrier only synchronizes all of the work-items within one work-group, leaving different work-groups to execute asynchronously with one another.

With the blocks in place, the computation proceeds with the loop over the local indices of a block (kloc). At the end of this loop is a second barrier. This barrier is important. It prevents any work-items in one work-group from proceeding until all the other work-items in the same work-group have finished with the loop over kloc. This is essential since we do not want a work-item to continue to the next iteration of the Kblk loop and begin the copies into *A* and *B* blocks for the next iteration until all the work-items are finished with the current block.

OPENCL AND THE INTEL XEON PHI COPROCESSOR

OpenCL programmers reason about performance by understanding how the platform model maps onto a particular system, considering how their data parallel loops might be transformed into kernels and mapped onto devices, and how data would need to flow up and down the memory hierarchy. Consider the platform model in Figure 22.1. On an SPMD-style architecture, such as a GPU, the hardware has more constraints than say a multiple instruction multiple data (MIMD) architecture such as an Intel Xeon processor or an Intel Xeon Phi coprocessor. As an open standard, OpenCL's goal was to enable efficient parallel programming on both SPMD and MIMD architectures, and even more diverse devices such as FPGAs and DSPs.

This creates an interesting situation for OpenCL on a CPU platform or a many-core platform such as the Intel Xeon Phi coprocessor, which is in much more akin to a many-core multiprocessor than a GPU coprocessor. There are many ways the OpenCL platform could be mapped onto these systems. And once a particular mapping has been selected, it can change since decisions are set in software not hardware.

At this time, the OpenCL platform model is mapped onto an Intel Xeon Phi coprocessor in the following manner. A compute unit is mapped onto the hardware threads on a core. The cores in a processor unit share the vector units. Processing elements are mapped onto the lanes in a vector unit. The number of OpenCL processing elements depends on the data types involved in the computation. For single precision matrix multiply kernels (as we have been considering in our example), the 32 bit float types permit each vector unit to support 16 processing elements.

To achieve high performance with the Intel Xeon Phi coprocessor, the processing elements must execute the kernel code as a set of uniform work-item control flows, one work-item to each lane of the vector units. Conditional instructions or a work-group size that is not a multiple of the number of lanes that can be supported by the Intel Xeon Phi vector unit will result in unused SIMD lanes and poor performance. In addition, the number of work-groups should ideally be an exact multiple of the number of hardware threads (compute units) in order to achieve best performance.

Consider an Intel Xeon Phi coprocessor with 60 cores. Each core has 4 hardware threads and a 512-bit vector unit (wide enough for 16 single precision floating-point numbers). Therefore, you need $60 * 4 * 16 = 3840$ work-items to run the OpenCL platform at full occupancy. A work-group runs on a single core so work-group sizes of 16 (dictated by the width of the vector unit for float type kernels) or $4 * 16$ (number of hardware threads times the lanes in the vector unit) should work well.

Currently for OpenCL on the Intel Xeon Phi coprocessor, the host program runs on a CPU and the OpenCL kernel runs on the coprocessor. Hence, data starts on the CPU in DRAM and must move onto the faster memory on the coprocessor card. In the OpenCL software development kit (SDK) for Intel Xeon Phi coprocessor, a working pool of memory is allocated on the coprocessor card when the program starts up. We found in our matrix multiplication kernels that it was important to make sure this pool was large enough to hold our matrices. If this pool was too small, the system would dynamically increase the size of the pool at runtime thereby increasing the time to transfer data from the host onto the coprocessor memory. The size of this work-pool can be adjusted by setting the appropriate environment variable.

```
CL_CONFIG_MIC_DEVICE_2MB_POOL_INIT_SIZE_MB
```

A link for more information about the OpenCL SDK for Intel Xeon Phi coprocessors is noted at the end of this chapter.

MATRIX MULTIPLY PERFORMANCE RESULTS

We report results for our matrix multiplication programs in Figure 22.6. We present results from a laptop class processor (dual core Intel® Core™ I5 processor @ 2.5 GHz), a GPU (Intel® HD graphics 5200 GPU), and an Intel® Xeon Phi™ coprocessor. Our intention is not to compare the performance of these very different classes of processors, but to demonstrate OpenCL's ability to run across a wide range of processors. The matrix size was fixed at order = 1000. This is considered a small size for a matrix used in performance analysis and serves to expose weaknesses in how a system manages memory movement relative to computation. Running a serial C implementation on a single laptop CPU core achieves 200 MFLOPS when compiled with optimization "-03." This level of optimization instructs the compiler to vectorize the program automatically. Moving on to our naïve, simple OpenCL matrix multiply (from Figure 22.2b), we achieved 800 MFLOPS on the same laptop CPU, although this time the OpenCL code will be using both of the CPU cores. The same OpenCL program ran at 13.6 GLOPS on an Intel Xeon Phi. The most compelling performance was achieved with the blocked algorithm (from Figure 22.5a). We fixed the block size at 16. It is impressive that a single program just recompiled (no source level customization) resulted in performance numbers of 12, 38, and 74 GFLOPS on the CPU, GPU, and coprocessor, respectively. Also note that, unlike performance numbers produced by hand-coded math libraries, our program did not resort to any assembly code techniques.

With both the GPU and the Intel Xeon Phi coprocessor we found significant overheads due to data movement. When we report matrix multiplication runtimes, we include the costs of moving data from host memory into global memory. This means we incur the cost of moving memory across the PCIe bus. We can see this in Figure 22.6 with the second, parenthetical numbers for the blocked matrix multiplication. To produce those numbers we ran the calculation twice and only reported the speed for the second case. In other words, the second instance of the computation was able to take advantage of the memory movement from the first instance. Not surprisingly, this had a much larger impact on the Intel Xeon Phi coprocessor due to its configuration as a coprocessor and the fact data movement occurs over the PCIe bus. It will be interesting to see what is possible in the next generation of Intel Xeon Phi

	Processor	GPU	Coprocessor
Serial C Program (code from figure 1-2A)	0.2		
OpenCL: one work item per C(I,j) … all global memory (code from figure 1-2B)	0.8		13.6
Blocked parallel (blksz=16) (code from figure 1-5A)	12	38 (53)	74 (126)

FIGURE 22.6

Matrix multiplication of order 1000 matrices, performance in GFLOPS for (1) Processor: Intel® Core™ i5-2520M CPU @ 2.5 GHz (dual core) Windows 7 64 bit OS, Intel compiler 64 bit version 13.1.1.171, OpenCL SDK 2013; (2) GPU: Intel Core i7-4850HQ @ 2.3 GHz with an Intel HD Graphics 5200 w/high-speed memory, ICC 2013 sp1 update 2; and (3) Coprocessor: Intel Xeon Phi SE10P, CL_CONFIG_MIC_DEVICE_2MB_POOL_INIT_SIZE_MB = 4 MB. Second numbers for GPU and coprocessor show the speed from running the matrix multiplication multiple times reporting only the time for the second run. Note that while not shown, the timing errors we observed are small relative to the number of significant figures reported in this table.

products, code named by Intel as Knights Landing, is able to operate as the processor in a system, or node, and eliminate these coprocessor data movement overheads.

One can see from the examples that OpenCL kernels themselves can be relatively straightforward. Much of the complexity associated with OpenCL comes from the parts of the program we have avoided up until this point; the host program. The program that runs on the host sets up the computations for the devices, manages the global memory, and coordinates execution of the kernels through a command queue. A typical host program will perform the following steps:

- Define the platform ... platform = devices + context + command-queues
- Create and build the program (dynamic library of kernel functions)
- Setup memory objects
- Define the kernel (attach arguments to kernel function)
- Submit commands ... transfer memory objects and execute kernels

The host functions are not difficult to write or understand, but they can be cumbersome. We will not discuss the host functions any further in this chapter. Instead, information about the OpenCL APIs and how they are used to create host functions can be found in the references.

CASE STUDY: MOLECULAR DOCKING

To demonstrate the effectiveness of OpenCL for developing performance portable applications on a real-world problem, we present a case study for BUDE (Bristol University Docking Engine), a molecular dynamics-based code. Dr. Richard Sessions and a team from Bristol University have been developing BUDE for many years. BUDE employs a novel atom-atom-based empirical free energy force field to accurately predict the relative binding free energies of interactions between two molecules. This ability means BUDE can be used to address three different problems: (1) *virtual-screening-by-docking* of millions of small molecules against a protein target (Figure 22.7);

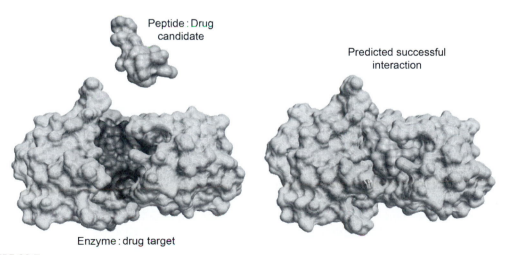

Peptide : Drug candidate

Predicted successful interaction

Enzyme : drug target

FIGURE 22.7

BUDE performing virtual screening by docking potential drug molecules (ligands) against targets (proteins).

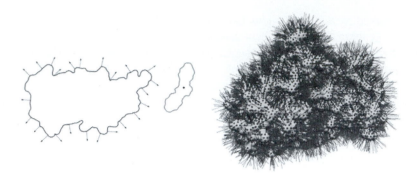

FIGURE 22.8

BUDE can perform binding site prediction by scanning the surface of a target protein with a target ligand (left). Potential binding sites are identified in the figure on the right.

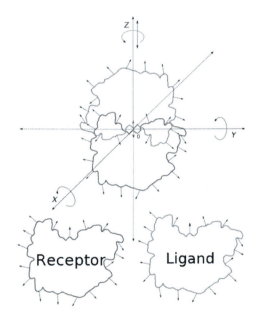

FIGURE 22.9

BUDE's third mode performs *protein-protein docking* in real space by the systematic scanning of one protein surface against the other.

(2) *binding-site detection* by scanning the surface of a protein with a ligand (Figure 22.8); and (3) *protein-protein docking* in real space by the systematic scanning of one protein surface against the other (Figure 22.9).

BUDE has been ported to OpenCL with the deliberate aim of delivering *performance portability* across a wide range of CPUs, GPUs, and accelerators. At this time, BUDE has been ported in its entirety to OpenCL. This deliberate policy means that only a single-source code needs to be developed and maintained, but it relies on achieving good performance for the OpenCL code on the default CPU target devices, as well as other devices including the Intel Xeon Phi coprocessor and GPUs.

One of BUDE's important characteristics is that it can exploit an enormous amount of natural data parallelism: many different molecule to molecule tests need to be performed, and they are all independent. BUDE is also compute intensive rather than memory bandwidth intensive. Both of these characteristics make BUDE easier to optimize for highly parallel architectures. Each molecule-molecule test has a unique configuration in terms of the relative positions and orientations of the molecules. Each such molecular configuration is called a *pose* in BUDE's terminology.

The approach taken for the OpenCL optimization of BUDE employed the following *principles for performance portability*:

1. *Expose maximum parallelism.* The main focus on development of the OpenCL code was to expose as much of the inherent parallelism as possible while minimizing any interdependencies (control and data). For BUDE this meant parallelizing at a relatively coarse level, assigning different molecule-molecule *poses* to different OpenCL work-items to be computed in parallel. There are many more molecular poses than say atoms in each molecule, so choosing pose-level parallelism exposed the highest degree of parallelism in the application.

2. *Apply well-known optimizations.* Once the maximum amount of parallelism was discovered and expressed in the OpenCL code, we then applied standard source code optimizations to improve performance on many-core architectures, such as those of the Intel Xeon Phi coprocessor and GPUs. These optimizations are well explained in the literature, and include such approaches as ensuring memory access patterns were as well-formed as possible for the device memory system (e.g., *coalesced*), removing as much conditional code as possible, making sure the compiler is provided all relevant information about pointers (such as the use of *const* and *restrict* keywords), and so on.

3. *Test across multiple devices.* During development, the code is repeatedly tested across multiple devices, including at least one multicore, multi-CPU system, one Intel Xeon Phi system, and one GPU system. Optimizations that improved performance across all the devices were kept. Optimizations that reduced performance significantly on any device(s) were investigated. If there was a device-specific reason for the performance degradation, the optimization was rejected. If the cause for the performance regression was a bug in a specific driver or compiler, then we worked with the relevant vendor to help fix the problem. When the problem was fixed, the optimization was integrated into the main code. It is very interesting to note that almost all optimizations improved performance on all our target devices, while only a very small number improved performance on one device while reducing it significantly on another device.

4. *Use the most extreme devices to drive development.* During the optimization, we would often focus on performance on the most parallel devices in our target set, such as the Intel Xeon Phi coprocessor or a high-end GPU. These devices require the most efficient parallel code designs, and we found that by focusing on these devices, we also improved the performance of the same code on the less parallel devices in our target set, such as the multicore CPUs.

5. *Avoid platform-specific optimizations.* Some potential optimizations exploit knowledge of specific architecture features, such as the size of one level of the memory hierarchy (private, local, global, host in OpenCL terminology), or the width of the work-item execution grouping on a certain device (i.e., AMD's wavefront size or NVIDIA's warp width). Generally these

optimizations only yield limited speedups on their intended platforms, and they often result in slowdowns on all other platforms. For BUDE we avoided all of these device-specific optimizations and instead focused on parameters such as work-group sizes that should work well on all devices (for example, small power of 2 work-group sizes such as 32, 64, or 128 often perform optimally or near optimally on all devices).

While BUDE is a complex scientific code, the atom-atom inner loop comes down to about 50 or so basic operations, around 20% of which are conditional branches. The remaining operations are single precision floating-point instructions (such as addition, multiplication, reciprocal, and square root), or load and store instructions. The branches were data dependent, and so *divergent* behavior was likely; that is, different work-items would have a high probability of branching in different directions. This is well-known to be a source of performance degradation in throughput-oriented processors, and so much effort was spent in replacing the data-dependent control flow with semantically equivalent, straight-line, predicated code. Predicated execution is an alternative to branch-based conditional behavior, where a sequence of straight-line instructions is executed but their results potentially ignored, depending on the value of some condition. Replacing conditional branches with straight-line predicated code in this way usually has a dual benefit: fewer branches means that the simple execution pipelines in many-core architectures suffer from fewer stalls, and decreased divergent branch execution reduces the length of the critical path. Overall we observed a 54.1% speedup for this optimization alone on an NVIDIA GTX 680 GPU. In the end we were able to optimize away all of the conditional control flow in BUDE's innermost loop, replacing it with straight-line, predicated code which gave much higher performance on all tested platforms including Intel Xeon Phi coprocessors, Intel Xeon processor, and GPUs from AMD and NVIDIA. Often we had to transform the OpenCL kernel code into a semantically equivalent version that was more compiler friendly in order to help the compiler generate predicated code instead of explicit branches—see Figures 22.10 and 22.11 for "before" and "after" examples from BUDE.

```
if (a > b)
{
  accumulator += (a - b*c);
}
```

```
        setp.gt.f32 %pred, %a, %b
@!%pred bra         $endif
        mul.f32     %t0, %b, %c
        sub.f32     %t1, %a, %t0
        add.f32     %accumulator, %accumulator, %t1
$endif:
```

FIGURE 22.10

A typical code fragment from BUDE prior to transformations to assist the compiler in generating straight-line code. The generated assembly instructions include a data-dependent conditional branch (the "bra" instruction).

```
temp = (a - b*c);
mask = (a > b ? 1 : 0);
accumulator += (mask * temp);
```

```
mul.f32      %t0, %b, %c
sub.f32      %temp, %a, %t0
setp.gt.f32  %pred, %a, %b
selp.f32     %mask, %one, %zero, %pred
mad.f32      %accumulator, %mask, %temp, %accumulator
```

FIGURE 22.11

The same code fragment after transformation to a semantically equivalent but more compiler optimization friendly version. The generated assembly code is now predicated straight-line code that will perform much better on most architectures.

RESULTS: PORTABLE PERFORMANCE

BUDE is known to be a compute-intensive code, and with the optimizations described in this chapter, we have a highly parallel implementation with good branching characteristics (minimize use of branching, and where conditional branches are unavoidable, minimize the occurrence of divergent branches) and a well-behaved memory access pattern. As a result, BUDE attains a high fraction of single precision peak floating-point performance on all the devices on which it has been tested.

Results for the Intel Xeon Phi coprocessor and Intel Xeon CPUs, when running identical OpenCL source code on both devices demonstrated a respectable 681 GFLOP/s sustained performance on a 61 core 1.1 GHz Intel Xeon Phi SE10P coprocessor, and 346 GFLOP/s on a dual socket Sandy Bridge system (two Intel E5-2687W 8 core CPUs at 3.1 GHz, 16 cores total). These results report sustained aggregate application performance across an entire run of BUDE, not just timings for an inner loop or kernel and represent a sustained performance of 32% of peak floating point on the Intel Xeon Phi coprocessor and 44% of peak on the 16-core Intel Xeon processor system. Remember that peak floating point for both systems is the peak *SIMD* floating-point performance. Given the high levels of peak that the code sustains across the whole run, Intel's OpenCL implementation had clearly been able to efficiently vectorize the OpenCL code for both the Intel Xeon Phi coprocessor and the Intel Xeon processors. The Intel Xeon Phi coprocessor performance also represents a 1.94X speedup over the high-end 16 core Sandy Bridge Intel Xeon processor system; see Figure 22.12.

Achieving a sustained overall performance this close to peak performance is significant and demonstrates the potential for using OpenCL to develop performance portable, single-source applications that do not need to rely on overly complex runtime code generation or source code auto-tuning.

Note, the exact same source code, when compiled to run on a wide range of different many-core platforms, such as GPUs from AMD and NVIDIA, also achieves similar high fractions of peak floating-point performance; see Figure 22.13 for more details.

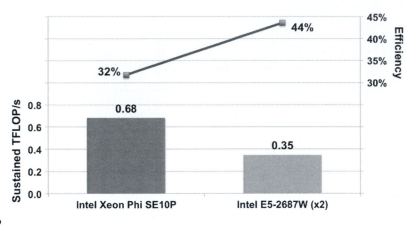

FIGURE 22.12

BUDE sustained performance on the coprocessor and processor test systems.

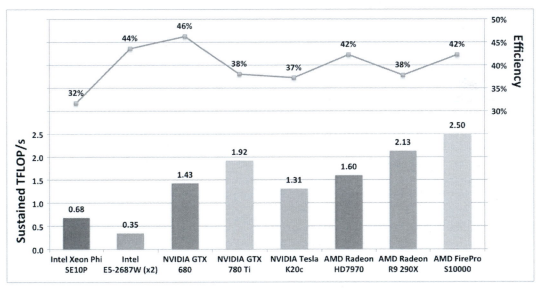

FIGURE 22.13

BUDE's sustained performance running identical OpenCL source code across a wide range of many-core and multicore devices. Performance is measured across a complete application run.

RELATED WORK

OpenCL and NVIDIA's CUDA are based on the same core ideas. They both are designed for throughput-oriented data parallel algorithms where the basic construct is a kernel instance running at each point in a 1, 2, or 3 dimension index space (an instance of the kernel parallelism design pattern). The jargon is different between the two programming systems, but the concepts are the same. The biggest difference between CUDA and OpenCL is that CUDA is proprietary and tied to NVIDIA GPUs while OpenCL is a portable, open standard supported by all major processor vendors.

While kernel parallelism is a great approach for programmers who like to get "close to the metal," and who are comfortable with managing detailed parallel platforms themselves, this approach can be too low level for many application-level programmers. The OpenMP Architecture Review Board has responded to this issue by defining a set of directives in OpenMP version 4.0 that target different devices. This basically integrates the high-level directive-driven approach to parallel programming that is already well known in OpenMP with the kernel parallelism pattern employed by OpenCL.

As with the OpenCL industry standard and NVIDIA's CUDA, there is a related standard to OpenMP 4.0 tied to a single vendor's products called OpenACC, which is also a directive-driven approach to programming heterogeneous platforms. Just as programmers interested in portable software that runs on platforms from multiple vendors should choose OpenCL over CUDA, it is likewise the case that programmers in the long run will be better served by choosing the OpenMP 4.0 industry standard over NVIDIA's OpenACC.

SUMMARY

OpenCL is a relatively new programming model designed to support programmers interested in writing portable and performant parallel programs for heterogeneous platforms. OpenCL might be too low level for many application-level programmers who would be better served using traditional MPI + OpenMP programming models. However, OpenCL offers a unique option, by embracing a view of a computer as a heterogeneous system, to support a diverse range of hardware that includes processors, coprocessors, GPUs, FPGAs, and other devices. As shown in this chapter, it is possible to write OpenCL programs that are both portable and perform.

FOR MORE INFORMATION

Here are some additional reading materials we recommend related to this chapter:

- Munshi, A., Gaster, B., Mattson, T.G., Fung, J., 2011. OpenCL Programming Guide
- Gaster, B., Howes, L., Kaeli, D.R., Mistry, P., Schaa, D., 2011. Heterogeneous Computing with OpenCL
- *Hands on OpenCL* tutorial and code examples by Simon McIntosh-Smith and Tom Deakin, with input from Ben Gaster and Tim Mattson, http://handsonopencl.github.io/
- McIntosh-Smith, S., Price, J., Sessions, R.B., Ibarra, A.A., 2014. BUDE paper: high performance in silico virtual drug screening on many-core processors. International Journal of High Performance Computing Applications. doi:10.1177/1094342014528252.
- McIntosh-Smith, S.N., Boulton, M., Curran, D., Price, J.R., 2014. On the performance portability of structured grid codes on many-core computer architectures. International Supercomputing, Leipzig. doi:10.1007/978-3-319-07518-1_4.
- OpenCL SDK for Intel Xeon Phi, http://software.intel.com/en-us/articles/opencl-design-and-programming-guide-for-the-intel-xeon-phi-coprocessor
- Download the code from this, and other chapters, http://lotsofcores.com

CHARACTERIZATION AND OPTIMIZATION METHODOLOGY APPLIED TO STENCIL COMPUTATIONS

23

Cedric Andreolli[*], Philippe Thierry[*], Leonardo Borges[†], Gregg Skinner[†], Chuck Yount[†]

[*]Intel, France, [†]Intel, USA

INTRODUCTION

This chapter describes a characterization and optimization methodology applied to a 3D finite differences (3DFD) algorithm used to solve a constant or variable density isotropic acoustic wave equation (Iso3DFD).

Time-domain finite differences, using an explicit solver, is a commonly used technique to simulate the seismic wave propagation for wave phenomena analysis or seismic acquisition design. The method is employed widely in seismic imaging through reverse time migration and full waveform inversion. Variations on the method include the treatment of waves as acoustic or elastic and the physical description of the ground taking care of anisotropy and density variations.

Additionally, the numerical stencils chosen to approximate partial derivatives have a strong impact on the performance of the implementation. These choices impact the *arithmetic intensity* (AI) (number of floating-point operations (flops) per byte of memory transferred) of the 3DFD algorithm. A given AI can be easily linked to performance expectations when using the Roofline model methodology. This technique helps when measuring the performance level of a given implementation with respect to its achievable performance on a particular hardware system. A Roofline model sets expectations for what performance gains can be achieved through source code optimization. Once the performance level predicted by a Roofline model has been achieved, performance can only be improved by algorithmic changes.

For any given computer, the hardware specifications define a peak capacity for computing flops and transferring data to and from memory (memory bandwidth). The achievable rate values can be obtained by running standard benchmarks such as the high-performance LINPACK and the Stream Triad benchmarks.

Starting from the most basic implementation of the 3DFD, we describe a methodology to estimate the best performance an algorithm can achieve based on algorithm and hardware characterization.

To obtain performance close to this expected value, we describe a series of tuning steps that range from the baseline version up to an implementation using hardware intrinsic functions. The tuning techniques described here include scalable parallelization (collaborative thread blocking), maximizing memory bandwidth (cache blocking, register reuse), and maximizing in-core performance (vectorization, loop-redistribution).

We then introduce an automatic tuning method to find the optimal set of parameters that might be required at either application build time and/or execution time. Choosing the best set of optimization parameters is difficult because of the many different characteristics of complex computer systems. Tuning parameters derive from manual tuning techniques, domain decomposition influence, compiler capabilities, and the impact of hardware. These parameters usually come from source code changes (e.g., loop blocking values), compiler driven options (e.g., loop unrolling factor), and hardware characteristics (e.g., cache sizes).

Often several dozen tuning parameters emerge—too many for simple trial-and-error search. Automatic tuning is an elegant solution to optimize source codes at compile time and run time. The main idea is to perform optimization of the input parameters and of the compiler flags without any automatic modification of the source code. We want to find a well-tuned set of parameters for a given application, whatever the level of optimization of the source code is.

We describe a *genetic algorithm* (GA) to search the space of available parameters including cache blocking sizes, domain decomposition shapes, prefetching flags, and power consumption. The resulting tuning method is considerably faster than traditional exhaustive search techniques.

From an unoptimized version to the most optimized, we achieved a six-fold performance improvement on Intel® Xeon® E5-2697 v2 processors and a nearly 30-fold improvement on Intel® Xeon Phi™ coprocessors. In addition to performance improvements, our automatic tuning methodology selects an optimal parameter set for any input workloads.

PERFORMANCE EVALUATION

Our *Iso3DFD* kernel solves an acoustic isotropic wave equation which is sixteenth order in space and second order in time. A standard implementation of this 3DFD kernel typically reaches less than 10% of the hardware system's peak floating-point operations per second (Flop/s). In this section, we will review how to obtain a *Roofline model* for the *Iso3DFD* kernel on both the processor and coprocessor. To identify the achievable application performance on a given platform, we require the following performance parameters:

- Theoretical peak computation: 2420 gigaflop per second (GFlop/s) single precision and 352 gigabyte per second (GB/s) for Intel Xeon Phi 7120A coprocessor; 1036 GFlop/s single precision and 119 GB/s for two Intel Xeon E5-2697 v2 processors with 1866 MHz DDR3 memory.
- Achieved values on Linpack (or DGEMM) and Stream Triad benchmarks give us an upper-bound performance for the platforms: 2178 GFlop/s and 200 GB/s for Intel Xeon Phi 7120A coprocessor; 930 GFlop/s and 100 GB/s for two Intel Xeon E5-2697 v2 processors with 1866 MHz DDR3 memory;
- Application AI calculated based on the number of floating-point ADD and MUL and on the amount of bytes transferred from the memory and defined by the number of LOAD and STORE operations.

This last point includes a strong assumption that the hardware has caches of infinite bandwidth and size with zero access latency. This defines a type of perfect memory subsystem where once data in memory is loaded into the cache, it is instantly available without stalling the program execution.

Several other factors may affect the performance of a complete application that would be using such a 3DFD kernel: the choice of boundary conditions, the I/O (input/output) scheme for time reversal, and the parallel programming model. For this analysis, we have not considered either boundary conditions or I/O. Also, a parallel implementation would use a hybrid parallel model combining domain decomposition for distributed memory parallelism using Message Passing Interface (MPI) standard together with shared-memory threading within a hardware node using the OpenMP® API. In this work, we consider a single SMP node processing one domain.

AI OF THE TEST PLATFORMS

Our testing system consisted of two Intel Xeon E5-2697 v2 (2S-E5) with 12 cores per CPU, each running at 2.7 GHz without turbo mode. These processors support the AVX extension with 256-bit SIMD instructions that can process 8 single precision (32 bits) numbers per CPU cycle. Thus the theoretical peak Flop/s is 2.7 (GHz) × 8 (SP FP) × 2 (ADD/MULL) × 12 (cores) × 2 (CPUs) = 1036.8 GFlop/s. The theoretical memory bandwidth is computed from the memory frequency (1866 GHz), the number of channels (4), the number of bytes transferred by channel per cycle (8), which gives 1866 × 4 × 8 × 2 (# of processors) = 119 GByte/s peak bandwidth for the dual socket 2S-E5 system.

We also need to measure real achievable values on the platforms to represent the application behavior. As a first approximation, let us consider that any real world application's performance can be characterized somewhere between totally memory bandwidth bound (represented by Stream Triad) and totally compute or Flop/s bound (represented by Linpack). The choice of these two benchmarks provides a strong hypothesis and we may argue that even if they remain far from ideal reference points, they represent a better approximation than the hardware theoretical peaks because they at least include the minimum overhead required to execute an instruction stream on the processing device.

On the 2S-E5 system, the Linpack benchmark gives 930 GFlop/s and the Stream Triad measures 100 GByte/s. We can then compute the AI for both theoretical (AI_{cpu}^{th}) and achievable peak (AI_{cpu}^{ac}), respectively, as

$$AI_{cpu}^{th} = \frac{1036.8}{119} = 8.7 \text{ Flop / Byte,}$$

and,

$$AI_{cpu}^{ac} = \frac{930}{100} = 9.3 \text{ Flop / Byte.}$$

With the above numbers, we can characterize a given compute kernel as: if the AI of the kernel is greater (respectively lower) than 9.3 Flop/Byte, we may define it as compute bounded (respectively memory bounded). On the Intel Xeon Phi 7120A coprocessors, Linpack and Stream Triad give 2178 GFlop/s and 200 GB/s, respectively, and 2420 GFlop/s, 352 GB/s are the theoretical peaks. Therefore, the arithmetic intensities become

$$AI_{\text{phi}}^{\text{th}} = \frac{2420.5}{352} = 6.87 \text{ Flops / Byte,}$$

and

$$AI_{\text{phi}}^{\text{ac}} = \frac{2178}{200} = 10.89 \text{ Flop / Byte.}$$

AI OF THE KERNEL

The *Roofline model* also requires computing the AI of the given application. This can either be done by counting the number of operations and memory accesses through visual inspection of the code or using dedicated tools accessing the hardware counters. Within standard FD kernels we can find 4 loads (*c*, *prev*, *next*, *vel*), 1 store (*next*), 51 additions (index computations are not accounted for), and 27 multiplications (Figure 23.4). The AI can be computed with the formula:

$$AI = \frac{\#ADD + \#MUL}{(\#LOAD + \#STORE) \times \text{word size}} \qquad (23.1)$$

This gives an AI of 3.9 Flop/Byte that we multiply by each platform memory bandwidth to obtain a first estimate of maximum achievable performance at 1372.8 GFlop/s on the coprocessor and 464.1 GFlop/s on the 2S-E5. However, as the peak flops considers two simultaneous pipelines (one for ADD, the other for MUL) a code that does not have a perfect balance between additions and multiplications will not be able to reach this peak. Therefore, this achievable peak must be weighted by:

$$\frac{(\#ADD + \#MUL)}{2 \times \max(\text{add, mul})} \qquad (23.2)$$

which represents the ratio of the total number of operations that can be done at 16 Flops/cycle over the maximum between the number of ADD and MUL that are done at only 8 ops/cycle assuming only one 256-bit AVX SIMD unit is used. It gives an achievable percentage of the peak Flops/s.

Figures 23.1 and 23.2 show the *Roofline model* with the upper bounds at 354.9 GFlop/s and 1049.8 GFlop/s for the 2S-E5 and for the coprocessor, respectively, as obtained by this weighted version of AI.

A more realistic roofline is obtained using the Stream Triad bandwidth multiplied by the AI of the kernel (390 and 780 GFlops/s, respectively) and even more realistic when considering the the ADD/MUL imbalance (Eq. 23.2) as shown by the line labeled Theoretical Bandwidth.

The new upper bounds are now around 298 GFlop/s for 2S-E5 and 596 GFlop/s on the coprocessor. As our model is based on a perfect cache system, we assume that those numbers are still high upper bounds. As demonstrated, one may also adjust to more realistic upper limits by adding other lower terms in the hardware characterization, such as cache level impact and limitations. The only missing information is the real optimization investment costs to get to those upper limits.

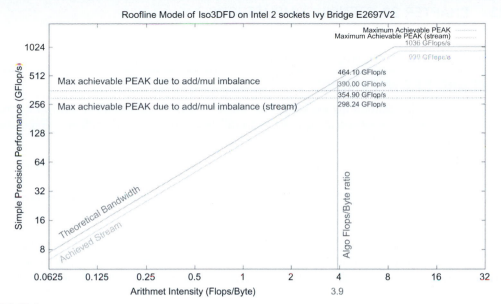

FIGURE 23.1

The Roofline model of Iso3DFD for Ivy Bridge 2S E5-2697 v2. The rooflines are represented here for the upper theoretical and the achievable limits of the platform, respectively. Horizontal lines represent the maximum achievable peaks when considering the ADD/MUL imbalance and when weighted by the Stream Triad bandwidth. The vertical line represents the arithmetic intensity of our Iso3DFD kernel. Intersection with the other lines gives the corresponding achievable limits.

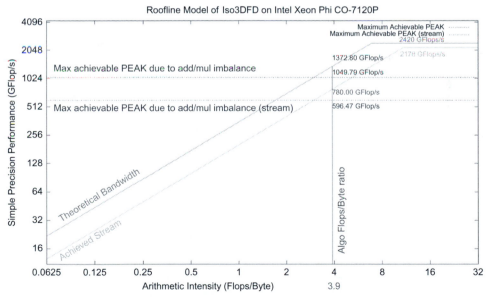

FIGURE 23.2

The Roofline model of Iso3DFD for Intel Xeon Phi 7120A coprocessor. The rooflines are represented here for the upper theoretical and the achievable limits of the platform, respectively. Horizontal lines represent the maximum achievable peaks when considering the ADD/MUL imbalance and when weighted by the Stream Triad bandwidth. The vertical line represents the arithmetic intensity of our Iso3DFD kernel. Intersection with the others lines gives the corresponding achievable limits.

STANDARD OPTIMIZATIONS

Standard optimization denotes the modifications done to improve parallelism, vectorization, and data locality. These three areas represent the most impactful elements on current multicore and many-core architecture optimization. We have implemented these in the following steps:

dev00:   The standard implementation. Pure 3D acoustic isotropic wave equation implementation including results validation (Figure 23.3).

dev01:   dev00 has a conditional branch in the innermost loop to avoid memory access errors on the boundaries. Starting with the AVX instruction set, such branches are implemented using masks, therefore removing the conditional tests does not change the performance on the 2S-E5, while a × 2 speedup can be observed on the coprocessor (Figure 23.11). As a matter of fact, it is always better to avoid branches in multilevel loops in case the copiler cannot perfectly handle it with masks because of the architecture complexity (out of order execution engine in the E5 processor versus in order execution in the coprocessor), instruction set, and vector length (256 versus 512 bits here).

dev02:   Cache blocking reduces the number of cache misses and only requires three new loops (Figure 23.4). The drawback of this technique is that it adds three new parameters controlling the block sizes. Even without optimizing those parameters, the performance is greatly improved here on the coprocessor, especially after remapping the index on the faster dimension from 0 to *ixEnd* to enable vectorization.

dev03:   To ensure that variables are private to the thread and not only to a single iteration we split the *#pragma omp parallel* and the *#pragma omp for* directives, properly declaring the private variables in between the two OMP clauses.

dev04:   The **#pragma ivdep** directive can be used to provide a hint to the vectorizer that the array variables within the loop are not aliased (assuming aliasing is the default behavior of the C/C++ compiler). Enabling vectorization can also be done by specifying compiler flags (-fno-alias) or by using C/C++ pragmas or Fortran directives. A riskier approach is to use the **#pragma simd**

```
for(int iz=0; iz<n3; iz++) {
for(int iy=0; iy<n2; iy++) {
for(int ix=0; ix<n1; ix++) {
  if((iz>=HALF_LENGTH && iz < n3-HALF_LENGTH) &&
     (iy>=HALF_LENGTH && iy < n2-HALF_LENGTH) &&
     (ix>=HALF_LENGTH && ix < n1-HALF_LENGTH)){
    int off = iz*n1n2 + iy*n1 + ix;
    float v = 0.0;
   v += prev[offset]*c[0];
    for(int ir=1; ir<=HALF_LENGTH; ir++) {
      v+=c[ir]*(prev[off+ir] + prev[off-ir]);
      v+=c[ir]*(prev[off+ir*n1] + prev[off-ir*n1]);
      v+=c[ir]*(prev[off+ir*n1n2] + prev[off-ir*n1n2]);
    }
    next[off] = 2.0f*prev[off]-next[off]+v*vel[off];
  }
}
}
```

FIGURE 23.3

Source code of the kernel without optimization (dev00).

```
for(int bz=HALF_LENGTH; bz<n3; bz+=n3_Tblock)
for(int by=HALF_LENGTH; by<n2; by+=n2_Tblock)
for(int bx=HALF_LENGTH; bx<n1; bx+=n1_Tblock) {
  int izEnd = MIN(bz+n3_Tblock, n3);
  int iyEnd = MIN(by+n2_Tblock, n2);
  int ixEnd = MIN(n1_Tblock, n1-bx);
  int ix;
  for(int iz=bz; iz<izEnd; iz++) {
  for(int iy=by; iy<iyEnd; iy++) {
    float* next = ptr_next_base + iz*n1n2 + iy*n1 + bx;
    float* prev = ptr_prev_base + iz*n1n2 + iy*n1 + bx;
    float* vel = ptr_vel_base + iz*n1n2 + iy*n1 + bx;
    for(int ix=0; ix<ixEnd; ix++) {
      float value = 0.0;
      value += prev[ix]*c[0];
      for(int ir=1; ir<=HALF_LENGTH; ir++) {
        value += c[ir] * (prev[ix + ir] + prev[ix    ir]);
        value += c[ir] * (prev[ix + ir*n1] + prev[ix - ir*n1]);
        value += c[ir] * (prev[ix + ir*n1n2] + prev[ix - ir*n1n2]);
      }
      next[ix] = 2.0f* prev[ix] - next[ix] + value*vel[ix];
    }
  }
}}}
```

FIGURE 23.4

Source code of the kernel with cache blocking (dev02).

directive which forces the vectorization but may lead to incorrect results if either aliasing or dependencies remain in the code.

dev05: Even if the compiler reports vectorized loops, enabling AVX (ymm registers) may be difficult, therefore, manual unrolling in association with directives as **__assume_aligned** can improve AVX vectorization (Figure 23.5). We created a C macro named CACHELINE_BYTES (equal to 64) to clarify the implementation (Figure 23.5).

dev06: The factorization of the FD coefficients (c1, c2, etc.) removes two MUL operations for each coefficient (Figure 23.6). On 2S-E5, this change may decrease the performance because it increases imbalance between multiplications and additions. However, with the coprocessor's in-order microarchitecture, removing the extra instruction has a direct increase on the performance as shown in Figure 23.11.

dev07: Nonuniform memory accesses (NUMA) are a well-known characteristic on multisocket platforms. For current operating systems, a typical dynamic memory allocation (e.g., **_mm_ malloc**) reserves the amount of space requested but the actual physical memory is only defined (or mapped) the first time the variable is written/read. This *first touch* policy, together with well-defined thread or process affinitization, enables developers to allocate physical memory pages in the same NUMA node in which the thread that consumes the memory page is running. The placement is done when data are first initialized within a parallel region that reproduces the same data splitting used later during the multithread computations. This optimization greatly improves the 2S-E5 results (Figure 23.11).

dev08: To optimize the use of registers, this version makes use of C/C++ support for hardware intrinsics programming. The drawback of this approach is that it makes the implementation more

```
__assume_aligned(ptr_next , CACHELINE_BYTES);
__assume_aligned(ptr_prev , CACHELINE_BYTES);
__assume_aligned(ptr_vel , CACHELINE_BYTES);
#pragma ivdep
for(int ix=0; ix<ixEnd; ix++) {
  v = prev[ix]*c0
  + c1 * FINITE_ADD(ix, 1)
  + c1 * FINITE_ADD(ix, vertical_1)
  + c1 * FINITE_ADD(ix, front_1)
  + c2 * FINITE_ADD(ix, 2)
  + c2 * FINITE_ADD(ix, vertical_2)
  + c2 * FINITE_ADD(ix, front_2)
  + c3 * FINITE_ADD(ix, 3)
  + c3 * FINITE_ADD(ix, vertical_3)
  + c3 * FINITE_ADD(ix, front_3)
  + c4 * FINITE_ADD(ix, 4)
  + c4 * FINITE_ADD(ix, vertical_4)
  + c4 * FINITE_ADD(ix, front_4)
  + c5 * FINITE_ADD(ix, 5)
  + c5 * FINITE_ADD(ix, vertical_5)
  + c5 * FINITE_ADD(ix, front_5)
  + c6 * FINITE_ADD(ix, 6)
  + c6 * FINITE_ADD(ix, vertical_6)
  + c6 * FINITE_ADD(ix, front_6)
  + c7 * FINITE_ADD(ix, 7)
  + c7 * FINITE_ADD(ix, vertical_7)
  + c7 * FINITE_ADD(ix, front_7)
  + c8 * FINITE_ADD(ix, 8)
  + c8 * FINITE_ADD(ix, vertical_8)
  + c8 * FINITE_ADD(ix, front_8)

  next[ix] = 2.0f* prev[ix] -   next[ix] + v*vel[ix];
}
```

FIGURE 23.5

Source code of the kernel dev04 and dev05. Here FINITE_ADD is a macro for the symmetric FD of the type `v[ix+off]+v[ix-off]`.

complicated and also multiple versions might be required due to differences in instruction sets. Thanks to C macros, the code can remain readable as shown in Figure 23.7. This optimization has more impact on the coprocessor than on 2S-E5 as shown in Figure 23.11. This is because on the coprocessor, the SHIFT_MULT_INTR is implemented with the instruction **_mm512_alignr_epi32** allowing a right shift on 32 bits values (single precision). Therefore, the finite difference on the faster dimension can be computed for a single vector with only three loads as shown on the Figures 23.8 and 23.9.

We are currently investigating the use of AVX2 instructions to enable equivalent optimization on the new Intel Xeon E5-2600 v3 architecture. We hope to provide some updated information on this investigation on http://lotsofcores.com in the future.

```
__assume_aligned(ptr_next, CACHELINE_BYTES);
__assume_aligned(ptr_prev, CACHELINE_BYTES);
__assume_aligned(ptr_vel, CACHELINE_BYTES);
#pragma ivdep
for(int ix=0; ix<ixEnd; ix++) {
  v = prev[ix]*c0
  + c1 * (  FINITE_ADD(ix, 1)
          + FINITE_ADD(ix, vertical_1)
          + FINITE_ADD(ix, front_1))
  + c2 * (  FINITE_ADD(ix, 2)
          + FINITE_ADD(ix, vertical_2)
          + FINITE_ADD(ix, front_2))
  + c3 * (  FINITE_ADD(ix, 3)
          + FINITE_ADD(ix, vertical_3)
          + FINITE_ADD(ix, front_3))
   ......
   ......

  next[ix] = 2.0f* prev[ix] -   next[ix] + v*vel[ix];
}
```

FIGURE 23.6

Part of the kernel on dev06.

```
#pragma ivdep
for(TYPE_INTEGER ix=0;ix<ixEnd; ix+=SIMD_STEP){
  SHIFT_MULT_INIT
  SHIFT_MULT_INTR(1)
  SHIFT_MULT_INTR(2)
  SHIFT_MULT_INTR(3)
  SHIFT_MULT_INTR(4)
  SHIFT_MULT_INTR(5)
  SHIFT_MULT_INTR(6)
  SHIFT_MULT_INTR(7)
  SHIFT_MULT_INTR(8)

  MUL_COEFF_INTR(vertical_1, front_1, coeffVec[1])
  MUL_COEFF_INTR(vertical_2, front_2, coeffVec[2])
  MUL_COEFF_INTR(vertical_3, front_3, coeffVec[3])
  MUL_COEFF_INTR(vertical_4, front_4, coeffVec[4])
  MUL_COEFF_INTR(vertical_5, front_5, coeffVec[5])
  MUL_COEFF_INTR(vertical_6, front_6, coeffVec[6])
  MUL_COEFF_INTR(vertical_7, front_7, coeffVec[7])
  MUL_COEFF_INTR(vertical_8, front_8, coeffVec[8])

  REFRESH_NEXT_INTR
}
```

FIGURE 23.7

Macros that are implemented with intrinsics in dev08.

FIGURE 23.8

Fast dimension vectorization on the coprocessor (coefficient c0).

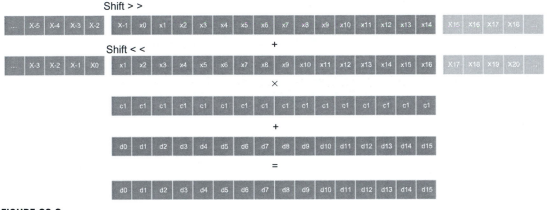

FIGURE 23.9

Fast dimension vectorization on the coprocessor (coefficient c1).

For the other two dimensions, vectorization is simpler. For a single coefficient, we only need four loads and then the vectors are summed and multiplied by the coefficient (Figure 23.10). This is accomplished within the macro MUL_COEFF_INTR (Figure 23.12).

dev09: On the coprocessor we can reduce the number of temporary variables and the register pressure if using the FMA instructions (fused multiply add). The coefficient can be stored in the same register throughout the computations (6 FMAs) and each FMA result is directly sent to the next set of computations limiting the data movement between registers (Figure 23.11). Investigation of FMA usage on AVX2 is ongoing.

AUTOMATIC APPLICATION TUNING

As microarchitectures become more complex, compilers are also becoming more difficult to use due to a growing number of tuning flags and pragmas or directives. While a few tuning parameters can be handled manually, working with a multidimensional parameter space can be made easier through mathematical optimization.

For that purpose, we are developing an automatic tuning framework based on GA optimization. Our tool acts as a compiler and uses the GA to find an efficient set of parameters.

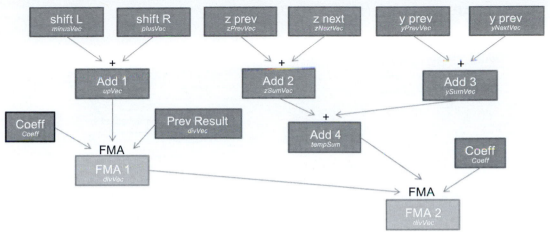

FIGURE 23.10

Operations process on dev08 for a single coefficient.

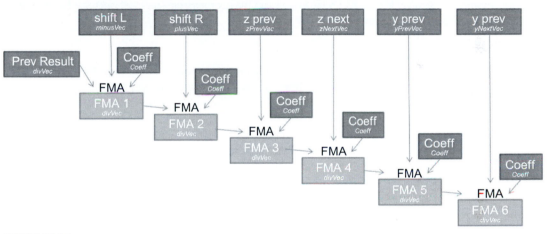

FIGURE 23.11

Operations process on dev09 for a single coefficient.

	Ivy Bridge		Coprocessor	
	GFlop/s	Peak %	GFlop/s	Peak %
dev00	36.73	3.95	12.32	0.57
dev01	35.97	3.87	22.36	1.03
dev02	42.49	4.57	141.88	6.51
dev03	42.58	4.58	147.90	6.79
dev04	45.16	4.86	148.14	6.80
dev05	90.45	9.73	156.14	6.45
dev06	91.58	9.85	182.39	8.37
dev07	137.96	14.83	176.09	8.08
dev08	125.40	13.48	208.46	9.57
dev09	132.48	14.25	208.97	9.59
dev09+GA	226.27	24.33	368.46	16.92

FIGURE 23.12

Performance in GFlop/s for ECC off/Turbo on for the coprocessor and Turbo on for Ivy Bridge.

FIGURE 23.13

The performance of each version on 2S-E5 Ivy Bridge and the coprocessor. The most optimized version *dev09* is also improved after genetic-algorithm auto-tuning.

Choosing the right technique for such an optimization problem is not straightforward and publications noted in Section "For more information" at the end of this chapter, such as as "Introduction to Stochastic Search and Optimization" (James, 2013) or "Metaheuristics—The Metaphor Exposed" (Sörensen, 2013), may help to better understand the quality of the metaheuristic research fields and of the stochastic optimization in general. Also we have provided links to open source library implementations of GA for creating similar frameworks.

Our objective was to select an optimization algorithm able to get to a good solution in the case of incomplete and imperfect information with less computational effort. As with any non-exhaustive optimization algorithm or iterative method such as simulated annealing, there is no guarantee that a global optimal solution will be found.

Many metaheuristics implement some form of stochastic optimization, so that the solution found is dependent on the set of random variables generated. The GA targets discrete and combinatorial optimization problems such as our 3DFD case.

A GA manipulates populations. Ideally, a GA selects the best individuals of a generation and creates a new generation including individuals with better characteristics than the previous generations. In our case, the first generation is randomly created and used for producing the second generation. This process can be repeated for as many generations as needed. A population is composed of individuals and an individual is described by a set of attributes such as compiler optimization flags, an unrolling factor, execution domain, cache block sizes, MPI domain shapes and size, power consumption, and so on.

We consider the original sizes of the input fields (velocities, density, anisotropic parameters) to be fixed since they are coming from prior processing steps. When distributing one or several seismic shot gathers per node, these input sizes cannot be changed. However, when considering a domain decomposition implementation, we can optimize the domain sizes per shared-memory nodes. For creating a new generation, the GA is articulated around four major concepts (Figure 23.14):

Evaluation: For each individual, an evaluation criterion must be provided. This evaluation criterion is called *fitness*. We may want to reduce the elapsed time (low evaluation of the fitness) or to increase the GFlop/s (high evaluation of the fitness).

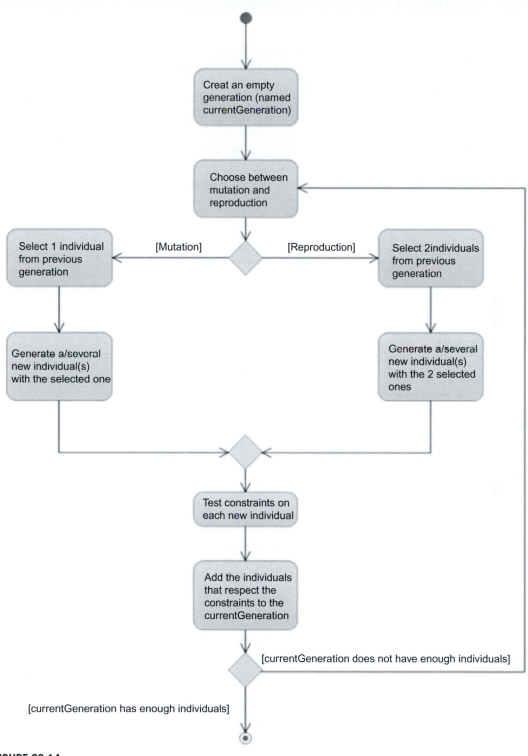

FIGURE 23.14

General flowchart of the genetic algorithm optimization. In our case we use evaluation criteria based on elapsed time reduction.

Selection: The selection allows us to choose some individuals among the existing ones for reproduction or mutation. The selection must favor the best individuals but must also select some "bad" individuals in order to avoid an overly quick convergence to a local optimum. Most of the time, selection is based on a random choice moderated by a nonuniform distribution. The *wheel selection* distributes the individuals with regard to their fitness (Figure 23.15). Therefore, an individual with a higher fitness has more chance to be selected than an individual with a lower one. The first step is to evaluate the fitness of each individual and the next step is to sort the individuals by their fitness. As a last step, a random number is picked between 0 and the sum of all individual fitness. The individuals are then superimposed and the one for which the fitness matches is selected.

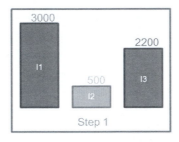

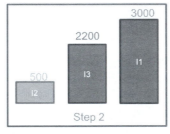

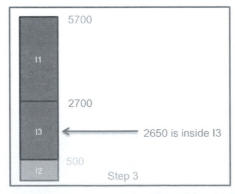

FIGURE 23.15

Description of the wheel selection which distributes the individuals in regard to their fitness. The selection favors the best individuals but must also select some "bad" individuals in order to avoid an overly quick convergence to a local optimum. In this case, in step 3, 2650 is a random number that selects Individual I3.

Reproduction: Reproduction is the process that allows the GA to converge toward a better solution. Two or more individuals from the previous generation(s) are merged to create one or more new individuals using a pivot technique. Given two parents, the pivot represents the index used for splitting and combining the attributes in a new individual. First we randomly choose the number of pivots, then we randomly choose the indexes for each pivots (Figure 23.16).

Mutation: Mutation ensures the exploration of the parameter space and avoid a too quick convergence to a local optimum. Here we randomly choose the attributes to modify and assign them some random values (Figure 23.17).

Among the four steps above describing the GA, the most compute intensive remains the **evaluation** step in which we build and run the application for each trial. This is a key point for any search algorithm because the time needed to evaluate a given set of parameters will also impact the choice of the optimization technique. As shown in Figure 23.18, we may need several thousands of trials and that would not be possible if the test case was not short enough even if our GA is running in parallel mode.

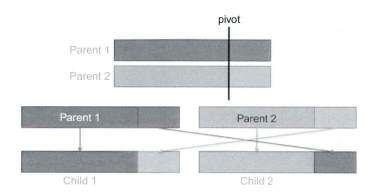

FIGURE 23.16

Illustration of the reproduction with one pivot. Reproduction is the process that allows the genetic algorithm to converge toward a better solution. Given two parents, the pivot represents the index used for splitting and combining the attributes in a new individual. First we randomly choose the number of pivots, then we randomly choose the indexes for each pivots.

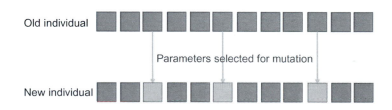

FIGURE 23.17

Illustration of the mutation. Mutation ensures the exploration of the parameter space and avoid a premature convergence to a local optimum.

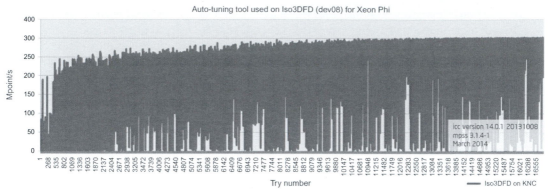

FIGURE 23.18

Auto-tuning tool used for optimizing the parameters of Iso3DFD on the coprocessor

For time-stepping applications where the same computation (intensively speaking) is done for each iteration, we can then reduce the number of time steps to evaluate the impact of the parameter tuning. A minimum number of iteration remain mandatory to leverage the impact of any initialization phase and to be sure that no cache effects impact the search.

Pragmatically speaking, we are in the same situation when doing optimization or benchmarking. The choice of the adequate test cases is extremely important to ensure any modifications would not take more than a minute or so to evaluate, but will remain representative of the application behaviors. Working in a single node is enough to work on the main parameters (cache block, compiler flags, etc.) and even on the MPI domain decomposition shape impacting the intranode communications. The same technique can be used at the cluster level to optimize the impact of domain decomposition shape or to tune the MPI default environment variable. The key would again remain the duration of a single representative test. Another approach to decreasing convergence time is to evaluate several individuals in parallel over a number of computing systems.

THE AUTO-TUNING TOOL

We are developing a tool to optimize the build and execution process of a program. Our auto-tuning tool uses a configuration file that allows us to:

- describe the project (path, working directory, number of generations, number of individuals, etc.);
- describe a set of "nodes." For each node, a thread is created on the machine that runs the auto-tuning tool. This thread launches the compilation and the program execution to optimize multiple nodes in parallel;
- define variables (`int`, `float`, `stringset`) and their allowed values that are used in the other parts of the configuration file; for example:
```
int v1[1, 100, 5]
float v2[0.1, 12.6]
stringset v3["This", "is", "an", "example"]
```

- Add background knowledge under the form of constraints or *a priori* information. An individual can be added to the current generation only if it satisfies all the constraints. Here is an example with a constraint that guaranties that n1, n2, and n3 will satisfy $n1 \times n2 \times n3 < 100,000$:

```
begin constraints
  n1*n2*n3 < 100000
end constraints
```

- define exports that are added to the bash environment before calling the compilation and execution scripts;
- setup and combine compilation or execution calls as,

```
begin buildcall
  "make clean; make"
end buildcall
begin programcall
  "./run_on_mic.pl";"bin/iso3dfd.exe";NODE;n1;n2;n3;cb1;cb2;cb3;nbThreads
end programcall
```

- Indicate a regular expression to retrieve the fitness from the program output. In our case, Iso3DFD outputs the speed in GFlop/s. The regex syntax uses Perl. The following sample shows how to match a numeric output in Iso3DFD.

```
begin regex
  "speed:\s*([0-9\.]+)\s*GFlop\/s"
end regex
```

RESULTS

Figure 23.13 presents the performance results on a $n1 = 256$, $n2 = 200$, and $n3 = 400$ dataset for the incremental code change optimizations on the 10 versions (*dev00* to *dev09*). Here we achieve about 6x to 30x improvement on 2S-E5 (24 threads) and on the coprocessor (244 threads), respectively, The auto-tuning tool has been applied only to the version *dev09* for clarity and it provided an extra 2x improvement compared to the original *dev09* version. Figure 23.18 shows the performance in GFlop/s for each auto-tuning tool attempt (higher is better). The overall performance increases progressively up to more than 350 GFlop/s. Figure 23.19 shows the parameters generated by the auto-tuning tool that provide improved performance results for dev02, dev07, and dev09+GA.

We reached about 70% and 60% of the achievable performance on 2S-E5 and the coprocessor, respectively, as defined in Section "Performance evaluation." This is a good result considering that the perfect cache assumption to develop our *Roofline model*. The efficiency is slightly less on the coprocessor due to the in-order microarchitecture and the larger number of threads. Typically, any of the optimizations impacted both platforms, but we notice that on the coprocessor, the most impactful were:

- Cache blocking and vectorization
- Instruction reduction with the factorization of the kernel
- Intrinsics

while on the 2S-E5, the best impact came from:

- manual unrolling and _assume_aligned directives
- first touch

Version	Platform	GA	Loop order	Affinity	Opti	Prefetching	nx	ny	nz	cbx	cby	cbz	#threads	Performance (Gflop/s)
Dev02	2 Sockets E2697 V2	No	"-DBLOCK_Z_Y_X"	compact	"-O3"	Not used	400	400	400	400	40	40	24	42.49
		Yes	"-DBLOCK_Y_X_Z"	compact	"-O3"	"-opt-prefetch-distance=84,48"	272	1105	1452	1392	12	199	24	48.16
	Xeon Phi 7120 C0	No	"-DBLOCK_Z_Y_X"	balanced	"-O3"	Not used	400	400	400	400	4	40	244	141.88
		Yes	"-DBLOCK_Z_X_Y"	balanced	"-O2"	"-opt-prefetch-distance=4,2"	368	316	1403	1488	3	12	183	217.39
Dev07	2 Sockets E2697 V2	No	"-DBLOCK_Z_Y_X"	scatter	"-O3"	Not used	256	256	256	256	2	40	24	137.96
		Yes	"-DBLOCK_Z_Y_X"	compact	"-O3"	"-opt-prefetch-distance=88,14"	208	1227	1305	1216	49	70	24	217.38
	Xeon Phi 7120 C0	No	"-DBLOCK_Z_Y_X"	balanced	"-O3"	Not used	400	400	400	400	4	40	244	176.09
		Yes	"-DBLOCK_X_Y_Z"	balanced	"-O3"	"-opt-prefetch-distance=4,2"	416	278	1427	1184	3	9	183	248.46
Dev09	2 Sockets E2697 V2	Yes	"-DBLOCK_X_Y_Z"	scatter	"-O3"	"-opt-prefetch-distance=78,24"	224	1222	1405	1376	48	93	24	132.48
		Yes	"-DBLOCK_X_Y_Z"	compact	"-O3"	"-opt-prefetch-distance=78,24"	224	1222	1405	1376	48	93	24	226.27
	Xeon Phi 7120 C0	No	"-DBLOCK_X_Y_X"	balanced	"-O3"	Not used	400	400	400	400	4	40	240	208.97
		Yes	"-DBLOCK_X_Z_Y"	balaced	"-O3"	Directly in Intrinsics	400	388	1432	400	2	48	244	368.46

FIGURE 23.19

Parameters generated by the GA auto-tuning tool for optimization steps dev02, dev07 and dev09+GA.

SUMMARY

Apart from discussing performance improvement techniques, the most important takeaway from this chapter is the three-step methodology for ensuring high efficiency:

- Estimate the best achievable performance, even before starting tuning.
- Tune the code for parallelism, data locality, and vectorization.
- Auto-tune the best set of parameters for both the building and the running-time phases.

Building a strategy to improve the performance is a complicated task which should not be started without a perfect knowledge of the application capabilities with respect to a given computing platform. It does not make sense to optimize a code by only referring to the total elapsed time without any idea of the best achievable performance, while computing a Roofline model is straightforward. Once done, the most time consuming tasks will of course remain in the manual optimizations phase. Many well-established strategies exist as the iterative top-down approach (see for example https://software.intel.com/en-us/articles/de-mystifying-software-performance-optimization).

We always have to keep in mind that at a first-order approximation, most of the high-performance scientific applications are in between the Flops/s and the Bytes/s limits, so called cpu and bandwidth bounds, at least at the node level. When moving to the cluster scale, the key factor to keep in mind are very well summarized by the Amdahl's law and by the need for perfect or dynamic load balancing to compensate for any workload or hardware imbalance.

Going deeper into the code, the vectorization (that may be called "SIMDization") of the code will play another mandatory role to achieve the best performance. But again, making the most of SIMD capability will rely on the FP and bandwidth capability of the platform.

After the "best optimizations" for parallelism have been implemented, we believe automated tuning will become a mandatory step to extract the best performance from computing systems. Once again, the definition of "best optimization" can be based on several other criteria than just simple performance ones. When we can position the application on its Roofline model, we are then able to estimate what would be the costs of pushing optimization further. If we refer to the ten versions of the same 3DFD kernel presented in this chapter, it is fairly clear that the development and the maintenance costs will differ between the original dev00 version and the intrinsics dev09 version.

Once the choice has been made based for example on industrial or R&D criteria, the use of an automatic tuning tool to get the optimal parameters without modifying the source code is a very elegant and easy way to extract considerable improvements, keeping portability and maintainability of the code. Also note, it is not necessary to run the GA auto-tuning tool for every change or code run, but only when the hardware or workload characteristics change significantly.

FOR MORE INFORMATION

Sörensen, K., 2013. Metaheuristics—the metaphor exposed. International Transactions in Operational Research. http://dx.doi.org/10.1111/itor.12001.

Spall, J.C., 2003. Introduction to Stochastic Search and Optimization, first ed. John Wiley & Sons, Inc., New York, NY.

Williams, S., Waterman, A., Patterson, D., 2009. Roofline: an insightful visual performance model for multicore architectures. Communications of the ACM. 52 (4), 65–76 http://doi.acm.org/10.1145/1498765.1498785.

A large variety of genetic algorithm software can be found on http://www.geneticprogramming.com/ga/GAsoftware.html and http://www.cs.cmu.edu/afs/cs/project/ai-repository/ai/areas/genetic/ga/systems/0.html.

Several genetic algorithm libraries for different programming languages can be found at http://geneticalgorithms.ai-depot.com/Libraries.html.

Download all codes from this, and other chapters, http://lotsofcores.com.

PROFILING-GUIDED OPTIMIZATION

24

Andrey Vladimirov
Colfax International, USA

Profiling-guided optimization is a method of increasing developer productivity through the use of application performance analysis (profiling) tools. Based on the reports of the profiling tool, the programmer learns where to make changes in the source code to improve application performance on processors and coprocessors. General-purpose profilers are well known for their ability to identify parts of the code that take the most time, "hotspots." In addition, a profiler with support for hardware-based performance event collection, such as Intel® VTune™ Amplifier XE, can point the programmer to general issues limiting application performance: lack of parallelism, load imbalance, long latency operations, etc.

This chapter demonstrates profiling-guided optimization on Intel architectures. The example code involves memory and cache traffic tuning in the problem of in-place square matrix transposition. Matrix transposition is a building block in a number of computational problems, including discrete fast Fourier transforms, numerical methods in linear algebra, image processing, and computational fluid dynamics. Because transposition involves no arithmetic operations, its performance is dependent upon the optimization of processor access to the memory and cache bandwidth. We demonstrate transposition bandwidth improvement through optimization of data locality (loop tiling and recursion), regularization of memory access pattern, and exposing additional parallelism. Our work is guided by the profiler Intel VTune Amplifier XE, which determines the strategies for optimization based on performance event collection on an Intel® Xeon® processor and an Intel® Xeon Phi™ coprocessor. Results and methods of this exercise are applicable to multicore Intel processor (CPU)-based platforms, as well as platforms based on many-core Intel Xeon Phi coprocessors, which use the Intel Many Integrated Core (MIC) architecture.

MATRIX TRANSPOSITION IN COMPUTER SCIENCE

The computational challenge that serves as test case for our discussion of profiling-guided optimization is matrix transposition. Transposition rearranges elements of a two-dimensional array so that rows become columns and columns become rows. This operation is commonly used to precondition multi-dimensional arrays in order to allow numerical algorithms to access data contiguously, rather than with a stride. For instance, in linear algebraic operations such as xGEMM, optimized implementations may transpose some of the operands in order to access data contiguously. Transposition is the basis of some of the methods of discrete fast Fourier transforms (see "The design and implementation of FFTW3" in "For more information" at the end of this chapter). Computational fluid dynamics uses transposition of multidimensional arrays, for example, in solvers represented by stencils that are applied in each of multiple array dimensions (see "A free, fast, simple and efficient total variation diminishing magneto-hydrodynamic code" in "For more information" at the end of this chapter). However, in order to be useful for preparing data to accelerate other algorithms, the transposition operation itself must be efficient.

This chapter's discussion is limited to optimization of in-place transpositions of square matrices in shared memory. In-place means that the result of transposition overwrites the original data, and a shared-memory transposition algorithm operates on data stored in a single compute node rather than distributed across a cluster. The discussion is restricted to square matrices; rectangular matrix transposition is a more complex problem; however, it can also benefit from accelerated computing (see "In-place transposition of rectangular matrices on accelerators" in "For more information" at the end of this chapter).

Mathematically, transposition is expressed by the following equation:

$$A_{ij} = A_{ji}, \quad i = 0, 1, \ldots, (n-1), \quad j = 0, 1, \ldots, (n-1)$$

In computer memory, matrix A is typically stored in a format where the address of the element A_{ij} is offset from the beginning of the matrix by $(i \times n + j)$ (the row-major format) or by $(j * n + i)$ (column-major format). Without loss of generality, either method can be discussed.

The difficulty with transposition of a matrix in row-major storage is that Intel Xeon processors and Intel Xeon Phi coprocessors achieve optimal memory performance by moving data in 64-byte chunks called cache lines. If double precision numbers (8 bytes each) are used, each cache line contains eight matrix elements. Therefore, even when only one matrix element is used by the application, this element is fetched from memory along with seven adjacent matrix elements. This is good only if all of the eight elements in the cache line are subsequently used by the core to perform computation or data rearrangement. However, if memory access pattern is such that the core uses only one element in a cache line and then proceeds to fetch data from other cache lines, the processor will have to move eight times more data than necessary. It is easy to see that this may occur in the transposition algorithm. Consider swapping the several elements A_{ij} and A_{ji} for a matrix in row-major format. If the algorithm contiguously increases the index j, then accesses to A_{ij}, $A_{i(j+1)}$, $A_{i(j+2)}$, etc. can all hit the same cache line, however, the corresponding A_{ji}, $A_{(j+1)i}$, $A_{(j+2)i}$ will all hit different cache lines (assuming double precision and $n > 8$). A similar argument applies if the algorithm contiguously increases the index i and/or matrix storage is column-major. This access pattern is illustrated in Figure 24.1.

Of course, processor caches can improve data access latency the next time that a cache line is used. For instance, when the algorithm swaps $(A_{i0} \leftrightarrow A_{0i})$, the cache line containing $\{A_{0i}, A_{0(i+1)}, \ldots, A_{0(i+7)}\}$ is loaded into processor caches. If the algorithm subsequently swaps $(A_{i1} \leftrightarrow A_{1i})$, $(A_{i2} \leftrightarrow A_{2i})$, etc., the data in the cache line $\{A_{0i}, A_{0(i+1)}, \ldots, A_{0(i+7)}\}$ is not reused. However, by the time the algorithm reaches the pair $(A_{i(n-1)} \leftrightarrow A_{(n-1)i})$ and proceeds to swap $(A_{(i+1)0} \leftrightarrow A_{0(i+1)})$, the second element in that cache line can be reused. If the cache line is still in cache, data access time will be shorter than if it was in the main memory.

Naturally, in order for caches to work effectively, the algorithm must be cache-aware. Specifically, if matrix size n is large enough, then by the time the algorithm traverses elements from A_{i0} to $A_{i(n-1)}$, the cache line containing A_{0i} will no longer be in processor caches. So, when the algorithm swaps the elements $(A_{(i+1)0} \leftrightarrow A_{0(i+1)})$, the processor will have to read the cache line containing A_{0i} from main memory again. A smarter algorithm should reuse that cache line sooner while it is still in cache.

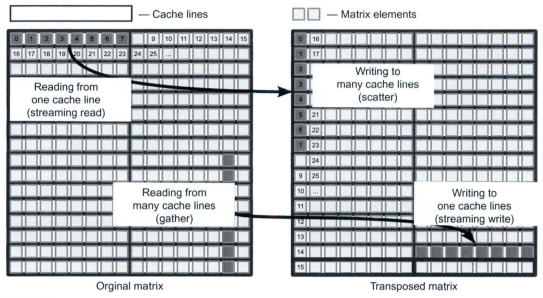

FIGURE 24.1

Transposing a matrix in a row-major format. As the algorithm traverses the data, scattered memory accesses will occur, causing the processor to touch multiple cache lines, but use only one of the eight matrix elements in each cache line.

The challenges discussed above are encountered and resolved in subsequent sections with the help of a performance profiling tool.

TOOLS AND METHODS

Even though the aim of this chapter is to create a portable, future-proof code, the evolution of software tools and microprocessors may change the results and best-known methods presented here. For the sake of reproducibility, below is a summary of the system configuration used in this work.

All examples shown below are executed on a Colfax SXP7450 workstation (see "For more information" at the end of this chapter), which is based on an Intel Xeon E5-2630 v2 two-way processor (a total of 12 physical cores at 2.6 GHz) with 128 GB of DDR3 RAM at 1066 MHz. There are two Intel Xeon Phi 3120A coprocessors in the system, each with 57 cores at 1.1 GHz and 6 GB of GDDR3 RAM. The system is running CentOS Linux 6.5 with kernel 2.6.32-431.el6.x86_64 and MPSS 3.2.3. Intel C++ Compiler XE version 14.0.2.144 (Build 20140120) and Intel VTune Amplifier XE 2013 Update 15 (Build 328102) are used.

We report the performance of transposition as bandwidth, in the units of GB/s. This bandwidth is calculated as

$$P = \frac{2 \times \text{size of (double)} \times n \times n}{10^9 \times T} \text{ GB/s,}$$

where n is the matrix size; the factor 2 accounts for the fact that in the course of transposition, $n \times n$ matrix elements are read from memory and the same number is then written to memory; size of (double)=8 bytes, the number 10^9 is the conversion factor from bytes per second to GB/s; and T is the transposition time in seconds. This metric is convenient because it allows comparison of achieved performance to its theoretical maximum set, for example, by the STREAM benchmark.

All performance results shown below are obtained by compiling different versions of the transposition code with the same set of compiler arguments: "-O3 -g -fopenmp." The argument "-O3" requests the highest optimization level, "-g" embeds code symbols into executable for use in VTune, and "-fopenmp" links the Intel OpenMP library for parallelism. Additionally, for native coprocessor applications, the argument "-mmic" is used.

"SERIAL": OUR ORIGINAL IN-PLACE TRANSPOSITION

In order to establish a baseline (and, in fact, to start with something simple), a C language code for in-place transposition of a square matrix is shown in Figure 24.2. In the source code archive for this chapter (lotsofcores.com), this corresponds to Step 1.

Here and in the rest of this chapter, the transposition routine is benchmarked using a matrix of size $n=4000$. In double precision, a 4000×4000 matrix is 122 MB in size, which is much larger than the 30 MB last level cache of the dual-socket CPU-based system, and also larger than the aggregate 28.5 MB Level-2 cache of the coprocessor. The benchmark procedure involves multiple calls to the transposition function. The first two calls are not included in the timing statistics as illustrated in Figure 24.3.

This code is benchmarked on the Intel Xeon processor and on the Intel Xeon Phi coprocessor in the native mode. Native mode means that the code is compiled with the argument "-mmic," after which the executable is copied to the coprocessor file system and executed there (see "Parallel Programming and Optimization with Intel Xeon Phi Coprocessors" in "For more information" at the end of this chapter).

The mean measured performance is shown in Figure 24.27 for this example and all subsequent code optimization examples. The results for the code in Figure 24.2 are reported in the bars labeled "Serial." On the host, the achieved performance is 4.3 GB/s while the coprocessor delivers a significantly lower 0.7 GB/s.

```
#define FTYPE double

void Transpose(FTYPE* const A, const int n) {
  for (int j = 0; j < n; j++) {
    for (int i = 0; i < j; i++) {
      const FTYPE c = A[i*n + j];
      A[i*n + j] = A[j*n + i];
      A[j*n + i] = c;
    }
  }
}
```

FIGURE 24.2

Serial implementation of in-place square matrix transposition.

```
const int nTrials = atoi(argv[2]);
const int skipTrials = 2;
for (int iTrial = 0; iTrial < nTrials; iTrial++) {
        // Perform and time the transposition operation
        const double t0 = omp_get_wtime();
        Transpose(A, n);
        const double t1 = omp_get_wtime();
        if (iTrial >= skipTrials)
                t[iTrial] = t1-t0; // Record benchmark result
}
```

FIGURE 24.3

Timing procedure performs multiple trials, excludes the first two from timing statistics.

Not only is it disappointing that the performance on the Intel Xeon Phi coprocessor is dwarfed by the performance on the processor but also the absolute value of this performance is very low compared to the STREAM benchmark "Copy" test. (The STREAM benchmark test suite is the industry reference for memory bandwidth performance.) On the benchmark system, we compiled and ran STREAM using the code and methods found in "For more information" given at the end of this chapter. In our tests, the processor (CPU) achieved 53.5 GB/s while the coprocessor ran significantly faster to deliver 124.8 GB/s.

The poor performance by the coprocessor on Figure 24.2 example code is readily explained by noting that this code is serial, meaning it only runs on one thread on one core even when hyper-threading is enabled. As a result, only a fraction of the available hardware memory bandwidth is utilized.

While the serial nature of the code in Figure 24.2 is easy to observe, a sequential bottleneck may be much more difficult to detect in more complex codes. For this reason, we will set up an Intel VTune Amplifier XE (hereafter, "VTune") project to learn how to detect serialization in a multithreaded environment.

In this chapter, the VTune GUI (Graphical User Interface) will be used to collect and analyze performance data. In Linux, the VTune GUI is invoked with the command "amplxe-gui." In practice, one may also choose to use the VTune command-line interface depending on preferences or operating environment (see "VTune documentation" in "For more information" at the end of this chapter).

VTune stores the application analysis setup and results in "Projects." Figure 24.4 shows the project properties of a sample project in the VTune GUI. The line "Application" points to the executable. Application parameters "4000 1000" are command-line arguments. In this example, they specify the value of $n=4000$ and the number of trials as 1000. The application must run long enough to collect good quality performance data, and for this reason, a large number of trials were chosen. Environment variables specified for this project direct the Intel OpenMP library to use as many threads as there are logical cores in the system and to pin the OpenMP threads to the respective cores.

Once the project is configured, the user can choose to run the application according to one of the preconfigured analysis types (see Figure 24.5). A particularly useful analysis type is General Exploration, which enables hotspot detection, as well as other general performance metrics. Clicking the Start button launches the application, and after execution, the results of analysis are shown in the same window.

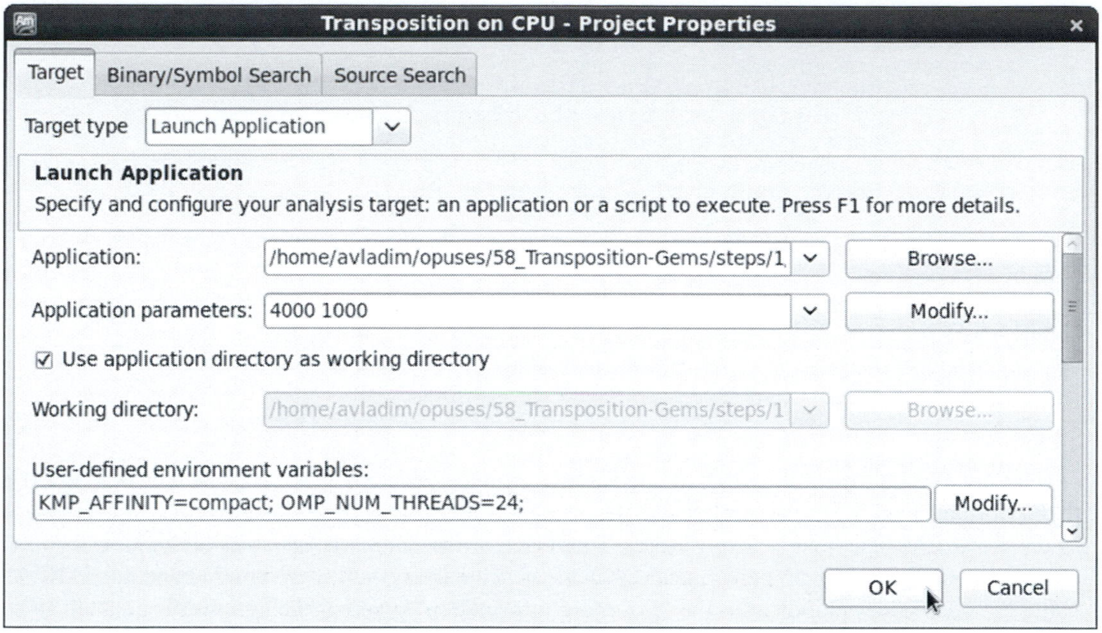

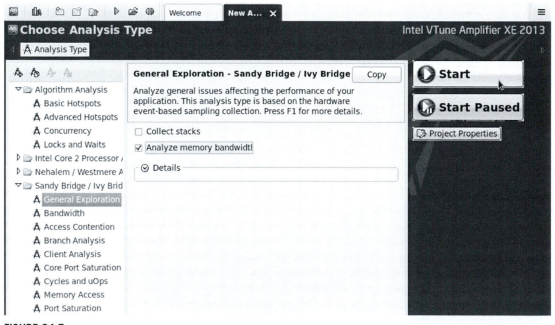

FIGURE 24.4

Setting up a project "Transposition on CPU" in VTune.

FIGURE 24.5

Starting a General Exploration analysis for the Sandy Bridge CPU architecture.

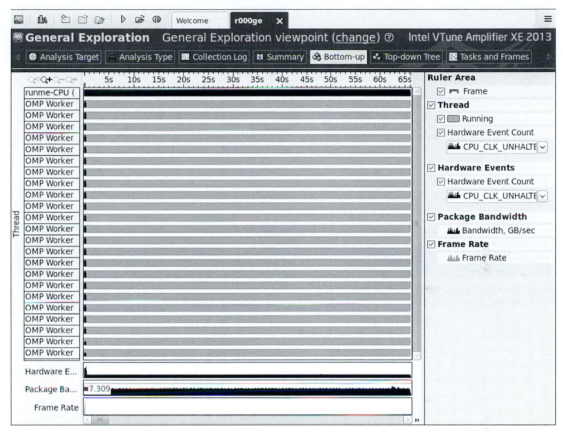

FIGURE 24.6

Analysis of results in the "Bottom-up" view, thread panel expanded, show unbalanced load. While one thread is performing all the work, all other threads are idling.

Figure 24.6 shows the results interface and the possible selection of one of several views ("Summary," "Bottom-up," "Top-down tree," etc.). The user can select which view they wish by clicking on the respective button at the top of the window.

Clicking the "Bottom-up" view brings up a threads panel containing the timeline of the load in each of the processor's 24 logical cores (this panel was expanded for the screenshot). The black-shaded region is present in only one of the 24 worker stripes, indicating useful workload in only one of the processor's logical cores. For an application that contains both serial and parallel stages, the pattern may look different (e.g., black stripes with worker patches). However, serial and under-parallelized regions will appear as green gaps. It is thus possible to gauge "by eye" how much performance is left out because of the serial parts of the application.

It is also possible to get a quantitative measure of the usage of parallelism by running a specialized analysis type called "concurrency." The corresponding entry is found in the side panel of VTune under the "Algorithm Analysis" folder (see Figure 24.7).

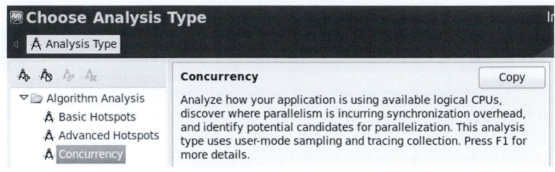

FIGURE 24.7

Starting the concurrency analysis.

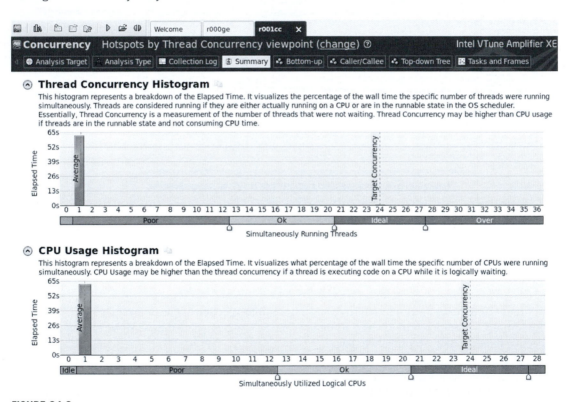

FIGURE 24.8

Results of the concurrency analysis, the Summary view, indicate poor utilization of parallelism.

Results of the concurrency analysis are shown with bar charts in the "Summary" view. Figure 24.8 shows there is only one bar at the x-value of 1, which means only one thread was running during 100% of the analysis time. In more complex applications, several bars may appear, showing the relative fractions of time spent in more and less parallel stages.

"PARALLEL": ADDING PARALLELISM WITH OPENMP

Now that VTune has been used to identify serialization as the cause of the poor transpose performance, it is time to fix it.

A parallel solution can be fairly simply implemented using OpenMP, which works both on Intel Xeon processors and Intel Xeon Phi coprocessors. The key observation is that every iteration of j in Figure 24.2 is independent of every other, which means one can distribute the for-loop in j across parallel threads. As shown in Figure 24.9, this is accomplished by simply adding a "#pragma omp parallel for" statement before that loop.

Figure 24.9 code corresponds to Step 2 in the source code archive that comes with this book. After rerunning the benchmark with the parallel code, we find that the performance on the processor (CPU) is now 28.6 GB/s, and on the coprocessor −20.0 GB/s (see the set of bars labeled "Parallel" in Figure 24.27), which represents an orders of magnitude improvement over the serial version.

Figures 24.10 and 24.11 show the output for the General Exploration and concurrency VTune analysis.

In Figure 24.10, the timeline is filled with black shading, which indicates useful workload in all cores. In addition, the timeline is shorter (see the time axis labels) than in the parallel code.

Likewise, in Figure 24.11, the thread concurrency histogram (top bar chart) has only one bar at a value of 24, confirming that all 24 cores were loaded 100% of the time. However, the CPU usage histogram has multiple bars, most of them clustered in the "Ok" zone, indicating a significant amount of idling time. This aspect of performance analysis indicates that further optimization of the code may improve performance.

Further improvement of the transposition code will deal with more subtle optimizations, as discussed in the remainder of this chapter.

"TILED": IMPROVING DATA LOCALITY

While the performance achieved by adding parallelism is significant relative to the serial code, the performance of the coprocessor is still disappointing as it performed worse than the CPU by a factor of 1.4.

```
#define FTYPE double

void Transpose(FTYPE* const A, const int n) {
#pragma omp parallel for schedule(static)
  for (int j = 0; j < n; j++) {
    for (int i = 0; i < j; i++) {
      const FTYPE c = A[i*n + j];
      A[i*n + j] = A[j*n + i];
      A[j*n + i] = c;
    }
  }
}
```

FIGURE 24.9

Parallel implementation of in-place square matrix transposition.

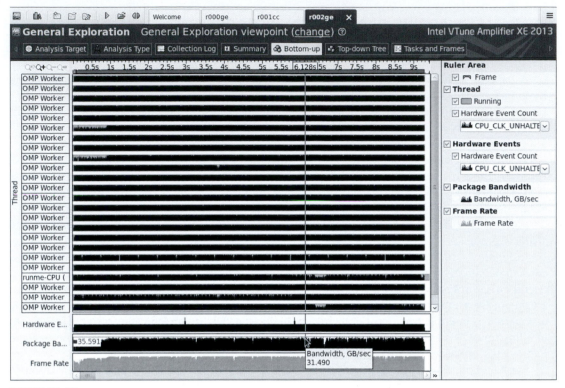

FIGURE 24.10

Results of the General Exploration analysis, the Bottom-up view, shows good utilization of multiple CPU cores.

In order to improve the coprocessor performance, we will use VTune to collect profiling information from the transposition code running on the Intel Xeon Phi coprocessor.

Prior to proceeding with performance analysis, a VTune project for the MIC architecture, "Transposition on MIC," must be configured. Figure 24.12 illustrates one way to configure a VTune project for a native Intel Xeon Phi coprocessor execution. The executable file in this case is the SSH client "ssh," and its command-line arguments set up the execution of the actual application. In "Application parameters," mic0 is the hostname of the coprocessor into which ssh is supposed to log in. The path name is specified as ~/runme-MIC, which is the path to the native coprocessor executable that is benchmarked. Again, "4000 1000" are the command-line arguments that specify the matrix size and the number of trials.

NOTE

Intel VTune Amplifier XE can run performance analysis of applications on Intel Xeon processors and Intel Xeon Phi coprocessors. For first generation Intel Xeon Phi coprocessors, choose the "Knights Corner Architecture" analysis types. For native MIC applications, it is possible to use "ssh" as the application and pass the name of the executable name as a command-line argument.

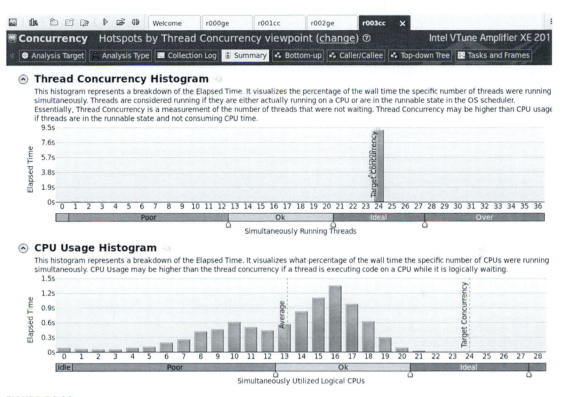

FIGURE 24.11

Results of the concurrency analysis, the Summary view, show a highly parallel code (top panel). A significant amount of idling time is revealed by the bottom panel, where CPU utilization is below ideal most of the time.

Additionally, as Figure 24.13 shows, in order to see the names of functions and the lines of the source code in VTune, one must point VTune to the directory on the host that contains the binaries for the MIC architecture.

Prior to running any native VTune analysis, the user must copy the executable file and all dependent libraries to the coprocessor. The only dependency in this example is the Intel OpenMP library that needs to be copied to the coprocessor, for instance, to mic0:/lib64/. Alternatively, NFS sharing can be used to share the appropriate libraries, executables and, if necessary, data with the coprocessor. Refer to "Parallel Programming and Optimization with Intel Xeon Phi Coprocessors" ("For more information" at the end of this chapter) for more details.

Once the project is configured and the native application is ready to run, analysis can be started. Just like the host, a good starting point is the General Exploration analysis albeit this time in the Knights Corner Platform folder (i.e., analysis on the Intel Xeon Phi coprocessor) (see Figure 24.14).

The results of profiling, as seen in the Summary view, are shown in Figure 24.15. A powerful feature of VTune is demonstrated in this view as performance metrics that look alarming are highlighted. In this case, the cycles per instruction (CPI) rate and Estimated Latency Impact are called out.

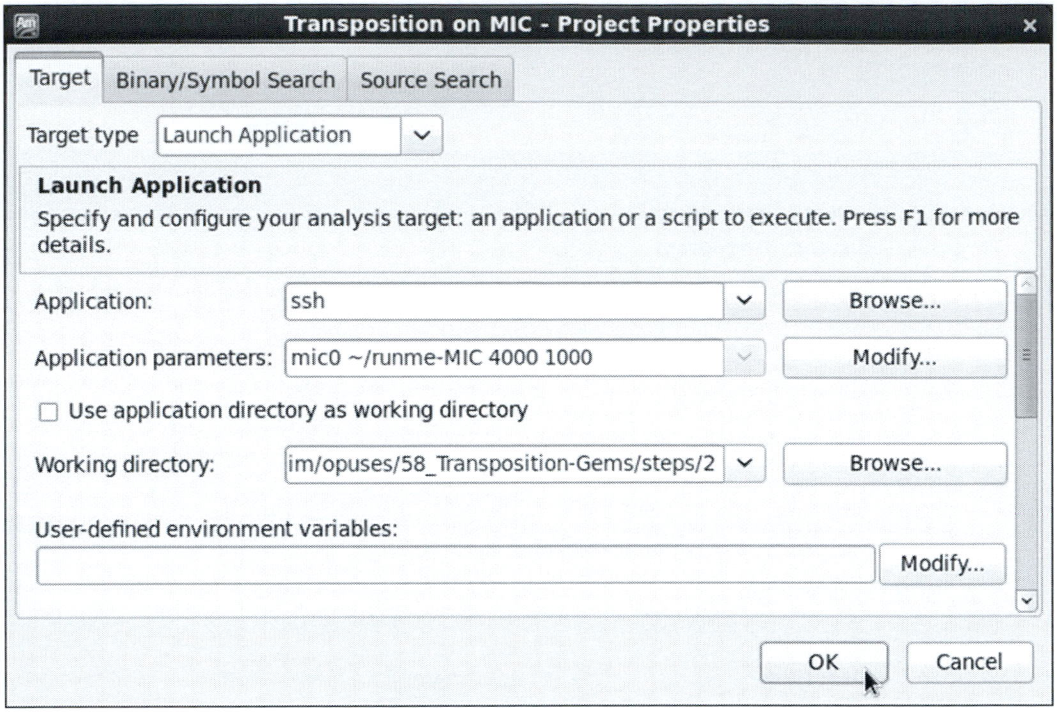

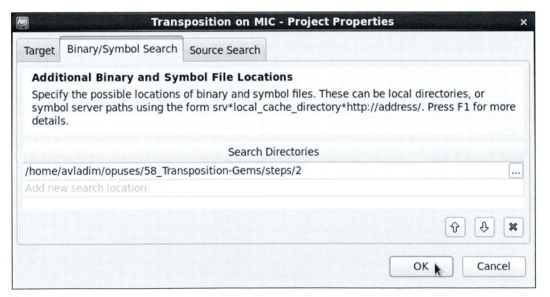

FIGURE 24.12

Setting up a VTune project to profile a native coprocessor application. The SSH client is used as the application, and the profiled executable is supplied as its command-line arguments.

FIGURE 24.13

In order to see the names of running functions and the source code in VTune, compile the code with the argument "-g," and point VTune to the directory on host that contains the executable file.

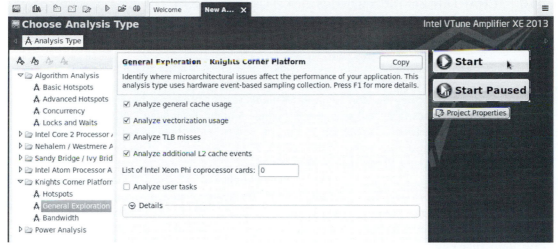

FIGURE 24.14

Launching General Exploration analysis in VTune on an Intel Xeon Phi coprocessor.

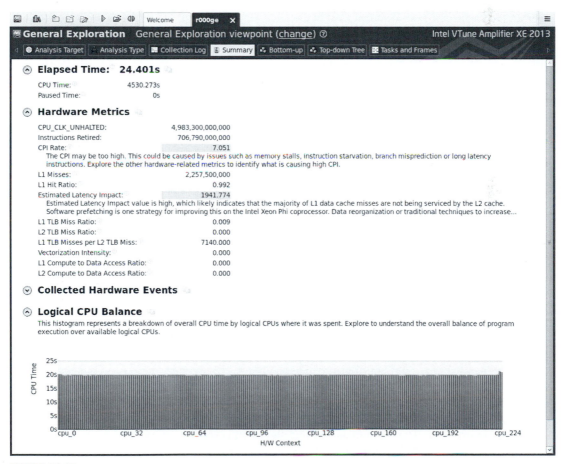

FIGURE 24.15

Summary of the General Exploration analysis in VTune on an Intel Xeon Phi coprocessor.

The CPI metric indicates how many cycles it takes on average to retire an instruction. It is a measure of the latency impact on performance. The reported metric in the Summary view is CPI per thread. With four threads per core, the Intel Xeon Phi Knights Corner processor has a theoretical minimum value of 2.0 because these are dual-issue in-order cores. A high CPI indicates a latency-related component in the application, which is not of much concern for bandwidth-bound applications such as matrix transposition. In fact, even the highly optimized STREAM benchmark of memory bandwidth on the MIC architecture shows a CPI rate over 8.2 in VTune.

The Estimated Latency Impact is another metric highlighted by VTune in Figure 24.15. This is actually important in our example. The Estimated Latency Impact is calculated from the number of Level-1 cache misses that are not serviced by the Level-2 cache and have to be serviced by the main RAM. The VTune GUI is filled with hints on most metrics and on the possible methods of resolution. In this case, the VTune information paragraph suggests the programmer to look into software prefetching and methods of improving data locality.

Methods of improving data locality are applicable here. A traditional, simple, yet effective locality optimization method is tiling. It involves reordering memory accesses so that data once fetched from memory to caches are reused sooner than in the plain loop algorithm.

From practical programming standpoint, tiling an algorithm with two nested loops involves strip-mining these loops and permuting the resulting loop to move the tiled loops outside. This procedure is illustrated in Figure 24.16. The three-code snippets in this code listing show (A) plain nested loops, (B) the same code with the loops strip-mined in preparation for tiling, and (C) tiled code obtained from the previous step by permuting two loops.

In the plain loop algorithm (A), the inner loop iterates in variable j, using the corresponding elements $B[j]$ in a "black box" function Compute(). Suppose that the size of the cache, the value of n, and the size of the elements of A and B are such that arrays A and B do not fit into cache. If that is the case, then, by the time that j is iterated from 0 to $(n-1)$, the value of $B[0]$ will be gone from cache. Then, when the algorithm increments i and restarts at $j=0$, the processor will have to load $B[0]$ from memory again, incurring a performance penalty. In contrast, in tiled loop (C), the value of $B[0]$ will be reused after TILE iterations, assuming that TILE is small enough that $B[0]$ will still be in cache.

The value of TILE must be empirically chosen for every computer architecture and algorithm and must be small enough so that the data used within a "tile" fits into the cache level for which optimization is performed. There may be additional restrictions on the value of TILE. For instance, if the inner loop in j is vectorized, then it is optimal for TILE to be a multiple of the SIMD vector length. For example, double precision calculations on the Knights Corner architecture have a vector length of 8, so the value of TILE must be a multiple of 8.

For the matrix transposition code seen in Figure 24.9, additional care must be taken when tiling. First, the inner loop in Figure 24.9 has upper bound dependent upon the variable in the outer loop. Therefore, the tiled algorithm must ensure the condition $(j < i)$. Second, there is no guarantee that the matrix size, n, is a multiple of TILE. Consequently, the tiled algorithm must be protected from accessing the matrix beyond its edges.

With the above considerations in mind, the tiled version of the matrix transposition algorithm is shown in Figure 24.17. The performance of this algorithm is shown in Figure 24.27 with bars labeled "Tiled." The performance boost on the CPU is marginal in this case, but in the coprocessor, performance increases by 30%.

```
// (A) Unoptimized case: plain nested loops
for (int i = 0; i < m; i++) {
    for (int j = 0; j < n; j++) {
        Compute(A[i], B[j]);
    }
}

// (B) The same exact code in a different form:
// strip-mined loops. This example assumes
// that m%TILE==0 and n%TILE==0.
const int TILE = 1; // This value is fine for now
for (int ii = 0; ii < m; ii += TILE) {
    for (int i = ii; i < ii + TILE; i++) {
        for (int jj = 0; jj < n; jj += TILE) {
            for (int j = jj; j < jj + TILE; j++) {
                Compute(A[i], B[j]);
            }
        }
    }
}

// (C) Optimized code: strip-mined loops are permuted
// to achieve better data locality. This is
// known as loop tiling.
const int TILE = 16; // Must be chosen empirically
for (int ii = 0; ii < m; ii += TILE) {
    for (int jj = 0; jj < n; jj += TILE) {
        for (int i = ii; i < ii + TILE; i++) {
            for (int j = jj; j < jj + TILE; j++) {
                Compute(A[i], B[j]);
            }
        }
    }
}
```

FIGURE 24.16

Illustration of practical loop tiling.

In VTune, the General Exploration analysis confirms that tiling improved application performance on the coprocessor (Figure 24.18). In the Summary view, the Estimated Latency Impact line shows 1082 as opposed to 1942 before optimization (Figure 24.15). Further optimization is still needed because the achieved performance on the coprocessor is still lower than on the host CPU and only 20% of the STREAM Copy bandwidth. The next section will continue with additional VTune analysis and code optimization.

"REGULARIZED": MICROKERNEL WITH MULTIVERSIONING

A very useful functionality of VTune that will help with further optimization is the ability to narrow the view of event counts down to a single line of code, or even down to a single assembly instruction. There are two situations in which this is useful:

```
const int TILE = 16; // Empirically chosen tile size

#pragma omp parallel for schedule(static)
for (int ii = 0; ii < n; ii += TILE) { // Tiling
    for (int jj = 0; jj <= ii; jj += TILE) { // Tiling

        // Do not go beyond matrix border
        const int jMax = (jj+TILE < n ? jj+TILE : n);

        for (int j = jj; j < jMax; j++) {

            // Do not go beyond main diagonal
            const int iMin = (ii > j ? ii : j+1);

            // Do not go beyond matrix border
            const int iMax =
                (ii+TILE < n ? ii+TILE : n);

            // Transpose the tile
            for (int i = iMin; i < iMax; i++) {
                const FTYPE c = A[i*n + j];
                A[i*n + j] = A[j*n + i];
                A[j*n + i] = c;
            }
        }
    }
}
```

FIGURE 24.17

Tiled implementation of in-place square matrix transposition.

(1) In complex programs, it allows to find functions and lines of code that take the most time (hotspots).

(2) When "hotspots" are known, users can view the assembly code that was executed. Even though assembly code can be studied without VTune (Intel C++ compiler argument "-S" produces an assembly listing), it is sometimes difficult, because the compiler generates different versions of some loops and statements, which can make it difficult or impossible to tell the version that was executed at runtime. VTune-annotated assembly makes it easy to determine which code branches were taken at runtime because the timing statistics are shown next to every line of assembly in the listing (Figure 24.19).

To view the assembly listing, the programmer should go to the "Bottom-up" view and double-click the name of the function of interest. The source code of the function should show up, and the button "Assembly" opens the corresponding assembly listing view as shown in Figure 24.19.

Even without a detailed analysis of the listing, it is clear that many instructions in the executed code are involved with swapping data between rows and columns. Indeed, the compiler implemented a number of "lea" instructions, which take addresses of its operands. The listing also shows a number of memory copy instructions, not all of which pertain to the swapping of elements.

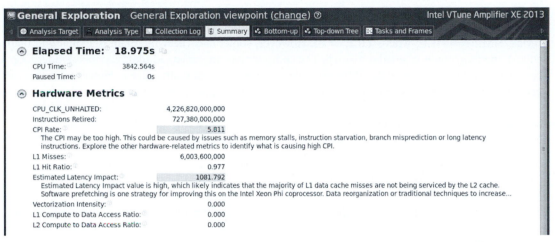

FIGURE 24.18

General Exploration summary with tiled code on the coprocessor shows reduced, but still high latency impact.

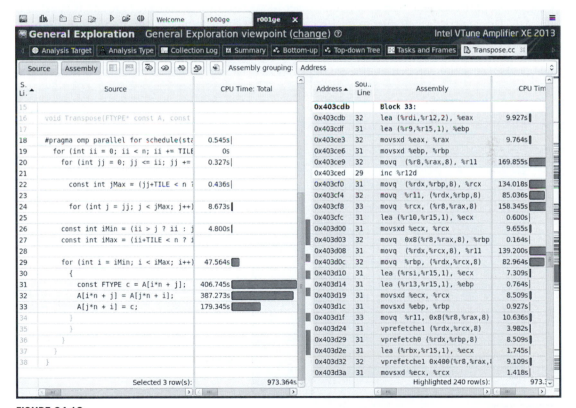

FIGURE 24.19

VTune allows the user to view event counts for every line of code or assembly. This allows identifying which branch of compiled code is taken most frequently at runtime.

The listing in Figure 24.17 shows why the compiler decided to implement this particular method of data movement. Note that the inner loop has the counter ranging from iMin to iMax. Most of the time, $(i\text{Max} - i\text{Min}) == \text{TILE}$, where TILE $== 16$. However, sometimes (near the main diagonal and matrix edges), the loop count is smaller than 16. The compiler has implemented multiversioned inner loop as best as it could to accommodate all the possible runtime values of matrix size n. However, in this case, generality of executable code comes at the cost of reduced application efficiency.

The programmer can express the code to take care of multiversioning, which can assist the compiler in generating efficient executable code, which should consist mainly of data-movement instructions. Namely, we can split the matrix into three regions (see Figure 24.20):

(a) The "body," where 16×16 tiles can be transposed without any checks for bounds,
(b) The "main diagonal" of 16×16 tiles, which will be transposed with a slightly modified microkernel, and
(c) The "peel" around the edges of the matrix, which will be transposed with its own nontiled code. This region exists only if the matrix size is not a multiple of TILE $== 16$.

With the matrix partitioned, the executable code for the transposition of each region can be simplified. The C language code implementing such approach is shown in Figure 24.21. Note that within the first parallel OpenMP loop, the loop count of the inner j-loop is known at compile time and is equal to the tile size. This allows the compiler to implement more efficient data-movement code.

Indeed, a benchmark of the multiversioned code yields 29.4 GB/s on the host CPU and 81.2 GB/s on the coprocessor. On the host, the performance is slightly greater than in the previous case, however, the standard deviation (around 1 GB/s, not shown) is large enough so that, in fact, there is no significant

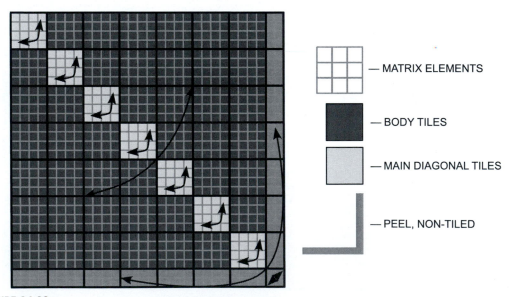

— MATRIX ELEMENTS

— BODY TILES

— MAIN DIAGONAL TILES

— PEEL, NON-TILED

FIGURE 24.20

Partitioning the matrix into three regions in order to eliminate bound checks from the code.

```
const int TILE = 16; // Empirically chosen tile size

// nEven is a multiple of TILE
const int nEven = n - n%TILE;

// Complete tiles in each dimension
const int wTiles = nEven / TILE;

#pragma omp parallel
{

// The main body tile transposition microkernel
#pragma omp for schedule(static)
for (int ii = TILE; ii < nEven; ii += TILE)
    for (int jj = 0; jj < ii; jj += TILE)
        for (int j = jj; j < jj+TILE; j++)
            for (int i = ii; i < ii+TILE; i++) {
                // Key to performance: the bounds of
                // this loop are known at compile time
                const FTYPE c = A[i*n + j];
                A[i*n + j] = A[j*n + i];
                A[j*n + i] = c;
            }

// Transposing the tiles along the main diagonal
#pragma omp for schedule(static)
for (int ii = 0; ii < nEven; ii += TILE) {
    const int jj = ii;
    for (int j = jj; j < jj+TILE; j++)
        for (int i = ii; i < j; i++) {
            const FTYPE c = A[i*n + j];
            A[i*n + j] = A[j*n + i];
            A[j*n + i] = c;
        }
}

// Transposing ``peel'' around the perimeter
#pragma omp for schedule(static)
for (int j = 0; j < nEven; j++)
    for (int i = nEven; i < n; i++) {
        const FTYPE c = A[i*n + j];
        A[i*n + j] = A[j*n + i];
        A[j*n + i] = c;
    }
} // End of OpenMP parallel region

// Transposing the bottom-right corner
for (int j = nEven; j < n; j++)
    for (int i = nEven; i < j; i++) {
        const FTYPE c = A[i*n + j];
        A[i*n + j] = A[j*n + i];
        A[j*n + i] = c;
    }
```

FIGURE 24.21

Multiversioned, tiled of in-place square matrix transposition.

different between these cases. Coprocessor performance is a very different story. Here, performance increased by a factor of 3 compared to the previous case, without multiversioning.

The VTune assembly listing of the main body tiles shows a much more regular stream of instructions (see Figure 24.22). Most of the time is taken by instruction "movq," which copies quad words of data.

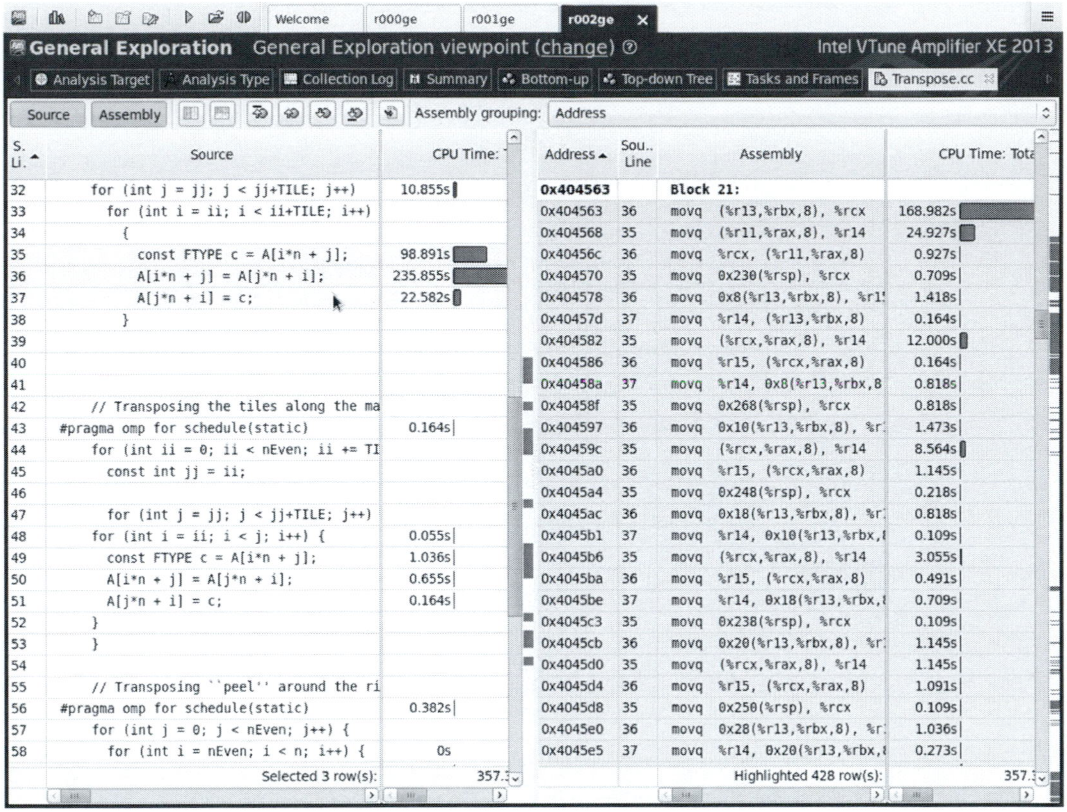

FIGURE 24.22

Assembly listing of transposition code with matrix partitioned into three regions. Once the programmer took care of multiversioning the transposition microkernel, the stream of instructions produced by the compiler becomes more regular.

Optimization with code multiversioning may be alien to coding styles that encourage abstraction. However, this practice is common in high-performance computing applications. Indeed, the code in Figure 24.17 is much more compact than the code in Figure 24.21. Moreover, "textbook" practices of programming are not followed in Figure 24.21 because redundant code is present at four separate locations. However, a performance boost by a factor of 3 is significant and provides both motivation and justification for introducing redundant code in order to assist the compiler.

The "rule of thumb" that can guide optimization in cases like this is to make the inner loop of performance-critical functions as simple as possible. For instance, it is best if array bounds are known at compile time. Additionally, if vectorization is used, then the loop count should be a multiple of 16 if possible.

In the last remaining optimization step, we will use VTune once again to diagnose and resolve a performance bottleneck related to insufficient parallelism.

"PLANNED": EXPOSING MORE PARALLELISM

There is one more low-hanging fruit that may be reaped with the help of profiling in VTune to optimize the matrix transposition code in this chapter.

The Bottom-up panel shown in Figure 24.23 shows that the majority of CPU cycles in the multiversioned code discussed in the preceding paragraphs belongs to the file [libiomp5.so], which is a part of the Intel OpenMP library.

Excessive amount of cycles spent in the OpenMP library usually indicates idling threads caused by load imbalance or serialization due to synchronization. Looking at the code in Figure 24.21, one can spot two important aspects:

1. The number of iterations in the first parallel for-loop of function Transpose(...) is too low. Indeed, for $n = 4000$ and TILE $= 16$, there are $4000/16 = 250$ iterations in that loop. With 240 hardware threads in this Intel Xeon Phi coprocessor, it is difficult to evenly distribute the load across threads.

2. Thread imbalance is present because smaller values of variable ii require less work than greater values. This is caused by the termination condition in the second loop ($jj < ii$) in combination with the OpenMP clause "schedule (static)." Even if the loop scheduling is changed from "static" (where all threads get the same number of iterations) to "dynamic" or "guided" (where iterations are distributed across threads at runtime), it would still be difficult to achieve load balance across threads because of the low number of iterations.

Finding situation with insufficient parallelism is a typical challenge faced when using the MIC architecture because of the large number of hardware threads available in Intel Xeon Phi coprocessors. The solution is to reduce the granularity of parallel work items in order to expose more parallelism to the compiler and OpenMP runtime library.

Function / Call Stack	CPU Time	Clockticks by Ha... CPU_CLK_UNHA...	Instructions Retired	CPI Rate	Cache Usage		
					L1 Misses	L1 Hi...	Estimate...
▷[libiomp5.so]	733.800s	807,180,000,000	140,460,000,000	5.747	36,000,000	0.999	18170.667
▷Transposeompparallel@24	373.582s	410,940,000,000	71,040,000,000	5.785	1,557,600,000	0.963	230.840
▷[vmlinux]	53.345s	58,680,000,000	10,440,000,000	5.621	102,000,000	0.976	454.588
▷[libc-2.14.90.so]	1.091s	1,200,000,000	0	0.000	0	1.000	0.000
▷[Import thunk __kmpc_barrier]	0.164s	180,000,000	0	0.000	0	0.000	0.000
▷[Import thunk __kmpc_for_stati]	0.109s	120,000,000	0	0.000	0	0.000	0.000
▷[micscif]	0.055s	60,000,000	0	0.000	0	0.000	0.000
▷[sep3_10]	0s	0	60,000,000	0.000	0	1.000	0.000
▷[libcrypto.so.1.0.0]	0s	0	60,000,000	0.000	0	1.000	0.000

FIGURE 24.23

Bottom-up view of the performance analysis of the code in Figure 24.21 shows that Intel OpenMP library functions constitute a significant fraction of execution time.

For matrix transpose, the granularity of work distribution is a row of tiles corresponding to a single value of ii (see Figure 24.24, left) resulting in $O(n/\text{TILE})$ work items. The solution is to shrink the grain on work distribution down to a single tile (Figure 24.24, right), which will result in $O((n/\text{TILE})^2)$ work items. For $n=4000$ and $\text{TILE}=16$, this is 3×10^4 work items which is plenty to keep 240 threads busy.

In order to change the granularity of work distribution in practice, a mapping needs to be created from a single index that spans the parallel iteration space to the location of the tile corresponding to that index. For tile enumeration expressed in Figure 24.21, it is possible to construct such a mapping using an arithmetic expression involving integer division and modulo operation. A more general solution is to precompute this map (planned). Precomputing a plan has several benefits. First, it eliminates integer math latency from the application, and second it is extendable to allow for more complex patterns of matrix traversal (for example, a recursive cache-oblivious method discussed in "Multithreaded Transposition of Square Matrices" in "For more information" at the end of this chapter).

The transposition code with planning is shown in Figure 24.25. Note that the user application must call the function CreateTranspositionPlan(…) prior to making the first call to the main function Transpose(…). After the last call to Transpose(…), the function DestroyTranspositionPlan(…) must be used to free memory allocated for the plan.

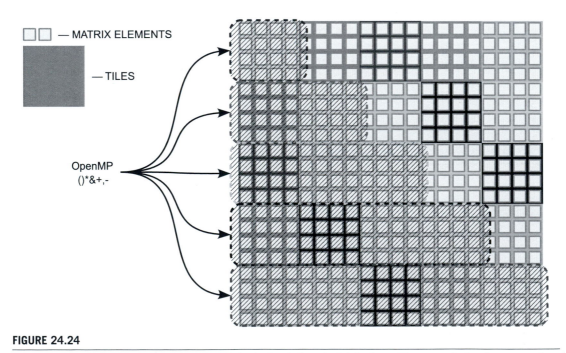

FIGURE 24.24

Expanding parallelism in the transposition code. Instead of work distribution with a granularity of one row of tiles, distributing work with a granularity of a single tile.

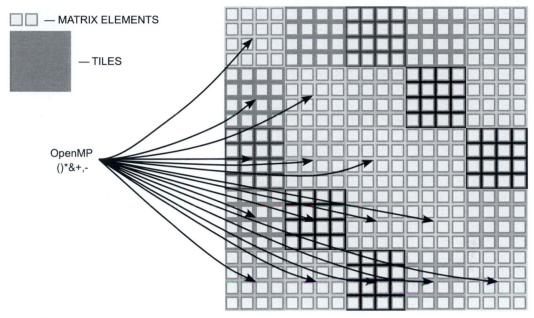

Figure 24.24—Cont'd

```
const int TILE = 16; // Empirically chosen tile size

void CreateTranspositionPlan(int* & plan, const int n) {

        // This function must be called prior to
        // calling the function Transpose()
        // to allocate and fill the array plan[],
        // which contains the tile traversal order.

        // Number of complete tiles in each dimension
        const int wTiles = n / TILE;

        // Number of complete tiles below the main diagonal
        // in the whole matrix
        const int nTilesParallel = (wTiles-1)*wTiles/2;

        // Order of tile traversal
        plan = (int*)
                malloc(sizeof(int)*(2*nTilesParallel));

        // Storing tile locations in the plan
        int c = 0;
        for (int ii = 1; ii < wTiles; ii++)
             for (int jj = 0; jj < ii; jj++) {
                    plan[2*c + 0] = ii*TILE;
                    plan[2*c + 1] = jj*TILE;
                    c++;
             }
}
```

FIGURE 24.25

Matrix transposition with a planning routine: expanding parallel iteration space.

```
void DestroyTranspositionPlan(int* plan) {
      // Free the memory allocated by
      // the function CreateTranspositionPlan()
      free(plan);
}

void Transpose(FTYPE* const A, const int n, const int*
const plan) {

      // nEven is a multiple of TILE
      const int nEven = n - n%TILE;

      // Complete tiles in each dimension
      const int wTiles = nEven / TILE;

      // Numer of tiles in the matrix body
      const int nTilesParallel = wTiles*(wTiles - 1)/2;

#pragma omp parallel
{

// Distribute work with single tile granularity
#pragma omp for schedule(static)
      for (int k = 0; k < nTilesParallel; k++) {
            // For large matrices, most of the work
            // takes place in this loop.

            // Pull location of the tile from the plan
            const int ii = plan[2*k + 0];
            const int jj = plan[2*k + 1];

            // The main tile transposition microkernel
            for (int j = jj; j < jj+TILE; j++)
                  for (int i = ii; i < ii+TILE; i++) {
                        const FTYPE c = A[i*n + j];
                        A[i*n + j] = A[j*n + i];
                        A[j*n + i] = c;
                  }
      }

      // The rest of the code in function Transpose(…)
      // is the same as in Figure 21. That code
      // is required to transpose the main diagonal tiles
      // and the "peel" around the matrix perimeter
      ...

}
}
```

Figure 24.25—Cont'd

Benchmarking confirms that expanding the iteration space and use of precomputed plans increases performance of the transposition code (Figure 24.26). On the host CPU, performance increases by 40%, reaching 41.4 GB/s, and on the coprocessor, the performance boost is 7%, achieving 87.0 GB/s (see Figure 24.27).

Examining the VTune performance analysis, we see that the contribution of [libiomp5.so] is considerably reduced, and now the hotspot is a parallel loop in function Transpose(),which was the intended result of this optimization step.

General Exploration   General Exploration viewpoint (change) ⑦

◁ | ⦿ Analysis Target | Ⓐ Analysis Type | Ⓜ Summary | ⦾ Bottom-up | ⦿ Top-down Tree | ⧈ Tasks and Frames

Grouping: | Function / Call Stack

Function / Call Stack	CPU Time▾	Clockticks by Ha... CPU_CLK_UNHA...	Instructions Retired	CPI Rate	Cache Usage L1 Misses	L1 Hi...	Estimate...
▷Transposeompparallel@24	605.945s	666,540,000,000	66,960,000,000	9.954	1,422,900,000	0.970	425.801
▷[libiomp5.so]	447.764s	492,540,000,000	89,580,000,000	5.498	24,000,000	0.999	17235.500
▷[vmlinux]	42.927s	47,220,000,000	4,440,000,000	10.635	0	1.000	0.000
▷mainompparallel_for@19	3.655s	4,020,000,000	0	0.000	0	0.000	0.000
▷[libc-2.14.90.so]	0.818s	900,000,000	180,000,000	5.000	0	1.000	0.000
▷[Import thunk __kmpc_barrier]	0.109s	120,000,000	0	0.000	0	1.000	0.000
▷[ld-2.14.90.so]	0.055s	60,000,000	0	0.000	0	0.000	0.000
▷[Import thunk __kmpc_for_stati	0.055s	60,000,000	0	0.000	0	0.000	0.000
▷[Import thunk __kmpc_for_stati	0.055s	60,000,000	0	0.000	0	1.000	0.000
▷mainompparallel_for@30	0s	0	120,000,000	0.000	0	0.000	0.000

FIGURE 24.26

Bottom-up view of General Exploration on an Intel Xeon Phi coprocessor with code from Figure 24.25. Exposing more parallelism improves performance by reducing thread idling, as reflected by the reduced contribution of [libiomp5.so].

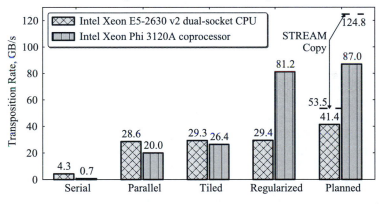

FIGURE 24.27

Performance values of the matrix transposition function on an Intel Xeon CPU and an Intel Xeon Phi coprocessor at different optimization stages. The theoretical best performance is the STREAM Copy bandwidth, indicated by dashed lines.

SUMMARY

This exploration of profiling-guided analysis of matrix transposition function is completed, and results are summarized in Figure 24.27.

Let us recap the steps performed in this chapter.

1. We started with a simple serial transposition code (Figure 24.2) and noted that the performance was disappointing on both the Intel Xeon processor and Intel Xeon Phi coprocessor (see bars

"Serial" in Figure 24.27). Using the VTune concurrency analysis, we saw that lack of parallelism was the cause of poor performance.

2. Performance increased after adding parallelism with an OpenMP pragma (shown in Figure 24.9), but not to the level expected for the MIC architecture (see bars "Parallel" in Figure 24.27). General Exploration analysis in VTune on the coprocessor highlighted issues caused by memory latency.

3. The impact of memory latency was reduced through the use of loop tiling (Figure 24.17) to improve data locality. This improved performance on the coprocessor; however, it was still lagging behind the CPU (bars "Tiled" in Figure 24.27). Studying the assembly code using VTune showed that the inner loop of the function had bounds determined at runtime, which caused the compiler-generated assembly code to be unnecessarily complicated in order to maintain generality.

4. A multiversioned C language code utilizing zones (Figure 24.21) was created that fixed the issue with the inner loop. This allowed the compiler to regularize data movement in the inner loop, which increased the Intel Xeon Phi coprocessor performance beyond that of the host (see bars "Regularized" in Figure 24.27).

5. The Bottom-up VTune view of the multiversioned application profile showed that the bottleneck of the application was in the OpenMP library. The excessive time spent in the OpenMP library was caused by constrained parallel iteration space, which did not allow for good load balancing. Shrinking the granularity of parallelism from a row of tiles down to a single tile with the help of planning (Figure 24.25) fixed this issue for both the processor and the coprocessor (bars "Planned" in Figure 24.27). At this point, VTune reports that the hotspot is now in the performance-critical data-movement loop, which we take as an indicator of adequate performance.

The achieved values of performance can be compared to the "Copy" test of the STREAM benchmark. On both platforms (processor and coprocessor), the optimized transposition code achieves 77% and 70%, respectively, of the STREAM bandwidth. STREAM is a simple, synthetic benchmark designed to measure sustainable memory bandwidth plus a corresponding computation rate for four simple vector kernels. Well-optimized STREAMS bandwidth is generally a good indication of the maximum achievable sustainable memory bandwidth for a platform, and reaching 70% is significant.

Further optimization of this application may be possible. The "tuning knob" that may help to further improve performance is software prefetching. In the Intel Xeon Phi coprocessor, for data movement from RAM to Level-2 cache, software prefetching is supplementary to hardware prefetching. For data movement from Level-2 to Level-1 cache, only software prefetching is available. Normally, the compiler estimates and implements prefetching in executable code. However, the programmer may alter the prefetching behavior using #pragma (no) prefetch and compiler arguments -opt-prefetch-distance. Additionally, explicit calls to prefetch intrinsics can be placed in the code in order to modify prefetching behavior. This kind of optimization is implementation-specific and is not as likely to scale directly to future implementations of Intel Xeon Phi designs such as the next generation known by the code-name Knights Landing.

In contrast, the portable, future-proof approach of high-level language programming achieved a coprocessor vs. processor speedup of 2.2, and reached over 70% of the theoretical best performance.

This chapter also demonstrated that the utility of a profiling tool such as Intel VTune Amplifier XE in optimization for the MIC architecture is two-pronged. First, it allows detection of the application's hotspots (even down to the level of identifying the branch of assembly instructions taken at runtime). Second, VTune also computes overall performance metrics such as latency impact, cache misses, vector instruction utilization, etc., and suggests directions for code improvement.

FOR MORE INFORMATION

Here are some additional reading materials that were mentioned in the text of this chapter:

- Vladimirov, A., 2013. Multithreaded Transposition of Square Matrices with Common Code for Intel Xeon Processors and Intel Xeon Phi Coprocessors. Colfax Research. http://research.colfaxinternational.com/post/2013/08/12/Trans-7110.aspx.
- Frigo, M., Johnson, S., 2005. The design and implementation of FFTW3. Proc. IEEE 93(2), 216-231. http://www.fftw.org/fftw-paper-ieee.pdf.
- Sung, I.-J., et al., 2014. In-place transposition of rectangular matrices on accelerators. In: PPoPP, pp. 207-218. http://dx.doi.org/10.1145/2555243.2555266.
- Pen, U.-L., et al., A free, fast, simple and efficient total variation diminishing magnetohydrodynamic code. Astrophys. J. Suppl. 149, 447. http://dx.doi.org/10.1086/378771.
- The STREAM benchmark code is available at http://www.cs.virginia.edu/stream/.
- Instructions for compiling and running STREAM on Intel Xeon Phi coprocessors are given in https://software.intel.com/en-us/articles/optimizing-memory-bandwidth-on-stream-triad.
- Colfax International, 2013. Parallel Programming and Optimization with Intel Xeon Phi Coprocessors. ISBN-10 0-9885234-1-8|ISBN-13 978-0-9885234-1-8. http://www.colfax-intl.com/nd/xeonphi/book.aspx.
- Colfax SXP7450 workstation specifications. http://www.colfax-intl.com/nd/workstations/sxp7450.aspx.
- Intel VTune Parallel Amplifier online documentation. https://software.intel.com/en-us/vtuneampxe_2013_ug_lin.

HETEROGENEOUS MPI APPLICATION OPTIMIZATION WITH ITAC

25

Vadim Karpusenko
Colfax International, USA

This chapter focuses on the workload balance of Message Passing Interface (MPI) applications running in heterogeneous cluster environment, consisting of Intel® Xeon® processors and Intel® Xeon Phi™ coprocessors, in a financial industry application that calculates Asian option payoffs. Three cases will be considered: unbalanced symmetric MPI code, manual balancing with precalculated performances of the cluster components, and dynamic workload balancing, implemented with Boss-Workers model, also known as master/slave communication model.

ASIAN OPTIONS PRICING

Options are contracts that allow one party (called the *beneficiary*) to buy (*call option*s) or sell (*put options*), on some future date (*options expiration date*), a stock market asset from/to the other party (the *grantor*) at a *strike price* agreed at the signing of a contract. A contract to buy is called a *call option*, and a contract to sell is a *put option*. Unlike a *futures contract*, an option gives the beneficiary the right to choose whether to exercise the transaction. This choice is typically made based on the market price of the asset at the option expiration date. For example, if at a call option expiration date, the stock market price of the asset is higher than in the option contract, the beneficiary will elect to buy the asset from the grantor, and sell it on the market, which yields a profit called a *payoff*. Otherwise, the beneficiary does not exercise the option, but the grantor retains the *option fee*. A style of options called *Asian options* has the feature that the payoff is calculated based on the mean price (arithmetic or geometric) of the asset, sampled at prearranged instances. This reduces the risks associated with market volatility and short-term market manipulations.

In order to perform risk analysis and to price an Asian Option, a Monte Carlo (MC) simulation method can be used. In this method, multiple stochastic histories of the asset price are simulated based on the available information on the asset volatility.

Variable *S(t)* is the price of the underlying asset for the option, which is assumed to evolve in time according to the stochastic equation:

$$dS(t) = \mu S(t)dt + \sigma S(t)dB(t).$$

In this equation, μ is the drift of the asset, σ is the option volatility, and $B(t)$ is a standard Brownian motion.

The solution of this stochastic differential equation can be written as:

$$S(t_i) = S(t_{i-1}) e^{\left(\mu - \frac{\sigma^2}{2}\right)\Delta t + \sigma \sqrt{\Delta t} \chi},$$

where χ is a normally distributed random variable with zero mean and unit standard deviation, and $\Delta t = t_i - t_{i-1}$.

In order to calculate the Asian option payoff for this asset, the asset price is averaged over the expiration time T at N instants:

$$\langle S \rangle_{\text{arithm}} = \frac{1}{N} \sum_{i=0}^{N-1} S(t_i)$$

$$\langle S \rangle_{\text{geom}} = \exp\left(\frac{1}{N} \sum_{i=0}^{N-1} \log S(t_i)\right)$$

for the arithmetic and geometric means, respectively, where $t_i = T \times i/(N-1)$. The corresponding payoffs for the *call* and *put* options for strike price K are:

$$P_{\text{put}} = e^{-rT} \max\{0; K - \langle S \rangle\}$$

$$P_{\text{call}} = e^{-rT} \max\{0; \langle S \rangle - K\}$$

where $\langle S \rangle$ can be either $\langle S_{\text{arithm}} \rangle$ or $\langle S_{\text{geom}} \rangle$, depending on the contract, and r is the risk-free rate.

In order to numerically determine the mathematical expectation of the Asian option payoff for a set of parameters $\{S, K, r, \mu, v, T, N\}$ and averaging rules (arithmetic or geometric), a MC simulation can be used. The simulation plays out a large number M of random paths, each of which stochastically evolves the option price from $t=0$ to $t=T$ according to the solution of the stochastic equation above, and computes the means over N time points. These means are then used to calculate the *put* and *call* *options payoffs*. Finally, these payoffs are averaged over the M random paths, producing a MC estimate of their mathematical expectation.

APPLICATION DESIGN

The MC method is an important tool in sampling the state space of a chosen statistical ensemble. It is *embarrassingly parallel* type of problem, because many independent stochastic processes are generated in parallel by many compute units simultaneously, and only a single reduction operation is required at the end of the calculation to collect the distribution of those independent pathways. Moreover, each generated pathway of asset price is averaged in predefined N instances over expiration time T, as was shown in the previous section. Therefore, the same arithmetic operation can be applied to many randomly generated pathways simultaneously, which allows to utilize the single instruction multiple data (SIMD) concept for this calculation. Therefore, the MC method of calculating Asian option pricing distribution can be easily parallelized on several nested levels, using vector processing units (VPUs), multiple threads, and even multiple machines in the cluster environment (Figure 25.1).

Intel Many Integrated Core (MIC) architecture combines many Intel processor cores onto a single chip. Each of 61 physical cores of Intel Xeon Phi 7xxx coprocessors have four hardware threads and one VPU. Independent parallel data can be processed with SIMD instructions by VPU (Figure 25.1; data parallelism), and parallel tasks/instructions can be distributed between total 244 (61 cores×4 hardware threads) logical threads (Figure 25.1; thread parallelism) on each Intel Xeon Phi coprocessor.

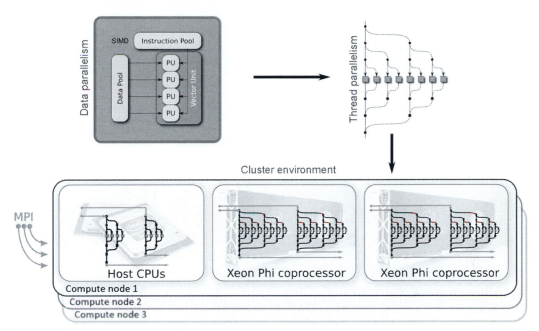

FIGURE 25.1

Three layers of parallelism.

Intel Xeon processor with the AVX instruction set has 256-bit vector registers. For Intel Xeon Phi coprocessors, the size of the vector register is 512 bits. This allows packing up to 16 single-precession floating point numbers or 32-bit short integers; and 8 double-precession floating point numbers or 64-bit long integers into each vector register and operate on them simultaneously. For the compute-intensive applications, multiple coprocessors, and host processors, can be used for the calculations. Communication between the devices and nodes in the compute cluster can be implemented by MPI.

To achieve high performance of Asian options pricing calculation, the application code should be designed accordingly to utilize data- and thread-parallelism. This will allow using wide vector registers of Intel Xeon Phi coprocessors, and also partition those parallel calculations to many cores. It can be implemented by writing two nested `for`-loops, with outer loop scaled between cores with thread-parallel library, and inner loop is automatically vectorized by the Intel C/C++ Compiler, which is one of the optimization techniques enabled at –O2 (default) compiler optimization level.

Source code in Figure 25.2 shows the OpenMP `parallel  for` pragma on top of the outer `i`-loop, which will distribute the iterations of this loop among all available threads, initialized by OpenMP. Three inner `k`-loops with `vecSize` iterations in each, proportional to size of the vector register, will be automatically vectorized by the compiler. The Intel Math Kernel Library implementation of the random number generator uses vector instructions as well.

Reduction of the final result across multiple vector lanes and across all OpenMP threads is automatically implemented by the compiler and by reduction operation of OpenMP library. Therefore, data parallelism of MC calculations of Asian option payoffs can scale over many cores and VPUs, operating on multiple independent vector lanes simultaneously.

```
/* The i-loop is thread-parallel, i.e.,
 distributed across the processor cores */
#pragma omp parallel for schedule(guided) \
  reduction(+: payoff_arithm_put)
for (int i = 0; i < nPaths/vecSize; i++) {
  for (int j = 1; j < nIntervals; j++) {
/* Intel MKL random number generator */
    vsRngGaussian(
      VSL_RNG_METHOD_GAUSSIAN_BOXMULLER,
      stream, vec_size, rands, 0.0f, 1.0f);
/* The k-loop is data-parallel thanks to
 automatic vectorization by the compiler */
    for (int k = 0; k < vecSize; k++) {
      spot_prices[k] *=
        exp2f(drift + vol*rands[k]);
      sumsm[k] += spot_prices[k];
    }
  }
  for (int k = 0; k < vecSize; k++) {
    arithm_mean_put[k] =
      K - (sumsm[k] * recipIntervals);
    if (arithm_mean_put[k] < 0.0f)
      arithm_mean_put[k] = 0.0f;
  }
/* Reduction across vector lanes and across
 OpenMP threads is automatically implemented
 by the compiler */
  for (int k = 0; k < vecSize; k++)
    payoff_arithm_put += arithm_mean_put[k]*
      expf(-r*T)/(float)nPaths;
}
```

FIGURE 25.2

Code listing of compute-intensive part of Asian options pricing calculation.

In the next section, we will discuss an additional level of parallelism, achieved by distributing sets of calculation parameters (strike prices) among multiple compute units: processors and coprocessors.

SYNCHRONIZATION IN HETEROGENEOUS CLUSTERS

MPI communication model allows using multiple machines and devices with distributed memory, uniting them for a parallel MPI application run, scaling the application for as many compute devices as available for a user in the cluster environment. This high-level MPI parallelism takes care of the communication between processes on multiple devices, but does not provide any automatic scheduler or load balancer. It is the developer's responsibility to implement these in the application. In particular, workload balancing is especially important in a heterogeneous cluster environment where the compute devices have different computational performance.

```
for (int iCalc=0; iCalc < nCalculations; iCalc++) {
  const int nStrikes = 100;
  const float strikeMin = 10.0f
  const float strikeMax = 20.0f
  for (int iStrike = myRank*nStrikes/(float)mpiWSize;
       iStrike < (myRank+1)* nStrikes/(float)mpiWSize;
       iStrike++) {
    const float K = strikeMin + (strikeMax - strikeMin)*
      (float)iStrike / (float)(nStrikes - 1);
    ...
  }
  MPI_Barrier(MPI_COMM_WORLD);
}
```

FIGURE 25.3

Code listing of unbalanced workload distribution.

We design our initial application (see Figure 25.3) to distribute 100 strike prices (`nStrikes`) among all available MPI ranks equally. Those calculations are conducted `nCalculations = 10` times with the explicit `MPI_Barrier` after each calculation step for the synchronization. Note that the Intel Xeon Phi coprocessors can generate and calculate corresponding Asian options pricing values faster than two Intel Xeon processors, which leads to coprocessors stall and an efficiency of only 79%, as shown in the application output in Figure 25.5.

The next section focuses on two aspects of MPI application optimization:

- Uneven workload distribution, or load imbalance, causing some MPI ranks to stall
- Finding communication bottlenecks - regions of the code that delay execution

For those optimization techniques, we will be using Intel® Trace Analyzer and Collector (ITAC), an MPI communication visualizer and performance analysis tool which is part of Intel® Cluster Studio XE. ITAC provides a convenient way to profile and analyze MPI traffic to find areas for performance improvement.

FINDING BOTTLENECKS WITH ITAC

Two components of ITAC—Intel® Trace Collector (ITC) and Intel® Trace Analyzer (ITA)—will be used to collect and visualize the trace data from our MPI example. The ITC library output contains a record of the MPI parameters plus a time-based record of all function calls and MPI communications including the time spent waiting on synchronization. Those MPI application stalls (e.g., time spent waiting on synchronization) are the first candidates for application performance improvement.

A simple method of using ITC with user's MPI applications requires loading the ITC library at runtime and specifying an additional `-trace` flag as an argument for `mpirun` script execution. The default behavior of the ITC library is to generate an individual trace file per each MPI process, but the format of the output files can be controlled by the environment variables. For instance, multiple trace outputs can be combined by ITC into a single trace file that contains the execution information for all the application MPI processes. This file (or files) will be generated by ITC at the end of the user's application run, and later can be analyzed in ITA.

SETTING UP ITAC

A heterogeneous cluster environment can contain processors and devices with different bandwidth and computational capabilities. Symmetric MPI applications will assign identical workloads to all participants in the application, which can cause load imbalance, as the execution time might be shorter on some devices due to their higher computational performance. MPI synchronization events will show this load imbalance because high-performance devices will be idle while they wait for slower devices to catch up. ITAC can visualize MPI communication and allows spotting those situation(s), where some MPI ranks must wait a significant amount of time for the synchronization with slower components of the heterogeneous cluster.

Before collecting the trace, the user needs to set the environment for MPI and load ITC library, using the following scripts:

```
source /opt/intel/impi/4.1.3.048/intel64/mpivars.sh
source /opt/intel/itac/8.1.4.0.45/intel64/itacvars.sh
```

ITC uses *structured trace files (stf)* format to collect individual timed MPI communication records per MPI process. For convenience, one may request ITC to combine the data into a single trace file by enabling the following environment variable:

```
export VT_LOGFILE_FORMAT=singlestf
```

At this point, everything is ready for the user's MPI application run; collect a single file of trace data.

Three Intel MPI environment variables are used to enable MIC architecture support, set the communication protocol to TCP/IP and pin the MPI processes with correspondence to OpenMP pin policy:

```
export I_MPI_MIC=1
export I_MPI_FABRICS=tcp
export I_MPI_PIN_DOMAIN=omp
```

The following execution line will run the MC Asian options pricing calculation across the devices specified in the machine file `machines-HETEROGENEOUS`, one MPI process per device, and generate a trace file containing all of the timed MPI calls made by the application, since we used `-trace` flag.

```
mpirun -trace -machinefile machines-HETEROGENEOUS \
-env I_MPI_PIN=0 ~/options &> results.txt
```

The content of `machines-HETEROGENEOUS` file includes hostname of the main node, and hostnames of the corresponding Intel Xeon Phi coprocessors:

```
c001-n003
c001-n003-mic0
c001-n003-mic1
```

Finally, ITA can be used to open the generated single trace file and begin the analysis:

```
traceanalyzer options.single.stf
```

In the following section, we will see the examples of the code optimization and visualization of MPI communication with ITAC.

UNBALANCED MPI RUN

The default graphical user interface view of ITA is shown in the Figure 25.4. It contains the time interval of the trace, timeline of MPI function calls, and execution/communication time information grouped together for all MPI processes.

The line, in Figure 25.4, labeled *Group Application* indicates total execution time summed over all MPI processes. For purposes of our discussion, this will be considered as time spent on useful calculations. The line *Group MPI* collects time intervals used by all MPI ranks on communication and idling due to synchronization. Therefore, to achieve better overall performance, this number should be as small as possible.

This particular MPI run used a single node (hostname `c001-n003`) containing two sockets of 8-core Intel Xeon E5-2687W v2 processors, hyper-threading enabled, and both simultaneously used by the `rank 0` MPI process. Total amount of memory was 128 GB in eight 1600 MHz 16 GB modules. Four Intel Xeon Phi C0PRQ-7120 passive-cooled coprocessors with 16 GB GDDR5 memory were installed in the system, but only the first two of them were used for the calculations as MPI `rank 1` and `rank 2`. The operating system was CentOS 6.5 with Linux kernel 2.6.32-431.el6.x86_64. MPSS version 3.2.3, MPI 4.1. 3.048, and ITAC 8.1.4.0.45 were installed.

Switching from **Flat Profile** tab to **Load Balance** shows the execution time per MPI process, as well as the time each process spent on MPI communication and synchronization (Figure 25.5).

Out of 44.3 s of total execution time (shown in the *TTotal* column) on Intel Xeon Phi coprocessors for processes 1 and 2, only 35.3 s were spent on useful calculations per process, and 9.1 s on average for MPI communications and idling (*TSelf* column for Application and MPI groups correspondingly).

The same ratio can be found from the application's output (see Figure 25.6). The first column contains the hostname of the device running the MPI process. The *performance* column indicates the number of random paths generated by the device per second. The last *Efficiency* column shows the ratio between the useful calculation time and total time spent on MPI communication idling due to workload imbalance, and synchronization between all three working devices. *Net performance* reports the sum

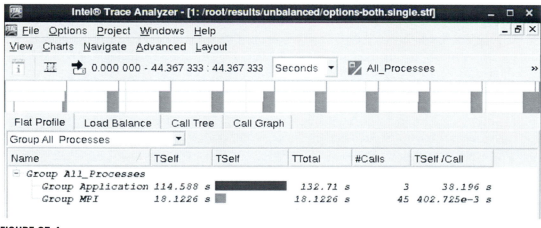

FIGURE 25.4

Intel® Trace Analyzer: default graphical user interface view.

Flat Profile	Load Balance	Call Tree	Call Graph				

Children of Group All_Processes ▼   Show Pies

Name	TSelf	TSelf	TTotal	#Calls	TSelf /Call
⊟ Group Application	114.588 s		132.71 s	3	38.196 s
Process 0	43.9788 s	████████	43.9849 s	1	43.9788 s
Process 1	35.1656 s	██████	44.3632 s	1	35.1656 s
Process 2	35.4435 s	██████	44.3624 s	1	35.4435 s
⊟ Group MPI	18.1226 s		18.1226 s	45	402.725e-3 s
Process 0	6.063e-3 s		6.063e-3 s	15	404.2e-6 s
Process 1	9.19765 s	██	9.19765 s	15	613.176e-3 s
Process 2	8.91892 s	██	8.91892 s	15	594.595e-3 s

FIGURE 25.5

ITAC: Load Balance view. Three MPI processes running Asian option pricing demo on host and two Intel Xeon Phi coprocessors.

```
#            Worker   Share  Performance    Effic.
         c001-n003    34.0%    8.19e+06    100.0%
    c001-n003-mic0    33.0%    1.06e+07     77.3%
    c001-n003-mic1    33.0%    1.05e+07     78.1%
# Calculation   7 of  10 took 4.356 seconds
# Net performance: 2.41e+07 paths/second
```

FIGURE 25.6

Output fragment of unbalanced Asian options pricing MPI run.

of all paths divided by the total time of the calculation including idling for all processes. Therefore, net performance will be always smaller than the sum of individual device performances and will be equal to the sum only for a perfectly balanced calculation.

By default, ITAC uses MPI process numbers (e.g., Process 2) to show the time statistics of the execution.

We can change the group names to be represented by the hostnames instead, by clicking menu **Advanced – Process Aggregation**, selecting **All Nodes** from the list and clicking **Apply** or **OK** button (see Figure 25.7).

The result of the manipulations above are shown in Figure 25.8, confirming that on c001-n003 host execution time was close to 44 s and on Intel Xeon Phi coprocessors c001-n003-mic0 and c001-n003-mic1 useful calculation times were close to 35 s, with the net efficiency of ~80%.

Using menu **Charts – Event Timeline** or keyboard shortcut **Ctrl+Alt+E,** we can visualize the communication between the devices of our unbalanced MPI Asian options pricing calculation. Since we previously modified the **Process Aggregation** method to **All hosts**, hostname groups will be shown here as well.

The **Event Timeline** chart shows a breakdown of what each rank or device is doing over the execution time of the application (see Figure 25.9). Navigation keys can be used to zoom in/zoom out and to move the selected time interval. Notice that, when zooming or shifting the interval, all charts except the Trace Map at the top will alter the data shown to only display information for the selected time frame.

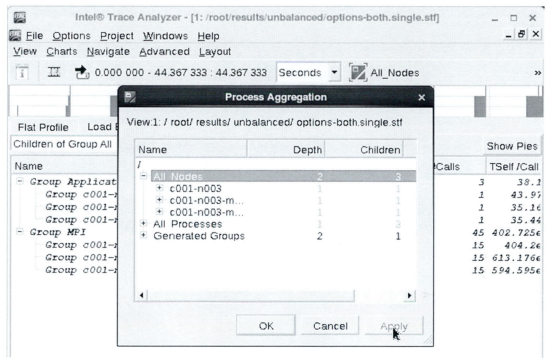

FIGURE 25.7

ITAC: changing Process Aggregation to "All Nodes" allows to see hostnames of the devices.

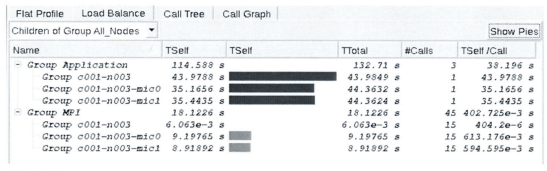

FIGURE 25.8

ITAC: Load Balance tab with executing times grouped by the hostnames of the devices.

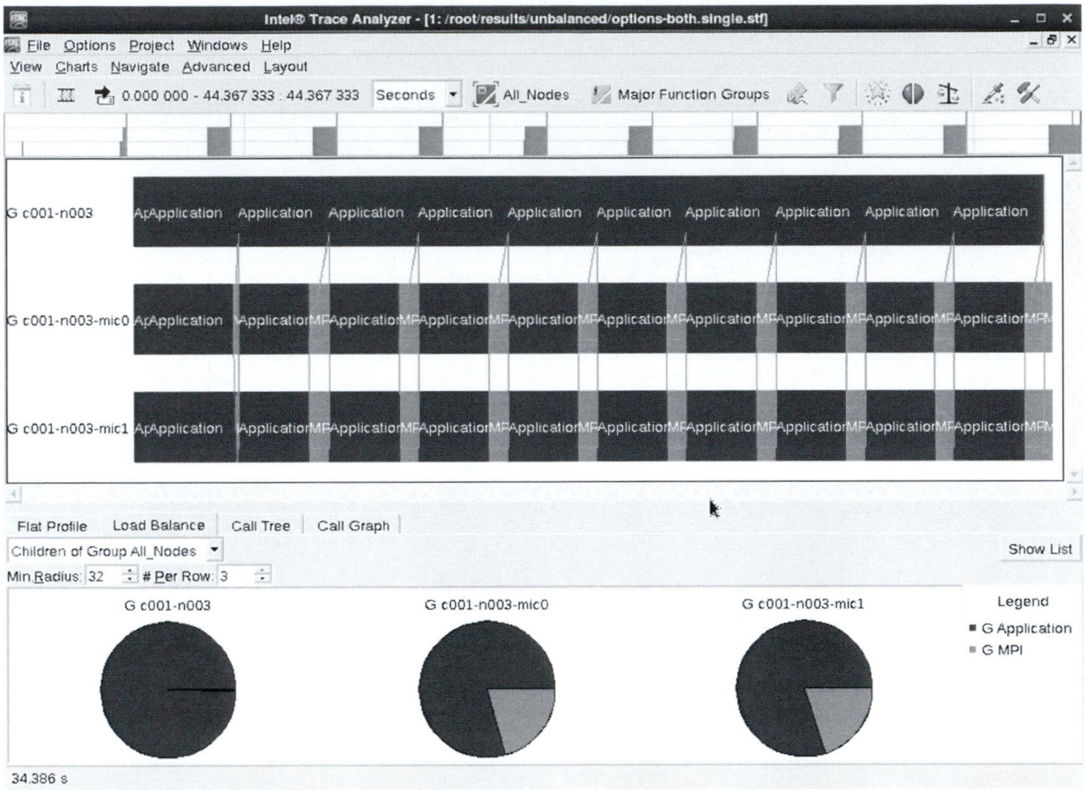

FIGURE 25.9

ITAC: Event Timeline of *unbalanced* MPI run.

All charts in ITAC use the following color scheme: blue color (dark gray in the print version) bars labeled with "Application" represents useful calculations, red color (light gray in the print version) bars with "MPI" label—MPI communication and idling time; point-to-point communication connects corresponding MPI groups with the black lines, and collective operations represented by the blue lines, which might be not very convenient to spot on the background of blue-colored (dark gray in the print version) "Application" bars. Therefore, corresponding colors can be modified by clicking the right mouse button on the Timeline chart and choosing **Event Timeline Settings…** menu, with the following modification of the corresponding parameters.

MANUAL WORKLOAD BALANCE

One of the ways to distribute the calculation workload of our example application is to assign more iterations of iStrike for-loop to faster devices. The following approach works only if all iterations take exactly the same amount of time to process, which is the case in this particular problem. If the

```
int arrStrikes[4] = {0, 28, 64, 100};
for (int iCalc=0; iCalc < nCalculations; iCalc++) {
  const int nStrikes = 100;
  const float strikeMin = 10.0f;
  const float strikeMax = 20.0f;
  for (int iStrike = arrStrike[myRank];
       iStrike < arrStrike[myRank+1];
       iStrike++) {
    const float K = strikeMin + (strikeMax - strikeMin)*
      (float)iStrike / (float)(nStrikes - 1);
    ...
  }
  MPI_Barrier(MPI_COMM_WORLD);
}
```

FIGURE 25.10

Code listing of manually balanced workload distribution.

execution time were to vary from iteration to iteration, for instance, due to nondeterministic nature, this approach may still lead to unbalanced workload distribution (Figure 25.10).

Iteration amounts were calculated based on the performance values from the application output (Figure 25.6). MPI run will use Intel Xeon processors as rank 0, and coprocessors as rank 1 and 2. Therefore, the first 28 iterations will be assigned for processors, and the following two blocks of 36 iterations (out of total 100) for each Intel Xeon Phi coprocessor:

$$N_{CPU} \approx \frac{8.19 \times 10^6}{8.19 \times 10^6 + 1.06 \times 10^7 + 1.05 \times 10^7} \times 100 \approx 28$$

$$N_{PHI} \approx \frac{1.05 \times 10^7}{8.19 \times 10^6 + 1.06 \times 10^7 + 1.05 \times 10^7} \times 100 \approx 36$$

Those iteration numbers can be stored in our application as values of array arrStrikes[4] and distributed among the participants of the calculation. For instance, the first coprocessor will process strikes from 28 to 64 (64 = 28 + 36), processing 36 strike iterations in total. Therefore, any modification of the calculation set-up will also require recalculation of those values and retuning of the code.

The **Event Timeline** chart for the manually balanced calculation is shown below in Figure 25.11. Less time were used on synchronization between the MPI processes, increasing overall performance of the application.

Click **View – Compare** to compare the new trace to the original unbalanced case. You can synchronize navigation keys and/or mouse zoom, as well as match time scaling between the two traces. You can see the improvements here, showing that the application is now spending more time doing actual computation (the blue regions; dark gray in the print version), rather than waiting in communications (Figure 25.12).

Output produced by the manually balanced MPI application run indicates that this implementation is running 22% faster than load unbalanced code (Figure 25.13).

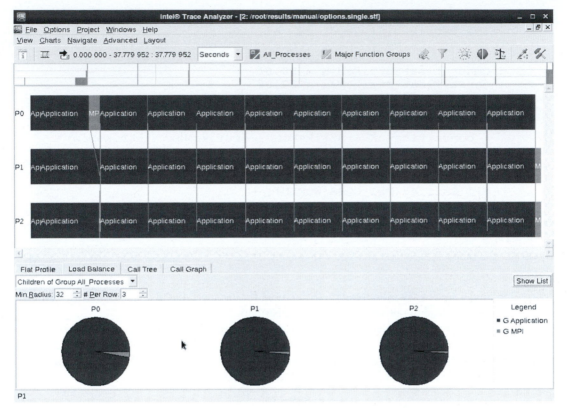

FIGURE 25.11

ITAC: Event Timeline of *manually balanced* MPI run.

DYNAMIC "BOSS-WORKERS" LOAD BALANCING

Load balancing usually requires changing the distributed workload across the MPI application. In this section, we look at dynamic load distribution across heterogeneous cluster components (see Figure 25.14).

Dedicated MPI `rank 0` (*Boss rank*) is playing the role of the dynamic scheduler, distributing parameters of the MC Asian options pricing calculation among heterogeneous cluster components (*workers*)—specifically the Intel Xeon processors and Intel Xeon Phi coprocessors. Each worker requests a new portion of the calculations upon returning the results of the previous computing step. As a result, faster components in the compute cluster simply perform more calculations than the slower components. No manual intervention is required and only a single thread is dedicated for the workload distribution (MPI `process 0` in Figures 25.15 and 25.16).

It should be noted that the communication between workers and the boss rank can become a bottleneck if the workload distribution at each request is very small. This can be fixed by increasing the

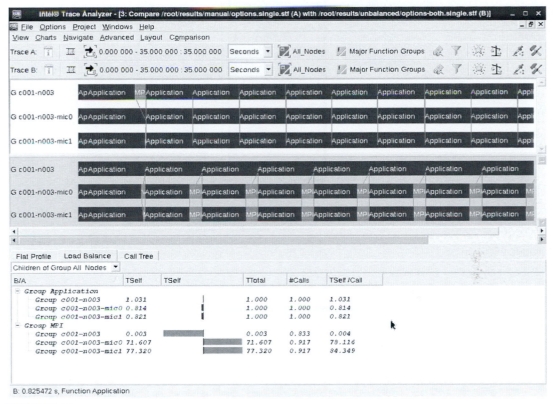

FIGURE 25.12

ITAC: Event Timeline Compare view of *manually balanced* and original *unbalanced* MPI runs.

```
#          Worker    Share  Performance   Effic.
       c001-n003    28.0%     8.26e+06    99.2%
  c001-n003-mic0    36.0%     1.06e+07    99.5%
  c001-n003-mic1    36.0%     1.05e+07   100.0%
# Calculation    4 of   10 took 3.587 seconds
# Net performance: 2.92e+07 paths/second
```

FIGURE 25.13

Output fragment of manually balanced Asian options pricing MPI application run.

amount of calculations assigned to each worker at a time. On the other hand, if the workload distribution is too coarse-grained, this may lead to unbalanced processing of the last requests. Therefore, we strive to find the right balance between the requests communication and the amount of workload assigned per each request.

Figure 25.16 shows zoomed-in communication between the Boss process 0 and three workers P1, P2, and P3, where the last two were running on Intel Xeon Phi coprocessors.

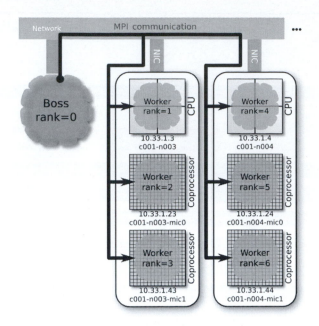

FIGURE 25.14

MPI communication scheme of *dynamically balanced Boss-Workers model* of load distribution.

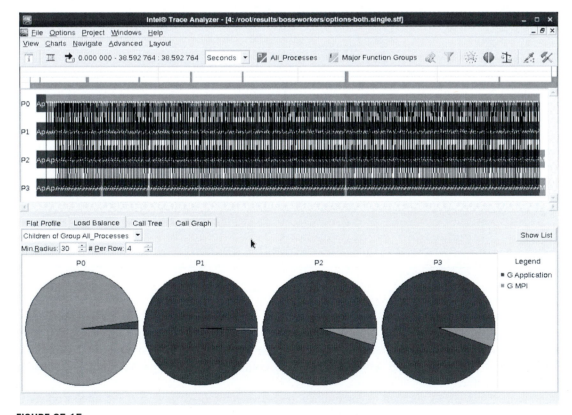

FIGURE 25.15

ITAC: Event Timeline of *dynamically balanced Boss-Workers model* implementation.

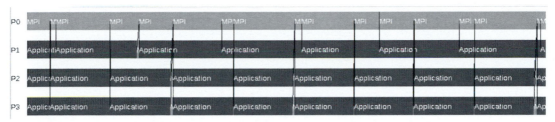

FIGURE 25.16

ITAC: zoomed-in Event Timeline of *dynamically balanced Boss-Workers model* implementation.

It should be noted that only one thread is needed for the Boss process. The rest of the available threads can be used as a worker. But MPI default behavior for two MPI processes running on the same device is to split available cores into two equal blocks, which provides only 50% compute capability of the device. With the following two environment variables, compute performance will be distributed proportional to number of OpenMP threads used by each MPI process:

```
export I_MPI_PIN_DOMAIN=omp
export I_MPI_PIN=0
```

Dynamic workload distribution by the Boss rank can be implemented with the code snippet shown in Figure 25.17.

Execution of dynamically balanced Boss-Workers implementation produces the result similar to one presented in Figure 25.18.

Figure 25.19 shows overall performance, represented by generated stochastic paths per second for the three implementations discussed in this chapter.

Performance results in this figure indicate that Boss-Workers dynamic load balancing for the MC calculation of Asian option payoffs has similar performance to static/manual workload balancing.

CONCLUSION

Unlike GPUs, Intel Xeon Phi coprocessors are able to execute native application in symmetric mode with the host processor. In this mode, the application runs in the operating system on the coprocessor, and does not require a host process executing on the CPU offloading data to the coprocessor. Therefore, for an application in the MPI framework, it is possible to run MPI processes directly on coprocessors, with the same code running on the host system processor (symmetric mode). In this case, coprocessors behave like independent compute nodes in the cluster, with an MPI rank, peer-to-peer communication capability, and access to a network-shared file system. With such a configuration, there is no need to instrument data offload in the application in order to utilize a heterogeneous system comprised of processors and coprocessors. That said, an MPI application designed for a CPU-only cluster can be used on coprocessor-enabled clusters without code modification.

For better overall performance of symmetric MPI applications, workload balancing is required, because compute units of the heterogeneous cluster—processors and Intel Xeon Phi coprocessors—have different computational capabilities.

```
if (myRank == bossRank) {
  int nR = 0; /* Number of processed tasks */
  int iP = 0; /* Next task to assign */
  while (nR < nPars) {

  /* Wait for any worker to report for work */
    float buf[msgReportLength];
    MPI_Recv(&buf, msgReportLength,
      MPI_INT, MPI_ANY_SOURCE, msgReportTag,
      MPI_COMM_WORLD, &status);
    const int iW = status.MPI_SOURCE;

    if (buf[0] > 0.0f) {
  /* If worker reports with results of a
     previous task, record these results */
      nR++;
      const int iR = floorf(buf[1]);
      payoff_arithm_put [iR] = buf[2];
    }

    if (iP < nStrikes) {
  /* Assign the next task iP to worker iW */
      float buf[msgSchedLen] = {iP,
        M[iP], N[iP], K[iP], S[iP], /*...*/};
      MPI_Send((void*)&buf, msgSchedLen,
        MPI_FLOAT, iW, msgSchedTag,
        MPI_COMM_WORLD);
      iP++;
    }
  }
}
```

FIGURE 25.17

Source code fragment of dynamically balanced Boss-Workers Asian options pricing MPI application (Boss rank).

```
#          Worker   Share Performance   Effic.
       c001-n003    28.0%     8.10e+06    99.5%
  c001-n003-mic0    36.0%     1.07e+07    96.9%
  c001-n003-mic1    36.0%     1.07e+07    96.6%
# Calculation   9 of  10 took 3.645 seconds
# Net performance: 2.88e+07 paths/second
```

FIGURE 25.18

Output fragment of dynamically balanced Boss-Workers Asian options pricing MPI application run.

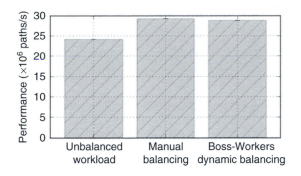

FIGURE 25.19

Performance results for tree load balancing techniques presented in this chapter.

Explicit or manual load balancing can be implemented by redistributing computational workload proportional to computational capabilities of the compute devices.

Dynamic workload balancing techniques (Boss-Workers model) can produce similar overall performance to manual workload distribution. There is the additional advantage of this approach: scaling of this MPI application will not require additional program tuning. Adding more compute nodes and populating the machine file will allow easy distribution of dynamic MPI application for faster calculations.

The techniques of finding and fixing workload imbalance in symmetric MPI applications presented here can be used to improve overall application performance running in heterogeneous cluster environment of the host processors and Intel Xeon Phi coprocessors. The consistent programming environment of such a cluster made our work very straightforward, and the resulting code has broad applicability even in homogeneous systems that experience execution variations node-to-node.

FOR MORE INFORMATION

Some additional reading materials we recommend related to this chapter:

- Vladimirov, A., Karpusenko, V., October, 2013. Heterogeneous Clustering with Homogeneous Code: Accelerate MPI Applications Without Code Surgery Using Intel Xeon Phi Coprocessors. Colfax Research. http://research.colfaxinternational.com/post/2013/10/17/Heterogeneous-Clustering.aspx
- Colfax International, 2013. Parallel Programming and Optimization with Intel Xeon Phi Coprocessors. ISBN-10 0-9885234-1-8|ISBN-13 978-0-9885234-1-8. http://www.colfax-intl.com/nd/xeonphi/book.aspx
- Download the code from this, and other chapters, http://lotsofcores.com

SCALABLE OUT-OF-CORE SOLVERS ON A CLUSTER

26

Eduardo D'Azevedo[*], **Ki Sing Chan**[†], **Shi-Quan Su**[‡], **Kwai Wong**[‡]

[*]*Oak Ridge National Laboratory, United States,* [†]*Chinese University of Hong Kong, Hong Kong,* [‡]*University of Tennessee, United States*

This chapter explains the implementation of a distributive out-of-core (OOC) solver for performing LU and Cholesky factorizations of a large dense matrix on clusters equipped with Intel® Xeon Phi™ coprocessors. The OOC algorithm combines both the left-looking and right-looking schemes aimed to minimize the movement of data between the CPU host and the coprocessor, optimizing data locality as well as computing throughput. The OOC solver is built to align with the format of the ScaLAPACK software library, making it readily portable to any existing codes using ScaLAPACK. A runtime analysis conducted on Beacon cluster that composed of 48 nodes, with Intel® Xeon®; processors and Intel Xeon Phi coprocessors, at the National Institute for Computational Sciences is presented. Comparison of the performance on the Intel Xeon Phi coprocessors and GPU clusters are also provided.

INTRODUCTION

The large-scale dense matrix computation is a backbone of modern numerical simulations, such as thermal analysis, analysis using the boundary element method, and electromagnetic wave calculations in fusion application. Many of the top-ranked supercomputers take advantage of PCIe-attached devices especially accelerators or coprocessors such as the Intel Xeon Phi coprocessor or NVIDIA graphics processing unit (GPU). For example, the number one spot in June 2014 Top500 list, Tianhe-2 supercomputer in the National Super Computer Center in Guangzhou China, uses Intel Xeon Phi coprocessors to achieve a LINPACK score of 33.86 PFlops and the second spot, Cray XK7 Titan at the Oak Ridge National Laboratory, uses NVIDIA K20 GPUs to achieve a LINPACK score of 17.59 PFlops.

Although coprocessors and GPU accelerators are very capable in performing numerical operations, there are several challenges in the effective use of these attached devices:

- A massive amount of parallelism is needed to fully exploit the accelerator or coprocessor. The Intel Xeon Phi coprocessors have over 60 physical x86 cores and each core is capable of 4-way multithreading. Thus, the coprocessor has the capacity to perform over 240-way parallelism.
- Attached devices have limited amount of device memory compared to the memory capacity on the host computer. For example, the coprocessor may have only 8 GBytes of on-board device memory but the host computer may have 32 GBytes or more of main memory. External memory or "OOC" algorithms are needed to solve problems larger than available device memory.

- Data transfer between the host, or host memory unit, and the device can be very costly. For example, on the Cray XK7 Titan supercomputer, the bandwidth for data transfer between GPU and CPU host is about 4 GBytes/s. Thus, substantial computation on the device is needed to amortize and justify the high cost of data transfer.

Therefore, a new parallel OOC solver is needed to fully take advantage of the new hybrid architecture of multicore CPUs with coprocessors or accelerators. There are a number implementations of dense linear algebra libraries for the heterogeneous systems (see Section "For more information"; Agullo et al., 2011, 2009; Barrett et al., 2010; D'Azevedo and Hill, 2012; Fogue et al., 2010; Humphrey et al., 2010; Jetley et al., 2010; Quintana-Orti et al., 2009; Song and Dongarra, 2012; Song et al., 2012). In general, the performance of these numerical library functions are tuned and optimized to attain maximum throughput. A new parallel LU solver that is compatible with the two-dimensional block cyclic distribution used in ScaLAPACK library had been developed to take advantage of NVIDIA GPU. The algorithm uses the OOC approach in treating the GPU device memory as the "fast" core memory and the host main memory as the "slower" secondary storage. The solver is able to handle problems several times larger than the available device memory. The OOC procedure adopts both the left-looking and the right-looking algorithms in the factorization steps. The left-looking algorithm minimizes the communication cost to update that part of the matrix on the coprocessor while the right looking one gives better computing performance.

This chapter describes the challenges and techniques used in porting the parallel OOC solver from NVIDIA GPU using CUBLAS to the Intel Xeon Phi coprocessor using offload directives and the Intel Math Kernel Library (MKL). First, in Section "An OOC factorization based on ScaLAPACK" we present the "OOC" approach to factorize the large dense matrix in parallel on hybrid multicore with a multi-GPU system and multicore with multiple coprocessor system. Next, in Section "Porting from NVIDIA GPU to the Intel Xeon Phi coprocessor," we describe the main challenges and techniques used in porting the parallel GPU solver to the coprocessor. Next, in Section "Numerical results," the numerical results on Beacon, including the performance data and timing result compared to that on Keeneland. Finally, Section "Conclusions and future work" highlights the conclusion and some of the future works in progress.

AN OOC FACTORIZATION BASED ON SCALAPACK

OOC factorization methods have been studied in the past in the context of inadequate CPU memory relative to the storage required for the large dense matrix. The ideas developed in these contexts can be applied to this case. In this work, we adapt the left-looking OOC algorithm for LU and Cholesky factorization described by E. D'Azevedo and J. Dongarra (see Section "For more information"; D'Azevedo and Dongarra, 2000) with a minor change that seeks to minimize the data transfer between the CPU host and the attached device memory. Central to this algorithm is the necessity for an in-core parallel LU and Cholesky factorization method that operates primarily on the device using the right-looking factorization scheme.

ScaLAPACK uses a distributed two-dimensional block cyclic storage scheme, shown in Figure 26.1. Data transfer is performed by the host using the Basic Linear Algebra Communication Subprograms (BLACS) over the message passing interface (MPI). The parallel LU algorithm has been described in detail in several papers (see Section "For more information"; D'Azevedo and Dongarra, 2000;

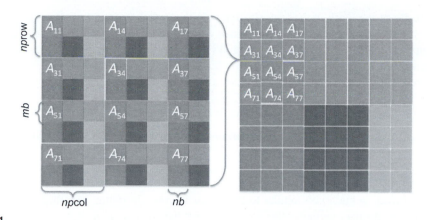

FIGURE 26.1

Two-dimensional block cyclic distribution in ScaLAPACK. Matrix *A* is decomposed by a grid of blocks of *nprow* × *npcol* processor grid, *nb* is the size of the block.

D'Azevedo and Hill, 2012). In this chapter, we extend the similar OOC algorithm to the Cholesky factorization.

IN-CORE FACTORIZATION

ScaLAPACK PDPOTRF uses a right-looking algorithm for Cholesky factorization, the same approach is applied to a distributed matrix residing in the device memory. Since the CPU host does not have direct access to memory of the attached device, any data residing on the device must be transferred to temporary buffers on the CPU to be available for communication by the MPI library. This transfer is one of the primary bottlenecks and must be minimized to achieve any performance gain using the device.

Consider a block partitioning of a symmetric positive definite matrix A:

$$A = \begin{pmatrix} A_{11} & A_{21}{}^t \\ A_{21} & A_{22} \end{pmatrix} = \begin{pmatrix} L_{11} & \\ L_{21} & L_{22} \end{pmatrix} \begin{pmatrix} L_{11}{}^t & L_{21}{}^t \\ & L_{22}{}^t \end{pmatrix}, \tag{26.1}$$

where A_{11} is a $k \times k$ square matrix. There are several steps for the factorization of matrix A:

1. Assuming the first k columns have already been factored, apply

$$\begin{pmatrix} A_{11} \\ A_{21} \end{pmatrix} \rightarrow \begin{pmatrix} \tilde{A}_{11} \\ \tilde{A}_{21} \end{pmatrix} = \begin{pmatrix} L_{11} \\ L_{21} \end{pmatrix} (L_{11}{}^t), \tag{26.2}$$

   where $\tilde{A}_{11} = L_{11}L_{11}{}^t$, $\tilde{A}_{21} = L_{21}L_{11}{}^t$. The factorization of the diagonal block A_{11} is performed on the CPU host using ScaLAPACK PDPOTRF. In our case, $k = $ MB was chosen to be the matrix block size.

2. Perform the symmetric rank-k update to $\tilde{A}_{22}$ on the device

$$\tilde{A}_{22} \leftarrow A_{22} - L_{21}L_{21}{}^t. \tag{26.3}$$

The majority of the work in the factorization is in the rank-k updating of $\tilde{A}_{22}$. The operation requires broadcasting L_{21} across the processor columns and $L_{21}{}'$ down the processor rows. This rank-k update can then be performed using DSYRK and DGEMM on the device without further communication.

3. Recursively factor the remaining submatrix

$$\tilde{A}_{22} = L_{22}L_{22}{}'. \tag{26.4}$$

A right-looking variant gives good load balancing and higher opportunities for parallelism.

OOC FACTORIZATION

The OOC factorization method is similar to that of the in-core algorithm described in Section "In-core factorization." The primary variant is that we assume that the portion of the matrix A belonging to a CPU processor is too large to be fully held in-core to the device. Thus, some data movement of the matrix between the CPU and the device will be necessary, but must be minimized to achieve good performance. The total I/O cost for the right-looking algorithm and the left-looking algorithm can be quantified as

$$\frac{M^3}{3n_b}(1+O(n_b/M))(R+W), \tag{26.5}$$

$$\frac{M^3}{2n_b}(1+O(n_b/M))R+2M^2(1+O(n_b/M))W, \tag{26.6}$$

where n_b is the block size of an $M \times M$ matrix A, and R and W are the times to read and write one matrix element, respectively. Assuming the cost of R and W are similar, the left-looking variant, Eq. (26.6), generates less data transfer compared to the right-looking variant, Eq. (26.5).

The OOC computation proceeds using two column panels. A large panel Y (in device memory) accumulates the updates from previously computed factors and a small panel X holds the previously computed factors. The computation steps are essentially similar to the in-core factorization and are described below.

1. Similar to the in-core factorization, $\tilde{A}_{12}$ and $\tilde{A}_{22}$ are copied into panel Y on the attached device. Parts of the previously computed factors in L_{11} and L_{21} are moved from the CPU into panel X on the device.
2. The triangular solve can be computed by copying part of panel Y back to the CPU host and then computed using PDTRSM in PBLAS.
3. The symmetric rank-k update to the lower part of panel Y is performed as a matrix-matrix multiplication. Similar to the in-core factorization, this requires broadcasting part of L_{21} across processor columns and broadcasting part of $L_{21}{}'$ in down processor rows. Then the rank-k update can be performed using DSYRK on the diagonal blocks and DGEMM on the off-diagonal blocks on the device without further communication.
4. After all previous updates are performed, the factorization of the lower rectangular part of panel Y ($\tilde{A}_{22}$) is computed using the all in-core algorithm described in Section "OOC factorization."
5. The computed factorization blocks in panel Y are then copied from the attached device back to CPU host.

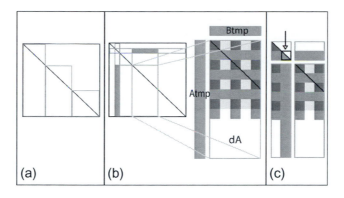

FIGURE 26.2

Schematic overview of the OOC algorithm of the Cholesky factorization. (a) Trailing part of Matrix *A* is decomposed into panels (left). (b) For each panel, compute left-looking updates. (c) Followed by right-looking updates.

The choice of the width of panel Y will affect the performance of the algorithm, but is also governed by the amount of device memory available. A wider panel Y will reduce the amount of passes and data transfer needed. A schematic overview of the OOC algorithm is shown in Figure 26.2.

If we choose the width of panel Y to be (N/K) columns such that the total size of panel Y is $N \times (N/K)$, or where the entire matrix is *k* times the width of panel Y, the factorization of the first Y-panel requires no previous factors. However, subsequent factorization of the *k*-th panel requires the transfer of the previous $k-1$ Y-panels. The volume of data transferred is thus $(1+2+\cdots+(K-1)) * (N * (N/K)) = (K-1)/2 * N^2$. Thus, the choice of *k* should be as small as possible to make the width of panel Y as large as possible. This will minimize the amount of data transferred between the device and the CPU. However, the width (N/K) will be limited by the amount of device memory available.

PORTING FROM NVIDIA GPU TO THE INTEL XEON PHI COPROCESSOR

The GPU code is written using Compute Unified Device Architecture (CUDA) with high-level library routines in CUBLAS to perform dense matrix operations in the Basic Linear Algebra Library (BLAS), manage data transfer, allocate and deallocate device memory. This use of high-level operations matches well with the offload model for the coprocessor using the Intel Language Extensions for Offload (Intel LEO) #pragma compiler directives. This method can also easily be adapted to use the OpenMP 4.0 "target" directives.

The first difference is in management of device memory. The offload model assumes an array in device memory is maintained as a mirror copy of the same array in host memory. The memory management is performed using `length()`, `alloc_if()`, `free_if()` options in the offload directive listed in Figure 26.3.

CUDA allows the extra flexibility of explicitly allocating (and deallocating) storage in device memory without the corresponding storage on host. Specification of a different length as used in Figure 26.4 will lead to errors.

```
double *Y = (double*) malloc(n*sizeof(double));
#pragma offload_transfer target(mic:MYDEVICE) nocopy(Y:length(n) alloc_if(1) free_if(0))
#pragma offload_transfer target(mic:MYDEVICE) nocopy(Y:length(n) alloc_if(0) free_if(1))
```

FIGURE 26.3

Code fragment to allocate and deallocate memory on the Intel MIC.

```
int *p = (int*) malloc(1*sizeof(int));
int *q = (int*) malloc(1*sizeof(int));
#pragma offload_transfer target(mic) nocopy(p:length(1000) alloc_if(1) free_if(0))
#pragma offload_transfer target(mic) nocopy(q:length(1000) alloc_if(1) free_if(0))
```

FIGURE 26.4

Unequal size offload allocation of memory may lead to errors.

```
intptr_t offload_Alloc(size_t size){
    intptr_t ptr;
    #pragma offload target(mic:MYDEVICE) out(ptr)
    {
        ptr = (intptr_t) memalign(64, size);
    }
    return ptr;
}

void offload_Free(void* p){
    intptr_t ptr = (intptr_t)p;
    #pragma offload target(mic:MYDEVICE) in(ptr)
    {
        free((void*)ptr);
    }
}
```

```
#ifdef USE_MIC                                          if (dAtmp != 0) {
    dY = (double*) offload_Alloc(isizeY*elemSize);          #ifdef USE_MIC
#else                                                           offload_Free(dAtmp);
    cublasAlloc( isizeY, elemSize, (void **) &dY );     #else
#endif                                                          CUBLAS_FREE( dAtmp );
                                                        #endif
                                                            dAtmp = 0;
                                                        };
```

FIGURE 26.5

Code fragment to perform allocate and deallocate memory on the Intel MIC.

A work-around is to allocate device memory using `memalign()` on the device but to transfer only the *value* of pointer address using long integer type instead of pointer type. The integer value is used only in the offload data transfer. The integer value is recast as pointer before use. This technique is illustrated in Figure 26.5 to implement the equivalent of `cublasAlloc()` and `cublasFree()`. Note that the `intptr_t` type is guaranteed in C99 standard to be sufficiently long to hold a pointer.

```
CUBLAS_DGEMM(
        CUBLAS_OP_N,CUBLAS_OP_N, mm,nn,kk,
        zalpha,  (double *) dA(lrA1,lcA1), ldAtmp,
                 (double *) dB(lrB1,lcB1), ldBtmp,
        zbeta,   (double *) dC(lrC1,lcC1), ldC );

                        |
                        v

offload_dgemm("N",  "N", &mm, &nn, &kk,
        &zalpha,  (double *) dA(lrA1,lcA1), &ldAtmp,
                  (double *) dB(lrB1,lcB1), &ldBtmp,
        &zbeta,   (double *) dC(lrC1,lcC1), &ldC );

                        |
                        v

void offload_dgemm(const char *transa, const char *transb, const MKL_INT *m, const MKL_INT *n, const MKL_INT *k,
                   const double *alpha, const double *a, const MKL_INT *lda, const double *b, const MKL_INT *ldb,
                   const double *beta, double *c, const MKL_INT *ldc){
/*
 * perform dgemm on the device. a,b,c pre-exist on the device
 */
    intptr_t aptr = (intptr_t)a;
    intptr_t bptr = (intptr_t)b;
    intptr_t cptr = (intptr_t)c;
    #pragma offload target(mic:MYDEVICE) in(transa,transb,m,n,k:length(1)) \
                                         in(alpha,lda,ldb,beta,ldc:length(1))
    {
        dgemm(transa,transb,m,n,k,alpha,(double*)aptr,lda,(double*)bptr,ldb,beta,(double*)cptr,ldc);
    }
}
```

FIGURE 26.6

Conversion of CUBLAS to Intel MKL.

Another difference is the offload directive allows transfer of only one-dimensional or contiguous region of memory, whereas CUDA cudaMemcpy 2D can perform data transfer of a two-dimensional submatrix. This operation is emulated by a loop that:

  (i) packs two-dimensional data into a contiguous one-dimensional buffer,
 (ii) performs contiguous data transfer by off-load directive,
(iii) unpacks data from buffer into two-dimensional submatrix on the device.

The translation of CUBLAS calls to using equivalent operations in MKL is quite straight-forward. Figure 26.6 shows a code fragment of converting a CUBLAS DGEMM call to equivalent MKL DGEMM. The offload directive transfers the pointers (as integers) then recast the integers back to pointers before use.

NUMERICAL RESULTS

The numerical experiments of the OOC Cholesky factorization solver were run on the Beacon cluster that includes coprocessors to determine the scalability and performance characteristics.

Beacon is a cluster, using both an Intel Xeon processors with Intel Xeon Phi coprocessors, at the National Institute for Computational Science and held the number 1 place in the November 2012 Green500 list. Beacon reached 71.4% energy efficiency (2.449 GFlops/W). The machine consists of 48 compute nodes. On each node, it has two 8-core Intel Xeon E5-2670 processors (total 16 physical cores), with *four* Intel Xeon Phi 5110P coprocessors. Each coprocessor has 8 GBytes of device memory with 60 cores at 1.053 GHz. There are 256 GBytes of CPU memory on each node. The machine has FDR InfiniBand interconnect between nodes. Each core on the node has full access to all coprocessors. GPU results were performed on the Keeneland machine (http://keeneland.gatech.edu/). Keeneland is a 264-node cluster delivering a total peak double precision performance of 615 TFlops. Each node has 32 GBytes of host memory, two Intel Xeon E5 processors and three NVIDIA M2090 GPUs. Each M2090 GPU has a peak performance of 665 GFlops and 6 GBytes of device memory.

Table 26.1 summarizes the performance of LU factorization on Beacon using four MPI tasks per node, so that each MPI task is associated with a coprocessor (mydevice = MOD(MPI rank,4)). About 6 GBytes of device memory was allocated to the OOC panels, and block size MB=NB=512. The performance of Cholesky factorization is shown in Table 26.2. The highest performance achieves 370 GFlops on each coprocessor.

Figure 26.7 shows the performance per coprocessor against the ratio between host memory and device memory on Beacon. We perform the computation on four nodes, two coprocessors, and two CPU cores on each node. We choose a 4 × 2 processor grid. The block size NB is 512. The memsize

Table 26.1   Performance of LU Factorization on Beacon

Processor Grid	N	Size per MIC (GBytes)	GFlops per MIC (GFlops)
8 × 8	176,000	3.9	140
8 × 8	250,000	7.8	172
8 × 8	350,000	15.3	208
10 × 10	250,000	5	124
10 × 10	350,000	9.8	171
10 × 10	400,000	12.8	177
12 × 12	250,000	3.5	112
12 × 12	500,000	13.9	141

Table 26.2   Performance of LLT Factorization on Beacon

Processor Grid	N	Number of Panels	GFlops per MIC (GFlops)
1 × 1	156,672	20	372
4 × 1	313,344	20	349
8 × 2	626,688	20	340
2 × 1	156,672	10	311
10 × 10	313,344	10	319
10 × 10	626,688	10	260
4 × 1	163,840	6	281
8 × 2	327,680	6	269
16 × 4	655,360	6	212
16 × 4	983,040	12	246

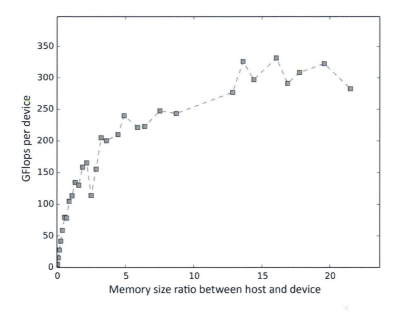

FIGURE 26.7

Performance via memory ratio ρ between host and device, on Beacon. The processor grid is 4×2. The ratio ρ can be up to 20.

is 737,280 fixed, which is equivalent to 5.625 GBytes device memory (1 MPI task per coprocessor). The largest matrix we compute is $N = 360{,}448$, resides on 948 GBytes host memory totally, which is 242 GBytes on each node. The maximum ρ can reach $(360{,}448 * 360{,}448)/(737{,}280 * 1024) = 20$. The curve shows the same trend that the larger the ρ is, the better is the performance.

Figures 26.8 and 26.9 show the performance via matrix size N, so we can compare to the computation that just calls the corresponding ScaLAPACK routine `PDPOTRF`. On Keeneland, we compute the matrix size up to 86,400. The performance comparison is on one GPU to one 8-core CPU. The GPU version shows better performance than the CPU version in the whole range. Especially the GPU version keeps gaining performance at the large N region, and the CPU version reaches its best performance at the intermediate N, and the performance decreases significantly at large N. On Beacon, the performance of the coprocessor version also keeps increasing at large N.

We show the performance data on fixed processor grids, we study the performance scaling behaviors on both platforms. We show the weak scaling and strong scaling studies on Keeneland in Figure 26.10. The processor grid is $4p \times 4p$. And we use $2 * p^2$ nodes. For the weak scaling, the matrix size $N = 84{,}352 * p$, each MPI task used about 665 MBytes of device memory, and the block size NB = 128. The total performance keeps increasing close to linearly to the processor grid size, and the performance per GPU is around 170 GFlops declines slightly in the whole range. For the strong scaling, the matrix size is fix at $N = 84{,}352$, each MPI task used about 665 MBytes of device memory, and the block size NB = 128. The total performance keeps increasing via increasing the processor grid size. The wall time of the factorization decreases in the whole range.

In Figure 26.11, we show the strong scaling study on Beacon. We have the similar results, the total performance keeps increasing via increasing the processor grid size $p * p$. The total time of the

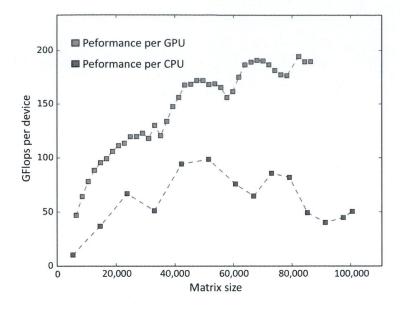

FIGURE 26.8

Performance via matrix size N, on Keeneland. The matrix size is up to $N = 86,400$, which equals to using 28 GBytes host memory per node. The comparison to the ScaLAPACK call using CPU only is also shown.

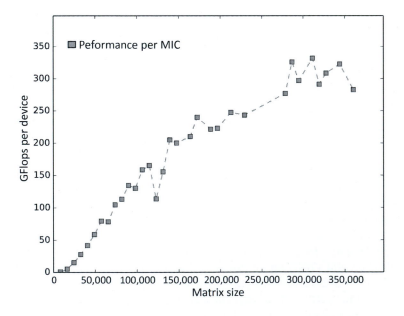

FIGURE 26.9

Performance via matrix size N, on Beacon. The maximum matrix size we compute is $N = 360,448$. The matrix occupies 242 GBytes of host memory on each node.

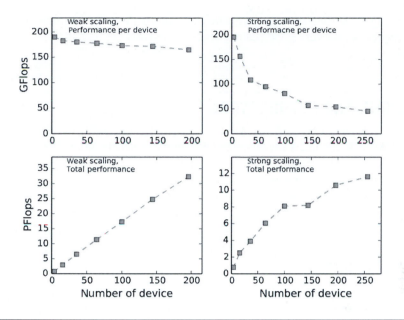

FIGURE 26.10

Weak and strong scaling study, on Keeneland. The processor grid is $4p \times 4p$. And we use $2 * p^2$ nodes. The p is up to 7.

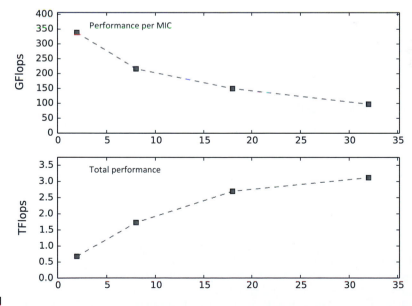

FIGURE 26.11

Strong scaling study, on Beacon. The processor grid is $2p * p$. And we use p^2 nodes. The p is up to 6.

factorization keep decreasing through out the range we reach. From the scaling studies, we can see that the OOC approach shows very good scaling behavior, and has the potential to scale up to very large processor grid.

CONCLUSIONS AND FUTURE WORK

In summary, we have described a distributed memory parallel LU and Cholesky solver that is compatible with ScaLAPACK and takes advantage of GPU and MIC accelerators. The OOC algorithm allows very large problems, several times available device memory, to be solved. The performance is higher as the ratio of data size to device memory (ρ) is increased.

Future optimization will consider use of asynchronous BLAS operations and concurrent data transfer to further improve the performance.

ACKNOWLEDGMENTS

This research project is supported by the National Science Foundation, Department of Energy, Oak Ridge National Laboratory, Chinese University of Hong Kong, and the University of Tennessee. This material is based upon work supported by the National Science Foundation under Grant numbers 0711134, 0933959, 1041709, and 1041710 and the University of Tennessee through the use of the Beacon computing resource at the National Institute for Computational Sciences (http://www.nics.tennessee.edu).This research used resources of the Keeneland Computing Facility at the Georgia Institute of Technology, which is supported by the National Science Foundation under Contract OCI-0910735. The submitted manuscript has been authored by a contractor of the U.S. Government under Contract No. DE-AC05-00OR22725. Accordingly, the U.S. Government retains a non-exclusive, royalty-free license to publish or reproduce the published form of this contribution, or allow others to do so, for U.S. Government purposes.

FOR MORE INFORMATION

Agullo, E., Augonnet, C., Dongarra, J., Faverge, M., Ltaief, H., Thibault, S., Tomov, S., 2011. QR factorization on a multicore node enhanced with multiple GPU accelerators. IPDPS 2011, Alaska, USA.

Agullo, E., Demmel, J., Dongarra, J., Hadri, B., Kurzak, J., Langou, J., Ltaief, H., Luszczek, P., Tomov, S., 2009. Numerical linear algebra on emerging architectures: The PLASMA and MAGMA projects. J. Phys. Conf. Ser. 180, 012037.

Barrett, R.F., Chan, T.H.F., D'Azevedo, E.F., Jaeger, E.F., Wong, K., Wong, R.Y., 2010. Complex version of high performance computing LINPACK benchmark (HPL). Concurr. Comput.: Pract. Exper 22 (5), 537–587.

D'Azevedo, E., Dongarra, J., 2000. The design and implementation of the parallel out-of-core ScaLAPACK LU, QR, and Cholesky factorization routines. Concurr. Comput.: Pract. Exper. 12, 1481–1493.

D'Azevedo, E., Hill, J.C., 2012. Parallel LU factorization on GPU cluster. Proced. Comput. Sci. 9, 67–75.

Fogue, M., Igual, F.D., Quintana-Orti, E.S., van de Geijn, R., 2010. Retargeting PLAPACK to clusters with hardware accelerators. FLAME Working Note 42.

Humphrey, J.R., Price, D.K., Spagnoli, K.E., Paolini, A.L., Kelmelis, E.J., 2010. CULA: Hybrid GPU accelerated linear algebra routines. SPIE Defense and Security Symposium (DSS), April 2010.

Jetley, P., Wesolowski, L., Gioachin, F., Kale, L.V., Quinn, T.R., 2010. Scaling hierarchical N-body simulations on GPU clusters. In: Proceedings of the 2010 ACM/IEEE International Conference for High Performance Computing, Networking, Storage and Analysis, SC10. pp. 1–11.

Quintana-Orti, G., Igual, F.D., Quintana-Orti, E.S., van de Geijn, R.A., 2009. Solving dense linear systems on platforms with multiple hardware accelerators. Proceedings of the 14th ACM SIGPLAN symposium on Principles and practice of parallel programming PPoPP '09, 121–130.

Song, F., Dongarra, J., 2012. A scalable framework for heterogeneous GPU-based clusters. Proceedings of the 24th ACM symposium on Parallelism in algorithms and architectures. ACM, 91–100.

Song, F., Tomov, S., Dongarra, J., 2012. Enabling and scaling matrix computations on heterogeneous multi-core and multi-GPU systems. Proceedings of the 26th ACM international conference on Supercomputing. ACM, 365–376.

SPARSE MATRIX-VECTOR MULTIPLICATION: PARALLELIZATION AND VECTORIZATION

27

Albert-Jan N. Yzelman, Dirk Roose, Karl Meerbergen

KU Leuven, Belgium

BACKGROUND

Sparse computations are ubiquitous in computational codes, with the sparse matrix-vector (SpMV) multiplication as an important computational kernel in software for simulation (e.g., computational fluid dynamics, structural analysis), optimization (e.g., economics, transport scheduling), data analysis (e.g., drug testing, social networks), and so on. A sparse matrix is characterized by having most of its elements equal to zero. To take advantage of the sparsity, such matrices are stored in specifically designed data structures so that meaningless multiplications with zeroes can be avoided.

Current hardware trends lead to an increasing width of vector units as well as to decreasing effective bandwidth-per-core. For sparse computations, these two trends conflict. In this chapter, we consider sparse matrix computations on multicore architectures with vector processing capabilities, and design a usable and efficient data structure for vectorized sparse computations.

An $m \times n$ matrix A has m rows and n columns and contains elements a_{ij}, with $i = 0,1,\ldots,m-1$ and $j = 0,1,\ldots,n-1$. Consider the matrix-vector multiplication $y = Ax$ with x and y vectors of dimension n and m, respectively. Each element of the output vector y is computed as the dot product of one row of A with the input vector x, i.e., $y_i = \sum_{j=0}^{n-1} a_{ij} x_j$; see Figure 27.1 for an illustration. When all values of A are stored in row-major order such that consecutive elements of a row of A are in consecutive memory locations, then both A and y are read contiguously and with stride-one accesses. Such stream accesses are very efficient and lead to high-bandwidth data movement. Nonobligatory cache misses then only occur on the input vector x, since its elements are read repeatedly.

Taking into account the sizes of the caches, storing A as a collection of blocks that fit precisely into cache can be highly efficient. Such *cache-aware* methods contrast with the development of storage schemes and algorithms that perform well regardless of the specifics of the cache hierarchy. Such *cache-oblivious* methods do not require setting architecture-dependent parameters, such as the size of the aforementioned blocks.

If A is sparse, only the elements $a_{ij} \neq 0$ and their location in the matrix should be stored. These sparse storage schemes are introduced in Section "Sparse matrix data structures." For operations on compact sparse matrix structures, the number of operations per data word (also known as the arithmetic intensity)

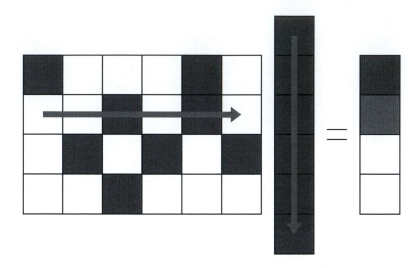

FIGURE 27.1

Illustration of a sparse matrix-vector multiplication $y = Ax$, at y_2. Colored squares represent nonzeroes, while empty squares represent zero values.

is very low; since the time to perform a floating point operation is much shorter than the time to read or store a data word, only a very small fraction of peak performance can be achieved during an SpMV multiplication. This is a characteristic problem for sparse computations and leads to the expectation that

(a) compressing the storage of sparse matrices increases performance and
(b) sparse computations cannot benefit from vectorization.

We show that the former is true even when compression results in additional operations, since the computation remains bandwidth-bound. The latter expectation, however, is *not* always true: vectorization *can* increase the performance of SpMV multiplication on the Intel® Xeon Phi™ coprocessor, despite its low arithmetic intensity.

We describe several sparse matrix data structures in Section "Sparse matrix data structures." Section "Parallel SpMV multiplication" then discusses various strategies to parallelize the SpMV multiplication on a shared memory system, followed by a section that shows how to benefit from vectorization on the Intel Xeon Phi coprocessor. Performance results are given in the final section in this chapter.

SPARSE MATRIX DATA STRUCTURES

A basic data structure for sparse matrix computations is the coordinate (COO) format, which stores a sparse matrix A using three arrays (i, j, v) of length nz each. Here, nz is the number of nonzero elements of A. COO stores the kth nonzero a_{ij} by setting $v_k = a_{ij}, i_k = i,$ and $j_k = j$. Note that the nonzeroes of A can be stored in any order. The following algorithm computes $y = Ax$ using COO.

Algorithm 1: COO-BASED SpMV MULTIPLICATION
1: **for** $k = 0$ to nz-1 **do**
2:     add $v_k \cdot x_{j_k}$ to y_{i_k}
3: **end for**

For the COO-based SpMV multiplication, the arithmetic intensity typically lies between 0.25 and 1, depending on the cache efficiency. To make full use of the compute power of current processors, however, a much higher arithmetic intensity is needed.

The Intel Haswell E3-1225 processor, for example, has four 3.2 GHz cores. The processor supports AVX 2 which allows simultaneous (vectorized) operations on four 64-bits data words, in particular also supporting fused multiply-add (FMA) instructions which executes two floating point operations (flops) per data word. The maximum peak performance assumes only FMA operations, multiplied with (1) the number of cores, (2) the number of data words that can be operated simultaneously on (the vector length), and (3) the processor speed: $2 \times 4 \times 4 \times 3.2 = 102.4$ Gflop/s. The bandwidth of a DDR3-1600 memory controller is 12.8 GB/s, or 1.6 giga-words per second. To make full use of the compute power of this processor, $1024/16 = 64$ computations must occur for each data word brought to the processor.

The Intel Xeon Phi 7120A coprocessor has 61 cores operating at 1.238 GHz, also supports FMAs, and contains vector units that can handle eight 64-bit data words simultaneously. Its peak performance therefore is $2 \times 61 \times 8 \times 1.238 = 1208$ Gflop/s. The coprocessor contains 16 GB of GDDR5 memory with a maximum bandwidth of 352 GB/s, or 44 giga-words per second. For algorithms to become compute bound on this processor, an algorithm must perform at least 28 operations per data word ($1208/44 = 27.5$).

Clearly, for both modern architectures discussed above, the required number of operations per data words lies several factors higher than those incurred for sparse computations such as the SpMV multiplication. Our problem thus is expected to be bandwidth-bound, with cores spending a relatively long time stalling while waiting for required data.

This problem can be alleviated somewhat by inducing more efficient cache behavior. While the access to the sparse matrix data structure itself is contiguous and stride-one, the access patterns of the vectors x and y are determined by the ordering of the nonzeroes: a row-major order induces contiguous stride-one accesses on y but random accesses on x, while a completely random order results in costly random accesses on both x and y. Random accesses (as opposed to contiguous accesses) have high latency cost, lower throughput, and may stall of compute cores. Optimizing the nonzero order such that the memory accesses to x and y are expected to be minimum leads to *fractal storage* schemes; there, space-filling curves impose an ordering on the nonzero coordinates (i, j). Figure 27.2 illustrates a cache-oblivious order of the nonzeroes based on the Hilbert curve.

A *matrix-aware* approach analyzes the nonzero structure of A and optimizes data storage according to this information. Automatic detection of small structured blocks, combined with cache-aware data structures, leads to auto-tuning approaches such as those in the OSKI and pOSKI libraries. For more information on cache- and matrix-aware methods, see, e.g., Vuduc et al. (2005). Alternatively, through sparse matrix partitioning, matrix rows and columns can be reordered such that an upper bound on the number of cache misses is minimized, in an improved cache-oblivious manner. The cost of auto-tuning or preprocessing of matrix-aware methods restricts the usability of this class of methods.

COMPRESSED DATA STRUCTURES

The COO data structure can be compressed in several ways. If we first impose a row major order on the nonzeroes, subsequent entries of i contain strings of the same row number. This redundant data may be compressed into an array s of size $m + 1$, where the value for s_i is set to the smallest integer $0 \leq k < nz$ for which $i_k = i$, for all $0 \leq i < m$; the value of s_m is defined as nz. The data structure (s, j, v), with the latter two arrays unchanged from COO with nonzeroes in row-major order, is the Compressed Row

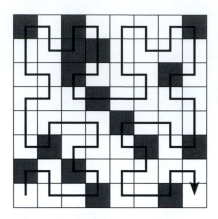

FIGURE 27.2

Traversal of a sparse matrix according to a space-filling Hilbert curve.

Storage (CRS) format. CRS is the *de facto* standard for storing unstructured sparse matrices.[1] Note that using CRS precludes cache-oblivious optimizations by using a fractal nonzero ordering such as in Figure 27.2.

A CRS-based SpMV multiplication loops over all rows first and over its nonzeroes second, as illustrated in the following algorithm:

> Algorithm 2: CRS-BASED SpMV MULTIPLICATION
> 1: **for** $i = 0$ to $m - 1$ **do**
> 2:   **for** $k = s_i$ to $s_{i+1} - 1$ **do**
> 3:   add $v_k \cdot x_{j_k}$ to y_i
> 4:   **end for**
> 5: **end for**

Similarly, imposing a column-major order and compressing j results in the compressed column storage (CCS). Note that CRS requires $\Theta(2nz + m + 1)$ of storage, which is a substantial reduction compared to $\Theta(3nz)$ for COO.

Compression without limiting the nonzero order to a row- or column-major one is also possible. Consider the COO data structure, with nonzeroes in an arbitrary order, and encode the differences of consecutive values in i and j in the "delta arrays" Δi and Δj, respectively, such that

$$(\Delta i)_k = \begin{cases} i_0 & \text{if } k = 0, \\ i_k - i_{k-1} & \text{if } k > 0. \end{cases}$$

and similarly for Δj. Figure 27.3 (left) illustrates this delta encoding.

When successive nonzeroes belong to the same row or column, strings of zeroes appear in Δi or Δj. This creates an opportunity for compression. Instead of storing Δi, we shall store the array $\widetilde{\Delta i}$, where $(\widetilde{\Delta i})_0 = (\Delta i)_0$ while omitting any remaining zeroes. To not lose information on which nonzero belongs to

---

[1]CRS is alternatively known as Compressed Sparse Rows (CSR).

$$\begin{pmatrix} & 6 & & & \\ & 7 & & & \\ 2 & & & 4 & \\ & & & & 2 \\ & 3 & 7 & 6 & \end{pmatrix} \rightarrow \begin{array}{l} i & = & [\ 0\ 3\ 4\ 4\ 4\ 2\ 2\ 1\ ] \\ j & = & [\ 1\ 4\ 2\ 1\ 3\ 3\ 0\ 1\ ] \\ v & = & [\ 6\ 2\ 7\ 3\ 6\ 4\ 2\ 7\ ] \end{array}$$

$$\begin{array}{rcl} \Delta i & = & [\ 0\ 3\ 1\ 0\ 0{-}2\ 0{-}1\ ] \\ \Delta j & = & [\ 1\ 3{-}2{-}1\ 2\ 0{-}3\ 1\ ] \\ v & = & [\ 6\ 2\ 7\ 3\ 6\ 4\ 2\ 7\ ] \end{array} \rightarrow \begin{array}{rcl} \widetilde{\Delta i} & = & [\ 0\ 3\ 1\ {-}2\ {-}1\ ] \\ \widetilde{\Delta j} & = & [\ 1\ \mathbf{8}\ \mathbf{3}\ {-}1\ 2\ \mathbf{5}{-}3\ \mathbf{6}\ ] \\ v & = & [\ 6\ 2\ 7\ 3\ 6\ 4\ 2\ 7\ ] \end{array}$$

FIGURE 27.3

Sketch of an example matrix (top left) and a COO representation of it (top right). By omitting zeroes from Δi of the COO delta encoding (bottom left), the BICRS data structure (bottom right) can be derived. A bold-faced element in $\widetilde{\Delta j}$ indicates that a row jump occurs at the corresponding nonzero; note that this means n was added to the corresponding column increment.

which row, we adapt the array Δj so that it marks whenever a row jump in Δi occurred, by adding n to the corresponding element in the column increment array. The resulting array $\widetilde{\Delta j}$ thus is determined by

$$\widetilde{\Delta j}_k = \begin{cases} \Delta j_0 & \text{if } k = 0, \\ \Delta j_k & \text{if } k > 0 \text{ and } \Delta i_k = 0, \\ \Delta j_k + n & \text{if } k > 0 \text{ and } \Delta i_k \neq 0. \end{cases}$$

Figure 27.3 (right) illustrates this approach. Note that the additional bookkeeping in the column increment array essentially costs a single bit per entry.

Similar to CRS and CCS, the roles of rows and columns could be interchanged with compression applied on Δj instead. These data structures are called Bi-directional Incremental CRS (BICRS) and BICCS, respectively. BICRS allows for efficient implementations, as shown in Algorithm 3. BICRS was introduced to make the use of space-filling curves feasible in terms of data movement. See Yzelman and Bisseling (2012) for details.

Algorithm 3: BICRS-BASED SpMV MULTIPLICATION
1: $c = 0, i = \tilde{\Delta} i_c, j = \tilde{\Delta} j_0$
2: **for** $k = 0$ to $nz\text{-}1$ **do**
3:      add $v_k \cdot x_j$ to y_i
4:      add $\tilde{\Delta} j_{k+1}$ to j
5:      **if** j indicates a row jump **then**
6:          add $\tilde{\Delta} i_c$ to i
7:          increment c
8:      **end if**
9: **end for**

Note that only $\Theta(\log_2 m)$ and $\Theta(\log_2 n)$ bits are required to store an element of $\widetilde{\Delta i}$ and $\widetilde{\Delta j}$, respectively. By using shorter integer types for storing these arrays, additional compression is achieved; we refer to this data structure as compressed BICRS.

BLOCKING

Using Compressed BICRS is synergistic with blocking of the sparse input matrix. We use a two-level approach where A is subdivided into small square blocks, and the blocks are ordered according to a space-filling Hilbert curve. Ordering the blocks this way increases cache efficiency, and can be efficiently stored using BICRS. Construction of this higher-level data structure is cheap since Hilbert COOs must now be calculated for each block, instead of for each nonzero, which also applies to the sorting of blocks (instead of nonzeroes) according to their Hilbert coordinates.

Within each block, nonzeroes are stored in row-major order. We optimize the dimensions of each block so that the elements of $\widetilde{\Delta i}$ and $\widetilde{\Delta j}$ can be stored in 16 bits (using `short int`). This enables the compressed storage of nonzeroes within blocks using Compressed BICRS; since most rows within sparse blocks are empty, BICRS is preferable to CRS since the latter requires $m + 1$ storage regardless of whether any of those rows are empty. By using compression via shorter integer types, this two-level scheme ensures that storing the blocked matrix requires less memory than storing the original unblocked matrix A using CRS. See Yzelman and Roose (2014) for more details.

PARALLEL SPMV MULTIPLICATION

To parallelize the algorithms above for shared-memory architectures, the work must be distributed over the available threads or processes. In general, data reside in the global memory, accessible by all threads. If the matrix and vectors are allocated in one contiguous chunk of memory, then each thread can access elements within that chunk according to the given work distribution. This way, the CRS-based SpMV multiplication can easily be parallelized using OpenMP compiler directives by adding the following pragma before the outer for-loop (statement 1) in Algorithm 2: `omp parallel for schedule(dynamic,8)`.

However, data can also be distributed explicitly by having each core allocates their own memory chunks, so that each thread allocates the data elements it operates during the parallel computation. There are two reasons for using explicit data distributions on shared-memory architectures: (1) to avoid data races and (2) to exploit data locality. The choice of distributing data explicitly or keeping all data globally available can significantly impact the performance. In the below, we describe two types of data distributions for the SpMV multiplication that apply explicit distributions in varying degrees.

PARTIALLY DISTRIBUTED PARALLEL SPMV

In the partially distributed approach, illustrated in Figure 27.4, the matrix A is partitioned row-wise, yielding submatrices A_s, $s = 0, \ldots, p - 1$, with p the number of threads. Each submatrix A_s is a rectangular matrix with less than m rows but with the full number of columns n. Each is stored in separate chunks of memory, conform the idea of explicit distributions. To ensure work balance, each A_s should contain approximately nz/p elements (although the number of rows may differ from m/p). Each A_s is divided into blocks with fixed row and column dimensions and uses (compressed) BICRS storage, as described in the earlier section on blocking. The blocks are handled in an order defined by the Hilbert curve. This ensures a cache-oblivious traversal that benefits data reuse on the high-level caches, while minimizing the amount of memory required for data storage.

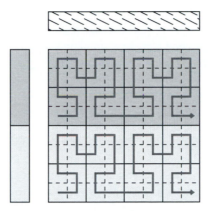

FIGURE 27.4

Illustration of the partially distributed method for $p = 2$. The upper and lower matrix regions are distributed to different threads. The distribution ensures each thread handles approximately the same number of nonzero elements; thus, in practice, the height of each region may differ. The output vector (left) is distributed according to the row distribution. The input vector (top) is not distributed explicitly. The Hilbert curve in the upper and lower regions indicates the cache-oblivious access pattern of the matrix blocks.

In accordance to the distribution of the matrix rows, the output vector y is also split in p contiguous and non-overlapping blocks, with the sth block allocated by thread s itself. Threads access only the y_s they allocated themselves, thus avoiding data races (concurrent writes) on the output vector, while simultaneously exploiting data locality on y. All threads still operate on the entire input vector x, which is stored in an interleaved fashion across the multiple memory banks that may be available. This happens automatically on the Intel Xeon Phi coprocessor, but requires manual intervention via the "libnuma" library on other shared-memory architectures. This prevents exploiting any data locality on x. By nature of this row-wise distribution and the global availability of the vector x, no explicit interthread communication or synchronization is required during SpMV multiplication. For a more detailed description, see Yzelman and Roose (2014).

The following algorithm sketches this approach. Note that the last line (statement 4) is optional, and only required when the application cannot work with a distributed output vector. To exploit data locality and for increased cache efficiency, however, efficient applications should phrase operations on y as thread-local operations on each y_s separately.

Algorithm 4: PARTIALLY DISTRIBUTED PARALLEL SpMV MULTIPLICATION
1: Partition A row-wise into local matrices $A_s, s = 0,\dots,p-1$ (see Fig. 27.4)
2: Create corresponding local arrays $y_s, s = 0,\dots,p-1$
3: Each core $s = 0,\dots,p-1$ executes $\text{SpMV}(A_s, x, y_s)$
4: Concatenate $y_s, s = 0,\dots,p-1$ into y

FULLY DISTRIBUTED PARALLEL SPMV

In a fully distributed scheme, we exploit data locality not only on A and y but also on x. In a preprocessing step, we first partition the sparse matrix by splitting the nonzeroes of A into p parts. These again form local matrices A_s, on which each thread can concurrently perform local SpMV multiplications $y_s = A_s x_s$. In this case, however, rows and columns of the A_s may overlap; the x_s and y_s thus are possibly overlapping subsets of the input and output vectors. A good matrix partitioning keeps the number of nonzeroes of A_s close to nz/p and minimizes the communication involving the overlapping parts of A_s, x_s, and y_s.

Figure 27.5 shows the partitioning of a matrix in the doubly separated block diagonal (SBD) form, as introduced by Yzelman and Bisseling (2009, 2011), for four threads. Such a partitioning can be obtained by (recursive) hypergraph bi-partitioning, which usually entails preprocessing the input matrix using a matrix partitioner. For examples of such partitioners, see Mondriaan by Vastenhouw and Bisseling (2005) or Zoltan by Devine et al. (2006). The partitioning also defines the reordering required to permute A into SBD form. This reordering results in p large local blocks (the squares in the figure), separated by $p - 1$ separator crosses. Thread-local multiplication of the local blocks requires no communication, while multiplications involving nonzeroes in separator crosses requires explicit inter-thread communication, and also incurs synchronization overheads to prevent data races on the output vector elements corresponding to matrix rows contained in the separator cross.

The thread-local multiplications do not use the explicit blocking scheme described in the earlier section on blocking, but instead rely on the blocks naturally created by the doubly SBD reordering. These local blocks and separator crosses are stored in separate Compressed BICRS data structures, for which the data types of the $\widetilde{\Delta i}$ and $\widetilde{\Delta j}$ arrays are auto-tuned at run time for maximum compression.

Explicitly distributing all data is mandatory on distributed-memory architectures: modern-day supercomputing requires fully distributed algorithms to parallelize over multiple nodes, while other methods may be used within nodes. The fully distributed SpMV multiplication method sketched here is efficient on both distributed-memory as well as shared-memory architectures, as demonstrated recently by Yzelman et al. (2014); when used on shared-memory multisocket machines, it is capable of

FIGURE 27.5

Illustration of the fully distributed and reordered SpMV multiplication for four threads. Each of the square blocks correspond to submatrices distributed to different threads. Between the square blocks separator crosses appear. Nonzeroes in separator crosses may be distributed to any thread the separator spans. Whenever an element of x overlaps horizontally with a separator cross, multiple threads may read that element; likewise, an element from y may be written to by multiple threads if its location overlaps with the vertical part of a separator cross. In practice, the blocks are usually not of equal size.

outperforming the partially distributed parallel SpMV multiplication described earlier in this section, as well as other state-of-the-art methods.

Since the cost of matrix partitioning is non-trivial and increases with the number of threads, this method will not be applied on the Intel Xeon Phi coprocessor. However, when work is to be distributed over multiple Intel Xeon Phi coprocessors, as in a classical distributed-memory supercomputing context, fully distributed methods are mandatory for good performance. For more detail on this method, refer to Yzelman and Roose (2014). For a high-performance implementation of this scheme, refer to its MulticoreBSP for C implementation by Yzelman et al. (2014).

VECTORIZATION ON THE INTEL XEON PHI COPROCESSOR

The vector units on the Intel Xeon Phi coprocessor operate on vector registers that each contain eight 64-bit floating point values. The low flop-to-byte ratio of the SpMV multiplication suggests that these vector units will not be usable for a bandwidth-bound computation; the computation is memory-bound, with processing units more often waiting for data to arrive than performing computations on said data. However, simply using the partially distributed parallel SpMV described in the previous section with an increasing number of threads p, up to $p = 240$, reveals an effective bandwidth use far less than the available 352 GB/s. This indicates that the SpMV on the coprocessor is not bandwidth-bound (nor did it turn compute bound). Instead, the multiplication on this architecture has become latency bound; using the full amount of 240 threads does not saturate the memory subsystem. A way to still be able to generate more data requests while using the same number of threads is to use vectorization.

Auto vectorization of a sequential SpMV multiplication using Compressed BICRS is, however, not possible. Pointer arithmetic and indirect addressing of vector elements prevents this. To enable vectorization, the BICRS multiplication algorithm is rewritten to operate on successive chunks of $p \cdot q$ nonzeroes, where $p \cdot q = l$ is the vectorization length, so that vector registers can operate op l nonzeroes simultaneously.

We refer to the different possible choices of p and q as the *blocking size*; on the coprocessor, $p \cdot q = 8$ and four possible blocking sizes thus appear: 1×8, 2×4, 4×2, and 8×1. These are illustrated in Figure 27.6. If $\mathbf{y}$, $\mathbf{v}$, and $\mathbf{x}$ are arrays of length 8 that correspond to vector registers, then the inner computation of the SpMV multiply, i.e., $y_i = a_{ij}x_j$, can instead be written as a single vectorized FMA $\mathbf{y} := \mathbf{y} + \mathbf{v} * \mathbf{x}$. Rewriting the BICRS SpMV multiplication algorithm to use this type of vectorization requires the use of gather and scatter instructions on the coprocessor; the gather allows loading non-consecutive

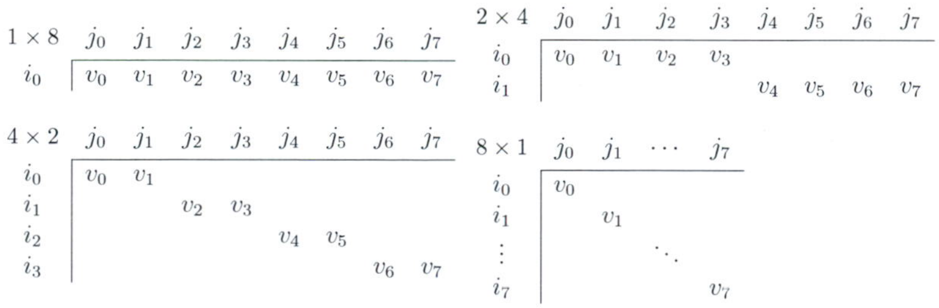

FIGURE 27.6

The four possible blocking sizes on the coprocessor: 1×8, 2×4, 4×2, and 8×1.

elements of an array into a vector register, while the scatter does the inverse. Using these primitives, the following pseudocode illustrates vectorized BICRS multiplication.

1: **while** there are nonzeroes remaining **do**
2:    get the next set of p rows to operate on
3:    gather the corresponding output vector elements in **y**
4:    **while** there are nonzeroes remaining on any of the current rows **do**
5:       get the next set of $p \cdot q$ (possibly overlapping) column indices
6:       gather the corresponding input vector elements in **x**
7:       retrieve the next set of $p \cdot q$ nonzero values **v**
8:       do the vectorized multiply-add $\mathbf{y} := \mathbf{y} + \mathbf{v} \cdot \mathbf{x}$
9:    **end while**
10:    scatter the cached output vector elements **y** back to main memory.
11: **end while**

Upon processing all nonzeroes on each of the p rows, the l entries of **y** need to be reduced by summation into p entries; e.g., for 2×4 blocking, the top half of **y** corresponds to i_0 in Figure 27.6, while the bottom half corresponds to i_1. The 1×8 case thus requires an allreduce into i_0, while the 8×1 blocking requires no reduction at all. Using other block sizes leads to partial reductions.

This algorithm requires a slight modification of the BICRS data structures as well; for each $p \times q$ block, the indices of the last $p \cdot q - 1$ nonzeroes are relative to the first element of that block. Figure 27.7

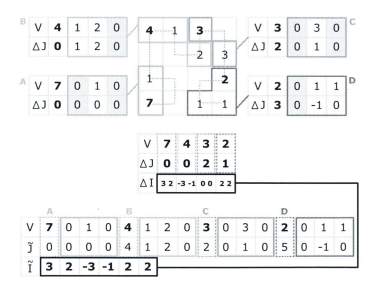

FIGURE 27.7

Illustration of the final vectorized BICRS data structure. It separates the relative encoding of $pq - 1$ nonzeroes in each block from the BICRS encoding of each of the leading nonzeroes of all blocks; these two encodings are then combined in the final vectorized data structure. The figure illustrates 2×2 blocking on an 4×4 matrix with 10 nonzeroes ordered according to a Hilbert curve. This results in 4 blocks, containing 6 explicit zeroes (fill-in).

illustrates this principle. When there are not enough nonzeroes in A to fill a block corresponding to a fixed set of rows, then explicit zeroes have to be stored; this *fill-in* results in additional storage and explicit multiplications using zeroes, an overhead which is hoped to be offset by the gain in effective bandwidth use.

IMPLEMENTATION OF THE VECTORIZED SPMV KERNEL

Figures 27.8 and 27.9 provide a generic C++ implementation of the vectorized BICRS SpMV multiplication. In these code snippets, the variables x,y,l,p,q are as defined in the text. The template variables _i_type and _v_type correspond to the index types and value types, respectively. Pointers to the arrays $\widetilde{\Delta i}$ and $\widetilde{\Delta j}$ are named row_index_array and col_index_array; a pointer to v is denoted by *value_array*. All other variables are declared within the code snippets. The code shown in the figures is functional and is directly derived from the production code distributed with the book.[2]

Specializing code for specific architectures and block sizes can lead to better performance than a compiler-optimized generic implementation would achieve. For cases where p is very small, for instance, it may not make sense to use gather and scatter primitives on the output vector. Figure 27.10 shows a specialized implementation for handling 1×8 blocks on the Intel Xeon Phi, optimized using

```
void spmv( const double *__restrict__ x, double *__restrict__ y ) {
    //declare buffers
    __declspec(align(32)) _i_type c_ind_buffer[ l ];
    __declspec(align(32)) _i_type r_ind_buffer[ l ];
    __declspec(align(32)) _v_type input_buffer[ l ];
    __declspec(align(32)) _v_type outputbuffer[ l ];
    __declspec(align(32)) _v_type outputvector[ l ];

    //shift input vector, output vector to first nonzero
    x += *col_index_array; y += *row_index_array;

    //fill buffers and load first l output elements
    for( size_t i = 0; i < l; ++i ) {
        c_ind_buffer[ i ] = *col_index_array++;
        r_ind_buffer[ i ] = *row_index_array++;
        outputbuffer[ i ] = 0;
        outputvector[ i ] = y[ r_ind_buffer[ i ] ];
    }

    //reset start column index, start row index
    c_ind_buffer[ 0 ] = 0; r_ind_buffer[ 0 ] = 0;

    //keep track of how many row blocks in outputvector were processed
    size_t blockrow = 0;
    ...
```

FIGURE 27.8

C++ implementation of the vectorized BICRS SpMV multiplication for generic architectures, data types, and block sizes. This is the kernel initialization code. The code listing continues in Figure 27.9.

[2]The latest code version is available from http://albert-jan.yzelman.net/software#SL.

```
...
//start kernel
while( value_array < value_array_end ) {
    //process row
    while( x < x_end ) {
        //fill input buffer (gather)
        for( size_t i = 0; i < l; ++i ) input_buffer[ i ] = x[ c_ind_buffer[ i ] ];

        //do FMA
        for( size_t i = 0; i < l; ++i ) outputbuffer[ i ] += value_array[ i ] * input_buffer[ i ];

        //shift nonzero vector
        value_array += l;

        //shift input vector
        x += *col_index_array;

        //fill c_ind_buffer
        for( size_t i = 0; i < l; ++i ) c_ind_buffer[ i ] = *col_index_array++;
        c_ind_buffer[ 0 ] = 0;
    }

    //reduce l outputbuffer elements to p row contributions
    for( size_t i = 0; i < p; ++i )
        for( size_t j = 0; j < q; ++j )
            outputvector[ p*blockrow + i ] += outputbuffer[ i*q + j ];

    //prepare for next block of p rows
    ++blockrow;
    for( size_t i = 0; i < l; ++i ) outputbuffer[ i ] = 0;

    //undo row change signal, shift input vector
    x -= n;

    //if all elements of outputvector were updated
    if( blockrow == q ) {

        //write back outputvector
        for( size_t i = 0; i < l; ++i ) y[ r_ind_buffer[ i ] ] = outputvector[ i ];

        //shift output vector to new row
        y += *row_index_array;

        //load new r_ind_buffer
        for( size_t i = 0; i < l; ++i ) r_ind_buffer[ i ] = *row_index_array++;
        r_ind_buffer[ 0 ] = 0;

        //read new outputvector
        for( size_t i = 0; i < l; ++i ) outputvector[ i ] = y[ r_ind_buffer[ i ] ];

        //reset block row counter
        blockrow = 0;
    }
    //write back any modified items outputvector may hold
    for( size_t i = 0; i < l; ++i ) y[ r_ind_buffer[ i ] ] = outputvector[ i ];
    }
}
```

FIGURE 27.9

C++ implementation of the inner kernel code of the vectorized BICRS SpMV multiplication for generic architectures, data types, and block sizes. The code was initialized in Figure 27.8.

```
void spmv( const double *__restrict__ x, double *__restrict__ y ) {
    __m512d input_buffer, value_buffer, outputbuffer;
    __m512i c_ind_buffer, zeroF;
         zeroF = _mm512_set_epi32( 1, 1, 1, 1, 1, 1, 1, 0 );
    outputbuffer = _mm512_setzero_pd();

    //load in column indices of the first block, and set c_ind_buffer[0]=0
    c_ind_buffer = _mm512_load_epi32 ( col_index_array );
    c_ind_buffer = _mm512_mullo_epi32( c_ind_buffer, zeroF );

    //shift vector pointers to the first nonzero position
    x += *col_index_array; col_index_array += 1;
    y += *row_index_array++;

    //start kernel
    while( value_array < value_array_end ) {
        //process current row
        while( x < x_end ) {
            //gather input vector elements
            input_buffer = _mm512_i32logather_pd( c_ind_buffer, x, 8 );

            //load (stream) nonzero values
            value_buffer = _mm512_load_pd( value_array ); value_array += 1;

            //do FMA; outputbuffer += value_buffer * input_buffer
            outputbuffer = _mm512_fmadd_pd( value_buffer, input_buffer, outputbuffer );

            //load in next block, shift input vector
            c_ind_buffer = _mm512_load_epi32 ( col_index_array );
            c_ind_buffer = _mm512_mullo_epi32( c_ind_buffer, zeroF );
            x += *col_index_array; col_index_array += 1;
        }
        //write out local contributions (via allreduce), and reset
                *y += _mm512_reduce_add_pd( outputbuffer );
        outputbuffer = _mm512_setzero_pd();

        //shift input vector back to a valid position
        x-= n;

        //shift output vector to next row position
        y += *row_index_array++;
    }
}
```

FIGURE 27.10

C++ implementation of the vectorized BICRS SpMV multiplication for the Intel Xeon Phi using ICC intrinsics. Assumes 64-bit floats, 32-bit indices, and 1×8 blocks.

ICC intrinsics for the AVX-512 instruction set. It assumes 32-bit index types (_i_type=**int32_t**), 64-bit floating point values (_v_type=double), and performs write-backs to y using scalar FMAs.

The Xeon Phi specific code, distributed with the book, employs shorter index types (_i_type=**int16_t**) to exploit the compression opportunities sparse blocking makes possible. A single load of c_ind_buffer thus reads in 16 integers instead of 8, since the 512-bit registers can contain 512/16 = 16 short ints. This requires the inner while-loop in Figure 27.10 to be unrolled in two parts, where the first part uses the upper half of c_ind_buffer. This is followed by code that handles a possible row jump, after which the upper half of c_ind_buffer is swapped with the lower half (which contains the remaining unhandled column increments), after which the inner kernel code is repeated. After the manual unroll ends, the loop continues and the next 16 column increments are read in. Such unrolls are also necessary when using gather and scatter instructions on the output vector while $p < l$: partial reductions needed when $1 < p < l$ require additional permutations and additions involving outputbuffer, while adding the thus obtained p contributions to outputvector requires masked vector additions that require unrolling for efficiency. For brevity, these codes are not included here; please refer to the distributed code to view the unrolled codes in detail.

EVALUATION

We have compared the execution speed measured in Gflop/s of three parallel SpMV algorithms, namely, (1) the OpenMP-enabled CRS SpMV multiplication, (2) the partially distributed parallel SpMV method (with local matrices stored using compressed BICRS) implemented using PThreads, and (3) a vectorized version of the partially distributed method (using the vectorized BICRS data structure as presented in the previous section), also implemented using PThreads. We compare the results to the CRS-based implementation from the Intel Math Kernel Library version 11.1.1. All code was compiled using the Intel C/C++ Compiler (ICC) version 14.0.1.

We ran tests using six matrices of various dimensions and sparsity patterns (see Figure 27.11). The selected matrices are representative of four generic classes: they are either small (so that the corresponding vectors fit into the combined caches) or large, and structured (so that the natural nonzero structure benefits cache reuse) or unstructured. See Yzelman and Roose (2014) for an application of this categorization on a much wider set of real-world matrices.

Small matrices	Rows	Columns	Nonzeroes	
nd24k	72,000	72,000	28,715,634	U
s3dkt3m2	90,449	90,449	1,921,955	S
Large matrices				
Freescale1	3,428,755	3,428,755	17,052,626	S
wiki07	3,566,907	3,566,907	45,030,389	U
cage15	5,154,859	5,154,859	99,199,551	S
adaptive	6,815,744	6,815,744	13,624,320	U

FIGURE 27.11

Matrices used in the experiments. The matrices above the horizontal separator line are considered small; their corresponding input and output vectors have sufficiently small combined dimensions to fit into most (combined) L2 caches of modern architectures. The right column indicates whether the sparse matrix has a beneficial structure (S for structured) with respect to cache reuse during a CRS-based SpMV multiplication, or whether the matrix has no such structure (U for unstructured).

ON THE INTEL XEON PHI COPROCESSOR

We ran our experiments on an Intel Xeon Phi 7120A coprocessor, which contains 61 cores at 1.238 GHz and 16 GB of memory. Each core comes equipped with a 32 kB L1 cache and a 256 kB L2 cache, supporting four hardware threads per core. We used all threads on all cores, except for the core reserved for the operating system, thus employing 240 threads.

Figure 27.12 shows the performance of the parallel SpMV multiplication using the partially distributed method with vectorized BICRS. We ran experiments on each matrix using all of the possible blocking sizes (1×8, 2×4, 4×2, or 8×1). These choices lead to different amounts of fill-in, which are reported in Figure 27.13. Comparing the results, choosing the block size that result in the least amount of fill-in almost always corresponds to the fastest execution among the possible block sizes; the only exception was on the matrix wiki07, where vectorization had an adverse effect compared to nonvectorized SpMV multiplication. The results indicate that vectorization is highly effective on the Intel Xeon Phi coprocessor, especially for small matrices (such as nd24k and s3dkt3m2), where thread-local parts of the vectors can reside in fast local caches.

The performance figures reported in Figure 27.17 exclude the time required for preprocessing. For the partially distributed methods, this overhead is negligible compared to the construction of a CRS data structure, since the latter requires sorting of all nonzeroes. Determining the fill-in for all possible block sizes *a priori* can be done by a single traversal of the input matrix before the actual matrix construction.

To assess the performance improvement of the various optimizations discussed above, we measured the performance of the OpenMP CRS implementation, successively augmented with

1. partial distribution of A and x,
2. sparse blocking with the Hilbert cache-oblivious order on the blocks, and
3. vectorized BICRS storage of the local A.

These results are reported in Figure 27.14.

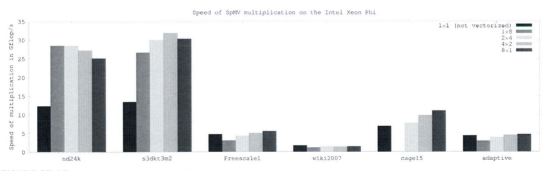

FIGURE 27.12

Performance of the partially distributed method using vectorized BICRS on each of the four possible blocking sizes 1×8, 2×4, 4×2, and 8×1. For reference, the results corresponding to the non-vectorized partially distributed method are included under the 1×1 block size. A value is missing for cage15 with 1×8 blocking; in this case, the extra amount of fill-in caused the coprocessor to run out of memory before the experiment could successfully complete.

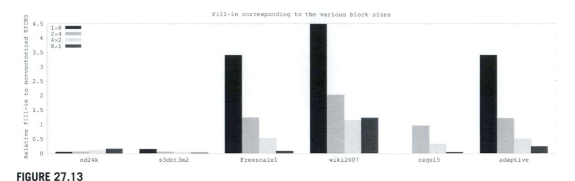

FIGURE 27.13

Relative fill-in corresponding to the matrices and block sizes in Figure 27.12. The reported figure is equal to the number of explicitly added zeroes divided by the number of nonzeroes contained in the matrix original. A value for the cage15 and 1×8 blocking is missing since the added fill-in (of presumably a factor 2) caused the coprocessor to run out of memory.

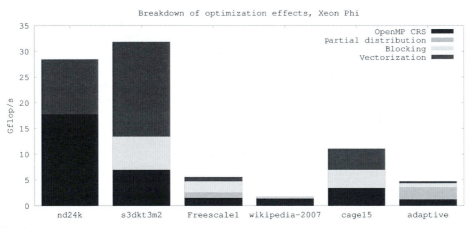

FIGURE 27.14

Performance improvement due to the various optimizations discussed in this chapter, on the Intel Xeon Phi. The performance baseline is OpenMP CRS, successively augmented with (1) partial data distribution, (2) sparse blocking with Hilbert ordering, and (3) vectorized BICRS.

Which optimizations are most effective strongly depends on both the matrix dimensions as well as its type. On the nd24k matrix, for example, partial data distributions and blocking do not improve the OpenMP CRS baseline performance, while vectorization speeds up its performance by about 50%. In contrast, the major performance increase on the adaptive matrix is due to partially distributing the data, while for the cage15 matrix, the main performance increase comes equally from blocking with Hilbert ordering as well as vectorization.

ON INTEL XEON CPUs

Another test platform is a dual-socket CPU-based machine, containing two Intel® Xeon® E5-2690 v2 "Ivy Bridge EP" processors. Each processor contains 10 cores equipped with 32 kB L1 and 256 kB L2 local caches, while the 10 cores share a 25 MB L3 cache. Both sockets connect to local memory banks containing 64 GB of DDR3 memory running at 1600 MHz, thus achieving a maximum bandwidth of two times 12.8 GB/s.

Ivy Bridge processors support vector instructions on 256-bit registers, hence $l = 4$ when using double precision floating point data. AVX does not support gather and scatter instructions, however, so the vectorized scheme on this architecture will likely be less effective than on the Intel Xeon Phi. Gather instructions are available in AVX2-enabled processors (the "Haswell" line), while scatter instructions are planned for AVX3.

Experiments were run using 40 threads, thus using the hyperthreading capabilities available on this processor. Figure 27.15 shows the performance of the vectorized SpMV multiplication on the dual-socket machine. Figure 27.16 illustrates the effect of the various optimizations on this architecture.

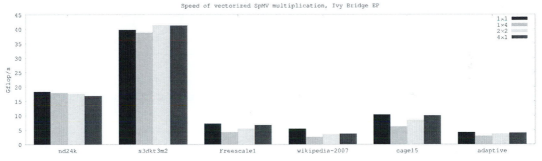

FIGURE 27.15

Performance of the partially distributed method using vectorized BICRS on a dual-socket Intel "Ivy Bridge EP." The performance of each possible blocking size (1×4, 2×2, and 4×1) is reported and compared against results obtained using nonvectorized BICRS (1×1).

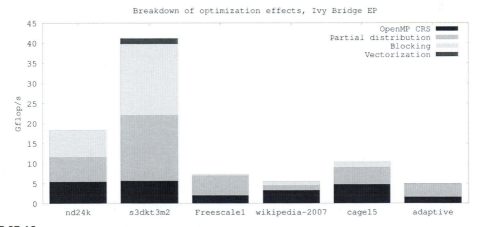

FIGURE 27.16

Performance improvement due to the various optimizations discussed in this chapter, on a dual-socket Intel "Ivy Bridge EP." The performance baseline is OpenMP CRS, successively augmented with (1) partial data distribution, (2) sparse blocking with Hilbert ordering, and (3) vectorized BICRS.

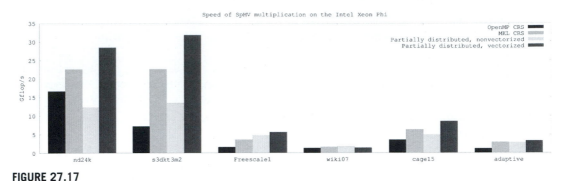

FIGURE 27.17

Performance of four implementations of a parallel SpMV multiplication using 60 cores (240 threads) on the Intel Xeon Phi 7120A coprocessor: (a) OpenMP-enabled parallel CRS, (b) MKL-enabled parallel CRS, (c) partially distributed method using compressed BICRS, and (d) partially distributed method using vectorized BICRS.

Similar to the results on the Intel Xeon Phi, the effect of each optimization largely depends on the size and type of matrix. In general, however, the effects of vectorization are noticeably less pronounced than on the coprocessor. This is due to the absence of hardware support for the gather and scatter instructions, and the fact that the SpMV multiplications are bandwidth-bound on CPUs (and not latency bound as on the coprocessor).

PERFORMANCE COMPARISON

Figure 27.17 compares the performance of the vectorized SpMV on the Xeon Phi to the following alternative methods: (1) the straightforward OpenMP CRS solution, (2) the partially distributed solution using nonvectorized BICRS, and (3) the SpMV multiplication code included with Intel MKL. For the larger matrices in our test set, the nonvectorized partially distributed algorithms and the MKL SpMV codes display a significantly better performance compared to the simple OpenMP-parallelized CRS algorithm. The performance of the partially distributed algorithm significantly increases with the introduction of vectorization, and outperforms the CRS SpMV multiplication from Intel MKL, with the exception of the unstructured wiki07 matrix.

Figure 27.18 makes a similar comparison for the dual-socket "Ivy Bridge EP" machine. As vectorization did not always lead to better performance on this architecture, the nonvectorized partially distributed method outperforms all other alternatives, except on the structured s3dkt3m2 matrix (where vectorization did result in increased performance).

SUMMARY

The difficulties in achieving a high performance for SpMV multiplication lie with a low flop-to-byte ratio and inefficient cache use. In the case of the Intel Xeon Phi coprocessor, an additional difficulty is the high-latency memory access.

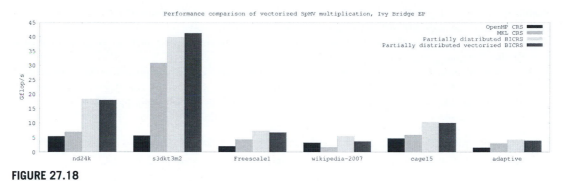

FIGURE 27.18

Performance of parallel SpMV implementations on 40 threads on a dual-socket Ivy Bridge machine. (a) OpenMP CRS, (b) MKL CRS, (c) partially distributed BICRS, and (d) partially distributed vectorized BICRS.

In this chapter, we discussed strategies that maximize data locality and data reuse for the parallel SpMV multiplication on shared-memory systems. We focus on data structures that support vectorized operations, in addition to arbitrary nonzero traversals for cache-obliviousness and advanced compression through blocking. Parallelization schemes for both shared-memory and distributed-memory platforms were discussed.

Experiments were performed on both the Intel Xeon Phi coprocessor and on a dual-socket Ivy Bridge shared-memory system. The results show that the shared-memory parallelization technique, in conjunction with sparse blocking, cache-oblivious traversals, compression, and vectorization, outperforms not only a CRS-based algorithm implemented using OpenMP, but also the SpMV-code available in the Intel MKL library; optimizing for the same programming model thus leads to efficient codes on both architectures.

ACKNOWLEDGMENTS

This work is funded by Intel and by the Institute for the Promotion of Innovation through Science and Technology in Flanders (IWT).

FOR MORE INFORMATION

Sparse Library: http://albert-jan.yzelman.net/software#SL.
MulticoreBSP for C: http://www.multicorebsp.com.

Devine, K.D., Boman, E.G., Heaphy, R.T., Bisseling, R.H., Catalyurek, U.V., 2006. Parallel hypergraph partitioning for scientific computing. In: Proceedings IEEE International Parallel and Distributed Processing Symposium 2006. IEEE Press, Long Beach, CA.

Vastenhouw, B., Bisseling, R.H., 2005. A two-dimensional data distribution method for parallel sparse matrix-vector multiplication. SIAM Rev. 47 (1), 67–95.

Vuduc, R., Demmel, J.W., Yelick, K.A., 2005. OSKI: a library of automatically tuned sparse matrix kernels. J. Phys. Conf. Series 16, 521–530.

Yzelman, A.N., Bisseling, R.H., 2009. Cache-oblivious sparse matrix-vector multiplication by using sparse matrix partitioning methods. SIAM J. Sci. Comput. 31 (4), 3128–3154.

Yzelman, A.N., Bisseling, R.H., 2011. Two-dimensional cache-oblivious sparse matrix–vector multiplication. Parallel Comput. 37 (12), 806–819.

Yzelman, A.N., Bisseling, R.H., 2012. A cache-oblivious sparse matrix-vector multiplication scheme based on the Hilbert curve. In: Günther, M., Bartel, A., Brunk, M., Schöps, S., Striebel, M. (Eds.), Progress in Industrial Mathematics at ECMI 2010, Mathematics in Industry. Springer, Berlin, Germany, pp. 627–633.

Yzelman, A.N., Roose, D., 2014. High-level strategies for parallel shared-memory sparse matrix-vector multiplication. IEEE Trans. Parallel Dist. Syst. 25 (1), 116–125.

Yzelman, A.N., Bisseling, R.H., Roose, D., Meerbergen, K., 2014. MulticoreBSP for C: a high-performance library for shared-memory parallel programming. Int. J. Parallel Programm. 42, 619–642.

MORTON ORDER IMPROVES PERFORMANCE

## 28

Kerry Evans
Intel Corp, USA

IMPROVING CACHE LOCALITY BY DATA ORDERING

Modern memory hierarchies do their best to keep your processors busy by providing the required data at the right time. But what if your data are not structured in a cache-friendly way? That is when we usually resort to some kind of data reordering, blocking, or tiling, and often end up with code that is very hard to understand (and maintain) and strongly tied to our target hardware. Developers are used to the idea of storing data in multidimensional matrices in either row- or column-major order. But what if your code needs to access data in a different order? What if you are really interested in the four or six nearest neighbors rather than 16 elements in a single row? What if you need to access a row-major matrix in column-major order? Worse yet, what if your data must be traversed in many different orders depending on previous calculations? Assuming all your data does not fit in cache, performance will suffer!

A large body of work exists on efficient mappings of multidimensional data along with algorithms to efficiently utilize these mappings. Many of the index calculations are complex and require special hardware or instructions to justify their usage.

In this chapter, we will examine a method of mapping multidimensional data into a single dimension while maintaining locality using Morton, or Z-curve ordering, and look at the effects it has on performance of two common linear algebra problems: matrix transpose and matrix multiply. Next, we will tune our transpose and multiply code to take advantage of the Intel® Xeon® processor and Intel® Xeon Phi™ coprocessor cache and vector hardware, add threading, and finally summarize the results.

IMPROVING PERFORMANCE

There are many facets to performance optimization but three issues to deal with right from the beginning are memory access, vectorization, and parallelization. Unless we can optimize these, we cannot achieve peak performance.

The fastest memory accesses occur when the needed data are already in cache. Since data transfers to and from cache occur in "cache lines" (not bytes or words), you may have poor cache efficiency, if the data you need are scattered among many cache lines, even though your data are in cache.

Consider the 512-bit vector registers found on Intel Xeon Phi coprocessors. A single cache line (64 bytes) contains enough data to populate a vector register. Therefore, it is possible to load 16 single precision floating point values with a single cache read. This is very efficient but, of course, it assumes the data you need resides within a single cache line. If not, then multiple reads are needed to load that vector register.

Efficient parallelization is also required to make the best use of the available hardware. If we can come up with an effective data-blocking approach that addresses memory access and vectorization, it may also provide a rationale for splitting computation across all of our hardware threads.

G. M. Morton introduced the Morton order (aka Z-order or Morton code) as a mapping of multi-dimensional data to one dimension that preserves locality of the data points. The mapping is done by interleaving the bits of the coordinates in each dimension. The code shown in Figure 28.1 accomplishes this for the 2D case. Figure 28.2 shows Morton order mapping for an 8×8 2D grid, further subdivided into 4×4 sub-blocks. In row-major order, the numbering would proceed from 0 to 7 along the first row, 8 to 15 for the second row and so forth. With Morton ordering, we see that good 2D locality (in terms of nearness to neighbors) is retained.

Something else interesting about each 4×4 sub-block is that each element is a single precision floating point value (4 bytes each). Therefore, the 16 floats in each sub-block fit in a single cache line of a processor or coprocessor and, if properly aligned, can be loaded into a vector register in one cache read.

MATRIX TRANSPOSE

Matrix transpose is defined as $A'[i,j] = A[j,i]$, so it is pretty simple to code up the naïve version as shown in Figure 28.3.

```
//split x leaving a zero bit between each original bit
int dilate_1(int x){
  x = (x ^ (x <<  8)) & 0x00ff00ff;
  x = (x ^ (x <<  4)) & 0x0f0f0f0f;
  x = (x ^ (x <<  2)) & 0x33333333;
  x = (x ^ (x <<  1)) & 0x55555555;
  return x;
}
//interleave row and column bits
int zindex2d (int column, int row) {
    return (dilate_1(row)<<1)|dilate_1(column);
}
```

FIGURE 28.1

Code to compute Morton index from row, column.

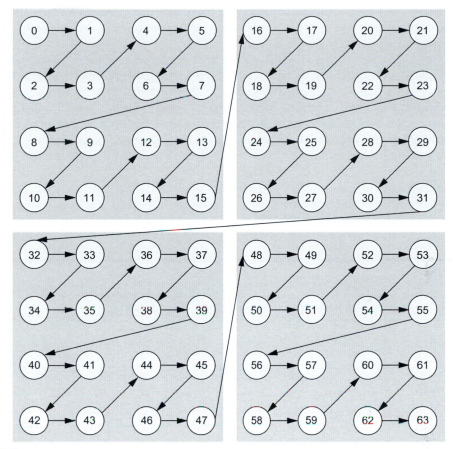

FIGURE 28.2

Morton order for 8×8 2D grid, subpartitioned into 4×4 blocks.

```
float a[N*N], at[N*N];
for(i=0; i<N; i++) {
  for (j=0; j<N; j++) {
    at[j*N+i] = a[i*N+j];
  }
}
```

FIGURE 28.3

Code for naïve matrix transpose.

This naïve version works but due to the rapidly changing index in the inner loop, our memory accesses are not even close to sequential and we know nothing about memory alignment. The compiler would not vectorize this loop either.

If we take a different approach using Morton ordering, we can do better. For illustrative purposes, look at the four 4×4 submatrices in Figure 28.2. From linear algebra we recall that we can accomplish the transpose operation by transposing the elements in each submatrix and then transposing the submatrices themselves. Since each submatrix is contained in a single cache line, we only need 4 reads to get all 64 elements of the 8×8 matrix. Transposing each 4×4 block just involves permuting 16 values and the permutations are the same for each 4× block. Figure 28.4 shows a portable implementation of the 4×4 transpose. An Intel Xeon Phi coprocessor can handle the permutation with a single _mm512_permutevar_epi32 intrinsic as shown in Figure 28.5.

All we have to do to have a full 8×8 matrix transpose is put some code together to call transpose 4×4 with the right input and output 4×4 blocks (Figure 28.6). Adding a bit more code in Figure 28.7 gives us a more general purpose matrix transpose. Since each submatrix can be transposed independently of all the others, we assign each to a thread using the OpenMP pragma on the outer loop.

NOTE

To keep indexing simple, the code forces matrix size to be a multiple of 4 and allocates matrix memory in square powers of 2. This is not required in general but let us ignore padding and/or cleanup handling.

```
void transpose4x4(float *a, float *at) {
    at[0]=a[0];
    at[1]=a[2];
    at[2]=a[1];
    at[3]=a[3];
    at[4]=a[8];
    at[5]=a[10];
    at[6]=a[9];
    at[7]=a[11];
    at[8]=a[4];
    at[9]=a[6];
    at[10]=a[5];
    at[11]=a[7];
    at[12]=a[12];
    at[13]=a[14];
    at[14]=a[13];
    at[15]=a[15];
}
```

FIGURE 28.4

Code to transpose a 4×4 block.

```
void transpose4x4(float *a, float *at) {
  __m512 oa;
  __m512 ta;
  __m512i pat={0,2,1,3,8,10,9,11,4,6,5,7,12,14,13,15};
  oa=_mm512_load_ps(a);
  ta=_mm512_castsi512_ps(
    _mm512_permutevar_epi32(pat,_mm512_castps_si512(oa))
  );
  _mm512_store_ps(at,ta);
}
```

FIGURE 28.5

Code to transpose a 4×4 block using intrinsics for the Intel Xeon Phi coprocessor.

```
int main(int argc, char **argv) {
  int i,j,k,iad;
  int uad,lad;
  int N=8;
  int N4=N/4;
  float *a=(float *)_mm_malloc(N*N*sizeof(float),128);
  float *c=(float *)_mm_malloc(N*N*sizeof(float),128);
  for(i=0; i<N; i++) {
    for(j=0; j<N; j++) {
      iad=zindex2d(j,i);
      a[iad]=j+i*N; //dummy data
    }
  }
  for(i=0; i<N4; i++) {
    for(j=0; j<N4; j++) {
      uad=zindex2d(j,i);  //offset of original submatrix
      lad=zindex2d(i,j);  //offset of transpose submatrix
      transpose4x4(&a[16*uad],&c[16*lad]);
    }
  }
  _mm_free(a);
  _mm_free(c);
}
```

FIGURE 28.6

Program to transpose 8×8 matrix using Morton ordering.

Comparing performance of the Morton order transpose to the naïve transpose for some larger matrices, we see that on an Intel Xeon Phi coprocessor (Figure 28.8) speedup for matrices larger than 1024×1024 single-threaded speedup is around 9×. For 244 threads, we do not see an advantage over the naïve implementation until our matrix size is 16,384×16,384 and larger.

```
int main(int argc, char **argv) {
  int i,j,k,iad;
  int uad,lad;
  int N=8;
  if(argc>1) {
    N=atoi(argv[1]);
    If(N>32768) N=32768;   // limit size
  }
// for now, N must be a multiple of 4
  i=N/4;
  if(N>(i*4)) N=(i+1)*4;
  int N4=N/4;
// for now, matrix size power of 2
  double l2=log(N)/log(2.0);
  int il2=(int)l2;
  if(il2<l2) il2++;
  int MSZ=pow(2,il2);
  printf("N=%d; N/4=%d; msize=%d\n",N,N4,MSZ);
  float *a=
    (float *)_mm_malloc(MSZ*MSZ*sizeof(float),128);
  float *c=
    (float *)_mm_malloc(MSZ*MSZ*sizeof(float),128);
  int iv=0;
// initialize faster as long as we're threading
```

FIGURE 28.7

Program to transpose more general matrix using Morton order and OpenMP multithreading.

Figure 28.9 shows results for an Intel Xeon processor. Single-threaded results show an advantage for most matrices of up to 2.6× for 32,768×32,768. With 32 threads, the speedup is more pronounced for most sizes and up to 4× for the largest size.

MATRIX MULTIPLY

Matrix multiplication is closely related to our transpose work in that we need to sum up the products of each row of the first matrix and each column of the second matrix:

Given $M \times L$ matrix A and $L \times N$ matrix B we compute $C = A*B$ as

```
      for (i=0; i<M; i++)
        for (j=0; j<N; j++){
          sum=0;
          for (k=0; k<L; k++)
            sum += A[i,k]*B[k,j];
          C[i,j] = A[i,k]*B[k,j];
        }
```

dim	naïve 1thread	Morton 1thread	speedup	naïve 244thr	Morton 244thr	speedup
256	0.0033	0.0014	2.46	0.0014	0.0037	0.38
512	0.0763	0.0066	11.60	0.0012	0.0155	0.07
1024	0.3304	0.0289	11.44	0.0114	0.0303	0.38
2048	1.2660	0.1499	8.44	0.0185	0.0476	0.39
4096	4.9433	0.5820	8.49	0.0359	0.0669	0.53
8192	20.1280	2.2590	8.91	0.1156	0.1477	0.78
16384	80.2921	8.9273	8.99	0.4316	0.3451	1.25
32768	328.4720	35.7564	9.18	1.8124	0.7410	2.44

FIGURE 28.8

Matrix transpose timing, in seconds, for an Intel Xeon Phi coprocessor, naïve and Morton order, single-threaded and multithreaded.

In this naïve implementation, we have little cache locality working for us. The usual way to improve performance is to perform some kind of blocking or tiling so why not use our Morton ordering and the basic 4×4 partitioning we used for matrix transpose? Considering one 4×4 block each from A and B, we see (Figure 28.10) we can compute partial values for C using all the values in each block. Since each block represents one cache line that is great efficiency. We do have to do some juggling of indices but that juggling is the same for every pair of 4×4 blocks.

Figure 28.11 shows a nice way to accomplish the 4×4 block multiply using intrinsics for the Intel Xeon Phi coprocessor.

Around this basic 4×4 block multiply, we just need to add some loops to iterate through all the pairs of blocks as we accumulate the results, also in 4×4 blocks. To keep things simple, once again, we are restricting ourselves to dimensions that are a power of 2 and multiple of 4. Since we know that each 4×4 block of the result can be computed independently, we have used OpenMP to add threading around the outer loop, similarly to what we did in the transpose code. Figure 28.12 lists the final program. Note the use of the #ifdef __MIC__ directive that selects intrinsics for Intel Xeon Phi coprocessor, builds, and uses plain C-language statements otherwise.

So how does it perform? Figure 28.13 shows timing results on an Intel® Xeon Phi™ coprocessor for matrix dimensions from 256 to 32,768. Compared to the naïve approach, the performance improvement is significant for all sizes and for 512×512 and larger, we see speedups in excess of 30×.

dim	naïve 1 thread	Morton 1 thread	speedup	naïve 32 thr	Morton 32 thr	speedup
256	0.0004	0.0003	1.52	0.0014	0.0037	1.73
512	0.0021	0.0009	2.26	0.0012	0.0155	1.00
1024	0.0067	0.0061	1.09	0.0114	0.0303	1.59
2048	0.0147	0.0282	0.52	0.0185	0.0476	0.59
4096	0.2043	0.1757	1.16	0.0359	0.0669	0.67
8192	0.8254	0.5219	1.58	0.1156	0.1477	2.30
16384	3.7540	1.7044	2.20	0.4316	0.3451	3.39
32768	18.4287	6.8835	2.68	1.8124	0.7410	4.07

FIGURE 28.9

Matrix transpose timing, in seconds, for an Intel Xeon processor, naïve and Morton order, single-threaded and multithreaded.

```
void zmatmul(float *a, float *b, float *c){
c[0]+=a[0]*b[0]+a[1]*b[2]+a[4]*b[8]+a[5]*b[10];
c[1]+=a[0]*b[1]+a[1]*b[3]+a[4]*b[9]*a[5]*b[11];
c[4]+=a[0]*b[4]+a[1]*b[6]+a[4]*b[12]+a[5]*b[14];
c[5]+=a[0]*b[5]+a[1]*b[7]+a[4]*b[13]*a[5]*b[15];
c[2]+=a[2]*b[0]+a[3]*b[2]+a[6]*b[8]+a[7]*b[10];
c[3]+=a[2]*b[1]+a[3]*b[3]+a[6]*b[9]*a[7]*b[11];
c[6]+=a[2]*b[4]+a[3]*b[6]+a[6]*b[12]+a[7]*b[14];
c[7]+=a[2]*b[5]+a[3]*b[7]+a[6]*b[13]*a[7]*b[15];
c[8]+=a[8]*b[0]+a[9]*b[2]+a[12]*b[8]+a[13]*b[10];
c[9]+=a[8]*b[1]+a[9]*b[3]+a[12]*b[9]*a[13]*b[11];
c[12]+=a[8]*b[4]+a[9]*b[6]+a[12]*b[12]+a[13]*b[14];
c[13]+=a[8]*b[5]+a[9]*b[7]+a[12]*b[13]*a[13]*b[15];
c[10]+=a[10]*b[0]+a[11]*b[2]+a[14]*b[8]+a[15]*b[10];
c[11]+=a[10]*b[1]+a[11]*b[3]+a[14]*b[9]*a[15]*b[11];
c[14]+=a[10]*b[4]+a[11]*b[6]+a[14]*b[12]+a[15]*b[14];
c[15]+=a[10]*b[5]+a[11]*b[7]+a[14]*b[13]*a[15]*b[15];
}
```

FIGURE 28.10

Multiply and accumulate code for 24×4 blocks.

```
void zmatmul(float *ain, float *bin, float *cout) {
__m512 a,b,c;
__m512 a0,a1,a2,a3;
__m512 b0,b1,b2,b3;
__m512i pa0={ 0, 0, 2, 2, 0, 0, 2, 2, 8, 8,10,10, 8, 8,10,10};
__m512i pa1={ 1, 1, 3, 3, 1, 1, 3, 3, 9, 9,11,11, 9, 9,11,11};
__m512i pa2={ 4, 4, 6, 6, 4, 4, 6, 6,12,12,14,14,12,12,14,14};
__m512i pa3={ 5, 5, 7, 7, 5, 5, 7, 7,13,13,15,15,13,13,15,15};

__m512i pb0={ 0, 1, 0, 1, 4, 5, 4, 5, 0, 1, 0, 1, 4, 5, 4, 5};
__m512i pb1={ 2, 3, 2, 3, 6, 7, 6, 7, 2, 3, 2, 3, 6, 7, 6, 7};
__m512i pb2={ 8, 9, 8, 9,12,13,12,13, 8, 9, 8, 9,12,13,12,13};
__m512i pb3={10,11,10,11,14,15,14,15,10,11,10,11,14,15,14,15};

a=_mm512_load_ps(ain);
b=_mm512_load_ps(bin);
c=_mm512_load_ps(cout);

a0=_mm512_castsi512_ps(
 _mm512_permutevar_epi32(pa0,_mm512_castps_si512(a)));
a1=_mm512_castsi512_ps(
 _mm512_permutevar_epi32(pa1,_mm512_castps_si512(a)));
a2=_mm512_castsi512_ps(
 _mm512_permutevar_epi32(pa2,_mm512_castps_si512(a)));

a3=_mm512_castsi512_ps(
 _mm512_permutevar_epi32(pa3,_mm512_castps_si512(a)));

b0=_mm512_castsi512_ps(
 _mm512_permutevar_epi32(pb0,_mm512_castps_si512(b)));
b1=_mm512_castsi512_ps(
 _mm512_permutevar_epi32(pb1,_mm512_castps_si512(b)));
b2=_mm512_castsi512_ps(
 _mm512_permutevar_epi32(pb2,_mm512_castps_si512(b)));
b3=_mm512_castsi512_ps(
 _mm512_permutevar_epi32(pb3,_mm512_castps_si512(b)));

c=_mm512_fmadd_ps(a0,b0,c);
c=_mm512_fmadd_ps(a1,b1,c);
c=_mm512_fmadd_ps(a2,b2,c);
c=_mm512_fmadd_ps(a3,b3,c);

_mm512_store_ps(cout,c);
}
```

FIGURE 28.11

Multiply and accumulate code using intrinsics for an Intel Xeon Phi coprocessor.

```
void zmatmul(float *ain, float *bin, float *cout) {

#ifdef _MIC_ //use intrinsics if an Intel Xeon Phi coprocessor
__m512 a,b,c;
__m512 a0,a1,a2,a3;
__m512 b0,b1,b2,b3;
__m512i pa0={ 0, 0, 2, 2, 0, 0, 2, 2, 8, 8,10,10, 8, 8,10,10};
__m512i pa1={ 1, 1, 3, 3, 1, 1, 3, 3, 9, 9,11,11, 9, 9,11,11};
__m512i pa2={ 4, 4, 6, 6, 4, 4, 6, 6,12,12,14,14,12,12,14,14};
__m512i pa3={ 5, 5, 7, 7, 5, 5, 7, 7,13,13,15,15,13,13,15,15};
```

FIGURE 28.12

Full matrix multiply program.

```
_m512i pb0={ 0, 1, 0, 1, 4, 5, 4, 5, 0, 1, 0, 1, 4, 5, 4, 5};
_m512i pb1={ 2, 3, 2, 3, 6, 7, 6, 7, 2, 3, 2, 3, 6, 7, 6, 7};
_m512i pb2={ 8, 9, 8, 9,12,13,12,13, 8, 9, 8, 9,12,13,12,13};
_m512i pb3={10,11,10,11,14,15,14,15,10,11,10,11,14,15,14,15};

a=_mm512_load_ps(ain);
b=_mm512_load_ps(bin);
c=_mm512_load_ps(cout);

a0=_mm512_castsi512_ps(
 _mm512_permutevar_epi32(pa0,_mm512_castps_si512(a)));
a1=_mm512_castsi512_ps(
 _mm512_permutevar_epi32(pa1,_mm512_castps_si512(a)));
a2=_mm512_castsi512_ps(
 _mm512_permutevar_epi32(pa2,_mm512_castps_si512(a)));
a3=_mm512_castsi512_ps(
 _mm512_permutevar_epi32(pa3,_mm512_castps_si512(a)));

b0=_mm512_castsi512_ps(
 _mm512_permutevar_epi32(pb0,_mm512_castps_si512(b)));
b1=_mm512_castsi512_ps(
 _mm512_permutevar_epi32(pb1,_mm512_castps_si512(b)));
b2=_mm512_castsi512_ps(
 _mm512_permutevar_epi32(pb2,_mm512_castps_si512(b)));
b3=_mm512_castsi512_ps(
 _mm512_permutevar_epi32(pb3,_mm512_castps_si512(b)));

c=_mm512_fmadd_ps(a0,b0,c);
c=_mm512_fmadd_ps(a1,b1,c);
c=_mm512_fmadd_ps(a2,b2,c);
c=_mm512_fmadd_ps(a3,b3,c);

_mm512_store_ps(cout,c);
#else
cout[0]+=ain[0]*bin[0]+ain[1]*bin[2]+ain[4]*bin[8]+ain[5]*bin[10];
cout[1]+=ain[0]*bin[1]+ain[1]*bin[3]+ain[4]*bin[9]+ain[5]*bin[11];
cout[2]+=ain[2]*bin[0]+ain[3]*bin[2]+ain[6]*bin[8]+ain[7]*bin[10];
cout[3]+=ain[2]*bin[1]+ain[3]*bin[3]+ain[6]*bin[9]+ain[7]*bin[11];
cout[4]+=ain[0]*bin[4]+ain[1]*bin[6]+ain[4]*bin[12]+ain[5]*bin[14];
cout[5]+=ain[0]*bin[5]+ain[1]*bin[7]+ain[4]*bin[13]+ain[5]*bin[15];
cout[6]+=ain[2]*bin[4]+ain[3]*bin[6]+ain[6]*bin[12]+ain[7]*bin[14];
cout[7]+=ain[2]*bin[5]+ain[3]*bin[7]+ain[6]*bin[13]+ain[7]*bin[15];
cout[8]+=ain[8]*bin[0]+ain[9]*bin[2]+ain[12]*bin[8]+ain[13]*bin[10];
cout[9]+=ain[8]*bin[1]+ain[9]*bin[3]+ain[12]*bin[9]+ain[13]*bin[11];
cout[10]+=ain[10]*bin[0]+ain[11]*bin[2]+ain[14]*bin[8]+ain[15]*bin[10];
cout[11]+=ain[10]*bin[1]+ain[11]*bin[3]+ain[14]*bin[9]+ain[15]*bin[11];
cout[12]+=ain[8]*bin[4]+ain[9]*bin[6]+ain[12]*bin[12]+ain[13]*bin[14];
cout[13]+=ain[8]*bin[5]+ain[9]*bin[7]+ain[12]*bin[13]+ain[13]*bin[15];
cout[14]+=ain[10]*bin[4]+ain[11]*bin[6]+ain[14]*bin[12]+ain[15]*bin[14];
cout[15]+=ain[10]*bin[5]+ain[11]*bin[7]+ain[14]*bin[13]+ain[15]*bin[15];
```

FIGURE 28.12—Cont'd

```
    #endif

}

int main(int argc, char **argv) {

 int i,j,k,iad;
 int aad,bad,cad;
 int N=16;

 if(argc>1) {
  N=atoi(argv[1]);
  if(N>32768) N=32768; // max dim for now
 }

 i=N/4;
 if(N>(i*4)) N=(i+1)*4;

 double l2=log(N)/log(2.0);
 int il2=(int)l2;
 if(il2<l2) il2++;
 int MSZ=pow(2,il2);
 int N4=N/4;

 printf("N=%d; N/4=%d; msize=%d\n",N,N4,MSZ);

// actual memory allocation must be power of 2 although N can be any // multiple of 4
 float *a=(float *)_mm_malloc(MSZ*MSZ*sizeof(float),128);
 float *b=(float *)_mm_malloc(MSZ*MSZ*sizeof(float),128);
 float *c=(float *)_mm_malloc(MSZ*MSZ*sizeof(float),128);

 int iv=0;
#pragma omp parallel for private (i,j,iv,iad)
 for(i=0; i<N; i++) {
  for(j=0; j<N; j++) {
   iv=j+i*N;
   iad=zorder2d_c2i(j,i);
   a[iad]=b[iad]=iv; //dummy data
   c[iad]=0;  //initialize output array
  }
 }


 for(i=0; i<N4; i++) {
#pragma omp parallel for private (aad,bad,cad,i,j,k)
  for(j=0; j<N4; j++) {
   cad=16*zorder2d_c2i(j,i); //offset for result block
   for(k=0; k<N4; k++) {
    aad=16*zorder2d_c2i(k,i); //offset for a block
    bad=16*zorder2d_c2i(j,k); //offset for b blocck
```

FIGURE 28.12—Cont'd

```
            zmatmul(&a[aad],&b[bad],&c[cad]);
         }
       }
     }
   }

   _mm_free(a);
   _mm_free(b);
   _mm_free(c);

 }
```

FIGURE 28.12—Cont'd

dim	naïve 244 thr	Morton 244 thr	speedup
256	0.02	0.003	6.67
512	0.26	0.008	32.5
1024	1.78	0.046	38.7
2048	12.87	0.4	32.18
4096	105.5	2.9	36.38
8192	105.5	23	36.74
16384	6597	181	36.4
32768	Too long	1468	--

FIGURE 28.13

Matrix multiply timing, in seconds, on a coprocessor, naïve and Morton order, 244 threads.

Intel® Xeon processor performance is shown in Figure 28.14. Morton order starts to pay off for matrices larger than 1024×1024, approaching 30× for larger dimensions.

SUMMARY

In this chapter, we looked at Morton ordering as an alternative to the usual row-major or column-major sequentialization of multidimensional data that preserves multidimensional locality.

dim	naïve 32 thr	Morton 32 thr	speedup
256	0.1	0.188	0.53
512	0.05	0.169	0.29
1024	0.62	0.366	1.7
2048	2.89	0.871	3.3
4096	211	7.92	26.6
8192	1850	60.2	30.7
16384	13695	473	29.0
32768	Too long	3989	--

FIGURE 28.14

Matrix multiply timing, in seconds, for an Intel® Xeon® processor, naïve and Morton order, 32 threads.

Techniques we examined were effective on Intel Xeon Phi coprocessors and Intel Xeon processors with the same programming. Two examples, matrix transpose and matrix multiply, were used to demonstrate the performance gains possible using such an approach. We restricted the examples to square, single precision matrices and the dimension of the matrices to powers of 2. In general, these restrictions are not necessary but the goal was to emphasize the value of Morton ordering in improving performance.

Morton order matrix transpose on the Intel® Xeon Phi™ coprocessor produced single-threaded speedups around 9×, compared to a naïve approach, for matrices larger than 256×256. Even in highly parallel implementations, the Morton ordering gives over 2× for larger matrices with 244 threads. The same implementation on an Intel Xeon processor resulted in single-threaded speedups over 2×, and slightly over 4× advantage through ordering when run with 32 threads.

Matrix multiply delivered even more impressive results ranging from 30× to almost 40× for matrices 512×512 and larger. This was not a big surprise since multiply is much more compute-intensive than transpose but the performance gains are clear.

Morton ordering was effective on both Intel Xeon processors and Intel Xeon Phi coprocessors, especially for large matrices, because of the importance of cache locality in getting the best performance out of a system. Since the processors have out-of-order execution, they are able to hide memory latency problems to some extent; the current generation of coprocessors have in-order execution and are more sensitive to memory latencies. However, for large matrices, both platforms suffer due to cache and TLB (translation look-aside buffer) misses. By arranging data in a way that utilizes all the elements on a cache line, Morton ordering greatly reduces the pressure on these limited resources.

Other data structures that may benefit from Morton or other locality preserving mappings include geometric models, rasterized or other discrete image data (pixel-based images, movies, animations, tomographic, and seismic data), coordinates, database tables, statistical data, and many more. And the concepts apply to any number of dimensions, not just 2D.

As mentioned earlier, a large body of research exists around the use of space-filling curves and other cache-agnostic methods for improving locality and reaping the performance benefits of doing so. The reading materials cited at the end of this chapter are good places to continue your own research.

FOR MORE INFORMATION

Here are some additional reading materials we recommend related to this chapter:

- Bader, M., 2013. Space-Filling Curves—An Introduction with Applications in Scientific Computing. Springer.
- Chatterjee, S., Sen, S., 2000. Cache-Efficient Matrix Transposition. In: Proceedings of the Sixth International Symposium on High-Performance Computer Architecture (HPCA-6), pp. 195–205.
- Valsalam, V., Skjellum, A., 2002. A framework for high-performance matrix multiplication based on hierarchical abstractions, algorithms and optimized low-level kernels. Concurr. Comput. 14(10), 805–839.
- Z-order curve, http://en.wikipedia.org/wiki/Z-order_curve.
- Decoding Morton Codes, http://fgiesen.wordpress.com/2009/12/13/decoding-morton-codes/.
- Download the code from this, and other chapters, http://lotsofcores.com.

Author Index

Subject Index

Note: Page numbers followed by *f* indicate figures, *b* indicate boxes and *t* indicate tables.

Edwards Brothers Malloy
Thorofare, NJ USA
November 6, 2014